Technique in Litigation

CW01418348

Technique in Litigation

ERIC MORRIS

SC BA LLB

Advocate of the High Court of South Africa

SIXTH EDITION

Revised and updated by John Mullins SC and Carlos da Silva SC

Advocates of the High Court of South Africa

JUTA

First Published 1969
Second edition 1975
Third edition 1985
Fourth edition 1993
Fifth edition 2003
Sixth edition 2010

© Juta & Co Ltd
First floor, Sunclare Building, 21 Dreyer Street, Claremont 7925

*This book is copyright under the Berne Convention. In terms of the
Copyright Act, No 98 of 1978, no part of this book may be reproduced
or transmitted in any form or by any means, electronic or mechanical,
including photocopying, recording or by any information storage and
retrieval system, without permission in writing from the publisher.*

ISBN 978 0 7021 8458 1

Typeset in 11½ on 12½ Point Bembo
Cover Design by Drag and Drop
Set by Helanna Typesetters
Print Management by Print Communications

The first edition of this book came into being through the suggestion,
encouragement and practical assistance of my wife June.
To her again I dedicate my work and no less than before
has she been my inspiration.

The sixth edition of this book is dedicated to the memory of Eric Morris SC
(author of the first three editions) and Judge Hekkie Daniels (who revised and
updated the fourth and fifth editions).

Preface to the sixth edition

This book is directed at fledgling litigation lawyers. It is intended to be a mentor which contains practical examples on how things are done, or should be done, in practice.

Morris' Technique in Litigation (then in its second and third editions) was the book on which we cut our teeth when embarking on our careers. We both fondly recall Eric Morris' inimitably dry humour, and the golden nuggets of practical advice that we found in the book. The book was extraordinarily useful for us as young advocates, and so for us the task of updating it has been both an adventure and a privilege. It has been a labour of love. We hope that the result is a book that still captures Eric's humour and timeless wisdom, while also being thoroughly practical and topical for the modern lawyer setting out as a courtroom specialist.

Where we have altered the original text, we have done this to reflect the current legal position and current norms. We have attempted as far as possible to refrain from changing Eric's individual and very personal style and approach. But that said, we have revised the book extensively, in terms of both structure and content. We have attempted primarily to do three things:

- To retain Eric's wisdom (of which a prime example is, perhaps, his timeless references to the importance of extracting the essence of a case) and dry humour (of which examples abound). For this reason, we have retained many of Eric's examples. Old they may be, but those that we have retained illustrate the point in question as well now as they did in Eric's time.
- To update the book, and to make it as practical as possible. To this end, we have reorganised chapters and the content of chapters. We have rewritten large portions of the book. We have replaced Eric's views with our own where we felt strongly enough about it. One example is the preparing of witnesses in chapter 8 where, in paragraph 8.3.6, we have adopted a more forthright approach than did Eric, suggesting that one not only may, but indeed should, prepare one's witness for the possible ordeal of cross-examination. Another example is the question of whether one should take the sting out of a problem in evidence-in-chief rather than leaving it to be dealt with by the other side in cross-examination where, in paragraph 11.9, we have in contrast with Eric suggested that the former is generally preferable.
- To build on not only our own experience, but the collected wisdom of colleagues, judges and so forth with whom we have dealt.

Whether we have succeeded in any of these aims, we leave to the reader to decide.

Although the text of the book is written in the singular, it reflects both authors' views.

We have opted to use the male gender in order to make the content of the book more streamlined. Even-handedly referring to both ('he/she', etc) is cumbersome, preferring the female gender struck us (perhaps wrongly) as pretentious, and so we settled on the male as a reference to both. Therefore, please be assured that although we refer to the male gender we are in fact referring to both genders.

In the illustrations given, other than by way of reference to the law reports, we have used fictitious names, as did Eric and Hekkie, both in regard to counsel and in regard to the parties where we have deemed it to be more tactful to do so. We have tried to be particularly careful on this point where counsel concerned is still in active practice.

This work is principally an approach to technique and is not intended to be a text book on some specialised legal field. Where we have referred to the law we have attempted to reflect the legal position as at December 2009.

Our thanks are also extended to our colleague and friend Johann Engelbrecht SC of the Pretoria Bar for his complete revision of Chapter 19 (Criminal Cases).

John Mullins SC and Carlos da Silva SC
Pretoria
December 2009

Table of Contents

Abbreviations

AD	Appeal Court
AD	Appellate Division
All ER	All England Law Reports
All SA	All South African Law Reports
BCLR	Butterworths Constitutional Law Reports
BLR	Building Law Reports
Buch	Buchanan's Reports
C & B	The Quantum of Damages in Bodily and Fatal Injury Cases, by Corbett and Buchanan
C & P	Carrington and Payne's Nisi Prius Reports 1823–1841
ChD	Chancery Division
Cox CC	Cox's Criminal Cases 1843–1945
CPD	Cape Provincial Division
EDL	Eastern Districts Local Division
IR	Irish Reports
Lloyds Rep	Lloyd's Reports
Lloyd's Rep PN	Lloyd's Reports Professional Negligence
Menz	Menzies Law Reports
NLR	Natal Law Reports
NPD	Natal Provincial Division
OPD	Orange Free State Provincial Division
PH	Prentice Hall
PNLR	Professional Negligence Law Reports
QBD	Queen's Bench Division
SA	South African Law Reports
SACR	South African Criminal Law Reports
SC	Supreme Court
SWA	South West Africa
TLR	Times Law Reports
TPD	Transvaal Provincial Division
WLD	Witwatersrand Local Division

Table of Cases

Table of Statutes and Rules of Court

CONSTITUTIONAL COURT RULES

MAGISTRATE'S COURT RULES

UNIFORM RULES OF COURT

UNIFORM RULES OF PROFESSIONAL CONDUCT FOR ADVOCATES

Bibliography

Advocate [formerly *Consultus* 1988—1999]. 2000

Beck, C A *The Theory and Principle of Pleadings in Civil Actions*. 6 ed (2002). Butterworths

Bullen, E & Leake, S M *Precedents of Pleadings in Actions in the Queen's Bench Division of the High Court of Justice*. 12 ed. (1975). Stevens & Sons

Butler, D & Finsen, E *Arbitration in South Africa — Law and Practice*. (1993). Juta

Carroll, Lewis *Alice's Adventures in Wonderland*

Ceram, C W *Gods, Graves and Scholars*. 15 ed (1967). Knopf

Chandos, John *Norman Birkett — Uncommon Advocate* (1963). Mayflower

Charlesworth, J *The Law of Negligence*. 7 ed (1983). Sweet & Maxwell

Churchill, Winston *English Prisons and Borstal Systems* (1952). Routledge

Cilliers, A C *Law of Costs*. 3 ed (Looseleaf). LexisNexis

Corbett, M M & Buchanan, J C *The Quantum of Damages in Bodily Injuries and Fatal Injury Cases*. 2 ed. (1964). Juta

Cox, E W *The Advocate: His Training, Practice, Rights and Duties*. (1852)

Daniels, H *Beck's Theory and Principles of Pleadings in Civil Actions* 6 ed. (2002). Butterworths

De Jongh, H M 'The Gatsometer and Stopwatch Speed Checking' *Tydskrif vir Hedendaagse Regsgeleerdheid* Vol 31 (1968)

De Villiers, J E & MacIntosh, J C *The Law of Agency in South Africa*. 3 ed. (1981). Juta

Dickens, Charles *A Tale of Two Cities*

Donovan, J W *Skill in Trials*. 2 ed. (1899). Williamson Law Book Co.

Donovan, J W *Tact in Court*. 6 ed. (1915). Sweet & Maxwell Ltd.

Du Cann, Richard *The Art of the Advocate*. (1993) Penguin

Du Toit, Etienne *Commentary on the Criminal Procedure Act*. (Looseleaf). Juta

Du Toit, Etienne *Straf in Suid Afrika*. (1981). Juta

Erasmus, H J & Van Loggerenberg, D E *Jones & Buckle The Civil Practice of the Magistrates' Courts in South Africa*. (Looseleaf). Juta

Erasmus, H J & Van Loggerenberg, D E *Superior Court Practice*. (Looseleaf). Juta

Evans, Keith *The Golden Rules of Advocacy* (1993). Blackstone Press Limited

Gilbert, Michael *The Oxford Book of Legal Anecdotes* (1986). Oxford University Press

Glissan, J L *Cross-Examination Practice and Procedure: an Australian Perspective*. (1991). Butterworths

Gordon, Gerald H *Criminal Law of Scotland*. 2 ed. (1967). W Green & Son

Grays Inn. Continuing Education Committee *Guidelines to pupil barristers*

Grisham, John *The Innocent Man*. (2006). Century Press

Hahlo, H R and Kahn, Ellison *The South African Legal System and Its Background* (968). Juta

Halsbury *Laws of England*. Butterworths

Harris, R *Hints on Advocacy*. (1943). Sweet & Maxwell Ltd.

Harris, Richard KC *Illustrations in Advocacy*. 5 ed. (1915). Stevens & Heyns.

Harms, L T C *Amler's Precedents of Pleadings*. 6 ed. (2003). LexisNexis.

Harms, L T C *Civil Procedure in the Superior Courts*. (Looseleaf). LexisNexis

Hastings, Patrick KC *Cases in Court* (1949). William Heinemann Limited

Herbstein, J & Van Winsen, L de V. *The Civil Practice of the High Courts in South Africa*. 5 ed. (2009). Juta

Hoffman, L & Zeffertt, D *The South African Law of Evidence*. 3 ed. (1981). Butterworths

Hunt, P M A *South African Criminal Law and Procedure* Vol II. (1970). Juta

Hyam, Michael *Advocacy Skills* 4 ed (1999). Blackstone Press Ltd

Jackson, Rupert M & Powell, John L. *Jackson & Powell on Professional Liability*. 6 ed. (2007). Sweet & Maxwell

James, William *The Principles of Psychology*. (1890)

Joubert, WA (ed) *The Law of South Africa*. LexisNexis

Keeton, G W *Harris's Hints on Advocacy*. 18 ed (1943), Stevens

Marnewick, C G *Litigation Skills for South African Lawyers*. 2 ed. (2008). LexisNexis

Mayne, J D & McGregor, H *Damages* 12 ed. (1961). Sweet & Maxwell Ltd

McGregor, H *On Damages* 17 ed. (2004). Sweet & Maxwell Ltd

McKenzie, H S *The Law of Building Contracts and Arbitration in South Africa*. 3 ed. (1977). Juta

McKerron, R G *The Law of Delict*. 7 ed. (1971). Juta

Merula, Paulus *Manier van Procederen in die provintien van Hollandt, Zeelandt en West-Vrieslandt belangende civile zaken*. (1741).

Midgley, R. *Lawyers' Professional Liability*. (1992). Juta

Moore, C C *A Treatise on Facts*. (1908). Edward Thompson Co

Morris, H H *In My Anecdotage*. (1953). Central News Agency

Morris, H H *The First Forty Years*. (1949). Juta

Morrison and Leith *The Barrister's World and the Nature of Law* (1992). Open University Press

Mortimer, John *Clinging to the Wreckage: a part of life*. (1982). Magna Print

Mozley & Whitely *Law Dictionary*. 3 ed. (1908). Butterworths

Munkman, John *The Technique of Advocacy* (1991). Butterworths

Nathan, C J M, Barnett, M & Brink, A *Uniform Rules of Court* 4 ed. (1987). Juta

Odgers, W B *Principles of Pleadings and Practice of Civil Actions in the High Court of Justice*. 22 ed. (1981). Stevens & Sons

O'Dowd, A P *The Law of Evidence in South Africa*. (1963). Juta

Osborn, A S *Questioned Documents*. 2 ed. (1946). Boyd Printing Co

Phipson, S L *The Law of Evidence*. 13 ed. (1982). Sweet & Maxwell Ltd

Pistorius, D *Pollak on Jurisdiction*. 2 ed. (1993). Juta

Pollak, W *The South African Law of Jurisdiction*. (1937). Hortors Ltd

Practice Manual: KwaZulu-Natal and the Eastern Cape: Rules of Practice

Pyemont, L O P *Company Law of South Africa*. 6 ed. (1953). Juta

Rubin, L *The Law of Costs in South Africa*. (1949). Juta

Salhany, Roger E *Cross-Examination: The Art of the Advocate*. (1988). Butterworths

Schwikkard, PJ & Van der Merwe, S *Principles of Evidence*. 3 ed. (2009). Juta

Scoble, C N *The Law of Evidence in South Africa*. 3 ed. (1952). Butterworths.

Shakespeare *Hamlet*

Shakespeare *Henry IV*

Shakespeare *Henry VIII*

Shakespeare *The Merchant of Venice*

Silke, J M *The Law of Agency in South Africa*. 3 ed. (1981). Juta

Spencer-Bower, G *The Law Relating to Actionable Non-Disclosure*. 2 ed. (1923). Butterworths

Van Blerk, P *Legal Drafting: Civil Proceedings*. (1998). Juta

Van der Keesell, D G *Praelectiones Iuris Hodierni ad Hugonis Grotii Introduction ad Iusprudentiam Hollandicam*. (1771).

Van der Merwe, S W et al *Contract — General Principles*. 3 ed. (2007) Juta

Van Leeuwen, S *Censura Forensis*. (1662). Petri Leffen & Francisci Moyardi.

Van Leeuwen, S *Commentaries*.

Van Zyl *The Theory of the Judicial Practice of South Africa*. 2 ed. (1902). Juta

Visser, P J & Potgieter, J M *Law of Damages*. 2 ed. (2003). Juta

Van Zyl, C H & Van Zyl, G B *Judicial Practice in South Africa*. 4 ed. (1931). Juta

Victor, Caius Julius *Ars Rhetorica*

Voet. Vols I & 2. (Gane's Translation). Butterworths

Voet *Commentarius ad Pandectas* Title III. (1955). Butterworths Gane's Translation.

Von Clausewitz, Carl *On War* edited by Howard & Paret. (1984).

Watts, Alaric Alexander *The Siege of Belgrade*. (1820).

Wellman, Francis *The Art of Cross-Examination*. 4 ed. (1948). Garden City Books

Wessels, Sir J W *History of the Roman-Dutch Law*. (1908). African Book Co. Ltd

Wigmore, J H *Anglo-American System of Evidence in Trials at Common Law* vol IV, IX. 3 ed. (1983). Little Brown & Co.

Wills, William *Principles of Circumstantial Evidence*. 7 ed. (1936). Butterworths

Woolman, S et al *Constitutional Law of South Africa*. 2 ed (Looseleaf). Juta

Wrottesley, F J *On the Examination of Witnesses in Court*. 2 ed. (1931). Sweet & Maxwell Ltd.

Zeffertt, D and Paizes, A *The South African Law of Evidence*. 2 ed. (2009). LexisNexis

CHAPTER 1

An Introduction

The primary aim of this book is to serve as a mentor to young lawyers as they embark on their careers in litigation.

The young lawyer qualifies after attending university and thereafter completing either his[1] candidate attorneyship within a firm of attorneys or his pupillage at one of the Bars followed, in either event, by passing the relevant professional examinations. Yet that is but the commencement of the voyage. He is now launched upon the world, theoretically qualified to appear in the appropriate court and perhaps to plead for the liberty of an accused or the financial survival of a litigant. He may (and, if an advocate, will) come to stand up in the High Court before a judge, than whom (to misquote the poet) 'no Austrian army was ever more awfully arrayed'.[2] He may mumble incoherently and be unaware whether his Lordship's or her Ladyship's forbidding countenance is caused by displeasure or dyspepsia.

But how does he learn the art of advocacy? The knowledge of the law which is acquired at lectures is only a starting point. He won't learn much from watching films or television serials, and anything he does learn from that source is as likely as not to earn him the judicial rebuke that he is addressing a judge and not a jury. Learning by watching others might have its charms, but it has its distinct limitations as well. Bitter experience is, of course, one of the best teachers, but bitter experience is apt to leave in its wake a trail of destruction, or a clutch of ghosts that ever and anon will return to haunt their creator. Nature in the raw, it is said, is seldom mild, but the practice of the law can make raw nature seem in comparison like a day in spring to one with a long memory and a keen conscience.

If I can help the fledgling to avoid swearing off litigation forever in reaction to his first case in court (a kaleidoscopic affair where witnesses rush into and out of the witness-box with a rapidity that leaves one breathless, perhaps to the point of incoherence), I shall have at least done something to atone for my multitudinous sins. Also it may possibly benefit clients and courts if this work can help younger practitioners to present their cases with a little more dexterity and polish, and if some of their stumbling and fumbling can be eliminated.

However, no book will produce a genius; no tome is a substitute for hard work and no words will ever convey all that can be learned from personal experience. With that chastening thought in mind and with a painfully

---

[1] See the preface, where the use of the one gender in this book is explained, with apologies.
[2] The misquote is from the first line of the poem *The Siege of Belgrade* by Alaric Alexander Watts (1820).

acquired consciousness of my own limitations, I venture to offer assistance to the young practitioner.

It is my sincere hope that even my more experienced colleagues will find something of value in these pages. I am not so presumptuous as to believe that I can either teach or advise them but rather I would suggest that they will look upon what I say — if they look upon it at all — as an offering of ideas. To the extent that I have learnt from them I thank them; to the extent that they have suffered at my hands I apologise. However, I feel that they, too, may profit from the collated wisdom of others which will be found in the following pages.

This does not pretend to be a general textbook upon civil procedure, nor upon the rules of court nor, indeed, upon any aspect of practice. Yet inevitably, in dealing with the development and conduct of cases, it becomes necessary to make brief incursions into those fields, with a few forays into the law of evidence. Such incursions and forays should not be regarded as pretending to greater dignity than they actually possess. They are made with the sole purpose of assisting the young practitioner by directing his attention, where it is pertinent, to decided cases upon any point. Thus, perhaps, the process could be called the distillation of experience rather than the citation of authority. When authority is needed recourse should be had to the recognised textbooks on whatever problem is plaguing the practitioner at the moment. I have made an attempt, however, to analyse those aspects of the law which touch upon the practitioner in his conduct of cases because I believe that the books on practice, procedure, evidence and various branches of substantive law do not deal with all the matters which may arise, both in and out of court, in the course of one's day-by-day practice.

My purpose is to provide assistance, guidance, illustration and example to practitioners in the work of commencing cases, drawing pleadings, preparing for trial and conducting cases in court. Everything which I suggest is designed as part of the application of the technique involved in persuading a court ultimately to give judgment for your client.

The issues are approached with the emphasis more on the Bar than the Side-Bar. This is only natural given my background. Because advocates generally appear in the High Court, the stress must inevitably be on 'counsel' rather than on 'attorneys'. I would suggest though, that there can be no difficulty in applying the suggestions made in the following chapters to the work of attorneys. As far as chapter 2 is concerned, where I deal with the law affecting the practitioner, I have done my best to deal as fully with the position of attorneys as with that of counsel. Thus, the word 'practitioner' is used to denote both counsel and attorneys.

There is one more thing to say, something born, perhaps, of experience, regret or cynicism. It is this: the day may well come, in your life, as it has in the lives of so many practitioners, when a decision goes against you, and you think that the judge has erred so grievously that either there is no justice in the world or you are a complete failure and should look for another job. My word of encouragement is that judges are human beings. Human beings err.

Sometimes, when human beings wear judicial robes, they may err beyond human comprehension and beyond the practicability of an appeal.[3]

If I must illustrate let me refer to a case decided by the Appellate Division in 1970.[4,5] This started as an ordinary application brought to enforce what was alleged to be a binding contract giving the applicant the sole distributorship of the respondent's synthetic fertiliser in the then Orange Free State. The respondent, Sentrale Kunsmis, took the point that the contract was not binding because it had been entered into before the applicant had been incorporated and the applicant had not brought itself within the provisions of the Companies Act of the time. To this the applicant replied that, even if this were so, the contract was a *stipulatio alteri,* the benefit of which it had duly accepted after incorporation. The matter was heard by a single judge in the Transvaal Provincial Division,[6] and then on appeal by a Full Bench of three judges.[7] Finally, the matter was decided by five judges in the Appellate Division, with a majority of three to two. In the result, of all the nine judges who were troubled with the matter, six held in favour of the respondent. Yet it failed in the final instance because the minority three judges out of the nine who decided against it happened to represent the majority in the Appellate Division! If Sentrale Kunsmis has ever troubled to analyse the judgments as I have done here it might be forgiven a measure of frustration at the result.

See also *Kessoopersadh and Another v Essop and Another*[8] where the Appellate Division allowed the appeal, also by a majority of three to two. The respondent lost, although he was successful in the initial proceedings[9] and a subsequent appeal to the Full Bench.[10] In the final event six judges held in his favour and three against, yet he lost.

So it may be with you. Perhaps, to take another metaphor, as your perspective lengthens your angle of vision will change so that you will see where you failed, and why you failed. For fail you will. Or yet it may be that you will have the joy of reading another judgment in another court — perhaps of higher jurisdiction — where your every argument is vindicated, where you now say: 'I was right, the judge was wrong!' And then you will ask yourself: Why was he wrong? Who was at fault — the judge or I? Nor will you ever know. *C'est la vie; c'est le droit.*

[3] See chapter 18 infra.

[4] *Sentrale Kunsmis Korporasie (Edms) Bpk v NKP Kunsmisverspreiders (Edms) Bpk* 1970 (3) SA 367 (A).

[5] Where, as here, examples of some vintage have been retained in the book, this is because notwithstanding their age they retain their force. This is explained in the preface.

[6] 1969 (1) SA 362 (T).

[7] 1969 (3) SA 82 (T).

[8] 1970 (1) SA 265 (A).

[9] 1968 (4) SA 610 (N).

[10] Unreported, but confirmed on appeal on 7 March 1969.

CHAPTER 2

The Law and the Practitioner

Before developing and utilising effective litigation technique, a legal practitioner must know his legal limitations. This chapter will deal with these limitations under the following list of topics:

1. The Authority of Attorneys and Counsel.
2. The Duty of Attorneys and Counsel to their Clients.
3. Liability for Negligence: Attorneys and Counsel.
4. Attorneys' Duty in Filing Papers.
5. Disagreement with Client.
6. The Drawing of Pleadings.
7. Admissions by Legal Representatives.
8. The Duty of Disclosure to the Court.
9. Evidence by Legal Representatives.
10. Freedom of Speech in Court.
11. Freedom of Counsel in Court.
12. Contempt of Court.
13. Recusal and Cautionary Rules.

2.1 THE AUTHORITY OF ATTORNEYS AND COUNSEL

2.1.1 Attorneys

An attorney's contract with his client is one of mandate.[1] The scope of the attorney's duties, and of his authority, is to be found in the contract. It is no broader, nor narrower, than envisaged by the contract. An English judge described these parameters thus:[2]

---

[1] Potgieter JA *Goodricke & Son v Auto Protection Insurance Co* 1968 (1) SA 717 (A) at 722H. See also *Eksteen v Van Schalkwyk en 'n Ander* 1991 (2) SA 39 (T) 42–3.

[2] Laddie J *Credit Lyonnais SA v Russell, Jones & Walker* [2003] Lloyd's Rep PN 7 (Ch) at 10. See also *Midland Bank Trust C. Limited v Hett, Stubbs & Kemp* [1978] 3 All ER 571 (Ch). The editors of the 6th edition of *Jackson and Powell On Professional Liability* say at 655 that the '*fons et origo* of a solicitor's duties is the retainer (or contract of engagement) between himself and the client', and it seems unlikely that an attorney could be held to owe his client a duty of care going beyond the duties which he has contractually undertaken. It is, after all, as illogical to suggest that an attorney can be held liable to his client for not doing something for the doing of which he would not have been entitled to charge a fee, as it would be to allow him to charge his client a fee for doing something which he was not contracted to do. Laddie J, for example, held in *Credit Lyonnais* that the solicitors in question ought to have informed their client of a fact which they came across in the course of carrying out their retainer, but he emphasised that this duty arose out of the contract of mandate, saying at 11 that the solicitor 'is under no general obligation to expend time and effort on issues outside the retainer. However if, in the course of doing that for which he is retained, he becomes aware of a risk

4

> In deciding what are the duties shouldered by a solicitor, the first step is to construe the terms of the instructions given by the client and accepted by the lawyer. In doing this, it must be borne in mind that in most cases the client is not a lawyer. He will ask the lawyer to carry out certain tasks for him, although the formulation of those tasks may not be expressed with the precision one would expect of a lawyer. The lawyer accepts the instructions on that basis. . . . The lawyer's duty . . . covers the width of the instructions given . . .

The filing of a power of attorney is not required, either in the High Court, or in the magistrate's court. However, if the authority of an attorney to act on behalf of a litigant is challenged, the onus is upon him to satisfy the court that he has authority so to act.[3]

Notwithstanding that a power of attorney is not required (unless and until there is a challenge), it remains an advisable step. There is no good reason why the attorney should not draft a detailed power of attorney outlining the nature of the instruction and of his powers, and even detail of his fees. The power of attorney should preferably cover the actual relief to be claimed in the summons, and should be authorised by a resolution in the case of a company, close corporation or public authority.[4]

Naturally, the attorney's mandate includes the power to do everything that is incidental to the carrying out of his instruction, unless specifically excluded. For example, in regard to proceedings instituted in the High Court it seems that an attorney has authority to brief counsel unless the parties have specifically agreed otherwise. Silke in *The Law of Agency in South Africa*[5] cites the case of *Bell & Hutton v Sassin*[6] as authority for the proposition that an attorney has authority to brief counsel. However, the attorneys there had in fact specifically been authorised to brief a particular counsel and the only question seems to have been whether the delivery of the brief was premature. The likelihood is that, if the matter is one in which the services of counsel might conceivably be employed (and that would include an action in the magistrate's court), the instruction to the attorney to conduct the proceedings tacitly includes the authority to brief counsel.

It should be remembered that in practice counsel generally looks to the attorney for payment of his fees,[7] so that the attorney would be well advised to

---

or a potential risk to the client, it is his duty to inform the client. In doing that he is neither going beyond the scope of his instructions nor is he doing "extra" work for which he is not to be paid. He is simply reporting back to the client on issues of concern which he learns of as a result of, and in the course of, carrying out his . . . instructions'.

[3] Rules 7 and 16 of the Uniform Rules of Court and rule 52(2) of the Magistrates' Court Rules. See *LAWSA* vol 14 2 ed part 2 para 305. In regard to inferred authority and discharge of proof, see *Administrator Transvaal v Mponyane and Others* 1990 (4) SA 407 (T).

[4] Cf *Town Council of Brakpan v Cohen and Others* 1938 WLD 146.

[5] 3 ed 158.

[6] 1928 EDL 445.

[7] *In re Rome* 1991 (3) SA 291 (A) at 306D, *Minister of Finance and Another v Law Society, Transvaal* 1991 (4) SA 544 (A) at 552D–553D, *Bertelsmann v Per* 1996 (2) SA 375 (T) at 380–3, and R Midgley *Lawyers' Professional Liability* 14.

make his client aware both of the fact that he is briefing counsel and of the likely costs implications of his doing so.[8]

Three aspects of the authority of an attorney in litigation which give rise to difficulties are the questions of whether power to conduct a law suit includes the power to note an appeal or to take further proceedings, whether an attorney has the power to submit a case to arbitration rather than to court, and the question of whether the attorney has the power to compromise the lawsuit.

It is well established that the attorney has the power to note an appeal, but that a separate or specific authority would be required to enable the attorney to prosecute the appeal.

Innes CJ made these observations at 498 of *D & DH Fraser Limited v Waller*:[9]

> It has not been the general practice of South African courts to apply a rigid interpretation to documents like the one before us and to hold that the authority of an attorney appointed to conduct a suit before a particular tribunal absolutely ceases *post latam sententiam*. It has been held to continue for supplementary purposes such as enforcing execution, or obtaining orders for sequestration or civil imprisonment; it has also been deemed sufficient to validate the service of notice of appeal. . . .

(The suggestion that a mandate to recover a debt includes authority to institute sequestration proceedings should perhaps be viewed with caution.)[10]

There is some doubt as to whether an attorney has the power to agree to submit a case to arbitration.[11] This seems correct. But every case will turn on its own facts. If the contract which the attorney is asked to enforce provides for arbitration, then logically the mandate includes the power to proceed to arbitration. If, on the other hand, the contract is silent on the point, then the

---

[8] *Howe v Church* 1941 TPD 611, *D & DH Fraser Limited v Waller* 1916 AD 494, *Pretoria City Council v Meerlust Investments (Pty) Limited* 1962 (1) SA 321 (A), and *Scottish Tube Co of SA Limited v Rodgers* 1966 (4) SA 526 (GW). Cf *Afglow Land & Cattle Co (Pty) Limited v Napier* 1972 (1) SA 430 (RAD).

[9] 1916 AD 494.

[10] JM Silke *The Law of Agency in South Africa* 3 ed 153 n15 states that: 'Authority to sue for a debt due does not include authority to institute sequestration proceedings'. The cases cited by the learned authors do not touch upon the dictum of Innes CJ, but there is considerable force in the proposition that an attorney should obtain his client's specific mandate before embarking on the relatively expensive and potentially far-reaching procedure of sequestration or liquidation. The words of De Villiers CJ in *Collett v Priest* 1931 AD 290 at 299 must not be overlooked: 'The order placing a person's estate under sequestration cannot fittingly be described as an order for a debt due by the debtor to the creditor. Sequestration proceedings are instituted by a creditor against a debtor not for the purpose of claiming something from the latter, but for the purpose of setting the machinery of the law in motion to have the debtor declared insolvent. No order in the nature of a declaration of rights or of giving or doing something is given against the debtor. The order sequestrating his estate affects the civil status of the debtor and results in vesting his estate in the Master. No doubt, before an order so serious in its consequences to the debtor is given the court satisfies itself as to the correctness of the allegations in the petition. It may for example have to determine if the debtor owes the money as alleged in the petition. But while the court has to determine whether the allegations are correct, there is no claim by the creditor against the debtor to pay him what is due nor is the court asked to give any judgment, decree or order against the debtor upon any such claim'.

[11] Botha J at 751G of *Inter-Continental Finance & Leasing Corp (Pty) Limited v Stands 56 and 57 Industria* 1979 (3) SA 740 (W).

attorney would probably require specific authority before choosing arbitration over the, at least theoretically, less expensive route of litigation.

In regard to compromise, the law appears to be in a state of some uncertainty. What is clear is that the attorney has the power of compromise where that power is included in the power of attorney, or where the attorney is otherwise specifically authorised to compromise.[12] As to whether the power to compromise is implied in the absence of a specific provision in a contract, there are two lines of cases: the one to the effect that it is,[13] and the other to the effect that it is not.[14] It seems that the former line of cases is based on principles of English law, and that the better approach is that founded in Roman-Dutch law to the effect that an attorney may not compromise his client's claim without specific authority to do so. *Voet* says the following in this regard:[15]

> **Attorney for suit has no power to compromise** — In this connection it should also be noted that an attorney appointed to sue cannot compromise . . .

The law, after all, is notoriously suggested not to resemble an ass and it would be, as Van Heerden J (as he then was) said in *Goosen v Van Zyl*,[16] 'surprising indeed' for a client who instructed an attorney to sue for a certain amount of money to be told that the attorney had settled without reference to him for a lesser amount.

As usual, the answer is a simple one: don't take a risk if you don't have to. Do not settle without the specific authority of your client. Even in an emergency, real or imaginary, an attorney should be most circumspect about compromising his client's case or he may find himself in the same position as the defendant in *Mfaswe v Miller*[17] whose articled clerk compromised a claim to avoid a probable

---

[12] *Glaser v Millward* 1950 (4) SA 587 (W) 590H — in fine, *Goosen v Van Zyl* 1980 (1) SA 706 (O) and *Hlobo v Multilateral Motor Vehicle Accidents Fund* 2001 (2) SA 59 (SCA) at 65I.

[13] *Dhlamini v Minister of Law and Order and Another* 1986 (4) SA 342 (D) at 346I–348A, *Ivoral Properties (Pty) Limited v Sheriff, Cape Town, and Others* 2005 (6) SA 96 (C) at 119D–F, and *MEC for Economic Affairs, Environment and Tourism v Kruisenga and Another* 2008 (6) SA 264 (Ck) 295D–296E. It is submitted that the comments of Plewman JA to the same effect at 65C–E of *Hlobo v Multilateral Motor Vehicle Accidents Fund* 2001 (2) SA 59 (SCA) are *obiter* because the attorney in that instance was in fact specifically authorised by his client to compromise the claim. See 64E and 65I of the judgment.

[14] Midgley *Lawyers' Professional Liability* 10 and 16, *LAWSA* vol 14 2 ed part 2 para 305 at 262, *Paramount Stores Limited v Hendry (1)* 1957 (2) SA 451 (W) at 452E–F, *Ras v Liquor Licensing Board, Area No. 11, Kimberley* 1966 (2) SA 232 (C) at 237, *Goosen v Van Zyl* 1980 (1) SA 706 (O) at 709F–H; *Transvaal Canoe Union v Butgereit and Another* 1990 (3) SA 398 (T) 409–410.

[15] *Voet* 3.3.18 (Gane's Translation, vol 1 at 533–534). In this regard the translator states at 511 that Voet's statement has led to some differences of opinion, and he sets out certain authorities at 533 fn(d). To these authorities should be added the cases listed here. See also Midgley *Lawyers' Professional Liability* 10: 'In Roman-Dutch law an agent (*gemachtigde* or *procurator*) could not compromise a suit on behalf of his principal. This rule was extended to attorneys [fn 106: *Voet* 3.3.18; *Van der Keessel* 3.4.2; *Huber* 4.17.20]'.

[16] *Goosen v Van Zyl* 1980 (1) SA 706 (O) at 709H: 'Dit sou inderdaad verbasend gewees het indien 'n prokureur met 'n blote opdrag om 'n skrywe ter invordering van 'n bedrag te rig, 'n inbegrepe volmag sou hê om enige mindere bedrag ter skikking van sy kliënt se vordering te aanvaar. Sodanige aanvaarding sou immers in stryd wees met die wese van die opdrag om die volle bedrag te vorder.'

[17] *Mfaswe v Miller* (1901) 18 SC 172.

judgment of absolution from the instance, only to find that the client would, apparently, have been prepared to suffer the latter fate with costs, rather than have his claim compromised. It would be unsound to believe that all clients are the acme of reasonableness, because experience teaches that even where a client puts his signature to the deed of settlement himself, he will afterwards deny all involvement and blame his attorney. Only a bold practitioner will take upon himself the responsibility of compromising his client's claim without a very clear authority (preferably in writing) to do so.

One must of course distinguish between actual and ostensible authority. It might well happen that the client is bound by an unauthorised compromise entered into by his attorney on his behalf, on the basis that the attorney was ostensibly authorised, ie, that the other side was fully entitled to assume that the attorney had been authorised.[18] But, although the client might in such circumstances be held bound by the compromise, he would have a claim against his attorney if the compromise was prejudicial.

There is, in addition, authority to the effect that an attorney should consult with his client before rejecting a settlement proposal, however much he might regard the offer as being beneath his contempt. In *Goldschmidt and Another v Folb and Another*[19] Botha J said:

> An attorney would be failing in his duty to his client if he did not consult with his client on a proposal for settlement coming from the other side before answering such a proposal. His answer to such proposal is a necessary and proper step in connection with the conduct of the action, and the preceding consultation with his client stands on the same footing.

2.1.2 Counsel

The reported cases offer less guidance in regard to the authority of counsel.

What the cases do affirm is that, within the limits of the brief and subject to any specific instructions, counsel has a complete discretion in the conduct of a case. Blackburn J put it as follows in *Strauss v Francis*:[20]

> Mr Kenealy has ventured to suggest that the retainer of counsel in a cause simply implies the exercise of his power of argument and eloquence. But counsel have far higher attributes, namely, the exercise of judgment and discretion on emergencies arising in the conduct of a cause, and a client is guided in his selection of counsel by his reputation for honour, skill and discretion. Few counsel, I hope, would accept a brief on the unworthy terms that he is simply to be the mouthpiece of his client. Counsel, therefore, being ordinarily retained to conduct a cause without any limitation, the apparent authority with which he is clothed when he appears to conduct the cause is to do everything which, in the exercise of his discretion, he may think best for the interests of his client in the conduct of the cause: and if within the

---

[18] See for example *Hlobo v Multilateral Motor Vehicle Accidents Fund* 2001 (2) SA 59 (SCA) at para [11] where Plewman JA pointed out that even had the attorney not been specifically authorised to compromise, he was ostensibly so authorised.

[19] *Goldschmidt and Another v Folb and Another* 1974 (3) SA 778 (T) at 781H.

[20] (1866) LR 1 QB 379 at 381.

limits of this apparent authority he enters into an agreement with the opposite counsel as to the cause, on every principle this agreement should be held binding.

Later at 382–3 he put it thus:

> I am therefore clearly of opinion that the withdrawal of a juror in the present case is binding. In so deciding, I do not mean to say that counsel can compel a client to enter into a compromise by consenting to the withdrawal of a juror against his will. If the counsel cannot induce his client to act on his advice in such a case, the proper course is to return his brief. Nor do we decide that, if the client's dissent were known to the other side, such a compromise would be binding. All we decide is that when a counsel, acting within his apparent authority, consents to withdraw a juror, the other side, acting fairly, may safely rely on the compromise being binding; and that, in order to invalidate the arrangement, not only must it be shewn that the counsel's authority was limited, but that the limitation was known to the other side at the time.

That counsel (and this would presumably apply equally to an attorney doing the work of an advocate[21]) has a complete discretion in the conduct of the case as such is logical: no counsel, certainly none with any self-respect, would be either able or willing to continually seek his client's consent for every one of the myriad small and large decisions which have to be taken in the running of a case (whether to plead a particular point or not, whether to call a particular witness or not, what to put to the witness, how to approach cross-examination, whether to object or not, what to argue, etc). As Schreiner JA said in *R v Matonsi*:[22]

> I have found no Roman-Dutch or South African authority which supports the view that the accused in a criminal case can question his counsel's conduct of the trial. . . . Such Roman-Dutch writers as I have consulted emphasise the importance and high status of the advocate and I see no reason to doubt that his authority over the conduct of the case which he has been instructed to fight on behalf of a client was quite as full as that of the English barrister (cf *Klopper v Van Rensburg* 1920 EDL 239 at 242). The English cases show that in general, trials cannot be conducted partly by the client and partly by counsel. Once the client has placed his case in the hands of counsel the latter has complete control and it is he who must decide whether a particular witness, including the client, is to be called or not. . . .
> . . . [O]n the assumption that the appellant was entitled at the close of the Crown case to withdraw the mandate of counsel, there is nothing on the record to suggest that he attempted to do so. It is true that in the case of an ignorant accused who wishes, contrary to his counsel's advice, to give evidence, it would be proper for counsel to satisfy himself that the accused understood that he was entitled to withdraw the mandate . . .

Notwithstanding the breadth of counsel's discretion, one aspect with regard to which counsel would be well advised to obtain specific instructions from the client — in writing if necessary — is whether the client is to be called as a witness. This is especially so in criminal cases. If your client wants to give evidence but you, unimpressed with his frank and open countenance and

---

[21] *Van der Berg v General Council of the Bar of SA* [2007] 2 All SA 499 (SCA) at para [14].
[22] *R v Matonsi* 1958 (2) SA 450 (A) at 456–7. See also *S v Mkhise* 1988 (2) SA 868 (A).

commanding mien, decide that he should not venture within ten kilometres of the witness-box, pray devoutly that you do not lose the case. Your client will be satisfied that defeat would have been turned into victory had you allowed him to testify, and that it was your blundering incompetence that lost the case. It will not avail you to point out precisely why the slaughter would have been the worse had he testified. In your client's eyes (and in the ears of everyone he talks to), you will be damned forever. Strangely enough, if against your better judgment you allow your client to testify and the slaughter which your better judgment predicted ensues, he will blame you for this as well. The best course is for you to remember that your purpose is to do the best you can for your client and if, in your judgment, that includes keeping him out of the witness-box, then that is what you should do — but only after canvassing it with him first.

Finally, although there is authority, following English law, to the effect that counsel's discretion includes authority to compromise in the absence of his client,[23] this authority must be approached with caution. Most clients would, I suggest, be shocked to hear that their advocate (who, after all, was chosen by their attorney and not by them) has the power to compromise their case without reference to them.

A distinction must, it is suggested, be drawn between the authority of counsel to make those *concessions* that, in his discretion, need to be made in the conduct of a case (that a point is not good, that an aspect of the claim cannot be proven, that proof might not be of the amount claimed but of a lesser amount, etc), and *compromise* of the claim as such. The former is, I suggest, authorised and the latter not.[24]

Defining the dividing line between those concessions which counsel may make in the course of his conduct of the case, and the compromising of his client's claim or defence which he may not, is difficult. But perhaps, like other things in life, the dividing line is easier to recognise than to define. Counsel who is asked, on his feet, whether a point is good or an item proven, is free in

---

[23] See, in England, *Matthews v Munster* (1888) 20 QBD 141 and, in South Africa, *Klopper v Van Rensburg* 1920 EDL 239 at 242, *Dhlamini v Minister of Law and Order and Another* 1986 (4) SA 342 (D) at 346I–348A, *Ivoral Properties (Pty) Limited v Sheriff, Cape Town, and Others* 2005 (6) SA 96 (C) at 119D–F, and the *obiter* comments of Plewman JA in *Hlobo v Multilateral Motor Vehicle Accidents Fund* 2001 (2) SA 59 (SCA) at 65C–E.

[24] This is also the view of Judge van Dijkhorst in his contribution to *LAWSA* vol 14 'Advocates' 2 ed part 2 para 144 at 152: 'Unless counsel receives instructions, either express or implied, to compromise, he has no authority to do so.' See also *Hawkes v Hawkes and Another* 2007 (2) SA 100 (SE) where Leach J allowed the client to resile from an undertaking which her advocate had given. The advocate no doubt thought that in the circumstances the undertaking was justified, but he had no mandate to give it, and in fact his instructions were to oppose the application in question. The learned judge held as follows at 104D–H: 'In the normal course of events the conduct of a party's case at a trial of an action is in the entire control of such party's counsel. However, although counsel has authority to compromise an action or any matter in it, no such compromise will be binding if it flies in the face of client's instructions to the contrary. . . . [T]he undertaking . . . amounted to a capitulation, which was contrary to his instructions to oppose the : . . relief. . . . This amounted to a failure of justice and in my view a court will not hold a party bound by an agreement concluded in such circumstances'.

his discretion to make the concessions which he feels are justified, but counsel who is asked whether his client ought not to give an undertaking which would compromise the case is not entitled to accede without his client's authority (the matter can be stood down for a discussion with the client). This, it is suggested, is the case no matter how much counsel might, at that moment and in the full glare of the Bench, feel that the compromise is justified.

The answer, again, is simple: like the attorney, the advocate also should not think of settling without the specific authority of the client.

2.2 THE DUTY OF ATTORNEYS AND COUNSEL TO THEIR CLIENTS

2.2.1 Attorneys

Clients are one of the occupational hazards of attorneys. The result is that in the law reports there can be found a fair amount of learning in regard to the duties of the latter to the former.

The relationship between an attorney and his client was discussed by Cillié J in *Goodriche & Son v Auto Protection Insurance Co Ltd (In Liquidation)*[25] where the learned judge pointed out that with the exception of advisory, consultative or similar functions the legal principles applying are those of the law of agency. There is a very full discussion of the relationship at 504–8 of the report which may be summarised as follows:

- despite the wishes of the client the attorney must not do or be party to anything tainted with fraud, or mean or dishonourable;
- although the client may not (is not entitled to) prescribe the manner in which the services are to be rendered, the attorney must at all times act subject to the proper instructions of the client;
- the attorney has a duty to report to his client when it is reasonable or necessary;[26]
- he owes his client a duty of good faith;
- he must manifest in all business matters an inflexible regard for truth, there must be a vigorous accuracy in minutiae, a high sense of honour and incorruptible integrity;[27]
- he is bound to keep the secrets and confidences of his client.

An attorney may not act in litigation against his client or former client where he may have acquired confidential information about the client. Should the

---

[25] 1967 (2) SA 501 (W) at 503. See also *Law Society of Transvaal v Matthews* 1989 (4) SA 389 (T) at 396 and *Barlow Rand Ltd T/A Barlow Noordelike Masjienerie Maatskappy v Lebos and Another* 1985 (4) SA 335 (T).

[26] Failure to do so, or to notify the client of particular steps in the litigation, such as a notice of bar, may be gross negligence: *Du Plessis v Tager* 1953 (2) SA 275 (O) at 280.

[27] Quoting Van Zyl *Judicial Practice in South Africa* 4 ed 33.

attorney do so or attempt to do so the client will be entitled to an interdict restraining the attorney from acting.[28]

Perhaps one of the most important duties owed by an attorney to his client is not to take advantage of the influence which, in many cases, he may be able to exercise over the client. Inevitably the client trusts his attorney, or one would find him taking his business elsewhere, and inevitably the attorney will become acquainted with the financial position of the client to an extent which goes beyond the bounds of the matter in hand. It is very easy for the attorney to be in a position to benefit himself by means of transactions with his client or to take advantage of his client's circumstances. For this reason, at any rate where the client has not had the benefit of independent legal advice, there is the risk that any transaction entered into between them may be set aside on the ground of undue influence.[29]

Within the limits stated by Cillié J, it is submitted that the attorney has a complete discretion as to the manner in which he will present the client's case, consistent with the exercise of due diligence, care and skill.

A matter which arises from experience is that pressure of work often causes attorneys to lose sight of time limits prescribed by the rules of the various courts, especially in regard to the noting and prosecution of appeals. The court will usually grant condonation for a failure to observe time limits but, as Steyn CJ said in *Salojee v Minister of Community Development*:[30]

> The court has on a number of occasions demonstrated its reluctance to penalise a litigant on account of the conduct of his attorney. . . . I should point out, however, that it has not at any time been held that condonation will not in any circumstances be withheld if the blame lies with the attorney. There is a limit beyond which a litigant cannot escape the results of his attorney's lack of diligence or the insufficiency of the explanation tendered. To hold otherwise might have a disastrous effect upon the observance of the rules of this court. Considerations *ad misericordiam* should not be allowed to become an invitation to laxity. In fact this court has lately been burdened with an undue and increasing number of applications for condonation in which the failure to comply with the rules of this court was due to neglect on the part of the attorney. The attorney, after all, is the representative whom the litigant has chosen for himself, and there is little reason why, in regard to condonation of a failure to comply with a rule of court, the litigant should be absolved from the normal consequences of such a relationship no matter what the circumstances of the failure are.

In *P E Bosman Transport Works Committee v Piet Bosman Transport*[31] the court found that even where 'virtually all the blame can be attributed to the applicant's attorney's, condonation ought not . . . to be granted'. This is an

---

[28] *Robinson v Van Hulsteyn, Feltham & Ford* 1925 AD 12, per Wessels JA at 21–3. See also *Dunbrody Mission v Cunningham and Others* 1926 EDL 264, where the interdict was refused on the ground of the tacit consent of the client.

[29] *Armstrong v Magid and Another* 1937 AD 260 and *Miller v Miller* 1965 (4) SA 458 (C) at 462–3. See, for the principles relating to undue influence in general, *Preller v Jordaan* 1956 (1) SA 483 (A) and *Patel v Grobbelaar* 1974 (1) SA 532 (A) at 533–4.

[30] 1965 (2) SA 135 (A) at 140–1.

[31] 1980 (4) SA 794 (A).

extreme example of negligence and dilatoriness on the part of the attorneys but serves to illustrate the point that attorneys and counsel are in duty bound to perform their duties with diligence and the utmost care.

Apart from statutory provision[32] the court has an inherent power to order an attorney to pay the costs of a case in certain circumstances. A list of the cases may be found in Cilliers *The Law of Costs*.[33] The author says that the 'court will in appropriate circumstances award costs *de bonis propriis* against an attorney', and cites a number of examples where this occurred.

2.2.2 Counsel

Counsel who desires to ascertain the extent of his duties towards his clients in the conduct of their cases would be well advised to read volume 14 of *LAWSA*. Counsel's duties may be summarised as follows: firstly, there is the requirement of loyalty to the client. This entails the advocate's duty of good faith and the obligation to further the client's cause to the best of his ability. Further, there is the requirement of candour to the court which entails not only frankness and truthfulness, but absence of deceit in any form and due respect for the judge. There is a requirement of fairness to the adversary, namely the opposite party, his witnesses and his counsel. There is the obligation to adhere strictly to the rules of the society of which he is a member and to which he has subscribed. Counsel is not a mere agent of his client; his duty to the court overrides his obligations to his client, subject to his duty not to disclose the confidences of his client.[34]

Counsel is in a better position than an attorney because he is required, and entitled, to act only when specifically and properly briefed thereto. The brief will indicate the particular purpose for which counsel has been briefed and his function is limited to his instructions. Of course counsel will not hesitate to draw the attention of the instructing attorney to any matter which he thinks requires consideration or action by the attorney and will not regard his instructions as metaphorical blinkers. All too often it happens that pressure of work (and the fact that counsel is to be briefed) may cause an attorney to overlook some matter that must be handled urgently. I doubt whether counsel would receive much sympathy at the wound-licking ceremony if he offered the defence that he had been briefed to draw a particular pleading and not to teach the attorney his job, much less to do it for him. No counsel should ever handle a brief without acquainting himself with every document and fact therein, and if counsel considers or discovers that something must be done, all that is needed is a tactful suggestion or inquiry.

Counsel, of course, is not specifically saddled with the burden of observing time limits in the filing of documents — not that he can disregard such time limits when he has been timeously briefed to draw a pleading or other

---

[32] Section 74 of the Insolvency Act 24 of 1936.
[33] A C Cilliers *The Law of Costs* 3 ed para 10.25.
[34] *LAWSA* vol 14 2 ed part 2 para 132.

document or to advise on a proposed course of action. It is suggested that the judgment of Cillié J[35] referred to earlier could fairly be read as laying down the duties of counsel to their clients, and that the previous summary of that judgment should be regarded as of equal application to counsel save that they are under no duty to report to their clients. Should any report become necessary that report will have to be made to the instructing attorney. However, in almost all cases, counsel's authority is defined on his brief, and so his memorandum on the brief will be a sufficient report.

A decision which should be engraved on the heart of every advocate is that of *Duncan v Roets*.[36] After a direction by the judge sitting in the Motion Court on a Thursday setting the matter down for hearing on the following Tuesday, application was made on the Tuesday for a postponement. The application was dealt with by Lucas AJ in the following terms:[37]

> I am informed by Mr B, who is briefed to apply for the postponement, that counsel who had been engaged for the respondent could not appear today. I do not think that is any reason why the case should be postponed. While the court will do its best to meet the convenience of counsel, convenience of litigants must have prior consideration. Counsel must make themselves available for the dates assigned or else surrender their briefs.

In that case the postponement was refused and, because counsel who moved the postponement had not been briefed on the merits of the application, he was forced to seek leave to withdraw from the matter. The client was left without representation, due solely to the fault of counsel who failed to surrender his brief when notified that the matter had been set down for a day on which he was not available. Perhaps this is not only a duty owed to the client; it is a duty owed to oneself also.

No doubt many cases will occur where one can retain two or more briefs for the same day and get away with it. After all, cases have the habit of becoming settled overnight. But, when one has gone through sleepless nights worrying what will happen if one of the cases is not settled, one is cured of the temptation to live dangerously. Naturally, sometimes counsel will be able to earn two fees on one day, but sooner or later there will come disaster, as in *Duncan v Roets* where the unfortunate respondent was ejected, perhaps rightly, but without his case being adequately presented to the court.

This problem is not a new one for in 1741 we find Merula stating:

> *De Advocaten en behooren geen meer zaaken aan te nemen, dan zy met gemak en goede commoditeyt konnen expedieren, en ten uyteneinde brengen, zonder der Partyen recht te zeer te verachte.*[38]

---

[35] *Goodriche & Son v Auto Protection Insurance Co Ltd (In Liquidation)* 1967 (2) SA 501 (W).
[36] *Duncan v Roets* 1949 (1) SA 226 (T).
[37] *Ibid* at 227.
[38] *Manier van Procederen* 17.5.1: 'The advocate also should not take on more cases than he can manage with ease and good comfort and can bring to finality without unduly prejudicing the parties' rights.'

2.3 LIABILITY FOR NEGLIGENCE: ATTORNEYS AND COUNSEL

In this section it is proposed to only discuss cases in which actions for damages have been brought by disgruntled clients against attorneys arising out of work done in the course of litigation. The reason is to be found in the title of this book.

Attorneys are most at risk, primarily because of their more direct relationship with the client, but also because the most fruitful source of professional negligence actions lies in the failure to timeously attend to the institution of actions or the filing of documents, conduct which is essentially within the realm of the attorney. It is probably for these reasons that section 40B of the Attorneys Act[39] provides primary layer cover to all practising attorneys.[40] Attorneys would be well advised not to rely only on this primary cover, but to pay for additional insurance as well.

Advocates are less vulnerable to such actions. Whether they have more skill in the conduct of actions is a point on which, no doubt, differing opinions are held. However, counsel specialises in trial work (leaving out matters such as opinions and consultations) as opposed to the mass of routine with which an attorney's practice is beset. Also, at least theoretically, counsel can devote more time and thought to the preparation of his cases and should consequently not as easily be guilty of errors of judgment. That said, counsel's responsibilities are as onerous as are those of attorneys, and although the reported cases in South Africa do not appear to reflect any matter in which counsel has been sued by his client, that is likely to change.[41]

2.3.1 Attorneys

The relationship between attorney and client is a contractual one, imposing upon the attorney the duty of exercising due skill and care in the conduct of the client's affairs.[42]

For an action for damages to lie against an attorney there must have been a want of the contracted-for degree of skill or care. The attorney will normally be

---

[39] Act 53 of 1979.

[40] Section 40B grants primary layer cover to all practising attorneys against legal liability 'arising out of the conduct of the profession by the insured'.

[41] The reported cases in England, for example, show that counsel are increasingly being sued, often in conjunction with their solicitors. See, for example, *Arthur JS Hall & Co v Simons* [2000] 3 All ER 673 (HL), *Green v Hancocks and Another* [2000] PNLR 813 (Ch), *Prettys v Michael John Carter* [2001] Lloyd's Rep PN 832 (Q), *Moy v Pettman, Smith and Another* [2005] PNLR 24 (HL) and *Williams v Thompson Leatherdale and Another* [2009] PNLR 15 (Q). See para 2.3.2 below, where the question of counsel's liability, and in particular the question of whether counsel are immune from suit at the hands of disgruntled clients, is considered in more detail.

[42] *Bruce NO v Berman* 1963 (3) SA 21 (T), per Vieyra AJ at 23. See also *Mouton v Die Mynwerkersunie* 1977 (1) SA 119 (A) at 142. The client can proceed against the attorney in contract and, in the alternative, in delict; see *Rampal and Another v Brett, Wills & Pinks* 1981 (4) SA 360 (D).

judged by the standard of the reasonably competent practitioner,[43] although he could be judged by a higher standard if that is the basis upon which the parties contracted. The latter would be the case where the attorney held himself out to be a specialist.[44]

No liability will arise merely because the attorney has committed an error of judgment falling short of negligence, whether on matters of discretion or of law. The task of an attorney is a difficult one, calling for him to exercise his judgment on many issues. The mere fact that his decision on a particular point or to adopt a particular course transpires later to have been wrong does not mean that it was necessarily negligent.[45] It may be of some assistance to quote a passage from the judgment of Goldin J in the case of *Honey & Blankenberg v Law*:[46]

> An attorney's liability arises out of contract and his exact duty towards his client depends on what he is employed to do. (See Charlesworth *Negligence* 4 ed paras 1032–42; *Clarke and Another v Kirby Smith* [1964] 2 All ER 835 (Ch) and *Bagot v Stevens Scanlen & Co* [1964] 3 All ER 577 (QB).) In the performance of his duty or mandate, an attorney holds himself out to his clients as possessing adequate skill, knowledge and learning for the purpose of conducting all business that he undertakes. If, therefore, he causes loss or damage to his client owing to a want of such knowledge as he ought to possess, or the want of such care he ought to exercise, he is guilty of negligence giving rise to an action for damages by his client (see Halsbury's *Laws of England* 3 ed vol 36 para 135). It has been said that —
>
>> no attorney is bound to know all the law; God forbid that it should be imagined that an attorney, or a counsel or even a judge is bound to know all the law, or that an attorney is to lose his fair recompense on account of an error, being such an error as a cautious man might fall into.
>
> (See *Montriou v Jeffreys* 1825 (2) C & P 113; 172 ER 51.) If an attorney considers a point to be difficult or doubtful he should, if instructed to do so, take counsel's

---

[43] Midgley *Lawyers' Professional Liability* speaks at 124 of 'the standard of the ordinary reasonably prudent practitioner'. See also *Mouton v Die Mynwerkersunie* 1977 (1) SA 119 (A) at 142 and *Green v Collyer-Bristow* [1999] Lloyd's Rep PN 798 (Q) at 809. Douglas Brown J described the standard by which an attorney is to be judged as follows in *Green v Collyer-Bristow* at 809: 'A solicitor should not be judged by the standard of a particularly meticulous and conscientious practitioner. The test is what the reasonably competent practitioner would do having regard to the standards normally adopted in his profession. A solicitor in advising is [for example] not expected to possess an encyclopaedic knowledge of the law'.

[44] See Megarry J in *Duchess of Argyll v Beuselinck* [1972] 2 Lloyd's Rep 172 (Ch) at 183–4 and *Green v Collyer-Bistrow* [1999] Lloyd's Rep PN 798 (Q) where the court, at 809, said that it was agreed that because the solicitor in question was, and held himself out as being, a specialist, he was to be judged by the standard of the reasonably competent practitioner specialising in the area of practice in question. See also *Jackson and Powell On Professional Liability* 6 ed 717, where it is suggested that 'the correct approach is to judge the defendant solicitor by the standard of "the reasonably competent practitioner" specialising in whatever areas of law the defendant holds himself out as a specialist'.

[45] *Honey & Blankenberg v Law* 1966 (2) SA 43 (R), *Mouton v Die Mynwerkersunie* 1977 (1) SA 119 (A).

[46] Ibid at 46–7. But note the important, and self-evident, qualification voiced by Wessels JA at 143A–B of *Mouton* that, just as an error of judgment is not necessarily negligent, neither is it necessarily not. The test remains whether the error is one which a reasonably competent practitioner might, or might not, have made.

opinion. If counsel's opinion is taken and acted upon he is generally under no liability for negligence. (See Charlesworth *Negligence, supra*.) Where an action is brought by the client against his attorney for negligence, the latter must prove that there was such a want of skill or care as to amount to a breach of contract. The test for establishing negligence is whether he has been proved to be guilty of such failure as no attorney of ordinary skill would be guilty of if acting with reasonable care. He will not be guilty of negligence merely because he committed an error of judgment whether on matters of discretion or law (Halsbury's *Laws of England (supra); Lewis v Collard* 139 ER 86).

A consideration of the case law, both here and, because of the legal similarities, in England, shows that attorneys have been held liable for allowing their clients' claims to prescribe,[47] for failing to join the correct parties,[48] for neglectful delay such that by the time litigation ensued the defendant was in financial difficulties and no longer able to meet the claim,[49] for failing to advise properly on settlement,[50] for failing to advise properly in respect of commercial transactions in which their clients were involved,[51] for negligent drafting of contracts,[52] for failing to consider the possibility of insurance,[53] and for a myriad of other failings.

More difficult to discuss is the assessment of damages against neglectful attorneys.

The starting point is that the attorney is liable to do no more, and no less, than to restore the client's patrimony to that which it would have been in the absence of the attorney's breach.

It follows that a client who wishes to sue his attorney for damages for negligence committed during the course of litigation must establish not only that there was a breach of duty on the part of the attorney, but also that the breach has caused him to suffer damage. This for example entails proof not only that he would have succeeded in the litigation in the absence of his attorney's negligence,[54] but that success would have been crowned with recovery.[55]

---

[47] *Mazibuko v Singer* 1979 (3) SA 258 (W) and *Slomowitz v Kok* 1983 (1) SA 130 (A).

[48] *Brinn and Jarvis v Russell, Jones and Walker* [2003] Lloyd's Rep PN 70 (Q).

[49] *Pearson v Sanders Witherspoon* [2000] Lloyd's Rep PN 151 (CA). It is important, of course, for the client to prove not only that the delay was neglectful, but that he would in the absence of the neglect have been able to successfully resolve the matter before the financial difficulties intervened.

[50] *Griffin v Kingsmill and Others* [2001] Lloyd's Rep PN 716 (CA), *McIlgorm v Bell, Lamb, Joynson and Another* [2002] Lloyd's Rep PN 101 (Q), *Moy v Pettman Smith* [2005] PNLR 24 (HL); *Hickman v Blake, Lapthorn and Another* [2006] PNLR 20 (Q), and *Luke v Wansbroughs and Another* [2005] PNLR 2 (Q).

[51] *Boateng v Hughmans* [2002] Lloyd's Rep PN 449 (CA) and *Pickersgill v Riley* [2004] Lloyd's Rep IR 795 (PC), [2004] PNLR 31 PC.

[52] *Mouton v Die Mynwerkersunie* 1977 (1) SA 119 (A).

[53] *McClain v Mohamed & Associates* [2003] 3 All SA 707 (C). See also the comment of Donaldson J in *Forney v Dominion Insurance Co Limited* [1969] 1 Lloyd's Rep 502 (Q) at 506 that a client who has a claim against a relative or friend but who might, for obvious reasons, not want to pursue the claim, might feel differently if he discovers that the relative or friend is insured.

[54] See *Dhooma v Mehta* 1957 (1) SA 676 (D), where Henochsberg J upheld an exception on the basis that a client suing his erstwhile attorney for failing to note and prosecute an appeal must allege (and in due course prove) that the appeal would have succeeded.

[55] See Midgley *Lawyers' Professional Liability* 177 and the authorities there cited, and Visser and Potgieter *Law of Damages* 2 ed 364. The latter point out that '[t]he question [in an action between

Where the attorney's negligence lies in failing to timeously institute an action so that a good claim is allowed to prescribe, or in failing to defend, or to properly defend, an action brought against his client so that his client is held liable to pay an amount which he would not otherwise have had to pay, the damages will be the whole amount which the client would have been awarded had his claim not been allowed to prescribe, or the whole amount for which the client is held liable (subject, of course, to the point already made that the client would also have to prove that the damages would have been recovered).[56]

If the attorney succeeds on behalf of the client (either in successfully instituting, or in successfully defending, the action) but his negligence results in adverse costs orders being granted against the client, the latter can hold him liable for those costs. If the attorney succeeds in his defence of the client but negligently failed to obtain adequate security for his client's costs and if those costs as a result cannot be recovered, he is liable for the irrecoverable costs.[57]

If the action which was allowed to prescribe, or the defence which was mishandled, is not so certain, then the court would probably have to estimate the chances of its succeeding (or, for example, being compromised) and assess damages on a percentage basis, provided the best evidence reasonably available as to how the action was likely to have turned out is placed before it.[58]

2.3.2 Counsel

Though almost every advocate who practises at the Bar must at some time or another in his career have mishandled a case, there is no reported South African decision on a claim against an advocate. This might be because of the assumption that the English rule of barristers' immunity applied here. Counsel at the English Bar were for at least two centuries considered to be immune from

erstwhile client and attorney] is, of course, not only how much the plaintiff would have been awarded, but how much he would actually have recovered from the defendant.'

[56] *McGregor On Damages* 17 ed 975.

[57] *Martin Boston & Co v Roberts* [1996] PNLR 45 (CA), and *McGregor On Damages* 975.

[58] That is the position in England. See *McGregor On Damages* 975 and *Jackson and Powell On Professional Negligence* 820–4. In South Africa, the basic principle is that the plaintiff must establish on a preponderance of probabilities *that* the attorney's negligence caused him to suffer damage and, if he overcomes this hurdle, may prove *the extent of that damage* by means of contingencies (ie percentage allowances). See *Burger v Union National South British Insurance Co* 1975 (4) SA 72 (W) at 74–5 and *Blyth v Van den Heever* 1980 (1) SA 191 (A) at 225–6. Thus, in South Africa, a plaintiff who establishes that the defendant attorney negligently allowed his claim to prescribe but fails to establish that there was any prospect that the action would have been successful (including being successfully compromised) would be non-suited. But a plaintiff who establishes negligence and establishes on a preponderance of probabilities that it is materially possible that his claim would have succeeded (or that an acceptable compromise could have been entered into), but not that it would certainly have succeeded might find that he is awarded damages based on the amount he would have recovered had the action succeeded, but subject to a contingency deduction for the risk that the action might have failed, or might have had to be compromised. See, in general, *De Klerk v ABSA Bank Ltd and Others* 2003 (4) SA 315 (SCA). (The case involved an attorney, but he was the plaintiff. It thus did not relate to the professional negligence of an attorney, but is otherwise analogous.)

claims for damages arising out of their professional activities. This immunity was grounded in considerations of public policy, it being thought that exposing barristers (and, since they gained right of court appearance, solicitors performing advocacy functions) to potential liability would impact on the proper discharge of their litigation functions and in particular their duties to the court, and would result in cases being collaterally re-litigated.[59]

This special immunity, though, was abolished by the House of Lords in *Arthur Hall & Co. v Simons.*[60] The court held by a majority of five to two that the immunity could no longer be justified. Extracting the essence of the reasoning of the majority is, as so often with the House of Lords, difficult but it probably lies firstly in the conclusion that the established reasons for the immunity do not stand up to scrutiny (an advocate's duties to the court ought not under any circumstances to cause him to act negligently towards his client; whether a case ought to be relitigated or not in order to establish whether the advocate was negligent will have to be decided on a case-by-case basis), and the illogicality of treating barristers differently from other professionals. After all, as Lord Steyn said at 682:

> . . . doctors have duties not only to their patients but also to an ethical code. Doctors are sometimes faced with a tension between these duties [and have to make decisions in that context]. . . . Such decisions may easily be as difficult as those facing barristers. And nobody argues that doctors should have an immunity from suits in negligence.

Jackson and Powell[61] say this of the state of this immunity in other jurisdictions:

> Immunity still exists in Scotland in relation to criminal proceedings. Elsewhere in the commonwealth, the position is more mixed. Immunity has recently been abolished in New Zealand. In Australia, a bare majority of the High Court of Australia supported immunity in *Giannarelli v Wraith*, on public policy grounds similar to those previously adopted by the House of Lords, and that decision has been recently confirmed by the High Court of Australia in *D'Orta-Ekenaike v Victoria Legal Aid*. . . . Immunity does not exist in Canada.

The issue of immunity has not arisen in South Africa, so there is no reported South African decision either confirming or rejecting the idea of an advocate's immunity from suit. Voet [62] says that advocates are liable for damages for fraud or ill-will, but not if 'through mere inexpertness or through some mistake either of fact or of law they have advised or done things by which loss falls upon the client'. Voet's basis for this statement appears to be that '[n]o obligation

---

[59] *Patience Swinfen v Lord Chelmsford* 157 All ER 1436 at 1448, *Rondel v Worsley* [1967] 3 All ER 993 (HL) and *Saif Ali v Sidney Mitchell & Co* [1978] 3 All ER 1033 (HL). As Lord Steyn pointed out in *Arthur Hall & Co v Simons* [2000] 3 All ER 673 (HL) at 678, the reasons given by courts for the immunity altered over the years but were ultimately distilled into the two core reasons of the courts' wanting to avoid the advocate being pressurised by the risk of liability into subordinating his duty to the court to his duty to the client and the undesirability of re-litigating issues already decided.
[60] [2000] 3 All ER 673 (HL).
[61] *Jackson and Powell On Professional Liability* 875.
[62] *Voet* 3.1.10, Gane's translation Volume 1 506.

arises for advice that is not fraudulent', and as authority he quotes Digest 50.77.47. In addition, Van Leeuwen[63] states that, in the absence of fraud, an advocate who commits an error is not responsible for it. However, one doubts that these statements can be said to accurately reflect the modern South African approach. It seems a foregone conclusion that South African courts will (and ought to) hold that advocates have no immunity. As the House of Lords said in *Hall v Simons*, an advocate should be subject to the same rules as other professionals, whether they are attorneys or medical doctors. There is no logical reason why an advocate should be protected from liability to a client to whom he causes harm by his negligence.[64]

The standard by which the advocate is to be judged is the same as that of the attorney: that of the average reasonably competent advocate (unless, of course, the advocate in question professes to have special skills and charges accordingly, in which event he would be judged by that higher standard which he has set for himself).[65]

That which was said earlier in relation to attorneys about distinguishing between a mere error of judgment and negligence is particularly apposite to advocates, given that so much of advocacy relates to thinking on one's feet and to matters of judgement where various courses, each often difficult to predict, have to be chosen considered.[66]

---

[63] *Censura Forensis* 5.7.5; *Commentaries* 4.33.11.

[64] It is suggested that the approach adopted by the majority in *Arthur Hall & Co v Simons* [2000] 3 ALL ER 673 (HL) accords with the basic principles of our law. To suggest that it is an implied term of the contract in terms of which the advocate is appointed that he is immune from suit for his negligence would not be in keeping with the principles on the basis of which one imputes an unspoken term into a contract. To suggest that the advocate owes no duty of care to his client (the negligent breach of which would expose him to delictual liability) would surely be in conflict with society's notions — enriched by the appropriate norms of the objective value system embodied in the Constitution — of what justice demands, which underpin the concept of wrongfulness. See *Carmichele v Minister of Safety and Security and Another* 2001 (4) SA 938 (CC) at 962, *Premier of the Province of the Western Cape v Fair Cape Property Developers (Pty) Ltd* 2003 (6) SA 13 (SCA) at 27–9.

[65] See *Jackson and Powell On Professional Liability* 874, where the authors quote two cases, *Matrix Securities Limited v Theodore Goddard* [1998] PNLR 290 (Ch) and *Estill v Cowling* [2000] Lloyd's Rep PN 378 (Ch), in which the standard adopted was respectively that of 'the rather small and select group of silks specializing in tax matters' (*Goddard*) and of 'a reasonably competent barrister in general Chancery practice, having experience in tax and trust matters, but not the standard of a barrister who specialised in tax' (*Cowling*).

[66] See Lord Hobhouse in *Arthur Hall & Co v Simons* [2000] 3 All ER 673 (HL) at 736, where the learned judge said the following: 'The standard of care to be applied in negligence actions against an advocate is the same as that applicable to any other skilled professional who has to work in an environment where decisions and exercises of judgment have to be made in often difficult and time constrained circumstances. It requires a plaintiff to show that the error was one which no reasonably competent member of the relevant profession would have made. This is an important element of protection against unjustified liability'. And see Lord Carswell in *Moy v Pettman Smith and Another* [2005] PNLR 24 (HL) at 441: 'In deciding [whether counsel's advice was negligently given] . . . I have to try and put myself into the position of [counsel] . . . at the time, and decide whether her advice fell outside the range of possible advice which reasonably competent counsel of her seniority and purported expertise could be expected to make'.

2.4 ATTORNEYS' DUTY IN FILING PAPERS

Anyone who raises his eyebrows in horror at the inclusion of a discussion on this point is advised to attend the motion court in Johannesburg or Pretoria to listen, in particular, to the calling of the return days of rules *nisi*. The return of service will not have been filed, the commissioner of oaths will have omitted to state his designation or the province for which he holds his appointment and affidavits were 'signed too late for filing'. And from there onwards it is in the lap of the gods. If the judge is by nature easy-going he will allow all these irregularities to be rectified, somehow or other. On the other hand he may be a precisian, or just have had a poor breakfast on that particular day. If so, a minor thunderstorm will break forth, particularly if the attorney is too busy to attend court for matters which are regarded as mere formalities. Perhaps the attorney will even find that his case is reported, with a comment such as the following:

> The affidavit by the doctor has been placed before me in a form so slovenly that it approaches disrespect for the court on the part of the defendant's attorney. I shall mark my disapproval of such conduct on the part of an attorney.[67]

A good deal of the difficulties mentioned will be avoided by the application of system, although I suppose most attorneys do apply system and would resent being told how to conduct their practice. But so many cases occur where it is obviously neglected that some timorous suggestion is not out of place. The system which one might propose is one of taking steps in advance of the due date and not on arrival of that date — and certainly not the day before the matter is to be heard in court. As an example of the consequences of oversight such as failing to ensure that the copy of the summons served on the defendant showed the registrar's signature, although the original was so signed, reference may be made to *Hawkins and Others v Pietersburg Town Council*[68] and the cases cited in it. The costs incurred and the worry occasioned must have been quite out of proportion to the error.

A further aspect of this topic relates to the prolixity of documents filed. Here the attorney steers a perilous course between those well-known characters Scylla (of prolixity) and Charybdis (of omission of material information). In the case of *Simoes v Hasewinkel and Another*[69] Colman J said:

> It is, in my view, proper for the court, in an appropriate case, to exercise its discretion as to costs in order to discourage and penalize wastefulness and undue prolixity.
>
> If an attorney out of cupidity or stupidity has burdened the record of an application with a substantially greater quantity of paper than was reasonably required for the presentation of the client's case, his or her opponent should not be ordered to bear the resulting burden of unnecessary costs.
>
> But that does not mean that the court will disallow the costs of every document which in the result turns out not to have been essential, or that the presentation of a

---

[67] *Textile House (Pty) Ltd v Silvestri* 1960 (4) SA 800 (W) at 802.
[68] 1955 (4) SA 147 (T).
[69] 1966 (1) SA 579 (W) at 583–4.

complete document of moderate length will necessarily be penalised merely because some portions of that document are irrelevant or inessential.

It must be remembered that the primary duty and concern of an attorney who is filing papers in an application is to ensure that his or her client's case is adequately presented. He or she cannot, at the time of filing, always foresee with certainty whether material which he or she has and which bears on the matter is going to prove important or not. It would be wrong, in my judgment, to exercise a discretion as to costs in such a way that an honest attorney is placed in a dilemma with regard to the presentation of a document which although not vital to his or her client's case, is one which in his view might help the court to obtain a full and true picture of some material aspect of the matter.

True abuses can be readily discovered and checked. But in the present case I see no abuses.

2.5 DISAGREEMENT WITH CLIENT

Donovan[70] describes an anxious client as being a thorn in the side of counsel. A slightly different version of the matter is given by Harris[71] in the following words:

> With many advocates the wish is to please the client — I mean the solicitor — *the very worst of all reasons* for putting any question at all. Your legal client (the solicitor) should be forgotten, and if he interrupts in your own well-considered line of cross-examination, he should be politely ignored.

Not always, however, does it prove possible to dispose of clients, legal or lay, as simply as that. In the main, of course, they realise their own limitations and would no more dream of telling their counsel how to run the case than of telling the physician which particular antibiotic to prescribe. Nevertheless sooner or later counsel will find himself in a position where his views conflict with the wishes of his client. This is particularly likely to occur in a criminal case where the client wishes to testify while counsel has reservations about his client's ability to answer certain awkward questions that may be put in cross-examination. The matter has already been mentioned in regard to counsel's authority.[72] According to the headnote of *Matonsi's* case:

> If an accused, in spite of his advocate's advice to the contrary, insists on going into the witness box and thereby makes it impossible for his advocate to exercise his legal ability honourably and faithfully, as required of him by his office, then the advocate must withdraw from the case rather than act contrary to the express wish of his client.

This quotation is translated from a passage from the minority judgment of Van Blerk AJA which was in any event *obiter*. With respect, it is not sought to question the wisdom of the statement made but it is submitted not to be quite

---

[70] *Tact in Court* (1915) 42.
[71] *Illustrations in Advocacy* (1915) 79–80.
[72] See the quotation from *R v Matonsi* in para.2.1.2 above.

so clear that it is counsel's duty to withdraw in all cases. Thus, in and after the passage quoted previously, Schreiner JA used these words:[73]

> Cases of disagreement between the views of client and counsel arise from time to time and counsel may find himself between the Scylla of precipitately, and therefore improperly, withdrawing from the case, and the Charybdis of unreasonably overriding his client's will. The decision may be particularly difficult where the accused is being defended on a capital charge by counsel who is acting *pro Deo* without other legal assistance.
>
> From the evidence that the appellant gave in mitigation of sentence, it may be inferred that counsel exercised a wise discretion *in not allowing him to give evidence*[74] that would in all probability have been rejected.

No doubt the two passages can be reconciled without much difficulty by saying that counsel will probably withdraw where his client overrides his advice and counsel feels that his position becomes untenable because, for example, he is of the opinion that questions which he would have to put in leading his client's evidence would produce answers damaging to his client's case. If counsel feels it right to disregard his client's wishes on such a matter, he may do so and will not be held to have acted improperly in so doing. It is suggested, however, that in every case in which counsel withdraws it is his duty to ascertain that his client understands the reason for the withdrawal and the consequences both of the withdrawal and the course of proposed conduct which has led to that withdrawal.

Counsel must, of course, withdraw when his brief is withdrawn.

2.6 THE DRAWING OF PLEADINGS

This topic is closely interrelated with the question of freedom of speech in court, dealt with in paragraph 2.10 below. Nevertheless it may be convenient to consider here the law on the subject of responsibility for allegations in pleading. At first sight it would appear that there is a substantial difference in the duties of attorneys and counsel. In reality the duty is the same but it is the manner in which the duty can be complied with that presents differences. The duty is not to make defamatory allegations which are reckless, irrelevant or scandalous, or which the pleader does not reasonably believe can be established by evidence. The nature of the difference, in practice, appears from the judgment of Wessels CJ in *Findlay v Knight*:[75]

> It has been argued by Mr Millin that when Findlay drew up the plea he was in the same position as an advocate. This is not so. There is an inherent difference between an advocate who draws up a plea on the instructions of an attorney and an attorney who draws up a plea on the information given to him by his client. The advocate does

---

[73] 1958 (2) SA 450 (A) at 457C.

[74] My own italics. See also, for a good example of the circumstances under which counsel might be obliged to withdraw, *Van der Berg v General Council of the Bar of SA* [2007] 2 ALL SA 499 (SCA) at para [20].

[75] 1935 AD 58 at 73. See also *Joubert and Others v Venter* 1985 (1) SA 654 (A).

not get his information from his client. He gets his instructions from the attorney and presumes that the latter has sifted the matter and that proof will be forthcoming. The attorney draws his plea from the instructions of the client. It is unnecessary in this case to consider to what extent an attorney who pleads a libellous charge can rely upon the instructions of his client. This might have been necessary if the action were founded on the allegations in the first plea. When, however, the second plea was filed, Findlay had obtained so much information that he knew or ought to have known that he would not be in a position to lay evidence before the court to support the more serious charges contained in the second plea. When he drew the second plea he did not know whether the charges were true or false and whether there was or was not evidence to support them. He made them recklessly, careless of the consequences. This the court cannot allow an attorney to do. If it did, it would allow the process of the court to be used to defame a litigant, not '*defendendi consilio*'[76] but '*impune convicia projiciendi causa*'.[77]

Perhaps practitioners are more circumspect in regard to the written word than the spoken, for the greater number of reported cases deal with utterances in court where tension mounts and tempers become understandably short.

In any event, reassurance may be found in a judgment of Schreiner J[78] to the effect that a pleading partakes of the nature of a submission that certain facts exist, rather than of an assertion which it is intended that the reader shall believe and act upon. As the learned judge stated:

It informs the court and the other party what the pleader means, if possible, to prove to the court's satisfaction. Whether the allegations are established or not is a matter for the court to decide upon the evidence. A pleader need not himself believe in the truth of the evidence that will be available to prove the allegations in the proceedings; it is enough that he does not know the evidence to be false. For if he does know it to be false he could not properly plead it, and it would therefore not be available to prove his case. Nor where proof rests upon a chain of reasoning need he himself be prepared to draw the requisite inferences; it is enough that he believes in the possibility of their being drawn by the court. Such inferences need not be mere steps in the proof of fact. If the defamatory allegations involve an element of legal definition the inferences may rest on propositions of law.

It was pointed out that a pleader should be held to be guilty of *animus injuriandi* only where he does not believe that there will be evidence available at the trial which might prove the allegations, or where he does not believe in the *possibility* of any requisite inference being drawn by the court. A practitioner who draws a defamatory pleading upon the instructions of his client and who has no reason to disbelieve those instructions, or to doubt seriously that any court could draw the inferences necessary to his case, need have no fear of a successful action for defamation being brought against him personally. If he performs an analytical process on the lines suggested in chapter 4, his reasoning should tell him whether he can safely plead what his client wishes.

---

[76] 'In the interest of defending.'

[77] 'For the sake of casting insults with impunity.'

[78] *Solomon v Van Leggelo* 1938 TPD 75 at 80, referred to without qualification in *Basner v Trigger* 1946 AD 83 at 106.

2.7 ADMISSIONS BY LEGAL REPRESENTATIVES

Admissions may be made deliberately and formally by an attorney or counsel at any stage of the litigation with the object of saving time and money by rendering it unnecessary to call witnesses to prove matters which are not really in dispute. The rules of court dealing with pre-trial conferences are designed for this very purpose and will be discussed later.[79] The framers of the rules considered that if the legal representatives were compelled to come face to face and discuss matters which the one or the other thought to be beyond dispute the process of litigation might be streamlined. Those meetings lead to admissions which are normally recorded and are the basis of the trial. Our present purpose, however, is somewhat different: it is to consider the effects of erroneous admissions or, perhaps, statements which are said to amount to admissions but which were not realised to be such at the time.

The following was said in this regard in an old English case:

> If the counsel says, 'I made a concession under a misapprehension', it never has been, and I trust it will never be, the course of the court to bind counsel to that mistake.[80]

This seems to be the attitude of the courts in South Africa as well when attempts have been made to rely upon concessions made loosely or incautiously by counsel during the litigation.[81] Of course, counsel must exercise his calling with care, skill and diligence and should be careful to refrain from making incautious concessions or admissions. But mistakes will happen and a counsel who realises that he has mistakenly made a concession should say so fearlessly and promptly.

Nothing is easier than the careless word and anyone who has listened to legal argument on the interpretation of a written contract will realise that there is no word that can be so plainly stated that ingenious argument cannot show that it bears a different meaning.

The English law on the subject is summarised as follows in *Halsbury,*[82] and probably accurately reflects the position in South Africa:

- statements by counsel in the presence of his client or his instructing attorney or the representative of the latter are evidence against the client unless repudiated;

---

[79] See chapter 6.

[80] Per Malins VC in *Holt v Jesse* 3 ChD 177 at 184.

[81] See Nicholas J (as he then was) in *Fisheries Development Corporation of SA Limited v Jorgensen and Another* 1979 (3) SA 1331 (W) at 1334C–H quoting with approval the passage in *Holt v Jesse*, and see also *Kevin & Lasia Property Investment CC and Another v Roos NO and Others* 2004 (4) SA 103 (SCA) at 108. Concessions relating to points of law can be withdrawn at any stage. See *Paddock Motors (Pty) Limited v Igesund* 1976 (3) SA 16 (A) at 23B — in fine, *Prinsloo & Viljoen Eiendomme (Edms) Beperk v Morfou* 1993 (1) SA 668 (T) at 669–70, *National Police Service Union v Minister of Safety and Security* 2000 (3) SA 371 (A) at 379I–J and *Ndlovu v Santam Limited* 2006 (2) SA 239 (SCA) at 243–4.

[82] 4 ed (2005 reissue) vol 3(1) 444 para 668.

- undertakings given by counsel without authority will not be accepted by the court;[83]
- undertakings given by counsel in court and accepted by the court or the opposing party should be as scrupulously observed as if embodied in an order of court;
- a communication by counsel outside court to the opposing party or his attorney[84] has not the same effect as one proceeding from the attorney who instructs counsel.

2.8 THE DUTY OF DISCLOSURE TO THE COURT

In the case of *Schoeman v Thompson*[85] Barry J said:

> Now it is the duty of counsel to inform the court of any matter which is material to the granting of an application, and of which counsel is aware. While I accept [counsel's] explanation that he did not wilfully keep back the information he had received, the fact that he had knowledge of the respondent's previous insolvency is knowledge that must be imputed to his client. The fact that it was known at the time of the application that the respondent was an unrehabilitated insolvent and that such knowledge was not disclosed is a good ground for the court to discharge the provisional order because there has not been a proper disclosure of all the facts.[86]

A further illustration of the extent of this duty is to be found in *Katzenellenbogen's* case.[87] That was a case where a decree of divorce was granted on the grounds of malicious desertion. At the time when the final order was sought there were in existence an agreement and other documents in respect of which the judge said that it was 'hard to escape the conclusion' that the plaintiff was confessing adultery. When the final decree of divorce was granted the existence of these documents was not disclosed to the court, although both counsel who then acted for the parties were aware of them. Millin J said:

> Neither counsel considered it his duty to inform the Court of the existence of two other documents of which both were aware and which were actually in the brief of counsel for the defendant.

Perhaps this lends point to the remark of Mason JP in *Ex parte Geffen*[88] that 'the court expects the advocate to be to a certain extent independent of the solicitor'. Counsel has a duty to the court which, subject to his duty not to

---

[83] *Hawkes v Hawkes and Another* 2007 (2) SA 100 (SE). The usual procedure is that the court will assume that counsel has authority for his undertakings and normally will not raise a query as to the existence or extent of that authority.

[84] Counsel, it is suggested, should never speak to the opposing party in the absence of the opponent's legal advisers. He should also be chary of speaking to the opposing attorney, eg, communicating with the opposing attorney to arrange a postponement, because this may be interpreted as touting or as 'performing the work of an attorney'.

[85] 1927 WLD 282 at 283.

[86] Compare paragraph 17.4.3 in chapter 17.

[87] *Katzenellenbogen v Katzenellenbogen and Another* 1947 (2) SA 528 (W) at 530. See also *Russell v Russell* 1946 WLD 35.

[88] 1923 TPD 373 at 376.

disclose the confidences of his client, over-rides his obligation to his client. In both *Schoeman's* and *Katzenellenbogen's* cases counsel were aware of facts which would have been fatal to their clients' causes. In both cases the opinion of the court was that those facts should have been disclosed.

This duty probably arises out of the fact that counsel and attorneys are officers of the court, and is consistent with Voet's description of the profession as an honourable one.[89]

The court will always accept and act on the assurance of counsel in any matter heard in court and, in order to deserve this trust, counsel must act with the utmost good faith towards the court. In *Ex parte Swain*[90] the applicant's application for admission as an advocate was refused because he failed to disclose material facts. The court held, as a consequence, that he had failed to show that he was a fit and proper person to practise as an advocate. During the course of his judgment James JP said:

> [I]t is of vital importance that when the Court seeks an assurance from an advocate that a certain set of facts exists the Court will be able to rely implicitly on any assurance that may be given. The same standard is required in relations between advocates and between advocates and attorneys. The proper administration of justice could not easily survive if the professions were not scrupulous of the truth in their dealings with each other and with the Court. [91]

No doubt this imposes a heavy burden on counsel. One cannot but sympathise with the client who can hardly believe his ears when he hears his counsel raise with the court (particularly in unopposed matters) some point which may be destructive of the whole case. And he is charging a fee! No doubt counsel will attempt to argue his way out of the point he has raised, but the client's sense of bewilderment will hardly qualify him to recognise the forensic mastery displayed by one who has bitten the very hand that fed him.

Neither attorneys nor counsel are mere agents for their clients: they have duties towards the judiciary to ensure the 'efficient and fair administration of justice'.[92]

It is suggested that the duty applies primarily, but not exclusively, in *ex parte* applications or in those matters where the party affected by the relief which is being sought is not yet before the court. In opposed or defended matters the duty might be stated as a duty not actively to mislead the court.[93] It would probably, almost certainly, not be held to require the disclosure of weaknesses in one's case, but might cover the suppression of a fact, unknown to the other side, which would completely disentitle the client to the relief claimed. This

---

[89] *Voet* 3.1.1, Gane's translation vol I 497–8.
[90] 1973 (2) SA 427 (N).
[91] At 434.
[92] *Cape Law Society v Vorster* 1949 (3) SA 421 (C), per De Villiers JP at 425. See also paras [14] to [18] of *Van der Berg v General Council of the Bar of South Africa* [2007] 2 All SA 499 (SCA).
[93] *Van der Berg v General Council of the Bar of South Africa* [2007] 2 All SA 499 (SCA) at paras [14] to [18].

includes a duty to refer the court to reported decisions which are clearly adverse to your case. See the comments of Leach J in *Toto v Special Investigating Unit and Others*.[94] The learned judge's words are well worth remembering:

> A legal representative who appears in court is not a mere agent for his client, but has a duty towards the Judiciary to ensure the efficient and fair administration of justice. . . . [which] could not easily survive if the professions were not scrupulous of their dealings with the Court. As a result of this, it has long been regarded as a practitioner's duty to inform the Court of a judgment within his knowledge material to the issues, even if such judgment is against the case which he is presenting: in which latter event he can then seek either to argue that it was wrongly decided or to attempt to distinguish it from the case being heard. For a practitioner to be aware of a judgment adverse to his case and not bring it to the attention of the Court amounts, in my view, to a gross breach of this duty.

Of course, it is not the duty of either counsel or attorney to mistrust his client, let alone to act as some sort of a guardian of the truth either by disclosing to the court or his opponent his doubts about his client's virtues, or by preventing his client from testifying to that version, no matter how improbable the counsel or attorney might view it as being. The dividing line is reached when he no longer *suspects*, but *knows as a fact and not merely as a matter of belief* that the version is false (either because the client has admitted this to him, or because he has come across incontrovertible evidence which undoubtedly disproves his client's version). In this regard I could not put it better than to quote from the judgment of Nugent JA in paragraphs [14] to [16] of *Van der Berg v General Council of the Bar of SA*:[95]

> Advocacy fulfils a necessary role in the proper administration of justice. . . . [which]. . . . would be seriously compromised if an advocate were to be required to believe the evidence of his client before being permitted to present it. That would mean that the rights of the litigant would be determined by the advocate rather than by the court. . . .
>   . . . An advocate is not called upon to believe, to any degree, the evidence that he is instructed to place before a court. Even if he believes positively that his client's evidence is false, he is entitled, and indeed obliged, to place it before a court if those are his client's instructions, and there can be no qualification in this regard. . . .
>   But it is a different matter altogether if an advocate knows (as a fact and not merely as a matter of belief) that evidence is false or misleading. For the role of advocacy in furthering the proper administration of justice also gives rise to duties that are owed to the court, primarily a duty upon an advocate not to deceive or mislead a court himself. . . .

Bear in mind also that, where counsel discovers (as, it must be thoroughly emphasised, a matter of fact and not merely of belief) that his client's version is false, counsel is barred by the ethics of attorney and client privilege from bringing the true facts to the attention of the court or his opponent. That he cannot do. What he can, and in those circumstances must, do is face his client

---

[94] 2001 (1) SA 673 (E) at 683.
[95] [2007] 2 All SA 499 (SCA).

with the awful alternative of either disclosing the truth (with the presumably calamitous consequences that would hold) or seeing his counsel withdraw. If the client declines the former option (as I have not the slightest doubt he will!), counsel has no alternative but to take the latter option: to withdraw, citing a conflict which has arisen between himself and his client the nature of which he is not at liberty to disclose, but which compels him to withdraw.

Counsel's duty towards the court extends beyond matters where he is actively involved in litigation before the court. In *S v Longdistance (Pty) Ltd and Another*[96] the appellants were charged with and convicted of contravening s 31(1)*(a)* of the Road Transportation Act 74 of 1977. After having obtained counsel's opinion to the effect that the conveyance was lawful they were unsuccessfully prosecuted on two occasions. Subsequently, however, they were convicted, hence the appeal. They relied upon a lack of knowledge of the unlawfulness of their actions, arising from the opinion. The court held that the professed reliance on a manifestly incorrect opinion was so unreasonable that it could not have been the basis for a belief that conveyance was lawful. In the course of his judgment McLaren J said the following:

> 'A legal practitioner who provides his client with an opinion must furnish such opinion with that degree of care and skill which is in general expected from members of his profession. A great responsibility rests on the shoulders of a legal practitioner who is asked to advise his client as to whether certain intended conduct of the client will be lawful or not. He also has a duty towards the court, and he ought to foresee that, if his client should be prosecuted because of such conduct, the latter would probably rely on a lack of knowledge of unlawfulness arising from the opinion.'[97]

The Appellate Division in another matter involving the same accused described counsel's advice as 'bizarre'; the reasoning contained in the opinion as 'a travesty' and the conclusion as 'palpably absurd'.[98]

2.9 EVIDENCE BY LEGAL REPRESENTATIVES

It has been stated in a number of cases since early in the last century that it is most undesirable for an attorney or counsel who is actually acting for a party in the litigation to give evidence as a witness.[99] The legal practitioner is not disqualified but, particularly where issues of credibility are involved, he should not put himself in the position, perhaps, of having to argue that his own evidence should be accepted. As De Villiers JP remarked in *Hendricks v Davidoff*,[100] '[t]his city is full of advocates and attorneys.' It matters not that, as in

---

[96] 1986 (3) SA 428 (N).

[97] At 444F–G (translated from the original Afrikaans).

[98] *S v Longdistance (Natal) (Pty) Ltd and Others* 1990 (2) SA 277 (A) at 283D and I–J.

[99] *Landers v Vogel* (1906) 27 NLR 590, *Becker v Rex* (1928) 12 PH H101 (AD), *Hendricks v Davidoff* 1955 (2) SA 369 (C), *Elgin Engineering Co (Pty) Ltd v Hillview Motor Transport* 1961 (4) SA 450 (D), *Hailmer v Hailmer* 1963 (2) PH F76 (C), *Wronsky en 'n Ander v Prokureur-Generaal* 1971 (3) SA 292 (SWA) and *Keetmanshoop Munisipaliteit v Uitvoerende Gesag van Suidwes-Afrika* 1988 (2) SA 819 (SWA).

[100] 1955 (2) SA 369 (C).

this same case, the legal practitioner turns out to be 'a very important, and . . . successful witness'. What would have been said had he not been so successful? After all, the legal practitioner takes on sufficient responsibility when he handles the case in his professional capacity and no reason can be suggested why he should accept the added burden of becoming an acceptable witness. Indeed it is not too much to suggest that there may be a conflict between the practitioner's duty to testify fearlessly without regard to the effect of his evidence and his interest (and duty) in trying to win his case for his client. Wessels J, as he then was, dealt with this question in the following way in *Elgin Engineering Co (Pty) Ltd v Hillview Motor Transport*:[101]

> I must digress at this stage to remark that in circumstances where his credibility may be in issue it would appear to be undesirable for an attorney who is to be an important witness in any matter, to act as the attorney of record. The fact that the witness is the attorney of record for one of the litigants does of course not affect his competence as a witness in any way. It is important that an attorney should at all times retain his independence in relation to his client and the litigation which is being conducted. If he is to give important evidence in the case in circumstances where his credibility may be called into question, his independence as a professional adviser to his client in the matter may, in my opinion, be affected.

The Uniform Rules of Professional Conduct for Advocates provide that counsel must avoid, as far as possible, putting himself in any position where he may have to make statements or give evidence in relation to matters which are in dispute in the case in which he is appearing.[102]

2.10 FREEDOM OF SPEECH IN COURT[103]

2.10.1 Defamation: Freedom of counsel's speech in court

> It is in accord with this oath that they (advocates) gave an assurance that they will not undertake the patronage of an unjust lawsuit, nor pursue one once undertaken when its injustice becomes evident; nor use false statements and lying charges in a just cause; nor either openly or covertly rave with invectives to the insulting of the opposite party beyond what the advantage of lawsuits demands[104]

An advocate or an attorney is protected when he makes a defamatory statement in the interests of his client (including the State) if it is shown *(a)* that the statement was pertinent and germane to the issue and *(b)* that it has some

---

[101] 1961 (4) SA 450 (D).

[102] See rule 4.5: 'Counsel must avoid, as far as possible, putting himself in any position where he may have to make statements or give evidence in relation to matters which are in dispute in the case in which he is appearing. In all cases, before counsel may make an affidavit or volunteer to give evidence concerning matters which become known to him while acting in his professional capacity, permission of the Bar Council must first be sought'.

[103] See also paragraph 2.6 above, dealing with the making of defamatory allegations in pleadings.

[104] This quotation comes from *Voet* 3.1.9 (Gane's translation vol I at 505–6). It concludes: 'nor purposely drag out lawsuits to their own foul profit or disgusting self; but will essay every path and catch at every chance of heightening their true honour.'

foundation in the evidence or circumstances surrounding the trial.[105] This applies to civil and criminal proceedings. However, a plea of privilege cannot prevail if the person claiming damages for defamation can establish malice on the part of the defendant.[106]

In *Pogrund v Yutar* Beyers JA said:[107]

> Kotze JP points out that, in formulating the rule in the terms stated, our law aims at the dignity and independence of the Bar, while at the same time safeguarding the character and reputation of third parties. The wide language used by Schreiner JA in *Basner's* case is possibly open to misconstruction. It would not, I consider, be in keeping with the dignity of the Bar, if the language were to be interpreted as allowing an advocate not only a considerable latitude in presenting his case to the court, but also a licence to speak ill of others in doing so. I do not think that the learned judge of appeal intended to convey this impression.

Perhaps this branch of the law is one of the most important, personally, to an attorney or advocate who has a busy trial practice. In court one develops an intensity of purpose and one is subject to pressures, stresses and tensions which render it difficult to exercise that calmness of purpose and detachment of judgment which prevail in chambers. Individuals, moreover, react differently to provocations and what may be a remark of little significance can very easily be interpreted as an insult demanding instant retaliation. Not only, therefore, must the practitioner school himself into a phlegmatic approach to every issue and an unemotional acceptance of every incident, but he must profit from the mistakes of others.

The Appellate Division once again considered the position in *Joubert and Others v Venter*.[108] In the course of his judgment Kotze JA said:

> As regards the qualified privilege afforded counsel in the conduct of legal proceedings, it has been said that the statement must *(a)* have been pertinent or germane to the issue (or, it is preferable to say, an issue in the case) and *(b)* have had some foundation in the evidence or circumstances surrounding the trial. The defendant must establish requirement *(a)* in order to be provisionally protected.

---

[105] *Joubert and Others v Venter* 1985 (1) SA 654 (A) at 702–5, *Van der Berg v Coopers & Lybrand Trust (Pty) Limited and Others* 2001 (2) SA 242 (SCA) and *Hardaker v Phillips* 2005 (4) SA 515 (SCA) at 524–6. The Uniform Rules of Professional Conduct for Advocates provide, in rule 3.3, firstly that counsel should not attack the character of a witness unless that issue is relevant to the main enquiry or, if not, he has reasonable grounds for thinking that the basis for the attack is well-founded or true, secondly that counsel is entitled to assume that the imputation is indeed well-founded or true where his attorney confirms that in his (the attorney's) opinion it is, thirdly that counsel should in this regard not accept the opinion of a person other than his attorney 'without ascertaining, so far as is practicable in the circumstances, that such person can give satisfactory reasons for his statement', fourthly that counsel must in any event be careful to ensure that the questions will or might materially affect the credibility of the witness, and finally that it is 'in all cases . . . the duty of the advocate to guard against being made the channel for questions which are only intended to insult or annoy either the witness or any other person'.

[106] *Basner v Trigger* 1946 AD 83 at 105, *Pogrund v Yutar* 1967 (2) SA 564 (A) at 570 and *Joubert and Others v Venter* 1985 (1) SA 654 (A) at 704E.

[107] 1967 (2) SA 564 (A) at 570.

[108] 1985 (1) SA 654 (A).

Counsel's protection is not confined to the opening addresses, the examination of witnesses, cross-examination and addresses to the Court, but also extends to pleadings drafted by him and 'other documents necessary to place his client's case before the Court'. This last category is clearly wide enough to include affidavits settled or prepared for motion proceedings. While counsel who drafts a pleading or affidavit on the instructions of an attorney is in a stronger position than the attorney, since counsel presumes that the matter has been sifted and that proof will be forthcoming, the position of counsel who accepts a brief to consult with witnesses and thereafter to draft pleadings or affidavits can, in principle, not differ from that of an attorney who acts on the instructions of his client.

With reference to the second of the requirements posed immediately above, it is true that in particular circumstances it may be required of a defendant pleading privilege to prove that he had reasonable ground for making the defamatory statement, but this is certainly not a rule of universal application. The incidence of the onus in the present context falls to be determined by considerations of policy, and what is of paramount and decisive importance is that the welfare of society demands that an advocate or attorney who pleads the cause of his client should have a large degree of freedom in laying his client's case before the Court, even though in so doing he defames the other party or even a third party. To give due effect to these considerations it is necessary to lay down that the privilege which counsel enjoys (and thus the provisional protection afforded thereby) is established on proof that the statement in question was relevant or germane to an issue in the legal proceedings in the course of which it was made, and that it is then for the plaintiff to prove that the defendant abused the occasion (and thus forfeited the protection of the privilege). The plaintiff can do this by, for instance, proving that the defendant did not have 'some foundation' in the evidence or surrounding circumstances for making the statement. The Court should not, however, be astute to find a lack of 'some foundation' (for reasonable cause) for counsel's statements. There are, of course, other ways of defeating the claim of privilege such as proof that the defendant was actuated by malice in the sense of an improper or indirect motive. As regards the relevance or otherwise of counsel's belief in the truth of the statement expressions can be found in some of the cases suggesting that an absence of (reasonable) grounds for believing in the truth of a statement is sufficient to attract liability. This is not a correct reflection of the law. In order to be afforded protection, counsel needs not believe in the truth of the statement and accordingly the absence of grounds for such belief is, *per se*, inconclusive. The absence of a subjective belief on the part of counsel in the truth of the statement does not defeat the privilege.

2.10.2 A distillation of the principles relating to counsel's freedom of speech in court

From all these cases, apart from the object lesson which they provide, it should be possible to distil a few principles.

•   Defamatory language may be used only if germane to an issue actually being tried by the court.
•   The advocate is not in all cases obliged to satisfy himself that the allegation is true. If he is an attorney he may accept the instructions of his client but, it is suggested, should consider himself as upon his inquiry as to the reliability of those instructions. If an attorney obtains his information from a person other than his client, he should satisfy himself that the

information is correct before using it. Counsel may act upon the instructions of his attorney and may reasonably assume that the attorney has taken all steps necessary to justify the use of the information. (Notwithstanding this, it is an elementary principle of common sense in all cases to take every reasonably possible step to verify defamatory matter which is to be put to witnesses in cross-examination — in the interests of one's own professional reputation.)

• The use of strong language or the couching of a proposition in terms wider than in fact justified will not normally be visited with pecuniary consequences upon the practitioner responsible.

• It is the occasion that is privileged not the capacity (of a lawyer). So outside court, indeed outside the actual hearing, counsel and attorneys talk at their peril.

• The nature of the tribunal is irrelevant; it is its capacity (of a forum) that creates a privileged occasion.

• Counsel is not required to usurp the functions of the judge and decide upon the truth of what he states; he is protected, to put it from the negative point of view, unless he knew the statement to be untrue or unless there was no reasonable ground to believe that it might be true.

2.11 FREEDOM OF COUNSEL IN COURT

Of course, counsel must exercise his calling with care, skill, diligence, restraint, fearlessness and dignity. It takes many years of painful practice to combine all these qualities in any one opening address, any one cross-examination or any one argument. During the course of a trial counsel will be pressed by his attorney who lauds the care, skill and diligence bit, but would like a little less of the restraint. The attorney may be unable to contain himself during a cross-examination and, if not actually tugging counsel's gown, is busy writing notes in capital letters saying: 'Ask him this . . .', and so on. No doubt many a valuable suggestion has been made in this manner, but all too often the suggestion is hastily conceived and ill-considered. It takes great courage for counsel to use the words of Sir Charles Russel and say: 'Sit down, sir; you know nothing about it'.[109]

Perhaps, to return to our theme, it may be the client who is impressed with counsel's quality of fearlessness but doesn't quite see the need for so much dignity when dealing with a treble-dyed scoundrel like his opponent. He demands more of the mailed fist and less of the velvet glove. Counsel who is torn between these distracting influences and his own carefully prepared plan of campaign is at risk of abandoning some of the caution with which he proposed to approach his case, and of pitching his remarks too highly, or of overplaying his hand. Nothing is easier than to give in to the exhortations of attorney and client. Don't do it. Trust to your judgment. If there is time and

---

[109] Quoted by Harris *Illustrations in Advocacy* (1915) 3.

opportunity, ask them for their views. But rely on yourself and your own judgment.'

2.12 CONTEMPT OF COURT

The administration of justice is founded not only upon that portion of the power of the State which is assigned to the courts, but also upon the preservation of the dignity of the courts. It is obviously the duty of practitioners to assist in upholding that dignity, and cases of contempt of court by practitioners are fortunately uncommon.

Not always, however, is it easy to maintain a standard of behaviour consistent with what is due to the court, particularly if the practitioner allows himself to develop strong feelings about a case. In this regard I would refer to the old saying: 'the lawyer who defends himself has a fool for a client'. When the lawyer identifies himself with a client, the client has a fool for a lawyer. Counsel can do justice to his client only if he retains that degree of detachment which will preserve for him an unimpaired power of judgment and discretion. If he maintains this attitude he will not misunderstand the questions or behaviour of the judicial officer nor suspect him of motives which do not exist. Moreover, he will be able to see the value or danger of the point which the judicial officer has in mind and will consider how to meet it, how to use it or whether it may be safely ignored.

The practitioner's particular temperament may be a factor predisposing him, if that is the correct phrase, to contempt of court. This rather rash generalisation arises from the fact that two practitioners who find themselves involved as defendants in respect of defamatory statements made in court may also find themselves as accused persons in contempt proceedings.

The magistrate's complaints about the accused (attorney, charged with contempt) in *R v Benson*[110] might be noted:

> His conduct of the cross-examination terrorised the witness and he ignored requests not to shout. The applicant's whole conduct was derogatory to the dignity of the court. He had shouted spasmodically for seven hours. On the two subsequent days of the trial, Benson never once raised his voice and everything went off very well indeed.

The culminating point in the conduct of the volatile Mr Benson was when he lost control of himself and thumped the table, shouting very loudly at the witness. When called upon by the magistrate to apologise he replied: 'The court must take its own course', which it did, fining him £3 or five days into the bargain.

The case of *R v Rosenstein*[111] shows how careful a practitioner may have to be. Of course the report cannot give the full picture of the case. The appellant,

---

[110] *R v Benson* 1914 AD 357, *Briscoe v Benson* 1914 TPD 598, *R v Luyt* (1926) 7 PH H69 (E), (1926) 8 PH H50 (AD) and *Preston v Luyt* 1911 EDL 298.
[111] 1943 TPD 65.

the late Victor Rosenstein KC, apart from being a very capable advocate, was a thorough gentleman. The incident which gave rise to his appeal occurred prior to his taking silk. Rosenstein was appearing in a criminal case in the magistrate's court. The prosecutor was questioning an accused in regard to questions which had been put to a Crown witness. Rosenstein interrupted saying: 'The witness never said that. The record is wrong. The record contains a number of inaccuracies. I have checked up on it. The record contains a number of inaccuracies.' He was called upon to apologise to the court but refused and, after an adjournment, persisted in his attitude maintaining that he had nothing to apologise for, inasmuch as, in drawing attention to alleged irregularities, he had merely stated his opinion. He was fined £5 for contempt of court and this was upheld on appeal. The court on appeal held that Rosenstein had imputed carelessness or incompetence to the magistrate and had not merely in a proper manner drawn attention to alleged inaccuracies in the record. Perhaps Rosenstein's manner was brusque and perhaps he could have said: 'The witness never said that. *I submit that* the record is wrong. *I submit that* the record contains a number of inaccuracies. I have checked it. *I submit that* the record contains a number of inaccuracies.' If Rosenstein believed, as he obviously did, that there were inaccuracies in the record, he was entitled to raise that point without being understood to impute more than error to the magistrate, and not carelessness or incompetence. Ramsbottom J in fact recognised this but held that Rosenstein acted improperly in going beyond the particular point in issue and brusquely alleging that the magistrate's record contained inaccuracies. In *Rosenstein's* case it was held that there need not be an actual intention to commit a contempt or to be disrespectful or insulting to the magistrate, and this was followed later in *Cape Times Ltd v Union Trade Directories (Pty) Ltd and Others*.[112]

With these authorities[113] to afford him warning and guidance, counsel ought to have sufficient material to enable him to act properly in court. He should never hesitate to apologise, even in the absence of reproof by the court, where he knows that his conduct has not strictly complied with what is expected of him. The apology should be prompt and sincere.[114]

Even unjustifiable words used by a judicial officer will not entitle counsel or attorneys to retaliate with impunity.[115] While a judicial officer is expected to behave with as much dignity as those who appear before him, the fact that he

---

[112] 1956 (1) SA 105 (N) 122. The case, in the reported arguments of counsel and in the judgment, contains a full and most valuable exposition of the authorities relating to contempt of court. Also see *Afrikaanse Pers Publikasie (Edms) Bpk en 'n Ander v Mbeki* 1964 (4) SA 618 (A). (These two references are *obiter*, because the cases do not deal with legal practitioners.)

[113] Other reported cases dealing with contempt by practitioners are: *Duffy v Munnik and Another* 1957 (4) SA 390 (T), *Duffy v Attorney-General, Transvaal and Another* 1958 (1) SA 630 (T), *R v Hawkey* 1960 (1) SA 70 (SR), *R v Pitje* 1960 (4) SA 709 (A), *S v Singh* 1964 (3) SA 106 (N), *S v Van Niekerk* 1972 (3) SA 711 (A) and *In re Chinamasa* 2001 (2) SA 902 (ZS).

[114] Cf *S v Tobias* 1966 (1) SA 656 (N) at 666. See also the exposition of the law generally in the same case at 659H–661H.

[115] *S v Tobias* ibid at 665E–H and the authorities quoted there.

might occasionally fail in those standards will merely create a greater need for restraint, courtesy and dignity on the part of counsel. If, by his conduct, counsel can make the court realise that unfortunate and unjustified words have been used then either a spontaneous apology will be elicited or else, and this is perhaps as effective a remedy, counsel will have proved to those present at the time that the court has erred.

Two useful judgments to read in regard to contempt of court are those of Kriegler J in *S v Mamabolo (E TV and Others Intervening)*[116] and Cameron JA (as he then was) in *Faki NO v CCII Systems (Pty) Ltd.*[117] The following aspects of these judgments are important:

•   The offence of contempt of court is defined as 'publications or words which tend, or are calculated, to bring the administration of justice into disrepute'. The interest served is not the private interest of the court concerned, but that of the public at large. It is not the self-esteem or dignity of any judicial officer that is protected, but the moral authority of the judicial process as such. The offence is a public injury and it exists to protect the integrity of the administration of justice.[118]

•   When one looks at an allegedly scandalising statement, one has to ask what the likely effect of the statement was. The test is an objective one. The test is, in short, whether the offending conduct, viewed contextually, was likely to damage the administration of justice.[119]

•   There is no pressing need for firm or swift measures to protect the integrity of the judicial process and, if punitive steps are indeed warranted by criticism so egregious as to demand them, there is no reason why the ordinary mechanisms of the criminal justice system cannot be employed. The alternative of a summary hearing is constitutionally unacceptable.[120]

•   The elements of the offence must be established on the criminal standard, ie beyond reasonable doubt.[121]

2.13 RECUSAL, AND A NOTE OF CAUTION

Sometimes the practitioner will find himself in the unenviable position of having to apply for the judicial officer to recuse himself. Where this is on the ground of kinship or of a previous connection with or decision in the same proceedings, the matter should present little difficulty. Where, however, the basis of the application has to be a possible bias on the part of the judicial officer, the utmost tact must be exercised to avoid remarks which might properly be regarded as contemptuous. In respect of submissions founded on fact and made in moderate language the advocate will enjoy a wide degree of protection, but

---

[116] 2001 (3) SA 409 (CC).
[117] 2006 (4) SA 326 (SCA).
[118] Paras 22 to 25 of *Mamabolo*.
[119] Paras 43 to 45 of *Mamabolo*.
[120] Paras 47 and 48 of *Mamabolo*.
[121] Para 42 of *Faki*.

exaggerated or reckless, even incautious, language may render him punishable for contempt of court as happened in *R v Silber*.[122]

In *Silber's* case the appellant, an attorney, asked a magistrate to recuse himself on the grounds that the 'defence [in a criminal case] seem to think that there is bias' against the accused. The attorney then proceeded to set out what he submitted were grounds for thinking that the court was biased. These were that the appellant's objections, despite his 'most earnest arguments', had been overruled without reasons being given. In fact, said the appellant, every ruling given had been 'against defence'. Furthermore the appellant said that the questions put by the magistrate to the witnesses led 'the defence' to think that the court had formed an opinion in the matter, an opinion adverse to 'the defence'. The appellant proceeded to say that, in addition, members of the public had spoken and written to him, and that those persons, too, shared the impression held by 'the defence'. The appellant went out of his way to stress the magistrate's honesty and integrity and his reputation as an impartial and conscientious judicial officer. The magistrate fined the attorney for contempt of court and the decision was confirmed in due course by the Appellate Division, because of the absence of any reasonable basis for the submissions.

It will happen to every advocate in the course of his career that in some case or the other he will feel that the court has formed an opinion adverse to his client. That, of course, may be true, and the opinion may be well-founded or erroneous. The court may be incautious enough to manifest that opinion, but naturally it is not necessarily a final opinion — especially if it is erroneous. The more intensely the advocate identifies himself with his client, the more prone he will be to assume that the ruling and questions of the court are indicative not of an opinion presently entertained, but of a closed or biased mind. Thus, the first cautionary rule is to preserve that degree of independence and detachment essential to the art of advocacy.

If the manifestation of the court's opinion is fancied, or merely the expression of contemporaneous feeling, then counsel's suspicions or concerns might well be allayed in the course of the trial, let alone by the outcome. Thus, the second cautionary rule might well be to wait, wherever possible, for the last word in the case.

Another possibility is that, cumulatively, the manifestations of a suspected bias or pre-judgment, are insignificant compared with the weight of evidence. Perhaps, also, the advocate in fact is wrong in his interpretation of the court's attitude. So the third cautionary rule is to be sure that you are right before making an application for recusal, and to be sure also that it is the only reasonably practical step to take.

Professional courtesy requires that a judicial officer whose recusal is sought should be informed that such an application will be made. Often an informal approach, made timeously, will avoid embarrassment both to the court and to

---

[122] 1952 (2) SA 475 (A). Compare also the grossly improper language used in *R v Luyt* (1926) 7 PH H69, (1926) 8 PH H50 (AD).

counsel. The usual procedure is to request the judge or magistrate to receive both your opponent and yourself in chambers, where you indicate tactfully the fact and grounds of your application. This can be termed the fourth cautionary rule. In all cases, application of the fourth cautionary rule will allow time for consideration and the informal approach will obviate the indignant reaction which may result from an unheralded application made in court.

Should you, nevertheless, decide that an application is necessary you will find both support and an admonition to caution in the words of Schreiner JA in *Silber's* case:

> Now the right of any litigant to ask a judicial officer to recuse himself is a very important right which must be given full protection so long as it is being honestly exercised. But if the right is abused and if, under the cloak of an application for recusal, the applicant is in truth insulting the court wilfully, summary committal may be appropriate.

CHAPTER 3

Preparing for Practice, and Aspects of Practising

3.1 AN INTRODUCTION

> . . . he is furnished with my opinion; which bettered with his own learning, the
> greatness whereof I cannot enough commend, comes with him, at my importunity,
> to fill up your grace's request in my stead. I beseech you, let his lack of years be no
> impediment to let him lack a reverend estimation; for I never knew so young a body
> with so old a head. I leave him to your gracious acceptance, whose trial shall better
> publish his commendation.[1]

With these sentiments, tempered in varying degree by our own individuality,
each one of us starts on his chosen profession of law, whether at the Bar or at the
Side-Bar.

3.2 STUDY AND EXPERIENCE

But let us go back a little, for it is not given to any of us to be admitted to
practice as dexterously as was Portia, nor is it given to us to discomfit the
opposition as adroitly as she did.

In reality today, admission requires qualifications, and to this end I address
the young practitioner thus:

We study and we learn. When we stop studying we have qualified; when we
stop learning we have retired.

So let us start where we should start — with the preliminary formality of
study.

By the time you consider my suggestions, the first problem that you meet
may have been disposed of. That problem is how best to fit yourself
academically for your career. Specifically, you will have debated whether to
study for the four-year LLB, or for a five-year BComm LLB, or perhaps a
five-year BA LLB. Let me start by suggesting that you should rule out the
first-mentioned, and rather choose between the latter two. Of these, the realists
will have selected BComm LLB, and I am told that it is a qualification that
offers more mobility in obtaining candidate attorneyship or other
employment. I hope they are right. If I err I believe myself to be in good
company when I suggest that a knowledge of your own language is somewhat
more advantageous than a course in economics, that the understanding of
history benefits you no less than a study of economic history, and that Accounts
III takes a very poor second place to Political Philosophy II or Psychology II in

[1] Letter of commendation from Bellario, learned doctor of Padua, to introduce Portia (as
Balthazar) in *The Merchant of Venice* Act IV scene i.

giving you the intellectual background that an advocate needs. I believe that you can learn to understand a balance sheet in the time it takes to prepare a case. I also believe that you can interrogate an insolvent on the information contained in his books without ever having attended a lecture in bookkeeping. I believe in literature and languages, in poetry and philosophy and in an understanding of humanity, whether that be gleaned from history, anthropology, sociology, psychology or just plain life experience.

Simultaneously with your later studies you may gain experience, whether as a candidate attorney or as a judge's registrar. My own timorous suggestion is that either of these courses is to be preferred to full-time academic devotion. The wear and tear on the stamina and constitution should be reasonably within the capacity of youth — provided you don't try to add an active social life to the mixture. As a complete outsider I would suggest your preference should be candidate attorneyship for various reasons: there is less temptation to spend the day reading novels while counsel drones on interminably in court, you will gain a good deal of practical experience and common sense for future use, you will establish a 'connection' that may prove beneficial should you join the Bar, and you will learn much about others' mistakes before you get around to making your own.

A passing observation is this: do not for an evanescent moment think that in this book you can find even a tithe of the technique taught by experience. For every illustration I have been able to provide there are a thousand that are unknown to me, and a thousand from which you can learn more than ever I could offer. In your conversations with your colleagues you will hear of their own experiences in court. From each anecdote you may pick up a lesson or at least a hint. For why do we recount our experiences in practice? Is it not because each experience holds something of a novelty, something out of the routine run of litigation? It may be what the magistrate said, it may be how a witness was outwitted, it may be how the wiles of the opposition were stultified; it matters not what it is, nor does it matter that the motive of the narrative is to glorify the narrator; it does not matter, for these trivialities are the atoms from which knowledge is composed.

From this topic one's thoughts turn naturally to one's own loquacity. I remind you that the law of professional privilege applies not only in court. What you might consider is whether it is ever permissible, let alone wise, to recount to *anyone* what your client has communicated to you in confidence.

Not all your clients will be pillars of rectitude. Sometimes you will be embarrassed at having to act for such scoundrels and you will envy your opponent, who seems to be briefed only for the right people. It is, in the circumstances, some consolation to your pride, but no service to your client, to speak disparagingly of him to the other side. By so doing you will but encourage them in their sanctimony.

Perhaps I have stated rather pompously and pedantically what has been written with pith and punch:

Do not run your client down or speak disparagingly of him to the other side. You only weaken your case and encourage them in theirs. You are paid to look after him.[2]

3.3 LIFE AT THE BAR

Before the discussion proceeds it is desirable to face up to one of the harsh realities of life at the Bar. It is this: a successful legal practice and a successful social life are irreconcilable. Why anyone would remain married to a successful barrister is one of the mysteries of life. He is in court or consultation all day, works until midnight on most nights of the week and spends weekends with senior counsel or preparing for 'a big case which starts on Monday'.

This is the life that faces you if you achieve success. But you will keep at it, because of the wonderful human drama that is litigation. There is probably no other profession in the world that can offer you quite what the Bar will, if you can make it there.[3] Each case will offer something new, often the opportunity to deal with specialists in interesting and varied fields. You will be part general, part gladiator, part gunfighter, part psychologist and part actor. You will, moreover, find at the Bar a camaraderie born of combat which no other profession can equal.

From the time of our entrance on to the forensic stage our careers are at the mercy of the laws of chance. To some extent we can withstand the operation of those laws by fitting ourselves for the conflict. We can study, for example, rules and hints for the conduct of civil and criminal trials. If we are gifted with insight and foresight we shall ask ourselves whether we have the personality required to achieve success. We shall go further and ask ourselves what sort of personality is needed. From that point the inquiring mind will ponder whether, in the course of practice, the right sort of personality can be developed. It is only the next logical step to study our colleagues to try to determine how they, individually, conform to the ideal personality.

After a few years, you will no doubt come to the reassuring conclusion that the yardstick of personality does not serve to measure success in the law. You may meet a colleague who appears to be on the verge of tears in almost every address to the court. He falters, stutters and apologises for the very submissions he is making. Yet in substance his arguments may be cogent, convincing and compelling. He wins and, in so doing, helps mould the law. You may meet others who leave their studies trailing clouds of glory. After a few short years they will return to the academic seclusion which is better suited to their own talents, and in which they can both fulfil themselves as lawyers and make their individual contributions to the growth and learning of the law as a whole.

You will find that physical attributes are of no consequence where the battle is one of intellects.

[2] HH Morris KC *The First Forty Years*.
[3] Morrison and Leith *The Barrister's World and the Nature of Law* (Open University Press, 1992) at 24 say that the 'initial problem of finding work of any sort usually disappears for the successful barrister: if it does not, the unsuccessful barrister disappears'.

Later, when reference is made to the conduct of trials, something will be mentioned of diction, but diction need only be precision acquired by training and not given necessarily by nature.

Intellect, voice, personality are all weapons in one's armoury, but to none can be ascribed any degree of dominance. There are, however, two qualities that can overcome any physical failing and, fortunately, they are qualities that are yours for the taking. The first is the quality of courage. It takes courage to argue a matter when the judge is against you. It takes courage to argue a matter before five or eleven judges. But if you have thought the matter through and have satisfied yourself that you are right, or even simply that you are obliged to argue the point, you can do so fearlessly. The second quality is conscientiousness. Counsel should strive to be known for this quality to their colleagues, to attorneys and even to the Bench. Judges will listen with more tolerance and more receptivity to an argument which they know has conscientious effort as its foundation. Attorneys will gain the respect of their clients if they display the same characteristic and, from that respect, will acquire the reputation upon which a successful legal practice is built.

One day junior counsel may be invited to sit as an assessor in a criminal trial, perhaps on circuit, perhaps even at his own Bar. From this lofty eyrie he will perhaps see two or three of his colleagues appear for various accused. He will mark the differences in personality and mannerisms of each. Ultimately, however, he will find that what weighs with him is not the personality of the man but the technical presentation of the case. *What* is said is far more important than *how* it is said. It is true that one must at all times speak convincingly, but not even the most righteous tone of voice will atone for a lack of substance in the argument. Nor will a glittering display of intellectualism outshine the laser beam of logic when that logic fastens on to the basic issue of fact or law.

Apart from the personal talents of the practitioner there arises the question of character. We should always remember that the law is an honourable profession. I would suggest that it should be the aim of every practitioner to acquire a reputation of honesty and candour among his colleagues, for you will find that it takes no more than one case for a man's worth in this regard to be known to the profession. Your word must be your bond; but beware of giving your word unless you are prepared to defend it even against your own client. How many of us make rash promises for the convenience of our colleagues and then try to retract them in the face of the wrath of our client? Your undertaking to a colleague should be sacrosanct; when you make an arrangement or agreement it should be honoured to the letter. Your attitude should be that your client has put his trust in your ability and conferred on you a discretion in the conduct of his case. That discretion should not be abused, but if you act on it you must have the courage to stand by your undertakings.

It must one day happen, to your bitter surprise, that you and a colleague with whom you have had negotiations have widely differing versions of the terms of your discussion. How is one to avoid this? The answer, in the case of discussions between attorneys, is simply that it is wise, and indeed proper, to write a letter confirming any arrangement or undertaking. The arrangement or undertaking may very well become the subject of litigation, and it is no doubt part of the attorney's duty to his client to ensure that there can be no room for dispute. I doubt whether any attorney would resent a suggestion that the terms of a discussion be confirmed in writing, nor would he take exception to a letter accurately recording such terms, even in the absence of a prior suggestion to that effect. The position with counsel is different, for, in the main, discussions between counsel pertain to the conduct of the trial rather than to matters which may be in issue at the trial. Moreover, in South Africa at least, the custom of the Bar would render offensive the writing of letters confirming the terms of discussions between counsel.[4] It would be well, perhaps, to make one's own memorandum immediately after any discussion. It may be your misfortune to be told that you have given an undertaking of which you have not the slightest recollection, which you *think* you had no authority to give, and which you *are certain* you would never have given without reference to your instructing attorney. Your opponent will be so adamant that even your instructing attorney will wonder whether you are lying to save your face — or your skin. You cannot avoid this; you can only try to guard against it by a process of careful concentration on the terms of your discussions and a meticulous system of making immediate notes of what was agreed.

There was a case some years ago where senior and junior counsel for both parties found themselves in the witness-box in a subsequent action arising out of a settlement which, it was said, had been agreed upon orally between counsel in the trial. Both senior counsel were men of the utmost eminence in the profession, men whose integrity was beyond doubt, whose ethical standards were such that nobody would have doubted the word of either of them. Nor did the juniors fall in any whit short of the standards of their leaders, save in their eminence at that time. Yet they differed as to whether they had settled the action. You, too, may have the distressing experience of having to cross-examine one of your respected colleagues or, worse still, of finding yourself in the witness-box undergoing the humiliating experience of being cross-examined at least as to the accuracy of your recollection.

All I can say is that if the circumstances permit you to make a note in collaboration with your colleague, but without affronting him, then do so.

Never be guilty of elaboration or concealment; whether with the court, with your opponent or with your instructing attorney. Of all things you must

---

[4] As Malan J said in *Murphy NO and Benjamin NO v Semphill and Others* 1954 (3) SA 450 (W) at 452D:

> 'Mr Oshrey states that the day before the hearing he informed Mr Suzman that it would not be necessary for him to appear at the hearing. I am not prepared to have regard to communications that pass between counsel unless they were intended to constitute an agreement binding upon the parties. Mr Suzman was not obliged to act upon Mr Oshrey's suggestion and was entitled to appear.'

gain and deserve the confidence of the court.[5] If you have erred (and who does not?) admit the error, suffer the wrath of the court but earn and preserve your reputation. And if you have done something of which your instructing attorney will not approve do not withhold your fault from him; you may lose his support by reason of that fault, but if you try to cover it up he will find out and you will certainly lose his support and respect as well as the support and respect of those to whom he cares to relate his grievance. As far as your colleagues are concerned, if once you deceive them they will know how to deal with you on the next and subsequent occasions.

Inevitably there will come the day when your opponent makes some mistake which may cost him his client's case. It may possibly jeopardise his practice. What does one do? The answer is not simple because the variety of circumstances is infinite. Your first duty is to your client but I, personally, have some doubt whether the duty of fair dealing may not override this. You are not, I would suggest, called upon to rectify the consequences of your opponent's ineptitude. Errors of a technical nature, however, are on a substantially different basis, and you should hesitate to gain what may be an unconscionable advantage. Or what are you to do when your opponent fails to appear in court at the appointed hour? In such cases it would be grossly unfair to snatch a benefit — or a judgment — and I would suggest your duty is to allow your opponent every reasonable opportunity to remedy that default. Is it really in the interests of the client to bring about further litigation designed to secure formal condonation of the error and to start the main case *de novo*? Perhaps some guidance may be obtained from a judgment of the Appellate Division, *Hladhla v President Insurance Co Ltd*,[6] where Van Blerk JA said:

> I see no reason why even at this stage of the proceedings a trial court should not on application have the power to allow in its discretion a witness to be recalled especially where, as in this case, it is clear that plaintiff's counsel inadvertently omitted to establish the identity of the vehicle which was involved in the accident. The defendant put the identity of the vehicle in issue, merely because it had no knowledge of the allegation that the insured vehicle was involved in the accident. It was never suggested that the defendant was in a position to adduce evidence to disprove the allegation. The nature of the evidence which the plaintiff now seeks to place before the court by recalling the witness is purely supplementary and almost of a formal nature. It is, on the view I take, to correct an error which may be described as a slip of the pen.

Heed the advice of the Duke of Norfolk to Buckingham in Shakespeare's *Henry VIII*:[7]

> Heat not a furnace for your foe so hot that it do singe yourself.

---

[5] *Haarhoff v Wakefield* 1955 (2) SA 425 (E) at 428A per Van der Riet J quoting James LS as to the signature of counsel being 'a voucher that the case is not a mere fiction'. The correct citation should be James LJ in *Great Australian Gold Mining Company v Martin* 5 ChD 1 at 10.

[6] 1965 (1) SA 614 (A) at 621–2.

[7] Act I scene i.

3.4 JUNIORS

Senior counsel may appear in court without a junior, but are generally briefed with one.

The first duty of the junior, I would suggest, is to call upon his leader immediately the brief is delivered. Sometimes there is a degree of procrastination which is unwarranted, while in other cases the procrastination is due to the junior's laudable desire to present senior counsel with whatever drafts or notes may seem to be indicated. Even the latter cause of delay should be avoided, because the senior himself may have embarked upon a similar course of research with a resultant waste of effort by one or other of them. If you present yourself at senior counsel's chambers without delay the responsibility thereafter is his to indicate what preparation he desires you to undertake and what drafts he requires you to prepare.

When you arrive at court it is your duty to have all the authorities available, properly marked, for use by your senior at the appropriate time. You are expected to know as much about the case as he does, although you will not necessarily be expected to act as his understudy where the case is difficult and involved.[8]

Even in your early days at the Bar you should not be hesitant about expressing your views or making suggestions, provided you have thought them through beforehand. There is no reason why you should be wrong, nor why your opinions should be of any less substance than those of your leader. As time passes you will be more able to tactfully tell him that he is in error, should the occasion arise.

My last offering will be unpopular. I suggest that it is your duty timeously to return your brief if your own commitments are such that you cannot give your leader the time he wants or give the brief the attention it deserves.

You might well, in your early years, find that you have more spare time on your hands than you would like. Use that spare time productively. Research areas of the law which you might reasonably expect to have to tackle in practice. For example, look again at the basic principles of the laws of delict and contract. Research the law relating to postponements and amendments, etc. If you do that, you will be better prepared when you do eventually receive a brief and, as a result, the impression you make will likely in turn assure you of more briefs and less spare time.

Another suggestion is that if you know that a really good silk is appearing in

---

[8] *Cosmetic Distributing Co v Industrial Products* 1944 WLD 201. This case dealt with the question whether the sudden unavailability of a party's leading counsel due to illness is a sufficient reason for granting a postponement. Should junior counsel be forced to proceed with the matter? In this particular case a postponement was granted. This decision was followed by Colman J in *S v Shepard and Others* WLD, 22 October 1966, unreported. Cf *S v Shepard* 1966 (4) SA 530 (WLD) and *S v Shepard* 1967 (4) SA 170 (WLD). The decision in *Cosmetic Distributing Company* was considered in *Van Staden v Union and South-West Africa Insurance Co Ltd* 1972 (1) SA 758 (E) and in *Centirugo A G v Firestone SA Ltd* 1969 (3) SA 318 (T).

a case in your division, go and listen. Study the manner in which he presents his case. We can always learn by the example of others.

3.5 IMPLEMENTING GOOD SYSTEMS

Later in this work I propose to discuss specifically the successive steps in the normal trial action, with principal reference to the High Court.

However, before you concern yourself with that, let us first consider the more practical matters of implementing systems in your practice that will make you a better trial lawyer, and how you should approach your cases generally.

3.5.1 The importance of having a good system

To achieve proper application to one's case, one requires *system* in one's practice.

There are few spectacles more awkward in court than that of counsel, who has been asked a question by the judge or who desires to confront a witness with a document, shuffling his papers and paging backwards and forwards through his brief in search of what he wants. He knows it is there, in fact he saw it this morning, or maybe it was yesterday afternoon, when he looked at the papers. He finds a document and picks it up with relief, scans it for a moment and then has to resume the rummaging. It is debatable who is more embarrassed by this sort of performance. Often it is the opponent who is sitting quietly, well aware of what is required but reluctant to intervene for fear of adding to the discomfiture of the moment. Counsel is expected to know his brief and he cannot expect the business of the court to be delayed while he looks for what he theoretically knows.

3.5.2 What system?

You will need to develop the habit of sorting the papers in your file if you are at the Side-Bar or your brief if you are at the Bar into systematic order so that you know at a glance what is to be found where. And you will need a system for collecting (and being able readily to retrieve) useful precedents and legal points.

Any system will do. In what follows, suggestions will be made as to systems which might be followed. These suggestions are no more than my own views on the topics. Other persons might have other views and probably have better systems. Work out your own system and aim at thoroughness, although not the thoroughness of junior counsel who once analysed 2000 pages of evidence into 3000 pages of summary.

When you have worked out your systems, turn them into routine. If you do this your energies will be available to their maximum effectiveness. You will be able to concentrate on *what* you are doing and not *how* you are to do it. Whenever possible do not rely on your memory; the witness easiest to cross-examine is the one who relies on his memory.

3.5.3 A system for sorting the documents in your file or your brief

It might be that some attorneys, and also some advocates, perform better when their files or their briefs are a hodge-podge of documents without any order or logic. But if that is so, they are by far the minority, and probably deluded. You might *think* that you perform best in the midst of confusion, but you are mistaken.

Attorneys would do well to have a file for every matter, and to have an order to every file with correspondence, notes of telephone calls, pleadings, notices and memoranda all bound in some or another fashion in separate sub-files in chronological order.

Advocates will do better if, on receipt of their briefs, they sort them into a logical order (perhaps correspondence with the attorney followed by the pleadings, followed by the discovery and important notices, expert reports and then the papers, and perhaps further divisions), and particularly if they sort the papers (contracts, correspondence etc; the evidentiary material that tells the story of the matter) into some sort of a chronological order.

3.5.4 A system for collecting the law

One of the most time-wasting features of legal practice is tracing the decided cases applying to any point. Careful use of digests, noters-up and law reports (electronic and other) is called for and will, of course, ultimately provide what is being sought. However, nobody likes to have to repeat the same performance time after time on points which, if not actually identical, are very similar. Systems which you might well consider in order to simplify your task are the following:

- A useful system is to keep your own set of notes covering the fields with which you are likely to deal in court, either because those are your fields of specialisation or because those are the fields with which you generally find yourself dealing. For example the various aspects of procedure, the law of evidence, delict or contract or both, the law relating to damages, estoppel, prescription, etc.

  As each monthly instalment of the law reports appears (these days there is a proliferation of law reports and you should at least subscribe to the South African Law Reports), incorporate into your notes those cases falling within the fields in question which strike you as being particularly useful or relevant. For example, under 'Evidence' you might have headings in your notes such as a general heading (where you collect useful items that do not fall within your other headings, such as authority relating to a court's discretion to allow affidavit evidence in trial actions, etc), absolution from the instance, the courts' approach to resolving factual disputes, inferences, the burden of proof generally, the implications of the failure to call a witness, cross-examination, the effect of a failure to cross-examine on a particular point, hearsay and so on. Where you find a case that seems particularly material, note it under the relevant heading.

Of course, this requires time, but it will pay dividends: you will find that you can draft opinions more systematically and in less time by using your notes, and you will often be able to use your system of notes to deal with an unexpected issue when it comes up in court without any delay or discomfiture.

• You will no doubt either prepare notes of your argument or Heads of Argument in every case, complete with references to the decided cases to be cited on points of law. When you have finished with your notes or Heads, preserve them carefully and file them in covers which respectively relate to the various topics of law in, say, alphabetical order. Of course, if you are more conscientious and painstaking you will prepare your own file of index cards onto which you will note the authorities you collect from time to time. If you object that you might as well look up the cases in the digest anyway, the answer might well be that your index cards can achieve a degree of collation and analysis not met with in any digest. The best time to start a system of index cards is at the beginning of your career. Do not lend your notes to anyone because the odds can safely be assessed at 33 to 1 that you will never see them again if you do so. Let your colleague make a list of the cases you have found, if you will, but guard your own notes as though they bore the signature of the governor of the Reserve Bank.

• Today with the modern computer it is easy to update your notes or Heads of Argument, or have your secretary update them. One simply inserts the latest case or article at the relevant place with the necessary comments. The advantage of such a system is that with the necessary 'cut and paste' you can swiftly produce a comprehensive set of Heads of Argument.

• Perhaps it might also be of value to preserve a record of unusual points of practice, whether of law, of fact or of procedure. Not all the points and decisions which might be of value can be reported or even come to the attention of the reporters. I have known a case where a lengthy and relatively important decision was not reported because the stenographer found it too much of a burden to transcribe his notes of a judgment that took nearly three hours to deliver. In that judgment the court declined to follow one of its previous decisions because it was satisfied that the earlier decision was wrong. The result is that the original erroneous decision remains on record in the law reports and may be followed in future cases. You cannot, of course, have a complete record of everything that happens in every court, but it is safe to assume that sooner or later you will profit from the notes you make.

• Either in the course of your regular reading of the law reports or in the preparation of cases, you will find passages in the judgments which contain useful observations or learning on rare points of law or practice. These may not be mentioned in the headnote, and may strike you as being well worth remembering for use should the occasion arise. One thing is certain: you will not remember them. Sometimes you will be able to trace them later, usually not. Examples are discussions on what is an *obiter dictum*, what use (if any) can be made of the claim for 'further or alternative relief', what the practical effect is of rejecting the evidence of a witness on a particular point, and so on. The only sensible thing to do is to make an immediate note of the point that has impressed you, whether in your notes or in your card index. The same system could be followed in regard to matters of tactics, problems of proof and, indeed, all the topics which are discussed in this book.

3.5.5 The importance of attorneys having a system

In the case of attorneys there are a variety of additional reasons for following a *system* in the course of practice. For example, a good deal of time is taken up with telephone discussions with clients or with attorneys for the opposing parties. Make it a habit immediately the conversation is finished to write, dictate or record a note setting out as fully as possible the terms of the discussion, recording particularly any instructions given or arrangements made. This will serve the triple purpose firstly of having an *aide-memoire* should any difference of opinion arise, secondly of having a reminder should further action be necessary, and thirdly of enabling you to charge properly for your time.

3.6 PREPARATION, AND APPLICATION

3.6.1 Preparation, preparation, preparation

The importance of proper preparation cannot be sufficiently emphasised. If there is a key to success in your practice, it is preparation, preparation, and yet more preparation.

3.6.2 Application

Application is the dedication of the mind and energies to the case in hand. It is not synonymous with *preparation*, although it must of necessity pervade the latter. Litigation, as every lawyer learns to his regret or his client's cost, is not the same as school or college. When the court adjourns at the end of a tiring day the lawyer's task is not finished. Often enough he may have to continue on the morrow.[9] If he is a busy attorney or junior counsel he may have clients waiting to see him, half a dozen telephone messages to be attended to and even pleadings to be drawn. These things *must* be done, and done they are. But the conscientious lawyer will, as soon as time permits, return to the trial that continues on the morrow. He will think over everything of importance that happened during the day. He will ask himself, for example, what the significance was of an apparently casual but incongruous question put to a witness by the opposition. His speculative thought process will abound in the iteration of two questions: What were they after? What have I overlooked?

---

[9] Unless his case is in the magistrate's court, where all too often it is heard in a fashion that makes the word 'piecemeal' appear as a comparative description of Einstein's space-time continuum.

Perhaps it is not an exaggeration to say that you should approach every case as though it is your first and, if not handled properly, may be your last. You make a living by selling your 'time', your labour. You have nothing else to offer. Your client buys these commodities. He is entitled to both — without reserve and without qualification.

By no means do I suggest that you should worry from night to morn, nor that you should pace up and down the corridor in front of your chambers in a frenzy of concentration until court begins again in the morning. What is called for is quiet contemplation and analysis, so quiet as to be almost subconscious. This feat, I have found, is often best performed during the course of a 30-minute drive from town to suburbs early in the evening, when the traffic grows quiet and the air becomes still.

One word of advice I would offer, on a topic discussed earlier. My own view is that counsel with a trial practice should make it a rule to have no social engagements whatsoever except on Friday and Saturday nights. Trials are of uncertain advent and of even more uncertain duration. It is an impossible situation to find that one is engaged to go visiting when the evidence in one's trial has finished on that day, and argument is to begin on the morrow. Rather one should regard the odd night that becomes available for social purposes as something in the nature of a windfall. You will, of course, be regarded as a social misfit and most of your friends won't believe you anyway, but your clients will get what they are entitled to and you may attain what you want — success, which does not always come merely from ability.

On the other hand you may well decide that the principle of application means application to your social life, with the object of using your personal charm to build up a large business connection. This way, too, you may make a success of your legal practice, but it requires a high degree of skill and you may find it easier to win your reputation in court.

Application, I hasten to add, does not relate only to the stage when a case is actually being heard in court. It refers to every aspect of legal practice and to every legal problem. It refers even to the drafting and despatch of letters on behalf of a client who has become involved in a dispute. It will be found, in any commercial case, that at least 75 per cent of the cross-examination will turn on incautious and inaccurate statements in letters which have passed between the parties and, far too often, that have been written by the attorneys on one side or the other.

If *application* is to be a thorough process it must include observation and perception. The lawyer, regrettably, is not equipped with eyes in the back of his head and one doubts whether a court would tolerate the use of a rear-view mirror. Yet often some of the most interesting action in a case takes place behind the back of counsel who are appearing for the parties and who are diligently attending to the papers or the witnesses in front of them. There may be the spectator who is affected with the wanderlust, the onset of which appears to be precipitated by an embarrassing question put to the witness in cross-examination and the pangs of which can be allayed by a communion with the next witness, who is patiently waiting outside the court. Nobody will blame counsel for not becoming aware of these peregrinations, but there is nothing like an eavesdropping attorney or candidate attorney to provide the assistance necessary in such cases. Counsel cannot afford to wear blinkers — literally or metaphorically. Counsel must see everything and must appreciate everything. Cross-examination is no easy task, as a few trial runs will show, and it demands every effort of concentration of which one is capable. Yet the cross-examiner, apart from thinking about the last question, the present answer and the next question, must also watch. He must watch the witness for any glimmering of physical reaction,[10] and he must watch the judge or magistrate in order to detect the all-too-easily provoked symptoms of boredom. And with all this he must also remain aware of everything out of the ordinary which is going on around him. With the exercise of proper observation one will become aware of many little matters which may not win the case for one but which can be turned to great advantage at the proper moment. You must also bear in mind that the judicial officer will also be conducting the same exercise, so be aware of what interests him.

I doubt whether you will ever observe your opponent surreptitiously supplying the answer to a witness, but be mindful of an anecdote related by senior counsel who, many years ago, consulted with a client prior to a trial and was a little disconcerted when this client asked him: 'Mr M, what are your signals?' Affecting surprise, Mr M asked for further and better particulars and learned that he was expected to supply a code indicating when the witness was to answer 'Yes', when 'No', and when he was to become afflicted with amnesia! Nor should you unreservedly accept the word of your client that your opponent is actually assisting the witness. After all, it is easy to misinterpret a nervous mannerism as a signal.

So much for the physical blinkers that you are not to wear. The mental blinkers are equally important. Throughout a trial you will be concentrating wholeheartedly on the realisation of the essence, as outlined below. But from time to time there will arise the odd point, whether of fact or law, which irritates the subconscious as a grain of sand irritates an oyster. Sometimes one reacts as does the oyster by covering the grain of sand with a smooth coating so that it no longer irritates; but, the lawyer not being a marine creature, the result of the coating is far from profitable. Too often the irritant produces an ulcer that erodes the whole case. I am fully aware of the difficulty of practising what I preach but I have learned that these little matters should never be ignored. Your self-training in application must be such that your mind turns every subconscious irritation into a conscious reaction. You must mentally stop — and when I say stop I mean no more than a pause to consider — and examine the irritant from every angle. From that point the procedure varies: the point may be discarded as insignificant, it may be filed for future reference and

---

[10] See paragraph 12.5.27 in chapter 12 'Cross-examination'.

discussion, or it may call for an urgent reconsideration of the tactical path you are following. Don't find yourself after the case is over in the unhappy position of saying: 'Well, I couldn't really have anticipated that on the pleadings.' Perhaps you could not, but if the warning was given and you missed it there is no possible excuse. Yours, it should be repeated, is a profession in which one's mistakes are one's opponent's advantages.

There are other, possibly gratuitous, suggestions on this topic:

- Every lawyer who is liable to develop a court practice should either learn shorthand, or a form thereof, or else develop his own system of abbreviations. No matter how experienced you may become, how brilliant you are or how retentive your memory you cannot remember every word uttered by every witness during a trial. Since electrical recording machines have greatly accelerated the tempo of court proceedings it is no longer always possible to take a leisured note whilst the long-suffering judge makes a handwritten narrative of the evidence. You may be assured that, no matter how simple the case, at some stage or the other everybody will be uncertain as to precisely what one of the witnesses has said on a particular point. There are two other certainties: firstly, the dispute will arise at the crucial point of your cross-examination, where a diversion will destroy the whole atmosphere that exists; secondly, if you are relying on memory or an inadequate note of the evidence, your question will be sufficiently inaccurate to have the same result and to leave you with an uncomfortable feeling that the court thinks that you are trying to mislead the witness.

- Counsel (and attorneys) are supposed to know the law. I doubt whether any practitioner can in fact 'know' the whole of the law. He will probably know the basic principles and a fair amount of detail but at least he should know where to find the rest. There are, however, two topics at least on which the lawyer must know the details. He must know the rules of court, usually both the High Court and magistrates' courts, and probably other courts as well. He must also know every principle and detail of the law of evidence. Only in this way is it possible to deal promptly and efficiently with the numerous little crises that arise from time to time during the course of a trial.

- The suggestion to the young practitioner that he learns how to use a computer may give rise to a wry smile. However, if you are old enough not to smile, but rather to nod, at the suggestion, why not register at one of the many local colleges that offer these courses?[11] Apart from learning the practicalities of using a computer such as creating and filing various documents and sending and receiving e-mails, you might also learn to type which always proves useful when you do not have a typist available.

---

[11] Adv Steve Kirk–Cohen SC has written a number of useful articles in 'Advocate' on how to use a computer in an advocate's practice. See 'Advocate' August 2004 at 46 and further additions.

You might also learn how to 'surf the internet' and to search for all those elusive law reports in England, America and elsewhere in the world.[12] The Constitutional Court, the Supreme Court of Appeal and other courts have very useful websites which enable one to download judgments as they are reported.[13]

- Another useful talent to acquire is the ability to 'speed read'. It is said that the average person reads at the rate of 250 words per minute. With a bit of practice you could at least double your speed. If you learn to speed read you should at the very least be able to quadruple it. Imagine what you could achieve then.[14]

Application does not relate only to preparation for trial for, as Oscar Wilde might have said, had he thought of it first: answers are given by those who don't understand the questions.

It was an unusual case, but the facts are irrelevant. Suffice it to say that provisional sentence was granted on a mortgage bond in the sum of R40 000. The defendant believed he had a good case — probably he did, but very few defendants can beat a mortgage bond on a balance of probabilities. The next step, therefore, was to go into the principal case, to which end the defendant raised a loan to cover the provisional judgment and costs. The money was handled by his attorney who knew that the successful plaintiff had to provide security for repayment of any amount received. The attorney then communicated with the plaintiff's attorneys saying, in effect: 'I have the money to meet the provisional judgment. Please let me have security for repayment.'

The attorney knew also that, in order to go into the principal case, his client would have to deliver a plea. So he went to senior counsel saying, 'Please draw me a plea'. But senior counsel was engaged in a trial and could not find time to draw a plea. 'Do not worry', said he, 'they have to serve a notice of bar and we shall then have five days to plead.'

Two mistakes were made. Firstly, in terms of rule 8(9) security has to be furnished only against payment and not against a statement that funds are available. Secondly, in terms of rule 8(11) certain times are stipulated for notice of intention to enter into the principal case and for plea. The stipulations in rules 22(1) and 26 as to notice of bar in the case of pleas do not apply to provisional sentence proceedings. I point to these mistakes in all humility, for only the brash pretend to infallibility. Yet both practitioners gave the answers without understanding the questions. And, as far as the unfortunate defendant was concerned, that was the end of the road. An application to condone late filing of the plea was refused, there having been no valid tender of payment and

---

[12] Section 39(1)(c) of the Constitution provides that a court when interpreting the Bill of Rights may consider foreign law.

[13] Constitutional Court: www.constitutionalcourt.org.za; Supreme Court of Appeal: www.supremecourtofappeal.gov.za.

[14] Once you are able to surf the net you should be able to locate several institutions that could teach you this talent. It is said that some people are able to read at a rate of 10 000 words per minute.

hence no right to enter upon the principal case. Perhaps the third mistake was in not reading rule 8(10) before applying for an extension of the times stipulated in rule 8(11). None of these mistakes need have been made if somebody had directed proper thought to the rules before writing letters or expressing opinions. Perhaps the lesson to be learnt is, whenever dealing with a rule of court or a principle of law, first to read it again and pause to consider its impact on your case.

Let us here have a true story — and you can work out the precept. The attorney issued summons against a municipality on a claim arising out of an assault by an employee. Notice had been duly given in terms of para *(a)* of s 2(1) of the then current Limitation of Legal Proceedings (Provincial and Local Authorities) Act 94 of 1970. When the 90 days prescribed in that paragraph had elapsed the attorney, mindful of the further time limit prescribed in para *(b)* of the subsection, caused the summons to be served upon the local authority (municipality) concerned. The legal adviser to the local authority, or maybe it was the municipality's attorney, then communicated with the plaintiff's attorney saying (in effect): 'Your action is defective because by issuing your summons before the 90 days prescribed had elapsed you fell foul of the stipulation that "no legal proceedings in respect of any debt shall be instituted" before the expiry of 90 days from your demand.' Plaintiff's attorney hit the panic button. She rushed off to counsel who had drawn the particulars of claim to find out what to do. Counsel agreed that the situation was grave. 'There is no doubt,' said he, 'that the summons is a nullity because it was issued despite a statutory prohibition. You had better withdraw, pay costs and start again — if you can.' So the attorney left and went to see another counsel about another matter. But for good measure — and at no extra cost — she thought that she would get a second opinion. Second counsel agreed that the situation was indeed grave. However, she (for so it was this time) idly turned the page of the statute and cast a casual eye at para *(a)* of s 2(2) where it was proclaimed, as large as life, that 'legal proceedings shall be deemed to be instituted by *service on the debtor* of any process . . . in which the creditor claims payment of the debt'. The day was saved — and the costs — there having been no *service* prior to 90 days.

And, to conclude, an attorney once handed a copy of *Jones & Buckle* to his newly employed candidate attorney with the words 'Make this your Bible'. Those words, in one form or another, as the circumstances demand, should commence the first lecture given to every student in the law of civil procedure and the law of evidence.

3.6.3 Preparation reprised

Perhaps little need be said on *preparation* as a separate topic, because it will be discussed in dealing with trials, criminal trials and opposed applications. It is to be regretted, however, that all too often counsel deems it unnecessary to do any work in preparation of unopposed applications in the motion court. Perhaps an example will illustrate what I mean — although an hour or so spent in the motion court will provide an object lesson — or perhaps a few such lessons.

The scene of our illustration opens in the Witwatersrand Local Division in the years known as the 'Mad Twenties'. It is a criminal trial and the prosecutor is a member of the Johannesburg Bar. For reasons which do not concern us, let us, in any event, refer to him as Smith. Counsel for the accused may be called Jones — to preserve the equities of anonymity. At the end of the case Mr Jones makes submissions on behalf of his client, including the raising of a point of law of some substance. Mr Smith is jolted out of the complacency engendered by being briefed on behalf of the big battalions and he realises that the Crown has a problem. Says Mr Smith: 'M'Lord. I must confess that the ingenious point of law raised by my learned friend has taken me somewhat by surprise. I had not anticipated that such a point would be raised and, ahem, m'Lord, I regret that I am not in a position to deal with the point. M'Lord, perhaps if your Lordship would grant me a postponement, a short adjournment . . . perhaps if your Lordship would allow the matter to stand down I could be in a position to deal with my learned friend's argument.' Says his Lordship: 'Mr Smith, counsel who appear in these courts must be prepared at any time to meet any point that arises in their cases. Your application is refused.'

The scene changes to the motion court in the Witwatersrand Local Division and the calendar moves on some 20 years or more. Mr Smith has now become Smith J, and he is sitting on the Bench for the purposes of this act in the drama. Mr Jones (junior of that ilk) has now been admitted to the Bar and is following in the footsteps, though far behind, of Mr Jones (senior). Jones (junior) has a brief. It is an application for the sequestration of a debtor who owes an attorney a goodly sum as, and by way of, fees for professional services rendered. Also on the roll at the same time is another application for the sequestration of the same chronic debtor, this one at the instance of an aggrieved merchant who has sold and delivered vast quantities of goods to him. Jones (junior) knows all about the competing application but he is not worried because the security bond in his case was taken out earlier than in the other case and also his petition was lodged first; likewise his case appears on the roll before the other matter. The case is called. Says Mr Justice Smith: 'Mr Jones, isn't there another application on the roll for the sequestration of this respondent?'

Says Mr Jones (junior): 'Yes, my Lord, but the security bond in this case was taken out first and also the petition was lodged first.'

Mr Justice Smith: 'Mr Jones, does your client's claim not require taxation before it becomes liquidated? And if that is so, have you any right to the order which you seek?'

Mr Jones (junior): 'M'Lord, the point hadn't occurred to me. It may well be that I can show that the applicant is entitled to claim the amount on which his petition is based. Would your Lordship be pleased to allow the matter to stand down for a while so that I can investigate and be in a position to make submissions to your Lordship.'

Mr Justice Smith: 'Mr Jones, 20-odd years ago your father took a legal point against me. I asked for a postponement to go into the matter. Your father objected. He said that counsel should be ready for any point at any time. The court upheld his argument. At that time I thought it was a wrong decision. I now think it was right. Your application for a postponement is refused.'

Suffice it to say that had Mr Jones (junior) approached his motion court brief as though it were a trial matter he would have been in a position either to make submissions on the law or to present a supplementary affidavit showing that the section did not hit his client's claim. At the very least, being only the second generation, he would have avoided having the sins of his father visited upon him.

Usually the presiding judge is a little more tolerant and will allow a matter to be 'mentioned later'. But many people may be inconvenienced and, in my view at least, it is no advertisement for counsel to be compelled in a crowded motion court to have to ask for a matter to stand down so that he can prepare a point which he did not anticipate or which he has neglected.[15] Of course matters may arise in which the judge raises points for which counsel is not prepared for the simple reason that the points in fact do not present a real difficulty but have occurred to the judge as possibilities in his reading of the papers. And if the judge troubles to prepare himself to deal with a motion roll consisting perhaps of two hundred or more matters the very least that counsel can do is to return the compliment.

It seems hardly necessary to say that *system* must include *preparation* as well as *preparation* being based on *system*. In fact most attorneys and counsel would resent being advised that they should prepare their cases. In the majority of cases such resentment would be fully justified, but, as will be seen in the chapter dealing with preparation for trial, there is a lot more to preparation than reading one's brief and looking up a few cases — perhaps performing the latter task in so perfunctory fashion that one merely quotes from a textbook.

3.7 A FEW FURTHER PRACTICAL SUGGESTIONS

I add a few further points. I hope they might be of some use to you.

3.7.1 Strive to be perfect

Never make a mistake. Accountants may make mistakes — and add up their figures again. Doctors may make mistakes — and either rely on nature to remedy (or bury) them, or call in a specialist. The mistakes of those professionals are their own and are usually reversible.

But the lawyer must realise that he is faced with an adversary who will seize on any mistake and will do his best not to allow it to be reversed. I do not refer here to technical mistakes, but to such tactical blunders as calling the wrong witness or not calling the right witness or error in any one of the ten to 50 decisions that one has to make in the conduct of a case.

It is well known that no one is perfect; what is not so well known is that counsel cannot afford to be less than perfect. Leave out an allegation in a

---

[15] Cf: *Groenewald v Conradie* 1957 (3) SA 413 (C) at 415.

pleading or a statement in an affidavit and that roaring noise about your ears will be the roof falling in. Fail to call evidence on a material point and that sudden chill down your spine will not be caused by the air-conditioning but by the court granting absolution. Cross-examine too liberally and you will find that you have consolidated the case for the opposition; cross-examine with too much economy and you will hear the judge say 'I accept the evidence, which was scarcely challenged in cross-examination'. On the other hand, if you would succeed, be ever watchful for such mistakes by your opponent, seize on them, capitalise on them, make them into weapons of attack in your own cause. And then, when the trial is over, consign them to limbo with a prayer of thankfulness that they were not your own.

3.7.2 Do not procrastinate

The topic of *procrastination* can be dealt with briefly.

For attorneys two suggestions are offered:

* Read chapter 2, paragraph 2.3.1 of this book.
* Take out a professional public liability policy.

For counsel two suggestions are offered:

* If you don't do it now you will have to do it all on the day before you leave on holiday.
* Attorneys may be impressed by the row of briefs paraded on your desk; but they will be more impressed by promptness[16] — and promptness pays.

3.7.3 Less haste, more speed

Strangely enough, *haste* is as reprehensible as *procrastination*, and, of course, the latter may lead to the former.

Haste is totally irreconcilable with the proper extraction of the essence of a matter. The practice of law requires the consideration of a problem from many angles, from every angle, and indeed from angles that Euclid never imagined. You may take it for granted that when you rush out a difficult pleading because the *dies* are expiring the pleading will be defective and require amendment later. If you draft an urgent application to anticipate a sale in execution or to stop a debtor from leaving the country it is a fair shade of odds that there will be a material non-disclosure.[17] Still less should an opinion or an advice on evidence have the characteristics of the urgent removal of a ruptured appendix (bodily not literary).

3.7.4 Be cautious in your optimism

The best of cases have foundered on unexpected obstacles. Witnesses who were confidently expected to say one thing have conceded another. And when

---

[16] *Morrison and Leith* say on p 66, on the strength of numerous interviews with barristers' clerks in England, that 'speed and efficiency are valued in the legal world . . . for healthy commercial reasons'. If anyone knows what qualities attorneys seek in advocates, it is English barristers' clerks.

[17] See chapter 17, paragraph 17.4.3.

that happens — and happen to you it will — the optimism with which you predicted success to your client will seem like nothing more than foolishness. If a hard look at the case leads you to a pessimistic view, tell your attorney and then, in your attorney's presence, your client. If on the other hand that same hard look at the case affords you the luxury of being optimistic, you would be wise to hedge that optimism with caution. Your attorney, and your client, will be far better served by knowing that there are no guarantees of success.

3.7.5 Remember that the law is indeed an honourable profession

Trial lawyers are gladiators. But although we might play the game hard, we play it by the rules and this we must never forget. We belong to a brotherhood and sisterhood and, whatever the differences between our clients, we must always be able to look our colleagues (and the presiding officer) in the eye knowing that we fight our clients' cases honourably.

For example, whilst surprise remains one of the most valuable weapons in our armoury, that weapon has its limits. If there is a point you propose taking *in limine* and you have no reason to believe that your opponent is aware of it, warn him beforehand. You will find that if the point is good it is no less good for the prior warning, and that your advocacy is the better for the fact that your colleagues and your judges know that you conduct your cases vigorously, well and honourably.

3.8 CONSOLATION

I quote from two judgments, separated in time by nearly three-quarters of a century.

The first:

> This Court has the greatest latitude in granting amendments, and it is very necessary that it should have. The object of the Court is to do justice between the parties. It is not a game we are playing, in which, if some mistake is made, the forfeit is claimed. We are here for the purpose of seeing that we have a true account of what actually took place, and we are not going to give a decision upon what we know to be wrong facts. It is presumed that when a defendant pleads to a declaration he knows what he is doing, and that, when there is a certain allegation in the declaration, he knows that he ought to deny it, and that, if he does not do so, he is taken to admit it. But we all know, at the same time, that mistakes are made in pleadings, and it would be a very grave injustice, if for a slip of the pen, or error of judgment, or misreading of a paragraph in pleadings by counsel, litigants were to be mulcted in heavy costs. That would be a gross scandal. Therefore, the Court will not look to technicalities but will see what the real position is between the parties.[18]

---

[18] Per Wessels J in *Whittaker v Roos and Another* 1911 TPD 1092 at 1102–3.

The second:

> I am of the view that litigation of this nature is not a game; that the object of all litigation is to arrive at the truth and at a fair, just and expeditious solution [19]

---

[19] Per Le Roux J in *Stein Bros Ltd v Dawood and Another* 1980 (3) SA 275 (W) at 282C, where the court held that it was entitled to look at a fourth and fifth set of affidavits and that it should not shut its eyes because of a mere technicality.

CHAPTER 4

How to Approach Cases: Probabilities, and Extracting the Essence

4.1 APPROACHING YOUR CASES

Your greatest cases will be those in which you call no witnesses; your finest cross-examination will be where you ask no questions; your soundest arguments will be where the facts speak for themselves. It is where these Utopian conditions do not apply that court-craft and trial technique are important, whether the tribunal be the High Court, a magistrate's court or any other tribunal — perhaps even more so in the two last-mentioned instances.

From the moment the client walks into your office if you are at the Side-Bar, or from the moment that a brief is laid upon your desk if you are at the Bar, you are engaged in an exercise of problem-solving aimed at achieving the best practicable result for your client. To enable you to do that, you must learn how to approach your cases. This can be considered in stages.

4.2 THE STAGES OF APPROACH TO A CASE

There are three stages to approaching any case. They are firstly applying your common sense to the facts of the case, secondly extracting the essence of the case, and finally preparation for the case.

In this chapter I shall deal with the first two stages.[1]

4.3 APPLYING COMMON SENSE TO THE FACTS OF THE CASE

It hardly helps to have a good grasp of the law if you have an inadequate grasp of the facts. The law only finds relevance in factual context. The vast majority of cases are decided not on the law, but on the facts.

It is therefore only logical that the first stage of approaching any case is the analysis of the facts. This in itself broadly involves two steps. The first step involves sorting the facts (including the disputes of fact) into some sort of chronological order. The second step involves applying common sense to those facts in order to determine the probabilities.

The first step, sorting the documents and allegations, and thus the facts, into chronological order, is relatively straightforward. So also, to a large extent, is the second. That said, perhaps the most important habit that you need to inculcate, is this second step of applying your common sense to the facts.

---

[1] For the third stage, preparation for the case, see chapter 8.

60

4.3.1 Probability

Civil cases are decided on a preponderance of probabilities. What this means is simply that a dispute of fact will be decided in favour of the party whose version is more probable than the other and, if neither is more probable than the other, then the party who bears the burden of persuasion (burden or onus of proof) will lose.

4.3.2 The importance of common sense

> 'One *can't* believe impossible things'.
> 'I daresay you haven't had much practice,' said the Queen. 'When I was your age, I always did it for half-an-hour a day. Why, sometimes I've believed as many as six impossible things before breakfast'.[2]

Weighing up the probabilities of a matter should rarely involve more than applying good common sense. Asking oneself which of two versions is more probable is really nothing more than applying one's common sense to the question of what, given the facts and the personalities involved and their history, is more likely than not.[3]

This is perhaps best illustrated by the following, no doubt apocryphal, story often quoted in Bar common rooms. It was a case, so goes the story, heard in the magistrate's court in Sasolburg. The plaintiff, a slight man, sued the defendant for assault. The defendant, a huge man ruddy of complexion, strong of hands and bald of pate, was an electrician. The plaintiff was the defendant's assistant. On the day in question, the defendant was working at the foot of a ladder and the plaintiff was on the ladder, welding a pipe. In the process, some of the molten chips fell onto the defendant's bald head. The plaintiff's version was that the defendant yelped, swore, pulled the plaintiff down from the ladder and administered a severe beating. The defendant's version was that he merely, and mildly, asked his assistant to please be more careful in future.[4]

What does your common sense tell you is the more probable of these two versions?

Another, perhaps more realistic, illustration of the virtues of applying simple common sense to factual disputes is to be found in the following extract from the judgment of Miller JA in *McWilliams v First Consolidated Holdings (Pty) Ltd*[5] dealing with the question of whether one would be entitled to infer acquiescence from a party's failure to reply to a letter asserting the existence of an obligation owed by that party:

---

[2] Alice and the White Queen, in Lewis Carroll's *Alice's Adventures in Wonderland*.

[3] This is, after all, precisely what the judge is going to do. Roger E Salhany, a judge of the District Court of Ontario, says in his work *Cross-Examination: The Art of the Advocate* (Butterworths, 1988) at 44 that in arriving at factual conclusions '[t]he trier of fact . . . relies upon his understanding of human nature and his common sense'.

[4] According to the story, the defendant's version in Afrikaans was 'Ag meneer, wil u nie asseblief kyk wat u doen nie?'

[5] 1982 (2) SA 1 (A) at 10F.

(I)n general, when according to ordinary commercial practice and human expectation firm repudiation of such an assertion would be the norm if it was not accepted as correct, such party's silence and inaction, unless satisfactorily explained, may be taken to constitute an admission by him of the truth of the assertion, or at least will be an important factor telling against him in the assessment of the probabilities and in the final determination of the dispute.

Behind the careful judicial phrasing lies one thing: simple common sense.

4.3.3 The broader significance of probabilities, and common sense

Determining the probabilities with regard to each dispute of fact has broad significance. It has value not only in the obtaining of evidence or documents. It enables you, from the start of the case, to assess what your prospects of success might be, and it also guides you in the overall direction of the case. If you apply the test of common sense to a dispute, it might leave you with nothing but a straight conflict. If so, you will embark on a search for facts or factors which will fortify the evidence on your side and weaken the evidence on the other side.

If, however, applying common sense indicates that your client's case is improbable, you will have been warned. There is no second prize in litigation.

4.3.4 The resolution of factual disputes

One can, on this subject, do no better than to close with the following masterful exposition by Nienaber JA in *SFW Group Limited and Another v Martell et Cie and Others*:[6]

> On the central issue . . ., there are two irreconcilable versions. . . . The technique generally employed by courts in resolving factual disputes of this nature may conveniently be summarised as follows:
>
> To come to a conclusion on the disputed issues a court must make findings on (a) the credibility of the various factual witnesses; (b) their reliability; and (c) the probabilities.
>
> As to (a), the court's finding on the credibility of a particular witness will depend on its impression about the veracity of the witness. That in turn will depend on a variety of subsidiary factors, not necessarily in order of importance, such as (i) the witness' candour and demeanour in the witness-box, (ii) his bias, latent and blatant, (iii) internal contradictions in his evidence, (iv) external contradictions with what was pleaded or put on his behalf, or with established fact or with his own extracurial statements or actions, (v) the probability or improbability of particular aspects of his version, (vi) the calibre and cogency of his performance compared to that of other witnesses testifying about the same incident or events.
>
> As to (b), a witness' reliability will depend, apart from the factors mentioned under (a)(ii), (iv) and (v) above, on (i) the opportunities he had to experience or observe the event in question and (ii) the quality, integrity and independence of his recall thereof.
>
> As to (c), this necessitates an analysis and evaluation of the probability or improbability of each party's version on each of the disputed issues.

[6] 2003 (1) SA 11 (SCA) at 14I–15E.

In the light of its assessment of (a), (b) and (c) the court will then, as a final step, determine whether the party burdened with the onus of proof has succeeded in discharging it. The hard case, which will doubtless be the rare one, occurs when a court's credibility findings compel it in one direction and its evaluation of the general probabilities in another. The more convincing the former, the less convincing will be the latter. But when all factors are equipoised probabilities prevail.

4.3.5 Moving on to the second stage

You have sorted the documents in your brief or your file into a chronological order, you have tested the factual allegations against the documents by applying your common sense to any conflict between the two and, having done that, you have applied your common sense to the factual matrix comprised of the documents and allegations, in order to determine where the factual probabilities lie. But you now have nothing but a bare terrain. It is a terrain which you can see more clearly than you could before you started, but a terrain through which you still have to negotiate a path.

This brings us to the second stage of approaching a case, that of extracting the essence.

4.4 EXTRACTING THE ESSENCE OF THE CASE

4.4.1 Introduction

If there is one ability that you need to develop as a lawyer over and above the ability to apply your common sense, it is the ability to see the wood from the trees, to be able to sort out the relevant from the irrelevant, and to extract the essence of a case.

A case, like a good novel, will have themes and sub-themes, story-lines interweaving with other story-lines. But it is no exaggeration to say that every case, like every good novel, has one dominant theme, its *leitmotif*, its essence.[7]

This second stage of preparation, like the first, involves two steps. The first step is the *identification* of the essence of the case, and the second is the *realising* of that essence, ie, *imposing it on the case*.

Of course, I must not be understood by this to be suggesting that there is only one point that needs be proven in a case — far from it. As we will see when dealing in the next chapter with the drafting of pleadings and again when dealing in chapter 7 with the drafting of an advice on evidence, there are invariably a number of aspects which need to be proven in any case. But, as a general statement, the great battle in every case, the true locking of horns, will

---

[7] A colleague speaks of every case having a slogan. That slogan might, in an aerial pesticide case, be 'What's your pesticide doing on my crops?', in an environmental poisoning case, 'What's your cobalt doing in my urine?', or in a brain-damage case, 'If he's so brain-damaged, how come he's doing so well?', and so forth. The idea is that having determined the slogan, one embroiders that into one's case preparation and presentation, continually returning to it in one way or another. All of this is just another way of approaching the question of extracting, realising and then imposing, the essence of a case, as dealt with in this chapter.

hinge on the outcome of one particular point, or theme: the essence of the case. Your task, in every case, is to find that essence.

4.4.2 The importance of extracting the essence

> It had once been noted at the Bar, that while Mr Stryver was a glib man, and an unscrupulous, and a ready, and a bold, he had not that faculty of extracting the essence from a heap of statements, which is among the most striking and necessary of the advocate's accomplishments.[8]

The first rule of practice for the beginner, the paramount rule for the experienced practitioner and the all-too-often forgotten golden rule for the leader at the Bar, is to look for one issue of law or fact which determines the matter.

In every case, in every problem, in every point there will be found an essence, indeed a quintessence, hidden perhaps, dissipated perhaps, but nevertheless there for the seeking. The successful trial lawyer is he who can recognise this essence, can pursue it and ultimately distil and capture it.[9]

In the process there will be encountered false scents, so alluring that they may for a while be mistaken for the reality. Fortunate indeed is he who has so discerning an olfactory nerve that he can distinguish the true from the false, and thrice successful is he who performs his differential analysis before the court utters the words 'There will be judgment for so-and-so, with costs'. If he can do this, he will increase the probabilities in his favour from the normal mathematical fifty-fifty to something closer to two-to-one. Perhaps in the following pages something can be said which will tell the reader not how in any given situation to extract the essence and cast aside the dross, but through what processes this abstruse feat of forensic chemistry may be induced to perform itself. There are no set rules to be applied in these tasks; the insight required cannot be taught, it must be gained by experience and by patience.

What I have been trying to say may be illustrated by a story which appeared many years ago in an American magazine relating to a lawyer who was selecting a clerk.[10]

The lawyer put a notice in an evening paper saying he would pay a small stipend for an active office clerk. The next morning his office was crowded with applicants — all bright, and many suitable. He bade them wait in a room

---

[8] Dickens *A Tale of Two Cities*, in the chapter 'The Jackal'.

[9] Chandos, in his biography of the leading English barrister Norman Birkett QC *Norman Birkett — Uncommon Advocate* (Mayflower, 1963), writes on p 59: '[o]ne of the rarest and most valuable [of the qualities that go to make up the complete advocate] is *strategic judgment*. Many experienced and gifted counsel deliver good speeches, score in cross-examinations, make the most of their opponents' mistakes and, in general, appear to fight their . . . battles ably, without appreciating, until perhaps it is too late, what is the central and crucial issue or what are the decisive engagements of the campaign or, above all, where a particular course, if followed, is *ultimately* going to lead'. Birkett, the author suggests, had this quality.

[10] Quoted by Donovan *Tact in Court* 115–16.

till all should arrive, and then ranged them in a row and said he would tell a story and note the comments of the boys, and judge from that whom he would engage.

> 'A certain farmer', began the lawyer, 'was troubled with a red squirrel that got in through a hole in his barn, and stole his seedcorn; he resolved to kill that squirrel at the first opportunity. Seeing him go in at the hole one noon, he took his shotgun and fired away; the first shot set the barn on fire.'
>
> 'Did the barn burn?' said one of the boys.
>
> The lawyer, without answer, continued: 'And seeing the barn on fire, the farmer seized a pail of water, and ran in to put it out'.
>
> 'Did he put it out?' said another.
>
> 'As he passed inside, the door shut to, and the barn was soon in full flames. When the hired girl rushed out with more water —'
>
> 'Did they all burn up?' said another boy.
>
> The lawyer went on, without answer. 'Then the old lady came out, and all was noise and confusion, and everybody was trying to put out the fire'.
>
> 'Did anyone burn up?' said another.
>
> The lawyer, hardly able to restrain his laughter, said, 'There, there, that will do; you have all shown great interest in the story'; but observing one little bright-eyed fellow in deep silence, he said, 'Now my little man, what have you to say?'
>
> The little fellow blushed, grew uneasy, and stammered out, '*I want to know what became of that squirrel! That's what I want to know.*'
>
> 'You will do,' said the lawyer; 'you are my man; you have not been switched off by a confusion and a barn's burning, and hired girls and water-pails; you have kept your eye on the squirrel'.

4.4.3 Identifying the essence: take your time, and think

The first step to this second stage, that of *identifying* the essence of the case, requires thought. Having in the first stage sorted through the facts, you now need to apply your mind to those facts in order to extract from them their essence, the issue or issues around which the case will revolve, and on the determination of which success or failure will hinge.

As Cato said, 'Grasp the subject; the words will follow'.[11]

4.4.4 Ensuring that you have correctly identified the essence

There arises from time to time in the career of every lawyer a case where the essence appears to possess the properties not of attar of roses but of quicksilver.

Counsel, for example, will have been briefed with the relevant documents and instructed to draw the necessary pleadings. After careful thought and analysis he will arrive at his own decision as to the true essence of the plaintiff's claim or the defendant's defence as the case may be. He will then proceed to draw the necessary pleadings, study his handiwork with perhaps pardonable pride, mark his fee on the brief and return the papers to his instructing attorney. Then there may come a telephone call, particularly if the attorney belongs to

---

[11] Cato The Elder, Roman Statesman (234–149 BC), quoted in *Ars Rhetorica* by Caius Julius Victor.

the conscientious and capable class of those who check counsel's work when it is returned. The attorney has a doubt; the pleadings have been shown to the client who is not happy about one paragraph; there is something which is not clear; or any one of a dozen or more inauspicious causes for reconsideration. If counsel is wise he will realise that the fault may be his own, but, more serious still, it may not. In the interest of certainty counsel may suggest a consultation with the client. The point in question will be discussed and after anything from five to 50 minutes counsel will feel that he now understands precisely what his client's case is. Counsel will feel somewhat embarrassed at his original stupidity. He will, after the captains and the kings have departed, sit at his desk, ears still burning with shame, to redraft the offending pleading, now surely setting out the client's case with skill and precision. The paragraph which gave rise to the difficulty is redrafted and produces an elegant epitome of the client's version. The pleading is retyped and, before sending it out, counsel studies it again with a little extra care. Now he may find the new paragraph to project like the metaphorical sore thumb, or to clash with some other paragraph which counsel believes to be undoubtedly correct. Again a consultation is arranged because only the client has sufficient knowledge of the facts to be able to provide the necessary explanation. To counsel's surprise it is now clear that not only did he originally extract the wrong essence from the brief, but he also misunderstood the client's instructions at the previous consultation, even to the extent of making inaccurate notes of what was said by the client. There is no par for this particular hole; it may be played until counsel realises that his client is on the wrong side. Then, I would suggest, it is counsel's duty to risk offending the client — whom he will never see again anyway — and perhaps to jeopardise his future business connection with the attorney by expressing firmly (and courteously if possible) the view that if the case has so many elusive properties in the calm of chambers it is fated to an unhappy end when subject to vigorous attack and cynical scrutiny in court. You may lose many attorneys this way, but in the process you will acquire something more valuable, and that is the respect of the attorneys whose support really matters.

If you are in doubt as to the accuracy of this exposition, put it to the test when you are confronted with a case which seems to fit the description given. But remember: you have been warned!

4.4.5 Realising the essence

Having *identified* the essence, and taken some trouble to *ensure that you identified it correctly*, the second step of this second stage involves the *realisation* of that essence, ie, *imposing it upon the case*.

It should not for a moment be imagined that the extraction of the essence is either the whole end of the exercise in advocacy or that it is all that is needed to enable justice to triumph. The trouble is that there are two sides to every case (some cases are even perfect cubes, but two sides will do for present purposes). On the other side is an individual who has been performing the same exercise as you. Theoretically this gentleman (or lady) has extracted the same essence and is intoxicated by the same aroma. But, human nature being what it is, you may safely wager that the odour now delicately titillating the nostrils of your opponent differs from yours as drastically as cooking cabbage differs from Chanel No 5. That is why there is litigation. The difference is not one which necessarily need cause you to doubt the reliability of your own mental processes, but it should serve to prevent complacency on your part. The difference lies in human nature: perhaps counsel's, perhaps the instructing attorney's but more probably the client's. It is hardly an exaggeration to say that every conversation, produced to the power of the witness-box, will yield two differing versions, each of which may vary to the power of two. Every motor accident produced to the power of the witness-box will deliver at least twice as many versions as there are witnesses.

So, while believing unswervingly in the accuracy of your own analysis, the reliability of the data from which you have distilled an essence and, above all, in the justice of your cause, be not complacent, do not underestimate your opponent and do not overestimate your case. No matter how strong your evidence or how righteous your cause, do not fall into the same error as counsel (who shall be nameless!) did when, soon after the Second World War, he appeared in the then Supreme Court in an action where his client, the plaintiff, was an officer and a gentleman. The defendant suffered from the disadvantage of being of German origin and doubtful political allegiance. The case was about an agreement to sell certain shares upon the occurrence of a certain event and, the war having been disposed of, that event had occurred. The agreement was denied, but counsel for the plaintiff was not troubled because all the letters were in his favour and, as has been remarked, the plaintiff was an officer and a gentleman. So when he chanced to meet his opponent in the robing-room he delivered himself as follows: 'If I lose this case, I'll eat my hat.' Well, plaintiff may have been an officer and a gentleman, but when he assumed the role of a witness matters began to look a little different. The defendant gave evidence and his explanations of the adverse correspondence found favour in the eyes of the judge. The plaintiff lost his case, and the counsel had to avoid the consequences of his rash statement in the robing-room by the ingenious plea that he never wore a hat anyway. Perhaps this explains why counsel for the defendant subsequently adorned the Bench, while counsel for the plaintiff had to work for a living.

This anecdote is not without its moral. It shows that, notwithstanding the extraction of the essence, the course of justice is beset with many obstacles which may conveniently be classified as imponderables. These include the reliability of one's witnesses, the reliability of the opposing witnesses, and the myriad quirks of human nature, not least those of the presiding judge. Thus at no stage in the preparation and presentation of a case can counsel afford to relax. Every effort must be directed to what may somewhat inelegantly be described as the realisation of the essence. What you have found to be the essence becomes, from the moment of its extraction, a goal, an object to be realised.

The process of realisation commences with a testing of the extraction in consultation with the witnesses. In this regard it must be remembered that it is a mistake, perhaps even the eighth deadly sin, to attempt to bend the witnesses to conform to the essence. A witness who is bent in consultation will inevitably snap back to his original attitude at one time or other when in the witness-box. And the legal practitioner who has bent his own code of ethics in the process of bending the witness will possibly find that he is dealt a stinging blow when the snapping-back occurs. If the witnesses do not support the results of your distillation then something is wrong. The most probable source of error is that you have omitted to take into account some insignificant point which blooms unseen in the forest of facts. Admit your error. Make a reappraisal of the case; modify your theory; do whatever has to be done to arrive at the true basis of the matter, but never fall into the trap of persuading the witnesses or clients to modify their statements in order to bolster your theory.

Assuming that the essence has survived the test of consultation, or that ultimately the true essence has been determined, then its 'realisation' must be the object of the lawyer in every subsequent stage of the litigation; that is, in the pleadings, the outlining of the case to the court, the leading of evidence, the cross-examination of witnesses and the final stage of argument. This theme will be revisited again and again when we discuss these topics in subsequent chapters.

4.4.6 Two examples of the identification and the realisation of the essence

Yours, then, is a case which has an essence which is discernible, extractable and neither evanescent nor elusive. I have said that the realisation of that essence must be your goal. That very essence must be brought home to the court trying the cause until the court can see nothing else but the essence and the truth and justice of that essence. Also I have spoken of the essence that will be determined by your opponent — an opponent whom you must deem to be as strongly armed as yourself and probably twice as capable. In the more pragmatic procedure of today there is little room for feats of eloquence or the creation of atmosphere. But, within the tactical limitations placed on you, you must strive to sway the case from an adjudication upon the 'essence' of your opponent, or a comparison even of 'essences', to a determination of nothing else but the justice of what your case is — the realisation of your 'essence'. This is not idle talk; it can be done and it has been done.

As a model of the approach which I have suggested I refer to an exquisitely phrased passage in a judgment of Holmes JA:[12]

> The quintessence of the cause of action averred may be stated thus: A buys from B a number of mining claims including some held by B's nominee C. It is an implied term that B will procure and deliver a power of attorney from C in order to effect

[12] *Atet Mine (Pty) Ltd v Tamasi & Herceg* AD, 18 September 1967, unreported.

transfer to A. Wishing to enforce the contract A sues B (joining C) for delivery of such power of attorney.

The essential *facta probanda* are: (i) the contract of sale, (ii) the existence of the nominee, and (iii) the implied term. As (i) is in writing and (iii) is plain, the real dispute relates to (ii), namely whether C's claims were held by him for his own benefit or as nominee for B. However, this crisp issue was overshadowed at the trial because A had sought delivery of a specific power of attorney which, it was averred, C had already signed — Both B and C denied this, pleading in effect that the company's representative had procured C's signature to an incomplete document under circumstances amounting to fraud; and the evidence roamed far and wide on this aspect. But this was an arid inquiry because even if, at the end of it, the existence of this power of attorney was not proved, A would still be entitled to delivery of a power of attorney (assuming that the nominee aspect were established) in order to enforce his contract. Hence it seems to me that the decisive point in this appeal is whether C held the claims as B's nominee. If he did, A is entitled to delivery of a power of attorney. If he did not, A must fail.

In view of what has been indicated at the outset of this judgment, the decisive issue is whether the trial judge was wrong in holding that it was not proved that the first respondent was the nominee of the second respondent in respect of the 100 claims in question. I proceed therefore to examine the available material with a view to checking the relevant estimates of credibility formed by the trial court.

At the outset there is the written contract which the second respondent admits he entered into with P on 9 March 1963. This contract receives a brief mention early in the judgment of the learned trial judge, but thereafter it does not appear to have been taken into account. No doubt an appreciation of its significance was blurred in the welter of controversial issues and the sombre labyrinth of averment, denial, and falsehood in which the elusive truth was lurking.

The cumulative effect of these provisions (of the contract) renders it inconceivable that the second respondent was disposing of the 100 claims in question on any basis other than that they were his to dispose of because the first respondent was merely his nominee in respect of them. In other words this vital evidence in writing, which was not fully dealt with in the judgment of the court *a quo*, transcends the learned judge's finding that the second respondent testified with reasonable consistency and with the appearance of honesty and sincerity. There is accordingly a firm basis for disbelieving his evidence that the first respondent was not his nominee.

On this approach it is not necessary to delve into the unprofitable issues whether the specific power of attorney by the first respondent in favour of the second respondent was infected with fraud by the company as the respondents pleaded. . . .

In my view all the aforegoing facts flow like a coherent river towards the conclusion that the first respondent was at all times the mere nominee of the second respondent . . .

It can be seen from this extract that the first exercise performed by Holmes JA was the distillation of the quintessence of the matter — exactly as an attorney or advocate should do. Then he made use of the quintessence in a manner similar to that suggested in the preceding pages. He determined the matter by testing the facts and the judgment in the court below against the quintessence. The facts acceptable were those reconcilable with the quintessence. All other facts fell by the wayside and played no part in the final judgment.

If further justification is required for this suggested method of approaching cases it may be found in the judgment of Stratford ACJ in *Armstrong v Magid and Another*[13] in the following terms:

> No distinction need be drawn in this case between the remedies of the plaintiff resulting from fraud or from undue influence. Mr Millin, for the defendants, admits the plaintiff's right to a *restitutio in integrum* and to a possible claim for damages. The present claim, he says, is bad because it asks for neither of these remedies, it asks for the substitution of a new agreement for the one obtained by fraud or under influence. That claim, he argues, is one, on the facts alleged, unknown to the law and supported by no legal principle or authority. After analysing the declaration and the claim made by the plaintiff, I now confess that I now think the problem presented to us is as simple as Mr Millin says it is and that his answer is correct, that is, that the plaintiff cannot claim an agreement with the first defendant which he was never willing to make.

This case merits a little further consideration in the light of the present theme because a good deal can be read between the lines. What had happened was that the plaintiff had retained Mr Magid as her attorney for the purpose of 'advising and assisting her from time to time in her affairs and in the investment of her money and in the recovery of moneys that were outstanding and due to her'. A company was formed for the purpose of constructing flats on two stands in Hillbrow, Johannesburg. Agreements were entered into between the plaintiff, Miss Armstrong, on the one hand, and Mr and Mrs Magid on the other, and also between the plaintiff and the company so formed. In terms of the two agreements Mr Magid was to be permanent managing director and chairman of the company and Mrs Magid was to have the right to occupy a four-roomed flat free of rent for twenty years. It is relevant to note that Miss Armstrong and Mrs Magid each subscribed £599 towards the capital of the company while Mr Magid subscribed £2. The capital required to build the flats was to be lent by Miss Armstrong. There were certain other benefits obtained by Mr and Mrs Magid under the agreement but they need not trouble us here.

Miss Armstrong complained that she had entered into the agreements with her attorney, Mr Magid, without independent advice.[14] She also alleged other grounds which would entitle her to the intervention of the court and claimed the transfer of Mr and Mrs Magid's shares in the company as well as an order declaring that the Magids were not entitled to their directorships and flat.

Counsel for the Magids were Phillip Millin (later a judge of the Transvaal Provincial Division) and Archie Shacksnovis (who was probably one of the most colourful — if not flamboyant — characters at the Johannesburg Bar for some twenty-odd years). One can imagine them in Phillip Millin's chambers preparing their brief; Millin somewhat staid in comparison with Shacksnovis, yet both gifted with penetrating insight into causes and humanity; Millin's

---

[13] 1937 AD 260 at 269.

[14] See chapter 2, paragraph 2.2.1, in regard to the question of an attorney's duty not to take advantage of the influence which he might have over his client.

approach being of the prosaic phraseology of the lawyer while Shacksnovis looked at life not only as a lawyer but as a sportsman and *bon vivant*. One can hear the result of their analysis, expressed with precise formality by Millin or colloquially by Shacksnovis that the issue could be determined by a simple legal point, irrespective of 'independent advice' and of all the other causes of complaint which Miss Armstrong had against Mr and Mrs Magid. Today, reading the law report after a lapse of more than half a century, the answer seems so delightfully simple that one wonders how the contrary could have been argued but, as will be seen, it was not as easy as that.

Step 1 had been performed; the essence had been identified. The result was that, instead of becoming involved in a lengthy trial, counsel decided to except to the plaintiff's claim on the ground that what Miss Armstrong was really asking was that the agreement should stand, shorn of the benefits which were going to the Magids. Now came step 2, the *realisation* of that essence, and the problems which Millin must have had in step 2 can be deduced from the words of the learned Acting Chief Justice:

> At first I was inclined to view the matter as if the plaintiff was entitled to her investment in the venture independently of the agreement with the first defendant (Mr Magid) to share in it.

Behind those words one can see the picture of the argument on appeal. When so eminent a judge of appeal states that at first he 'was inclined to think' it means that counsel arguing the contrary has been the target of a barrage of questions from the Bench, questions so probing that they usually destroy any defective argument, questions so pertinent that they require all of counsel's skill and ability to meet them. Yet one can also see Millin in step 2 of this operation — 'realising' the essence which had been identified, persisting in the theme until the majority of the court of appeal had accepted its correctness. When a judgment contains the words which I have quoted it means that counsel has done his job.

4.5 APPLYING COMMON SENSE AND EXTRACTING THE ESSENCE, STEP-BY-STEP

4.5.1 The papers, and the first consultation

Some there are, indeed, who would condemn as trite and banal — even nonsensical — this dissertation on the extraction of the essence. I, however, join issue with them. When there arrives on one's table a brief containing dozens of letters, half a dozen statements of witnesses and 'Instructions to Counsel' prepared with great labour and care it is very easy to become overwhelmed with the masses of allegations and retorts, charges and counter-charges until one feels that one is emulating the bold knight at the court of King Arthur who leaped onto his steed and galloped off in all directions. When this occurs, the time has arrived politely to terminate the consultation, usher out the attorney and his cohorts, and spend time quietly extracting the essence of the case.

4.5.2 A good starting point

Having ushered the visitors out, the following physical (or other) exercises should be performed.

- Lock the door.
- Take the brief in the left hand and the red or green tape in the right — or *vice versa* in appropriate cases.
- Tie the tape around the brief.
- Sit in an easy chair and relax.
- Spend the first ten minutes thinking of absolutely nothing.
- Now start on the facts and issues of law with the simple rhetorical and unuttered question: 'How did this all start?'

You then ask yourself three more questions:

'Now, what is it all about?'
'What does my client want?'
'How do I — or we — get what he wants?'

These questions are the foundations of every case. They, too, may seem trite, not worthy of recording because they are so self-evident. Perhaps, however, the day will come when you are confronted with a case which resembles a jigsaw puzzle of a thousand pieces in indistinguishable blues and greys, every piece the same and some of them missing. It is then that you may ask yourself that first question: How did it all start? And your reflective process will continue until you can add the last and vital question:

How will it end?

No book can tell you how it started, nor how it will end. But you will know — or if you don't know at that moment, you may find that you know when the soft light of sunlight creeps through your bedroom window and prods your subconscious into wakefulness.

4.5.3 Start with the facts

The first two questions ('How did this all start?', 'What is it all about?') are factual questions. And that is where you start — with the facts. Law is nothing without reference to the facts. If you have the facts wrong, you will probably have the law wrong.

Go through the papers. Sort the documents into their chronological order. Juxtaposing two documents in their correct chronological order will often reveal the answer to a factual conundrum.

Having done this, draw up a chronology of the facts, incorporating all facts which might possibly have any relevance to the matter.

When collating the facts in their proper chronological order, you will find that you come across disputes. Your client says that one thing happened, the other party another thing. You will test these disputes against the background of the chronology exposed by the documents and of that which the parties did and did not say in letters, etc. You will bring your common sense to bear on these disputes of fact.

4.5.4 The law

Having established what the facts of the case are, carefully consider what areas of law apply. Is this a contractual, or a delictual dispute? If the former, was the contract one of deposit or some other type of contract? What are the principles of law that apply?

4.5.5 The last two questions

Now, having established what are the probable facts of the case, and having considered the legal implications of the probable facts, you are in a position to start answering the last of the questions: 'What does my client want?', and 'How do I get what he wants?'.

Having done all this, ask yourself again what the case is all about? If, having done so, you arrive at the same answer, you will have extracted the essence of the case.

4.5.6 Keep your eye on the squirrel

Once you have thought the case through, once you have extracted from it its factual and its legal essence, you should follow the example of that young fellow in the story. Amidst all the confusion and all the distractions, he kept his eye on the squirrel. You must do the same. Do not be distracted. Allow the other side to be distracted, to follow false leads. You keep your eye on the essence. That is how you achieve the solution to the problem with which you started.

CHAPTER 5

The Technique of Pleading

5.1 GENERAL DISCUSSION[1]

The greatest fear of all lawyers is that their pleading will invite an exception. Their second greatest fear is that the exception will be upheld.

Both in the High Court, and in the magistrate's court, it is not competent to except to a pleading on the ground that it is vague and embarrassing without first giving the offending pleader an opportunity to rectify what you, as the excipient, consider his mistake to be.[2] The notice calling on the pleader to remove the cause of complaint must clearly and concisely specify the grounds on which the pleading is claimed to be vague and embarrassing.[3] Because counsel who signed the pleading would hardly have done so unless he thought it was a good one, the normal reaction is to indignantly wonder how fault could be found with such an elegant pleading, but in a few instances second thought may lead to an amendment removing the cause of complaint.

Of course, such an exception is always a somewhat perilous matter, as appears from the following anecdote:[4]

> The late Mr Justice Stratford, Chief Justice of the Appellate Division, and the late Mr Tielman Roos, also a judge of the Appellate Division, when they were at the Bar, frequently met in mortal combat. There came the time when Tielman was briefed to draw a declaration in a Supreme Court action. The drawing of that document in this case was by no means an easy matter for reasons which we need not go into. The task of replying to this declaration was entrusted by the defendant to Mr James Stratford. He gave it one look — smote his head and said, 'Good God, what is Tielman talking about?' Then he drew his reply. The burden of his song was that the declaration was vague and embarrassing — meaning that it was so badly drawn that no one could understand what it was about. At last the parties got into court and here they argued for four hours as to whether it was a good declaration or an embarrassing one. Stratford maintained that this document could only be likened to a pool of mud and he never ceased emphasising the point that it was the most embarrassing declaration he had ever seen. Tielman said it was a perfectly lucid and transparent document that would embarrass no one who had the slightest smattering of the English language. At length the court decided, perhaps wrongly, for Stratford was rarely at fault, that the declaration was a good one. As they walked into the robing room Stratford said: 'But Tielman, why did you draw your declaration in that way?'

---

[1] For useful precedents of pleadings, see Harms, LTC *Amler's Precedents of Pleadings* 7 ed. Also Daniels, H *Beck's Theory and Principles of Pleadings in Civil Actions* 6 ed; Marnewick, CG *Litigation Skills for South African Lawyers* 2 ed, and Van Blerk, P *Legal Drafting: Civil Proceedings*.

[2] Uniform Rule 23(1), and magistrate's court rule 17(5)(c).

[3] Wessels, CJ in *Molteno Bros v South African Railways* 1936 AD 408 at 417.

[4] HH Morris *In my Anecdotage* (Central News Agency 1953) referring, no doubt with 'poetic' licence, to *SA Railways & Harbours v Landau & Co* 1917 TPD 485.

'Oh, only to embarrass you', said Tielman.

Courts justifiably tend to adopt a sensible and, as far as possible, non-technical approach to pleadings and exceptions to pleadings.

Innes CJ said this in *Robinson v Randfontein Estates GM Co Ltd*:[5]

> The object of pleading is to define the issues; and parties will be kept strictly to their pleas where any departure would cause prejudice or would prevent full enquiry. But within those limits the court has a wide discretion. For pleadings are made for the court, not the court for pleadings. And where a party has had every facility to place all the facts before the trial court and the investigation into all the circumstances has been as thorough and as patient as in this instance, there is no justification for interference by an appellate tribunal, merely because the pleading of the opponent has not been as explicit as it might have been.

As De Villiers JA stated in a subsequent case:[6]

> While listening to him however, I could not but ask myself what the substantial issue was between the parties in the court below. The importance of pleadings should not be unduly magnified.

With all these reassuring principles and decisions behind him counsel's responsibility for faulty pleadings is greatly minimised and perhaps this might lead to hasty or defective workmanship. To obviate this the words of Schreiner JA should be borne in mind:[7]

> Generally speaking the issues in civil cases should be raised on the pleadings and if an issue arises which does not appear from the pleadings in their original form an appropriate amendment should be sought. Parties should not be unduly encouraged to rely, in the hope, perhaps, of obtaining some tactical advantage or of avoiding a special order as to costs, on the court's readiness at the argument stage or on appeal to treat unpleaded issues as having been fully investigated.

Apart from this authoritative warning there are several considerations which experience teaches one to bear in mind in the drafting of pleadings. I offer them to you as follows:

- The pleading you draw is the foundation of the case you intend to make on trial. If the foundation is weak because it was not thought through properly, the case is going to be weak. Take time to think about the case you want to make before you draft the pleading and, when you have finished with it, check it to ensure that it meets your case.
- Defective pleading may even lead to the failure of the action. Pray that

---

[5] 1925 AD 173 at 198.

[6] *Shill v Milner* 1937 AD 101 at 105, applied in numerous cases subsequently including *Collen v Rietfontein Engineering Works* 1948 (1) SA 413 (A) at 433 and *Trans-African Insurance Co Ltd v Maluleka* 1956 (2) SA 273 (A) at 278. See also *Imprefed (Pty) Ltd v National Transport Commission* 1993 (3) SA 94 (A) at 107, where it was stressed that '[t]he whole purpose of pleadings is to bring clearly to the notice of the court and the parties to an action the issues upon which reliance is to be placed'.

[7] *Middleton v Carr* 1949 (2) SA 374 (A) at 386.

what Lord Denning said in *Rondel v Worsley*[8] of the case of the barrister Rebutter, is not in 130 years' time said of you:

> Fifty years later, in *Perring v Rebutter*, a certificated special pleader, appropriately called Rebutter, drew the pleading in an action so badly that the defence failed.
>   With the wide powers of amendment exercised by the courts today, such cases might be rare but they are possible.

•   In many cases an amendment, even if effected without opposition, either affords material for cross-examination or may create an atmosphere which will taint the whole case. This is particularly so where the amendment seeks to advance a new version of the facts, whether by way of claim or defence. Unfortunately, this often results from the fact that, in the careful preparation that precedes a trial, counsel reconsiders his brief and finds perhaps more, perhaps less in it than he first thought. It may become apparent that the evidence and the pleadings must be reconciled, and this can be done only by an amendment. No matter how much of the responsibility counsel may bear there is always a residual blot on the client's escutcheon.

5.2   THE APPROACH TO PLEADING

The aim in drafting pleadings is this: your pleadings must be concise, the allegations must be pertinent, and the object must be to state issues succinctly, crisply and effectively.

As far as counsel is concerned, his first introduction to a case may be the drawing of a pleading. For the attorney and counsel the first pleading which they have to draw in any particular case should be regarded as a step of even greater importance than the final argument. At the risk of repeating myself, everything that develops in a case, as far as either the plaintiff or the defendant is concerned, flows in a direct sequence of causation from that first pleading. Under pressure of work it may well happen that pleadings have to be turned out as soon as possible, particularly when there has been notice of bar, or the threat of it, or prescription is nigh. This does not make for good pleading, nor does it promote the successful conduct of cases.

I would suggest that the approach to pleadings should be that outlined in chapter 4 of this book. There should be a calm analysis of the case, an unhurried and contemplative examination of all the facts of the matter in order that the essence can be extracted.

One is, perhaps, misled by the ease of pleading routine items such as particulars of claim in undefended matrimonial cases, or even in running-down cases. No pleading should really be regarded as a routine matter; if that approach does become habitual there is a reasonable possibility that one day the little quirk that makes a routine matter into a *cause célèbre* will be overlooked, with consequences that may be embarrassing if not actually disastrous.

---

[8] [1966] 3 All ER 657 (CA) at 662.

The suggested approach to the problem of pleading is based on applying the principles of analysis to the two matters that form the basis of litigation: fact and law. In other words the facts, consisting of instructions, statements, correspondence, plans, photographs and the opinions of experts, must be considered and then the same process has to be performed in regard to the law. This is no idle exercise in philosophy because the nature of the relief claimable depends often on a proper assessment of the legal classification of the cause of action. Thus in 1948 Price J said:[9]

> The ordinary reader of this declaration would be puzzled to know whether the action is based on delict or on breach of contract or on both. The declaration does not boldly and unequivocally select either line, nor does it plainly and unmistakably purport to base the action on both. It seems to balance itself precariously on the tight rope of division between the two, now threatening to fall on one side, now on the other, and in the end it recovers its balance and staggers awkwardly still balanced dangerously on the tight rope of division. Such a declaration is, in my opinion, more embarrassing than a declaration which embarks boldly upon one or other of the two actions, or that boldly asserted that the claim was based on both actions.

The learned judge had in mind a number of practical consequences which he stated as follows at 352:

> In this case there are two defendants, one of whom is not liable and is not sought to be made liable in contract. Then the damages may be quite differently calculated in each of the two actions. Furthermore, the causes of the two actions are based on altogether different facts; in the one case on a contumacious holding over, in the other, on a breach of contract. Wilfulness is necessary in the one case, and is not necessary in the other. A knowledge of special circumstances is necessary in the case based on breach of contract and is not necessary in the case based on tort.[10]

The specific steps to be taken will vary with the type of pleading drawn, and these steps will be discussed in successive sections of this chapter. When, however, the essence of the facts and the essence of the law have been determined for the purpose of pleading, the two must be collated in order to decide what facts are to be alleged in the pleadings, and how they are to be alleged.

5.3 HINTS ON DRAFTSMANSHIP

5.3.1 Drafting pleadings generally

A pleading should ordinarily set forth neither law nor evidence.[11] Nevertheless it may sometimes be not only permissible but also necessary to plead evidence

---

[9] *Wellworths Bazaars Ltd v Chandlers Ltd and Another* 1948 (3) SA 348 (W) at 350–1.

[10] See *Thoroughbred Breeders' Association v Price Waterhouse* 2001 (4) SA 551 (SCA) at 580–3, Christie, RH *The Law of Contract in South Africa* 5 ed 542–3, Van der Merwe, Van Huyssteen, Reinecke and Lubbe *Contract – General Principles* 3 ed 425–6 and Visser and Potgieter *Law of Damages* 2 ed 282.

[11] For a discussion in regard to both the pleading of evidence and to the law see the judgment of Horwitz AJP in *Edwards v African Guarantee & Indemnity Co Ltd* 1952 (4) SA 335 (O) at 339F.

in order to inform the opposing party of the case which he has to meet. This may be because, for example, the pleader seeks to draw inferences from certain facts.[12] Normally the inference would be what we describe as a 'fact' while the facts from which that inference is to be drawn are 'evidence'. So, too, it is permissible to plead 'history' for the sake of clarity as an introduction to allegations founding the cause of action.[13] This may not be done if the purpose of pleading historical facts is not merely as explanatory but to strengthen the cause of action relied upon.[14]

Subject to these considerations, a pleading will be divisible into two principal concepts: the allegations of fact which go to make out the party's case, and the conclusions of law which flow from those facts. The statement of the conclusions of law may be so terse as to amount almost to an anticlimax, and may be no more than: '(i)n the premises the plaintiff is entitled to judgment in the said sum from the defendant.' Nevertheless the facts and the conclusions of law are to be kept separate in the pleadings.[15]

Of course, the first elementary precaution to be taken in the proper drafting of pleadings is to refer to the relevant rules of court with regard to the particular pleading which one is drawing. Eventually you will know the rules of court by heart (at which stage they will promptly be amended).[16] It is not proposed at this stage to embark upon an exposition of the Uniform Rules of Court, or the rules of the magistrate's court as this has been done in the standard textbooks which every practitioner will no doubt have as the cornerstone of his practice.

Apart from the consideration of defining the issues, pleadings are inevitably used as tactical weapons in the dispute between the parties. The objectives may be varied, such as drawing the opponent on to your own particular ground; creating a position in which the opponent may be forced to call a particular witness or himself to testify; or to give away as little as possible. It must be remembered, however, that fencing with pleadings is a dangerous occupation. The dangers are:

- the pleading may be so cautiously drawn as to be excipiable, either disclosing no cause of action or no defence or being vague and embarrassing;

---

[12] *Van Biljoen v Botha* 1952 (3) SA 494 (O) and *Union Free State Mining & Finance Corporation Ltd v Union Free State Gold & Diamond Corporation Ltd* 1960 (4) SA 547 (W).

[13] *Ahlers NO v Snoeck* 1946 TPD 590 and *Du Toit v Du Toit* 1958 (2) SA 354 (D).

[14] *Myburgh, Krone & Kompagnie Bpkt (In Liquidation) v Ko-operatieve Wijnbouwers Vereeniging van Zuid-Afrika Bpkt* 1923 CPD 389.

[15] Broome JP in *Prinsloo v Woolbrokers Federation Ltd* 1955 (2) SA 298 (N) at 299D–E. Exemplified also in *Henry Tayler & Ries Ltd v Naidoo and Others* 1960 (3) SA 207 (D) at 210G–211A.

[16] Even if you think you know the rules by heart, look at the particular rule or rules again before you finalise your pleading.

- the matters withheld may have to be pleaded later, and if the court is of the opinion that an allegation has deliberately been withheld for tactical reasons it may refuse to allow any amendment;[17]
- the tactical advantage sought may not be attained, and the tactical pleading may become a boomerang instead of a rapier.[18]

5.3.2 Everything must have a purpose

A sub-theme that you will hopefully discern in this book, is the need in everything that you do to determine the *purpose* of what you are doing, and then to *tailor your technique to meet that purpose*. An opening address, for example, is not simply a nice way to get proceedings rolling; when we come to deal with opening addresses in chapter 10, we will see how your address must be tailored to its purpose. Likewise cross-examination is not simply a matter of asking every question you might be able to think of; it has a purpose and effective cross-examination is tailored to that purpose.

So too with the drafting of pleadings and, for that matter, notices of motion and affidavits. You should always ask yourself what the purpose is of what you are doing, and you should tailor what you do to meet that purpose.

The corollary of this is that you should jettison that which serves no purpose but is simply done because it is 'always done that way'.

I can best illustrate this with three examples. The first relates to simplified structure and grammar, the second to allegations relating to jurisdiction, and the third to the interesting question of the customary prayer for further or alternative relief.

- Firstly, the simplification of structure: It is virtually inevitable that certain items will be referred to repeatedly in a pleading. For example, in a contractual action it is likely that the pleader will need to refer to the contract on more than one occasion. In a collision action, there will be more than one occasion to refer to the vehicle in respect of which the plaintiff claims, and to the collision in which it was involved. In a more complex contractual action there might be more than one contract, so that the pleader will find it necessary to distinguish one contract from another. So often one finds phrases like 'the aforementioned contract', 'the aforementioned motor vehicle', or even 'the contract referred to in paragraph 4 above' (to distinguish it for example from 'the contract referred to in paragraph 8 above'). Would it not be so much easier to

---

[17] *Florence Soap & Chemical Works (Pty) Ltd v Ozen Wholesalers (Pty) Ltd* 1954 (3) SA 945 (T). Counsel sought to justify the delay in applying for the amendment on the ground that one of the witnesses for the opponent was an astute person who might have fabricated evidence to meet the allegations in question had it been placed on record at an earlier stage. The application for an amendment was disallowed, Neser J saying (at 948): 'The object of pleadings is to define the issues in the action and the failure by a party to plead causes of action or defences of which it is aware cannot be condoned if the only reason for the failure is a desire to cross-examine witnesses before the issues are pleaded.'

[18] As in *Joseph v Black* 1930 WLD 327, *Black v Joseph* 1931 AD 132.

simplify one's structure and grammar by giving the particular item a label, and then using that label thereafter? In the simple contractual matter one would, for example, after the first occasion in the pleading in which one describes the contract add '("the contract")', enabling one thereafter to simply refer to the contract in question throughout as 'the contract'. In the more complex contractual action one might find one's self referring to 'the first contract' and then 'the second contract', in the collision matter to 'the plaintiff's vehicle', and so forth, without the need for the repeated and sometimes confusing use of the word 'aforementioned'. This is not simply a matter of style. It is also a matter of achieving your purpose of drafting an unambiguous, crisp and effective pleading.

- Secondly, as to jurisdiction, it is a requirement of the rules of the magistrates' courts that specific averments be made in the particulars of claim where the plaintiff relies for the court's jurisdiction on the fact that the cause of action arose wholly within the district or on the immovable property in question being within the district.[19] But there is no such requirement in the High Court. Yet one often finds allegations in particulars of claim in the High Court to the effect that the court has jurisdiction for such-and-such reason. Surely if it is evident from allegations already made in the particulars of claim (and which need to be made for purposes of making out the case) that the court has jurisdiction because, for example, the defendant's address is within its area, or the contract was entered into or had to be performed there, or the collision occurred there, it is entirely unnecessary to add a further allegation that the court has a jurisdiction which it already evidently has? Surely in such cases it serves no good purpose to add this further allegation about a jurisdiction which is already evident? Of course there are other instances where jurisdiction is by no means self-evident and, in fact, where jurisdiction could be an issue. In those instances it would indeed be necessary to add pertinent allegations relating thereto so that potential issues in that regard are properly raised. But not otherwise.

- The third example of jettisoning a purposeless piece of pleading relates to the so-called *clausule salutaire* of the prayer for further or alternative relief, described by Coetzee J of the Transvaal Provincial Division in *Johannesburg City Council v Bruma Thirty-Two (Pty) Limited.*[20] With his customary forthrightness as 'in modern practice redundant and mere verbiage', it seems from the relevant authorities[21] that the learned judge's

---

[19] Rules 6(5)*(f)* and 6(5)*(g)*.

[20] *Johannesburg City Council v Bruma Thirty-Two (Pty) Ltd* 1984 (4) SA 87 (T) at 93F. Bliss and Weyers AJJ concurred.

[21] See *Queensland Insurance Co. Limited v Banque Commerciale Africaine* 1946 AD 272 at 286, *Johannesburg City Council v Bruma Thirty-Two (Pty) Limited* 1984 (4) SA 87 (T), *Port Nolloth Municipality v Xhalisa and Others, Luwalala and Others v Port Nolloth Municipality* 1991 (3) SA 98 (C) at 112D–F, *Combustion Technology (Pty) Limited v Technoburn (Pty) Limited* 2003 (1) SA 265 (C) at 268, *Meihuizen Freight (Pty) Limited v Transportes Maritimos de Portugal LDA and Others* [2004] 3 All SA 289 (SCA) at

reasoning that '[w]hatever the Court can validly be asked to order on papers as framed, can still be asked without [the] presence [of the prayer for further or alternative relief]' might well be correct, in that relief has only been granted under the *clausule salutaire* where it was substantially similar to the relief specifically sought and was sufficiently foreshadowed in the papers.[22] After all, it is for precisely the reasons outlined in *Bruma* that one does not need to ask for an amendment or to rely on the *clausule salutaire* to ask for judgment for a lesser amount than that stated in the summons, and the cases[23] illustrate the point that, where relief is granted under this prayer, it is inevitably lesser relief than the primary relief specifically sought in the papers:

> The answer seems to be that the prayer probably no longer serves any useful purpose but that, ours being a profession in which discretion is by far the better part of valour, caution in the interests of one's clients probably dictates that one retain the practice. It serves to illustrate, and to define, the dividing line between that which serves a purpose and should be retained, and that which serves no purpose and should be jettisoned: because there are cases in which relief has been granted under the prayer it seems safest to retain its use notwithstanding that the same relief would probably have been granted in each of those cases in the absence of the prayer.

5.4 ON DRAFTING THE PARTICULARS OF CLAIM

5.4.1 Particulars of claim (and declarations), generally

Particulars of claim are required in all actions in the magistrate's court and, in the High Court, in all actions in which the claim is unliquidated. In such latter actions, the first step is the serving and filing of a combined summons, almost identical in form with the ordinary summons in the magistrate's court. In the High Court, even in those cases in which action is instituted by way of a simple summons because of the liquidated nature of the claim, the plaintiff is required to file a declaration if, as usually happens, the defendant is able to avert summary judgment. Apart from the procedural differences, the principles of technique which apply to particulars of claim are equally applicable to declarations. For convenience, both particulars of claim and declarations will in what follows be referred to as 'particulars of claim'.

Particulars of claim must, of course, be such that the defendant can reasonably plead thereto.[24] The object is to state the plaintiff's case and to define

---

para [23] and *Kiliko and Others v Minister of Home Affairs and Others* 2006 (4) SA 114 (C) at 127. See also the useful discussion of the subject in Daniels' *Beck's Theory and Principles of Pleading in Civil Actions* 71–2.

[22] See Tindall JA *Queensland Insurance Co. Ltd v Banque Commerciale Africaine* 1946 AD 272 at 286 to the effect that 'the prayer for alternative relief is limited by the statement of fact in the declaration and by the terms of the express claim, and . . . a plaintiff cannot get, under the prayer for alternative relief, anything that is inconsistent with those two things.'

[23] See fn 21 above.

[24] *White v Moffett Building & Contracting (Pty) Ltd* 1952 (3) SA 307 (O), and Uniform Rule 18(4).

the issues which he wishes to raise. In drafting your particulars of claim, apart from the personal question of pride and reputation, you will, no doubt, have a wary regard for the *dicta* of Erasmus J in regard to amendments:[25]

> It seems to me that the wide discretion a court thus has should not be liberally exercised in favour of the party responsible for the pleadings in collision cases. In matters of contract, for instance, it may sometimes be difficult to ascertain precisely the extent to which the evidence is covered by the cause of action made out on the pleadings and there is greater scope for allowances. This to my mind is so because of the technicalities of contract itself and the shades of thought in the minds of the contracting parties which may lead to a genuine dispute in a court of law. In such cases the court may less sparingly exercise its discretion. Cf *Angath v Muckunlal's Estate* 1954 (4) SA 283 (N) at 284. When, however, one deals with collision cases, one is mainly concerned with outward manifestations and observations — signs, signals, speed, conditions of the road, vehicles using it and the performances of drivers. Objects and acts were seen, or acts performed, and the pleadings tell and inform the court and the opposite party what they were and whether they constitute the negligence complained of. It follows, I think, that such facts produced in evidence and which are in conflict with facts stated in the pleadings and based on observation should not lightly give rise to an amendment of the pleadings, and especially so where the opposing party has during the hearing objected to a submission or an amendment, unless of course a reasonable explanation is given in evidence for the incorrect statement of facts in the pleadings.

No doubt there are statements in this passage which are *obiter dicta* or which may fruitfully be discussed further. For present purposes, however, the quotation is offered as a valuable guide in the approach to pleadings, and to particulars of claim.

5.4.2 How to go about drafting particulars of claim

Your starting point, as outlined above, is to determine what the facts of the matter are. There will often be competing allegations. What does your client say are the facts? Having obtained some idea of what the facts are, the next step is to consider the law. What branch or branches of the law apply to these facts? What relief does your client want? Applied to the facts, does the law afford him that relief, and if so on what basis? Having determined the issues of law you then determine what the essential elements are that have to be proved, and you then proceed on the basis of your analysis to set out an allegation covering every one of those elements. This sounds simple, but when you study the law reports relating to exceptions you will find a great many cases in which it would appear that counsel had drawn his pleading on some other system and consequently omitted a material allegation.[26]

---

[25] *John William Motors Ltd v Minister of Defence and Another* 1965 (3) SA 729 (O) at 732–3.

[26] Further examples of exceptions based on the omission of material averments include: *Hiscock v Mallinson* (1923) 44 NLR 105 (malicious proceedings; want of reasonable and probable cause); *Union Whaling Co Ltd v Union Government* 1942 NPD 320 and also *United Canners Ltd v Deepfreezing & Preserving (Pty) Ltd* 1960 (1) SA 852 (C) (fulfilment of a condition precedent); *Cullen v Zuidema* 1951 (3) SA 817 (C) (that purchaser ignorant of defect in property at date of purchase); *Minister of Defence v*

5.4.3 An example: a collision case

To illustrate the process let us take the average collision case in which one party claims from another for damage to his motor vehicle.

You study your brief and extract the essence of the case as follows: your client was driving her car on a main road, on the correct side of the double white lines, when the defendant came over a blind rise at a high speed, straddling the lines. A collision occurred and your client's vehicle was damaged.

Your analysis of the facts will tell you that this appears to be a good case: the collision was on your client's correct side of the road. Turning to the law, you will have little difficulty in concluding that the branch of law which applies is that of delict. Relying perhaps on your unerringly good knowledge of the law or, if you are more cautiously minded, on the text books to which reference was made in the beginning of this chapter, you will determine that the essential elements of your client's case relate to whether your client has *locus standi* to sue (is she an adult? If she is, is this one of those rare but by no means inconceivable cases where your adult client is cognitively impaired — perhaps by injuries sustained in the collision — such that she is unable to comprehend the litigation and requires assistance?[27] If she is not yet an adult, who will represent her?), whether the papers identify the defendant sufficiently in order to enable you to cite him properly (do you have a physical address for him where summons can be served? Is he an adult and if not, who should you cite as assisting him? Are there any suggestions that he sustained injuries in the collision such that he is unable to comprehend the litigation and requires assistance?), whether she has *locus standi* to sue in respect of the damage (she says she was the owner. Was she? Or do the papers or would further enquiry show that in fact the owner was her husband, or her father? Or, as often is the case, does it transpire that she wasn't in fact the owner but the possessor by virtue of a credit purchase or lease agreement?), wrongfulness (your splendid knowledge of the law, or your research, will tell you that because this is an instance of physical damage caused by positive conduct, and thus neither of omission or of economic loss, wrongfulness is assumed and need not be alleged),[28] negligence on the other driver's part (he veered onto his incorrect side of the road), and damage to your client's vehicle (do you have sufficient detail of the cost of repairs? Did the vehicle have to be towed away, and then stored, at additional expense?).

Commercial Properties Ltd and Others 1955 (3) SA 324 (D) (acts constituting expropriation); *Saffer Clothing Industries (Pty) Ltd v Worcester Textiles (Pty) Ltd* 1965 (2) SA 424 (C) (that special damages claimed were in the contemplation of the parties at the time of the contract — and, of course, that the contract was entered into on the basis of liability for such damages); *Natal Fresh Produce Growers' Association v Agroserve (Pty) Ltd* 1990 (4) SA 749 (N) at 754–5 (failure to plead sufficient grounds to give rise to a duty of care in delict); and *IS & GM Construction CC v Tunmer* 2003 (5) SA 218 (W) (failure to allege that the plaintiff builder was a registered home builder as defined in the Housing Consumers Protection Measures Act 95 of 1998).

[27] See, for example, *Jonathan v General Accident Insurance Company of South Africa Limited* 1992 (4) SA 618 (C) et seq and *Santam Insurance Limited v Booi* 1995 (3) SA 301 (A) at 309.

[28] *BOE Bank Limited v Ries* 2002 (2) SA 39 (SCA) at 46 para 13.

You will then note, physically or mentally, the following elements which are material to your cause of action:

- the plaintiff's detail;
- the defendant's detail;
- the plaintiff's ownership of the vehicle (or, if those are the facts, her possessing same by virtue of a credit purchase agreement in terms of which she bore the risk of loss of or damage to the vehicle);
- the detail of the collision;
- that the collision was caused by the defendant's negligence;
- that the vehicle was damaged in the collision, and the amount of the damages and their composition;
- demand (not essential, but it might play a role in claiming interest[29] or costs).[30]

Before drawing the particulars of claim you will, of course, satisfy yourself that the action has not prescribed. Moreover, and this is a point which should be considered very carefully in every case no matter how straightforward the answer usually is, you will ask yourself which court has jurisdiction and why.

You will now proceed on the basis of your analysis of the elements constituting the cause of action, and will set out in successive paragraphs a statement of the facts constituting your case in relation to each element. In the case which we are discussing you will find a fascinating compromise between the pleading of evidence and alleging facts. It is this: in a limited class of matters it is the practice to set out particulars constituting the allegation of fact.[31] However, the failure to set out these particulars will not render the particulars of claim excipiable if it contains a paragraph in the following terms, more or less:

> The collision was due to the negligence of the defendant.

If the details are omitted there will probably be a request for further particulars for purposes of trial. The particulars, whether pleaded originally or furnished in response to a request, will no doubt contain a number of allegations of negligence after the introductory phrase that the defendant was negligent 'in all, a number or one of the following respects'. This will not be held to be embarrassing to the defendant.[32] In the present case your claim is based on the existence of a blind rise, double white lines and the fact that the defendant was partly on the wrong side of the road. Therefore, you will probably find yourself pleading along the following lines:

---

[29] See s 2A of the Prescribed Rate of Interest Act 55 of 1975.
[30] See Cilliers *Law of Costs* 3 ed para 2.29.
[31] Negligence should be particularised.
[32] *Middelburg Coal Agency v Johannesburg Municipality* 1916 TPD 224. See also *Coetzee v Van Rensburg* 1954 (4) SA 616 (A).

3.

At all times material hereto, and more particularly on 1 January 2008, the plaintiff was the owner of a 1956 model Volkswagen Beetle bearing the registration letters and numbers SZT314GFP ("the plaintiff's vehicle").

4.

On 1 January 2008 and on the road between Polokwane and Sesiteng, a collision occurred between the plaintiff's vehicle and a motor vehicle bearing the registration letters and numbers BRZ417GP driven by the defendant ("the collision").

5.

The collision was caused by the negligence of the defendant, who was negligent in all, a number or one of the following respects:

5.1 He failed to keep a proper lookout;
5.2 He failed to keep BRZ417GP under any, alternatively sufficient, control;
5.3 He failed to remain on his correct side of the road;
5.4 He crested a blind rise in the road without remaining on his correct side of the road;
5.5 He veered over double white lines which prohibited him from doing so;
5.6 He veered onto his incorrect side of the road;
5.7 . . . .

5.4.4 A more challenging example: a supermarket case

Let us then take a second, more challenging, example.

You study your brief and extract the essence of the case as follows: your client was visiting a supermarket. Whilst ambling in the aisles viewing the wares, she slipped on an oily substance on the floor, fell and broke her hip. The floor manager who came to her assistance exclaimed that 'I am so sorry. I told the packers to clean that up'.

Your analysis of the facts will tell you that this appears to be a good case: the oil spill was evidently there for some time, it had been noted by the floor manager, and not only did the packer (who will have been an employee of the supermarket and for whose conduct the supermarket will be vicariously liable) not do as ordered, but on the face of it the floor manager never checked that this potentially dangerous situation was cleared up. Turning to the law, you will have little difficulty in concluding that the branch of law which applies is that of delict. Relying again on either your unerringly good knowledge of the law or the text books, you will determine that the essential elements of your client's case relate to whether she has *locus standi* to sue, whether you have been given sufficient detail of the supermarket to be able to cite it, wrongfulness (in this case, because one is relying on an omission on the part of the supermarket to keep the floor area safe, facts will have to be alleged on the basis of which it can be concluded that the supermarket owed your client a duty of care in that regard),[33] negligence and the defendant's vicarious responsibility for that

---

[33] See fn 28 above. See also *Seaharvest Corporation (Pty) Limited v Duncan Dock Cold Storage* 2000 (1) SA 827 (SCA) at 837–8.

negligence,[34] injury and consequent damage on the part of the plaintiff (do you have sufficient detail as to what injuries your client suffered and what her consequent damage amounts to, to enable you to comply with the requirements of Rule 18(10) of the Uniform Rules?).

You will then note the material elements:

*   the plaintiff's detail;
*   the defendant's detail;
*   the material facts giving rise to the defendant's duty of care;[35]
*   the incident;
*   that the incident was caused by a negligent breach by the defendant's employees, acting in the course and within the scope of their employment with the defendant, of its aforesaid duty of care. You will outline the respects in which you suggest the employees to have been negligent;
*   the bodily injuries sustained by the plaintiff as a result of the incident;
*   the damage sustained by the plaintiff (complying with the requirements of Rule 18(10) of the Uniform Rules);
*   demand.

5.4.5   Contractual claim or misrepresentation?

As a further illustration of drawing particulars of claim, let me give an example of a differential analysis, this one in a case relating to a written contract. I do not say 'arising out of contract', for a reason which I hope to clarify. Let us postulate the sale of a property or a business where the transaction takes the form of a sale of shares. It often happens, in all good faith, that the seller makes an inaccurate statement regarding the expenses relating to the property or the business, or regarding the assets of the business. What is the cause of action? And what difference does it make?

Of course the first point to be investigated is whether the inaccurate statement is incorporated in the contract. If it is, the action is based on a breach of a term of the contract, and, if the breach is material, the claim is either for rescission or for damages for breach of that term. If the statement was not incorporated in the contract, the plaintiff will have to rely upon a material misrepresentation which led him into the contract. Here, there may be a right to avoid the agreement; if the plaintiff does not wish to avoid, his claim is not

---

[34] The supermarket wasn't negligent. Employees of the supermarket, for whose acts and omissions it can be held vicariously liable, were.

[35] See fns 28 and 33 above for the concept of a duty of care. You will ask yourself why the defendant owes a duty of care. You will find that not everyone is his brother's keeper, but that if one opens a supermarket to the public for reward, one incurs a duty to that public to keep the supermarket reasonably safe for their use. From that thoughtful examination you will establish what facts you need to allege, viz. that the defendant operated the supermarket, that in doing so it opened same to the public, that in the circumstances it owed members of the public patronising the supermarket a duty to take reasonable care to ensure that the supermarket was safe for their use, that the plaintiff was on that day a member of the public patronising the supermarket, and that in the circumstances the defendant owed her a duty of care.

for damages but is one for a reduction of the purchase price by way of an *actio quanti minoris*. What is relevant is not a difference of nomenclature, but the basis of the claim and a consequent difference in its computation.

If the seller has made a fraudulent misrepresentation, he may be sued for damages on the basis of fraud, even though the fraudulent misrepresentation has become embodied in a warranty.

The cases from which you may ascertain the principles, and from which you may sort out what I have set out in the preceding paragraphs are *Maennel v Garage Continental Ltd*,[36] *Evans & Plows v Willis & Co*,[37] *Phame (Pty) Ltd v Paizes*[38] and *Prima Toy Holdings (Pty) Ltd v Rosenberg*.[39] Remember, of course, that I am merely trying to give an illustration of how to approach a differential analysis having regard to the cause of action and the appropriate basis of the claim.

5.4.6 General points about particulars of claim

It is not my present purpose to set out what the material allegations for any other cause of action are. This can be ascertained from the text books which I have mentioned. However, it may be far more advantageous if you make your own analysis of the essential aspects of the issue of the law involved and draw up your list of essential allegations before looking up a precedent in the text books.

Nevertheless there are a few topics that should be mentioned.

- The particulars of claim must show that the court has jurisdiction over the defendant, and in the magistrate's court also that there is jurisdiction in regard to the subject matter of the claim.[40] Failure to allege facts which disclose that the court has jurisdiction may lead to an exception,[41] or a special plea.

- In cases where the plaintiffs join in an action under rule of court 10 and, it is suggested, equally where the defendants are joined under the rule, you should have careful regard to the disclosing of causes of action in favour of all the plaintiffs (or against all the defendants) even alternatively. In this connection reference is made to the remarks of Ogilvie Thompson JA in *Trust Bank of Africa Ltd and Another v Western Credit Ltd*.[42]

- A tacit term[43] upon which reliance is placed must be specifically pleaded but, in terms of rule 18(7), it is not necessary to plead the circumstances

---

[36] 1910 AD 137.

[37] 1923 CPD 496.

[38] 1973 (3) SA 397 (A).

[39] 1974 (2) SA 477 (C).

[40] The question of jurisdiction in the High Court is discussed in Pistorius *Pollak on Jurisdiction* 2 ed. See also ss 6, 7 and 19 of the Supreme Court Act 59 of 1959 as amended.

[41] Cf *Appleby (Pty) Ltd v Dundas Ltd* 1948 (2) SA 905 (E) and *Viljoen v Federated Trust Ltd* 1971 (1) SA 750 (O).

[42] 1966 (2) SA 577 (A) and especially at 591F–592H.

[43] The tendency is now to refer to 'tacit' terms, leaving the epithet 'implied' to cover terms implied by law. See the remarks of Corbett JA in *Alfred McAlpine & Sons (Pty) Ltd v Transvaal Provincial Administration* 1974 (3) SA 506 (A) at 532.

which show that the term must be implied. However, the circumstances giving rise to a tacit contract must be pleaded.[44] It would seem to be unnecessary to plead terms that are implied by law.[45]

- Also, in regard to claims based on contract, where this is contained in a bulky document, the method of pleading is indicated in *Bantry Head Investments (Pty) Ltd and Another v Murray and Stewart (Cape Town) (Pty) Ltd*.[46]

- If reliance is placed on a statute, you as the pleader must either (and preferably) state the statute and the section or sections upon which you are relying, or formulate your client's claim or defence sufficiently clearly so as to indicate to the other side precisely what statutory provision is being relied upon.[47] In regard to statutory regulations or by-laws, the position appears to be that there must be specific reference to the regulation or section relied upon.[48]

- Where the relief which your client claims is dependent on the performance of a reciprocal obligation to the other party the pleading must contain a tender of performance of your client's obligation,[49] for example, in terms somewhat like the following (in the case of the sale of land):

    Wherefore against payment of the sum of R12 500 tendered as aforesaid, the plaintiff claims:
    (a) transfer of the said stand 12345 in the township of Valleyvlei, Johannesburg;
    (b) an order that should the defendant fail to effect such transfer within a period of. . . .

- It is necessary to allege circumstances which show that a reasonable time has lapsed in cases where the plaintiff's right to relief depends on that factor.[50]

- If, in your pleading, you rely on a contract, you must comply with the requirement of Rule 18(6) that you 'state whether the contract is written or oral and when, where and by whom it was concluded, and if the

---

[44] *Roberts Construction Co Ltd v Dominion Earthworks (Pty) Ltd* 1968 (3) SA 255 (A).

[45] *Clarke v Durban and Coast SPCA* 1959 (4) SA 333 (N) at 336.

[46] 1974 (2) SA 386 (C). The headnote reads as follows: 'A pleader who relies on a written document is required to do one of three things: (a) annex the document on which he relies; or (b) set forth the material portions thereof; or (c) "refer to" the material portions thereof. . . . (s)ufficiently . . . so as to inform the other party of the case he has to meet. . . '.

[47] *Yannakou v Apollo Club* 1974 (1) SA 614 (A).

[48] *Brandfort Munisipaliteit v Esterhuizen* 1957 (1) SA 229 (O) at 231G–232B, *Serobe v Koppies Bantu Community School Board* 1958 (2) SA 265 (O) at 269A–271D, and also authorities cited in these passages.

[49] See *Crispette & Candy Co Ltd v Oscar Michaelis NO and Leopold Alexander Michaelis NO* 1947 (4) SA 521 (A). In *Lafrenz (Pty) Ltd v Dempers* 1962 (3) SA 492 (A), however, it was held that the absence of an express tender was not a fatal defect where the nature of the order prayed necessarily implied a willingness to deliver.

[50] See Miller J *Credit Corporation of South Africa Ltd v Roy* 1966 (1) SA 12 (D) at 13, and also *Rustenburg Platinum Mines Ltd v Breedt* 1997 (2) SA 337 (A) at 353D.

contract is written a true copy thereof or of the part relied on in the pleading shall be annexed to the pleading.'

- If your client is claiming damages for personal injury you must comply with the requirements of Rule 18(10) in that you must specify the claimant's date of birth and outline the damages in such a manner as to enable the defendant reasonably to assess the quantum thereof. You would be well advised, in drafting such a pleading, to study the specific requirements of Rule 18(10). But note that the requirement that you apportion the claim between pain and suffering, loss of the amenities of life and disfigurement is, understandably, generally honoured only in the breach. It is usual (and, indeed, advisable) to claim a global figure in respect of general damages for pain and suffering, loss of the amenities of life, disfigurement and the other aspects of general damages that might arise in the particular case, adding a formula along the following lines:

11.

11.1 The amount claimed in paragraph 8.4 above in respect of general damage is a global figure in respect of pain, suffering and discomfort, emotional shock and trauma, loss of the enjoyment and of the amenities of life, disfigurement and the non-pecuniary aspects of disability.

11.2 It is not reasonably practicable for the plaintiff to apportion the amount claimed in respect of general damage amongst the components thereof.

On the other hand, where there are separate and distinct claims against the defendant, based on different causes of action, it is wrong to claim a global amount arising out of all of the claims.[51]

- In claiming damages you will no doubt have regard to two propositions, one of which is no excuse for casualness or inattention, and the other of which calls for caution and analysis. In the first place, even where by statute there is a limit to the amount which can be claimed from a particular defendant, a mere *plus petitio* will not ground an exception.[52] Secondly, a grossly excessive claim may result in a special order for costs being made against the party responsible, even if he should succeed in the action.[53]

- If you set out alternative claims in your particulars of claim you must ensure either that the facts in the main claim are sufficient to support the alternative or that additional facts are alleged for that purpose.[54] The alternative claim does not have to be consistent with the main claim,

[51] Eg, *Armitage v Estate Armitage* 1932 NPD 358.

[52] *Dharumpal Transport (Pty) Ltd v Dharumpal* 1956 (1) SA 700 (A), *Van Diggelen v De Bruin and Another* 1954 (1) SA 188 (SWA) at 195, *Thornton v Royal Insurance Co Ltd and Another* 1958 (4) SA 171 (C), and *Saffer Clothing Industries (Pty) Ltd v Worcester Textiles (Pty) Ltd* 1965 (2) SA 424 (C).

[53] *Naidoo v Auto Protection Insurance Co Ltd* 1963 (4) SA 798 (D) and *Palmer v SA Mutual Life & General Insurance Co Ltd* 1964 (3) SA 434 (D).

[54] See *Marney v Watson and Another* 1978 (4) SA 140 (C) at 144H–145A.

provided that it is clearly couched in the alternative.[55] In this regard one should bear in mind that there may arise cases where inconsistent allegations could render the pleading excipiable.[56]

• In regard to the prayer for further or alternative relief, see the discussion in paragraph 5.3.2 above. It does seem advisable to add a further prayer for 'further or alternative relief' after setting out the specific claims.[57]

5.4.7 Aim for perfection: one last check

Finally, when the particulars of claim have been drawn and typed, but before the claim is sent out, study it again, with a dispassionate absence of pride in your handiwork. Ask yourself whether it is intelligible,[58] whether it clearly conveys your client's case[59] and whether it discloses a cause of action.

5.5 ON DRAFTING THE PLEA

The drafting of a plea requires the performance of three preliminary analyses, as against the two required for the particulars of claim. Moreover, the pleader must also have regard to two pitfalls which exist to trap the unwary — failure to plead to an allegation and the making of an admission. Subject to these differences and to special considerations relating to the pleading of specific defences, the approach to the drafting of a plea is similar to the approach to drafting particulars of claim. It is not proposed to discuss the question of tenders in terms of rule 34 here. This is dealt with in the next chapter.

The three analyses which require to be made relate to:

• plaintiff's particulars of claim;
• the issues of law pertaining to the defendant's case;
• the issues of fact constituting the defendant's case.

You will note that, in regard to the particulars of claim, the phrase used was 'allegations of fact', whereas it now becomes 'issues of fact'. This is not carelessness, and indeed the very fact that this change is made should be a warning in regard to pleading generally. The warning is this: if you change your phraseology it may be contended, justifiably, that you have done so deliberately, to express a different intention or to create a different interpretation. After which digression it should be explained that the phrase

---

[55] *United Dominions Corporation (Rhodesia) Ltd v Van Eyssen* 1961 (1) SA 53 (SR) and *Kragga Kamma Estates CC and Another v Flanagan* 1995 (2) SA 367 (A) at 374I.

[56] See *Heydenrych v Colonial Mutual Life Insurance Society Ltd* 1920 CPD 67, *Florence v Criticos* 1954 (3) SA 392 (N), *Lloyds & Co (South Africa) Ltd v Aucamp and Another* 1961 (3) SA 879 (O) at 881–2 and *Pillai v Pillai* 1962 (3) SA 867 (D) at 870. The accuracy of the judgment in *Heydenrych's* case was doubted in the *United Dominions Corporation (Rhodesia)* case, see fn 55 (*supra*).

[57] See the authorities referred to in the discussion of this subject in paragraph 5.3.2 above.

[58] *Edwards v African Guarantee & Indemnity Co Ltd* 1952 (4) SA 335 (O), per Horwitz AJP at 344.

[59] The opposing party should not have to sort out a jumble of facts and fit them together: *Roberts Construction Co Ltd v Dominion Earthworks (Pty) Ltd* 1968 (3) SA 255 (A).

'issues of fact' is chosen because it embraces the denial of an allegation in the declaration as well as confession and avoidance.

After the first analysis, and before troubling yourself with your own case, you inquire of yourself whether the plaintiff has placed sufficient allegations of fact on record to justify the conclusion of law set out in the particulars of claim. If a material allegation is missing you will be entitled to take exception in terms of rule 23(1). The problem is to determine whether the allegation is missing because of poor draftsmanship on the part of your opponent or because his case does not support the allegation. If it is a case of poor draftsmanship and if the exception should succeed, your opponent will probably be given leave to file an amended pleading. Usually, nothing will have been achieved, except an order for costs, a feeling of superiority and the entry of your name in your opponent's mental blacklist. If the allegation is missing because your opponent cannot make it, either for want of evidence or simply because the facts do not support it, then it is your duty to except and so to dispose of the matter as cheaply as possible.

The topic of exceptions will be discussed later in this chapter.

When the question of an exception has been settled one way or the other you next consider your own case in order to draw the plea. This is done in the same general way as the approach to the particulars of claim, but certain special problems arise for your consideration and must be discussed a little later.

Subject to what has been said previously about the perils of using pleadings as tactical weapons, you will have to make up your mind precisely what objectives you wish to attain with your plea. Ideally, one would wish simply to be able to plead 'The defendant denies the plaintiff's allegations of fact and conclusions of law and prays that the plaintiff's claims be dismissed with costs'. However, even in 1830 a pleader had misgivings when he pleaded 'that he does not owe the sum demanded or any part thereof', for he covered himself by adding 'and that the writing obligatory, alleged to have been signed by G Rossouw, was not the deed of the said G Rossouw'. Even that did not avail him because the court held that, after evidence had been led, he could not argue a number of special defences which had not been pleaded.[60] As Krause J also put it:[61]

> Now the object of all pleadings is to inform the opponent, whether plaintiff or defendant, of the case which he has to meet, and in order to prevent a defendant from evading the issue it has been laid down that a mere general denial, as it is called, will not be permissible, and that the defendant is obliged specifically to deny each and every material allegation which appears in the declaration, so that the plaintiff may ascertain from the manner of his denial the case that the defendant sets up and, therefore, the case which the plaintiff has to meet.

---

[60] *Horn v Loedolf et Uxor* (1830) 1 Menz 403.
[61] *Hillman Brothers Ltd v Kelly & Hingle* 1926 WLD 153. See also rule 22(2).

More recently Smalberger AJ in *Rumanal (Pty) Ltd v Hubner*[62] said:

> There is *prima facie* a contradiction between the body of the defendant's plea, and the prayer thereto. It is apparent from the body of defendant's plea that he admits liability to plaintiff in respect of portion of the amount claimed by plaintiff. Yet the prayer asks for dismissal of plaintiff's claim with costs. *Prima facie* the prayer relates to the whole of plaintiff's claim, in which case it is in conflict with the admissions contained in the body of the plea. The prayer could also possibly be construed, as Mr Jones who appeared for the defendant suggested that it should be, as relating only to the disputed portion of plaintiff's claim, and not the whole thereof. The purpose of pleadings is to crystallise and clearly define the issues between the parties. It is incumbent upon a defendant in his plea to apprise the opposing party fully of his defence, and to this end he must deal specifically with every allegation of fact which he intends to put in issue. In determining whether or not a plea fulfils this function it should be read as a whole. If this is done then it is apparent that defendant's plea, despite its inelegance arising from the conflict referred to, suffices to inform plaintiff precisely what is in issue between the parties.

That some degree of latitude is allowable to the draftsman of a plea appears also from the case of *AA Mutual Insurance Association Ltd v Nomeka*,[63] where Viljoen AJA said:

> The weight of the decisions is, therefore, that provided that plaintiff's fault is put in issue an apportionment need not be specifically pleaded or claimed. This is the correct view, in my opinion.
>
> The effect of the Uniform Rules of Court has been to clarify the requirements of pleadings (if previously any doubt existed). Thus in regard to the plea rule 22(2) stipulates that the defendant must either admit or deny or confess and avoid all the material facts alleged or state which of the said facts are not admitted and to what extent, and shall 'clearly and concisely state all material facts upon which he relies.'

This rule requires a plea to consist, therefore, of statements (answers) falling into one of four categories, although in the same plea, of course, all four categories may be employed. The matters now to be discussed arising out of rule 22(2) are:

- admissions;
- denials;
- avoidances;
- non–admissions.

5.5.1 Admissions

Admissions may be expressly made or they may result from rule 22(3) which provides that every 'allegation of fact — which is not stated in the plea to be denied or to be not admitted, shall be deemed to be admitted. If any qualification of any denial is necessary, it must be stated in the plea.'

---

[62] 1976 (1) SA 643 (E) at 645B–E.
[63] 1976 (3) SA 45 (A) at 55D.

Admissions are easy. They require no thought. The only reservation is that they are too easy and may be caused by no thought. They may be made in error and the problem then arises how to avoid their consequences.[64] The court has a discretion to relieve a party of the consequences of an admission made in error, and:

> it does not seem to me that such a discretion could be exercised, in a case where the admission has been made in a pleading, in any other way than by granting an amendment of that pleading.[65]

The attempt to withdraw an admission understandably provokes a strong reaction from the opponent who seeks to take advantage of it, nor do the courts incline lightly to granting the necessary amendment. It becomes necessary to explain adequately, sometimes by means of evidence, how the admission came to be made in error before the court will allow it to be withdrawn.[66] Also you, as the party responsible, will have to satisfy the court that there will be no prejudice to the other side if the admission is withdrawn.[67]

There are two interesting illustrations of the effect of admissions in a plea which might bear discussion:

In *South British Insurance Co Ltd v Glissan*[68] the defendant company had been sued under the Motor Vehicle Insurance Act 29 of 1942. The plaintiff in his declaration alleged that the defendant was the insurer of the motor vehicle which had been involved in the collision giving rise to the action. The defendant admitted this allegation in its plea. On the 'eve of the trial', and well after the expiry of the two-year period of prescription provided by the Act, the defendant applied for the amendment of its plea by withdrawing the admission made. The amendment was refused, not on the ground that the erroneous admission had not been properly explained,[69] but because the amendment would prejudice the plaintiff who could no longer sue the Motor Insurers Association for damages, the period of prescription having expired. If in fact the defendant company was not the true insurer of the vehicle its erroneous admission saddled it with a liability which it should not have borne.

---

[64] Section 15 of the Civil Proceedings Evidence Act 25 of 1965 provides: 'It shall not be necessary for any party in civil proceedings to prove nor shall it be competent for any such party to disprove any fact admitted on the record of such proceedings'. Cf *Whittal v Alexandria Municipality* 1966 (4) SA 297 (E).

[65] Davis AJA in *Gordon v Tarnow* 1947 (3) SA 525 (A) at 532. Compare *Mamojee v Pillay* 1948 (1) SA 212 (N).

[66] See *Bellairs v Hodnett and Another* 1978 (1) SA 1109 (A) at 1150E–1151B, *Levy v Levy* 1991 (3) SA 614 (A) 622A–D and *JR Janisch (Pty) Ltd v WM Spilhaus & Company (WP) (Pty) Ltd* 1992 (1) SA 167 (C) at 169–170.

[67] See for example *Workmen's Compensation Commissioner v Crawford and Another* 1987 (1) SA 296 (A) at 307, where a party was not allowed to argue a point on appeal because 'if the point had been taken . . . timeously, whether in the pleadings or otherwise, the possibility cannot be excluded that the respondents' conduct of their case would have been different, for example in relation to the cross-examination. . . .'

[68] 1963 (1) SA 289 (D).

[69] Although Miller J at 295 is reported as saying that the plaintiff's submissions on this point did have 'some substance'.

In *Dinath v Breedt*[70] an order had been granted ejecting the defendant from certain property at the instance of the plaintiff who alleged that he was the owner of the property. There was no denial of the plaintiff's allegation in this regard. In fact at the date when summons was issued the plaintiff was not the owner of the property and he would not have been entitled to an ejectment order. On appeal the court was concerned with the question whether an ejectment order had rightly been granted, one answer to such an order being the plaintiff's want of title. In giving the judgment of the court Colman J said:[71]

> I am driven to the conclusion, therefore, that, on a proper construction of the pleadings in the court *a quo*, it was admitted that the plaintiff was the owner of the property at the time of issue of his summons. The appeal must therefore be decided on that footing notwithstanding our knowledge that the averment so admitted was not in accordance with the facts. The argument based on the absence of ownership at the time of issue of the summons, must, therefore, be rejected.

With these two cases before you the need for caution in making admissions should be apparent. The need for caution in pleading denials will appear a little later.

When you are minded to make an admission, you will usually find that a simple 'This is admitted' will suffice or, if you incline to the more verbose, 'The allegations contained in this paragraph are admitted'. But there will be instances where you find nothing of substance in the paragraph of the particulars of claim with which you are dealing which you are not prepared to admit, but are uncomfortable with the way in which the allegations are put. You would have put it differently, and you perhaps wonder whether by admitting the allegations in the language in which they are couched, your admission will not go further than you would like. An example might be where you are quite satisfied that your client owed a duty of care and are prepared to admit it, but have the uncomfortable feeling that the plaintiff might have couched the ambit of that duty of care a bit more broadly than you would yourself have done. In those circumstances, the safer course is to follow the procedure of what I would call 'admitting and denying'. Rather than simply admitting the allegations, you couch them in a first sub-paragraph in language with which you are comfortable, and then insert a second paragraph denying everything else. For example:

4.1   As owner of the supermarket, the defendant owed to patrons making use of the supermarket a duty to take reasonable care for the safety of such patrons.
4.2   Save as aforesaid, these allegations are denied.

5.5.2 Denials

If you are in doubt about an admission the natural reaction is to plead a denial. In other circumstances a denial may be pleaded if the defendant thinks that the

---

[70] 1966 (3) SA 712 (T).
[71] Ibid at 717F.

plaintiff may be unable to prove a material allegation in his case, or where the pleader knows that the plaintiff will be able to prove the allegation, but prefers to deny it in order to force the plaintiff to testify. Such denials are referred to, with varying degrees of disrespect, as 'tactical denials'. These tactical denials do not always endear themselves to the court,[72] nor do they always achieve the desired result. An instance of the latter misfortune is to be found in *Joseph v Black*[73] where an attorney sued for damages for defamation. In order to compel him to enter the witness-box and subject himself to cross-examination, counsel for the defendant denied the plaintiff's status. However, the plaintiff's status was proved by other means, presumably the court record of his admission to the Side-Bar, and he was not called to testify. Perhaps it is a wise precaution not to make tactical denials unless one is certain that their purpose may not be frustrated by the opposing party. Very little purpose is served by pleading 'tactical denials'. Mostly they serve only to raise the ire of the court — never a good thing to do unnecessarily.

A denial is a sufficient answer to an allegation, and there is no need to set out facts in support of the denial. The denial must be specific, that is to say it must relate to a specific allegation and must not leave the plaintiff in doubt as to what is in fact being placed in issue.[74] A reference to the cases quoted shows how easily plaintiffs can become confused on this topic. The point to watch for seems to be whether an allegation of fact made by the plaintiff really consists of two or more constituent elements or whether it can properly be treated as a single allegation.

Sometimes the temptation to plead a denial must be strenuously resisted and put behind one. In place of the denial must be substituted an admission. Thus in *SA Railways & Harbours v Landau & Co*[75] De Villiers JP said the following regarding a denial:

> But the same cannot be said of the general denial of par 5 of the declaration — namely, 'The defendant refuses, and persists in his refusal, to remove the said buildings from the plaintiff's said land'. Such a denial is clearly absurd. In the face of his denial that he had erected the building, and that the building was on the plaintiff's land he ought to have admitted this paragraph, at the same time referring to his previous denials as regards the erection of the building and the ownership of the land. It is, therefore, clear that the plea is ambiguous and consequently embarrassing.

5.5.3 Confession and avoidance

Speaking very generally, pleading a confession and avoidance is the same as the raising of a specific defence such as fraud, waiver, payment, *ultra vires* and so on.

---

[72] See, for example, the remarks of De Villiers JP in *SA Railways & Harbours v Landau & Co* 1917 TPD 485 at the top of 488; also *Ebrahim v Excelsior Shopfitters & Furnishers (Pty) Ltd* (II) 1946 TPD 226 at 239 and *Suzman Ltd v Pather & Sons* 1957 (4) SA 690 (D).

[73] 1930 WLD 327, upheld on appeal *sub nom Black and Others v Joseph* 1931 AD 132.

[74] See *Schultz v Nel* 1947 (2) SA 1060 (C) 1066 and *Sterling Consumer Products (Pty) Ltd v Cohen and other related cases* [2000] 4 All SA 221 (W).

[75] 1917 TPD 485 at 487.

It is not my purpose to discuss these defences in detail or even to list them because that would go to the merits of cases rather than the technique of pleading.

It seems to be principally in the present context that the rule to the effect that the pleader must 'clearly and concisely state all material facts on which he relies' becomes applicable. The pleader cannot, for example, simply say 'The plaintiff is not entitled to judgment because he has waived his rights'. It will be necessary to plead when, where and how a waiver was effected. Such considerations apply to all the special defences and all grounds of confession and avoidance.[76]

The previous suggestions made in connection with the drafting of particulars of claim would seem to be valid in regard to the manner of pleading special defences in confession and avoidance. Sometimes, should you misconceive the law applicable, for example, it may be possible to argue alternative propositions of law if the facts have been pleaded and established in evidence. This occurred in *Nel v Louw and Another*[77] where, in answer to a claim for damages, the defendant pleaded that a right of public trekpath had been created by prescription. On appeal it was held that the right could not be so created, but that the pleadings and evidence were wide enough to cover creation by *vetustas*.

5.5.4 Non-admissions

The debate as to whether there is a distinction, other than merely of emphasis, between the denial and the non-admission of a fact and, if so, precisely what that distinction is, has been played out in the Cape courts, with De Vos J in *Wilson v South African Railways & Harbours*[78] kicking-off by holding that it is in order to plead a non-admission as opposed to a denial, but that the non-admitter must also plead the reason for his unreadiness to admit the allegation in question. That reason, he pointed out, is usually an absence of knowledge. Marais AJ (with whom Schock J concurred) declined in *Standard Bank Factors Limited v Furncor Agencies (Pty) Limited and Others*[79] to express an opinion on whether a non-admission must indeed always be accompanied by an explanation (it was unnecessary: the non-admission in the case before him was explained) but went on, *obiter*, to outline the distinction between the two forms as follows:[80]

> To my mind, there is a clear notional distinction between these two stances. A plaintiff faced with a positive denial must anticipate and prepare for the leading by

---

[76] Compare *Peacock v Hodges* 1876 Buch 65 (remarks of De Villiers CJ during argument as reported at 68), *Dreyer v Van Reenen* (1845) 3 Menz 375, and cases at 365 et seq, *Harrison v Colonial Motors Ltd* 1934 NPD 168, and *Naude v Bredenkamp* 1956 (2) SA 448 (O), especially at 452. As to the degree of particularity which may be required in specific cases, see *Lieberthal & Lieberthal v South British Insurance Co Ltd* 1959 (3) SA 81 (W), *Kliptown Clothing Industries (Pty) Ltd v Marine & Trade Insurance Co Ltd* 1960 (1) SA 446 (W) and *Swart v De Beer* 1989 (3) SA 622 (E).

[77] 1955 (1) SA 107 (C).

[78] *Wilson v South African Railways & Harbours* 1981 (3) SA 1016 (C).

[79] *Standard Bank Factors Limited v Furncor Agencies (Pty) Limited and Others* 1985 (3) SA 410 (C).

[80] At 417I–418C.

defendant of rebutting evidence which contradicts the allegations he has made. A plaintiff faced with a non-admission need not anticipate and prepare to meet contradictory evidence to be adduced to the defendant. Indeed, there is authority for the proposition that he need not even anticipate a limited challenge by way of cross-examination. . . . While that may conceivably be going too far . . ., I think, with respect, that [it] . . . is undoubtedly correct insofar as . . . a plea of non-admission . . . because of a lack of knowledge, will not entitle the leader to contradict the plaintiff's averments by leading evidence to the contrary at the trial. In my view a plaintiff is entitled to know which of these two stances a defendant is adopting and a plea which leaves that in doubt is vague and embarrassing.

Van den Heever J was in due course in *N Goodwin Design (Pty) Limited v Moscak*[81] confronted with the consequences of *Furncor Agencies*, when it was argued before her that the defendant which had pleaded a non-admission of the allegation that the plaintiff's charges were fair and reasonable was precluded from cross-examining thereon, and from leading evidence in contradiction.[82] The learned judge rejected this contention, preferring at 163H to relegate the distinction between denial and non-admission to 'simply a matter of emphasis, a denial being more emphatic than a non-admission'.

Let me suggest to you that there *is* room in our system for the accepted distinction between a denial and a non-admission, that it is not and ought not to be a distinction without a difference, and that the distinction does indeed lie in the suggestion in *Wilson* and *Furncor Agencies* that —

* when you dispute a fact it would be the correct form of pleading to say that you deny it;
* where, however, you consider that it is an allegation which the plaintiff ought to be made to prove, and which you reserve the right to test by cross-examination but have no intention of leading contradictory evidence on, it is best to employ a non-admission furnishing the reason for the non-admission, along the following lines:

> The defendant has no knowledge of the allegations contained in this paragraph, can consequently neither admit nor deny these allegations and puts the plaintiff to the proof thereof.

However, this ought not to be done where it is apparent that the defendant must have the knowledge which he disclaims as, for example, where he himself was a party to the very contract to which he is now pleading.[83] Marais AJ in *Furncor Agencies* drew a distinction, at 416, between the technical adequacy and the ethical legitimacy of a plea of non-admission on the strength of lack of

---

[81] 1992 (1) SA 154 (C).

[82] Interestingly, one gathers from the judgment that this argument was raised not as an objection to the cross-examination or to the leading of evidence by the defendant, but in final argument. Therein lies a further lesson: it is elementary that if you intend objecting to a line of cross-examination or to the evidence of a witness, you should object at the time and not later, after the horse has bolted. It is possible that this played a role in the learned judge's decision on this point.

[83] *Behm v Newmarch* (1915) 36 NLR 560.

knowledge in circumstances where there is likely to be knowledge. He pointed out that the question of whether the defendant in fact has knowledge of that which he denies knowing is something that can rarely if ever be tested by way of exception. If of course it should emerge at trial that the party in fact had knowledge, he might be mulcted in costs.

5.5.5 An example: a plea in a defamation action

In pleading in defamation actions, you will, of course, remember the law lecturer who explained that the 'rolled-up' plea, unlike an umbrella, cannot be used to cover a wide area of subject-matter, and you will carefully separate the defence of 'justification' from that of 'fair comment'.[84] A plaintiff is entitled to know whether the facts are being justified or the comments are being defended. The problem which arises is that there is no defence of 'fair comment' if the facts upon which it is based are false.[85] If in doubt you will probably consult the authorities and those textbooks which set out precedents of such a plea. Using the analysis method of pleading which is suggested in this chapter, there should be no doubt because you will ask yourself: what essential elements enable one to confess and avoid by raising the defence of fair comment? You will find that the comment must be based on facts which are true, it must be relevant, it must not be inspired by malice, it must be fair and the matter must be of public interest. To ensure you do not place a 'rolled-up' plea on record you perform a differential analysis with the defence of justification and you find that the elements of the latter defence are that the statement must be true and its publication must have been for the public benefit. The analysis shows the following which can be expressed in a comparative table:

Fair Comment	Justification
It must be comment.	It must be fact.
It must be based on correct facts.	The facts must be true.
It must be relevant.	
It must not be inspired by malice.	
It must be fair.	It must be true.
The matter must be of public interest.	The matter must be for the public benefit.

From your analysis you will then proceed to give your plea that degree of nuance which makes it clear that you are defending your comment and not attacking the plaintiff. You will also be careful to distinguish between 'public interest' and 'public benefit', although oft-times you will be hard pressed to do so.

---

[84] *Steenkamp v Laurence* 1918 CPD 79 and *Davies and Others v Lombard* 1966 (1) SA 585 (W).
[85] Compare *Crawford v Albu* 1917 AD 102.

5.5.6 General considerations relating to pleas

- It will not avail you to make an allegation in your plea if evidence would not be admissible to support it.[86] The converse also holds good,[87] that is, an allegation cannot be struck out as irrelevant if evidence on it could be led at the trial.
- It is not competent to couple with a main plea disputing liability an alternative plea making a tender, nor to tender in the alternative.[88] The reason is that the plaintiff does not know whether, by accepting the tender, he will be putting an end to the action. The point raised, however, may well be more academic than real because of the provisions of rule of court 34 and in particular the system of a 'secret tender', being an offer or tender made without prejudice. In terms of rule 34(10) the fact that such a tender has been made may not be disclosed, and accordingly it cannot be referred to in the pleadings. An unconditional offer or tender is exactly that, and obviously if the tender is made unconditionally and is accepted, it puts an end to the case.
- The principle of separating the defences, so that a plaintiff does not have to ponder over which of several defences set out in a paragraph the defendant relies upon, is of general application and is not confined to defamation actions. The fact that a plea can be read a number of ways makes it embarrassing.[89]
- Defences may be pleaded in the alternative. If there are several alternative answers to a particular allegation in the particulars of claim, it would be appropriate to employ alternative paragraphs. Such answers do not have to be consistent with one another provided they are specifically pleaded in the alternative.[90]

5.5.7 Conclusion

When the plea has been drawn it should be reconsidered with four points in mind:

- Does it comply with rule 22(2)?
- Does it contain whatever allegations of fact may be relevant to the particular defence pleaded (and none that is irrelevant)?
- Are any of the allegations inconsistent with one another when subjected to the test of logic, save where they may properly be pleaded in the alternative?

---

[86] See, for example, *Wells v SA Alumenite Co* 1927 AD 69 and *SA Sentrale Ko-op Graanmaatskappy v Shifren* 1964 (4) SA 760 (A).

[87] *Golding v Torch Printing & Publishing Co (Pty) Ltd and Others* 1948 (3) SA 1067 (C).

[88] *Li Kui Yu v Jamieson* 1906 TS 469, *Van Coller v Bukes* 1912 OPD 113 and *Kam NO v Udwin* 1939 WLD 339.

[89] *Quinlan v MacGregor* 1960 (4) SA 383 (D) at 390 and *Nasionale Aartappel Koöperasie Beperk v Price Waterhouse Coopers Ing en Andere* 2001 (2) SA 790 (T) at 797.

[90] *SAR & H v Lennon Ltd* 1945 AD 157 at 167.

- Can the plea be stigmatised as 'evasive'?

Examples of these topics abound in the law reports but it would hardly seem worthwhile to do more than draw attention to the principle.

When all this has been verified there remains one last elementary precaution: the plea must contain a prayer, either for judgment against the plaintiff or for the dismissal of the plaintiff's claim, presumably with costs.

5.6 SPECIAL PLEAS

It will sometimes be found that a point arises which is not apparent from the particulars of claim and which, if successful, will dispose of the whole case without it being necessary to go into the merits. Or else it may be that there is some error in the plaintiff's procedure which renders it temporarily unnecessary or incompetent to deal with the main dispute. The defence, in such instances, is raised in the form of a preliminary plea, called a 'special plea'. It is suggested that if the requirements set out in the first paragraph of this section are satisfied then a special plea ought to be filed, bearing in mind the views of Claassen J expressed as follows:[91]

> When it comes to special pleading, I think it is a mistake to give such a plea a heading such as plea in bar or plea in abatement, and then to argue that such a heading would be a basis for an argument for which no proper basis has been laid in the body of the pleading. It is perhaps much wiser to call such a pleading a special plea and then to set out specifically in the body thereof the grounds to be relied on.

Amongst defences to be raised by way of a special plea since it destroys the cause of action, are for instance: extinctive prescription, non- or misjoinder and *res judicata*. A plea of *lis alibi pendens* although merely postponing the action, has to be pleaded specially.

5.7 EXCEPTIONS

5.7.1 Exceptions, generally

There is one more matter which merits mention at this stage. That is the exception. In your earlier years the exception will sit on your shoulder watching every pleading you draw and waiting, vulture-like, for you to fall by the wayside. With experience you will come to look on the exception as a useful ally in securing a quick, neat and comparatively inexpensive decision in appropriate cases. The menace of the exception is the utter sense of shame and degradation which it instils. Yet it must be met philosophically. If the exception is due to your oversight there is nothing for it but to concede graciously and amend your pleadings. You may conceivably convince a court that what is not there is in fact conveyed by what is there or that it need not be there anyway. If you fail in your tilt at this windmill you will only have increased the wasted

---

[91] *Van der Westhuizen v Smit NO and Another* 1954 (3) SA 427 (SWA) at 430. See also *Dease v Minister of Justice* 1962 (3) SA 215 (T).

costs tenfold or more and you will then concede ungraciously and amend your pleading.

I suggest that, from the point of view of both the potential excipient and the potential respondent, the matter can be reduced to a few basic rules, with the proviso that, if you are the potential respondent, the fact that your opponent does not apply the 'rules' should never induce you to follow his example.

- You can except where a pleading lacks an averment which is essential to the cause of action,[92] whether that averment be a positive one or a negative, such as those that are to be found in an action on a dishonoured cheque: 'there being no duty on the said bank, as between itself and the defendant, to honour the said cheque'.

- You can except when the pleadings up to the date of your exception contain sufficient averments or admissions by your opponent to justify the court in deciding the case against him assuming all his averments to be true.

- You can except when, despite due notice under rule of court 23(1), your opponent does not remove the cause of complaint and you believe that you can satisfy the court that the pleading is vague and embarrassing.[93]

- Professional courtesy dictates, whether your opponent is a fellow advocate, a fellow attorney or on the other side of the professional divide, that if you intend excepting you first contact him informally, tell him what your difficulty with his pleading is, and invite him to amend.

- Always ask yourself, before excepting, whether it is really necessary, ie, whether what you perceive as the abysmal state of your opponent's pleading is indeed such that you need to except, or whether you ought not simply to plead and in particular, whether an exception promises to finally dispose of the matter.

- In the last-mentioned case, as in the case of the 'jump shift' at contract bridge, the response is mandatory. You must except or expose your client to liability for costs.[94] When I refer to 'deciding the case against him' I mean to convey that the decision will be a final one based on law and not based on any technical deficiency in the pleading. There must be no possibility that the hearing of evidence would lead to any different decision.[95] Generally, on the scope and purpose of exceptions see

[92] See rule 23(1) and for example the cases cited in fn 26 above.
[93] *Wilson v South African Railways & Harbours* 1981 (3) SA 1016 (C).
[94] As in *Myers v Shraga* 1947 (2) SA 258 (T), *Scheepers v Vermeulen* 1948 (4) SA 884 (O) and *Laingsburg Afdelingsraad v Luyt* 1959 (3) SA 679 (C).
[95] Compare *Verstuis v Greenblatt* 1973 (2) SA 270 (NC) where 'an exception was taken by the plaintiff that the plea disclosed no defence and it appeared that the whole matter was interwoven with the evidence which would be led at the trial'. The court ordered the exception to stand over until the trial.

Dharumpul Transport (Pty) Ltd v Dharumpal[96] and *Lewis v Oneanate (Pty) Ltd and Another.*[97]

5.7.2 How to respond to an exception

*   If you receive a notice under rule 23(1) inviting you to rectify your pleading, take another look at your pleading. Is it clear and unambiguous; is it a fair reflection of the principles of law on which your allegations are based; is there any inconsistency or contradiction? It will not avail you to argue that your pleading conveys a perfectly lucid case and that it will support either version A or version B. If you do this your opponent will gratefully acknowledge your assistance in making his point for him. He wants to know what the case is, not what it could be. If you have any doubt about the cause of complaint your safest course is to accept the invitation and amend. Even if you can see no fault in your pleading, you must still ask yourself whether your client's interests are best served by risking an argument. It is sometimes best to bend with the wind where meeting the point will not harm your case and will save your client from being exposed to the costs, the delay and the risk of an exception. Even where you are convinced that your opponent's point is crass and wrong.
*   If the exception is that your particulars of claim disclose no cause of action or your plea no defence then I suggest that you repeat the process of analysis set out earlier in this chapter.
*   If you believe or are told that the exception is in the third category previously described you should welcome it — provided that there is no further averment which could possibly be made in support of your client's case. Again, I suggest that you submit your pleading to the analytical process. The temptation will be great to read through the document and mentally reconcile the allegations of fact with your view of the law. That, however, will not do. Your testing process, therefore, should be capable of serving as the written notes of the argument which you will present to the court. You proceed by reconsidering the law and making a tabular exposition of the elements essential to your case. When this has been done, opposite each item in the table you write your particular allegation of fact. The analysis will then show that you are right, or it will show why you are wrong, or it will show the essence of the contention of law which arises in the exception. If you are satisfied that no possible amendment can be made in your allegations of fact then you have a true exception.

5.8 REPLICATING, DUPLICATING AND SO FORTH

Remember what was said about the need for everything that you do to have a purpose, and to be tailored to meet that purpose.

---

[96] 1956 (1) SA 700 (A) at 706D–E.
[97] 1992 (4) SA 811 (A) at 817F–G.

You replicate if the plea raises issues to which you need to respond, and which are not covered, or are not adequately covered, in your particulars of claim. If that is necessary, then you do the necessary. If it is unnecessary, then you do not replicate.

In those rare instances where the replication raises new issues to which you must respond, and where your response is not covered, or is not adequately covered, in your plea, then (and only then) do you duplicate; otherwise not.

CHAPTER 6

Pre-trial Procedure

6.1 PRE-TRIAL PROCEDURE, GENERALLY

Once the pleadings have closed, whether by action or inaction, a stage best described as 'the period of pre-trial procedure' arrives.

There is much to be done after the pleadings close — so much with so little time for it that it is fatal to wait until the case is set down for hearing before one commences with preparation. Advocacy is often hampered through a failure to take the steps prescribed. It is frustrating in the extreme to be unable to call for particulars for purposes of trial, or to use certain documents simply because the rules regulating documents have been overlooked.

Pre-trial procedure must be put into operation on the day after the pleadings become closed, and not on the day when notice of trial is received.

Indeed, as you will see, pre-trial procedure commences even before the pleadings close.

6.2 THE PURPOSE OF PRE-TRIAL PROCEDURE

Before I discuss the pre-trial rules individually, it might be well to ask what one sets out to achieve in pre-trial procedure. The objectives can be succinctly stated and I shall venture to summarise them:

*   to be able to prove every element of your case without undue inconvenience and without foundering on formality;
*   to learn what your opponent's case will be on the issues arising from the pleadings;
*   to know every relevant document in your opponent's possession;
*   to ascertain precisely what documents he proposes to use against you;
*   to attempt to establish how your opponent will prove his case;
*   to be able to test your 'case theory' against the case your opponent intends to prove.

With that I turn to discuss the rules, which must be invoked with a sense of timing that has nothing to do with court days or formalities or anything like that. It has to do with the tactics of the case, with the order in which information must be sought and with the action which must be taken to assemble information despite the reticence of the opposition. But nothing that I shall say about particular rules will be of the slightest assistance unless immediate attention is given to every document, notice or reply received from the opposing party. One soon tires, I might remark, of hearing the excuse: 'I am sorry that this was overlooked, but when it was received the typist filed it.' It would seem that attorneys' offices are staffed with typists who have nothing to do but to hide documents as they are received — usually underneath the draft power of attorney where nobody will ever look for them again.

6.3 THE VARIOUS PRE-TRIAL RULES OF COURT

The various pre-trial rules, and the chronological order in which you will probably have regard to them, is as follows:

Rule

36(4)   Production of medical and other reports etc.
35(14) Inspection of documents for purposes of pleading.
35(1)   Discovery.
35(3)   Further and better discovery.
35(6)   Inspection of discovered documents.
35(8)   List of documents intended to be used.
35(9)   Notice of avail.
36(10) Photographs, plans, diagrams etc.
35(10) Notice to produce.
35(11) Production of documents.
35(12) Inspection of certain documents.
35(13) Applicability of provisions to applications.
36(1) and 36(5A) Medical examination.
36(5)   Second medical examination.
36(6)   Inspection of things.
36(9)   Expert witnesses.
33(4)   Separation of issues.
21(2)   Particulars on trial.
34   Tenders.
37(1)   Pre-trial conference.
38(1)   Subpoenas.
38(2)   Evidence on affidavit.
38(3)   Evidence on commission.
62(4)   Paginating the pleadings.

From the point of view of effectiveness there will be variations in the sequence in which these rules should be invoked, depending on the type of case with which you are dealing and on the permutations that may occur in such cases.

Since the problem concerns the attorney more than counsel, and since an attorney's practice must either be conducted on a basis of a system or of chaos, I would suggest that the attorney might consider spending a few rand to have duplicated pages prepared reflecting:

Column 1. Rule number.
Column 2. Gist of the rule.
Column 3. Number of court days before trial limiting the application of the rule or required in terms of the rule.
Column 4. Last date, calculated on the basis of column 3, available in terms of the rule.

Column 5. Date on which action taken.

Such a sheet could be fastened inside the file dealing with each matter and would do much to ensure timeous attention to the terms of the relevant rules.

6.4 RULE 36(4): PRODUCTION OF MEDICAL AND OTHER REPORTS

A party may serve a notice requiring any person claiming damages for bodily injury to make available in so far as he is able to do so medical reports, hospital records, X-ray photographs, or similar documentary information relevant to the assessment of the damages. This rule supplements rules 35(6) and 35(12) but may be invoked at any stage in the proceedings.

Where you represent a defendant you will take advantage of this rule either in order to make a payment into court under rule 34, or for the purpose of enabling your own medical experts to become aware of the plaintiff's relevant medical history for the purpose of their own examination. It is also useful for trial purposes.

Sometimes a defendant will strike oil — so to speak. Some efficient medical practitioner will have noted, of a motorist who has been involved in a collision, that on admission to hospital he smelt of alcohol. And a smell of alcohol to a defendant is as manna to the tribes of Israel in the desert. Usually, however, complications set in. When the file is eventually found the handwriting will be almost illegible. If decipherable the note will be unsigned and no one will know who wrote it. If there is a signature it will be that of a houseman who is no longer at the hospital, and who is known only as Dr Smith. And if you find Dr Smith even his own note will not spur his memory to more than a recognition of his handwriting.

From this you will learn. One thing you will learn is to serve your notice under rule 36(4) as soon as possible. And, since the plaintiff does not have possession of his own hospital file and you may elicit nothing more than a radiological report, you will learn how to obtain a written consent to supplement the rule and enable you to try to persuade the hospital officials to let you have an early sight of the claimant's file.

As usual, time is of the essence.

6.5 RULE 35(14): INSPECTION OF DOCUMENTS FOR PURPOSES OF PLEADING

Rule 35(14) entitles any party to an action, after appearance to defend and for purposes of pleading, to require from any other party to make available for inspection 'a clearly specified document or tape recording in his possession which is relevant to a reasonably anticipated issue in the action' and to allow him to make a copy thereof. In effect, the rule applies to parties who must plead to other parties' allegations, such as defendants, third parties, etc. The rule can be usefully employed in for instance an action for defamation where the plaintiff relies upon publication of the alleged defamatory words in a newspaper and alleges an innuendo contained therein. By obtaining a copy of the publication, tape recording, sound track etc, the defendant can view the words in their full context, so as to be in a position to plead his case properly.

The rule is limited to circumstances where, in the first place, the defendant knows of the document and can describe it precisely[1] and where, secondly, sight of the document is essential, and not merely useful, in order to enable the party to plead.[2]

6.6 RULE 35(1): DISCOVERY

Rule 35(1) relates not only to the discovery of documents, but also to the discovery of tape recordings, which in terms of rule 35(15) include 'a sound track, film, magnetic tape, record or any other material on which visual images, sound or other information can be recorded'. Accordingly, wherever reference is made to 'a document' in this section, such reference includes the other material referred to in rule 35(15).

The notice to make discovery shall not, save with the leave of a judge, be given before the close of pleadings and has to be replied to within 20 days of delivery.

Discovery must be made of all documents 'relating to any matter in question in such action'. Notwithstanding this broad ambit, our courts have applied the English practice of requiring disclosure only of those documents which tend to impeach a party's own case or to advance that of his adversary,[3] but with the added requirement that a party must also discover all documents which he intends using on trial.[4] Effectively, this means that you must make discovery of all documents to which you might need to make reference at the trial,[5] as also all other documents which might harm your case or advance that of your adversary irrespective that you have (perfectly understandably) no intention of making use of them yourself.[6]

It is accordingly well worth your while to submit all your client's documents to careful scrutiny in order to determine which of them must be disclosed under rule 35(1).

Some practitioners seem to adopt the attitude that they will not discover if they have not been asked to do so by way of rule 35(1). Perhaps on a literal

---

[1] *Durban City Council v Mndovu* 1966 (2) SA 319 (D), *Mgudlwa v AA Mutual Insurance Association Ltd* 1967 (4) SA 721 (E), *Goldberg v UNISWA* 1980 (1) SA 160 (E), and *Cullinan Holdings Ltd v Mamelodi Stadsraad* 1992 (1) SA 645 (T).

[2] *Cullinan Holdings Ltd v Mamelodi Stadsraad* 1992 (1) SA 645 (T) at 647F and *The MV Urgub v Western Bulk Carriers (Australia) (Pty) Ltd and Others* 1999 (3) SA 500 (C) at 515E–I.

[3] See *Carpede v Choene NO and Another* 1986 (3) SA 445 (O) at 452 et seq and *Copalcor Manufacturing (Pty) Ltd v GDC Hauliers (Pty) Ltd* 2000 (3) SA 181 (W) at 191–2.

[4] See *Copalcor Manufacturing (Pty) Ltd v GDC Hauliers (Pty) Ltd* 2000 (3) SA 181 (W) at 191–2.

[5] Ie, all documents which are needed to prove your case.

[6] The result of all of which is, as Harms *Civil Procedure in the Supreme Court* points out in para B35.3, that 'the proviso [that all documents which you might want to use on trial have to be discovered] renders the exception [that you do not need to discover that which tends only to advance your case] virtually useless'.

interpretation of the rule they may be correct, and practitioners are advised to religiously deliver rule 35(1) notices. But it must be borne in mind that discovery is not only triggered by rule 35(1), but also by the provisions of rule 37(1), which provide that a party who receives a notice of a trial date and who has not yet discovered shall within 15 days deliver a sworn statement which complies with rule 35(2). In other words, if the party who receives notice of a trial date has not yet discovered, he must do so.

Conversely, the sooner you ask for discovery, and insist on it, the less will your opponent be equipped to consider the precise value of documents in his possession, and the more likely that he will disclose documents about which he might later have had second thoughts. Naturally, I do not suggest that your client should use these documents to fabricate answers to meet anticipated difficulties, but the proper evaluation and preparation of your case requires you to be aware of every contingency that may arise.

I do not discuss the technical details pertaining to discovery because my purpose is to consider the tactics and not the practice of the matter. The reason for asking for discovery is to enable you to prepare your case. You ask for discovery in order to see documents. I do not know why I should have to write this, but write it I must: the attorney's duty does not end when the opponent's affidavit of discovery is served upon him. His duties in fact start then, for the documents must be inspected in terms of rule 35(6), considered, compared with his own documents and (where necessary) copied. Nor yet is that all, for arising out of the perusing and considering may come the laborious business of following up information gathered in that process. It is all part of the technique of knowing everything there is to be known about your own case and finding out everything that you can legitimately ascertain about your opponent's case.

There is one more observation. As important as is the active aspect of discovery, so too is the passive. Too often the discovery affidavit is merely a recapitulation of the correspondence between the attorneys, sometimes merely formal acknowledgments. The documents of importance are extracted from the client only when consultations on trial begin. The result is a supplementary discovery affidavit and often even a number of such supplementary discovery affidavits. That is all very well if you are the defendant and are prepared to face with equanimity the prospect of a postponement. But for a plaintiff who wants a judgment so that he can get his money, a postponement is by no means the balm that is Gilead. Either party, however, takes the risk that late discovery in most cases will entitle the aggrieved opponent to a postponement. And opponents aggrieve very easily. Also, the party making late discovery will usually have to pay the wasted costs.[7]

---

[7] *Associated Musical Distributors (Pty) Ltd v Big Time Cycle House* 1982 (1) SA 616 (O), *Webster v Webster* 1992 (3) SA 729 (E) and *Terminus Centre CC v Henry Mansell (Pty) Ltd and Others* [2007] 3 All SA 668 (C) para 34. Note, though, the point made by Mullins J in *Webster* that a party who delivers a rule 35(1) notice cannot simply adopt a supine attitude if the other party has not discovered, and

6.7 RULE 35(3): FURTHER AND BETTER DISCOVERY

The opportunity to use rule 35(3) by definition arises only when the other party has made discovery.

The rule is one of the most useful of the pre-trial rules and, I would suggest, was introduced to overcome the problem, derived from English practice, that an affidavit of discovery is almost conclusive and that it is only in a limited number of instances that the court will be induced to go behind the oath of a litigant and compel him to make further and better discovery. This may not have actually placed a premium on dishonesty or even superficiality but it often would prevent a party from becoming aware of documents which were of value to his case. Most litigants, I have no doubt, do honestly direct their minds to the disclosure of relevant documents, and very few practitioners would consciously withhold documents on the pretext that these were not relevant if they did not genuinely believe so. Yet views on relevance differ, and the difference is not alleviated by the fact that opposing parties may desire the use or withholding of documents for reasons not apparent to each other. With the procedure of rule 35(3) at your hand you can largely cut across the adversary's oath both as to possession and relevance. Relevance, if I may coin a phrase, becomes largely irrelevant. All that you have to do is to specify the document and, provided you have reasonable grounds for believing that it might be relevant to the issues in the matter, you are entitled to see it. When you have seen it you can decide how to make it available for the purposes of your case if you wish to use it. On the other hand the opponent who in fact is not in possession of a document need, in effect, tell you no more than where it was when he last saw it. His original oath on possession (although he should have said that he did have, but no longer has, the document) still has a substantial measure of protection, for rule 35(3) cannot be used as a means of cross-examination in order to show that what was stated on oath was not correct. Here you may be driven to an application for further and better discovery if you can show that, despite his silence, the opposing party must be in possession of a document or documents.[8] Failing this, if his attitude remains one of denial that he possesses any specified document, rule 35(3) will not help you.

In a previous edition of this work attention was drawn to the decision of Kannemeyer J in *Richardson's Woolwasheries Ltd v Minister of Agriculture*[9] where the learned judge held that the rule 'clearly envisages the demand for production of specific documents for inspection'.

This expression of opinion, however, was disapproved by the Full Bench of the Natal Provincial Division, which pointed out that the remarks 'in any event

should if necessary bring application to compel discovery. His failure to do so could result in postponement being refused, or in each party bearing their own costs of the postponement.

[8] Rule 35(7).
[9] 1971 (4) SA 62 (E) at 67–8.

appear to have been obiter'. The case is *Rellams (Pty) Ltd v James Brown and Hamer Ltd.*[10] In his judgment at 560 Van Heerden J said:

> Rule 35(1) contemplates the discovery of all relevant documents, specific or otherwise, and indeed provides that a document shall be deemed to be sufficiently specified if it is described as being one of a bundle of documents of a specified nature which have been initialled and consecutively numbered by the deponent. If such a bundle of documents existed but was not discovered there could be no valid reason why it should not be permissible to obtain its production under Rule 35(3) which is certainly couched widely enough to allow the production of 'a vast number of documents covering a long period'.

There is some doubt as to whether this reasoning shows that the *obiter dictum* of Kannemeyer J was incorrect. The latter did not suggest that a bundle of documents could not be 'specified'. What he in fact was dealing with was a request for the production of a large number of unspecified documents described by category. What Van Heerden J seems to have had in mind was a bundle of definable documents which could be specified although there may have been a large number of them. Anyhow, you can work this one out for yourself when you think that there is ground for invoking rule 35(3).[11]

Before you risk an application to court to compel further and better discovery, consider the cases of *Federal Wine & Brandy Co Ltd v Kantor*[12] and *Continental Ore Construction v Highveld Steel & Vanadium Corporation Ltd.*[13]

6.8 RULE 35(6): INSPECTION OF DISCOVERED DOCUMENTS

Rule 35(6) should be read with rule 35(12) which, from a practical point of view, has a similar effect, albeit somewhat wider. Prompt inspection and copying of documents is essential for the purposes of advice on evidence and even more so for the purposes of trial. The sanction provided, however, may not always be an effective weapon, and is possibly subject to sub-rule (7) which is provided for the recalcitrant or neglectful party who fails to give discovery or to comply with a notice under sub-rule (6). In case of such default the party requiring discovery may apply to court to order compliance with the rule and, failing such compliance, to dismiss the claim or strike out the defence.

You may think that I am obsessed with the importance of documents. Naturally, there are some cases where they do not matter at all, usually in running-down cases or even in defamation actions. Yet even in these instances

---

[10] 1983 (1) SA 556 (N) at 560A–F.

[11] See also *Swissborough Diamond Mines (Pty) Ltd and Others v Government of the RSA and Others* 1999 (2) SA 279 (T) at 323B–C, where Joffe J held that rule 35(3) is not limited in its application to specific documents, but that the documents must be described with sufficient accuracy to enable them to be identified.

[12] 1958 (4) SA 735 (E) particularly at 748B–749H. Applied in *Lenz Township Co (Pty) Ltd v Munnick and Others* 1959 (4) SA 567 (T) (a Full Bench decision). See the discussions in Erasmus *Superior Court Practice* at B1–257 and Herbstein & Van Winsen *The Civil Practice of the High Courts of South Africa* 5 ed (Vol 1) at 813–6.

[13] 1971 (4) SA 589 (W).

a party's financial records may have to be inspected in order to meet his case. The sub-rule is, in my view, a weapon of great value when properly employed. The problems that arise result usually from the time transformation that I have mentioned, and the understandable tendency of the busy practitioner to leave everything until the last moment and so even to deprive him of the opportunity to use the weapon.

Bear with me, then, if I declare pontifically that no document should remain un-inspected.

As you will see later, perhaps the best way to master any series of documents, evaluate any miscellany of facts or cross-examine (almost) any witness is to deal with the matter chronologically. When documents are inspected and copies taken it is usually because the party who is performing this exercise is not himself in possession of the documents. It then may become of importance, when the documents are subsequently arranged in chronological order for purposes of comprehension and convenience, to know which party disclosed a particular document. Of course, you can check through two discovery affidavits until you find the answer and if this has to be done in court the judge may be very patient — or he may not. It is thus often of great value to mark on each document as it is copied for the benefit of counsel a reference to the party disclosing it and the number which the document bears on the schedule — thus — 'Pf 21' or 'Def 17'. Where both parties have disclosed the document it is advisable that both references should be marked on the document. Of course, it means work and attention to detail, two attributes that are reeling under the onslaught of the modern world.

6.9 RULE 35(8): LIST OF DOCUMENTS INTENDED TO BE USED

Rule 35(8) seems to have given rise to very few reported judgments. One of these, at least, is *Bank of Lisbon & South Africa Limited v Tandrien Beleggings (Pty) Ltd and Others (1)*[14] where Van Dijkhorst J was concerned principally with the question of a party who acquires possession of further documents after he has complied with a notice under rule 35(8). The learned judge held that the mere fact that there has been compliance within the time laid down by the rule does not excuse such party from supplementing the reply 'should he obtain possession of or gain knowledge of a further document which he intends using'. He held further that the wording of the rule does not deal only with documents in the possession of strangers to the proceedings but '[p]rima facie [the] wording is wide enough to encompass documents in the possession of the party giving the notice'. A passage from the judgment might well be of interest, and also afford some insight into the purpose or effect of the rule:[15]

[14] 1983 (2) SA 621 (W).
[15] Ibid at 623F–G.

Counsel for the defendants eloquently argued that in fact the plaintiff was after the fruits of his labour, that these documents should have been disclosed by the plaintiff in the first place, that the plaintiff could not be surprised by the use thereof against it and that to list the documents copied would hamper his cross-examination. That the order requested would cause a sharing of the fruits of counsel's week-end toil is clear. I can also appreciate that the revelation of the document copies may blunt the rapier of the adroit cross-examiner and deprive him of that rare joy which arises from the carefully planned and gracefully executed thrust. I must, however, interpret and apply the Rule.

This passage emphasises that the rule could provide a very powerful means of protecting oneself from being taken by surprise at the trial. It would seem to be capable of being used to counteract the effect of the decisions which hold that documents which do not damage one's own case or advance that of the adversary need not be disclosed.[16] Even if these decisions do reflect the proper interpretation of the words 'relating to any matter in question' as set out in rule 35(1) it is difficult to extend their effect to rule 35(8), quite regardless of the stipulations in rule 35(4). The framers of the rules, no doubt, wished to eliminate completely the element of surprise at the trial, a desire which is understandable although debatable. If all litigants were honest and all cases to be decided on stated facts, the rules could not be challenged. But litigants are not always honest and one of the challenges of advocacy is to establish the true facts despite the mendacity of witnesses. In this regard the occasional surprise has always been the ideal means, although far too rarely available. I suggest that in many cases the cause of justice may suffer as a result of the limitations placed on tactics and cross-examination by rule 35(8), and I deferentially express the view that the older practice was an adequate safeguard in preventing the suppression of material documents.

Another criticism of the rule is that it ignores the fact that the tactical situation in a case can change from day to day, before trial as well as during the trial. It can hardly be in the interests of litigants if time and money are spent in obtaining the leave of the court where additional documents have to be sought to meet new situations. Moreover, some problems may arise because the recipient must comply with the notice not less than 15 days before the trial, but the party giving the notice is at large to do so when he wishes to invoke the rule. Of course, the court would probably come to the assistance of the recipient if he were not afforded adequate time in which to file his replying list of documents, but a rule which has so much potential for dispute perhaps should be reconsidered. Nor does the multiplicity of lists and notices assist in any way in reducing the cost of litigation. The standard response, referring to all documents in the discovery affidavits of each party without more detailed specification, does also tend to reduce the rule to a farce.

Rule 35(8) is extant, however, and no practitioner should neglect it, because it is designed to cover documents which were not subject to discovery because

---

[16] See paragraph 6.6 above.

they were in the possession of third parties but which are to be used at the trial. On this basis there is considerable justification for the rule, and only your own experience will determine whether this justification outweighs the criticisms.

6.10 RULE 35(9): NOTICE OF AVAIL

This is a very useful rule.

There are usually two hurdles which you must overcome if you propose relying on a document to prove something: you must authenticate the document (ie, prove that it is the genuine article), and you must prove the correctness of its content.[17] The rule assists you in overcoming the first-mentioned hurdle (without the overcoming of which, the second will not arise).[18] It enables you to call upon the opposing party to admit that any particular document which you specify is in fact what it purports to be, and that it was properly executed. If he emulates Br'er Fox[19] (or whichever character it was who lay low and '*sed nuffin*'), all you have to do is to prove, firstly, that the document was listed in the notice and, secondly, that no objection was made to the notice (both of which you can do from the bar, by simply handing up the rule 35(9) notice, identifying the document in question as listed in the notice, and confirming that no objection was received. It would then be for your opponent to either contend that the document in question is other than that identified in the notice, or to surprise you by producing a notice of objection which your attorney never troubled to draw to your attention.) If, instead, your opponent is cagey and actually files a notice objecting to the document, then it has to be proved in the ordinary way. But if you succeed in your efforts, your obstreperous opponent pays the costs.

---

[17] See *Da Mata v Otto NO* 1971 (1) SA 763 (T) at 769, *Knouwds v Administrateur, Kaap* 1981 (1) SA 544 (C) at 551–2, *Selero and Another v Chauvier and Another* 1982 (2) SA 208 (T) at 216 and *Swart v Santam Bpk* 1986 (2) SA 377 (T) at 380–1. Of course, you might want to authenticate the document for its own worth only, such as proof that the opposing party sent a letter, without wanting to prove that what was said in the letter is true. In that event, only the first hurdle need be overcome. Where, on the other hand, you want to use a document in order to rely on the correctness of its content, both hurdles must be overcome. Usually, in that event, the person who can authenticate the document (eg, its author) can also speak to the truth of its content, so that both hurdles are overcome simultaneously. But there will be instances in which you are not so fortunately placed, and have to rely on rule 35(9).

[18] Overcoming the second-mentioned hurdle involves either calling the author or someone who can authoritatively speak to the correctness of the contents of the document (such as, in the case of authenticated photographs of a collision scene, for example, a person who was there and who, although he did not take the photographs himself, can confirm from memory the freshness of the marks shown thereon, etc.) or relying on the various provisions allowing hearsay evidence, such as Part VI of the Civil Proceedings Evidence Act 25 of 1965 and s 3 of the Law of Evidence Amendment Act 45 of 1988, as also (to the extent not subsumed into s 3) the recognised common law exceptions to the hearsay rule. A full discussion of these provisions is beyond the scope of this work. For more detail, see (dealing with s 3 of the Law of Evidence Amendment Act) *Makhathini v Road Accident Fund* 2002 (1) SA 511 (SCA) at 520 et seq and (dealing with Part VI) *Da Mata v Otto NO* 1971 (1) SA 763 (T) at 769 and *Shield Insurance Company Ltd v Hall* 1976 (4) SA 431 (A) at 436–9, as also the various recognised text books dealing with the law of evidence.

[19] An animal character from *The Tales of Uncle Remus*.

I would recommend that you use rule 35(9) in respect of all documents save the following:

- where you perceive that there might be some sort of tactical advantage in actually proving the document in evidence;
- where the document is in any event deemed to be authentic, such as where the original of the document is listed in the other side's discovery,[20] or is one of which a court might properly take judicial notice,[21] or where you utilise the provisions of Parts IV and V of the Civil Proceedings Evidence Act 25 of 1965, to prove documents.[22]

6.11 RULE 36(10): PHOTOGRAPHS, PLANS, DIAGRAMS, ETC.

If a party proposes to prove in evidence any plan, diagram, model or photograph he must, not less than fifteen days before the hearing, deliver a notice of his intention to do so, offering inspection thereof and requiring the party receiving notice to admit the same within ten days.

Notwithstanding that rule 36(10) requires the party receiving the notice to *admit* the documents in question, in practice a rule 36(10) notice is an invitation to object, or hold one's peace. If the recipient fails to file written notice of objection within ten days of receipt, the plan, diagram, model or photograph can be received in evidence upon its mere production. If the recipient does file timeous notice of objection, then the document in question (plan, diagram, model or photograph) must be proved in the ordinary way, with a penalty as to costs upon the party who has necessitated such proof.

The plain purport of this rule is that you may not use a plan, diagram, model or photograph unless you gave timeous notice in terms of rule 36(10). Strictly speaking, should you fail to comply with rule 36(10), you would have to apply in terms of rule 27 for condonation and only if you do so successfully, could you use the particular plan, diagram, model or photograph of your desire. In practice, this is something which you might profitably resolve in the course of a pre-trial conference.[23]

Note, though, that proof of the plan, diagram, model or photograph does not of itself and without more ado constitute proof of the correctness of that which is portrayed therein. See *Shield Insurance Co. Ltd v Hall*.[24] Here, as with rule 35(9), one must distinguish between the first hurdle of proving the authenticity of a document, and the second hurdle of proving the correctness of

---

[20] See *Knouwds v Administrateur, Kaap* 1981 (1) SA 544 (C) at 551, and see also *Howard & Decker v De Sousa* 1971 (3) SA 937 (T). See also rule 35(10).

[21] *Howard & Decker v De Sousa* 1971 (3) SA 937 (T) at 940.

[22] See Parts IV and V of the Civil Proceedings Evidence Act 25 of 1965, which make provision for the admissibility of certain documents under certain circumstances. There is no need for rule 35(9) where documents are admissible in terms of these provisions, provided that the procedures outlined in Act 25 of 1965 are followed.

[23] See paragraph 6.25 below.

[24] 1976 (4) SA 431 (A) at 436–439.

its content. Rule 36(10), just like rule 35(9), serves only to overcome the first hurdle.[25]

6.12 RULE 35(10): NOTICE TO PRODUCE

Not later than five days before the hearing, you may give your opponent notice to produce at the trial any non-privileged document specified in his discovery affidavit. With the leave of the court such notice may be given during the course of the trial. In accordance with the common law rule to the effect that a party need not prove the authenticity of a document produced by his opponent under discovery,[26] the rule provides that the document shall be 'receivable in evidence to the same extent as if it had been produced in evidence by the party to whom notice is given'. This rule affords a convenient means of proving useful documents which are in the possession of your opponent without having, perhaps, to call the other party as a witness in order to produce the document.

6.13 RULE 35(11): PRODUCTION OF DOCUMENTS

The court is empowered in any proceedings[27] to order any party to produce under oath any documents relating to the matter under consideration. There is no time limit and rule 35(11) seems to be designed for invocation during evidence or even during argument. It does enable you to deal with the gentleman whom we may term 'the reluctant discoverer'. Seemingly the advice in the old cookery book, 'first catch your hare', is valid, because until you catch him you cannot jug him — or whatever one does with hares. You catch your hare either when he goes into the witness-box or when you can prove from the evidence or affidavits, or even from letters, exhibits and annexures, that the documents exist. I doubt whether a court would invoke this rule as a mere repetition of rule 35(1), particularly in the light of rule 35(3) which has already been discussed.

Strictly speaking, rule 35(11) should be regarded as part of the technique of conducting trials (chapter 9) or arguing opposed applications (chapter 17), so I pray that you read these comments as if in those chapters duly inserted and contained.

---

[25] But, as illustrated in *Shield Insurance v Hall* 1976 (4) SA 431 (A), reference to other provisions such as Part VI of the Civil Proceedings Evidence Act 25 of 1965, might enable one to overcome the second hurdle.

[26] See the authority quoted in fn 17 above. This is logical: the other side will have listed the document in its discovery, which by definition means that it agrees that the document is precisely what it was purported in the discovery affidavit to be.

[27] Including motion proceedings. See *Pieters v Administrateur, Suidwes-Afrika en 'n Ander* 1972 (2) SA 220 (SWA) at 228. See, however, *Transgroup Shipping SA (Pty) Ltd v Owners of MV Kyoju Maru* 1984 (4) SA 210 (D) and more recently *Loretz v MacKenzie* 1999 (2) SA 72 (T).

6.14   RULE 35(12): INSPECTION OF CERTAIN DOCUMENTS

A party may at any time before the hearing give a notice to any other party in whose pleadings or affidavits reference is made to any document to produce such document for his inspection and to permit him to make a copy. Any party failing to comply with such notice may not, without the leave of the court, use the document in the case. The document called for must, however, be in the possession of the other party; it must be relevant and obviously not a privileged document.[28]

As stated previously, rule 35(12) should be compared with rule 35(6), although it confers on the litigant the additional benefit of being able to obtain a limited form of discovery even before the close of pleadings. It is often of value where you have doubts as to the accuracy of the version of the document given by the opposition or where you have no copy of the document yourself. Under rule 35(12) you may inspect the document and then, if so advised, place on record your own version in your answering pleading or affidavit. The rule applies to an 'action or proceeding'. It has, however, been held more recently that the rule applies to motion proceedings only where a special order of court in terms of rule 35(13) has been obtained.[29]

Not in every case will rule 35(12) need to be invoked. Nor does every document have to be inspected. One instance of its application may serve as an example. This was an application by a company for an interdict to restrain an ex-employee from taking up employment in breach of a covenant in restraint of trade. For present purposes one need not trouble about the general validity of such covenants as between employer and employee, for the applicant's case was that the employee had also been a managing director of the company, that he had enjoyed access to confidential information and confidential documents of the company. It was also alleged that he had been present at meetings of directors where this information and those documents had been discussed. His proposed new employment, it was alleged, would result in a competitor being given the benefit of what was confidential to the applicant company. It was also alleged that the respondent had, as a matter of routine, received copies of the minutes of those meetings. Extracts from some of the minutes, with excision of matter said to be confidential, were attached to the applicant's affidavits.

The respondent was not slow to seize the opportunity of invoking rule 35(12) and calling for inspection of the minutes. This was a simple, logical and necessary step, for only an inspection of the minutes could enable the respondent to test or rebut the allegation that the information and documents were confidential. The applicant now faced a dilemma. If it did not disclose the

---

[28] *Gorfinkel v Gross, Hendler & Frank* 1987 (3) SA 766 (C) where it was also held that the onus was on the recipient of the notice to set up facts relieving him of the obligation to produce the document. See also *Unilever plc and Another v Polagric (Pty) Ltd* 2001 (2) SA 329 (C).

[29] *Loretz v MacKenzie* 1999 (2) SA 72 (T), *Afrisun Mpumalanga (Pty) Ltd v Kunene NO and Others* 1999 (2) SA 599 (T), *Premier Freight (Pty) Ltd v Breathetex Corporation (Pty) Ltd* 2003 (6) SA 190 (SE) and *African Bank Ltd v Buffalo City Municipality* 2006 (2) SA 130 (Ck).

minutes and documents in full the court could hardly judge whether there was the element of confidence so necessary to justify the interdict. If it did disclose the documents then they would be disclosed not only to the new employer, who had been cited as a second respondent, but also they would be disclosed to the world — or such a portion of the world as was interested in the matter which the applicant sought to protect. In these circumstances would not the whole basis of the interdict be destroyed?

This tactical use of the rules is an object lesson to other practitioners. The present illustration, however, is not quoted for that purpose, nor to decry rule 35(12), but merely to show what circumstances may call for the invocation of the rule and also the very reason for its existence.

If you are minded to invoke rule 35(12) it will be a profitable preliminary to read the judgment in *Moulded Components and Rotomoulding South Africa (Pty) Ltd v Coucourakis and Another*.[30] Three important propositions are dealt with in the judgment. Firstly, and this may well be the most significant of the three, rule 30(5) applies when a notice given under rule 35(12) has not been complied with. The former rule provides that if a party fails to comply timeously with a request made or notice given in terms of the rules, the aggrieved party may apply, as the case may be, that the claim or defence be struck out. Secondly, it was held that rule 35(12) applies also to documents which are not in a party's possession, although if it appears that such party is unable to produce the document the court 'would obviously not make an order' in terms of the rule. Thirdly, it was held that the court can order a party to produce for inspection documents not referred to in that party's affidavits, and can order a party to produce for inspection items of machinery, 'ie objects not being documents'. What is interesting in regard to the last proposition is that Botha J did not refer in his judgment either to rule 35(11) or to rule 36(6), although he may well have had these rules in mind. In any event, the judgment is one which merits the most careful consideration in regard to cases dealing with infringement of industrial or other designs.

6.15   RULE 35(13): APPLICABILITY OF PROVISIONS TO APPLICATIONS

In so far as the court may direct, the rule relating to discovery applies to applications. Rule 35(13) is self-explanatory.

6.16   RULES 36(1) AND 36(5A): MEDICAL EXAMINATION

A party to proceedings in which damages for bodily injury are claimed has the right to require any party claiming such damages to submit to medical

---

[30] 1979 (2) SA 457 (W), and amongst the many annotations to this authority *Loretz v MacKenzie* 1999 (2) SA 72 (W), *Krygkor Pensioenfonds v Smith* 1999 (3) SA 459 (A) and *Absa Bank Ltd v The Farm Klippan 490 CC* 2000 (2) SA 211 (W). As to rule 30(5) see also *Khunou and Others v M Fihrer & Son (Pty) Ltd and Others* 1982 (3) SA 353 (W).

examination. The same applies to a loss of support claim where the claimant's state of health might be relevant to the determination of damages. This is to ensure that a litigant is not taken by surprise in regard to matters beyond his power or control and in which he could not otherwise prepare for trial.[31]

A problem that both rule 36(1) and rule 36(5A) have created is that many doctors feel that their medical knowledge and surgical skill qualify them to function as private detectives or claims assessors in the wider sense of the expression. They slip in the odd surreptitious question on the merits and, in their medical reports, endeavour to present the insurers at whose behest they perform the examination with material for cross-examination. And when complaint is made, comes the sanctimonious reply: 'Well surely your client would not tell lies.' Of course the client would not tell lies, but a doctor extracting factual information from a litigant is about as deft as an advocate removing an appendix. Nor is there any reason to believe that the 'Hippocratesian' is any more reliable than the average newspaper reporter in remembering and recording what is said.

I suggest that the practice of interrogating a claimant on the facts of a collision, where such facts are not directly relevant to explain medical symptoms, is an abuse of the process of the court.

It was initially an open question whether an attorney may attend such examination with his client in order to see that the latter is not over-reached.[32] In *Feros and Another v Rondalia Assurance Corporation*[33] Kotze J considered that such right to legal representation does exist, whether in terms of the rule or not. The question was finally resolved some ten years later by Howie J in *Goldberg v Union and SWA Insurance Co Ltd*[34] where he found that a plaintiff has a right to legal representation at a rule 36 medical examination.[35]

In *Mgudlwa's* case it was also held that where a qualified practitioner is available close to the place most convenient to the person to be examined the services of that practitioner should, as a rule, be utilised.[36]

## 6.17	RULE 36(8): REQUIRING A REPORT OF THE EXAMINATION

An often overlooked provision is rule 36(8), which entitles the party at whose instance the rule 36(1) examination was carried out to cause the examining doctor to bring out 'a full report in writing of the results of his examination and

[31] *Cullinan Holdings Ltd v Mamelodi Stadsraad* 1992 (1) SA 645 (T).
[32] *Mgudlwa v AA Mutual Insurance Association Ltd* 1967 (4) SA 721 (E).
[33] 1970 (4) SA 393 (E).
[34] 1980 (1) SA 160 (E).
[35] See also *Selamolela v President Versekeringsmaatskappy Bpk* 1981 (3) SA 1099 (T).
[36] One wonders, though, whether this is still good authority in modern times. I would think that provided a good reason can be given why the defendant wishes the plaintiff to be examined by a medical practitioner at a place elsewhere than the town or city of the plaintiff's residence, a court would be prepared to order compliance with the rule 36(1) notice. For example, the leading expertise of the expert in question might justify the inconvenience to the plaintiff.

the opinions that he formed as a result thereof' and entitles the examinee to a copy of that report on request.

This means that unlike the plaintiff, who can if he so chooses wait until the eleventh day before trial before producing his expert reports in terms of rule 36(9)*(b)*, the defendant who has the claimant examined can be forced to disclose his expert hand much earlier.

Rule 36(8) is an important but, as I say, often overlooked, weapon in the armoury of a plaintiff.

6.18 RULE 36(5): SECOND MEDICAL EXAMINATION

If it appears that any further medical examination by another person is necessary or desirable on matters relevant to the assessment of damages a party may require a second and final medical examination.

Sometimes, of course, two or three specialists have to make reports on different bodily conditions or injuries and also, where the question of improvement or deterioration is material, each may have to make two examinations. The matter is usually determined by the dictates of reasonableness and common sense, because a plaintiff who sheltered behind the strict terms of the rule might well find himself at the wrong end of an order for a postponement and wasted costs if his doctors started testifying about something which had been put beyond the power of the defendant to test.

In terms of rule 36(5) the provisions of the rule shall also apply to a party who claims damages resulting from the death of another, provided that it is alleged that his own state of health is relevant in determining the damages.

6.19 RULE 36(6): INSPECTION OF THINGS

If it appears that the state or condition or any thing whether movable or immovable may be relevant in an action any party thereto may at any stage before the hearing give notice requiring the party relying upon the existence of such state or condition of that thing or having it in his possession or under his control to make it available for inspection or examination and may require that the thing or a fair sample of it remains available for inspection or examination for a period of not more than ten days, from date of receipt of the notice.

The rule, I suggest, speaks for itself and its application is obvious. In regard to the duty of the recipient of the notice see *SA Neon Advertising (Pty) Ltd v Claude Neon Lights (SA) Ltd*.[37]

In what was then Rhodesia it was held[38] that inspection is not limited to a superficial examination, and that examination may be of such a nature (in that case sinking test holes into a driveway) as to cause actual physical interference with the property affected. In that case, of course, the damage was capable of

---

[37] 1968 (3) SA 381 (W). See also *Crown Cork & Seal Co Inc and Another v Rheem South Africa (Pty) Ltd and Others* 1980 (3) SA 1093 (W).

[38] *Caltex Oil Rhodesia (Pty) Ltd v Perfecto Dry Cleaners (Pty) Ltd* 1970 (2) SA 44 (RS).

being repaired, but what of chemical analysis which may conceivably lead to the total disappearance of the subject-matter? I suggest that the balance of convenience will be found to be the decisive test, and that any form of examination necessary to do justice between the parties will be allowed.

If the 'matter at issue' can be identified before the close of pleadings there seems every justification for invoking this rule. Why should things be more sacrosanct under rule 36(6) than human beings under rule 36(1)?

6.20 RULE 36(9): EXPERT WITNESSES

Where a party proposes to call any person to give evidence as an expert witness he must, not less than fifteen days before the hearing, deliver a notice of his intention to do so, and not less than ten days before the trial deliver a summary of the expert's opinions and the reasons for that opinion.

Guidance in drafting the summary of the expert's opinions (and the reasons for those opinions) is to be found in the cases of *Coopers (South Africa) (Pty) Ltd v Deutsche Gesellschaft Für Schädlingsbekämpfung mbH*,[39] *Boland Construction Co (Pty) Ltd v Lewin*[40] and *Uni-Erections v Continental Engineering Co Ltd.*[41] It is to be observed that in the *Boland Construction* case Vos J suggested that the concept 'summary' might not have received sufficient weight in *Coopers'* case.[42]

There are essentially two ways in which the rule 36(9) can be complied with: the expert can produce his own summary in which he expresses his opinion on the various areas falling within his expertise and, in each case, gives his reasons for those opinions and this summary can then be attached to a notice in terms of rule 36(9)*(b)*, or the attorney (or counsel) can, as it were, translate the expert's report (or, in what I would think would be rare cases, the upshot of a consultation with the expert in which the expert's opinions and the reasons for those opinions were extracted) into a formal rule 36(9)*(b)* summary. For my part, I would generally recommend the former route. There are a number of reasons for this. In the first place, where the expert examined the claimant in terms of rule 36(1), or an object in terms of rule 36(6), on behalf of the defendant, the astute opponent will in any event be able to get at the expert's report by way of rule 36(8),[43] so that there seems little point in opting for the second route in those circumstances. In the second place, the second route poses the danger (which the first does not) that the expert might distance himself from the language or terms used in his summary when he testifies. In the third place, having the expert produce his own report probably accords more closely with the ideal expressed by Lord Wilberforce in *Whitehouse v Jordan*[44] 'that expert evidence presented to the court should be, and should be

---

[39] 1976 (3) SA 352 (A). See also *Visagie v Gerryts en 'n Ander* 2000 (3) SA 670 (C).
[40] 1977 (2) SA 506 (C).
[41] 1981 (1) SA 240 (W).
[42] 1977 (2) SA 506 (C) at 506A–B.
[43] See paragraph 6.17 above.
[44] [1981] 1 All ER 267 (HL) at 276.

seen to be, the independent product of the expert, uninfluenced as to form or content by the exigencies of litigation'.

This rule places a premium on early preparation for trial and, in particular, early advice on evidence. Perhaps it could be better said to penalise late preparation. It illustrates the need for early briefing of counsel for an early advice on evidence. In his advice on evidence, counsel should have indicated what expert evidence will be required, so that the rule can be adhered to timeously.

The case of *Klue and Another v Provincial Administration, Cape*[45] affords an illustration of the use of rule 36(9) as well as an unusual and instructive approach to cases involving expert evidence. The claim was for damages alleged to have been suffered through injuries sustained when the plaintiff slipped and fell on a floor at the Uitenhage hospital. The plaintiff's counsel at the trial stated that he proposed to lead expert evidence on the composition of various floor polishes used by the defendant at the hospital and on 'the characteristics of such polishes to minimise slipping on the part of persons walking on the hospital floors'. Counsel for the defendant objected on the ground that the summary of the witness's evidence had been delivered less than ten days before the trial.

Before quoting from the judgment I would remark that the fact that expert evidence was tendered affords an excellent example of 'application' which was discussed in chapter 3. In many cases plaintiffs have failed in their claims for damages when they have slipped on polished floors and, no doubt, counsel for the plaintiff was mindful of these cases and desirous of succeeding where others had failed for want of proof of proper negligence. How the matter proceeded appears from the judgment of Addleson AJ at 562–3:

> [Plaintiff's counsel] thereupon applied for leave, under rule 36(9), to lead Professor N's evidence . . .
>
> In the first place, it should be noted that, as far back as 19 August 1965, the defendant itself gave notice under rule 36(9)(a) of its intention to call expert evidence on
>
> > 'the floor of the hospital corridor on which the second plaintiff is alleged to have slipped and fallen and matters relating thereto'.
>
> No such evidence was however called, nor was any summary of such proposed evidence provided, by the defendant under rule 36(9)(b). On 28 August 1965 the plaintiff had given similar notice to the defendant.
>
> It appears from the summary of events . . . that it was only on 1 March 1966 that the plaintiff obtained sight for the first time of documents which revealed that at various times the defendant had used different floor polishes in the hospital, some of which polishes were described as 'non-slip' and some of which were not so described. It was through no fault of the plaintiff that this information was obtained so late and the change in polishes could well have been a material factor in the case. As soon as the information was available, further consultations were held with Professor N and

[45] 1966 (2) SA 561 (E) at 562–3.

it was decided to call him and a summary of his evidence was made available to the defendant at the earliest opportunity.

In the light of these facts above, it was my view that this was an appropriate case in which to grant leave to the plaintiff to call the expert evidence. It seems to me that it would be quite wrong to preclude a party from calling expert evidence when his failure to comply strictly with rule 36(9)(b) was not due to default on his part but was in fact caused by the conduct of the defendant, however *bona fide* the latter's conduct may have been. . . . In any event it seems to me that in this case the defendant could not really have claimed to be taken by surprise. On the pleadings, one of the main issues was whether the floor in question had been polished to a dangerous degree of slipperiness and the defendant had specifically indicated its intention of calling expert evidence relative to the condition of the floor.

A party is not entitled to wait for the other side's rule 36(9)*(b)* summary before filing his own: the rule is there for both parties, and each must comply therewith. See Addleson AJ at 563 of *Klue and Another* above:[46]

I do not think that rule 36(9)(b) was designed to encourage one party to wait ten days before a trial in order to satisfy himself that his opponent does not intend to call expert evidence, before himself deciding whether or not to call expert evidence on a material issue on the pleadings. Such an approach would in many cases result in a situation of stalemate and would in my view be contrary to the spirit of the rule.

It may well be that one of the purposes of this rule is to remove the element of surprise from a trial; but I think that it was also intended to enable the experts to exchange views before giving evidence and thus to reach agreement on some, if not all, of the issues, thereby limiting the duration of the trial and consequently the costs. Certainly the rule could not have been designed to enable the parties to play cat-and-mouse in the sense that neither need prepare his expert evidence until the other furnishes the summary envisaged by rule 36(9).

6.21 RULE 33(4): SEPARATION OF ISSUES

Rule 33(4) provides for the court either in its own discretion or on the application of either or both of the parties, to order that one or more issues either of fact or of law be separated out from the others and decided separately. The following points need to be made in this regard:

•   The test to be applied is one of convenience in the broad sense of the better administration of justice: if there is a crisp point which if decided in favour of one or another of the parties might put an end to the matter and, by the same token, if evidence on the extent of the plaintiff's damage will be extensive and will be obviated if the plaintiff is unsuccessful on the merits (and if, in addition, there is a material risk that he will be so unsuccessful), then it would probably be better for all concerned and for the administration of justice if the crisp point or the merits, as the case might be, were decided first.[47]

---

[46] See also, to the same effect, *Doyle v Sentraboer (Cooperative) Ltd* 1993 (3) SA 176 (SE) at 183.

[47] See *Minister of Agriculture v Tongaat Group Ltd* 1976 (2) SA 357 (D) at 362 et seq, *Braaf v Fedgen Insurance Ltd* 1995 (3) SA 938 (C), *ABSA Bank Beperk v Botha* 1997 (3) SA 510 (O), *Lappeman*

- Although the rule can conceivably be applied in a manner such that evidence on the separated-out point is led or, if it is a pure point of law, argument thereon is presented, and the matter is then adjourned for a decision thereon whereupon it proceeds before the same judge on the remaining issues if the point was not decisive, this seems impractical. In the first place, it would require the presiding judge to commit himself to a swift decision on the point, which seems neither feasible nor advisable. In the second place, it would moreover involve wasted expense in terms of standing time whilst a decision is being arrived at. In practice, then, the rule invariably means that if there is a separation, the trial will relate only to the separated-out issue. If the decision on the point is decisive then, subject to the appeals process, that is the end of the matter. If on the other hand the decision is such that the remaining issues now have to be determined, then the matter will have to be enrolled anew for determination of the remaining issues.
- This brings me to the next point, which is that separation is not something that should be decided upon without careful reflection. The rule:

   is aimed at facilitating the convenient and expeditious disposal of litigation. It should not be assumed that that result is always achieved by separating the issues. In many cases, once properly considered, the issues will be found to be inextricably linked, even though, at first sight, they may appear to be discrete. And even where the issues are discrete, the expeditious disposal of the litigation is often best served by ventilating all the issues at one hearing, particularly where there is more than one issue that might be readily dispositive of the matter. It is only after careful thought has been given to the anticipated course of the litigation as a whole that it will be possible properly to determine whether it is convenient to try an issue separately . . .[48]

- Where issues are to be separated, it is important to give careful thought to the definition of precisely which issues are to be decided.[49]
- Where there is a separation of issues, it logically impacts on the application of the various other rules. A defendant who insists that merits be decided separately from the quantum is hardly in a position to insist that the

---

Diamond Cutting Works v MIB Group (No.2) 1997 (4) SA 921 (W) 927 et seq, and *Internatio (Pty) Ltd v Lovemore Bros Transport* 2000 (2) SA 408 (SE).

[48] Nugent JA at 484–5 of *Denel (Edms) Beperk v Vorster* 2004 (4) SA 481 (SCA). See also Lord Scarman's comment in *Tilling v Whiteman* [1979] 1 All ER 737 (HL) at 744 that preliminary issues are 'too often treacherous shortcuts. Their price can be delay, anxiety and expense'. Remember that either party might appeal against the outcome, possibly resulting in years of delay.

[49] See *Denel (Edms) Beperk v Vorster* 2004 (4) SA 481 (SCA): Nugent JA at 485 emphasised the importance of clearly circumscribing the issues to be tried, and added the following: 'The ambit of terms like the "merits" and the "quantum" is often thought by all the parties to be self-evident at the outset of a trial but, in my experience, it is only in the simplest of cases that the initial consensus survives. Both when making rulings in terms of Rule 33(4) and when issuing its orders, a trial court should ensure that the issues are circumscribed with clarity and precision.'

plaintiff make full discovery of all documentation relating to the quantum.[50]

•   Rule 33(4) should not be, and should most certainly not be allowed to be, a disguised attempt at costless postponement in the hands of an ill-prepared litigant.[51]

6.22   RULE 21(2): PARTICULARS ON TRIAL

Particulars on trial are limited to details which are 'strictly necessary' for purposes of trial preparation.[52] They should be sought when you wish to ascertain what case your opponent intends to make in regard to the allegations in the pleadings. For example, when an allegation could be based upon, or justified by, any one of various sets of circumstances, or where you suspect that you are dealing with a tactical denial and that your opponent might well concede the point if pressed in terms of rule 21(2). The authorities show also that particulars will not be refused merely because to some extent the party furnishing them will have to disclose his evidence.

The principles underlying this branch of forensic fencing were stated by Galgut J as follows:[53]

> [The] purpose of further particulars for trial [is]
> 1.   to prevent surprise;
> 2.   that the parties should be told with greater precision what the other party is going to prove in order to enable his opponent to prepare his case to combat counter allegations?;
> 3.   having regard to the above nevertheless not to tie the other party down and limit his case unfairly at the trial.

As you prepare your advice on evidence (dealt with in the ensuing chapter), it will become apparent to you that there are matters in regard to which the issues are nicely defined. The contentions of each party will have been delimited with precision and the point to be decided admits of no uncertainty. What you now seek to elicit is information as to the manner in which your opponent proposes to establish his case, or the manner in which he seeks to combat yours. These are the matters on which it is permissible to ask particulars. The pleadings have

---

[50] See Flemming DJP at 673 of *Rubico (Pty) Ltd v Pawell (Pty) Ltd* [2001] 2 All SA 671 (W): 'The object of separation of issues is to avoid the costs of preparation for and hearing of the stayed issues.'

[51] Kirk-Cohen J in *Dreghorn v The Fund* (unreported TPD Case No 13758/87 17 October 1989 at 6 and further).

[52] See *Jonnes v Anglo-African Shipping Co* (1936) *Ltd* 1974 (2) SA 561 (D), *South African Railways & Harbours v Deal Enterprises (Pty) Ltd* 1975 (3) SA 944 (W), *The Wanson Company of South Africa Ltd v Establissements Wanson Construction de Material Thermieque Societe Anonyme* 1976 (1) SA 275 (T) at 281B–D and *Swissborough Diamond Mines v Government of the RSA* 1999 (2) SA 279 (T) at 317.

[53] *Thompson v Barclays Bank, DCO* 1965 (1) SA 365 (W) at 369, *Lotzoff v Connel and Another* 1968 (2) SA 127 (W) at 129, *Swart v De Beer* 1989 (3) SA 622 (E), *Schmidt Plant Hire (Pty) Ltd v Pedrelli* 1990 (1) SA 398 (D) and *Swissborough Diamond Mines (Pty) Ltd and Others v Government of the Republic of South Africa and Others* 1999 (2) SA 279 (T).

defined the contentions; particulars on trial should be used to define the respective cases.

Always bearing in mind the words 'strictly necessary' in the rule, you might well seek particulars on trial in instances such as the following:

- where your opponent is not committed to a specific allegation on an issue of importance;
- when you do not know what evidence you will require to establish or to meet a particular point;
- where there is ambiguity or uncertainty in the issues;
- where you suspect that you are dealing with a tactical denial, and want to ask your opponent whether he persists with it.

A word of caution: do not overdo it. Over the years, a practice appears to have developed of always seeking particulars on trial no matter what the circumstances. Remember what was said earlier about tailoring your technique to the purpose of what you are doing. If you do not really need to ask particulars on trial, why do so? If you ask unnecessary detail, you not only invite the sting of rejection. You also run the risk of drawing your opponent's attention to aspects of his case that he might otherwise have overlooked.[54] My advice is: *don't utilise rule 21(2) unless you actually are convinced that you need the information in order to prepare for trial, or that by asking for it you will force the other side into a useful admission that would obviate an otherwise necessary line of preparation.*

6.23 FURNISHING PARTICULARS

Welcome it when your opponent asks for further particulars for trial. It might not be pleasant, it might be an irritant to have to answer them, but *what your opponent has done is to invite your attention to those aspects of your case which are important to him, and which you might otherwise have overlooked.* Paying careful attention to his request for further particulars will undoubtedly assist you in preparing your case, whether in the ultimate analysis you answer his questions or not.

The reply is a matter of some nicety. Particulars may be refused if they relate to matters which are irrelevant. You should think twice before refusing particulars merely because the request amounts to a request for evidence. After all, your opponent is entitled to know what your case is. You must tell him what you intend to prove. It is of no avail to say, 'What I intend to prove is a matter of evidence and you are not entitled to know'. He is entitled to know not who your witnesses are, nor what they will say, but what your case is.

It would seem somewhat paradoxical if a party who has pleaded something were to be entitled to refuse particulars on trial because he did not know the answer. In this latter event, what would he think that he was going to prove

---

[54] Your opponent might, whilst curtly rejecting your request as unnecessary, silently be thanking you for drawing his attention to weaknesses in his case that he might otherwise not have noted until it was too late. See also paragraph 6.23 below.

anyway? In the exceptional case such a reply may be permissible, but the party making such reply must be able to show (by allegations *prima facie* probable) that he cannot by use of reasonable diligence find out.[55] Such a case might occur if the only witness to a material fact declines to afford information and says that he will do so only when subpoenaed and put into the witness–box.

Also, I think, a refusal is often a tactical blunder. Can you imagine the aggrieved tone of your opponent who addresses the court on these lines:

> My Lord. We had some difficulty in understanding the defendant's case on this point, and if your Lordship will bear with me while I briefly analyse the pleadings I shall show your Lordship what I mean. . . . At page 72 is the plaintiff's request for particulars on trial. For some reason the defendant did not wish to take us — or the court — into his confidence, and the particulars were refused. It would have been interesting to know what the defendant really is trying to say on this point. But he has been most reticent. We have — short of spending time and money on interlocutory applications to compel — no option but to respect his reluctance to tell us what his case is and to proceed in the hope that sooner or later he will favour the court with his version of the matter.

From an opening address like this you do not recover. You start off a loser and you will end up in second place. Which means that, generally speaking, you should not refuse particulars on trial except on grounds of relevancy, or where the whole request is in fact vexatious or oppressive. After all, sooner or later your client will have to answer the question — and he should not have the added burden of explaining why, if his answer was so innocuous, he did not furnish it in the first instance.

6.24 RULE 34: TENDERS

A defendant who is likely to be held liable to the plaintiff operates under the disadvantage and the plaintiff operates under the corresponding advantage, that both interest and costs run against the defendant.

Rule 34 comes to the assistance of a defendant in these circumstances, particularly where liability is likely but where the *amount* of that liability is debatable.

In these circumstances, the defendant's legal team should give careful and early consideration to the making of a good tender in terms of rule 34.

Permit me to make the following points in this regard:

---

[55] *Snyman v Monument Assurance Corp Ltd* 1966 (4) SA 376 (W) and *Lotzoff v Connel and Another* 1968 (2) SA 127 (W). See also *Von Gordon v Von Gordon* 1961 (4) SA 211 (T) and *Hardy v Hardy* 1961 (1) SA 643 (W). In both these cases the request for further particulars was refused because the court was of the view that the relevant information could be secured by cross-examination, ie, related to matters of evidence. However, in regard to marriages subject to the accrual system it may be wise to consider the provisions of s 7 of the Matrimonial Property Act 88 of 1984, which obliges a spouse to furnish full particulars of the value of the estate.

- Rule 34 provides for two types of tender: a secret tender (one made 'without prejudice as an offer of settlement'),[56] or an unconditional tender.
- The difference between a secret and an unconditional tender is that the former may not be disclosed to the court until after judgment has been given, whereas the latter is fully disclosed, from the moment it is made.
- A defendant will in the vast majority of cases be advised to make a secret tender. But, remembering the point made earlier about every step you take being tailored to the *purpose* for which you are taking it, do not discount the idea of making unconditional tenders in some instances. Depending upon the circumstances, there might be an advantage to be gained by openly tendering to pay an amount or to perform an act, so that the court is made aware of your client's willingness and, perhaps, of the plaintiff's bloody-mindedness.
- I would suggest that, in arriving at an appropriate amount to tender by way of a secret tender, the key is to ask yourself two questions. The first is whether your client's interests will be well served if the tender is accepted? After all, litigation is expensive and even if the tender errs on the side of generosity, that might still be economically sensible. The second is to ask yourself what the prospects are of the plaintiff beating the tender if it is not accepted? If you can answer the first question in the affirmative and the second in the negative, it is a good tender.
- A secret tender will only be disclosed to the court after judgment has been delivered, and then only if judgment is given for a lesser figure or the same amount as was tendered.[57]

  Beware, in this regard, of the need to offer the plaintiff's costs during a reasonable *spatium deliberandi*, ie, a reasonable opportunity to consider the tender whilst still continuing with trial preparation.[58] Attorneys often in their tenders offer costs only 'up to and including the date of this tender'. That might be in order where the tender is made many months before trial, but the closer the tender is made to the trial date, the greater the risk that the tender will be held to have been robbed of its effectiveness by the failure to offer a reasonable *spatium*.[59] The difficulty lies in determining what reasonable *spatium* to offer. I suggest that the way to overcome this is to offer costs along the following lines:

---

[56] See sub-rules (1), (4) and (5)(*a*) of rule 34.

[57] See sub-rules (11) and (12) of rule 34.

[58] See *Omega Africa Plastics (Pty) Limited v Swisstool Manufacturing Company (Pty) Limited* 1978 (4) SA 675 (A) at 678G–679E. This concept of a *spatium deliberandi* must be distinguished from the period of fifteen days for which a tender must lie open for acceptance in terms of rule 34(6).

[59] This is precisely what happened in *Godfrey NO v Santam Insurance Company Limited* 4 C&B A4–96 (SE). The court concluded that the plaintiff was justified in rejecting the tender for a number of reasons. One of those reasons was the fact (see A4–116 to A4–117 and A4–120) that costs were offered up to the date of the tender only, whereas a reasonable *spatium* would, so held Jones J, have been a further two days.

together with the plaintiff's taxed or agreed party and party costs to date of delivery of this tender as also during a reasonable *spatium deliberandi* thereafter (the duration of which is either to be agreed between the parties or, if they are unable to reach agreement thereon, to be determined by the court on application to it) . . .

- Remember that a tender differs from its common law counterpart, an offer to settle, in at least two material respects: in the first place, a court will have regard to the former (in terms of the provisions of rule 34) but not to the latter,[60] and in the second place, unlike an offer which can be withdrawn at any stage before it is accepted, a rule 34 tender may not be withdrawn and the plaintiff has an absolute right to accept same at any stage within the fifteen days allowed for in rule 34(6) and even to do so thereafter if a court on application to it so orders.[61]

6.25 RULE 37(1): PRE–TRIAL CONFERENCE

The psychological importance of pre-trial conferences should not be under-estimated. This is the first time you and your opponent look one another in the eye. It is an opportunity to assess how your cases, your preparation and indeed the two of you, match up to one another.

The rule requires a pre-trial conference to be held on a number of specified matters. Aspects which should be covered at such a conference include, but should generally go beyond, those listed in rule 34(6). They include the following:

- prejudice: this is the opportunity for a party who feels aggrieved at the other's non-compliance or late compliance with the rules to raise this, specifying what is complained of, and the nature of the prejudice;
- settlement discussions (note that, unless either party makes a settlement proposal on a with prejudice basis and insists that it be recorded, the actual content of any settlement discussion is by its nature privileged, and should not be disclosed in the minute. In such event, and on the assumption that the settlement discussions were fruitless or have at the time of minute-ing the discussion not yet borne fruit, it should simply be recorded that the parties did discuss possible settlement, but were unable to reach agreement);
- the possibility of referring issues to mediation, arbitration or decision by a third party;

---

[60] See for example *Naidoo v Marine & Trade Insurance Co Limited* 1978 (3) SA 666 (A) and *Tshabalala v President Versekeringsmaatskappy Beperk* 1987 (4) SA 72 (T) at 75F–G. Evidence of a settlement offer is inadmissible.

[61] See sub-rule (6) of rule 34, and see also *Turboprop v Croock t/a Honest Air* [1997] 1 All SA 181 (W). Clearly, where application is made to court for permission to accept the tender out of time, the court has the power to punish the plaintiff with an adverse costs order.

- whether a case which is being heard in the High Court ought not properly to be transferred by agreement to the magistrates' court;
- whether there is scope for separate decision of issues in terms of rule 33(4), and if so what issues?
- the asking of the other side to make specified admissions;
- whether there is agreement on the duty to begin or the burden of proof;
- whether agreement can be reached regarding the production of proof by way of affidavit in terms of rule 38(2);
- obtaining agreement as to the making up of bundles of documents, and the status of those documents. The parties are for example often able to agree on a formulation along the following lines:

> The plaintiff will make up a bundle of the documents which the plaintiff proposes using at trial, and will provide this bundle to the defendant within five days of the date of the pre-trial conference. The defendant will have the right to supplement the bundle within a period of a further five days. Subject to the right of either party to object to specific documents within fifteen days of the date of the pre-trial conference, the parties are agreed that the documents so to be contained in the bundle are what they purport to be, that copies may be used instead of originals, that e-mails or telefaxes were sent by the addressor and received by the addressee on the dates and at the times reflected therein, that letters were sent by the addressor on the dates specified thereon and were received by the addressee within two days of such date (unless there is a date-receipt stamp thereon, in which event the date of receipt is that reflected on the stamp), and that neither party necessarily hereby admits the correctness of the content of any of the documents contained in the bundle.

- the plans, diagrams, photographs, models and the like to be used at the trial;
- the holding of any inspection or examination;
- the exchange between parties of the reports of experts, and meetings of experts, including issues of whether the legal teams are to agree an agenda for the experts to discuss, whether the lawyers are to be present at the meeting of the experts, who is to arrange the meetings, precisely which experts are to meet, etc;[62]
- the giving of any further particulars reasonably required for the purposes of trial;

---

[62] A matter to which you might give thought, is whether to seek agreement to the effect that the parties will be bound by the minute produced by the experts who meet. Although a party who repudiates an agreement reached by his expert is, indubitably, in a difficult position, that is not to say that a party is necessarily bound by that agreement unless he has agreed to be so bound. See *Dladla v President* 4 C&B J2–7 (T) at J2–12 and *Marais v Road Accident Fund* 5 C&B C3–12 (C) at C3–66, but see *Mautla v Road Accident Fund* 5 C&B B3–1 (T) at B3–4. HHJ Newey QC, in *Richard Roberts Holdings Ltd v Douglas Smith Stimson Partnership and Others* (1989) 47 BLR 117 (Q), concluded at 127–8 that the parties had intended their respective experts to have authority to bind them when they directed them to meet. But whether that would or would not be so would depend upon the particular facts of the case, and is thus perhaps something to which you would rather specifically direct your mind beforehand.

- the possible consolidation of trials;
- discussion of, and possible agreement on, the quantum of damages or aspects thereof;
- the likely duration of the hearing;
- where the trial is anticipated to be lengthy, perhaps the obtaining of a running record;[63]
- agreement on counsel's costs of attending the pre-trial conference (rule 37(9)*(b)* provides rather thoughtlessly that the costs of counsel's attending the pre-trial conference are not to be allowed on a party and party basis where the conference was held more than ten days before the hearing. This notwithstanding that rule 37(3)*(a)* requires the conference to be held at least six weeks before trial. This arguably qualifies as the silliest provision in the rules. A pre-trial conference without counsel is usually a meaningless affair. Although there is no guarantee of this, the likelihood is that if the parties agree to this effect, the provisions of rule 37(3)*(a)* can be overcome.

The various Divisions of the High Court each have their own specific requirements as to when the pre-trial conference is to be held by, and often as to what is to be discussed at the conference. You will no doubt be familiar with the requirements of the particular Division in which you practise. If you are conducting a matter in a Division with which you are not fully familiar, you are advised to establish at an early stage precisely what the requirements relating to pre-trial conferences are in that particular Division.

The object of this rule is to expedite proceedings and to reduce costs by eliminating evidence on matters which are not really in dispute.

Very often practitioners attend a pre-trial conference simply because the rules require it and without any specific objectives in mind. The rule, however, was designed to achieve certain very useful purposes and it would be well to take advantage of its provisions wherever possible. In *Grasso v Grasso*[64] Berman J commented upon the practice which has evolved of practitioners honouring rule 37(1) in the breach only, by holding a short telephone conversation and 'agreeing that nothing can be agreed'. He describes this as 'nothing short of a gross abuse of a Rule of Court'.

The problem is that the rules of your Division might require you to hold a very early pre-trial conference, sometimes even before applying for a trial date. If a conference is held at such an early stage, it is certain that the issues will not yet have been fully analysed and evaluated. I would suggest that where possible the pre-trial conference (or, perhaps, a second and more meaningful pre-trial conference) is best arranged for a date after the furnishing of advice on evidence, ie, closer to the trial date, at a stage when all relevant minds are properly concentrated. To some it may seem that this is a transparent attempt to

---

[63] See paragraph 9.5 below, where this is discussed.
[64] 1987 (1) SA 48 (C) at 61–2.

circumvent the rule. Perhaps it is, but the rule appears to raise practical difficulties which the framers did not appreciate. It is suggested that, subject to the practice rules of your particular Division, the general sequence of events should be as follows:

- close of pleadings;
- notice to disclose documents;
- notice under rule 37(1);
- request for trial particulars;
- set-down;
- inspection of documents;
- advice on evidence;
- pre-trial conference;
- securing attendance of witnesses.

By the time the advice on evidence has been written and digested, everyone should have a clear idea of the issues which really matter and those which, on the contrary, are only going to waste time, money and patience. You can then attend the pre-trial conference armed with a list of points on which you think the other side may be willing to make admissions. By then, both parties ought to have a fair idea of what has to be proven in the case and whether there is really any merit in placing various points in issue any longer. In other words you should brief yourself beforehand on the items which I have suggested be covered at the pre-trial conference, both from your own point of view and that of your opponent.

One thing that must be borne in mind is that admissions made at a pre-trial conference may be more in the nature of agreements than admissions. As Van Winsen AJA said in *Price NO v Allied-JBS Building Society*:[65]

> The pre-trial conference conducted under the terms of Rule of Court 37 is designed to afford an opportunity to the parties, among other matters, to find ways of curtailing the duration of the trial by redefining the issues to be tried. One of the methods of doing so is by way of admissions of fact which could lead to the elimination of one or more of the issues raised in the pleadings.

In that case an agreement at the pre-trial conference and a concession at the trial that the contractual claim had become prescribed precluded consideration of that claim. Ordinarily if a person makes an admission in error, he is entitled to give evidence to explain the error and to counter the admission.[66] If an admission is held to be a judicial admission, as it would seem is the case in regard to admissions made at a pre-trial conference[67] then, at the very least, the

---

[65] 1980 (3) SA 874 (A) at 882E. See also *Filta-Matix (Pty) Limited v Freudenburg and Others* 1998 (1) SA 606 (SCA) at 614.
[66] Wigmore 3 ed vol IV s 1058–9; Phipson *The Law of Evidence* 13 ed s19–08 at 372.
[67] Wigmore 3 ed vol IX s 2588.

withdrawal of such admission would appear to require the same degree of formality and proof as in the case of an admission in a pleading.[68]

Quite a useful technique has evolved of using the pre-trial conference as a form of interrogatory, and although this has not yet been tested, I think that the practice will receive judicial approval. Often the pleadings result in a number of denials of matters which are disputed merely for tactical reasons. The consequence is that some facts have to be proved (at the cost of inconvenience) not because they represent real disputes between the parties, but merely because of a hopeful denial by the opposing party. In these cases the legal team of the party who has to prove these facts would do well to compile a list of topics which they require to be admitted and, at the conference, ask the other side whether they are willing to make admissions. Any admission is recorded as a matter agreed upon.

What is equally effective is the recording of the refusal to make any specific admission. This can cast the recalcitrant party in a poor light, and you might find that all that is needed to persuade the other party to do a *volte-face* and offer the admission, is the sonorous recording of the refusal in your opening address.

One of the problems which you may face when you attend a pre-trial conference is that you are endowed with a natural, even an admirable, degree of caution. You may be reluctant to make admissions because it is sometimes difficult to calculate precisely how damaging an admission may be. Just to put your mind at rest, let me give you an illustration of what happened to a party who refused to make an admission when called upon to do so. The claim, in the Supreme Court, was for the purchase price of goods sold and delivered to a character whom we will call Klitznit. He carried on business in some small town in the Orange Free State under the style of Klitznits. When sued for the purchase price of these goods he pleaded that although the business was being carried on under the name of Klitznits it was not his business at all and in fact he had sold it some time previously to his daughter and son-in-law. It was they, he solemnly averred, who had purchased the goods in question and it was they to whom the plaintiff should look for payment of the purchase price. The financial situation of the daughter and son-in-law was not such as to afford any consolation to the plaintiff and, uncharitably enough, it persisted in its claim against Mr Klitznit himself. It so happened that the plaintiff desired to prove, as part of its case, that during the year in which the goods had been purchased no trading licence had been taken out in respect of the business known as Klitznits. Accordingly, at a pre-trial conference, or at a discussion between counsel before the hearing (it matters not), the request was made that this fact should be admitted. The objective position was either that there was a trading licence or that there was none. It seems not unreasonable to suppose that Mr Klitznit was either personally aware of the position, if the business were in fact still his, or he could ascertain what had happened by the rather elementary procedure of

---

[68] See chapter 5 above, and particularly paragraph 5.5.1.

asking his daughter and son–in–law. Be that as it may, a great degree of caution (you might well call it obstreperousness) was displayed and the desired admission was not made. The plaintiff was accordingly compelled to seek elsewhere the evidence which was desired. This evidence, it so happened, was not difficult to obtain and all that was necessary was to issue a subpoena on the local Receiver of Revenue to produce the relevant file at the date of the hearing. When the file was in fact produced in court the joy of counsel for the plaintiff knew no bounds, for within those unprepossessing covers was found a note by a policeman who had gone to the business and had interviewed Mr Klitznit in order to ascertain why a licence had not been taken out. Mr Klitznit, indeed, had vouchsafed an explanation to the constable, but, sad to say, that explanation was not the one raised in his pleadings, namely that the business was no longer his. Counsel for the plaintiff accordingly took the next and logical step of calling the constable as a witness to prove the statement and Mr Klitznit, in his turn, was driven to denying that he had ever said the things which the constable had contemporaneously recorded in the file. You will not be surprised to learn that the court disbelieved Mr Klitznit and accepted the evidence of the constable without hesitation. This little dispute of fact was an important element in leading the court to the conclusion that Mr Klitznit should be disbelieved and he suffered the fate of having a judgment given against him.

What the motive of Klitznit or his legal advisers could have been is a matter of speculation. As I have said, the fact was simple and capable of objective ascertainment. Had Mr Klitznit admitted that there was no licence taken out for that year, his explanation would have been the simple one that it was not his duty anyway to take out the licence. I find it almost impossible to conceive how it could have been of any value to refuse the admission which had been requested. I would suggest to you that, when you attend a pre-trial conference and are asked to make an admission, you bear in mind the horrible fate of our friend Klitznit and you ask yourself whether, if the admission is refused, you will ultimately be able to dispute the fact. If you cannot dispute the fact then you should think twice, indeed several times, before declining to make any admission.

6.26 EVIDENCE (RULES 38(1), 38(2) AND 38(3)), AND DOCUMENTS IN POSSESSION OF NON-PARTIES

Rules 38(1), 38(2) and 38(3) deal with the method of obtaining evidence for use at the trial. I do not think that in this book it is necessary to set them out or discuss them, largely because they are matters of practice and procedure.

What does deserve discussion is the question of employing rule 38(1) in order to obtain sight of documents which are in the possession of a non–party to the litigation.

The rules of court have elaborate provisions, many of which have already been discussed, to enable a litigant to become aware of documents in the possession of his adversary or which his adversary proposes to use against him.

Where there is a problem, and no mean problem at that, is in getting hold of documents to use against the aforesaid adversary, where those documents are neither in the possession of your client, nor in that of the other party. The position used to be that one had, in such an event, to subpoena the party in whose possession the documents are *duces tecum* (ie, to bring the documents with him), and the courts differed as to whether one could have insight into those documents without having to depose the witness in question.[69]

This issue has been resolved by the provisions of rule 38(1)*(b)*, in terms of which a witness who is subpoenaed *duces tecum* must, unless he claims privilege in the document, 'hand it over to the registrar as soon as possible [whereafter] . . . the parties may inspect such . . . document . . . and make copies . . . thereof, after which the witness is entitled to its return'.[70,71]

6.27 PAGINATING THE PLEADINGS (RULE 62(4))

The attorney for the plaintiff should ensure that the pleadings in the court file are properly paginated and indexed, and that all parties are supplied with a copy of the index.

Many attorneys fail to understand that pagination of the pleadings means exactly what it says. They paginate all conceivable documents in unconceivable order, so that at the end of their labours all that they have achieved is to number pages.

A paginated set of the pleadings should consist of the following documents, in the following order: summons, particulars of claim, plea, replication (if any), request for particulars for trial (if any), particulars on trial (if any), notices of set down.

Where pleadings have been amended, it is the pleadings *as amended* that are included. The notices of amendment can be paginated separately, if desired, in a bundle of notices. They play no part in the bundle of pleadings.

---

[69] *King v Margau* 1949 (1) SA 661 (W) and *Picked Properties (Pty) Ltd v Northcliff Townships (Pty) Ltd* 1972 (3) SA 770 (W) were to the effect that one may not, and *Bladen and Another v Weston and Another* 1967 (4) SA 429 (C) was to the effect that a two-stage approach could be adopted in terms of which the witness was deposed, he stated whether he had objection to producing the documents and if he didn't, the matter stood down whilst the calling party examined the documents.

[70] See *Trust Sentrum (Kaapstad) (Edms) Bpk v Zevenberg and Another* 1989 (1) SA 145 (C) in which Berman J at 148–9 pointed out that rule 38(1)*(b)* was clearly intended to obviate the very difficulties outlined in *King v Margau, Picked Properties* and *Bladen* above. *Trust Sentrum* involved an application by the defendant in an action to compel a witness to produce certain documents to the registrar prior to trial, so that the defendant/applicant could study the documents. Berman J upheld the application, rejecting the witness' contention that the documents were confidential. He ordered the witness to deliver the documents to the registrar within twenty four hours for the defendant's inspection.

[71] See paragraph 7 of Appendix A: it is often a good idea to accompany a subpoena *duces tecum* with a courteous letter explaining the need for the documentation, apologising for the inconvenience and even suggesting that if the recipient would prefer, the documentation could be collected and copied without any need for it to be deposited with the registrar.

6.28 HOMILY

It seems to me that in writing this chapter I have also written most of the
following two. This observation is very true if someone — yourself it may be
— regards each of the rules I have discussed not as a stage in a forensic
countdown, but as an exercise in assembly of the craft (abstract or concrete
noun as you please) that is to be launched into court. What is done should not
be done merely because there is a rule of court to cover it. It should be done
because it is part of the construction process, designed to yield information
which is part of the case itself. If each stage is given thought and utilised
teleologically the result will be that your mind will be equipped for its task in
court. You will know the facts, the pros and cons of each point of fact, the
documents and evidence bearing upon each point of fact. The remainder of
your preparation will be the analysis and collation of the documents and
evidence, with one eye upon the issues and the other on the essence.

When you are invoking the procedures or sanctions of the rules, moreover,
you might consider the remarks of Flemming J in *SA Metropolitan Lewensversekeringsmaatskappy Bpk v Louw NO*:[72]

> (T)he exercise of the Court's discretion has been consistently led [sic] by the presence
> or absence of prejudice in relation to the exercise of a party's procedural right or duty
> to respond to a communication received, or to partaking of a next step in the
> sequence of permissible procedures to ripen the matter for properly orderly hearing.
> Where such prejudice is absent, a decision to set the irregular proceeding aside will
> not be given. On the contrary, the irregularity may be overlooked . . . Rules of Court
> should not only be interpreted but also applied in such a manner that the parties come
> to grips on the real dispute without undue delay and expense.

---

[72] 1981 (4) SA 329 (O) at 334A–E.

CHAPTER 7

Advice on Evidence

7.1 INTRODUCTION

An army, it is said, marches on its stomach. That is probably metaphorically true, and what it reflects is the importance of planning in military strategy. When an army launches an offensive, or when it defends territory against an enemy, it will do so in accordance with detailed planning. The more complex the manoeuvre, the more careful and detailed the planning should be. Not everything — perhaps in the fog of war not anything — will go according to plan. But I have heard it said in this military context that 'A plan is the basis for change'.[1] In other words, one is better placed to adapt to changed circumstances when one has a plan to adapt in the first place.

Litigation is not much different. It is a battle between two or more parties, albeit fought on more genteel lines (perhaps) than war. And just as it is inconceivable that the modern army would embark on manoeuvres without detailed plans in place, so is it inconceivable that litigation should be conducted without a plan.

And the best way to plan, is by way of an advice on evidence.

The advice on evidence is often neglected but, with exceptions of course, it should be the most important step in litigation. The written document is privileged from disclosure and, if properly conceived and executed, should form the basis of every subsequent step of any importance in a trial matter. The case can be outlined to the court from the pattern of the advice. Witnesses will be called along the lines drawn in the advice. It may be used as the framework of cross-examination. And finally, if you have planned and built well, the matter may be argued from the self-same blueprint.

See, in this regard, Schutz JA at 326G–H of *De Klerk v ABSA Bank Limited and Others*:[2]

> One strongly suspects that when De Klerk's case was being prepared an advice on evidence was not sought nor given. Such an advice focuses the minds of the legal team *before* the trial commences, on what facts have to be proved and how they are to be proved. An advice is not simply an item in a bill of costs, but is vital to the preparation of all but the simplest cases. If a proper advice had been given there would have been no need for a postponement, while running repairs were effected to

[1] One of General Dwight Eisenhower's favourite sayings was, apparently, that 'In preparing for battle I have always found that plans are useless, but planning is indispensable'. Litigation is not unlike war, so that perhaps it could accurately be said that in litigation, plans are useful, and planning indispensable.

[2] 2003 (4) SA 315 (SCA) at 326G.

the case, and there would almost certainly have been no [successful] application for absolution and no appeal.

Of course, an attorney who is to conduct his own case in either the High Court or the magistrate's court will probably not have the time to draw up a formal written advice on evidence, unless of course he specialises exclusively in litigation. Inevitably, however, he will have to follow the procedure suggested (or perhaps some improvement on that procedure) if he desires to present his case adequately.

7.2 THE IMPORTANCE OF HAVING A PURPOSE: THE PURPOSE OF AN ADVICE ON EVIDENCE

As I have had occasion to say before, everything that you do as a lawyer must have a purpose, and must be so adapted as to best suit that purpose. So the first thing is to consider the purpose of the advice on evidence.

It is suggested that the purpose of the advice is, to continue with the military metaphor, to carefully think out one's strategy, one's battle plan: to determine the issues which will arise in the case, the incidence of the onus, and the evidence which will be required in the conduct of the client's case. Mention will also be made, in this context, of the issues of law which must be debated, procedural steps and the general tactical approach. The advice, moreover, should be used for a calm contemplation of every aspect of the matter, for a dispassionate evaluation of every issue and as the foundation for the ultimate preparation and presentation of the case.

7.3 ATTORNEYS — WHERE COUNSEL EMPLOYED

Counsel does not expect that, in your instructions, you will write the advice. He does (or should), however, welcome your assistance, not only in the manner in which the brief is placed before him, but also in your suggestions, comments and queries.

The preparation of the brief 'on advice on evidence' is no sinecure. Perhaps it is an extreme case, but the following quotation from an advice furnished only a few years ago shows how touchy counsel can be in this regard (including senior counsel who should be a paragon of self-control):

> Before discussing the evidence which will be required by the defendant, we must draw attention to two matters which we think of some importance in regard to the presentation of the defendant's case. In the first place, for the purpose of drafting this advice on evidence, we have had thrown at us an ill-assorted and unsorted mess of documents. In the second place, although the plaintiff's attorneys have filed and served an index to the pleadings, nobody has taken the trouble to ensure that our briefs are properly paginated in accordance with the index. If the defendant requires his case to be presented to the court as it ought to be presented, it will be necessary for the instructing attorneys to facilitate the task of counsel as far as lies in their power. We suggest, therefore, that the pleadings be properly paginated in accordance with the index, and that thereafter an effort be made to introduce some sort of system into the document in the brief. We suggest that all the correspondence relating to the

insolvent estate of the late J Caesar, whether such correspondence is disclosed by the plaintiffs or by the defendant, be sorted into chronological order and a bound copy of such correspondence be made available for each counsel acting on behalf of the defendant. The originals and carbon copies of the original letters may have to be handed into court and the instructing attorney should be in possession of a file corresponding exactly with the files of counsel and containing all the originals and carbon copies of originals of the letters to which we have referred. The same system should be adopted in regard to correspondence in the estate of Marc Antony (Pty) Ltd because it appears that certain of the correspondence in that estate may be relevant on some of the issues arising in the present case.

There should be a separate file containing the bills of costs in each estate in order that, when the original bills are handed into court, counsel may be in possession of copies thereof. Finally, there should be a separate file containing the statements of the defendant and his witnesses.

Before leaving this point we should remark that at the end of the junior counsel's brief is a typed copy of a bill of costs which relates to an interrogation in an insolvent estate. The interrogation, and the estate, appear to have nothing whatsoever to do with this case. We assume that this document was inserted only in order to mystify counsel.

It is suggested that the onus which rests on the attorney is not a light one. The matter must be submitted to counsel with as much material as possible and after some consideration for the problems which may arise.

A proper advice on evidence depends in many cases upon prompt attention to other procedural steps in the litigation. In a great many cases discovery is important, and probably in most cases it should precede the advice on evidence. If the sequence is reversed the result may be additional cost when the advice has to be reconsidered in the light of documents obtained from the other side.

It is suggested that attorneys (and counsel) may find it convenient if the instructions set out the attorney's views on the issues and also the problems he encountered in the preliminary business of advancing and preparing his client's case. Although it is very tempting to hand to counsel two bundles of documents, described respectively as 'Plaintiff's Discovery' and 'Defendant's Discovery', with or without a third bundle called 'Attorney and Client', this merely adds an unnecessary burden to those shouldered by counsel. In most cases — if not all — the true picture emerges from the chronology. For this reason it would be advantageous to arrange all documents chronologically in their respective categories such as correspondence or statements, or whatever it might be. In doing this you may feel that some of the effect created by discovery may be lost. One method that some attorneys adopt to overcome this — and for other reasons — is to make copies of documents for counsel and, in an appropriate place on each document, to endorse the relevant numerical reference to the plaintiff's and the defendant's discovery affidavits. There is a great deal to commend this practice, which has its value at every stage of the actual trial.

The same treatment could well be applied to the variety of other documents which go to make up a trial action, but the important things are always chronology, classification, consideration and comment. From there onwards counsel can look after himself.

7.4 COUNSEL

7.4.1 Introduction

A brief 'on advice on evidence' may vary from the formal to the formidable. The formal may be in the ordinary motor collision claim where you have to call as witnesses one plaintiff, one policeman and one panel-beating foreman. The formidable may beggar description, particularly at first sight. However, the job must be done, it must be done promptly and it must be done effectively.

There is no standardised method of drawing an advice on evidence. It does not have to comply with the rules of court. You will therefore find that the advice and the treatment of the case vary as much as counsel's personalities vary. Whatever suggestions are made in these pages are therefore no more than they purport to be — suggestions. They are surely susceptible to improvement or modification. Perhaps they may be discarded entirely — but not unless something better comes along.

Obviously the recommendation on this topic will follow the lines set out in chapter 4. The analytical process must be performed, a system must be adopted and counsel must apply himself to his brief — in the fear that the next time he will see it will be a scant four days before the trial date, if not less.

7.4.2 Appendix A

In Appendix A you will find a framework which it is suggested you can adapt to meet the requirements of all from the most simple to the most complex cases.

The system which is recommended in Appendix A has two merits: it facilitates the extraction of the essence, and it presents the entire case in convenient form for purposes of advice, outline, evidence, cross-examination and (almost) argument. If there are demerits then, no doubt, you will discover them for yourself. The theory behind this system is that the case must develop in chambers, as far as practicable, exactly as it should develop before the judge. You must put yourself for the nonce in the judge's position and understand the case as the judge will have to understand it. From that understanding will develop your tactics and your advice.

7.4.3 How you go about drafting an advice: the starting point

The first contact that the judge will have with the case will be the pleadings — and perhaps you will be good enough, from this point, to regard the judge as a constantly implied term in the discussion. You will read the pleadings which you perhaps last saw a few months previously. If you are acting for the plaintiff you may very well never have seen the defendant's plea. That reading of the pleadings will give you a broad picture of the case — either a masterpiece or a snapshot, or something in between. The principal object of this exercise is merely to refresh the memory and to get the general impression.

The procedure is not terrifying: indeed it is simple, even though what I recommend may be laborious.

Whether you choose to do the sensible thing and to adopt the format outlined in Appendix A, or to be perverse and to follow a format of your own design, the starting point is not to tackle the advice head-on: it is to analyse the pleadings, and to think.

As Euclid was wont to remark, more or less: that's how to do it.

Having pre-read the pleadings, you disabuse your mind of preconceived notions. Your half-formed ideas, born of the pre-reading of the pleadings, however, are not to be dismissed. They are to be preserved and developed during your consideration of the advice. The procedure now becomes mechanical, tedious and more precious than rubies. An ordinary examination book will do. The first page may be used to note those paragraphs in the particulars which have been admitted and on which no evidence will be required. For the sake of continuity do not be in too much of a hurry about recording paragraphs which are not in dispute. What I mean is that counsel who drafted the particulars of the plaintiff's claim will usually have set out to present a logical and chronological reflection of his case. If one paragraph is pulled out of context simply to be recorded on the first page of your preliminary analysis it may introduce incoherence where none existed previously. Far better it is to record on the first page of your examination book the gist of the undisputed paragraphs up to the point where you reach the first point of difference between the parties.

It may now be assumed that you reach a paragraph which is in dispute. Turn the leaf of the examination book so that a double page presents itself invitingly to your pen. Then on the left-hand page commence to summarise, or state the pleadings, on the first point in issue. The result will be that you will have in sequence on the left-hand page the paragraph from the particulars of claim, the request for further particulars for purposes of trial (if matters have progressed that far) and the reply (combined as one statement if necessary), the plea and so forth. This process is repeated with each paragraph or even sub-paragraph that requires such treatment.

When the analysis is done —

- you will be alive to all the issues;
- the essence of the case will usually proclaim itself too unmistakably to be lost;
- the work of analysing the facts can begin.

Some cases depend on correspondence, some on documents and some on witnesses. Which of these you consider next is a variable on which no positive rule can be stipulated. Often it will be better first to analyse correspondence and documents, because from this it is easier to detect inconsistencies between the statements of the witnesses and the contents of the documents. Whatever procedure you select the next suggested step is to note on the right-hand page pertaining to each point in issue a reference to the relevant correspondence, document or witness's statement. You may, if you wish, merely make the cryptic memorandum 'Letter 12/4/68 Pf to Def'. If your memory is better than average — much better — that will be enough. Usually you will be better advised to give the significance of the letter in a few words such as 'denying goods according to sample'.

It seems unnecessary to go through a detailed elaboration of the theme. When, however, the analysis is finished you will be able to follow the matter point by point and determine —

- where the general onus lies;
- which party ought to prove any particular point;
- the nature of the evidence required to prove or rebut each point on behalf of your client;
- to what extent the statements in your brief are inadequate or what additional evidence will be required;
- the strength or weakness of your case.

If this system is followed you will not find yourself in the position of Dr Knight who failed in his claim for fees for professional services rendered, because, in one of the cases leading to the defamation action, his attorney failed to prove in the magistrate's court that Dr Knight was on the register of medical practitioners when the debt was incurred.[3]

You have now fully drawn the basic plan from which the advice on evidence, and the case, is to be constructed. From here the process becomes one of mental effort and of design. This is now the most important stage in the litigation, where your degree of skill as a tactician and as an advocate in the broad sense of the word, may determine, if not the success, then the failure of your case. The points in issue must be considered in turn and in conjunction; the significance of each must be determined; the whole future structure of the case must be visualised to the last metaphorical screw or nail. Do not begrudge a couple of hours spent in thought on the little problems that arise; equally do not hesitate to sleep on the problems—whether this is imagination or not, I cannot say, but problems sometimes seem to dissipate overnight; either because they were never problems or because the unconscious thought processes are more effective than the conscious.

7.4.4 Proceeding from the thinking process to the process of actually drafting the advice

From the analysis, and from your deliberations, you proceed to prepare the final written advice on evidence, presenting it scientifically and coherently, and usually following your analysis in the same sequence as the issues in the pleadings. You endeavour to convey to those whose duty it is to study and act on your advice precisely what considerations underlie your recommendations, what the problems are and what the hundred and one nuances in the case

---

[3] *Findlay v Knight* 1935 AD 58 at 66.

signify. That the system requires painstaking application is manifest; the labour, however, will return dividends at the stage of preparing for trial as at the other stages mentioned.

Your task is, we have now decided, to consider, *seriatim*, the issues that present themselves as the focus of consideration travels downwards on the successive pages of the basic exposition which I have described. Whether each issue is to be treated in splendid isolation or whether it should more fittingly be considered in homogeneity with other aspects of the case is not for me to say. This is dependent upon the idiosyncrasies and dictates of the particular case. Whatever your decision may be, your subsequent cogitation and advice will be conditioned by tactical as well as practical considerations. The tactical aspects demand that you do not lose sight of the fact that you have an opponent. Your advice on evidence is not a thesis. It is a practical document to be used by your instructing attorney or whosoever is to do the leg-work. You are concerned not only to advise how to prove a case, but also how to counter the opposition, how to anticipate their thrusts and how to forestall their stratagems. You are required to consider the witnesses whom you think should be called, so that, for example, a potentially dangerous witness may be disarmed, or a timorous witness may be cajoled into a state of co-operation. Again, however, it is not possible to do more than to draw your attention to the fact that lawsuits are mostly won or lost by tactical planning.

The practical side of advice is severely practical. As each successive issue is analysed and considered, the basic elements of the required evidence will present themselves to view — and the whole process will yield up the true essence of the case if you care to discern it. But for the elements themselves it is well to make now the notes from which your advice will be written. So on each issue a note may be made — perhaps no more than a single word — and next to each such word or note you record the practical aspects of proof.

What I have in mind will be specifically illustrated in the subsequent discussion of a few of the matters which are more regularly dealt with in advising on evidence. The process will produce what I describe now as a skeleton.

It may be that I am obsessed with the importance of advice on evidence. Perhaps it is possible to take a bundle of pleadings, letters and statements of witnesses and from these to conduct a case to a successful conclusion. Remember, however, that the cases which appear overwhelming in court are more often than not the product of careful planning and painstaking attention to detail.

7.4.5 Does one deal with issues of law in the advice on evidence?

One question which inevitably arises from the suggested method is what to do about the issues of law.

The answer: of course, but only to the extent necessary. If you go back to the suggestions made in regard to pleading you will find that the first stage was an analysis of the elements of law going to make up the cause of action or the defence. It was after this preliminary analysis that the pleader set about determining what allegations of fact had to be made to support his conclusions of law. Why, it might be asked, should an advice on evidence be any different? It is only when one determines the elements of the cause of action that one can determine the allegations of fact that have to be proved by evidence. What, moreover, would be the point of producing reams of detail about the evidence needed if, on your view of the law, there are no realistic prospects of that evidence leading to success? If the point is in your view at best only debatable, then surely if one has regard (as in all things one must) to the *purpose* of an advice on evidence, one will conclude that you should mention *that* the legal point with regard to which the evidence is required is at best only debatable, *why* it is at best only debatable, and *what* needs to be done evidentially to get to debate the point if, after reading the advice, your attorney and your client remain of the view that they would rather debate it than settle or if, having tried without success on the strength of your advice to settle, your attorney and your client decide that they have no alternative but to debate the point?

But don't go into too much detail: this is an advice, not an opinion. The attorney, no doubt, is a busy practitioner. He is content to leave the law to counsel, and is fully justified in this attitude. It takes up a good deal of valuable time if he has to read, study and consider the discussions on the law before he is told what evidence he must seek and what general preparation of the facts is required.

The advantages of including this discussion are overwhelming as far as counsel is concerned.

7.4.6 Step-by-step

Having, then, conducted a careful analysis of the issues on the pleadings and having assessed those issues against the background of the available factual evidence, having thought the matter through and, if necessary, slept on it, you ought now to be in a position to actually draft the advice.

7.4.7 Every story has to start somewhere: an introduction

An advice on evidence (and a court case presented to a judge) is a legal story. It is intended primarily for the instructing attorney, but will often best also be shown to, and discussed with, the client. It should read plainly, logically, and well. Like any well-written story, it should start with an introduction in which the essential facts, or the origins, of the case, and the relief claimed and perhaps also the essence of the defence, is mentioned. Avoid a lengthy discussion of the issues at this stage.

7.4.8 Analysis of the pleadings

Whether you follow the format of Appendix A or not, this is the logical next step.

Here you deal with the issues on the pleadings. You start by listing that which is common cause and need not be proven. You then deal, point for point, with the disputed issues. Some of the disputed issues might be quite immaterial and if so, you say so (an example is the date of the collision in a collision case: unless prescription has been raised, the precise date on which the incident occurred ought to be quite irrelevant). Some of the disputed issues will be easily established through the plaintiff's evidence, and are unlikely to be contradicted. If so, you can say so here, and not deal with those issues again. Other issues will be more complex, and these you can mention will be discussed when you come to discuss the issues in more detail.

7.4.9 Jotting down other points, whilst you are analysing the pleadings

It must be evident that other points of evidence will occur to you whilst you are outlining the disputed issues. There will be points of discovery, of formal notices that are required, and of witnesses.

For example, in a collision case you might note that the plaintiff's *locus standi* to claim in respect of the vehicle is in dispute. It will, if you are applying your mind to the matter, have occurred to you then that the documentary proof relating either to the plaintiff's ownership of the vehicle or the fact that he was at the relevant time the risk-bearing credit purchaser or lessee thereof, will be required, and precisely what that documentation might be? You should logically then jot this down in that place in the advice where you will deal with discovery (paragraph 5.1 if you are following the format of Appendix A). As a matter of progressive logic it will also have occurred to you, with reference to the discussion of rule 35(9) in paragraph 6.10 above, that it might be a good idea to give rule 35(9) notice of those documents as well, and this you will have jotted down in the appropriate point in your outline (paragraph 6, if you are following the format of Appendix A). And so forth.

In this way, when you come to the parts of your advice on evidence where you deal with discovery and formal notices, you will already have noted these points and will merely have to flesh them out.

7.4.10 A discussion of the issues, and the incidence of the onus with regard thereto

This is, to continue with the military metaphor, the *schwerpunkt* (the central gravitational point) of the advice on evidence. It is where you will prove your mettle in being able to clearly and concisely extract the essence of the case, analysing the probabilities in order to be able to advise your instructing attorney and your client as to how the matter is likely to proceed, and how it is likely to end. This is not an opinion as such, but it comes close to it.

In some (indeed most) matters, it is self-evident that the burden of proof rests with the plaintiff. In other cases, the question of where the burden of proof lies might be less obvious. In either event, it is always a good idea to deal in your discussion with the incidence of the burden of proof.

With reference to what was said in paragraph 7.4.5 above, to the extent that it is necessary for you to discuss the law in order to discuss the issues you should do so, but not in the detail of an opinion. *Always remember the practical nature of an advice on evidence.*

Of course, to revert to the point that was made in paragraph 4.4.1 above when dealing with extracting the essence, you will here deal not only with what you have determined to be the essence of the case. You will deal with *all* aspects of the matter on which your client bears the burden of proof, and also those (if any) with regard to which the other side bears the burden of proof. Each and every item will be discussed, and in each respect you will deal with whether your client is able to succeed on the point and, if so, how you suggest he should go about succeeding on the point.

In this section of the advice, you will therefore discuss (as briefly as necessary) not only the issues themselves, but also the steps which you recommend taking in order to prepare properly for trial. Certain of these steps, such as supplementary discovery, the furnishing of formal notices etc. will also be discussed elsewhere in the advice, but to the extent that they are material to the discussion of the issues, they are best also discussed here. For example, if you believe that certain persons must be consulted with and certain documents in their possession studied and, if found to be material, copied, then you will mention all of this here whilst, as per paragraph 7.4.9 above, jotting the points down at the appropriate portions of your advice (discovery, notices, witnesses, etc.).

7.4.11 Separation of issues in terms of rule 33(4)

You will advise on whether, in your view, issues ought to be separated in terms of rule 33(4) and, if so, how your instructing attorney is to go about it.

You will, in this regard, consider what tactical approach will best suit the interests of your client.[4]

See in this regard paragraph 4 of Appendix A.

7.4.12 Discovery

Ideally, both parties will already have discovered by the time you come to draft your advice on evidence.

But even so, the issue must be addressed. You will often (indeed usually) find that your careful analysis of the issues in the case has exposed other documents which were omitted from the discovery affidavit, and which must now be supplementarily discovered. You will have analysed the other side's discovery against the background of your analysis of the issues and of the facts, and will quite possibly have identified documents which the other side have not discovered and ought to have, and which need to be listed in terms of rule 35(3). And so on.[5]

---

[4] See the discussion of rule 33(4) in paragraph 6.21, in chapter 6.

[5] See particularly paragraphs 6.6 and 6.7 in chapter 6.

See paragraph 5 of Appendix A.

7.4.13 Notices

You will need to advise your attorney on the various notices which need to be delivered.

Rules 35(9), 35(3), 36(9) and 36(10), and notices in terms of ss 22 and 30 of the Civil Proceedings Evidence Act 25 of 1965 come to mind.[6]

7.4.14 Witnesses

Here, you will deal not only with *what* witnesses you propose be called, but also with *their likely order of testifying*. There can be few things more annoying than being called to testify under power of a subpoena and then having to sit for days on the hard litigation-discouraging benches that seem to be a feature of all courts, before it is your turn. I do not want to suggest that the experience might induce a witness to lie, but it certainly won't engender the deepest empathy. Far better that a witness is subpoenaed but, on the basis of counsel's careful planning, warned rather to be on standby for a particular day or days on the basis that he will be told closer to the time precisely when he will be required to present himself for his evidence.

Here you will also deal with witnesses who should be subpoenaed *duces tecum* in terms of rule 38(1). See paragraph 7 of Appendix A.

This is also where you will deal with expert witnesses: whether experts are required, if so on what points and of what expertise, etc. If experts are required, you will in the portion of your advice dealing with formal notices have dealt with the provisions of rule 36(9) and in particular the time limits.

7.4.15 The estimated duration of the hearing

This is to a large extent a factor of the preceding discussion. In order for you to clear your diary sufficiently, in order for you to be able to advise your attorney as to which witnesses should be reserved for approximately what days and, in some Divisions, in order to meet procedural requirements, it is necessary for you to give thought to the likely duration of the hearing. Remember that matters have a way of running less smoothly than planned, and of taking longer.

7.4.16 Pre-trial conference

You need to advise on the pre-trial conference: when it should be held, and issues that need to be addressed in the course of it.[7]

---

[6] See, in general, chapter 6 and the discussion there of the various notices provided for in the rules. Section 22 of the Civil Proceedings Evidence Act 25 of 1965 facilitates proof of facts ascertained by way of processes requiring skills in chemistry, physics, pathology and so forth by affidavit a copy of which must be delivered to the other side at least seven days before the date of hearing, whilst s 30 of that Act provides for proof of entries in bankers' books by way of at least ten days' written notice.

[7] See the discussion of rule 37(1) in paragraph 6.25, in chapter 6.

7.4.17 Tender

If representing the defendant, you might in light of your discussion of the issues need to advise on the making of an offer in terms of rule 34.[8]

If representing the plaintiff, you might need to advise on whether any offer which the defendant might already have made in terms of rule 34 places the plaintiff on risk or not.

If following the format of Appendix A, this is something which could best be discussed whilst analysing and discussing the issues, in paragraph 3 thereof.

7.4.18 A summary of the steps that need to be taken

This is not essential. But it is useful. You could, in a final paragraph or in an appendix, outline each and every one of the steps which your discussion so far has indicated your attorney must take. See paragraph 10 of Appendix A and the discussion therein.

7.5 THE DEFENCE

7.5.1 Introduction

In advising a defendant, the same exercise will be performed and the same approach adopted.

It may happen that you decide not to call expert witnesses, but to cross-examine on the relevant issues only. In order to cross-examine with any measure of confidence the cross-examiner will have to be briefed properly. With this end in view, it is advisable to at least consult with experts so as to be able to cross-examine effectively.

7.5.2 Tender

One aspect that often calls for consideration when you are advising on evidence on behalf of the defendant is whether a tender should be made. Usually this involves a fairly neat evaluation of the merits and an even more precise assessment of quantum. I would suggest that, even if not specifically requested to do so, counsel, in his advice, should not hesitate to discuss the desirability of making a tender.[9] In the High Court this will be in terms of rule 34 and in the magistrate's court it will be in terms of rule 19, both of which have provisions for secrecy, thus ensuring that the court is not influenced one way or the other by the fact or amount of the tender. There are two objects in tendering: firstly, to terminate the litigation (for the benefit of the defendant) by assessing the damage at a figure which the plaintiff will hesitate to reject; and secondly, to protect the defendant against further liability for costs by assessing accurately the amount which will be awarded by the court.

---

[8] See the discussion of rule 34 in paragraph 6.24, in chapter 6.
[9] See the discussion of rule 34 in paragraph 6.24, in chapter 6.

Neither of these objects is easy to attain, and one thing is certain, namely that tenders for 'nuisance value' are seldom likely to assist. (The word 'tenders' here refers to formal tenders in terms of the relevant rules and not to the extrajudicial bargaining 'without prejudice' that goes on from the time the demand is made.)

7.5.3 Mitigation of damage

From the defendant's point of view an important factor is the plaintiff's duty to mitigate his damage, whether his claim results from breach of contract or from delict.[10] The onus of proof is on the defendant.[11] Accordingly, assuming the matter to have been placed in issue on the pleadings, you will have to set about advising the defendant how to prove his contention. Not only must you show that the plaintiff could have taken steps which would have reduced the damage, but you must also show firstly that he ought reasonably to have taken such steps, secondly that had he done so the damage would likely have been reduced, and thirdly by what extent it would likely have been reduced. The question is one of fact, which must be decided by reference to all the circumstances of the case.[12] It is usually a question which will require expert evidence.

7.6 CONCLUSION

You cannot successfully advise until you have determined what is required. From the cases, and the errors of others, you may learn what your case must be, and with your preliminary analysis of the law you can be aware of what must not be overlooked.

As with a pleading, step back, think about the case again, and then revisit your advice on evidence. Ensure that the product which goes out is, firstly, the result of a careful and comprehensive thought process and, secondly, a document which your attorney and, if appropriate, your client, will be able to read, understand and act upon. To revert to the analogy with which we started, it is your battle plan. A battle plan which cannot be understood by those who must implement it is less than useless.

---

[10] *Enslin v Meyer* 1960 (4) SA 520 (T) and *Janeke v Ras* 1965 (4) SA 583 (T).
[11] *De Pinto and Another v Rensea Investments (Pty) Ltd* 1977 (4) SA 529 (A) and *Jayber (Pty) Ltd v Miller* 1980 (4) SA 280 (W) at 282 et seq.
[12] Per Roos JA in *Kinemas Ltd v Berman* 1932 AD 246 at 253.

Preparation for Trial

If we then ask what sort of mind is most likely to display the qualities of military genius, experience and observation will both tell us that it is the inquiring rather than the creative mind, the comprehensive rather than the specialised approach, the calm rather than the excitable head to which in war we would choose to entrust the fate of our brothers and children and the safety and honour of our country.[1]

8.1 THE GOLDEN RULE: LOOSE TALK COSTS TRIALS

The golden rule in regard to preparation for trial is a simple one: do not talk. There is something about the last two or three weeks before the trial that seems to infect attorneys and counsel alike, counsel often being more susceptible to the virus than attorneys. Perhaps it is a substitute for the polite meteorological formalities that are exchanged in England. When one is in the throes of preparation it seems that the case becomes an obsession which, in large measure, is probably a good thing. This obsession brings a narrowing of horizons and seems to inhibit the ordinary pointless chatter with which our social intercourse is studded. One bursts (figuratively) to impart information. The impulse is to talk about what fills one's thoughts; and what is more natural than to discuss a subject in which the listener has an equal interest? Let us study a hypothetical conversation and, if you are a beginner at the game, I suggest that you show this passage to your more experienced colleagues, asking them to confirm its accuracy. If you have had some years in practice you will be able to recall a great many similar incidents. The characters, as usual, are fictitious. The scene is immaterial.

> 'Hullo, Henry.'
> 'Hi there, Monty.'
> 'You keeping fit?'
> 'Yes, fine thanks. And you?'
> 'Yes, full of beans.'

Now follows an interval which varies between three and five seconds. Monty, having commenced the greetings, is in the position of *dominus loquendi*, so he proceeds thus:

> 'We've got that case against each other next Wednesday.'

This gives Henry a chance for what is well described as 'one-upmanship' and he replies:

---

[1] The Prussian general who wrote on military strategy after the Napoleonic Wars, Carl von Clausewitz, *On War* edited by Howard & Paret (1984) 112.

'Which one is that?'

Monty rallies, to pretend for a moment that the name of one or other of the litigants has escaped his memory, the better technique being to recall only the name of your own client. Once the case has been identified to the satisfaction of both parties the next gambit is open to either of them, usually to the one who is a little more confident of success than the other. He says:

> 'Ought to be quite an interesting case.'
> 'How long do you think it will last?'
> 'I should say about four or five days. We are calling quite a lot of witnesses.'
> 'I don't think it can take as long as that. Seems quite a simple point really. Anyhow I've got another case on Monday.'
> 'Well, you don't want to run into trouble. Why don't you try to postpone the other matter?'
> 'Perhaps I should. But I still don't see how it can take more than two days.'
> 'Oh, yes, it will. We know all about your chap. He seems to make quite a habit of this sort of thing.'

Now, let us take it no further than these few superficial pleasantries, and let us see how counsel, whose client has been described as 'your chap', ought to react. He will, if he is clever enough, avoid any obvious sign of intelligence, and will remark that perhaps the case will be settled so that he can keep his brief for the following Monday after all. When the chatter is over he will telephone his attorney and ask him to investigate with the client the suggestion that there have been other similar transactions which, even if not admissible in evidence to prove a course of conduct, may well be used with devastating effect in cross-examination on credibility. The 'chap' will be forewarned, the element of surprise will be lost, explanations will be prepared and, perhaps, counsel himself will be adequately armed with authorities to stifle the particular line of cross-examination entirely.

Regrettably the common room, which is such an admirable institution of the Bar in South Africa, provides the ideal climate and culture for the growth of this particular inactive organism. When the disease has been contracted it is most difficult to eradicate and, in specific cases, the effect may be fatal. One should determine never to discuss one's case with an opponent save on a basis of the strict formality required to reach agreement on some matter pertaining directly to the conduct of the trial.

It does not cease to amaze me that so many juniors, and may their ebullience be cloaked in anonymity, cannot resist the temptation. In the robing room, during adjournments or at any other inopportune moment, they cannot resist the display of superiority and feeling of power thereby engendered in saying to the opposition:

> 'How are you chaps going to get over *mora*?'

For *mora* you may substitute any of a million and one topics, points, principles, maxims, judgments or dicta.

You may include the triumphant announcement that the proclaimer intends to call a particular witness. This, he says by his demeanour, is something that will show them. It does. It shows them how to prepare.

Now there are three possibilities:

- The opponent has not thought of it and is grateful for the reminder.
- The opponent is smarter than you think. He has the answer but leads you to think he hasn't — so you miss the vital point.
- He is also loquacious and gives you the answer, enabling you to react appropriately.

If I were a betting man I would lay the odds on the second possibility.

A further danger arises from conversations with colleagues who are not concerned in the actual case. It is one of the blessings of our system of practice at the Bar that one can discuss difficult points with one's colleagues or those colleagues more experienced in law and practice. Inevitably the risk is incurred of disclosing matters, which, even if not covered by professional privilege, ought to be kept from the knowledge of the other side. Human nature being what it is, a confidence shared becomes a confidence betrayed. That horticultural phenomenon known as the 'grapevine' flourishes no less in legal practice than anywhere else in society.

8.2 ATTORNEYS' PREPARATION FOR TRIAL

8.2.1 Introduction

Where counsel is employed the function of the attorney is not confined to the immediate preparation for the appearance in court. Often there is so much to do that the metaphysically minded attorney must wonder whether he is expiating the sins of a previous incarnation. Counsel will usually have erred on the side of caution in drafting the advice on evidence and suggested an investigation of such a nature as to leave no loophole in your case. In fact this is the only way to approach litigation, for the incautious oversight may well cost the success of the whole venture.

Once again, therefore, the attorney finds himself with inadequate time for all that has to be done, because simultaneously with executing the advice on evidence, he must attend to the formalities of pre-trial procedure, keeping up the requisite pressure on the opposition and also ensuring that he complies with the various notices served upon him.

8.2.2 Filing and pagination

I might here digress and mention a topic, that of the court record, which is no less pertinent to trials than it is to applications. (See chapter 17.) The rules require that the pleadings or the affidavits be collated, numbered consecutively and suitably secured. Now it has happened more than once that a judge has held aloft, delicately clasped between forefinger and thumb, a wad of papers, and has inquired of counsel (mindful, of course, of rule 62(4)):

'Mr Klitznit, is this "properly secured"?'

The quotation marks enclosing '*properly secured*' hang momentarily in the air above the registrar's head before speeding as air-to-ground missiles to transfix counsel before he can attain take-off speed. Incurring the judge's displeasure is a minor occupational hazard, as I shall have occasion to remark in chapter 20. What is a major hazard, however, is that the judge may rightly refuse to hear the matter and (even more rightly) refuse to adjourn for the bookbinding process to take place. And why should he when there may be any number of other matters awaiting their turn and only a limited number of days in the week? So he postpones the matter and grants an order for wasted costs in favour of your self-righteous opponent.

Bear with me. If I pontificate I do so out of despair. I well know the intense pressure under which attorneys work. I know that candidate attorneys are a carefree lot. But I have seen so much indifference and neglect — even ignorance — on the part of those who should be skilled in their profession that I must plead a cause to save you from yourself. Perhaps you will not win a case merely because of neatness of the documentation; you will, however, never lose a case because of precision and meticulous attention to rules and to detail and at least you will have started off on the right foot with the judge.

I have pleaded.

8.2.3 Briefing counsel

When counsel comes to be briefed on trial, it is a very unusual case which has precisely the same aspect as that presented on the client's first visit or even at the stage when the advice on evidence was returned. There will by now have been the tactical interplay between the parties. Sometimes counsel will have been consulted in the interim but very often he has completely lost touch with the matter and with its development and so must be reinstructed.

I would thus suggest that the attorney, save perhaps in the more simple cases, has a good deal of work to do in order to facilitate the final preparation which counsel undertakes prior to trial. It may be necessary to draw detailed instructions to counsel informing him what has been done in pursuance of his advice on evidence and to explain any inability to obtain the witnesses or evidence suggested. In such cases, no doubt, the attorney will have his own proposals for surmounting the problems that arise. Documents must be classified and sorted, and, in the case of documents which will be used as exhibits, it is essential that copies be available for counsel's own use.

One of the discouraging elements of the clerical aspect of the attorney's work is that counsel, when he gets the brief, will either shuffle the documents into a confused mass of confetti or else dissect it into his own favourite arrangement. Be that as it may, it is always appreciated when the attorney has troubled to arrange the brief in coherent form, with the copies of correspondence in chronological order, copies of documents which may be used as exhibits, the pleadings paginated and indexed, and statements of witnesses provided on the various matters which have to be proved.

8.2.4 A suggested schedule for attorneys

The following is a suggested schedule of preparation for trial on the part of the attorney, to be read concurrently with the pre-trial procedure discussed in chapter 6:

- Obtain copies of relevant documents disclosed by other party — rules 35(6), 35(12).
- Call for a notice specifying the documents which the other party intends to use at the trial — rule 35(8).
- Ensure that all notices served by the opposing party have been complied with.
- Ensure that all subpoenas have been issued and served — rule 38(1).
- Arrange for an interpreter if necessary — rule 61.
- Ensure that sufficient copies have been made of documents which will or may be used as exhibits.
- Ensure that the documents in counsel's brief have been classified and arranged in chronological order.
- Where appropriate, a chronological bundle of documents to be used at the trial should be made up at an early stage and provided to counsel, with the attorney retaining two copies, one for himself and another for use by witnesses in consultations.
- Generally, and whatever the nature of the matter, a bundle of trial documents will have to be made up before trial. This is usually agreed on at the pre-trial conference.[2]
- Attend to notices under rules 36(9), 35(9) and 36(10).
- If plans and photographs are going to be used ensure that a key has been compiled.
- If acting for the plaintiff prepare an index of the court file and copies for all parties — rule 62(4).
- Ascertain dates when witnesses will be available for consultation and arrange consultations.
- Where counsel is employed, draw instructions for counsel, setting out what has occurred since he gave his advice on evidence and drawing attention to difficulties which exist or are anticipated. Send the brief to counsel.
- (Such items as medical examinations, examinations of things and inspections *in loco* and expert witnesses are amongst those deliberately omitted from the list. They pertain to particular cases and have been discussed already, in chapter 6.)

---

[2] In a simple trial with an advocate on either side, six copies of the trial bundle must be prepared, one for each advocate, one for each attorney, one for the witness box and one for the judge. The original documents must be in the judge's bundle. See also, with regard to the content of the trial bundle, the discussion of the documents in paragraph 8.3.5 below.

8.2.5 Attorneys and consultations with witnesses

Many attorneys have the habit of telephoning counsel and saying: 'When can you minute statements from the witnesses?' A consultation is arranged and counsel will sit and write down the witnesses' statements. I have no hesitation in condemning this practice on at least two practical grounds: in the first place counsel should be assumed to be a little slow-thinking and to require time to consider the implications of what the witness is saying; in the second place it is not unknown for the necessity to arise of having to put to the witness, when he ultimately testifies, the fact that he has made a prior inconsistent or perhaps consistent statement. If counsel has to vouch for the prior statement a delicate situation may arise. Far more effective it will be if the attorney takes the statement, obtaining a signature if so advised. (Note that it has been held to be improper to take the statement on oath.)[3] Counsel will then consider the statement in the course of his preparation and, in consultation with the witness, elucidate matters which may require further explanation. I suggest that not even the most experienced and capable attorney or advocate can always be sure that his first investigation of a topic with a witness is comprehensive and adequate.

Sometimes it will be necessary to interview witnesses who may be called by the other party. Your client might for example be a plaintiff in a third-party claim who suffered concussion in the collision with resultant retrograde amnesia sufficient to render the evidence of the plaintiff himself valueless in establishing negligence. Or the claim may be by a widow whose husband has been killed in a collision on a country road with no indication as to which vehicle was on the incorrect side. The Road Accident Fund will usually have placed negligence in issue. In such circumstances counsel's advice in regard to proof of negligence can usually be carried out only by interviewing the insured driver and finding out whether his evidence-in-chief will establish such a clear case of negligence that it will not be destroyed by co-operative cross-examination. In such a case, and indeed in almost every case, it is permissible to interview the witness and to take a statement from him.[4]

---

[3] *Hersman v Angilley* 1936 CPD 386, *Boshoff v Manack* 1937 NPD 192, *Muller v Nel* 1942 CPD 337, and *Kolia v Secretary for the Interior* 1969 (1) SA 287 (C) at 294C; and rule 4.4 of the Uniform Rules of Professional Conduct for Advocates, which reads that 'Affidavits should ordinarily not be obtained by legal practitioners from prospective witnesses, except in cases in which their evidence is intended to be presented by means of the production of affidavits deposed to by them'.

[4] There is an alternative, though, presaged by the discussion of rule 35(9) in paragraph 6.10 above: the plaintiff might, as an alternative to the risky manoeuvre of calling the insured driver, consider proving (either by way of an uncontested rule 35(9) notice, or by way of formal proof thereof by for example calling the commissioner of oaths to whom the affidavit was deposed) the insured driver's statutory affidavit if, in his view, negligence can fairly be inferred from a reading thereof, and seek to put the document in as permissible hearsay evidence in terms of s 3 of the Law of Evidence Amendment Act 45 of 1988. See, for an example of this, *Makhathini v Road Accident Fund* 2002 (1) SA 511 (SCA) at 520–1. What this illustrates is the need for careful thought in the preparation of one's case.

In a letter written many years ago by the then Judge President of the Transvaal Provincial Division to the Johannesburg Bar Council it was stated that the opinion of all members of the Transvaal Bench was:

> that a litigant or an accused are entitled to interview any person who they have reason to believe is in the possession of information which may assist their client in his case, and cannot be deprived of this right by the fact that the other side has subpoenaed or taken a statement from such person, or that he has been called by the Crown as a witness at a preparatory examination, but that the other side should be notified. It is felt that to avoid any suggestion of impropriety the notification should precede the interview.[5]

Such an interview should be held only for the purpose of deciding whether to call that person as a witness or to obtain information which may lead to the obtaining of other evidence. It should not be used to obtain material for cross-examination of the witness should he be called by the opposing party.

Here I should mention an interim ruling in *S v Hassim and Others*[6] which pertains, of course, more properly to chapter 19 as the case was a criminal one. Nevertheless the warning may well be applicable also in the present context. In that case witnesses had testified for the State in a trial in Pietermaritzburg and had been released from further attendance at the trial. Counsel for the defence then suspected one thing and feared another. He suspected that the police had exacted evidence improperly from those witnesses, by use of the draconian powers of detention and control of persons under the powers at that time available to them. He feared that if he requested the Attorney-General to agree to an interview the police would take good care to frustrate it. In consequence he went to Cape Town personally over a weekend and there took statements from the witnesses. It is not for me to debate the justification for or wisdom of his decision, for the court, James JP, had this to say at 203:

> I have no doubt that in doing so he committed a serious error of that professional judgment which the court is entitled to expect from an advocate and that his conduct fell far short of what the courts have a right to expect from one of its [sic] officers.

I would think that, even in civil cases, it would be impermissible to interview a witness who has already testified in order to find out whether he has somehow been influenced or coached in his testimony. At 201F–G James JP remarked that the accused's legal representatives have 'an unrestricted opportunity of testing the truth of the evidence of a State witness by cross-examining him in open court'. So have you, in any case where your opponent calls witnesses. I cannot pretend that you will always find the right questions for the purpose. If you fail, well, perhaps there were no right questions after all.

---

[5] Quoted by Clayden J in *International Tobacco Corporation (SA) Ltd v United Tobacco Co (South) Ltd (1)* 1955 (2) SA 1 (W) at 12E. See also rule 4.3 of the Uniform Rules of Professional Conduct for Advocates, which is largely to the same effect.

[6] 1972 (1) SA 200 (N) referred to in *Shabalala and Others v Attorney General, Transvaal and Another* 1996 (1) SA 725 (CC) at 753C.

Let me not discourage you, however, from seeking an interview with any person you choose when you are seeking evidence for a civil case, provided only that the niceties are observed. Moreover, and this I can vouch from unhappy experience, there is nothing like an interview with opposing counsel to restrain a witness whose willingness to provide testimony far outstrips the accuracy of his recollection. A witness who was once prepared to support one up to the hilt seems suddenly to acquire a purity of heart that would make Sir Galahad a libertine by comparison.

8.3 COUNSEL'S PREPARATION FOR TRIAL

8.3.1 Introduction

As far as counsel is concerned, preparation may vary from a cursory glance at the pleadings and statements to three or four months of detailed analysis of documents and research of the law. I have heard of counsel whose practice flourished so that he was never able to look at a trial brief until the night before the case. His ability was such, or so he implied, that if he could not destroy the opposing witnesses in cross-examination upon such preparation then the case was a poor one and could not have been won by his client anyway. For the first ten to twenty years of your practice, at least, this method is not recommended.

There are certain basic assumptions to be made when you receive your brief on trial, assumptions that must continue to be regarded as valid until the final ringing tones of the plaintiff's replying peroration have faded into that tense hush in which his Lordship will speak. These assumptions are:

- your opponent is no less capable than yourself, probably more so;
- each party to the litigation believes himself to be in the right; your opponent is therefore equipped with ammunition to destroy your case and weapons wherewith to advance his own;
- someone is waiting to take advantage of any mistake you may make;
- nothing contained in your instructions, your client's statement or the information given by your witnesses can be taken for granted.

If you ponder on these propositions for a while you will no doubt realise that cases are won by preparation and application. A little practical experience will satisfy you that system, too, must play its part. It therefore becomes of some moment to apply in this chapter the theoretical discussions set out in chapters 3 and 4. Let us, then, consider the elements involved in preparation for trial, whether in the magistrate's court or the High Court, and whether or not the attorney will be appearing personally in the former or the latter case. Perhaps it will be useful to enumerate the elements first and to discuss them in turn thereafter.

- Clerical or routine work.
- The issues.
- The facts.
- The documents.

- The witnesses.
- Preparation, generally.
- The tactics.
- Calculated risks.
- Time to meditate.
- Preparing for the cross-examination.
- The law.

8.3.2 Clerical or routine work by counsel

It seems the ultimate in contempt to try to make suggestions to counsel, learned in the law, on clerical work. But the law must always be subservient to the facts, and the facts are where you find them. You may never actually lose a case because you cannot recall where you put any particular documents but, on the other hand and very indirectly, you may. You may lose the psychological advantage in cross-examination if your question to the other side's star witness, 'Mr Klitznit', is put as follows:

> 'Now let me put it to you, Mr Klitznit, that your answer cannot possibly be correct because on . . . (to the attorney) what was the date of that note? . . . Well anyway you signed a memorandum, a minute. . . . (To the attorney, again) Where is it? You gave it to me?. . . . Just let me look. . . . Will your Lordship just bear with me a moment, I must find the document in my papers, in fairness to the witness. Let me see . . . Now Mr Klitznit, I put it to you . . . (to the attorney, again) No, it's not this one; it's the one with the corner torn off . . . Oh yes, here it is. . . . Now Mr Klitznit, on 18 February 1967 you wrote a letter to the plaintiff in which you said.'

By this time Mr Klitznit, if he is worth his salt as a witness, will have three answers and four alternative explanations together with an assorted variety of denials. How much easier if counsel could open a folder, pull out the relevant document and say:

> 'If that is so, Mr Klitznit, listen to what you wrote to the plaintiff on 18 February 1967. (Reads crucial portion of document.) Was that false?'

There is no excuse for lack of system in preparation or in the conduct of cases. Either you make yourself fully conversant with the method of arrangement of the brief as adopted by the attorney or you have your own system, basically constant but permitting of slight modification with the exigencies of the case.

One method I would suggest is to sort the documents in your brief into one or more lever-arch files with labelled cardboard dividers and arranged, for example, in alphabetical order. The following is a possible list of titles:

- Pleadings — arranged and indexed.
- Discovery, Plaintiff — the affidavit.
- Discovery, Defendant — the affidavit.
- Notices — for the mass of formal notices in terms of the rules.
- (Plans, Diagrams, Photographs.)
- Argument — for notes of argument.
- Correspondence — chronologically!

- Documents — to be used in the case.
- Evidence — for notes of evidence.
- Exhibits — for copies of exhibits as handed in.
- Notes — working notes and memoranda.
- Previous Proceedings — such as inquest, criminal trial, preliminary application and so on.
- Pre-trial minute.
- Statements of witnesses.

It may be useful to put in the discovery files copies of documents, other than correspondence, disclosed by each party.

While the titles and order of files are always subject to personal preferences, whatever system is adopted must be memorised and followed unswervingly. You will find that there will be a vast improvement in the mechanical efficiency with which you conduct cases.

Another suggestion, which may be helpful in cases with many involved issues of fact (or even law) is to prepare index cards on which can be noted all references to any particular point of fact. This method is useful when there have been lengthy preliminary proceedings and it is necessary to have an analysis of all the evidence, point by point. It may involve a lot of work, but I have been at pains not to convey the impression that the Bar is a rest-cure.

8.3.3 The issues

Until you know the issues with pellucidity you will not know where you are going, or why, or how. This matter has thrice been discussed before: in regard to the extraction of the essence of a case, in regard to pleadings and in regard to advice on evidence. Your task, therefore, should be no more than refreshing your memory either from the pleadings or from the advice. The latter, of course, is to be preferred because the laborious aspect of the exercise will not have to be repeated.

From an understanding of the issues you proceed to the further branches of preparation; without an understanding of the issues you take the chance that the final score will be: played one, lost one.

Sometimes, by the time everyone has finished asking for, supplying and refusing further particulars, the pleadings become a little involved, with the result that it is necessary to page back and forth to find out precisely what the parties have to say on any specific point. In these circumstances it may be of great assistance, time permitting, to prepare what I call a 'consolidated exposition' of the pleadings. This is done on a clean sheet of A3 paper, which you divide horizontally into sufficient columns to accommodate all the documents comprising the pleadings. The headings along the top of the double page will be thus:

- Particulars of claim;
- Plea;
- Particulars for trial (Plaintiff);
- Reply;

- Particulars for trial (Defendant);
- Reply.

You may, of course, use the narrative form of setting out the pleadings, taking the paragraphs in the particulars of claim in turn. In this method you deal with the first paragraph in issue, and then go through the pleadings in regard to such paragraph.

This gives a fair idea of what it is all about.

8.3.4 The facts

No sermonising is needed.

When you wrote an examination in history you spent many wearisome hours swotting the facts. Every trial is an examination in history — an examination with a difference, because there is no 'pass' mark. It is 100 per cent or fail.

The facts come from many sources: statements of witnesses, correspondence, documents, plans, photographs and sometimes sheer deduction. Whether you study the statements first or the correspondence depends on the particular case. It does not really matter. What is essential is that your preparation must acquaint you with every single statement in every single document. You must know what every witness will say, and conversely, on every single point you must know exactly which witness can testify on that point.

In many cases the locality may be a factor of some importance, particularly in collisions. In such instances it is always worth the trouble to have an inspection *in loco* as part of your preparation:[7] not only will this acquaint you with aspects of the terrain which might not otherwise be apparent to you, but it will mean that you will have the inestimable advantage of having the scene in your mind's eye when you lead and cross-examine witnesses. Let your attorney arrange for your client and witnesses to be present at the inspection. Most people can point more coherently than they can talk — and if that does an injustice to the intelligence of the average witness then put it on the basis that his recollection will be far more vivid and easily stimulated by the surroundings in which his observations were made. More important, you will understand what they are talking about. Finally you will know what attitude to adopt should an application for an inspection *in loco* be made at the trial.

8.3.5 The documents

In preparing your case, of whatever type it may be, whether a civil trial, an opposed application, or a criminal appeal, you will make a habit of marking the important passages in the documents comprising your brief. It helps if you adopt a code which is quickly intelligible when you are on your feet and, perhaps, being questioned by the court. Thus it conveys an instant message if,

---

[7] In fact, experience teaches that consultations at the scene are invaluable, not just in trials but even in applications. One understands, and remembers, so much better when one has been to the scene of where it all happened, or what it is all about.

for example, you underline in red, passages which are adverse to your case; in blue those which support your case; and in green those which afford points of criticism of the person affected by the document. Your own artistic temperament, of course, may well suggest a more modern colour scheme, such as orange, purple and whatever else you please. But whatever colours you choose, elevate them into a system until, like Pavlov's dogs, you almost salivate when your brief is liberally lined with blue — or your substitute for that colour.

I have already emphasised, and will continue to do so, the importance of ensuring that documents are placed in a chronological order. You will understand things so much better once you have the chronology.

The following observation relating to bundles, and their usefulness, is that of an English Circuit Judge, Michael Hyam J:[8]

> Make sure that the bundles of documents are not too large; it helps to keep the judge at a low irritability level if he can handle the bundles easily, if they are arranged logically, if the bundles from which the advocates are working have the same page numbers (how often they do not!), if plans are of a convenient size to handle, if photostats are legible and if there is a comprehensive index. . . . It is a good idea also, if there are a . . . number of bundles, to have the covers of each bundle in a different colour.

8.3.6 Counsel and consultations with witnesses

It is essential that you consult beforehand with every witness whom you intend calling, and that you discuss with that witness the content of his evidence, the procedure to follow and terminology to use in the witness-box, and the likely lines of cross-examination.

As indicated above, it is often useful and usually imperative that you also consult with the witness at the particular scene.[9]

It is also essential that counsel consults with witnesses in the presence of his instructing attorney or, at the least, a competent representative of his instructing attorney. The primary reason for this is to avoid counsel having to testify about the content of the consultation, should that become necessary.[10]

Explain to the witness (particularly witnesses who, like most witnesses, are entirely unfamiliar with court procedures) the procedure of swearing-in (establish from the witness whether he has an objection to taking the oath; if he has, explore that with him, and reassure him that this can be dealt with by way of admonition. This will also enable you to clarify this with the court at the

---

[8] Michael Hyam *Advocacy Skills* 4 ed (Blackstone Press Ltd) 15.

[9] See paragraph 8.3.4 above, where the importance of consulting at the scene was emphasised.

[10] It might for example become necessary to put to the witness that his present evidence differs from that which he relayed in consultation. You would be at something of a disadvantage if the witness were to deny your recollection of the consultation. You either cannot testify or must withdraw as counsel in order to testify. Neither option is particularly attractive. Thus the need firstly to ensure the presence of your attorney or his representative at the consultation, secondly to ensure that the attorney or representative confirms your recollection of the consultation, and thirdly to be able to call the attorney or representative if necessary to refute the witness' version.

outset, without the witness being taken by surprise), court procedure insofar as it will pertain to him (ie, the process of evidence-in-chief followed by cross-examination and then possibly re-examination, and so forth), and what areas you intend covering with him in his evidence. Discuss his evidence in some detail so that, by the time the witness testifies, both he and you have at least some assurance that he has been prepared for the ordeal.

Explain to the witness the importance of keeping eye-contact with the court (what I usually suggest is that the witness should look at the person who is asking the question and then, when it is time to answer, should turn to the judge, look him or her in the eye and deliver the answer).[11]

The value and purpose of consultations with witnesses, even though there are limitations, are illustrated in two reported cases. In *O'Reilly v Lakofski*[12] the following was said:

> The attorney in this case contended that it would not be in the interests of his client to depend only on the consultations which he had with the witnesses when he took their statements, but that it was necessary and reasonable for him to have consultations shortly before the trial; in other words, if it were not for these consultations the plaintiff would have gone to trial without his counsel and attorney having seen these witnesses and having had consultations with them shortly before the action was heard . . . Mr R has admitted that the value of the consultations with counsel is to have a living impression of the facts so as to assist counsel in conducting the case before the court. Well, I think Mr R will have to admit that a busy counsel, dealing with many other matters in court in the meantime, cannot after six months carry in his mind the impressions and the conclusions to which he came in consultation, and that it is necessary to have a further consultation shortly before the action is heard.

The second case is *Bertish v Standard Bank*[13] where Herbstein J made the following remark:

> The second example of misconception is that . . . one of the purposes of pre-trial consultation is 'to prepare the witness for cross-examination' or, as it was later put, 'to examine with the witness the possible approaches during cross-examination'.

Without in any way venturing to criticise this latter pronouncement I am of the view that it is not just legitimate but, indeed, imperative in consultation to ascertain what the evidence of the witness will be on matters which will probably be raised in cross-examination. Equally, I suggest it is not just permissible but imperative to prepare the witness in a general sense for cross-examination possibly in the following terms: 'Listen to the question before you answer. If you do not understand it, say so. If you don't know any answer don't guess, just say that you don't know. Don't worry about what the man has in mind when he asks his question, just give a direct answer. Answer

[11] See also the discussion of preparing witnesses to testify in criminal trials, in paragraph 19.5.2 of chapter 19. The suggestions there contained apply with equal force to civil trials.
[12] Per De Wet J *O'Reilly v Lakofski* 1933 WLD 145 at 152.
[13] Per Herbstein J in *Bertish v Standard Bank of SA Ltd* 1956 (4) SA 9 (C) at 12F.

the same way to his questions as you would have answered mine: just tell the simple truth. And if the simple truth is that you don't know, say that you don't know. But if the simple truth is that you do know, say what you know. Don't make speeches.'

There is in my view nothing whatever wrong about preparing a witness for cross-examination by raising with him those issues which you believe the other party might or will want to raise in cross-examination, and seeing how he deals with it.[14] You can even, along the aforegoing general lines, assist in advising how to deal with issues. What you must of course never do, is to coach the witness by suggesting answers that do not come from the witness.

It is, in my view, equally right to warn your witnesses about the legitimate (and illegitimate) tricks and traps employed by your opponent in cross-examination. One particular counsel makes a habit of putting his questions, when he fears that the witness will not give him the information he wants, in the following form:

'Now, Mr Klitznit, please help us.'

Very few witnesses can resist a little flattery, and they glow with inner pride to think that this kind man is not cross-examining them but is really relying on their assistance so that the court can 'know all about it'. That is perfectly fair and proper, but the trap is that the witness is so obsessed with the idea of assisting that he forgets that he is testifying. He guesses, adds the little bit of garnishing where he really does not know, makes speeches and volunteers irrelevant and ill-considered information.

Until someone authoritatively pronounces to the contrary I suggest that it is quite permissible to warn a witness of the stratagems used by one's opponent, because this is not in the nature of working out the answers to anticipated questions.

The most important point regarding pre-trial consultations is that you must never accept as reliable any statement made by any witness, especially your client. When the statement is repeated in the witness-box your opponent will be affected by a degree of scepticism amounting almost to disrespect. He will test each statement, and if it is inaccurate, the damage may be irreparable. Thus,

---

[14] Roger E Salhany *Cross-Examination – The Art of the Advocate* (Butterworths 1988) makes the point at 25 that '(w)here a witness is likely to come under a strong attack it is best for him to realise this in advance. You should safeguard the case he is being called to support and, where possible, shield him from unpleasant shocks and surprises'. This is only logical. Willem Gravett of the New York State Bar says in an article in the December 2007 edition of *Advocate* on p 45, it 'is absolutely ethical — I would even say essential — for the trial lawyer to intensely prepare his . . . witness to give truthful testimony in a persuasive manner. . . It is justified on the theory that witnesses . . . are entitled to the lawyer's help in overcoming the intimidating and artificial environment of the courtroom and ensuring that their testimony is presented accurately and persuasively. A witness left to his . . . own devices might be forgetful, inarticulate, or unaware of the significance of the facts that he . . . relates or omits. People come to lawyers precisely because they want, and are entitled to, assistance in presenting their claims and defences. In . . . trial practice it smacks of abandonment to submit a client [or, for that matter, a witness] to examination without first reviewing the potential testimony'.

when you are acquiring your 'living impression of the facts' the question which you will ask most frequently will be:

'Why do you say that?'

Naturally there are a great many variations on this theme, one of the stronger ones being:

'But, Mr Klitznit, can that be so?'

You will probe and test until you are satisfied that every statement which will be made by the witness is accurate and is supportable in the context of the documents and the statements of the other witnesses. Your consultation consists neither of coaching the witness nor of reading through his statement with him. It consists of a testing and a filling-in — the latter being elicited from the witness with no assistance from any other witness, nor from the client, nor from the attorney, nor from you.

I would suggest that the *desideratum* in consultation is that you should be able to face with equanimity the prospect that, in cross-examination, your client elects to waive privilege in regard to what took place in your chambers while at the same time no statement made by him or the witnesses is exposed as being without foundation.

It may often require a good deal of tact to test your client's story in consultation without causing him to think that you consider him to be a liar. Very often he will resent what seems like cross-examination. This resentment may be shared by the attorney.

Ultimately, though, the interests of your client and of your attorney will not be served by your unquestioningly accepting what the client says. Cross-examination is, if I may be permitted a colloquialism, not for sissies, and you do not prepare your client for the rigours of cross-examination by being a sissy yourself. I find that the only clients who do not accept the simple explanation that what you are doing is in their interests and that if they think it is tough being cross-examined by their own counsel they are going to find cross-examination by your opponent excruciating, are clients whose evidence is so poor that no amount of preparation can save it.

8.3.7 Consultations with expert witnesses

Just as counsel must consult with the factual witnesses, so too must he consult with the expert witnesses.

The approach to consulting with expert witnesses should involve the following:

- Do not make the mistake of thinking that it is your stupidity which prevents you from understanding the point the expert believes he is making to you in consultation. Stupid you might be, but so might the judge be stupid. Rather work on the principle that if you don't understand what the expert is saying, nor will the judge. Insist on discussing, and debating, the point until you understand it.

- Do not abandon your critical faculties. *Debate* points with your expert. If you are not convinced, tell your expert that you are not, and why you are not. It might be that your point is good, and that the matter needs to be looked at anew. If so, that is hardly good news for your case, but even worse news would be to find this out during the trial.
- There will usually be an opposing expert. Deal not only with your expert's report and views, but also with the views expressed by the opposing expert in his report.
- Ensure, through this process of consultation, that by the time you lead your expert and cross-examine the expert on the other side, you have a full understanding of all of the expert views.
- It will usually be a good idea, if not actually required by the presiding judge, that the experts meet beforehand and bring out a joint minute of their areas of agreement and disagreement. Prepare your expert for this. Let him understand that he should not compromise simply for the sake of compromise but that, if his opponent makes a point which he genuinely believes is good, then he should feel free to concede this, but only after careful thought.[15]

8.3.8 Remember to rely on your ally, common sense

Now satisfy yourself that evidence has been obtained on all the matters raised in your advice on evidence, and show your mastery of your profession by working out how to adjust your case on the matters where your advice could not be implemented. Plan as you may, you have a forest of imponderables to contend with, such as flu, forgetfulness, fatality, fickleness, falsehood and just plain perversity. The good advocate is the one who can overcome these problems, if not at a moment's notice, then at least when a postponement would be inconveniently expensive.

Nor should it be assumed that expert witnesses are necessarily more reliable than others, as a true story will show. A plaintiff sued a defendant for damages done to his car in a rather unusual accident. On the main road between Klerksdorp and the then Orange Free State goldfields is an old-fashioned bridge across the Vaal River. It is wide enough, on a clear day, for only one vehicle to cross and is a structure made of strong steel girders. On the day in question the plaintiff was proceeding from Klerksdorp to the former OFS in a fairly new and fairly expensive motorcar. His car was driven by a chauffeur. They found the bridge to be free of traffic and proceeded on their lawful way. When the plaintiff's car was about a quarter way or more across the bridge the defendant's car, of a make no longer on the market, was seen to be entering upon the self-same bridge from the opposite direction. The chauffeur hooted furiously, but the defendant's only response was to put his arm out of the

---

[15] It is an open question whether, and if so to what extent, the parties and the court are bound by agreements reached between the experts at such a meeting. See the discussion of this issue in paragraph 6.25 in chapter 6 above, particularly in fn 62.

window and to wave equally furiously. The plaintiff's car came to a standstill. The defendant's did not. In the resultant action the defence, which seems highly probable in the circumstances, was brake failure. For reasons which are not relevant to this topic the condition of the footbrakes need not trouble us for the moment. The vital issue was whether the car could have been brought to a standstill by use of the handbrake had the defendant taken prompt steps when the need became apparent.

In the course of preparation counsel for the defendant advised that an ounce of practice was worth a ton of theory, and a demonstration *in loco* was arranged. Tests showed that a collision was unavoidable and counsel advised that an expert witness be employed to repeat the test. It is material to record that the defendant stated that he had been travelling at 50 kph; and also to note that the road down to the bridge had a gradient of, say, 1 in 40, this being the crucial factor in making it impossible to stop the car. The expert was duly briefed with these facts, given the motorcar, and told to determine the stopping distance. He duly submitted a report as to the distance in which the car could be stopped, that distance being sufficient to acquit the defendant of negligence.

When the expert testified counsel for the plaintiff rose to cross-examine. His first questions brought results which he could hardly have anticipated. The cross-examination proceeded thus:

> 'Now, Mr Expert, at what speed do you say the car was travelling when you applied the handbrake?'
> 'Fifty kilometres an hour.'
> 'Why do you say it was 50 kph?'
> 'I am an experienced driver and I can judge the speed of a car.' (This, of course, being far easier than looking at the speedometer!)
> 'Now you say that you conducted your test on a road with a gradient of one in forty?'
> 'Yes.'
> 'How do you know it was one in forty?' (Emboldened, no doubt, by his previous success.)
> 'I measured it.' (Excellent answer.)
> 'How did you measure it?'
> 'With my eye.'

That was the end of the expert as a witness (or vice versa).

You, yourself, may judge whether counsel for the defendant should have put these same questions to his expert witness in consultation.

Perhaps one further incident may be recounted from the same case, with the same lesson, but not on the same topic.

During the trial counsel for the plaintiff asked the court to examine the car, which was available for that purpose. The application, being unopposed in any event, was duly granted. At this inspection the plaintiff's own expert witness was called upon to demonstrate to the court just how the handbrake lever operated. He sat in the driver's seat, with the judge next to him, and pulled out the lever in the manner of one applying the handbrake. He succeeded in making the lever travel about three centimetres, drawing the judge's attention specifically to this fact. Counsel for the defendant, not being able at that moment to comprehend the significance of this fact, decided to verify it for himself in case it became important. Politely he asked the expert to allow him to take the driver's seat and he seated himself next to the judge. He seized the handbrake lever and, with no appreciable difficulty pulled it out another six centimetres. This caused the judge no small degree of surprise and he asked counsel a question to which counsel could suggest no answer: 'Why couldn't Mr Expert do that?'

History does not record why the plaintiff's expert tried to mislead the court because, whatever he may have had in mind, it was never made the subject of any evidence or argument in the case.

You might, with this type of expert on either side, be wondering who ultimately won? Emergency treatment salvaged the case for the defendant.

Both these instances show the importance of verifying — to the best of your own ability — everything that even expert witnesses say.

8.3.9 The tactics

The tactical planning and conduct of a case commences no later than the first pleading filed on behalf of your client and continues until the conclusion of argument. I say 'no later than' because often letters may have to be drafted with a view to the effect that will be created in subsequent litigation. No textbook has ever been written containing precedents of letters — nor do I intend to attempt the impossible. Equally, when you study precedents of pleadings you will bear in mind that those precedents are drafted to set out the essentials of a claim or defence, and without an attempt to achieve any tactical objectives. Those objectives are infinitely variable and not within the scope of precedents. Equally, though the objectives pertain to the topic of technique, it is impossible to do more than discuss the matter generally.

At the stage of preparation for trial there are two aspects of tactics:

*   How do I propose to present and conduct my case?
*   How will my opponent present and conduct his case?

By this time you will have made at least one complete analysis of the issues and the evidence required on those issues. Now you must determine such matters as the order in which you will lead your witnesses, how many witnesses you will call on any particular issue and what weaknesses your individual witnesses may have. You will sometimes have to decide whether to call a witness who, for one reason or another, is potentially dangerous, or whether to improvise, gamble or economise. An illustration will show what I mean, and, since it is a precursor of what will happen to you some day, sooner or later, it is worth quoting in some detail.

The plaintiff was a man whom we may call MacTavish. One Friday evening MacTavish stood on a street corner in, say, Welkom, trying to get a lift to the goldmine where he was due to go on shift at 8 o'clock. MacTavish had had a drink, although he maintained that it was one and no more. Along came a car driven by Conradie, who had finished work and was returning home. Finding that his journey would take him near to MacTavish's goldmine, Conradie obligingly gave MacTavish a lift. Seventeen kilometres along the route, it being dark at the time, a truck, driven by one Solomon, was taking furniture along the same road. Solomon missed his turn-off to the right and in order to get back to the road junction, decided to turn his vehicle around and retrace his path. This he did. Unfortunately there came a stage when the truck blocked the whole of the roadway, at which precise moment Conradie's car collided with the right rear corner of the truck. The collision occurred more or less in the middle of Conradie's correct side of the road.

Conradie died without regaining consciousness. MacTavish sustained severe injuries and came to his senses in hospital. The result of his injuries was that he was unfit for underground work as a miner and probably totally unemployable.

In due course MacTavish sued the Road Accident Fund for damages under the then applicable legislation.

In the plaintiff's particulars of claim a specific allegation was made that the truck turned to its right across the path of Conradie's car. This was denied by the defendant which, for its part, pleaded that the collision was due solely to the negligence of Conradie. One of the particulars of negligence given was that Conradie drove whilst under the influence of intoxicating liquor or of narcotic drugs.

Counsel were duly briefed on trial, a task somewhat hampered by the fact that the attorney had not troubled much about the pre-trial procedure which is discussed in chapter 6. However, this was a matter of no more than inconvenience in that particular case — largely because of the co-operative attitude of the defence (co-operative on technicalities, and to a limited extent only). Counsel then set about the question of witnesses and tactics and found themselves in the following position.

Issues:
- whether the furniture truck did in fact turn across the road;
- negligence of the insured driver;
- injuries etc.

Witnesses:
- whether the truck turned.

At this stage counsel considered whose name was to be put on the list of witnesses and this is how the matter developed, counsels' notes being based upon the record of an inquest into the death of Conradie:

MacTavish: Remembers travelling at 60 kph. Suddenly saw 'something' in the road ahead. Thinks it was about twenty metres away. Conradie shouted and then there was a collision. Next recollection was waking up in hospital. *N.B. No use on this point.*

Carpenter: Driving along road at about 100 kph when a car of the same make as Conradie's overtook him. Estimates speed about 140 kph. This car passed several others, weaving in and out. Then came on scene of collision and found this car had collided with lorry. *N.B. Of no use whatsoever; probably will be called by defendant to prove defendant's contention that collision due solely to negligence of Conradie.*

Fisher: Same as Carpenter.

Van der Merwe: Same as Carpenter.

Sgt Marais: Called to scene to investigate. Found MacTavish and Conradie still in car. Strong smell of liquor about both. Empty beer bottles and brandy bottle in car. Also two tumblers. Packet of dagga in cubby-hole. Asked for blood test to be performed on Conradie but, perversely enough, the doctors had started their attempt to save Conradie's life before anyone got around to taking a sample of blood. Prepared plan of scene. Could clearly distinguish the tracks of the truck making a wide sweep to turn across road. At inspection *in loco* told us that driver informed him that he had missed the turn-off and had decided to turn his truck round and go back. *N. B. Vehicles were found some distance from point of impact so that the tracks across the road are dissociated from the final position of the truck. A very hostile witness but of great value to the defendant on the allegation that Conradie was driving under the influence of liquor or a narcotic drug.*

Insured Driver: Declined to make a statement.

Summary: *The plaintiff cannot even create a prima facie case of negligence. The three other motorists do not help and, indeed, tend to lend some support to the defendant's contentions, if their evidence is admissible. Sgt Marais is most hostile. His observations create a prima facie case that the truck turned across Conradie's path — this would amount to negligence. He affords the defendant valuable evidence in support of its case. What happens if we call the plaintiff and Sgt Marais? The defendant will apply for absolution. This will be refused. Suppose the defendant then closes its case without giving us a chance to cross-examine the insured driver. His statement to Marais, on the greater weight of authority, might be held not to be admissible in evidence. Will we have proved on a balance of probability that the wheel tracks onto and commencing to cross the road belonged to the truck which was found twenty metres away facing in the opposite direction? We can't trace the wreck of Conradie's car and have no evidence about what part of the lorry was damaged. There seems to be no clear balance of probabilities in favour of our version.*

This analysis led counsel to one tactical conclusion. The insured driver would have to be called as a witness for the plaintiff. This would make it possible to dispense with the evidence of Sgt Marais. The reasoning was that the truck driver would certainly agree that he had turned across the road. He had admitted this not only to Sgt Marais but also to Carpenter, adding in the latter case that he had looked in his rear-view mirror before turning and had seen car lights but they were a long way off. Counsel hoped with some degree of conviction that, without the pressure of cross-examination, the driver would state that he could not say how far away the lights were when he saw them, and that he could not say how fast they were travelling. His preliminary swing to his left would take the lights out of his field of vision, while he would have to describe what the position was when he again swung to his right and commenced to travel across the road. The time of his journey up to the moment of impact was calculated to be about four seconds. Even at 140 kph Conradie's car would have been less than 160 metres away when the truck commenced to move across the road, which made the crossing a dangerous one at night when speeds and distances are notoriously difficult to judge.

After complying with the requisite ethical formalities, counsel proceeded to interview the insured driver.

From this point, subject to the anxiety that must always arise when one is dealing with unknown quantities, matters developed very much as had been hoped. In view of the certainty that the insurance assessors had taken a statement from the insured driver, and in view of the fact that the defendant's own legal advisers had promptly consulted with him upon receipt of notification of the plaintiff's intention, the decision was taken not to put anything remotely resembling a leading question to him at the interview. He was to be allowed to convict himself of negligence without any assistance from counsel. By this method counsel could be reasonably sure that his statements would be in close conformity with those made earlier.

In anticipation of the interview a list of questions was written out and spaces left for the filling in of the answers. This is how the statement looked after the interview:

Question: Did the collision take place before, at or after the place where the roads join?

Answer: About fifty metres after. It was about 6.30 p.m. It was already dusk. (The last two answers being in relation to supplementary questions.)

Question: What did you decide to do?

Answer: I decided to make a 'U' turn. I turned off the road and stopped.

Question: Is it possible to turn your lorry at that point without going off the tar?

Answer: It is necessary to go off the tar because the lorry is 'vreeslik lank' (terribly long).

Question: And what did you do?

Answer: I looked in my rear-view mirror and saw nothing. I then put my head out of the window and looked again to make sure that the road was clear. I again saw nothing coming. I then moved forward. When the front wheels of my lorry were just about to go on to the tar I

stopped and put my head out of the window to make sure that it was
safe to cross the road.

Question: What did you see?

Answer: The bright headlights of a car. I estimated that they were far away
          and I moved forward.

Question: Where, in relation to the centre of the roadway, were the lights?

Answer: I could not see where they were on the roadway.
          (The thin edge of the wedge.)

Question: Can you say how far away they were?

Answer: About two (city) blocks.
          (Later found to be about 200 metres. The wedge is being driven in.)

Question: How fast were those lights travelling?

Answer: I could not see how fast he was travelling because it was at night and
          the lights were on bright.
          (The job is done. Negligence has been established.)

From this summarised version of the consultation the technique should be
apparent.

   But do not use this weapon over-enthusiastically. In the actual case both
senior and junior counsel for the plaintiff were men with nearly thirty years of
experience behind them. After the idea had germinated, it was carefully
considered for several days before the final decision was taken. There were
doubts and counter-arguments. The effect of calling the insured driver as the
first witness was overwhelming and, because his evidence must have
corresponded closely with his statements to the defence, cross-examination
was greatly inhibited. Eventually a settlement could be negotiated on the true
monetary value of the claim. The plaintiff was not compelled to accept less than
he should have, for fear that he might lose the case and get nothing.

8.3.10 Calculated risk

During the discussion backwards and forwards that takes place in the course of
preparation for trial, a phrase which is often bandied about refers to 'taking a
calculated risk'. Sometimes, it is to be feared, those who use this phrase are
doing no more than deluding themselves that there is some chance of
succeeding in a hopeless case. This piece of jargon should not be used, I would
suggest, as an opiate nor yet as a stimulant. The problems which arise in the case
must be examined carefully and must not be obscured with the suggestion that
by taking a calculated risk something may develop and lead to success. On the
other hand there are cases in which the calculated risk must be taken because no
alternative presents itself. One such case has been mentioned already. It is the
case of *Joseph v Black and Others*.[16] All of the counsel who appeared in that case
were men who had achieved or who later achieved a high reputation and great
standing in the profession. One indeed later became a judge of appeal. Since

---

[16] 1930 WLD 327, upheld on appeal *sub nom Black and Others v Joseph* 1931 AD 132.

this case affords quite an interesting illustration in tactics and the calculated risk it is well worth careful reading. Joseph, now deceased but then in practice as an attorney, had been defamed in a newspaper published by Black. The details of the defamation are irrelevant beyond noting that there was a serious reflection upon Joseph in his professional capacity. Black's problem was to minimise damages and to force Joseph to submit to cross-examination not only on the defamation in issue, but also on his practice generally. To achieve this objective counsel, in their plea, denied Joseph's allegation that he was an attorney. Everyone knew that he was an attorney but it was calculated that Joseph would have to enter the witness-box to prove it. And that, it was hoped, would be the end of Joseph's case. However, Joseph avoided the trap and called other witnesses as to his qualification. Indeed, the subsequent argument against him that he was afraid to submit to cross-examination was held to have aggravated the damages.

Your immediate reaction will be that counsel for the defendant had been guilty of errors of judgment or indiscretions in their pleadings and tactical preparation of the case. Perhaps, however, when you have thought about it for a while you will see the case as a study in tactical manoeuvre and counter-manoeuvre. It is interesting to speculate as to how the defendants could have presented their case otherwise than as they did. Perhaps your own experience will have made you realise how difficult it is, even where you know your facts are correct, to prove that a fellow-practitioner has been guilty of conduct that deserves censure. Whether there was any reason to believe that the plaintiff in that case had been guilty of anything improper is impossible to say after the lapse of so many years. Certainly he had a 'nose' for a technical point, but there was never a suggestion subsequently that he was anything but a thoroughly respectable member of the profession. Perhaps counsel for the defendants had given their clients advice which was unacceptable to them and perhaps they had received specific instructions to take the 'calculated risks' which they did. The reports do not record these details, but those reports go to show what may result from tactical manoeuvres and how history may (or may not) misjudge the tactician.

This case will show that, even in the hands of the most experienced and capable counsel, the 'calculated risk' is something which ought to be avoided if at all possible. It will also show how careful planning and counter-planning are required in considering the tactics to be adopted at the trial because one must not lose sight of the ultimate effect of any tactical move where that effect may extend beyond the immediate and limited tactical advantage which is desired. Thus you plan not only your own tactics, but also those of your opponent; in the latter regard contriving to anticipate what moves he will make.

You should never cease to ask yourself: '*How will he prove (or meet) this?*'

There should then follow a sequence of questions which, naturally, vary from case to case.

8.3.11 Time to meditate

The busier you become, the more difficult it will be to attend properly to the tactical planning of your case. There is, however, hardly any matter which will not be better presented if you devote the occasional half-hour to meditation, introspection, contemplation or whatever you may prefer to call it. You will be surprised at how many points, factors, considerations and arguments present themselves to your mind in these half-hours. Let me warn you, however, that you must learn to recognise the spurious; for every sound idea that comes to you there will be twenty that are without substance. An impulsive reaction to an impulsive flash of 'genius' may be more than wasted effort; it may be positively dangerous, leading to an embarrassing letter, an unnecessary notice, or a rash subpoena. It may then wake up a dog which, being sleeping, should be let lie. Wherever possible, discuss your inspirations with somebody before you act on them, preferably with your instructing attorney.

8.3.12 Preparing your cross-examination

One of the problems of preparing cross-examination is that you do not always know who the witnesses will be or what they will say.[17] In matrimonial cases there is no problem; you may safely assume that in 90 per cent of cases what the wife says is true, subject only to feminine exaggeration. In running-down cases, the pedestrian will always say that he was on the pavement when struck, and the motorist will always say that it was dark and that the pedestrian was in dark clothing and intoxicated. Outside these matters there is a wide range of the unknown and the barely predictable.

The first step is to equip yourself with a complete knowledge of every statement in every document and of every fact in the statements of your own witnesses. You must know and understand the theory of the case (which we discussed in chapter 4 above) so that your cross-examination can be directed towards its verification or demonstration.[18]

The reason for this advice is far removed from empty idealism. As will be seen later, one useful device in cross-examination is the confrontation of a witness with an incongruity. The mental processes necessary to 'pick up' the incongruity cannot take place except on a foundation of fact. The facts must be known before you yourself can superimpose the witness' statement on them in order, as Euclid was wont to do, to decide whether the result is 'QED' or 'which is absurd'.

The second step in your preparation is to ensure that the facts are where you can find them. It is often useful to prepare a list of the statements, points, topics,

---

[17] See also chapter 12, dealing with cross-examination, and also paragraph 19.9 of chapter 19, where cross-examination is dealt with in criminal context.

[18] Salhany op cit says at 12 that '[t]he effective cross-examiner is one who has thoroughly examined and re-examined every facet of his case. . . What exactly must I attempt to achieve? Where do the strengths and weaknesses in the case lie? What kind of damage can I expect from each witness, and what advantages can be elicited from their testimony?'

letters and miscellaneous matters that pertain to each witness. The list should, if necessary, be rewritten in a chronological order so that each item noted can serve as a mnemonic or as an index to the full context which is to be put to the witness. Thus a note reading 'Letter of 12/3/67 re advertising' could provide the material for cross-examining a witness who denies that a contract was entered into on the basis that time of delivery was of the essence of the contract. The example is a trivial one, but there must be created some system which you can utilise for the comparison process. When you are on your feet you will be conscious of many things: of the problem of accurate phraseology; of the witness who is no novice in the art of evasion; of the court, polite, patient but not too long-suffering; of your client or attorney who is either passing you notes or else listening with a critical ear. In the midst of this you will not have time to think or to search; you must know.

The third step is one which is best served by the stillness of the night. It is what is really the theme of this book — the extraction and realisation of the essence. You prepare your notes for cross-examination. I have seen very experienced and capable counsel do it like this:

> 'When your attention was drawn to the letter of 12 March 1967 did you think that there had been some misunderstanding on the part of the plaintiff? If so, what steps did you take?'

By all means, if you enjoy working until 2 a.m., follow this precedent. From the clerical point of view it is more economical to make your notes in this form: 'Letter 12/3/67 — reaction? Steps?'

That, however, is not what I have in mind as the utilisation of the stillness of the night. What I mean is the conscious or subconscious process of meditation when you have determined the essence of each case and you are considering the witnesses who will be called for your opponent. Adopting your particular sequence of chronology or logic you inquire how the successive topics bear upon the case of each party and what questions must be put to the witness on those topics. Your thoughts may go thus:

> We say that the machine had to be delivered not later than 27 April 1967. It is our word against his. Why do people make oral contracts? What about this letter of 12 March? He knew we were advertising for work with the machine. What did he think when we told him that our advertising campaign was to start on 20 April? Why should we write to him like that unless he had to deliver by the fixed date? Must ask him what he thought. Surely he would have phoned to say we were taking a chance, unless he had committed himself: must ask him what he did. Not conclusive, but it may lead to something.

Of course, in many cases and with experience, it is possible simply to arrange the documents in order and cross-examine from these. In very few instances, however, is cross-examination really effective where there could have been preparation and there was none.

You will now ask: 'How do I deal with what was described as — "the unknown and the barely predictable"?' The answer is that your preparation can seldom proceed past the stage of knowledge and arrangement of the facts. The exact points to be put to unknown witnesses defy cataloguing. It is in the meeting of the unknown that the true art of cross-examination is to be found. This art is learned by experience and not from books. Books can give hints or provide illustrations. They can never recreate the atmosphere and magnetic tension of a trial where the witnesses exhibit the properties of quicksilver rather than the qualities of puppets.

In civil cases much of the difficulty has been eliminated from the cross-examination of expert witnesses by the provision of rule 36(9). But where an expert has to be cross-examined your preparation must qualify you, too, as an expert on whatever branch of the subject is to be examined. You will consult textbooks, explained if necessary in discussions with your own expert witnesses. You will make whatever inspections or arrange whatever demonstrations may be necessary. You will prepare a theory to counter the opinions of opposing experts or establish a schedule of considerations which are destructive of those opinions. Until you know *why* an expert is wrong, you have very little chance of proving that he is wrong.

8.3.13 The law

The time for research into the law is not on the night between the conclusion of evidence and the commencement of argument. You would have researched the law at the time when the particulars of claim were drafted, or when the plea was considered. In cross-examining a witness you will want to establish those facts which will fit in with your argument on the law also. The topic is discussed fully in chapter 12 dealing with cross-examination.

This profundity, and many of my suggestions in these pages are perhaps illustrated by an impassioned *cri de coeur* I received some time ago from a junior colleague who had been briefed as junior to another and far more senior junior. The point involved, if I am to believe my informant, was estoppel. Now I don't pretend to understand estoppel, and the more the doctrine is evolved by decisions of the courts the less I understand it. Perhaps the learned leader shared my deficiency.

'Go to the library', he commanded, 'and get me every case on estoppel.'

For my part, the process would leave me in a state of utter confusion, but from it I can at least offer a suggestion. Research is commendable, and as one is making one's way along the labyrinthine paths of practice one must devote a good deal more time to research than is needed when one's skill is surer and one's knowledge broader. You — if I may now adopt again the personal form of address — cannot know all the authorities, all the principles and all the answers. At the beginning of your career you will search widely lest there be principle or point that may have to be considered, met or adopted. Especially must your research prepare you for what may be met. However, I cannot suggest that you must find all the cases on any topic. What I do suggest is what I have discussed in particular in regard to pleadings and what I have tried to convey in my discussion of the essence. It is no more than this: every problem and every question of law can be resolved into basic or constituent elements. Those elements must be isolated. Your research into the law, I would say, is then to find the authorities which establish the basic elements and govern the application of those elements to the particular facts of your case.

Sometimes, I concede, a line of cases must be found, followed and cited to establish or illustrate a principle. Sometimes a number of cases must be quoted to affirm the acceptance of a proposition. More often, however, a minimum of cases will be no less effective and far less wearying to the court. Even if the highest court in the land has not yet pronounced authoritatively on the topic you will in most cases find a minimum of pertinent cases is pungently effective.

Let me not decry the value of quantity in a proper case — and for an example I refer you to *Daniels v Daniels; Mackay v Mackay*[19] where counsel's researches covered reports over more than a hundred years. But even here, research was confined to a basic principle.

So, with my unhappy colleagues, there must have been a basic point giving rise to the estoppel. There must have been a basic element of words or conduct that fell to be tested. There is a handful of leading cases in which the principles have been worked out. Usually, I would think, the task of the researcher is to study that handful of leading cases and to confine the proliferation to the particular feature which brings his own case into one or other of the propositions laid down in them.

8.4 CONCLUSION

In the hope that the foregoing suggestions will be reinforced by the citation of authoritative judicial pronouncement, I quote the words of Van Blerk JA:[20]

> Counsel for the appellant rightly pointed to the absence of important basic information which the plaintiff should have placed before the court. The manner in which the plaintiff's case was presented to the trial court is deplorable. No evidence was given as to the width of the road or as to the width of the truck; nor was a sketch plan of the scene of the accident produced. It appeared from Daniel's evidence that the day after the accident police officers took measurements at the scene of the accident. Before the trial the plaintiff's counsel inspected the scene. No doubt plaintiff's advisers were seriously hampered by lack of funds; but the preparation of a rough sketch depicting the road and the situation thereon of the relevant houses in relation to one another, as also the measuring of at least, the width of the road, could all have been done at negligible cost. Counsel for the plaintiff who also appeared at the trial, was invited to explain why none of this was done. Apart from mentioning the shortage of funds, his only 'explanation' was that it was anticipated that the defence would, at the trial, place evidence of all relevant measurements, etc. before the court. Such an anticipation is quite inadequate to excuse practitioners from the performance of what can only be described as elementary duties in the presentation of plaintiff's case in litigation of this nature.
>
> In the present case the court does not wish to apportion blame for the unsatisfactory manner in which the plaintiff's case was put before the court; there

[19] 1958 (1) SA 513 (A).
[20] *Minister of Justice v Seametso* 1963 (3) SA 530 (A) at 536–7.

may be factors of which this court has no knowledge and there is no proper opportunity to investigate the question. But it must be emphasised that the possible indigence of the client is no excuse for the failure to make available to the court trying such issues as were here involved, data which are easily available at little expense and which are usually vital and at any rate always of great assistance in the solution of the questions to be decided. The plaintiff's case was unnecessarily subjected to a considerable risk of being decided against him because of the failure to place before the court evidence which was readily obtainable.

Let it be remembered that behind the phrase 'Counsel . . . was invited to explain' lie an unpleasant ten to fifteen minutes during which counsel wishes that the floor would indeed open to swallow him up. The courts can and do make their displeasure painfully apparent to counsel. Also I suggest that you read the last sentence quoted, that you study it carefully and that it becomes engraved upon your memory.

CHAPTER 9

Technique in the Conduct of Trials, Generally

I love the smell of napalm in the morning . . .
Colonel Kilgore, in *Apocalypse Now* (Francis Ford Coppola, 1979).

9.1 INTRODUCTION

In this chapter I will deal with overarching aspects of conducting trials which do not naturally fall within the succeeding chapters (on opening addresses, leading and cross-examining witnesses, etc).

9.2 YOUR APPROACH TO TRIALS, GENERALLY

Beware
Of entrance to a quarrel; but, being in,
Bear't that th' opposed may beware of thee.[1]

So spake Polonius several centuries past, but that sentiment — or, let us say, the latter part of it — should serve you well in litigation. The next two lines of the speech are offered, with a respect that is tinged with despair, to the judiciary:

Give every man thy ear, but few thy voice:
Take each man's censure, but reserve thy judgment.[2]

On the assumption that the Bench will heed this advice as dutifully as did Laertes, the next exhortation is that you must know where you are going, and why, and you must keep going there. One of the things a judge is entitled to do is to put questions to witnesses. Another is to put questions to counsel. Sometimes the questions put to counsel may be very difficult to answer. Some of them may be so difficult that counsel may feel that he is being harassed. Sometimes the judge forms a strong view about the case. Sometimes he is wrong. Sometimes when he is wrong he puts questions to counsel. Sometimes they are difficult questions. Sometimes the judge, if he has formed a wrong view, cannot appreciate a good answer to a difficult question. Sometimes counsel may feel that he is being harassed. In fact the entire proceedings may develop that degree of incoherence and repetition that I have tried to attain in this paragraph.

In these trying circumstances counsel must learn to keep his head and, if he feels that he is right and the judge wrong, he must not allow himself to be

[1] Shakespeare's *Hamlet* Act I scene iii, Polonius' advice to his son Laertes.
[2] Ibid.

diverted from his path.[3] This is very easy to recommend, but often difficult to achieve. The man or woman who can think on his or her feet is destined to succeed in this profession. The man or woman who cannot had better note an appeal and make sure that the answers are ready when he or she gets to the appellate tribunal, where, as likely as not, a completely different catechism awaits. One method of learning to think on one's feet, of course, is by experience. The other is by system, application and preparation. Counsel who knows his brief and has asked himself, both in relation to fact and law, what can be urged against him will know the answers because he knows the questions.

Beyond this it is necessary to achieve a rigid degree of self-control. Even if the judge appears not to realise it you must never be conscious of the fact that you are no longer 'you'. You are 'counsel for the plaintiff (or defendant)'. That interrogation is not directed at 'you'; it is directed at 'counsel for the plaintiff (or defendant)'. It is not 'you' who has to answer the questions; it is that black-robed figure representing your client. The questions are, no matter how aggressive the judge may seem, to be regarded as exercises in forensics, the application of the science of logic to hypothetical facts. In other words give him a patient hearing, wait for your opportunity and submit your answer. If you become engaged in an exchange of words with the judge you may not help your client, your case or yourself. He may be right, in which case you lose. He may be wrong, and if you do not retain sufficient detachment to see where and why he is wrong you still lose.

Your behaviour to your opponent should not be any different from your behaviour towards the court. Both are entitled to courtesy and respect. If you think that your opponent has forfeited that right you will advance your case not a whit by letting him know what you think. After all, the only reason why you are in court is to advance the case of your client. When Polonius counselled Laertes to beware of entrance to a quarrel I doubt whether he referred to squabbles between counsel in court any more than he referred to litigation as such. It is to the former, however, from the advocate's point of view, that the exhortation is especially apposite. The latter is, of course, by no means to be discouraged.

Subject to what has been stated in the preceding paragraphs you should go in fighting and you should never stop fighting.[4] Whether you liken it to boxing, fencing or wrestling, the simile will be apt. The only difference will be the courtesy and detachment of the fight. Let it be said of you, if nothing more, that you stood out for your moral courage.

---

[3] Whatever happens, do not lose your temper with the judge. Your function as counsel is to persuade the judge that you have a good case. By losing your temper, you lose the judge and your case.

[4] The great English advocate FE Smith (later Lord Birkenhead) is said to have responded to Wrigley J's sour statement that 'I have read the pleadings and I do not think much of your case' with 'Indeed, I am sorry to hear that, My Lord, but Your Lordship will find that the more you hear it, the more it will grow on you'.

So, with these few precepts in your memory, you enter court and fight your cases, not opposing counsel.

Perhaps somewhere there is an advocate who can go into court without a preliminary sensation of semi-apprehension. At least, one's opponents always appear unruffled. I doubt, however, whether anyone can honestly say that he is ever free of that feeling of inadequacy and worry.

You must be tense, for you are to fight. You have a brief which is analysed into points of fact and law. You are determined to establish the essence of your case and to overwhelm the opposition. The very formalities of court procedure are calculated to foster impatience, particularly when it may take days to develop the simple point which you have determined to be the essence of this case. How then to restrain yourself? How then to maintain equilibrium, patience, calmness, courtesy? How then to do all these things with an attorney tugging at your gown, a client forever sending notes, an opponent bent on destroying your case and a judge who is so slow in responding to your efforts that your blood pressure could rise a swift 30 points with each question that he puts? There can be only one effect of this unless you have a firmly developed self-control. You will be tempted to elide, to omit, to improvise. Resist. That plan which has been days or weeks in maturing should be modified only when the development of the tactical situation makes such modification imperative. It should not be varied on hasty impulse, at a moment when the critical faculties are subordinated to the aggressive. Still less should it be altered because what may be a passing whim, whether of witness, judge or opponent, seems to render unsound what in chambers appeared to be incontrovertible. That you must be capable of adaptation and improvisation is not to be gainsaid. But before you adapt, modify or improvise be sure that your decision is sound and has been given all the consideration that the circumstances permit.

9.3 THE PROCEDURE OF TRIALS, GENERALLY

It is perhaps best to say a few words here for the very uninitiated about how a trial generally develops.

Assuming you are for the plaintiff, you might have had a hand in drafting the particulars and you might even have viewed the plea and considered whether to replicate or not. You will hopefully have drafted an advice on evidence along the lines outlined in chapter 7 above, trial-preparatory steps will have been taken as outlined in the advice and along the lines outlined in chapters 6 and 8 above and there will, in all probability, have been the odd skirmishing in the form of applications to compel this or that, attempts to resist being compelled, and so forth.

The matter has been set down for trial, you have consulted (perhaps more than once) with your witnesses lay and, if applicable, expert, also. You have conducted such inspections, whether of the scene or of the machinery or whatever, as the circumstances may have required. You have ensured that the evening before trial is spent not in last-minute consultation with witnesses, but in quiet and careful solitary contemplation of the battle on the morrow.

Procedures differ from Division to Division, and in what follows I shall conveniently assume that you are litigating in Johannesburg or Pretoria, where procedures are similar and in particular where one is not allocated to a particular judge for the day, but where rather there is a 'running roll' presided over by the Deputy Judge President of the particular Division (who will then allocate a judge to hear the matter).

You will meet your attorney and the client and whomever else you might think appropriate (perhaps one or more other witnesses who might be required on the first day) at, say, 09h15 at court or perhaps earlier elsewhere for a contemplative cup of coffee, knowing that the roll will be called at 09h30. By 09h30 you will be in your place at court. You will not speak unnecessarily to your opponent, lest your loose talk cost you your case.[5] To the extent that the two of you do speak, you will be the epitome of civility. The matter will be called. You will briefly tell the Deputy Judge President what the case is about, how long the matter is likely to run for, and that (hopefully) you are ready. Your opponent will (equally hopefully) confirm. A judge will (the hope continues) be available and allocated. You will all proceed in procession to his court. There you will take your place. If you have never had the pleasure of making the judge's acquaintance, you will ensure that you go together with your opponent to his chambers beforehand, to introduce yourself. Even if you have made his acquaintance, it is often a good idea for you and your opponent to go through (accompanied by attorneys or not as you judge best; there is something to be said for counsel going and attorney staying to keep the client's nerves calmed) as a courtesy. Having done so, you and your opponent will return to the court and await the judge's entrance.

The judge will get, and ask, no more than an opportunity to briefly glance through the pleadings so as to minimally acquaint himself with the issues; you will all wait in court for him to do that, and he will then make his appearance.

The matter will be called and, because you have the privilege of appearing for the plaintiff, you will rise first. You will record that you appear for the plaintiff. You will then sit down, and your opponent will rise and record his appearance for the defendant and sit down. You will wait for the judge to invite you to speak, whereupon you will again rise to open the plaintiff's case. You will have arranged with your attorney to ensure that whilst the witnesses on your side may be present in the course of the opening (usually a good idea: it will acquaint them with the atmosphere of court, and might help to calm the inevitable nerves), all lay witnesses other than the parties themselves should absent themselves thereafter. [6]

---

[5] See paragraph 8.1 above.

[6] See, as to the convention that factual witnesses should, if one or the other party so asks, remain outside the court after the opening address and may only remain in court after they have testified, *S v Moletsane* 1962 (2) SA 182 (E) at 182 and *S v Mphofu* 1993 (3) SA 864 (N) at 867. The court in

When you have finished your opening address, you will say that unless there is anything which His Lordship would like you to clarify, you propose calling your first witness, who will in all probability be the plaintiff.[7]

There is usually no call for counsel for the defendant to respond to your opening, but he may with the leave of the judge do so (briefly) if he judges this to be necessary. For example, he might feel that you have (no doubt quite innocently) misrepresented a point, or not made something sufficiently clear which ought to be made clear at this point, and so forth. It is most certainly not an opportunity for the defendant's counsel to counter your opening with his own. That is not permitted. Many judges follow the perhaps commendable habit of, at the end of your opening, asking your opponent whether he has anything which he wishes to add. Where that happens it is, again, only an invitation to add that which is *necessary*, and most certainly *not* an invitation to defendant's counsel to conduct his own opening.[8]

If the witness has an objection to taking the oath, explain this to the judge, so that the witness need not do so ('the next witness for the plaintiff, my Lord, is Mr Klitznit. Mr Klitznit has a religious objection to taking the oath, and will have to be admonished to tell the truth').

The plaintiff steps forward into the witness-box (which you will have shown him beforehand, again to assist with calming of his nerves) and is sworn or admonished. You lead the plaintiff. If your opponent objects in the course of your leading, you sit immediately he rises. Immediately he sits having made his objection, you rise. And so forth. When you have no more questions for the plaintiff, you say so, sit, and your opponent rises to cross-examine. When your opponent announces that he has no further questions and sits down, you wait to see whether the judge has any further questions. He might or might not. In either event, either after asking a few questions or without asking questions, the judge will enquire as to whether you wish to re-examine or not. You might, or you might not. See the chapter on re-examination.[9]

And so the process is repeated, witness after witness until, perhaps with some inner trepidation wondering whether you have done enough to prove your case, you close.[10] If the trepidation was justified and sometimes even if it was not, your opponent might apply for absolution.[11] If he does, you will oppose it, hopefully successfully. Your opponent might then close his case, hoping to argue that whilst your evidence might have been sufficient to escape absolution

---

Moletsane spoke of the 'usual and common practice, especially in criminal cases, also in civil trials, for one of the parties, if not both of them, to ask the presiding judicial officer to order the witnesses to leave the court until after they have given their evidence', saying that 'the object of this request is to prevent witnesses from hearing the evidence and therefore changing their evidence or trimming their evidence so as to agree with a prior witness'.

[7] See paragraph 9.7 below, as to the order of calling witnesses.
[8] See the chapter on the opening address in civil cases, chapter 10.
[9] Chapter 13.
[10] See the chapter on closing your case, chapter 14.
[11] See the chapter on applying for absolution, chapter 15.

at the close of your case, it was not sufficient to establish your case on a preponderance of probabilities. If so, it will be time for argument and because you commenced with the evidence you will commence with the argument, followed by your opponent answering and your (briefly) replying.[12] If on the other hand your opponent chooses to lead evidence, then of course the procedure outlined above is reversed, with his leading each of his witnesses, your cross-examining, and his re-examining, each of them in turn.[13]

Whilst it is permissible for your opponent representing the defendant to make an opening address before commencing with the leading of his evidence, it is only on the rare occasion that he will do so. The reason for that is obvious: if he has not made plain through his cross-examination of your witnesses what his case is, then he is unlikely to have done his job and if he has done his job, then he is unlikely to have to make an opening address (remember the point made above about everything having a purpose and being suited, and limited, to that purpose).

Once your opponent has led all of his witnesses, he closes his case, and you argue in the order in which witnesses were led, ie, you argue, your opponent argues and you respond.[14]

Judgment is usually reserved, hopefully for not too long, and hopefully when it is given, it is given in your favour — as simple as that. But it is of course within the cracks and stresses of 'that', that you will apply your technique to the object of winning your case.

9.4 THE ONUS AND THE DUTY TO BEGIN

Sometimes a good deal of tactical manoeuvring takes place in order to obtain the supposed advantage of forcing one's opponent to begin, or the right to lead rebutting evidence in terms of rules 39(13) and 39(14).

There is, I would think, no small advantage in being able to begin, even if this involves a recognition that the onus rests upon your client. One of the points to bear in mind is that the opposing party will have to put his version to your witnesses in cross-examination. There is usually a fair chance that, when the witnesses themselves give evidence, the version they give will differ from that put in cross-examination.[15]

---

[12] See the chapter on argument, chapter 16.

[13] What I have related, is the normal course of the normal trial. It can get a bit more complicated than that, where the plaintiff bears the burden on some issues and the defendant on others (with regard to which see Uniform Rules 39(13) and 39(14) and Magistrate's Court Rule 29(9)), or where there are more than two parties, such as multiple plaintiffs or defendants, or joined third parties. But I shall leave that type of complexity to books on civil procedure or evidence.

[14] See chapter 16, where the topic of argument is dealt with.

[15] A respected colleague maintains that one should speak not of the *right*, but of the *privilege*, to begin. He who begins gets to poison the judge's mind first, hopefully beyond redemption. R du Cann *The Art of the Advocate* at 65 describes the right to begin as 'a priceless and too often squandered asset'.

The disadvantage of being the first to lead evidence is that to some degree, the evidence which will be led by the other side is an unknown quantity. Your witnesses will enter the witness-box and, no doubt, be taken by surprise at some of the facts that are put to them (it may be a little cynical to say this, but the odds are that you yourself will be taken by even greater surprise when you find out what the witnesses have not told you). When one has heard the case for the opposition one has a better idea of how to lead one's own witnesses and also of what evidence will be required to meet the case made out.

The balance is not an easy one to strike and, in the majority of cases, the problem does not arise because the burden of proof is very clearly determined on the pleadings and there is little room for tactics.[16]

Note the provisions of rule 39(11), entitling either party to apply at the opening of the trial for a ruling on the onus of adducing evidence. This rule can be resorted to where there is material dispute between the parties.[17]

In regard to the calling of rebutting evidence, this is often a cumbersome procedure and, if the onus is on you on one or more of the issues, you being the plaintiff, it is as well to deal with all issues during the course of your case.[18] I also have the feeling that courts are not over-enthusiastic in regard to the invocation of rule 39(14) and the leading of rebutting evidence or evidence on issues where the onus is on the other party. A further disadvantage of this procedure is that you may have to call the same witnesses twice, once to deal with issues where the onus is on you, and once again to deal with issues where the onus is on the other party (usually the defendant). Very few witnesses enjoy one session of cross-examination, let alone two, and, in any event, there is nothing to stop your opponent from cross-examining the witnesses on the other issue when he has them in the witness-box for the first time.[19]

9.5 TAKING NOTES AND RECORDING THE PROCEEDINGS

Both for the purposes of cross-examination or argument you must know what has been said. Of course you will be keeping a note, everyone knows that.[20] The purpose is not only to know what has taken place; it is to provide a

---

[16] See, as to the determination of the burden of proof on the strength of the pleadings, *Mobil Oil Southern Africa (Pty) Ltd v Mechin* 1965 (2) SA 706 (A), *Nieuwoudt v Joubert* 1988 (3) SA 84 (SE), and *During v Boesak* 1990 (3) SA 661 (A).

[17] Rule 13(11) speaks of 'a ruling as to the party upon whom [the] onus [of adducing evidence] lies', and provides further that the ruling 'may thereafter be altered to prevent injustice'. Claassen J *Intramed (Pty) Ltd v Standard Bank of South Africa Limited* 2004 (6) SA 252 (W) at 255–7 held that the ruling referred to in the rule can relate not only to the duty to begin, but also to the burden of proof subject, of course, thereto that the ruling can be revisited, and is thus provisional only.

[18] Beware of the sting contained in rule 39(14) to the effect that a plaintiff who, before closing his case (perhaps inadvertently) called evidence on a point on which he does not bear the burden of proof 'shall not have the right to call any further evidence thereon'.

[19] See rule 39(15), which entitles the defendant to cross-examine 'any witness called at any stage by the plaintiff on any issue in dispute'.

[20] You will obviously be on your feet when leading a witness. This makes it difficult to record the witnesses' actual evidence. You will, though, have prepared the topics on which you intend leading

permanent stimulus to the memory. It is not only what *has* been said, but also *what you have to say about what has been said* that is important. So the function of your note is to record the points which have to be attacked in cross-examination or answered in argument.

Despite your careful preparation, because cross-examination has to take place *instanter,* you must evolve a system that will enable you to find the important points while you are on your feet. Some advocates make use of a mark in the margin of their notes, with or without a note of the question which they have in mind. Others divide the page into two columns, writing the evidence or argument on one side together with the question and comment in the adjoining column. Others yet, in recording evidence, trouble only to record the statement upon which they propose to cross-examine, leaving the remainder of the witness' remarks to their memory or to chance. Anyhow, there are three systems. Take your choice.

In the longer cases, or where technical experts will be giving explanations, you may indulge in the luxury of a running transcript.[21]

9.6 THE WITNESSES

The first problem in court is presented by the supporters. By this I do not mean those members of the public who have nothing better to do and who find court cheaper than a cinema. Since only a few civil cases have an element of sex it is very rare to have a gallery of those spectators whose delight it is to see that justice is done. By 'supporters' I mean the witnesses who will be called in due course and who, for want of direction to the contrary, like to sit in court until their turn comes to enter the witness-box. Almost without exception the interests of your case demand that opposing witnesses be kept out of court until they are to testify. It is arguable that they should not even hear counsel's opening address, although the usual procedure is to make the application for their exclusion only when the first witness is called.[22]

9.7 THE ORDER OF YOUR WITNESSES

It may happen that a case presents some nice points of timing, even in South Africa where one is not dealing with the psychology of a jury. Judges are less

---

the witness, and as he testifies you will simply tick the topics off one by one. Apart from following this method, the easiest way of recording the witnesses' evidence is to ask your attorney to take a note.

[21] Mechanical recording of proceedings is the order of the day in all South African courts. But if one requires the transcript, that has to be arranged and, usually, paid for. A running transcript is one that is made available in the course of the trial as it progresses (usually on the basis that each day's proceedings are transcribed overnight and made available the following day, at some expense). Where this is likely to be required, it is best to try to reach agreement between the parties beforehand on some sharing of expenditure, and on the principle that the shared costs will, in the final analysis, be recoverable as party and party costs (see the suggestion in paragraph 6.25 in chapter 6 above that, where appropriate, this be discussed at the pre-trial conference). Obtaining a running record can be expensive, but that expense is more than offset firstly by the advantages of all parties (judge and the parties) having the record ready to hand, and secondly by the fact that it ought to facilitate the speed of the matter in that the presiding judge need not take such detailed notes.

[22] See the authorities cited in fn 6 above.

susceptible to, but not entirely immune from, the subtle approach or the creation of 'atmosphere'. No doubt you will have taken this matter into account when you outlined the case, shaping that outline according to the known, or reputed, personality or whimsicalities of the judge. So far as has been considered prudent you have told him what your evidence would be. Now you lead your evidence and you must consider whether there is any merit in calling the witnesses in any particular order.

The litigant (plaintiff or defendant) should, for the reasons outlined in paragraph 9.6 above, generally be the first to testify in his cause, although by no means necessarily so.[23] That done, you have to decide on the best order of your witnesses after the plaintiff (or, if you are on the other side, defendant).

Some of the writers suggest that the 'best' witness be called first in order to achieve what in the advertising world would be called 'impact'. You must consider whether the 'impact' must be made at the outset or whether the 'best' witness should be kept until the end when he can tie up loose ends, atone for imperfections in his predecessors and leave the court with a final favourable impression of the case.

One cannot generalise on this tactical question but I would suggest that 'impact' is better than 'cover-up'. At the beginning of the case the judge's mind should be largely a blank canvass unaffected by *prima facie* impressions. If you act for the plaintiff you will be in the better position to take advantage of this, and it would be a folly to sacrifice your advantage with a 'low key' or 'piano' opening. Also, no matter how skilled your opponent, he will still be a little uncertain and will not yet have settled down to the atmosphere of the case. Cross-examination may be a little less effectual than it will be on the morrow when he may have had time to ask himself a few rhetorical questions on the significance of some of your witness' statements.

A second advantage is that, should your 'best' witness go well under cross-examination, he, to a certain extent, answers for later witnesses and takes the edge off their own ordeal. Remember, however, that there is no certainty about the best of witnesses and the old cliché 'gym form is not the same as ring form' is as aptly used in litigation as in fisticuffs. Since you cannot run your practice by fear alone you must merely keep the cliché for your own consolation when things go wrong.

The application of this suggestion should you choose to apply it, will be seriously hampered in those cases where you have a host of miscellaneous witnesses such as policemen, doctors, registrars of hospitals, secretaries of

---

[23] The reason why the litigant testifies first, is to avoid the imputation that he has tailored his evidence in order to suit that given by his witnesses (something less likely if his evidence precedes that of his other witnesses). But this is not to say that the rule is immutable. You might decide, for good reason, that your client should be preceded by one or more witnesses. If so, ensure that you have a good reason, consider in your opening address disclosing that reason, ensure that your client does not attend court until he testifies, and beware of the overwhelming likelihood that your opponent will suggest to your client in cross-examination that, even if he wasn't in court during the earlier evidence, he was kept up to date on it, and has trimmed his sails accordingly.

companies, accountants and so on. Not always can they be dispensed with at the pre-trial conference, for sometimes the other side wishes to establish a few facts for its own benefit through their evidence even if this is not seriously challenged. So, on the morning of the trial, you will be besieged by a crowd of gentlemen whose clamorous cry of 'when can you take me' is not without justification. You can be ruthless and let them wait while you present your case as you think it should be presented, or you can accommodate them, with the result that your 'best' witness finishes his evidence-in-chief just as the court adjourns for the day and your opponent goes home to indulge in that most dangerous of pastimes — thinking. It is temptingly easy to suggest that your client's interests come first and if the witnesses have to wait for a day or so that is their own misfortune. This one you must solve for yourself and exhibit your tactical skill in improvisation by filling in the time so as to avoid giving the opposition time for leisurely cogitation.[24]

If there are more issues than one in the case it may be advisable to present each issue, as far as possible, as a coherent whole. Sometimes a witness will cover more than one topic — he may deal with the whole lot — and he cannot pop into and out of the witness-box like the proverbial jack-rabbit.[25] With due allowance for this it certainly helps the court in forming a proper appreciation of your case if there is a systematic grouping of witnesses. It can do no harm to inform the court that your next witness is so-and-so, who will testify in regard to such-and-such topic. In this way you ensure that the court keeps track of the evidence. Too much is made of tactics. The object remains to place before the court a coherent story, and to present it in such a fashion as to make your client's case understandable to the judge or magistrate and, as far as possible, persuasive. By calling witnesses 'out of turn' you could very well create confusion. Once it has been decided to call a particular witness, allow him to testify where and when his evidence makes the most sense. The fact that it might also assist the opposition is one of the hazards of litigation. Moreover, by this method you will be less likely to omit to prove some minor but vital point. What the consequences of such an omission may be is not a constant but an unknown; the only constant is the personal reaction, yours, your attorney's or your client's. This will be discussed in the section dealing with the leading of witnesses.

[24] Of course, much of these difficulties can be avoided by careful planning. See paragraph 7.4.14 above and paragraph 7 of Appendix A. Witnesses who will not be called until the second or further days can be warned as to when they will likely be called, and kept on standby, rather than having to cool their heels outside the courtroom for hours or even days on end.

[25] Subject to the esoterics of rule 39(13) and (14), the evidence of a witness once called must, save with the leave of the court, be finished. It can happen that this dictate has to be departed from. A witness might, for good reason, only be readily available on a certain day and you might find yourself having to ask your opponent, and the court, to allow you to stand a witness down and interpose the evidence of this other witness. Provided that the reasons are good and that you furnish a full explanation, and in the absence of real prejudice, your opponent and the court ought to agree.

9.8 OBJECTIONS

In criminal cases it is the duty of the judge to exclude inadmissible evidence,[26] but in civil cases counsel is on his own. Sometimes there can be very little doubt that objection must be made, and made promptly at that. On other occasions it is difficult to weigh up the psychological balance between objection and inadmissible evidence. There can be little doubt that over-indulgence in objections creates an adverse impression in the mind of the judge, particularly in the case of trivial objections or those which are misconceived. Such conduct may create that subtle 'atmosphere', the existence of which has received judicial recognition time and time again in appeals on fact.

Thus, *think* before you object. Notwithstanding that your decision has to be taken in the wink of an eye, it must be based on two considerations: whether the objection is *technically good* and, if so, whether it is *necessary*. And in that same wink of the eye, having answered both questions in the affirmative, you need to formulate your objection so that you can object effectively when you stand up. By the same token, if either of these questions either is, or should be, answered in the negative, then of course you should refrain from objecting. An over-ruled objection does nothing for your confidence, enhances that of your opponent and, most importantly, might well impact adversely on the confidence your witness has in you (if your objection takes place in the course of cross-examination).

You may for example find that your opponent is putting leading questions to his witness during the evidence-in-chief. This may be due to inexperience, inadvertence or intent. The former two merely need to be rectified by a whispered remark such as 'Please don't lead'.[27] The last one is important, for it is usually an indication that the witness is not very reliable and that your opponent is keeping him on the right lines. Usually you will have no difficulty in determining the reason and, if you believe that leading questions are being put with intent, there can be no doubt that it is your right and duty to voice a formal objection.

---

[26] Cf *R v Perkins* 1920 AD 307 and *R v Noorbhai* 1945 AD 58. See also paragraph 19.10 in chapter 19, where this aspect is dealt with in more detail.

[27] A delightful anecdote which encapsulates the art of deciding whether and, if so, when to object and, indeed, how to do so, is related in Michael Gilbert *The Oxford Book of Legal Anecdotes* (Oxford University Press 1986) 149–150. The renowned American Supreme Court judge, Justice Felix Frankfurter, sat in on a sensational case being heard in London in 1934, *Youssoupoff v Metro Goldwyn Mayer Pictures Ltd* (reported at (1934) 50 TLR 581). Hastings KC led for the plaintiff, and Sir William Jowitt KC for the defendant. Frankfurter was struck by the differences between English and American procedure. Jowitt, he says, asked a series of irrelevant questions. In Frankfurter's words, 'Hastings sat there, nonchalantly . . . [eventually he] got up and instead of doing the conventional American thing, "your honour, I object, immaterial, irrelevant, impertinent, calling for a conclusion and opinion", and all the other stuff, he just got up. Before he said anything Jowitt said, "My Lord, it's the last question I'm putting to the witness." Hastings didn't even put his objections . . . He didn't even open his mouth. Jowitt saw, and knew what objection he was going to make, and he bent before the storm.'

Although objections to improper questions ought to be made before the answer has been given, this is of little value in the case of leading questions, because it is a poor witness who cannot respond to his cue. In other cases where there is in fact doubt as to the admissibility of evidence as a matter of law, it is permissible to raise the objection at any stage during the trial,[28] although counsel will often have to explain why he did not object at the time.

Evans *The Golden Rules of Advocacy* offers this useful advice in relation to objections:[29]

- Keep your objections to a minimum.
- Seem reluctant when you make them.

A good objection is one which is both technically sound and of some substance, ie, one which *needs* to be made and which, when made, is recorded briefly and succinctly.

As pointed out in paragraph 9.3 above, objections involve a jack-in-the-box routine: immediately the objecting counsel rises, the other counsel sits and immediately the former sits, the latter rises and so forth. Do not remain standing when your opponent rises to object.

To summarise:

- The purpose of objecting is to preclude the judge from hearing the evidence that is about to be tendered. So make certain firstly that you do not object before your opponent has finished asking his question (lest the objection be seen as premature), and secondly that you object before the witness furnishes the answer.
- Stand up, tell the judge that you are objecting. If necessary, look at your opponent to force him to sit, then return your gaze to the judge.
- Be clear and firm. State the ground or grounds of your objection (if necessary, repeating the objectionable question), and set out the legal position in regard to the ground.
- When you have made your objection, sit down, thereby allowing your opponent to rise to defend his question.
- You have the right to reply after your opponent has answered. Insist on that right.
- It might be that your opponent's answer explains the question, and is sufficient to overcome your objection. If so, withdraw the objection quickly and with good grace.
- Bear in mind that good objections can be devastating. If you have one, three or four good objections, your opponent might not only feel defeated, but look it.
- Not all objections will follow this pattern. Some will be so obvious that

---

[28] As in *Langham and Another NNO v Milne NO and Others* 1961 (1) SA 811 (N).
[29] K Evans *The Golden Rules of Advocacy* 60.

the judge will interject before you have addressed him, or that your opponent will concede even while you are in the act of rising.

• It might be appropriate for you to ask the court to require the witness to leave the courtroom and wait outside whilst you make the objection. This would be the case where you fear that your objection, and the debate around same, will simply serve to make the witness alive to a particular issue. In that event you rise, tell the court that you are making an objection (without at that stage furnishing any detail of the objection), and ask the judge to have the witness leave the courtroom whilst you make the objection. A competent judge ought immediately to appreciate that you have your reasons, and to acquiesce.

9.9 EXPECTING THE UNEXPECTED, AND PRESENTING YOUR CASE WITH INTEGRITY

One of the fascinating aspects of litigation is the occurrence of the unexpected. One need not be as cynical as an eminent senior counsel, from Johannesburg, who was briefed in a matter in Durban. On a mild afternoon when the day's work was over he and his junior, a Durban man, took a stroll along the Esplanade. Said senior counsel: 'Doesn't the Casino look impressive in the sunset?' Said his junior: 'That's not the Casino. We don't have one. That's the High Court.' Said the senior: 'I know!'

On a more serious level I would suggest that you may expect anything to happen. You can never relax, but withal you must never allow your feelings to show themselves. I have deliberately phrased the last sentence in the form of the feelings being the subject of the subordinate noun clause. It would have been simpler to have said: You must never show your feelings. If you are a good actor you may show your feelings — at the proper time and with the proper degree of expression and restraint. If you cannot act, do not try. You will only succeed in showing the artificiality which I am actually preaching in this context. Almost anybody can see through artificiality.

That is the negative side of presenting your case: to be prepared for the unexpected, to show no reaction whatsoever and to be able to meet the occasion with the speed of a boxer who is ducking a straight left and in return administering a smart jab in the solar plexus.

The other side calls for little in the way of additional positive suggestions. It would be well, however, to notice one or two decisions which should shape your professional conduct.

A case which arose in England in the sixties[30] affords an interesting illustration of the problems that can face counsel in the presentation of a case, and of how even senior counsel can err in his assessment of the factors which are to shape his tactics. It is easy, after the lapse of many years, to read the judgments in the Court of Appeal, and say that the tactical decision, for which

---

[30] *Meek v Fleming* [1961] 3 All ER 148 (CA).

senior counsel ultimately accepted full and sole responsibility, was so obviously erroneous that it is incomprehensible. What must be remembered is that problems of tactics are like clover-leaf highway intersections. From above the pattern is clearly discernible; when one is on them the path is not always apparent, and even if there are pointers one is usually travelling too fast to read these. Ask yourself then, what would you have done in the circumstances, but do not accept your own answer as being more than one which might reasonably be true.

On 5 November 1958 the plaintiff, a press photographer, was present in his professional capacity in Trafalgar Square, London, where a disorderly crowd was commemorating an event that might well have taken place some three hundred years previously. For some reason the defendant, a chief inspector of police, arrested the plaintiff and took him to a police station. On arrival at the police station, according to the allegations made by the plaintiff, he was assaulted by the defendant and other police officers. The defendant, for his part, sought in his pleadings to justify the arrest on the ground that the plaintiff was obstructing the police in the execution of their duties. (Reading between the lines one might infer that the plaintiff was getting in front of the police and taking photographs of the celebrators being hauled off to the police vehicles.) The assault was also denied, or, alternatively, said to be justifiable self-defence.

The plaintiff was convicted of obstructing the police and fined five pounds. In turn he sued the defendant for damages for assault and battery, trespass and false imprisonment. The matter was tried by a judge and jury, and the plaintiff's claim was dismissed after the jury had spent some four hours in deliberation.

The problem which had confronted counsel arose because, while the action was still pending, the defendant had appeared before a disciplinary board charged with offences involving the deception of a court of law. He was reduced in rank from chief inspector to station sergeant. This fact was known to his legal advisers. One can conceive how this event could have been used in cross-examination by counsel for the plaintiff, somewhat on the following lines, perhaps with more skill and subtlety, perhaps more elegantly or perhaps even more brutally:

> 'You say that the plaintiff is lying when he says that you assaulted him?'
> — 'Yes.'
> 'That he is trying to mislead the court?'
> — 'Yes.'
> 'Of course, you are not trying to mislead the court?'
> — 'No.'
> 'If it suited your purposes would you, in giving evidence, try to mislead a court?'

At this stage there would no doubt be an outburst from defendant's counsel and a flurry of objections to the 'form of the question'. Even if the question was disallowed as being hypothetical, opinion, or what have you, plaintiff's counsel would return to the attack in a simpler and more direct manner, on these lines:

> 'On 5 November 1958 you were chief inspector of police?'
> — 'Yes.'

'You are now merely a station sergeant?'
— 'Yes.'
'Why did this reduction in rank take place?'

It is not overstating the position to suggest that the defendant's credibility could have been completely destroyed in five minutes' cross-examination.

Precisely what considerations moved counsel do not appear from the report but the facts appear from a letter written by his instructing attorney:

> The learned Queen's Counsel instructed by me was throughout, as I believe you are aware, in full possession of all the facts relating to my client's past and present status and the reasons for the reduction in rank, and conducted the case in full knowledge of these facts in the manner he felt was consistent with his duty to his client and the court, and he is fully prepared to defend and justify his handling of the case at the proper time if called upon to do so.

What was decided by senior counsel was not to reveal to the court the facts referred to in the letter. Moreover, when the defendant entered the witness-box he was in civilian clothes and not in the uniform of a sergeant. When his evidence was led he was addressed, not by reference to his rank, but as 'Mr'. The defendant's evidence commenced with a brief summary of his career up to the time when he was chief inspector at the police station concerned, but made no reference to his reduction in rank. Logically this could be done quite simply because, the defendant having been established in office at the relevant police station and on the relevant date, he could next be led on the events of Guy Fawkes' night.

From the defendant's point of view, trouble came fairly soon in cross-examination with an innocuous question:

'You are a chief inspector, and you have been in the force, you told us, since 1938?'[31]

The answer was untrue, the defendant simply saying: 'Yes. That is true.'

The difficulty in which counsel found himself in trying to withhold information, rather than actively mislead, is illustrated in the judgment of Holroyd Pearce LJ at 152 of the report where he said:

> Nor was the defendant's counsel prepared to forgo the advantage to be derived from the status in the police force of his witness in general. The parties have, fortunately, in the interests of economy, been able to use the reports of the case in The Times newspaper. These show that in his opening speech for the defence, counsel stated that the jury had not yet had an opportunity of listening to persons against whom it was at times fashionable to make wild hysterical allegations, but who could not have reached their positions unless they had shown to those who controlled the Metropolitan Police a substantial degree of responsibility. They were not concerned here with some newcomer to the force who had only just finished his course, and was out on the street full of enthusiasm to arrest the first person he could. The Times report of the final speech of the defendant's counsel shows what he said in reference to the allegations of the plaintiff:

---

[31] See paragraph 12.5.7 in chapter 12, where the 'double-barrelled question' is discussed.

'That was un-English, and not what the jury would expect of any police officer
who had passed through the sieve, been trained and risen to any rank in the
Metropolitan Police'.

I accept from counsel that he was intending to refer to the generality of his seven or
eight witnesses, all of whom had attained some rank above that of constable.
Nevertheless, such references must inevitably have connoted in the minds of judge
and jury a reference to the status of the defendant, who was the leading person in the
case and held (in their erroneous belief) the highest rank of all the witnesses.

Notwithstanding that the fresh evidence (of the defendant's offence and
punishment) which the plaintiff wished to lead went only to credibility, the
Court of Appeal ordered a new trial.

It may well be that counsel's decision as to the manner of presenting his case
was influenced by the words of Denning LJ:[32]

The duty of counsel to his client in a civil case — or in defending an accused person
— is to make every honest endeavour to succeed. He must not, of course, knowingly
mislead the court, either on the facts or on the law, but, short of that, he may put such
matters in evidence or omit such others as in his discretion he thinks will be most to
the advantage of his client.

But, to quote again from the judgment of Holroyd Pearce LJ (at 154):

I appreciate that it is very hard at times for the advocate to see his path clearly between
failure in his duty to the court, and failure in his duty to his client. I accept that in the
present case the decision to conceal the facts was not made lightly, but after anxious
consideration. In my judgment the duty to the court was here unwarrantably
subordinated to the duty to the client. . . . It may well be that it was not so clear in
prospect as it is in retrospect how wide the web of deceit would be woven before the
verdict came to be given; but in the event it spread over all the evidence of the
defendant. It affected the summing-up of the learned judge, and it must have affected
the deliberations of the jury.

The other decision which bears mention is *Abraham v Jutsun*[33] I quote it
because almost every advocate will have the experience of being asked by his
more junior colleagues: 'should I take such-and-such a point? What do you
think of it?' It is only natural to desire not to be wrong. It is understandable that
younger counsel stand in awe of the judges, an awe not always shared by their
contemporaries. To appear in a crowded motion court and argue a point of law
amidst one's more learned colleagues can be a most unhappy experience. It is
for this reason that junior counsel is reluctant, even in civil matters, to take a
point unless he is sure that it is right. I say 'even in civil matters' because in
criminal matters there is no additional penalty of costs should the point be a bad
one. However, if you read judgments of the Supreme Court of Appeal where
the court is divided three against two and where, finally, adding the judges in
the court *a quo*, you get a 50/50 balance of opinion, you may begin to ask
yourself what is right and you may sympathise with senior counsel who

---

[32] In *Tombling v Universal Bulb Co Ltd* (1951) 67 TLR 289 at 297.
[33] [1963] 2 All ER 402 (CA).

confused Durban with Monte Carlo. In law it is not always possible to dogmatise and say that this must be correct and that must be incorrect.

Abraham v Jutsun, then, is a little vignette in the true Gilbertian tradition. On 9 January 1961 Mr Eric Jutsun incurred the displeasure of the law by allowing his brother Peter to drive a Ford motorcar without a licence or an insurance certificate. It is not clear whether the offence would have been more or less heinous had the car been a Jaguar XJ6. However, justice took its course and twelve months later the unrepentant Mr Jutsun found himself before the justices of the peace, being prosecuted by Mr Abraham, who was a superintendent of police, and defended by a solicitor, Mr Puntan. When the case for the prosecution was closed Mr Puntan took a point. He contended that the proceedings were out of time because of a statutory provision that such proceedings had to be *brought* within six months, and another statutory provision that the information had to be *laid* within six months. Mr Puntan argued that these words meant *brought* or *laid* before the court. After a whispered colloquy between the justices of the peace and their clerk, the point was upheld and Mr Jutsun left the court full of admiration, one imagines, for the fairness of the law. Mr Abraham, however, did not view the matter in the same light and appealed to the Divisional Court. Such was the celerity of English justice that the case came before the Divisional Court on 25 October 1962. The Divisional Court, on the facts, found that the proceedings were brought and the information laid within six months, although the case got to court only a year after the offences were committed.

Now, it seems that the Divisional Court looked askance at solicitors who took clever points and they promptly put a penalty on ingenuity by ordering Mr Puntan to pay fifteen guineas towards the costs of the prosecution.

The matter came before the Court of Appeal by way of a case stated at the instance of Mr Puntan and, in the course of setting aside the award of the Divisional Court, Lord Denning MR said at 403:

> But I think it only fair to the appellant to say that his evidence on affidavit, which is not challenged, makes it quite plain that he was not in the least degree guilty of any misconduct. The points which he took were fairly arguable. The one point on the word 'brought', had a good deal to be said for it. The other point on the word 'laid' had much less to be said for it; and the appellant said much less. The long delay gave merit to points which would otherwise appear unmeritorious. As it turned out, both points were bad points; but the appellant was not the judge of that. The magistrates had their clerk to advise them on the law. He was to advise them whether the points were good or bad. It was not for the advocate to do so. Appearing, as the appellant was, on behalf of an accused person, it was, as I understand it, his duty to take any point which he believed to be fairly arguable on behalf of his client. An advocate is not to usurp the province of the judge. He is not to determine what shall be the effect of legal argument. He is not guilty of misconduct simply because he takes a point which the tribunal holds to be bad. He only becomes guilty of misconduct if he is dishonest. That is, if he knowingly takes a bad point and thereby deceives the court.

I would suggest that there can be little doubt that these words would be as valid in South Africa as they are authoritative in England. There can equally be little doubt that they apply no less to civil than to criminal cases. There is, nevertheless, only the cautionary advice that in civil litigation the consequences of an imprudent point of approach may be very expensive for the unfortunate client who pays for his counsel's opinions and tactics. For this reason you will, no doubt, consider the contentiousness of points more narrowly than in criminal cases where the client usually has nothing to lose and everything to gain.

9.10 BE AS BRIEF AS YOU CAN AFFORD TO BE

An important additional consideration is brevity. Another is coherence. The third is vigilance. The fourth is determination. The judges welcome the first and second. You will benefit from the third. The client will appreciate the fourth. If you concentrate on the essence of your case you will find that your presentation will have these four desirable qualities and you will gain sufficient finesse and discretion to enable you to disregard the tempting bypaths that abound in litigation but usually end up nowhere in particular.

9.11 CONCENTRATE ON YOURSELF, AND YOUR CASE

I have been at pains to point out, from time to time, the need to always be aware of the fact that you have an opponent who is intent on destroying your case.

Thus the need for constant vigilance, asking yourself why your opponent has taken certain pre-trial steps, why your opponent is adopting a certain line of questioning, etc.

But allow me now to contradict all that I have just said.

Ultimately, if you win your case it will, and it must, be because of you, and the way you presented your case and dealt with your opponent's case, and not because of your opponent. You have prepared well. You have extracted the essence. Granted, it no doubt looks and smells different to the essence which your opponent has extracted but if you are to win, you must be right. If you have prepared properly and you have arrived at the considered decision that your essence hardly smells as sweet as that of your opponent, then you will have advised your attorney and your client accordingly, and the matter will hopefully have settled. If you find yourself in court, then your task is to win, and all of your efforts must be concentrated to that end, provided of course that you can do so within all the bounds of honour and propriety. Now it is up to you. When you rise to open, when you rise to lead or to cross-examine, be intent on yourself, and your case. Avoid constantly, if ever, looking across to your opponent to see what reaction your words have provoked. If you are cross-examining, the only persons to whom you should have reference should be yourself, the witness and the judge, in that order. Likewise if you are leading.

Whilst you must be vigilant in detecting all of the developments in the case, ultimately what you must concentrate upon is your case, not that of your opponent.

9.12 STAY CALM

A trial can be an exceedingly stressful event. All the more is this the case for counsel, on whose shoulders lie the burdens of planning, execution and the continual adjustments and split-second decisions involved in a trial.

Inculcate in yourself the habit of dealing with matters clinically and calmly.[34]

9.13 YOU ARE ON SHOW ALL THE TIME

This was alluded to in paragraph 9.9 above. Evans[35] makes these three very valid interrelated points. I heartily endorse all three:

- The human animal, he says, is more video than he is audio. What he means by this is that human beings (judges, witnesses) rely both on what they *hear* and on what they *see* and that, to the extent that one overrides the other, it is the latter.
- On p 33:

    The court is theatre. It should be professional theatre.

    By this he means that counsel should take care to ensure that his appearance, the way he acts when on his feet and the way he acts when in his chair listening to his opponent or to the witness, creates an impression which is consistent with the impression he wants to create in order to win his case. He adds on the same page that —

    you wouldn't want to be an advocate if there weren't something of an actor inside of you.

    I could not agree more.
- On p 12, of the fact that you are on show all the time, and not just when you are on your feet:

    You never appear surprised unless you intend to, you never appear troubled unless you intend to, and you must never seem to be expending effort unless you want to create that impression.

    Remember that the judge surveys all that is before him from his lofty eyrie. He sees the witness, he sees your opposing counsel and, if you are not on your feet, he sees you perhaps out of the corner of his eye. If your opponent scores a palpable hit in cross-examination, there is no good reason why you should reinforce that with a visible wince. Rather, if you can, affect a look of total unconcern, in the (probably vain) hope that the judge might, on reflection, share that unconcern.

9.14 USE GOOD VISUAL AIDS, IF THEY ARE RELEVANT

This ties in with the point made in paragraph 9.13 to the effect that the human animal is more video than he is audio.

---

[34] Munkman speaks at 167 of 'the ability to wait coolly and without undue alarm until [you are] able to appreciate the situation thoroughly'.

[35] *The Golden Rules of Advocacy* 8–33.

A judge will far more easily follow the evidence, and witnesses (particularly expert witnesses) will testify with far more force, if visual aids (maps, photographs, scale models, etc.) are used.

But, when using visual aids, remember the point made in paragraph 9.16 below re the record.

9.15 MATTERS OF DRESS

Jokes about the lawyer who wears polyester bearing the burden of proof aside,[36] what was said in paragraph 9.13 above about impact on the eye being, if anything, more important than that on the ear, and about the court as a form of theatre, applies equally to this topic: you are a professional, you are in court with a purpose, and that purpose is to bring all your abilities to bear in favour of your client. If you can *fill* the part, *dress* the part.

As Byles J is reported to have said to the late Lord Coleridge when the latter was at the bar:

> I always listen with little pleasure to the arguments of a counsel whose legs are encased in light grey trousers.[37]

9.16 REMEMBER THE RECORD

When a witness testifies that the vehicle was 'so far' away, or that the assailant went 'like this', demonstrating distance or action, all in court understand what is being portrayed. But the record doesn't show it.

Your job, in such instances, is to follow the question with a further question or questions in which you tease out what the witness showed, eg, you suggest that what the witness described was a distance of approximately three metres, say, or you describe the action to which the witness referred. It is then for the judge and your opponent to record whether your description for the record of what the witness portrayed was accurate or not.

9.17 MATTERS OF STYLE, ADDRESS AND MANNERS

Pointers regarding matters of style, address and manners are conveniently collected in Appendix B. This is not to suggest that they are unimportant. Quite the contrary, and the reader is directed to Appendix B before moving on to the next chapter.

---

[36] Evans *The Golden Rules of Advocacy* 11.
[37] Glissan *Cross-Examination — Practice and Procedure* 3.

CHAPTER 10

The Opening Address in Civil Cases

10.1 OPENING ADDRESSES, GENERALLY

What has been discussed up to now is the unspectacular, prosaic but highly important business of getting the case to court, to which I have added a few comments about appropriate technique in the conduct of cases in court generally. It is the trial itself, however, which must now take up our attention and, in particular, the first step in the trial itself, the opening address.

The trial commences usually with an opening address by the advocate for the plaintiff.[1]

The primary object of the address is to give the court an outline of what the case is all about. In practice it may be used with advantage for wider purposes. Remember, though, that you are not addressing a jury. Judges do not like being addressed as though they were jurors and will, not to put too fine a point on it, react a little brusquely to addresses of that type. Eloquence must be tempered in exposition but, with restraint, may still be used effectively in outlining the case.

To some extent the judge must be affected by the picture presented in the opening address. He will now have an idea of what the matter is about, and may even have formed a 'view', the firmness of that view varying with the judge as much as with the case. The whole of the subsequent proceedings may then, in the judicial mind, be devoted towards ascertaining whether that 'view' or the original picture is to be maintained. The difference is subtle but there is a vital distinction between a trial in order to establish which view is correct, and a trial in order to establish the correctness of the view. Whatever the initial reaction of the judge may be, he should not close his mind against either party; but the one who is fortunate to obtain the advantage of that initial reaction will find his task considerably lighter. Moreover, the Newtonian principle that every action produces an equal and opposite reaction can assuredly be relied upon to transfer the burden proportionately from one party to the shoulders of the other. Of course, you will read chapter 20 first, and you will adapt the advice that follows in these paragraphs in the light of the personality of the judge, and you may even utilise the proverbial pinch of salt in regard to the remarks in this paragraph.

It cannot be denied, if these observations are justified, that our system of legal procedure confers an advantage upon the litigant who has the right to begin. This is inevitable, because it is difficult to listen to two litigants simultaneously.

---

[1] See the discussion of the procedure of trials in paragraph 9.3 above.

It also explains why there is sometimes some jockeying for the right to begin, which, of course carries with it ordinarily the right of final reply.[2]

The technique of the outline can be conveniently stated firstly with reference to the purpose of the opening, and secondly in fourteen propositions together with an *obiter dictum*.

10.2   EVERYTHING YOU DO MUST HAVE A PURPOSE, AND THAT INCLUDES YOUR OPENING ADDRESS

This is something to which I have already referred.

All cases require opening addresses. That is not just a matter of form, it is because of the practical advantage of letting the judge know sufficient about the case to enable him to follow the evidence with understanding from the start. Some cases require the briefest of openings, others require lengthy openings.[3] At the start of your career, you are likely only to know the former. In either event, bearing in mind the purpose of the opening address as outlined in paragraph 10.1 above, determine what you need to cover in the opening address, and then cover it clearly and succinctly.

Bearing the *purpose* of an opening in mind, what you will want to cover in your opening address, as a minimum, is this:

•   Start by basically outlining what type of case it is.
•   Take the judge through the pleadings, as succinctly as you can, to show the judge what is in issue, and what is not.
•   Then give some idea of the evidence that will be led on the disputed issues, so that when the judge hears the evidence he will immediately be able to follow its relevance.
•   It might, or it might not, be necessary for you to deal with the burden of proof. In most cases, the incidence of the burden of proof is clear, and need not be (and, indeed, for that reason *should* not be) dealt with in the opening. But where it is unclear, or in dispute for all that it is clear, you should touch on the issue in your opening address.
•   Where there are documents (a bundle of documents, a bundle of plans and photographs, bundles of expert reports perhaps), at least explain to the judge what bundles there are, more or less what is contained in the bundles and, critically, whether there is or is not agreement as to the status of those documents and, if there is, what that agreement is.

---

[2] See the discussion of the onus and the duty to begin in paragraph 9.4 above.

[3] See rule 39(5), which prescribes that counsel for the plaintiff may 'briefly' outline the facts. Do not take that too literally. The opening address must be as brief, or as lengthy, as is necessary. Although the laudable motivation behind the word 'briefly' in rule 39(5) is apparent, it is a word that should not have been used. The judge has the power, the discretion and the ability to stop a prolix dissertation by counsel. Timorously I suggest that the word is an unfortunate manifestation of the tendency to prescribe by over-regulation. The same word is used in rule 39(7) which deals with the defendant's right to make a statement before the opening of his case. I do not, however, advocate undue verbosity.

This will enable the judge from the start to know whether reference can be had to the documents or not.

- You have extracted the essence of the case. You have planned how you are going to realise that essence. This is your first opportunity to subtly poison the judge's mind with that essence. But be careful. Do not overstate your case. Far better to *suggest* what the essence of the case might be through the language you use, than to spell it out in painstaking detail at this stage.
- Do not bore. Always remember the purpose of the opening. An opening must be only so long as is necessary to achieve that purpose.

Against that background, I proceed to the fourteen propositions.

10.3 FOURTEEN PROPOSITIONS

- Make sure that each fact is understood before you deal with the next. Remember that you have been preparing your case for days or weeks. The judge may have read the pleadings, or he may not. Think of the attorney who consults, gives you a five-minute summary of his file without pausing for breath and then asks you to confirm his opinion. The facts must be absorbed; then they must be understood. Cases must *start* on time; there should be no limitation at the other end. For want of appreciation of one simple fact by the judge a case may be lost.
- No matter how sorely you are tempted to assist the court — and your opponent — by providing a written summary of your opening address, resist the temptation. A quick reading of such a document may make no more than a superficial impression on the court. When the judge has to listen, to weigh up what you are saying and to make his own written summary you can be sure that he is in fact concentrating on the picture you are painting.
- Commence with the broadest possible statement of the case. This is as much for your own benefit as for that of the court. It may be dramatic enough to commence:

  'M'Lord, on 18 March 1965 certain discussions took place.'

  However, you are an advocate, not a journalist and, although the judge may know it if he has read the pleadings, I suggest that perspective is maintained if you open in words such as:

  'M'Lord this is an action for damages for breach of contract.

  This can be used as a subtle feeler because it will often provoke a response such as:

  'Mr Brown, I have read the pleadings and unless there is anything in particular to which you wish to draw my attention you may assume that I have a general idea of the issues between the parties.'

  This statement, of course, will justify you in proceeding to the next point which you need to cover in your opening, tailoring it to the fact that you can now be assured that the judge has at least read, if not necessarily understood, the pleadings.

- It is probably as well at this stage to identify for the court all of the various bundles which might be before it (paginated pleadings, one, two or more bundles of expert summaries, a bundle of trial documents, perhaps a bundle of photographs and plans, and so forth), dealing with the status of the documents in the bundles (eg, either identifying the rule 35(9) notice which was delivered without objection or referring the court to the passage or passages in the pre-trial minute where agreement was reached on the status of the documents, or even saying that although the documents have not yet been proven, they will be proven in the course of the evidence).

  It might, depending upon the circumstances, be that you would want to first simply identify the bundles, and then say that you will revert to these bundles after discussing the pleadings (as to which, see the next proposition).

- The next logical step is to discuss the issues in the pleadings. From your general statement the nature of the issues will have become apparent to the court and the first thing is to state with clarity what has been admitted and need not trouble the judge further. Thereafter, point by point, the disputed issues should be enumerated. There will be a tendency to launch into discussions as one or other issue is mentioned. Whether this should be done will depend on the circumstances, but, as a rule, it is better to adhere to your prepared plan than to obey spontaneous impulses. No serious damage should result from diversions, but there may be a loss of emphasis, or some loss of impact.

- As indicated above, you either will or will not deal with the incidence of the burden of proof, depending upon whether this is an issue of any importance, or not. It should, for example, be entirely unnecessary for you to tell the judge in a collision case that the plaintiff bears the burden of proving his *locus standi* and damage and negligence on the part of the defendant, whereas the defendant bears the burden of proving negligence on his plea of contributory negligence. These are obvious propositions which even a judge of the meanest stature should be fully aware of.

- You have now commenced 'Operation Essence'. The judge must be made to think as you want him to think. The case is no longer an action for damages for breach of contact, or an action for damages arising from a traffic accident. It will be something like this (to take a simple example):

  'M'Lord, in this multitude of allegations and denials, of contentions and explanations, it is my submission that the essence of the matter is whether a motorist, whose vehicle has broken down at night through no fault of his own, and who cannot move that vehicle off the roadway, is entitled to rely on its rear light and reflectors as an adequate warning to other motorists. This issue is naturally dependent upon the fact that we are concerned with a national road whose width is limited by the banks of a cutting . . .'

This aspect of the opening address cannot be over-emphasised. If your analysis of the matter is correct it will make a powerful impression on the judge whose mental processes thereafter will probably be more of the nature of testing the evidence against the essence rather than the reverse.[4]

One sometimes has the feeling, when outlining the case, that one is wasting time. This is because of the silence that prevails and because the attention of everyone in court is turned to the speaker. Nothing seems to be happening and, because the back-and-forth of ordinary conversation is missing, one feels that one is the club bore. Time, of course, should never be wasted. But time taken in presenting the case concisely, accurately and completely is never wasted. Any misapprehension caused by the omission to explain a point properly may cost time and money later when elucidation becomes necessary.

- Conduct your analysis in systematic order; avoid wandering aimlessly back and forth amongst the points and issues. Mention each in turn, discuss it as concisely as possible, link it logically with the next point and leave it.[5]
- In dealing with the issues, you should explain briefly what evidence is to be called on each aspect. *But do not go into detail.* After all you are *outlining* the case, not reading the statements of the witnesses.
- *Be conservative in your description of the evidence.*[6] It is neither necessary nor wise to say, for example:

[4] See, for a fine example of how counsel might as it were impose his essence upon the judge from the start of the case, the chapter entitled 'The case of the diamond syndicate' in Patrick Hastings KC's *Cases in Court* (William Heinemann Limited 1949). Hastings represented a small diamond miner against the forerunner of the De Beers Diamond Syndicate. The matter was to be heard by a jury. Opposing Hastings for the Syndicate was a large team which had mustered a frightening amount of documentation towards which the jurors were looking with trepidation. To Hastings' mind, the essence of the case was whether the valuations of the plaintiffs' diamonds by one Mr Otto Oppenheimer had been honestly made or not. As Hastings relates it at 139–140 he in his opening to the jury 'explained the story in a few words . . . and then told the jury that in the view I had put before them there was only one short point in the case which it would not take them more than a few minutes to understand and decide. Mr Oppenheimer's certificate was either honest or not. If it was not, they would have no difficulty in [arriving at a verdict for the plaintiff]. . . . I told the jury that they would have to listen to hours and possibly days of cross-examination upon matters which in my view would be absolutely irrelevant. At some time or another the defendants would have to explain Mr Oppenheimer's certificate. If they succeeded, they would win; if they failed, they would lose.' As it transpired, Oppenheimer was not called, and the Syndicate settled with the plaintiff for a handsome amount. Hastings was dealing with a jury, but he could just have well have been dealing with a judge. This is a near-perfect example of counsel's extracting the essence and placing it before the judge in the opening in such a way that it pervades the entire case.

[5] JL Glissan *Cross-Examination — Practice and Procedure* at 33 says, correctly, that the two essentials of a good opening are clarity and conciseness.

[6] I could not agree more with the advice of John Munkman *The Technique of Advocacy* at 150 that 'openings are pitched moderately, in case witnesses do not come up to expectation'. Glissan *Cross-Examination — Practice and Procedure* advises at 33 'not [to] open high. . . . That is, do not put in your opening facts that you are not in a position to prove', and adds at 35 that 'the more detail you give of a witnesses' expected evidence, the likelier it is that he will not agree with what you have [predicted] . . . when he comes to give that evidence.'

> 'The plaintiff will call a Mr Jones, who will say that while he was parked alongside the road and listening to the radio in his car he happened to look to his right. He will tell your Lordship/Ladyship that at this moment . . .'

This type of advance information not only gives your opponent additional time to consider his cross-examination, but if Mr Jones is as reliable as the average witness it may be assumed that the details of his narrative will not be the same as your outline. How much better to say:

> 'In order to establish his case on this point the plaintiff will call an eyewitness who will describe the collision. From his description the plaintiff will ask the court to find, etc . . .'

- If you intend to make admissions by all means do so. If you do not intend this then choose your words with caution. They probably will not be held against your client in any event,[7] but they may leave an indelible impression.

   One should never be in a hurry to make admissions upon contentious matters; the pleadings and the pre-trial conference should have established all the admissions that are necessary.
- Avoid humour. Litigation is a serious business. The result of every case is that someone gets hurt. It may be your client. He briefed you as counsel not as a comedian. The younger you are the less kindly will your humour be received by the court. Humour has its place in court — carefully used. Its function is not to provide paragraphs for the press, nor to enable you to establish your reputation as a punster or raconteur. It may be used — and the utmost skill is required — to soften the adverse mood of the judge or to turn aside the awkward question. In the opening address it is unnecessary and does not ring true.
- Avoid comment. The judge is not interested in your view. Your comment, moreover, may be belied by fact as the case progresses.
- *Avoid argument.* You will be arguing not a half a case, not a quarter of a case but no case at all. The object of your outline is to present the framework on which the facts will be filled in by the witnesses and cemented by argument.[8]

10.4 AN *OBITER DICTUM*

The *obiter dictum* is that the opening address may be used to achieve an ulterior purpose. An illustration will show what I mean. The action was one in the

---

[7] Carey J in *Standard Bank of SA Ltd v Minister of Bantu Education* 1966 (1) SA 229 (N) at 242H–243B and *Engel v Race Classification Appeal Board* 1967 (2) SA 298 (C) at 302B–E.

[8] This is not to say that there will not be cases in which you would be well advised to draw the court's attention at the outset (ie, in your opening address) to certain relevant decided cases. Where the case is going to turn on an interpretation of one or two decisions, or principles enunciated in a particular decision, it might be best to make all of this plain to the court at the outset, referring to the decisions so that the judge can study the cases at his ease in the course of the trial.

Natal Provincial Division against an insurance company, arising out of a collision between a motor cycle and a bicycle. The cyclist had been seriously injured, so seriously that he could give no evidence as to how the collision occurred. The motor cyclist had made a short statement to the police explaining how it happened. His version was that the cyclist suddenly turned across his path. This was recorded on the accident report form for all to see — including counsel for the plaintiff. There were no other witnesses. The plaintiff was confronted with a fair chance of suffering absolution from the instance. If his counsel could have the opportunity of cross-examining the 'insured driver' (the motor cyclist) there was very little doubt that there would be an apportionment of damages of at least 50/50. It was a case which had to be settled — or lost.

The problem was how to achieve a settlement without the direct approach, for there was no doubt in this case that any approach would accurately be interpreted as a sign of weakness. Senior counsel for the plaintiff set out to get what his client ought to be paid but might never get.

The technique adopted was to ignore the merits completely. Naturally counsel first made the broad statement suggested in the third proposition which is set out in the preceding discussion. From there on the object was to create the atmosphere that the actual dispute between the parties was in regard to medical matters and *quantum* rather than in regard to liability. The plaintiff's injuries were discussed in some detail. Reference was made to the opinions of the plaintiff's experts who included a neurologist and an ear, nose and throat specialist. There was some deliberation on the deafness with which the plaintiff had been left as a result of the accident. From this point it was only right and proper to tell the court what the medical witnesses for the defendant company had to say about the matter. Not without justification counsel suggested casually to the court that the differences of opinion between the two sets of experts were more apparent than real, and that, if the eminent gentlemen could get together, he was sure that they could arrive at consensus, so relieving his Lordship of the difficult task of giving judgment on medical matters. Learned senior counsel was to some extent artful in this suggestion in view of the circumstances that all the professional men, counsel, attorneys and doctors were from Johannesburg and he knew that the defendant had not incurred the expense of bringing its own witnesses to court — at that stage at any rate. As was expected, his Lordship welcomed the proposal with alacrity. The timing of the opening address had been perfect and it was shortly before the morning adjournment that the suggestion was put forth. What was more natural than to 'take the adjournment now and you can let me know when you are ready to go on'.

This manoeuvre gave the plaintiff a tactical advantage and what was more natural than that the defendant's difficulties should develop into discussions of a settlement. Counsel for the plaintiff was content not to overplay his hand. He manifested his spirit of sweet reasonableness by assuming as indisputable that the motor cyclist was negligent and by conceding a reasonably high apportionment of fault against the plaintiff. On this sound footing the medical evidence took its place as the prime issue for discussion and within an hour counsel were on their way to Durban for a much-needed recuperative holiday.

10.5 OPENING FOR THE DEFENDANT

When it comes to opening the case for the defendant, different considerations apply. The issues have been stated by counsel for the plaintiff. The relevant evidence has been led. The contentions of the defendant will have been put to the witnesses in cross-examination. Accordingly it will only be rarely that the defendant will find it necessary to take advantage of the right conferred by rule 39(7) and 'briefly outline the case'.[9] Where there is something in particular which has to be brought to the attention of the court then the right should be utilised. Otherwise not.

One example was to be found in a case where an application was made by shareholders in a company for an order in terms of s 103*ter* of the Companies Act 46 of 1926. The issues had been fully canvassed by counsel for the plaintiffs in opening the case on their behalf, evidence had been led, and the documents had been discussed in some detail. The defendant, whose case was that the transaction was perfectly *bona fide* and proper, proposed to call witnesses, and its objectives were stated by its counsel in the exercise of his right under rule 39(7). You will see from the following extracts how counsel placed before the court both the reasons for calling witnesses and also his contentions as to the 'essence' of the matter:

> This is one of the rare cases in which I think I ought to say something on behalf of the defendant before calling witnesses. I want to tell your Lordship at once that I propose to call Mr A, who was the chairman of the company until the takeover. He resigned, I think, on 6 October 1965. I am going to call Mr B, who was a director of the company at all material times. He was chairman of the defendant and he is now chairman of the company. I am going to do this because a great deal has been made in this case of the unfairness and inequity of the *scheme*. I hope your Lordship will not misinterpret me if I use the word scheme in a loose sense because, of course, legal argument will be addressed to your Lordship later as to the meaning of the word *scheme* in s 103*ter*.
>
> These were the two principal people concerned in the scheme, and I think it is right, in view of the criticism that has been uttered in this court and elsewhere about the fairness of the scheme, that these two gentlemen should go into the witness-box and tell your Lordship the reasons why this scheme was adopted; and that they should expose themselves to any legitimate questions which my learned friend may have to ask . . .
>
> Your Lordship is aware, of course, of the section in the Companies Act which provides that if a company goes into liquidation and if there has been fraudulent trading, the directors of the company themselves may be made personally liable for any losses that may be suffered. Your Lordship knows that the authorities, and I shall

---

[9]   See also the general discussion of the procedure of trials in paragraph 9.3.

cite them later, say that a company which is in insolvent circumstances ought not to incur further debts unless there is a reasonable prospect of repaying them.

This was the situation with which the company was confronted in 1965: This company had this enormous loan indebtedness, it was operating at a loss, and the problem that confronted the directors was, what to do about it . . .

They embarked upon the scheme — and again I say the word without prejudice, although it is, of course, perfectly clear, and it is common cause that all these arrangements were part of a single plan — and they entered into the agreement with the loan creditors in June 1965 for the reconstruction of the capital of the company. They did so with a view to the ultimate takeover . . .

It will be submitted that, when your Lordship comes to consider whether a scheme of this sort is fair or not, your Lordship will consider the matter from both sides: Your Lordship will, of course, consider the interests of the dissenting shareholders, but your Lordship will also consider whether the transferee company was getting an unconscionable bargain. And this was not the case in regard to this takeover bid.

This takeover bid was a rescue operation . . .

The *case for the defendant*, therefore, basically is that here was a scheme which was fair and honest and just: here was a scheme which was in fact advantageous to the shareholders, because if this scheme had not gone through, there would probably have had to be a liquidation and the shareholders would not have got a single cent.

I don't want, at this stage, to traverse the various questions of law — my learned friend has fairly outlined these on the pleadings: he has said something about the onus, he is going to make some contention about the onus of proof being upon us, and I shall contest that in due course, but I do accept the responsibility of putting into the witness-box the two chairmen of these two companies in order not only that they may explain to your Lordship the reasons for this scheme, but in order also that representatives of the dissatisfied shareholders may have an opportunity of asking these two gentlemen any questions . . .

CHAPTER 11

The Leading of Witnesses

11.1 INTRODUCTION

There are seven basic aspects to the topic of leading witnesses listed below. They will be discussed under nine different headings with the topics of non-leading questions and the leading of evidence-in-chief receiving more specific attention.

- Determining the issues.
- Determining the witnesses to call.
- Determining which witnesses not to call.
- Preparing for the leading of witnesses.
- Actually leading the evidence–in–chief.
- Volunteering an explanation.
- Making sure everything has been covered.

11.2 DETERMINING THE ISSUES

Your advice on evidence and your preparation for trial will have provided you with a list (physical or mental) of the issues pertinent to your case and of the witnesses required on each issue. The list, however, should not be regarded as final because you may find it necessary to call additional witnesses to rebut evidence led by the other side, or to meet suggestions made during the course of cross-examination of your own witnesses.

11.3 DETERMINING THE WITNESSES TO CALL

How many witnesses does one call, seeing that justice is not determined by a counting of heads?

Firstly, there must be evidence to establish every point which has to be proved as part of your case. If you call your witnesses in such a manner as to deal with each issue in turn,[1] you will minimise the risk of failing to prove a

---

[1] Which of course does not mean that you do not finish the evidence of a particular witness before going on to the next; as a general statement, the evidence of a witness should not be interrupted by the evidence of another, so that each witness must finish his or her evidence before the next is called. What I refer to, here, is the technique of so structuring your calling of the witnesses that, as a general statement, all of your witnesses on a particular point are called first, you then call your witnesses on the next point, and so on. There will obviously be overlap because some witnesses will have to testify on more than one point.

comparatively minor but essential point. The consequences of such an omission are illustrated in *Epstein v Arenstein and Another* in which Millin J said:[2]

> But [counsel for the applicant], in the event that I take this view of the evidence, desires to recall his decision to close his case and to lead further evidence, and the ground on which he does this is, as he tells me, that when he closed his case he was of the opinion that he had put all the necessary evidence before the court; but from the argument on the point now raised against him he now realizes that it is possible he has not established his case and he wishes to change his mind and tender more evidence. . . . As appears from the case of *Du Plessis v Ackermann* (1932 EDL 139), this is the kind of case in which the court ought not to allow the case to be reopened. The court ought to allow it where the evidence in possession of the party who intended to lead it was by inadvertence omitted, but it is quite a different position when the party, having the evidence at his disposal, deliberately elects not to put it before the court because he is of the opinion that it is not necessary. . .
>
> For these reasons I must refuse [the] . . . application to reopen the case and I hold that at the conclusion of his case he has not proved his allegations against the first respondent.
>
> As far as the first respondent is concerned the petition against him must be dismissed with costs.

Secondly, when you are satisfied that you are in a position to prove or rebut what is required for the purposes of your case you may turn your attention to deciding how many witnesses to call on each point. Do not make the mistake of regarding every witness as a further nail in the metaphorical coffin or case of the opposing party. One witness may contradict himself. Two can contradict each other. Three, it is said, is a crowd.

If you have one good witness on a point and two middling others, call the good one and keep the others in reserve. If your good witness turns out to be middling or worse, you are going to have to make a judgment call as to whether either or both of the middling witnesses will turn out to be good, or make middling look good by comparison.

Subject to these considerations, the courts will not readily fetter the discretion of counsel who calls four witnesses to prove a single point, when he might have called only three, or even possibly one.[3]

11.4 DETERMINING WHICH WITNESSES NOT TO CALL

The uncomplimentary remarks made in the preceding pages about the reliability of witnesses may or may not derive support from the manoeuvring

---

[2] 1942 WLD 52 at 61–3. See also *Stern and Ruskin NNO v Appleson* 1951 (3) SA 800 (W) at 809, *Guggenheim v Rosenbaum* (2) 1961 (4) SA 21 (W) at 28–9 and *Benjamin v Gurewitz* 1973 (1) SA 418 (A) 427–30.

[3] Compare *ITC (SA) Ltd v United Tobacco Co (South) Ltd* (2) 1955 (2) SA 29 (W) at 37.

that takes place in order to force the opposition to call somebody or other as a witness. The risk taken is to be found in the headnote in *Elgin Fireclays Ltd v Webb*:[4]

> It is true that if a party fails to place the evidence of a witness, who is available and able to elucidate the facts, before the trial court this failure leads naturally to the inference that he fears that such evidence will expose facts unfavourable to him. But the inference is only a proper one if the evidence is available and if it will elucidate the facts.

In *Webranchek v L K Jacobs & Co Ltd*,[5] when it was sought to make something of the plaintiff's failure to call a certain witness, Van der Heever JA remarked that the witness was available to both parties and had actually been waiting outside the court during the trial.

Whether an adverse inference should be drawn from a party's failure to call a witness is to be determined in the light of all the circumstances, including the incidence of the burden of proof, the availability or otherwise of the witness, whether the witness falls into the camp of the party against whom the inference is sought to be drawn, the likelihood or otherwise that the witness would indeed have been able to elucidate the facts, the strength or weakness of the opponent's case (an adverse inference should not readily be drawn against a party who fails to call evidence in refutation of a weak or an improbable case), and the strength or weakness of the case of the party against whom the inference is sought to be drawn.

One method of avoiding the drawing of any inference is to show that the witness cannot testify. This was done in *Gouws NO and Another v Montesse Township and Investment Corporation (Pty) Ltd and Another* (2)[6] by calling medical evidence that his memory had been impaired through old age, and by actually putting him in the witness-box. The subsequent objection that the expenses incurred in this procedure should not be allowed as part of the costs was overruled.

11.5 PREPARING FOR THE LEADING OF WITNESSES

The following are the essential requirements in your preparation for the leading of witnesses:[7]

- You must yourself have prepared properly, and understand your case. You must intimately know all the relevant facts of the case, you must have

---

[4] 1947 (4) SA 744 (A). See also *Webranchek v LK Jacobs & Co Ltd* 1948 (4) SA 671 (A) at 682, *Gleneagles Farm Dairy v Schoombee* 1949 (1) SA 830 (A) at 840–1, *Munster Estates (Pty) Ltd v Killarney Hills (Pty) Ltd* 1979 (1) SA 621 (A) at 624–5, *Ntsomi v Minister of Law and Order* 1990 (1) SA 512 (C) at 525, *Broude v McIntosh and Another* 1998 (3) SA 60 (SCA) at 76C–E, *Mkhatswa v Minister of Defence* 2000 (1) SA 1104 (SCA) at 1116G–H, *Nock v Road Accident Fund* [2000] 2 All SA 436 (W) at 445–7, and *Certain Underwriters of Lloyds of London v Harrison* 2004 (2) SA 446 (SCA) at 451.

[5] 1948 (4) SA 671 (A) at 682.

[6] 1964 (3) SA 609 (T).

[7] These are points that have been discussed in more detail in chapter 8.

extracted from those facts the essence of the case, and you must have thought through a plan as to how you are going to realise that essence through the witnesses.

- You must know the law relevant to your case. That means you must know what the issues are on which you intend calling evidence, and what evidence is and is not admissible on those issues. A simple example of the latter which comes to mind is calling a witness on the interpretation of a clause in a contract. Such evidence is, save perhaps in certain esoteric circumstances such as where technical terms bear a particular meaning in a particular trade, inadmissible.[8]

- You must, as discussed in chapter 8, have consulted with each witness whom you intend calling, so that you and the witness know more or less, if not entirely, what to expect from one another.

- Where the location is important (a collision scene; an operating theatre and its environs; a building site, even if what was once a building site is now a completed building, etc), you must have been there (preferably with the relevant witnesses) so that you can, at all material times, see points and places in your mind's eye.

- Where visual aids (photographs, scale plans, models etc) would be useful to elucidate the witness's evidence, you should have seen to it that these are available, that rule 36(10) notice thereof was, where necessary, given and that you and the witness are both familiar with the photographs, plan, model etc.

- You must have a plan for the specific witness in mind. You must know exactly what you want to lead the witness on, including what aspects of the witness's evidence are more important, requiring more attention, than others.

- Draw a list of the witnesses you intend to call, enumerating the topics on which each particular witness is going to testify with, if appropriate, complete references after each topic to the page or pages of the court bundle to which you are going to refer each witness.

11.6 NON–LEADING QUESTIONS

The object of leading evidence-in-chief is to prove the various elements of your case. Should you fail to do this it is only infrequently that the opposition will do it for you in cross-examination.

Your problem (and, surprisingly enough, serious problems can arise on so simple a proposition) is that you cannot put leading questions, while the witness often proves quite incapable of understanding words of one syllable unless that syllable is to be 'yes' or 'no'. The reason for the difficulty is one

---

[8] Harms DP in para [39] of *KPMG Chartered Accountants v Securefin Limited* 2009 (4) SA 399 (SCA): 'Interpretation is a matter of law and not of fact and, accordingly, interpretation is a matter for the court and not for witnesses . . .'

which cannot be properly appreciated by those of us who spend day after day in court. The average citizen regards a court with a proper degree of awe, and regards the witness-box as an ordeal. Those mental faculties which come into play in ordinary conversation or even in argument are submerged in the pervading sense of unreality and of fear. I doubt whether more than a few witnesses are able to rid themselves of a feeling of self-consciousness and of awareness of strange surroundings so that they can devote their whole attention to the questioning.

Because failure in the leading of evidence has more irreversible consequences than failure in cross-examination it follows that skill in the leading of evidence-in-chief is certainly no less important than skill in cross-examination. Because of the limitations imposed by the law on the manner in which evidence-in-chief may be led it follows that the skill required is certainly no less difficult to acquire.

How do you frame a non-leading question, as opposed to a leading one? The start of the answer lies in the distinction between the two. A leading question is one which either suggests the answer, or assumes a fact not already established. A non-leading question is, by definition, the opposite. Very useful guidelines to pupil barristers provided by the Continuing Education Committee of Grays Inn (one of the four English Inns of Court[9]) suggest the following methodology, which I wholeheartedly support. Firstly, that almost all questions which begin with 'Do/Did' or 'Is/Was/Were' will inevitably be leading questions, whereas questions beginning with words like 'What/When/How/Where/Why' will invariably not be; secondly that one should think of the answer one wants from the witness and then ask the simple question necessary to get that answer; and thirdly that one should 'piggy-back' one's questions, ie, sequence each of one's questions on the basis of the preceding answer. For example, a first question might be *where* the witness was at a particular time, the second might be *how* he knows that this was the time, the third might relate to *why he was there at the time*, the fourth *what* he then saw, the fifth to *what* his response was, a sixth to *why* that was his response — and so forth.

11.7 THE KEYS TO GOOD EVIDENCE-IN-CHIEF

The keys to good evidence-in-chief are the following:

- You must yourself have a plan. You must know *what* you want out of the witness, you must know *why* you want it out of the witness, and you must have a good idea of *how* you propose going about getting it out of the witness.
- Start by asking leading questions on the uncontroversial issues (introducing the witness, and dealing with background issues that cannot

---

[9] Gratitude is expressed to the Continuing Education Committee of Grays Inn for their kind permission to utilise their material in this book.

be controversial, such as common cause issues), before moving on to the controversial topics, on which you ask non-leading questions.

- See your task as that of painting a clear and understandable picture for the judge, using your questions and the witness's answers as your brush-strokes. Start by painting in the witness, and a background. Then, when you get to the controversial issues, paint the picture in far more detail, but see that detail against the background that you have already painted.

- As a general statement, follow a logical and, where that is appropriate, a chronological, progression, dealing with each topic in an orderly fashion before moving on to the next. This makes it easier for the judge to follow the evidence and, in fact, it makes it easier for the witness to follow your questions as he comes to understand the logic of your progression.[10]

- Because you have prepared well and have extracted the essence of the case from all of the facts, you will know which facts are particularly important, which are merely important, and which are unimportant. Your leading of the witness will follow a consonant temper, in which the amount of time spent on a subject is largely commensurate with the degree of importance or unimportance of the subject, relatively speeding through that which is relatively unimportant, slowing down as one gets to the important subjects, and then slowing fully on the very important.

    There is, in this regard, nothing wrong with your telling the witness (and thus also the court) that you are now going to move on to a different topic, and what that topic is. Essentially, you are holding a somewhat formal conversation in the presence of an audience of whom only one member of that audience (the judge) is particularly important.

- I can think of no better description of evidence-in-chief than that given in the aforementioned Gray's Inn guidelines:

    > There tends to be a great mystique about examination-in-chief. It is essentially simple. It is a private, somewhat formalised, conversation between counsel and the witness being conducted for a public audience.

- You will where appropriate be careful when dealing with something that happened quickly, such as an accident, to convey in the evidence that although the witness observed things, these observations were the observations of seconds, or milliseconds.

- You will, where the witness is unable to accurately measure a time or a distance (as will usually be the case with collisions, for example: a witness can say it happened 'very quickly', but not how many seconds or milliseconds it took, and he can say that the other vehicle was 'very close' when he first saw it and more or less where it was and where he thinks he

---

[10] Michael Hyam *Advocacy Skills* 4 ed 73 says that dealing with each topic completely and in an orderly fashion before passing onto the next topic in evidence-in-chief 'is an important element in good examination [firstly because it is easier for the witness, secondly because it is easy for the trier of fact] . . . A third reason is a psychological one; when a topic is dealt with fully there is a feeling that it is convincing because it is complete.'

was when they first saw one another, but to pretend to be able to accurately estimate the distance would usually be fallacious),[11] have ensured in your preparation of the witness that he or she knows that furnishing accurate estimations of time or distance is virtually impossible.

11.8 GENERAL COMMENTS ON THE LEADING OF EVIDENCE

See Appendix C for examples of the leading of evidence of both lay and expert witnesses.

The leading of evidence is a play with only two characters in it — counsel and witness. Occasionally a third character, the judge, will intervene, but if the play is properly acted and the judge possessed of a proper degree of patience he will seldom have lines to speak. Like a play, the evidence of the witness is designed to tell a story. Like some plays, there will be a 'lead' and a supporting cast. In fact, if the analogy may be pressed a little further, the play should be of the nature of a monologue, with counsel in the prompt box. This is how the play should appear to the audience — which is the court.[12]

As between yourself and your witness, your roles differ. You may well play the lead, or, to put it more conservatively, you must be the player who provides the right cue at the right time.

Thus your manner to the witness must be a confident one, for confidence inspires self-reliance. No matter whom he thinks he is or who you think he is, you must display courtesy and respect, for courtesy and respect inspire co-operation. Your diction must be clear, for clear speaking inspires clear response. Most important of all is clarity of phraseology. An ambiguous question may well bring out the wrong answer. You can be certain that of the three people who have to consider your question, namely judge, witness and opponent, at least one will misunderstand it. Your opponent matters not, for his misunderstanding may damage his case or embarrass himself. If the judge misunderstands it may damage your case and will embarrass you. If the witness misunderstands it may ruin your case and will embarrass him. An embarrassed witness is not a good witness. Not only, then, must your phraseology be precise, but you should make it a habit never to invite a response on more than one point in any one question. It is true that pressure of work when dealing with a long list of undefended divorce cases leads to a double-barrelled (indeed, in this example, quintuple-barrelled) question something like this:

---

[11] See the point made by Ogilvie Thompson AJ (as he then was) in *Van der Westhuizen v SA Liberal Insurance Co Ltd* 1949 (3) SA 160 (C) at 168 that the mathematical calculations which one so often sees in collision cases 'so vitally depend on exact positions and speeds, whereas in truth these latter are merely estimates almost invariably made under circumstances wholly unfavourable to accuracy'. And see *Lambrechts v African Guarantee* 1955 (3) SA 459 (A) at 465F, *Johannes v SWA Transport* 1994 (1) SA 200 (NmHC), *Tshikomba v Mutual & Federal Insurance Co Ltd* 1995 (2) SA 124 (T) at 129, and *Nock v Road Accident Fund* [2000] 2 All SA 436 (W) at 442–3.

[12] As to undue participation in the play by the court see, for example, *Hamman v Moolman* 1968 (4) SA 340 (A), *Solomon and Another NNO v De Waal* 1972 (1) SA 575 (A), and *S v Rall* 1982 (1) SA 828 (A) at 832C–F.

'You are the plaintiff in the action and you married your husband the defendant in Johannesburg on 14 August 2006 with antenuptial contract; is this a certified copy of your marriage certificate?'

Counsel then pauses for breath and nine out of ten witnesses look as though they are quite overcome with this torrent of sound. Of course, in undefended matrimonial cases it doesn't matter very much and, admittedly, the example is an extreme one. Nevertheless it shows what can happen.

Virtually all witnesses will be nervous to greater or lesser extent, particularly at the commencement of their evidence and whether they betray this nervousness or not. For the purposes of evidence-in-chief, therefore, it is wise to assume that every witness needs a little time to forget his surroundings and to get into the mood of the case. To that end, it is good to commence with a few innocuous preliminary questions in which you as it were introduce the witness to the audience. This you not only can, but should, do by way of leading questions (because the topic will by its nature be uncontroversial), put calmly and confidently. The judge, however, very soon tires of listening to innocuous questions so be careful not to overdo the introduction.

There will usually be no objection to the eliciting of non-contentious matter by suggesting the answer to the witness through leading questions, but it is wiser to inform the court and your opponent that this method is being adopted. It should be made clear that it is not your intention to transgress in regard to matters in fact in issue between the parties.

From this introduction, and once you have a sense that the witness is more at his ease, you proceed towards establishing the surrounding circumstances in which the witness must testify. Not only does this actually pertain to the issue, but it has two valuable effects: the court is given the broad picture in which to appreciate the evidence; the witness's attention is directed from the present surroundings and taken back to the events themselves. The witness is reminded of the details comprising the broad picture and, by process of association, can more readily and easily recall the minutiae in regard to which he must testify. So, wherever possible, tread warily until you have established communion with the witness and he or she has adjusted himself to what I have already, and rightly, described as an ordeal.

I have already remarked on the need for precision in framing the questions in order to avoid the misunderstandings which arise on the slightest provocation. Without disrespect to the court in which you are appearing you should, as has been pointed out already,[13] keep one eye on the court of appeal by keeping an eye on the record. You should not question a witness in the following manner:

'Mr Klitznit, when you saw this letter, what did you do?' (shows witness letter).

The question should be something like this:

---

[13] See paragraph 9.16 above, where it was pointed out that you should always ensure that the purport of both your questions and the answers are apparent from the record.

'Mr Klitznit, when you saw the letter of 15 July 1967, Exhibit 21, what did you do?'

It is suggested in one of the books on this topic that, in leading the evidence of a witness-in-chief, the advocate should endeavour to create an atmosphere of naturalness and spontaneity. The witness should appear to be telling a story, not giving evidence in answer to carefully prepared questions. As a contribution towards this atmosphere it was suggested that the advocate should not hold his brief in his hands, nor appear to be reading from a document on which is already written the dress-rehearsal version of the evidence. Instead counsel should stand naturally and, as it were, in conversation with the witness, obtaining from him or her a living presentation of the event concerned. Whether you care to adopt this advice is up to you. In many cases it will undoubtedly be effective. There are, however, two qualifications: Can you depend upon yourself? How far does it impress the judge?

Yourself: you must select the right witness, you must be sure that you do not omit a material detail from the evidence and you must be able to follow the logical order of the evidence. The judge, whatever his idiosyncrasies, is not a bucolic jury; he knows you have a statement and knows there has been a consultation. Let it not be thought that I decry the technique suggested. All that I say is that it must be used carefully. You will find, for example, that you may invite the witness, after you have led him up to the very *res gesta*, to tell the court in his own words what then took place. Sometimes he will do this, and do it well. Mostly, however, you find that human memory being what it is, he will omit something which is significant which will have to be established in any event. You will have to intervene and prod his recollection. By the time the two of you have finished, any appearance of naturalness will effectively have been destroyed and, contrary to your plans, the witness will create a poor impression in the mind of the judge. It is usually safer to remain in control and to be as unobtrusive as possible in guiding the evidence-in-chief.

Sometimes a witness will give an answer that causes counsel to wonder how much the other side have paid this man. It is of considerable importance in the majority of cases that counsel should reflect no emotion whatsoever. The probable cause of the bombshell is that the witness in fact did not understand the question. The most improbable cause is that he has been paid by the other side. Any abnormal behaviour by counsel will convince the opposition that something disastrous has happened (that is if they were not aware of it already). It will make the judge wonder whether any credence should be given to the witness's evidence. Worst of all it will destroy the delicately balanced equilibrium of the witness himself. You must ask yourself *why* the witness gave the answer which he did. And you must think fast, deciding whether the error should be dealt with at once or whether it should be handled a little later when the topic is approached afresh from a different angle so that a different light will illuminate the points and make the witness see them as he did not see them before. Whatever your decision in this regard may be, it is usually essential that you clarify the matter before the next adjournment of the court. If you do not, the impression will be created that someone (you) has talked to the witness; or else someone (your client) will in fact have talked to the witness, and between them they can be relied upon to make confusion worse confounded. If you believe that you know the reason for the mistake and that it can be rectified then approach the matter again, perhaps with different phraseology, so that the correction can be established. When you have acquired the necessary skill you will be able to do this, and do it in such a manner that it is apparent that the previous answer was due to a misconception by the witness.

When the topic of cross-examination is being discussed reference will be made to the 'sixty-four dollar question' and the leading question. For the purpose of evidence-in-chief the two are combined into the exhortation: your case may depend on the 'direct question'. Let me give an example, in some detail because it can also be regarded as a study in tactics.

The plaintiff was a woman who had an artificial leg. She had occasion to visit her doctor who had his consulting rooms on the upper floor of a building in town. The plaintiff went up in the lift, and later, after her consultation, called the lift in order to go down again. The lift, it may be remarked, was an automatic one but of somewhat dubious vintage. When the lift arrived the plaintiff opened the outer door intending to enter the car. However, she fell and was later rescued from the floor of the lift, her legs having prevented the doors from closing again. She sued the building-owner for damages, her case being that, to his knowledge, the lift was dangerous and that it would stop out of alignment with the floor of the hallway, the difference in levels varying, according to the evidence later given, from half an inch to two inches.

The defendant denied negligence and, as part of its case, proposed to prove that the lift was regularly serviced, maintained and overhauled by the local representatives of the manufacturers.

The first witness for the plaintiff was the doctor whom she had consulted. He described how the doors of the lift opened, how in his experience the lift would come to a standstill with its floor out of alignment with the floor outside, and how he had discussed this matter with the building-owner. He also stated that opening the outside door of the lift was difficult, and that the light in the lift was poor. Perhaps this evidence was led to explain why the plaintiff did not immediately notice the alleged difference in levels.

The plaintiff herself testified and the following is how her evidence proceeded:

> 'Now, was that difficult to pull it to one side?'
> — 'When I pulled the gate, I had to put my stick and my bag in this hand.'
> 'Which hand?'
> — 'In my left hand.'
> 'Where do you normally keep your stick?'
> — 'In my right hand.'
> 'In your right hand?'
> — 'In my right hand, because you couldn't sort of do it otherwise.'

'Now, let's take it stage by stage. You walked to the lift with your stick in your right hand?'

— 'Yes.'

'And then opened the door with the right hand?'

— 'That's right. I opened the door, pulled it back and the next thing I was on the ground. That's all I could remember.'

'Did you enter the lift at all?'

— 'I couldn't say if I entered it or not, I opened the door, as far as I remember.'

'Well, first of all, do you remember opening the outside door?'

— 'Yes, I remember pulling the door.'

'The inside door, does that work automatically?'

— 'It is an automatic door.'

'So do you remember whether that inside door automatically opened, when you opened the outside door?'

— 'Well, it must have, otherwise I couldn't have got in the lift.'

'And do you remember entering the lift?'

— 'No, I just remember falling on the floor.'

'Can you describe how you fell?'

— 'Well, I don't know. I went right across, flat down, I can't describe it.'.

'Flat across?'

— 'Yes, it was very sudden, I couldn't describe it.'

'Yes, then what happened? Do you remember anything more?'

— 'I lay on the floor and thought to myself whether the lift goes up or down, I didn't quite know, and then I heard footsteps.'

To anticipate, this evidence was insufficient to connect the plaintiff's fall with any negligence on the part of the defendant, and the plaintiff lost her case. It is suggested that when the plaintiff did not respond to the question '*Can you describe how you fell?*' counsel should have appreciated his dangerous position. He should have asked the direct question: '*What made you fall?*' I doubt whether any witness would have failed to respond: '*My foot caught against the floor of the lift.*'

The tactical exercise, although not relevant to this particular context, might well be noticed now instead of later having to repeat the facts of the case. It so happened that counsel for the defendant was able to spend the next half-hour cross-examining on medical matters and the lunch adjournment was taken without cross-examination being concluded. Moreover, cross-examining counsel had been very careful not to ask any silly questions such as: 'Did you look to see whether it was safe before you entered the lift?' In fact he had not reached the cause of the fall at all and deliberately so.

Over lunch counsel for the defendant conferred earnestly with his instructing attorney and a decision was reached in the following terms:

No cross-examination on the merits. Apply for absolution.

If absolution is refused then consider seriously abandoning the prepared defence case and stake everything on the strongly-held view that the plaintiff had really proved nothing.

In fact everything went as planned. Absolution was sought and refused. The attitude of the judge made it reasonably clear that his view of the case coincided with counsel's. So when absolution was refused the defendant closed his case without leading evidence. Counsel for the defendant, some months later, had the professional pleasure of hearing the judgment on appeal, when it was said that he had 'prudently refrained from asking any questions on this point'.

What the result would have been if counsel for the plaintiff had asked the direct question is another matter.

Also I invite you to consider the whole passage which I have quoted and, as an exercise, criticise each question in the light of what counsel was really trying to prove. Look at the 'leading' questions and especially consider whether the whole sequence of questions was the flawless examination-in-chief that would paint a picture to the court. In this case the picture should have been three-dimensional, even if not in colour.

There is no doubt, of course, that the need, or desire, to avoid leading questions causes even experienced counsel to become unnecessarily subtle, and it is not every witness who is so attuned to the case that he can respond to subtleties. In the example just quoted one can see that it would have been useless to rely on the general question: 'Now tell the court in your own words what happened after you left the doctor's rooms.' It became apparent that there had to be a 'direct question' on every step (literal and metaphorical) in the plaintiff's progress. Let me hasten to spare you the trouble of looking for judicial or other authority on the 'direct question'. I do not think that you will find it. By 'direct question' I mean one that draws the attention of the witness to the precise point on which an answer is required so that he has that point pertinently in mind, but one that does not actually suggest the answer. Now, in the case quoted, the witness had proved that she fell. The very proper, but too subtle, invitation to describe her fall was misunderstood or unavailing. Her case was based on negligence. Negligence included the difference in floor levels and a fall in consequence. She had to be told that her evidence must deal with this point. Counsel, however, had to avoid suggestion. So the 'direct question' which focused her attention on the cause of the fall or on to the floor of the lift was the proper technique to employ.

Nobody would attempt to give a list of direct questions; indeed, one is fortunate to be able to point to a single one from the mass of trial records that will never again see the light of day and in which many valuable lessons in blunders and technique lie buried.

It would seem very probable that with the average run of witnesses, evidence-in-chief should consist of 'direct questions' on every point in issue. Remember your consultation, where perhaps you took down a statement yourself or made notes on a statement taken by somebody else. How often did you have to put two or three questions and ask for two or three explanations before you wrote a particular sentence? When the witness gets into the witness-box this cannot be done. You know the answers; use them as the framework for your questions.

The next suggestion is that you should avoid providing material for cross-examination.

The object of leading evidence is to establish facts. The facts which you should prove are those which are material to your case, and nothing more. It may well be over-simplification to the degree of distortion to say that the witness's motives and reasons have nothing to do with the case, but in general the statement is correct. If the witness has to testify, say, that the public has been in the habit of using a certain roadway for sufficient years to establish a right of way, it has nothing to do with the case that he remembers use 32 years ago because 'that was the year when Fly-by-Night won the Durban July'. The opposing attorney sends his candidate attorney to make a quick telephone call and finds out that this equestrian achievement actually took place six years later. That is the end of the mnemonic, probably of the witness and possibly of the case. Perhaps the example is a little *outré* and could be met with the objection that counsel who led the evidence would certainly have asked the same question in consultation and would have taken steps to ensure verification of the witness's claim. Conceding all this, I ask you to look on this example as an analogy by way of a *reductio ad absurdum*. It is meant to found the dogmatic statement that any unessential matter in evidence-in-chief serves only to provide material for cross-examination. It is bad enough for a witness to be tested on matters of moment; there is no need to add to this ordeal by having the witness called upon to justify irrelevancies.

11.9 THE VOLUNTEERED EXPLANATION

An extension of the topic just discussed, avoiding providing material for cross-examination, is what may elegantly be referred to as the volunteered explanation. It will sometimes happen that you have to call a witness — often your own client — who, in dealing with the point in issue, has to disclose to the court some conduct on his part which, if not actually meriting the raised eyebrow, militates against his case in one way or another. The problem is whether to offer the excuse in evidence-in-chief or to leave it as a topic for cross-examination.

The answer, as with so much else, is that it depends. It depends on the conduct in question, your estimation of whether your opponent or the judge will identify the point if you don't, and your estimation of whether the witness can deal with the point with any degree of credibility or not. Evaluating these factors, and whatever other factors might come into your mind on the point, you might decide not to volunteer the point in chief, and rather to hope that it doesn't come out in cross.

Each case must be decided on its own merits, but let me suggest that as a general statement, volunteering the explanation in chief rather than running the risk that the point is raised in cross is the lesser, and thus the preferable, of two evils. As Evans[14] says, it is generally best to 'get to your difficulties before

[14] *The Golden Rules of Advocacy* 58.

anyone else does. You will handle them so much more sympathetically than your opponent'.

11.10 MAKING SURE YOU HAVE COVERED EVERYTHING

The last suggestion on this topic is that you must be sure, before concluding the evidence-in-chief, that the witness has dealt with every material point on which he is required to testify. One experience you will frequently have is that, in recounting a conversation, the witness will omit something which was said to you in consultation and which is of some value for the purposes of the case. This provides a nice dilemma, a curious beast this one, with three horns instead of two. One horn is the omission of an important fact; the second is that you must not put leading questions; the third is that if the method of the fresh approach is adopted the witness may remember what you are trying to establish but, in the process, omit something else. The last one is the most dangerous of the horns because it may be used effectively in cross-examination to establish that the witness has at best a confused or vague recollection of the discussion. It will require a very deft touch to be able to elicit what you want without telling the witness what he has to say. Often you will be able to ask: 'Was anything said about such-and-such a point?' This is the 'direct question', very close to the 'leading question' but, I suggest, sufficiently different to be permissible. The answer may be 'Yes' or 'No' but that is meaningless without the next explanation: 'What was said?' From this example you can work out your own technique for special circumstances.

11.11 AN EXAMPLE

See Appendix C for an example of evidence-in-chief opening with leading questions on non-contentious issues, and then switching to non-leading questions on contentious issues, using the techniques described in particularly paragraph 11.6 above, as also an example of the leading of expert evidence.

CHAPTER 12

Cross-examination

12.1 AN INTRODUCTION

I think it is fair to say that there is no part of the trial, except possibly the verdict, that raises tension to the heights as when counsel rises to cross-examine an important witness for the other side. He is suddenly thrust to the forefront of the proceedings. His skill and ability is put to the test — a test that may make or break the case.[1]

12.2 THE OBJECTIVES OF CROSS–EXAMINATION

Harris[2] defines the objectives of cross-examination in these words:

It should be borne in mind that the objects of cross-examination are three, the first positive, and the other two negative. They are: to obtain evidence favourable to your client, to weaken evidence that has been given against your client, and finally, if nothing of value which is favourable can be obtained, to weaken or destroy the value of the evidence by attacking the credibility of the witness.[3]

I would suggest that your objectives in cross-examination should be:
*   to elicit facts favourable to your case;
*   to elicit facts which may be used to cross-examine other witnesses;
*   to show that adverse evidence is unacceptable;
*   to show that the witness himself is not worthy of credence;
*   to put your case to the witness so that it may be known and commented upon.

In fact, if you analyse the quotation and my own restatement you will conclude that cross-examination has two, and only two, principal purposes: get what you can; destroy everything else.

All this sounds very impressive until you enter the lists, clad in shining armour (your robes) with, at the ready, a jousting lance (your technique). The witness, however, is a strange character who does not always fit into the moulds cast in the manuals. No sense of chivalry sparks in him the impulse to do fair battle. When you ride at him, he is not there. Those weapons that you have so carefully sharpened to accomplish the witness's destruction are wont to waste their worth on the empty air. Nothing can convey to you the surprise you will

---

[1] Roger Salhany *Cross-Examination – The Art of the Advocate* (Butterworths, 1988) 7. The author is a judge of the District Court of Ontario. He adds on the same page that the challenges of cross-examination have 'caused many a young aspiring counsel to abandon the bar for solicitor's work.'

[2] GW Keeton *Harris' Hints on Advocacy* 18 ed (Stevens, 1943) 75.

[3] Munkman, John *The Technique of Advocacy* (Butterworths, 1991) at 50 suggests four objectives, viz, to destroy the evidence of the witness, if that cannot be done to weaken it, to elicit new evidence helpful to your case, and to undermine the credibility or reliability of the witness.

feel when, after noting six untruths, fifteen improbabilities and a host of inconsistencies, you find that the witness is not even dented in his dirty coat of mail, while you lie breathless on the field, dismounted, discomfited and disconsolate. It is not as easy as all that; nothing goes according to plan. It will take a lot of defeats and a lot more practice for you to learn how to cross-examine. You must learn to know where you are going and why before you really can understand how you can get there. Moreover, if you are scrupulously proper in your technique, you will find that the truthful witness is most difficult to cross-examine except perhaps to obtain his assistance on facts which you need for your case. Fortunately, however, although many witnesses are truthful, few are reliable.

12.3 FAILURE TO CROSS–EXAMINE

You are, of course, not obliged to cross-examine anyone, but you fail to do so at your peril. As Claassen J said in *Small v Smith*:[4]

> It is, in my opinion, elementary and standard practice for a party to put to each opposing witness so much of his own case or defence as concerns that witness and if need be to inform him, if he has not been given notice thereof, that other witnesses will contradict him, so as to give him fair warning and an opportunity of explaining the contradiction and defending his own character. It is grossly unfair and improper to let a witness's evidence go unchallenged in cross-examination and afterwards argue that he must be disbelieved.
>
> Once a witness's evidence on a point in dispute has been deliberately left unchallenged in cross-examination and particularly by a legal practitioner, the party calling that witness is normally entitled to assume, in the absence of notice to the contrary, that the witness's testimony is accepted as correct. More particularly is this the case if the witness is corroborated by several others, unless the testimony is so manifestly absurd, fantastic or of so romantic a character that no reasonable person can attach any credence to it whatsoever. (See the following authorities: *Brown v Dunn* (1893) 6 The Reports 67 (HL); *Phipson on Evidence* 7 ed 460; *R v M* 1946 AD 1023 at 1028.)

The learned judge's next remark (which I quote below) is best introduced by way of the following example.

MacIlwaine, once attorney-general of Southern Rhodesia, and later a judge, was a heavily built man, with a strong sense of humour. He was prosecuting M for arson. The defence was that at the time of the fire, before, during and after, and at all times material and relevant, the accused was sleeping at the house of Ali H, six miles from the scene of the fire, and that therefore he could not have been a party to this fire. Ali H went into the box to support the alibi. MacIlwaine knew the witness. They had met before in court. The attorney-

[4] 1954 (3) SA 434 (SWA) at 438. See also *Pezzutto v Dreyer* 1992 (3) SA 379 (A), *President of the Republic of South Africa and Others v South African Rugby Football Union and Others* 2000 (1) SA 1 (CC) at 36J–38C and *Dexion Europe Ltd v Universal Storage Systems (Pty) Ltd* 2003 (1) SA 31 (SCA) at 39 and, in the criminal context; *R v M* 1946 AD 1023 at 1028 and *S v Boesak* 2000 (3) SA 381 (SCA) at 397–8.

general grasped the arms of his chair and began to hoist himself to the perpendicular. With each jerk he spoke: 'What-did-you-say-your-name-was?' 'Ali H my Lord.' Then, as he started on the downward journey, MacIlwaine added: 'Are-you-sure-it-is-not-alibi?'

That was the end of the alibi and of Ali H.

However, if you prefer it judicially stated, I quote what Claassen J said in *Small v Smith* dealing with the duty to challenge a witness's evidence:

> (U)nless the testimony is so manifestly absurd, fantastic or of so romancing a character that no reasonable person can attach a credence to it whatsoever. . . . (s)ome latitude is to be allowed in criminal cases and particularly when the defence is an alibi.

Another excellent example of what might be termed the art of not cross-examining is to be found in Michael Gilbert's *The Oxford Book of Legal Anecdotes*.[5] It relates to the *Youssoupoff v Metro Goldwyn Mayer Pictures Ltd* case referred to in chapter 9.[6] Princess Youssoupoff had instituted libel proceedings against MGM, claiming that the 'Princess Natasha' depicted in an MGM film as having been seduced by Rasputin was, to anyone who knew anything about Russian society, Princess Youssoupoff and that this was defamatory of her. Sir William Jowitt KC for the defendants, for reasons best known to himself, chose to call a Welsh domestic servant to say that she had seen the film and had made no connection with Princess Youssoupoff. This, of course, established nothing other than that the witness didn't know Princess Youssoupoff (put differently, it established nothing more than that the witness was a Welsh domestic servant). Patrick Hastings KC for the plaintiff could have chosen not to cross-examine her at all. Instead, he chose to make a point. Gilbert relays proceedings as follows:

> Sir Patrick Hastings rose slowly to his feet to cross-examine and there was a hushed expectancy in court.
> 'I see your name is Gwyneth Jones.'
> 'Yes, sir.'
> 'You have come from Llanelli?'
> 'Yes, sir.'
> 'I imagine you like Llanelli and are happy there?'
> 'Yes, sir.'
> 'It's a very long way from Llanelli to here, is it not?'
> 'Yes sir, it is'.
> 'And I imagine you are very anxious to get back there, are you not?'
> 'Yes sir, I am.'
> Sir Patrick slowly resumed his place and, with a wave of his hand towards the witness box said, 'Well, you run along then.'

[5] *The Oxford Book of Legal Anecdotes* (Oxford University Press, 1986) 149.
[6] See paragraph 9.8, fn 27.

In this regard, however, it is of interest to consider a passage from a judgment of Coetzee J.[7] What the case was all about was a fire. The Koster Ko-op said the SA Railways, by means of its locomotive, had caused a fire which spread on the plaintiff's veld and destroyed stacks of mealies to the value of R25 000. The routine reports disclosed by the Railways referred to a time of 2.45 pm as being when the fire was observed. From about 1.25 pm to 2.30 pm a large number of trains passed through the station adjoining the plaintiff's land. Opportunity to cause the fire was there in plenty. Evidence of one or two eyewitnesses was led; they testified to seeing the fire at about 2 pm; and the plaintiff closed its case. Then, and somewhat to the surprise of counsel (Mr X) for the plaintiff, the defendant let slip the dogs of war and called a number of witnesses who, on one pretext or another, averred that there was some incident four years ago by which they could fix the time of the fire. By some happy chance, they all referred to some event occurring about 1.00 to 1.15 pm — before a locomotive was even on the horizon — and at which stage the fire was already a veritable inferno. Mr X was cross. His complaint was that in dealing with the plaintiff's witnesses his opponent, Mr Y, had not disclosed that these pillars of rectitude and memory were to be called to prove that the fire started more than ninety minutes before the first time recorded in the Railways documents. Mr X, for his part, paraded his own cohorts, with such effect that a mass of counter-testimony was available. And he besought the presiding judge to allow him to adduce this testimony. Said Coetzee J:

> After C (at that time also a scholar at Koster High School) had testified and supported J in regard to the time at which scholars who were to travel in the school bus on the Fridays of home week-ends were allowed out of class, Mr X for the plaintiff applied to reopen his case on this point, ie, in regard to the time when the fire started. His application was based on the contention that the plaintiff had been taken by surprise by this evidence and had been prejudiced since there was nothing in the defendant's discovered documents to indicate anything but positive acceptance of the fact that the fire broke out after 2 pm. Moreover, he said, absolutely nothing had been said during cross-examination which in any way could warn him that evidence of this nature would be tendered and accordingly he had led no evidence, as he was now able to do, to prove that at 2 pm there was still no fire visible.
>
> Mr Y, for the defendant, took up the attitude that he was entitled to surprise the plaintiff — an element of surprise which is unloosed strategically, at the right moment and right time, is always part of the advocate's armoury. That is so, but if language which refers rather to physical combat is used to give a picturesque description of this aspect of the forensic art, I could add in the same idiom that it is my task to see that the Queensberry rules are not transgressed in the course of the match in court. Mr Y argued in regard to dicta in authorities cited by Mr X (*R v M* 1946 AD 1023 at 1027; *Small v Smith* 1954 (3) SA 434 (SWA) at 438E; and *R v Scoble* 1958 (3) SA 667 (N) at 669A–D), that it was not necessary for him to put the defendant's case concerning the

---

[7] *Koster Ko-operatiewe Landboumaatskappy Bpk v SA Spoorweë en Hawens* 1974 (4) SA 420 (W) at 422–3 (translated).

time of the occurrence since he was obliged to put to a particular witness only so much of his case as affected the evidence of that witness. And, so he proceeded, no witness had testified to the time of the events from his own memory. Thus he was not obliged to expose his coming knock-out blow in advance. . . . I am of opinion that Mr Y is correct in his general attitude regarding cross-examination and what must be put at the time thereof.

The learned judge discussed certain of the evidence before saying that, if the plaintiff's being taken by surprise arose solely from the failure to put the contrary in cross-examination, he doubted whether he would (although in fact he did) allow the plaintiff to reopen its case.

In this passage and in this incident are to be found lessons of inestimable value in the conduct of cases, let alone in the technique of cross-examination. For the purposes of the latter the principles of disclosing one's own case are more explicitly defined. For the former there is an object lesson in the degree of alertness required of the advocate. Nothing may be assumed from the silence of one's adversary. If a fact is material to your case it must be proved. In the *Koster Ko-op* case, it might be added, the relevance of the fact might have escaped notice entirely (strange though that may seem) had counsel not studied documents extracted from the defendant by means of rules 35(3) and 35(11) and drawn from these documents an inference as to why the defendant had sought unexpectedly to establish a time for the fire some two hours earlier than its other discovered documents had showed. The key lay in a 'train register' which recorded the times when trains passed through Koster station. If the fire could be placed two hours earlier than appeared from the documents it would show that no train had passed through the station for at least an hour and a half, and so it was impossible for a locomotive to have been the cause of the fire. Although I quote this case in regard to cross-examination, you can see how its implications must be borne in mind in those aspects of litigation discussed in chapters 4, 6, 7 and 8.

12.4 FUNDAMENTAL PROPOSITIONS

There are certain fundamental techniques in cross-examination, whether the objective is to destroy the force of the testimony, or to force an admission or statement of facts favourable to your case. Any one or more of these techniques may be employed in the cross-examination of a single witness, perhaps all of them will be required. It depends on the nature and details of the evidence and the circumstances. It depends, also, on the nature, condition and personality of the witness.

I offer the following eight fundamental propositions (together with numerous other aspects of the technique of cross-examination), with which I deal more fully in the ensuing paragraph:

•	prepare for, and then listen to, the evidence carefully, deciding in the light of the objectives of cross-examination discussed in paragraph 12.2 above *whether* you need to cross-examine and, if so, *what you need to cross-examine on, and how to go about it.*[8]

- generally, *use only leading questions in cross-examination;*[9]
- where you anticipate difficulty with a witness, ask yourself what escape routes the witness might choose if confronted with the proposition with which you intend confronting him, and first close off those escape routes before confronting him;[10]
- test the evidence in the light of common sense. Look for incongruities of fact or, more usefully, of conduct;[11]
- compare the evidence with established or clearly demonstrable facts;[12]
- test the evidence in the light of what the state of mind of the witness was or would have been at the time;[13]
- cross-examine on facts, not conclusions;[14]
- *always remember to put your case to the witness.*[15]

12.5 TECHNIQUES OF CROSS–EXAMINATION

12.5.1 Generally

I have already drawn attention to the question of preparing for cross-examination, and suggested that you can often anticipate what witnesses will be called and what evidence they can be expected to give.[16] In these cases you will have, at least, a list of topics on which to cross-examine the witness. Mostly, your list will follow a logical or chronological order. There will be instances where such order ought not to be followed, but effective cross-examination usually follows a logical or chronological order, so as better to be followed by the judge.

Ensure that you have fully researched, and understand, all of the relevant case law before you even enter the courtroom. You cannot properly cross-examine a witness unless you know beforehand what your case is, what you need to establish, and what you need to prevent the other side from establishing.

Sometimes you cannot anticipate or prepare and must improvise. In these cases, and indeed in all instances, you should adapt some method of recording the evidence that lets you note the point on which you wish to cross-examine, to find it quickly, and to recall what you had in mind when you made the note.

---

[8] See paragraphs 12.5.1 and 12.5.2 below.
[9] See paragraphs 12.5.6 to 12.5.8 below.
[10] See paragraph 12.5.10 below.
[11] See paragraph 12.5.15 below.
[12] See paragraphs 12.5.16 and 12.5.20 below.
[13] See paragraphs 12.5.17 and 12.5.18 below.
[14] See paragraphs 12.5.13 and 12.5.14 below.
[15] See paragraph 12.5.37 below.
[16] See the discussion of preparation for cross-examination in paragraphs 8.3.12 and 8.3.13 of chapter 8.

For the normal course, see the discussion in paragraph 9.5 in chapter 9 above on taking notes of what the witness is saying whilst at the same time preparing your cross-examination. Where the evidence is recorded electronically, one very quick method is to make an arrow in the margin next to the point which has aroused your interest. If time permits, a quick keyword might be added as a mnemonic. Another system is the underlining of relevant passages, while a third is to use a differently coloured ink to record what you intend to deal with.

Of course, you may be content to take your note of the evidence-in-chief and to go through it sentence by sentence for cross-examination. This may waste time and it may interrupt or disturb any ascendancy that you have been able to establish over the witness. The best cross-examination is free from the punctuation that occurs while counsel scratches through the brief looking for the subject-matter of his efforts.

12.5.2 Deciding whether to cross-examine and, if so, what to cross-examine on

The first decision you have to make is *whether you need to cross-examine the witness at all.*

In arriving at this decision, you will have regard to the objectives of cross-examination described in paragraph 12.2 above. Do you think that you will be able to elicit facts favourable to your case from the witness? Do you think that you will be able to elicit from the witness facts which may be used by you in cross-examination of other witnesses? Has the witness said something which necessitates your having to put your client's case to him? Has the witness said something which in one way or another is harmful to your client's case, so that you have to attack his evidence? Do you have a basis for attacking the credibility of the witness? If you do, do you need to launch that attack? It is only in the answering of these questions that you will be able to arrive at a reliable decision as to whether you need to cross-examine at all and, if so, what avenues you need to take up with the witness.

If the witness has not harmed you, then let him go unless he can provide material for your case or for the cross-examination of other witnesses. Beware of attacking for the sake of attack. You may succeed only in antagonising the witness and putting on to his evidence an edge that was not there before.

As an example of cross-examination where silence might have been prudent the following will illustrate the point: a witness had been called to establish a negative, namely that if a surveyor and his assistant had been responsible for causing a veld fire on a certain date it could not have been he, for he was on the land only some three to four weeks later. Of course, as cross-examining counsel well knew, this witness was also called as part of a case designed to establish that no surveyor whatsoever could have been on the land when the fire broke out. So counsel had this dilemma: not to cross-examine at all with the result that the evidence (otherwise acceptable) stood undisputed; or cross-examine without any positive facts with which to challenge the witness. He chose the latter course but was unable to challenge the fundamental and personal elements of the evidence, while the broader attempts to probe could never achieve direction and purpose. Indeed it might not be overstating the position to contend that the principal effect of cross-examination was to further the cause of the other party.[17]

The second decision you have to make, assuming that the first was decided in the affirmative, is *whether you want anything useful from the witness*. If you do, your procedure should be on the lines indicated in paragraphs 12.5.3 to 12.5.8 and (most importantly) paragraph 12.5.12.

If you want nothing useful from the witness but need to destroy (or at least make meaningful inroads into) his evidence, then read all of the paragraphs which follow.

These decisions are not easy. There is usually a mere matter of moments available when, ideally, you would welcome a transcript and adequate time to evaluate every answer in the light of your own case and its own potential or portent. Think, think fast and pray that you think lucidly.

From there onwards, in either case, the method varies with the witness and the case. If your plan is of the first sort indicated, that is, to get something from the witness, when you have squeezed him dry you can set about the task of destroying his evidence or discrediting him as a witness. One particular attorney delights in telling his counsel to 'smash' the witness. Sad to say, the improvements noticeable in the materials available to the glassmaker seem to have spread to witnesses also, and some of them are very close to shatterproof. Still, if you hammer away, a crack will eventually appear and your task may be done. On the contrary, the advice has been well given by Judge Donovan as: drop a bad witness.[18] A bad witness is one who withstands all your efforts. If you cannot break him it might be better to use other techniques to draw a veil over him. Anyhow, your basic decision must be made before you ask a single question.

12.5.3 Your manner: The art of cross-examination is not the art of examining crossly

Cross-examination is not a matter of opening your shoulders and hitting the witnesses all over the place.[19] True enough, in the course of your practice, you will meet many witnesses who are such strangers to the truth that they need be accorded no respect and can be treated as I have described. These you will

---

[17] See also 'Failure to cross-examine', in paragraph 12.3 above.

[18] *Tact in Court* 118.

[19] Salhany *Cross-Examination – The Art of the Advocate* (Butterworths, 1988) attributes the well-known *dictum* that 'the art of cross-examination is not the art of examining crossly' to an English judge, Baron Alderson, speaking to an advocate Smith in the late 1800s. See also the celebrated author and playwright John Mortimer, himself a QC, in his book *Clinging to the Wreckage* (1982): 'The art of cross-examination is not the art of examining crossly. It's the art of leading the witness through a line of propositions he agrees to until he's forced to agree to the one fatal question [or deny it, and look ridiculous].'

recognise without too much trouble. Until the mendacity of the man in the box is clear, however, you will exercise a delicate degree of restraint.

In all cases the witnesses should be treated with courtesy and respect — even if the latter is only simulated. In fact I would suggest that the more untruthful the witness and the more inadequate the explanations, the greater degree of courtesy and respect should be accorded. There is, of course, a subtle reason for the naive advice; in fact there are two subtle reasons. In the first place the very dignity of your own manner may serve by contrast to emphasise, more than argument could do, the utter unacceptability of the witness's evidence. In the second place the witness will gain confidence if accorded a respectful hearing and may be encouraged into flights of fancy or ventures of rashness that he or she might not essay if he or she were bullied into defensiveness.

Do not misunderstand this suggestion. The stage will no doubt come when your manner can change, when, so to speak, you may remove the velvet glove and wield the mailed fist with might and main. But be content to bide your time. Your training will tell you, in each case, just when to cry havoc and let slip the dogs of war.

It might be useful to have in mind the remarks of Snyman J in *S v Azov*[20] (whether you agree or not with all the observations of the learned judge):

> I think it must be made clear to him, and perhaps to others, that witnesses who come into court, be they police witnesses or any other kind of witnesses, are entitled to the ordinary courtesy one extends to decent people. Witnesses who give evidence are assisting the court in arriving at the truth and in carrying out the administration of justice. No cross-examiner is entitled to insult a witness or to treat him in the manner in which these witnesses were treated, without there being a very good reason for it. Witnesses must be treated with courtesy and respect. They are doing a public duty in coming to court: That must be borne in mind by both cross-examiners and by presiding officers. It was clearly the duty of the magistrate here to protect these witnesses. I do not wish to be understood to say that a witness may never be attacked, but before you can attack a witness you must at least lay a foundation to the satisfaction of the presiding officer that you have grounds for attacking the witness. Otherwise witnesses must be treated with respect and with the same courtesy that you would extend to a man in civilized society. One is not rude to people when you speak to them during ordinary social intercourse, so why should it be any different in a court of law? Here this cross-examiner really shocked me in regard to the manner in which he treated these respectable men. He starts off by attacking them without any reason. He seems to assume that they are dishonest people and that he is entitled to attack and insult them. When the magistrate intervenes to protect them he does not hesitate to attack even the magistrate. I cannot find any justification for his conduct and I think that the magistrate's strictures of him were fully justified.

In all cases address the witness by whatever title he or she enjoys, such as 'doctor', 'professor', 'Mr Mmutle', 'sir', 'Mrs Mmutle', 'inspector' or 'constable', etc.

---

[20] 1974 (1) SA 808 (T) at 810–11. See, also, to the same effect, Jones J at 865 of *Tshona and Others v Regional Magistrate, Uitenhage and Another* 2001 (8) BCLR 860 (E).

12.5.4 Gain the witness's co-operation

There are many witnesses whose evidence you will ask the court to reject but who are the very embodiment of honesty and candour. You will try to show that they are mistaken in their testimony, for want of proper observation or for defective recollection or for whatever other cause there may be. Sometimes such a witness can be made to concede that he may or must be mistaken. With these witnesses, just as with those from whom you want something, an atmosphere of co-operation must be established and the antagonism of the witness avoided.[21] You must show that you are frank, fair and firm. The witness must be made to trust you and to realise that he can safely make concessions without their being abused or distorted.

In other cases it is often of great help to disarm the witness first, particularly where you contemplate having to assault him later. His confidence should be won in the same manner because he will be twice as vulnerable when his truthfulness is attacked. I have already referred, in regard to the topic of preparing for trial, to counsel whose favourite gambit is 'Please help us, Mr K', and mentioned my views on the psychological effect of this approach. I would be very distressed if I were to cause a rash of counsel saying, 'Please help us' to every witness in cross-examination, so I merely offer the phrase as an illustration of how to win witnesses and influence answers.

12.5.5 Generally, cross-examine chronologically

In general you should cross-examine chronologically. The butterfly method, flitting from flower to flower, is picturesque but often carries no more punch than the average butterfly. There is a very good reason for this advice. Human existence is chronological. Human behaviour is chronological. Just as every event is the progenitor of its successor, so every human act is the progeny of its predecessor. Litigation mainly involves the analysis of the acts of human beings. Evidence is an alleged narration of those acts. *Cross-examination is mainly the testing of that narration by examining an act in the context of its predecessors and successors.* Forgive the italics, but I believe that this one sentence may well epitomise everything that can be written about cross-examination. Where the events do not flow logically the narrative is suspect. You can seldom show that they do not flow logically if you pick them at random and examine them individually.

But that is not all. The understanding of a narrative is easier when the narrative is chronological. The 'flash-back' should usually be left for the television. You who have studied your case for days, even weeks, must convey to the tribunal the understanding which you have of that case, and you are

---

[21] Salhany says this at 47: '[M]any witnesses can be persuaded to accept suggestions put to them, if done fairly and politely. It is only natural for a witness, inexperienced in the trial process, to believe that the cross-examiner's goal is to make a liar or a fool out of him. He will be apprehensive, and probably defensive in his responses. But if the questions are put fairly, and if they demonstrate a recognition of the witness's desire to tell the truth, surprising results can be achieved.'

trying to do so by attacking evidence which is inconsistent with your case. How better can you achieve your objective of destruction than by using the method which is easier to comprehend?

You will, of course, have noticed that I use the expressions 'in general' and 'usually'. Many times you will take a vital event out of sequence because the effectiveness of later cross-examination depends upon an analysis of that event. Or there may be cases where you have a 'sixty-four dollar' question of the type discussed in succeeding pages. Perhaps there are a few escape routes to be dealt with in the manner I suggest later. There may even be something in the latest conduct of the witness which will influence the court in the consideration of his or her earlier conduct. In these cases the chronology can wait. But experience has taught me — often to my sorrow — that to depart from the chronological sequence is a grievous error.

12.5.6 Ask leading questions!

One of the privileges of the cross-examiner is that he may put leading questions. It is surprising how often this privilege is neglected. After all, if you want some evidence to be on record what is easier than to give the evidence yourself? If you leave it to the witness he may give some or most of what you want, but not enough. You then struggle to get the remainder, against an increasingly obstinate witness who could hardly have dissented from the proposition if it had originally been put as a leading question.

In fact, *if there is one key to effective cross-examination other than good preparation in the form of a thorough knowledge of your case and thus of what you can expect to get out of the witness, it is this: as an almost invariable rule, you should ask only leading questions in cross-examination.*

See the example of cross-examination contained in Appendix D, and note the invariable use of leading questions to steer the witness in the intended direction.

12.5.7 Diction and phraseology, and asking short and simple questions

Of the utmost importance, I suggest, is the topic of diction. You do not need the voice of an Anthony Hopkins. Nor will an acquired artificiality do much more than fool some of the people some of the time. Your enunciation should be precise, your phraseology should be consistent with the intellect of the witness and your questions should be framed concisely and accurately. There must be no room for misunderstanding between yourself and the witness and no prospect of your opponent arguing that the answer meant something else because the witness might have understood the question in some form other than that contended for by you. Maybe I am harping on this topic unduly; this is because I have seen so many instances of this and I feel that they should have been avoided. I join with Marc Anthony in his lament that 'twere a grievous fault and grievously hath [counsel] answered it'.

I have seen counsel who cross-examined at tremendous speed and with tremendous noise. Yet the most effective cross-examinations that I have observed have been conducted in quiet level tones, free of emotion, free of histrionics, but charged with dynamite. This is purely a matter of personality, for other cross-examiners, amongst the best who have appeared in our courts, had the knack of making every question sound like an indictment. Until you are sure of yourself no harm will befall you if you conduct cross-examination as though you were doing nothing more than converse with the witness. When you have mastered every facet of technique then you may glitter with the brilliance of the diamond.

In the heading to this paragraph I spoke of 'asking short and simple questions'. That would, with reference to that which was said in paragraph 12.5.6 above, be better rephrased as 'putting propositions shortly and simply'.

Avoid the 'double-barrelled' question, ie, the 'question' comprised of two or more questions. Sometimes it is used deliberately as a trap; that is unfair. Sometimes it is used nervously or for want of patience; that is a snare, for ultimately it may prove that neither question has been answered. Sometimes it is used in ignorance that the question does in fact contain two parts; that is excusable, but should be realised and rectified without delay.

12.5.8 Remain in control

Throughout your cross-examination, whether you are trying to elicit facts through co-operation of the witness or attacking his evidence or credibility, you must remain in control of the witness. If the witness takes over the cross-examination and you allow the roles to be exchanged you will almost inevitably end up as the subject of ridicule. That is unimportant, because in your lifetime you will learn to survive a lot more than ridicule. What is important is that from that position you cannot hope to destroy or damage the testimony against your client.

Succinctly the matter could be put: never argue with the witness, and never, ever, answer a question. If the witness does put a question which shows that his object is to obtain clarification of the meaning or intent of your own question then clearly it is your duty to restate that question in a clear unambiguous form, phrased so that it could reasonably be understood. When this has been done, should the witness feign a lack of comprehension, you may reasonably assume that the court understands both the question and the witness's motives. You simply say:

'Mr K . . . the question is perfectly clear, will you please answer it.'

If Mr K runs true to form he will pretend to have forgotten the question and will ask you to repeat it, hoping that this time you will phrase it slightly differently and thus let him off the hook.

When you are satisfied that the witness is merely hedging or trying to gain time, don't trouble to repeat the question but merely use the formula I have suggested, or some appropriate variation on the theme.

From this it follows that you should be cautious of all bait offered by the witness. As an example I offer the following anecdote, in which the characters, although no longer with us, shall remain anonymous, being referred to by pseudonyms.

This was a case where a young man's venture into the world of business had ended in sequestration with the inevitable aftermath of prosecution for contraventions of the Insolvency Act. One of the witnesses was the principal creditor, a wholesaler who had in some measure contributed to the insolvent's overstocked and unsold position. His manner was hostile, not only to the accused but also to counsel. When the court adjourned for the day counsel spoke to him about his attitude and said that the following morning he would ask only a few short questions to which the answer would be 'Yes', or 'No'.

The next morning, as counsel was about to continue cross-examination, the witness said:

> 'Mr Green, I have read literature and I know of a character that matches yours.'
>   Said counsel: 'Mr Black, I have read your bond and I know a character that matches yours.'

The next witness was the trustee who had been appointed at the instance of the principal creditor aforesaid. He and counsel had been friends for many years. In the course of his cross-examination the trustee said, *apropos* of nothing: 'Mr Green, I am sorry for your client.'

Counsel held his peace, but, in the course of addressing the court, pointed out that his client had been over-reached. He stressed the fact that the trustee, who was conversant with the insolvent's affairs, was sorry for him. In due course, and for various reasons, the accused was acquitted.

The trustee invited counsel to join him and partake of coffee. Said he: 'Do you know why I said I was sorry for your client?'

Counsel did not.

So the trustee enlightened him.

> 'Some years ago,' he said, 'I had a chap prosecuted under the Insolvency Law. Bobby Ngobeni appeared for him and he was very rude to me. So I said: 'Mr Ngobeni, I am sorry for your client.' He asked me why and I said: 'Because he has you as his attorney.'

Counsel avoided the fate of the unfortunate Mr Ngobeni because he was not inquisitive, he did not let the witness take control of the cross-examination and because he declined to be diverted from the main course. In the case of both witnesses had counsel asked silly questions he would have ended up as the subject of ridicule. Nor do I have to stress the ingenuity of the manner in which counsel turned both attempts to his own advantage.

12.5.9 The attack, and the sixty-four dollar question

There comes a time when you and the witness must part company. In the majority of cases it will be when you rise to your feet in response to the court's invitation. In other instances it will be when the cross-examination passes from the phase of eliciting facts to that of attacking the evidence. When this moment arrives your purpose must be to find an opening question from which the witness can never recover. If you can do this then give grateful thanks; if you cannot, then you must achieve your results the hard way. It may well be that the process of eliciting information will detract from the force of what we may inelegantly but colloquially describe as the 'sixty-four dollar question'. In these cases it may even be profitable to reverse the order; hit first and ask questions afterwards. In other words, don't trouble about securing co-operation; destroy the effect of the testimony against you and then extract concessions, admissions, facts or what you will.

Once again, an example will show how the technique should be employed.[22]

The plaintiff was suing the defendant for damages for breach of promise of marriage. Both parties were no longer in the first bloom of youth. The plaintiff was a divorcee whose home was in the Midlands of England. The defendant was a manufacturer who resided in Johannesburg. They met when the defendant visited Birmingham to purchase equipment for his factory — let us call him Mr R. On the first meeting the parties spent the night together, and from then onwards Mr R spent all his spare time with the plaintiff. He then left for the United States of America and Canada, where he continued his search for suitable machinery. His progress was marked with a flow of letters written to the plaintiff in very affectionate terms, discussing his progress and expressing his anguish at their enforced separation. The plaintiff, too, contributed to the correspondence, her rare foresight being indicated by the fact that she typed her letters for easy reading and kept a copy for future reference.

The plaintiff's case was that before she left England the defendant had proposed marriage and she had accepted the proposal. It was arranged that she would give up her employment in Birmingham, sell all her furniture and other belongings, and come to South Africa where the parties were to marry.

In due course Mr R returned to South Africa, and soon the plaintiff was winging her way south to join him. The reunion was celebrated by a sojourn in Durban, where the rapturous excitement of those weeks in Birmingham was to be recaptured. Whatever the cause may have been, Mr R showed no enthusiasm regarding marriage and he even denied that any promise had been made. The result was the action under consideration.

Naturally the plaintiff testified first and fared moderately well under cross-examination. She had some difficulties but at least she made out a *prima facie* case. The defendant then entered the witness-box. His defence was a simple one, quite reasonable and quite logical. He said that there had been no promise to marry. There had been discussions about marriage but they both realised the problems. They were no longer young and had become set in their ways. Life in South Africa would be vastly different from life in Birmingham and the plaintiff might be unhappy. Thus they had arranged that she should come to

[22] One suspects that Eric Morris, the author of the first three editions of this book, based this example on a case in which he was involved, *Guggenheim v Rosenbaum (2)* 1961 (4) SA 21 (W).

South Africa to see whether she liked the country and whether, when they met in different circumstances, they might be interested in getting married.

Counsel for the plaintiff rose to cross-examine and his first question, a quite unpretentious question, was utterly destructive:

> 'Mr R, were you in love with the plaintiff?'

Consider that question for a while — because Mr R saw its import within moments. If he said 'Yes' then whose version was the more probable? People in love don't make calculated arrangements of the type described — apart from the fact that the plaintiff sold up her home. If he said 'No' then he was going to experience some difficulty in explaining the affectionate letters he had written — difficulties of which he was only too aware from his consultations with his own counsel. He tried to compromise by conceding an infatuation, but, as I have indicated, his testimony never recovered from the impact of that first question.

See, for a similar example, Sir Rufus Isaacs' opening questions in cross-examination of Frederick Seddon in the Old Bailey in 1912.[23] Seddon was charged with the murder by poisoning of his wealthy lodger, Miss Barrow, from whom he had extracted the agreement that, in return for her worldly wealth, he would give her free lodgings for the rest of her life. The shorter her life, the better for Seddon and, as things turned out, her life after the contract was remarkably short. But medical forensics were at that time in their infancy, and everything depended on cross-examination.

The questions (and their answers) were these:

> 'Miss Barrow lived with you from 26 July 1910 until the morning of 14th September 1911?'
> 'Yes.'
> 'Did you like her?'
> 'Did I like her?'
> 'Yes, that is the question.'

Seddon was unsettled, and this set the tone for his further cross-examination and conviction.

What, you may ask, makes a sixty-four dollar question? How do I find it? How do I recognise it when I see it? Very good questions, indeed. My suggested answer is that such a question is one which permits of at least two answers, either of which (or all of which) can be used to show that the witness's evidence is untruthful or biased, or in conflict with his conduct. Before the question can be employed, however, you must be sure of the possible answers and you must know how each answer can be used to destroy the evidence-in-chief.

---

[23] Quoted in Salhany *Cross-Examination – The Art of the Advocate*. Judge Salhany suggests at 40 that Isaacs' opening questions were probably the most famous of all time. They were, he says, 'obviously planned carefully to achieve the maximum effect. [They] caught Seddon off guard and, in the end, led to his downfall'.

The object of the sixty-four dollar question is to take advantage of that psychological moment when the witness does not know what is coming. He is apprehensive (unless he is an experienced habitué of the witness box) of the ordeal that awaits him. The witness knows neither your strength not your limitations, and before he can ascertain the latter he must be made aware of the former. Thus I suggest that, wherever possible, this technique should be employed. You note, of course, the words 'wherever possible'. There are three possibilities: you find the 'sixty-four dollar question'; there is no such question; there is such a question but you don't find it. Usually a quiet turning over of the case in the mind will lead you to your desired bonanza. At other times it will force itself before you too powerfully to be ignored. When, however, it neither obtrudes nor emerges from quiet introspection do not think that all is lost. The following paragraphs should contain sufficient hints to enable you to do your job properly — with practice.

12.5.10 Closing off the escape routes

It is far easier to suggest this point than to illustrate it. Subject to that qualification, the point is this: be wary of the direct question in cross-examination, if you have not first adequately prepared the ground for that direct question.

If you want to put to the witness that his statement on point X cannot be true because of fact Y, the direct question is a simple algebraical or geometrical formula: 'I put it to you that X cannot be true because of Y.' When you have had the sorry experience of hearing countless witnesses evade the direct question by offering, say, a factor known as Z, you begin to think that some technique should be devised to meet this propensity of witnesses. You find yourself breathlessly pursuing Z while the witness craftily hops to A, B, C and right through the alphabet.

Now this is not examination-in-chief where the 'direct question' was recommended as a means of establishing the material facts. This is cross-examination, where the witness must not be left at liberty to give whatever answer he pleases; the witness must be forced to meet the problem you pose and to give the answer you want. You must therefore eliminate in advance all the answers you do not want. Since the witness must be assumed at least to have as much insight as yourself the process of elimination must be carefully done. What you have to do is to work out for yourself the possible escape routes from the proposition 'that X cannot be true because of Y'. When you have decided on the escape routes you seal them up by getting the witness to agree to the direct opposite of every proposition that he would urge in his escape. Thus he should agree 'not Z', 'not A', 'not B' and so on. When you put the direct proposition in the form stated previously, ideally the witness should either have to say 'I concede that', or remain silent, or offer an unpersuasive answer which in any event confirms that he ought to have conceded the point, and which in addition damages his credibility.[24]

This technique can be used with the 'independent witness' in traffic cases. This is a most dangerous witness, because he is usually believed by the courts, although he never in fact saw what he says he saw, or believes he saw.

It is useless to say to him: 'I put it to you that there was no reason for you to pay any attention to the scene of the collision.'

He immediately becomes defensive, to such an extent that it appears that his only reason for not using a movie camera and tape recorder on this occasion was that he had lent them to his cousin for the weekend. Instead the matter is approached more obliquely.

> 'How long have you lived in Johannesburg?'. . .
> — 'All my life.'
> 'Do you know the street well?'
> — 'Oh yes.' (Begins to feel a little more self-important and reassured.)
> 'Is it very busy at that time of day?'
> — 'Oh yes.'
> 'Do you always use it at that time of the day?'
> — 'Yes.'
> 'On this particular day the traffic was the same as usual?'
> — 'Yes.'
> 'You were walking home?'
> — 'Yes.'
> 'You had had a very hard day at the office?'
> — 'Yes.'
> 'What were you thinking about?' (This question will annoy everybody else concerned with the case but it is useful — press it.)
> — 'I can't tell you now what I was thinking about, it is eighteen months ago.'
> 'And then you heard this collision?"

From this point it is a case of theme and variation, but the basic fact seems to have been established that the witness saw a little and imagined a lot.[25] Naturally, you will find many witnesses who candidly admit that the first thing that drew their attention to the scene was in fact the sound of the collision, in which case you need not waste time establishing what has been conceded.

But note, in this regard, the cautionary rule outlined in paragraph 12.5.12 below to the effect that you should never try to improve on a favourable answer. The principle can be stated thus: if the witness has committed himself

---

[24] See fn 19 above, and particularly John Mortimer QC's description of the art of cross-examination: '[T]he art of leading the witness through a line of propositions he agrees to until he's forced to agree to the one fatal question [or deny it, and look ridiculous].'

[25] Munkman *The Technique of Advocacy* at 20 points out that '*Interest* and *attention* are pre-conditions of accurate observation. Every day, numerous things are said and done in our presence which we hardly notice. . . It follows that evidence given by a witness about matters in which he took no interest at the time [or, one might add, in which one would not *expect* him to have taken an interest at the time] is likely to be vague: positive statements by such witnesses are likely to be unreliable, as they may have been built up after the event by inference and imagination'.

to a proposition, never afford him the opportunity of adopting an alternative and more favourable proposition. Naturally, when you have attacked and destroyed the proposition in all its facets the witness will be anxious to seek that alternative, and, again, you do not afford him the chance. It is so tempting to try to crush the witness and display your own forensic skill by a question such as:

> 'Now you have given three reasons for your proposition, we have examined them all and found each one insupportable. How can you say [whatever it is]?'

You are not sealing an escape route, you are opening one. The witness will be only too anxious to explain — usually a lot more completely and skilfully and successfully. Nor will it help to say accusingly: 'Why didn't you mention that earlier?' He will say 'I forgot' and the court may well believe that. Whereas if you say in argument: 'The witness was invited to state reasons for the proposition. He gave these. Each was examined and found insupportable', this is almost unanswerable.

12.5.11 As a general statement, don't ask a question to which you don't know the answer

No question should be asked which may produce an unfavourable answer. This has also been expressed by saying that you should never ask a question unless you know the answer or are indifferent to it.[26] In the stress and strain of the trial, you may ask, how can one know the answer to each question or know which question will produce an unfavourable answer? To some extent careful preparation will help you to decide what must be asked and what is dangerous.

12.5.12 Better is the enemy of good

Never try to improve on a favourable answer. If you do, the probabilities are so overwhelming as to amount to certainty beyond reasonable doubt that you will destroy what you have achieved. The impulse is almost irresistible and, as in the defence of irresistible impulse in criminal law, you will be in no better position to withstand the impulse and refrain from asking the question than if some physically stronger person had by mechanical compulsion directed your tongue. In pursuance of the analogy it might be well to become aware of the psychological factors which produce the impulse. The principal cause, I would suggest, is the absence of reaction from the judge who listens patiently, or writes diligently. He does not throw down his pen, lean back and order the witness to 'Just say that again'. Subconsciously you are troubled. Has the point got home? Has the judge even heard it? Is it as crystal clear as you believe? So you decide to make sure, with the result I have described. The other psychological factor is the witness, who appears unmoved by the enormity of what has been said. 'The enemy faints not, nor faileth, and as things have been they (seem to) remain.' My suggestion on this point is that witnesses do not

---

[26] Francis Wellman *The Art of Cross-Examination* 4 ed at 42 puts it thus: 'Certainly no lawyer should ask a *critical* question unless he is reasonably sure of the answer.'

collapse in the witness-box merely because they have been caught out in a lie or have given a fatal answer — at least, not often. In fact the happier you are with the answer, the less you should show it,[27] and, equally, the less you should be disappointed when the witness returns the compliment.

This point has been effectively put in the vernacular as follows: 'When yer strike ile, stop borin. Many a man has gawn on an' bored right through.'

An interesting example of boring right through occurred in a case, the name of which is irrelevant and the performers in which may remain anonymous. The court was concerned with rather a complicated engineering contract which contained a provision that if the cost of the works exceeded the stipulated contract amount by a certain percentage some result had to follow. The precise result, also, is irrelevant and it is sufficient to say that either the contract itself came to an end or, more probably, the engineer appointed by the employer became entitled, subject to certain conditions, to revise the rates under the contract. It was the plaintiff's case that the relevant provision had come into operation only at the end of the contract. The defendant, who was the employer, pleaded, on the other hand, that the operative clause had taken effect on one of two dates, depending upon which of one of two alternative events was regarded as the precipitating factor. The employer then went on to contend that if the provision had come into operation on either of the dates alleged by it the contractor had failed to comply with certain provisions in the contract pertaining to the giving of notices and that, accordingly, the contractor had disentitled himself from calling upon the engineer to fix new rates — rates, it may be added, which would apparently have been more favourable to the contractor than were the stipulated rates in the contract. The contractor's reply to this, apart from a denial, was that the question of excess could be determined only when everything was completed and all work had been finally measured up and quantities agreed between the parties. In the light of this exposition it is interesting to see how the matter went when counsel for the defendant (the employer) cross-examined the contractor's managing director.

When you read the following passages I ask you to bear in mind that the precipitating event stipulated in the contract was either that the total contract amount was exceeded by more than 20 per cent or that the value of any particular item in the contract, where that item itself was worth no less than seven per cent of the total contract amount, was exceeded by 25 per cent. I should also remark that the contractor's case was pleaded in the alternative, relying upon the fulfilment of both of the effective provisions. As the matter developed in evidence, however, the contractor placed no reliance upon the

---

[27] Wellman puts it as follows at 42: 'If . . . you obtain a . . . favourable answer, leave it and pass quietly to some other inquiry . . . He is indeed a poor judge of human nature who supposes that if he exults over his success . . ., he will not quickly put the witness on his guard to avoid all future favourable disclosures.'

seven per cent item but contended that the total contract amount was exceeded by 20 per cent and that this event did not occur earlier than 1 December 1969. For the employer, on the other hand, the contention was raised that an excess had occurred in respect of a specific item as early as October 1968 and that, by failing to give the relevant notices, the contractor had in some way disentitled itself from relying upon either provision of the relevant clause. Whether this contention would have been sound need not concern us now, but the contractor's managing director was being cross-examined in order to establish the basic fact essential to the employer's case. This, then, is how cross-examination proceeded:

> 'In your pleadings or in the plaintiff's pleadings, reliance is also placed on a vitiation of the contract by virtue of the fact that item 13(5)(b) of the Schedule of Quantities, which in itself was more than seven and a half per cent of the total contract value, had been exceeded by more than 25 per cent. Do you remember that?'
> — 'Yes.'
> 'Have you got the Schedule of Quantities at hand, Mr C?'
> — 'No.' (Document is handed to witness.)
> 'That is item 13(5)(b): Cut and borrow to fill, common material.'
> — 'Yes, I have it.'
> 'Is my note correct that the original volume under that item was 870 000 cubic yards?'
> — 'Yes.'
> 'Is that right?'
> — 'Yes.'
> 'According to the payments certificate for the period from 26 September 1968 to 25 October 1968 the total volume reached under that item was 1 144 408 cubic yards. Would you like to check that on your copy of the payments certificate?'
> — 'No, I take your word for it.'
> 'I am just hoping that I am not making a mistake, I would rather you checked it.'
> — 'Yes, that is right.'
> 'That shows then that by that time the volume of this particular item had been exceeded by more than 25 per cent, is that correct?'
> — 'That is correct.'
> 'So one of the matters referred to in clause 49(1) was actually satisfied as early as October 1968, is that right?'
> — 'Yes.'
> 'Were you in charge of the administration of this contract? Generally speaking.'
> — 'Generally speaking, yes.'
> 'Were you informed of the monthly certificates, did you go through them and check them, and so forth?'
> — 'No. We had a quantity surveyor.'
> 'But the plaintiff must have been aware, generally speaking, by virtue of the payments certificate, that this situation had been reached in October 1968?'
> — 'We should have been aware of it, yes.'

One would have thought that counsel would be satisfied with the concession that the relevant vitiating fact had occurred during October 1968, for it was really common cause between the parties that no notice in terms of the contract had been given before 23 December 1969 and this was far too late to be a valid notice in the circumstances. However, counsel returned to the attack when cross-examination of the witness resumed on the following day. This is how the matter proceeded and you will see that their attempt to gild the lily resulted in the probability that the point would be completely destroyed:

'Mr C, I would just like to return briefly to two matters we discussed yesterday. You will remember we referred to the increase in item 13(5)(b) of the Schedule of Quantities, and you will remember that we found that the volume of that item had been exceeded by more than 25 per cent in October of 1968?'
— 'That is right.'
'I just want to put it to you that, I think it is obvious, that — in case you have other views about it — that this was an irreversible increase, it could never be reduced subsequently?'
— 'No, it could be reduced subsequently.'
'Could it?'
— 'Yes. The engineer has the power to vary or change.'
'No, I think we might be at cross-purposes. We established that in the payments certificate of October 1968 the actual volume, the cubic yards under item 13(5)(b) had already, in respect of the payments certificate, been exceeded by more than 25 per cent in relation to the original volume as specified in the contract documents. Now what I am putting to you is — that could never have been reversed because the work had been done?'
— 'It could be reversed and in fact in later correspondence you will find that the consulting engineer tried to do exactly that.'
'But how, if there is 1 440 000 — something like that — cubic yards under this specific item, and you were paid for it in October, how could that be reduced? This I don't follow. It is work that has been done, it is an actual cubic yards volume work that has been executed?'
— 'If you read the later correspondence you will find that the consulting engineer tried exactly to do that. He said the increase in the volume and the extra work done was not done on his authority, it was done on the authority of the resident engineer who had no authority. So he was hinting that all the extra work we had done and for which we had been paid, would be reversed. It is all in the correspondence, you will find it in the letters, and this goes back to my point yesterday that we couldn't be sure that 20 per cent had been exceeded.'
'In relation to this specific item?'
— 'In relation to all items.'
'No, I am talking specifically of this item. Was there ever any query about this specific item? What was the item described as?'
— 'It doesn't have to be specific, he says all the additional work ordered by the resident engineer is not authorized, and later on in the pleadings it was admitted. But it was as late as the pleadings when it was admitted that they would pay for and accept all the extra work done, and this earthworks was one of those things.'
'Just let's get this straight. Was there ever any query as to this specific item having been duly authorized or not?'
— 'On the specific item, no. On all items, yes, of which this item was one.'

12.5.13 Don't argue with the witness

This is related to the next topic, the need to cross-examine on facts, not conclusions.

Ask questions. Do not make speeches. Do not make statements. Do not comment (especially do not comment, if for no other reason than that comments are like chickens: they come home to roost). Do not argue.

Your task is to get in there, extract what you can, and get out. You are in the advantageous position that you ask the questions; the witness has to answer them. Do not abandon those strategic heights for the equality of argument. An argumentative question ('So, you weren't looking ahead of you, were you?') virtually invites counter-argument. Far better to put the *facts* to the witness, and argue with the judge about the appropriate *conclusion* to draw from those facts.

Note that, invariably, a question which begins with 'so' is going to be argumentative and unnecessary.[28]

12.5.14 Cross-examine on facts, not conclusions

This topic is interwoven with the preceding topic. Cross-examine on *facts*, not *conclusions*. If you want to establish that the witness was negligent, cross-examine him on the *facts* from which you intend arguing his negligence. It is neither necessary, nor relevant, nor by any means advisable, for you to go on and debate with him whether those facts constitute negligence or not.

An example which encapsulates this would be the following:

> 'You had a clear view to your left for over 100 metres as you approached the intersection.'
> — 'Yes, I did.'
> 'We know the plaintiff entered the intersection from your left, not so?'
> — 'Yes.'
> 'The first you saw him was when he was right in front of you.'
> — 'Yes.'

So far, so good. Extremely bad would be to add the following argumentative, unnecessary and irrelevant question:

> 'So, you couldn't have been keeping a proper lookout.'
> —'Oh, I was. The reason I didn't see him until just before the accident, was because there was this big truck in front of him and although I could see the truck, and I kept my eye on it, it obscured him entirely until the last minute.'

12.5.15 Test the evidence in the light of common sense

See what was said in chapter 4 above about the importance of common sense, and see in particular Nienaber JA's exposition in *SFW Group Limited and Another v Martell et Cie and Others*[29] of the courts' approach to factual disputes.

The courts' approach must be your approach. You must, whilst listening to the witness and taking note of what he says, yourself be applying the approach outlined by the learned judge. What do you think of the witness's demeanour?

---

[28] Somehow, the word 'so', when beginning a question, inevitably proclaims that an argumentative question is about to follow, ie, a proposition with which the witness is invited to agree or disagree. He will inevitably opt for the latter.

[29] 2003 (1) SA 11 (SCA) at 14–5, as dealt with in paragraph 4.3.4 of chapter 4.

Is there reason to believe that he is biased? Does his evidence contain internal contradictions? How does his version measure up to established fact and what we know of his own conduct? How probable is it that he would have acted as he says he did, or been able to observe what he says he did?

You will ask yourself all of these questions, and it is on your answers to them that you will construct your cross-examination.

12.5.16 Test by comparison

Sometimes, and all too often it must be confessed, counsel finds that he makes no impression on a witness. Particularly is this the case where the witness has to depose to one simple fact free of motive, involvement, bias, mental reaction, self-contradiction or anything else. In such a case you will have to look for a consolation prize, if one there be. The consolation may lie in the other witness, if any, who will be called to testify on the same point. If none, there is nothing to be done but to hope that your own witnesses are as good as or better than the one with whom you failed.

The idea is to elicit from the witness as much collateral detail as possible. Later witnesses can then be cross-examined on the details of the matter and the comparison will reveal whether there are any important conflicts. Minor discrepancies are of no value and, in fact, are indicative of naturalness in the testimony. If you can achieve nothing of substance in the comparison then perhaps the witnesses are telling the truth after all.

12.5.17 Test by mental reaction

In some cases cross-examination can usefully be conducted with judicious use of the question: 'What did you think?' This is not an easy device to use, it does not arise with every witness, nor can it necessarily be used in every case. Properly regarded it is a particular instance of the test of fact, for it has been said that the state of a man's mind is as much a fact as the state of his digestion.

The technique consists in establishing a path from one fact to another by way of the witness's state of mind. Given the proposition, one asks oneself what state of mind that proposition would have created in the witness. Then one asks oneself how he would have reacted. The answer to the second question should coincide with the evidence of the witness. When it does not so coincide then there is a proper case in which to cross-examine applying the test suggested.

The value of this method is that, provided only that your reasoning is sound, the witness must destroy his own evidence. If he answers truthfully as to what he thought, his subsequent conduct will be incompatible with what his conduct would have been had he thought as he did. If he answers untruthfully as to what he thought, his untruthfulness should be apparent or easily demonstrable.

In using this technique you must be sure that there can be only one acceptable answer to the question: 'What did you think?' Of course, the witness will often see where this answer may take him, and will be anxious to have thought everything but what he did really think. Or else his memory of this mental process will have become clouded with the passage of time. In the former case your process of reasoning must be so sound that ultimately the court will say: 'The witness could only have thought what counsel suggests.' In the latter case the problem is both easier and more difficult. It is easier in that you can put to the witness that he must have thought what you expect the answer to be and this very forgetfulness is a tacit admission of your question. It is more difficult in that the court may very well listen favourably to an argument that the witness is not called upon to speculate but to testify. The answer to this argument is that you are really testing the credibility of the witness when he pretends not to recall his mental reaction. In this regard it might be well to quote a passage from *Moore on Facts:*[30]

> It is a reasonable supposition that a person should have a good memory of his or her own thoughts or feelings at a particular time. 'We remember our own theories, our own discoveries, combinations, inventions, in short whatever "ideas" originate in our own brain, a thousand times better than exactly similar things which are communicated to us from without,' says Professor James.

Bearing in mind all these comments, I suggest that you make a careful study of this point of technique. It is one of the most useful methods of cross-examination in those cases where it can be used and you should make it a habit to listen to the evidence-in-chief with the object of finding whether yours is such a case. I pass this suggestion on with a great deal of confidence because I have heard the test by mental reaction used frequently and effectively by advocates and attorneys who were renowned for their skill in cross-examination.

It is not only the mental reactions of the witness that may be examined, but also the probable mental reactions of those whose conduct he is describing. Perhaps 'motives' would be a better epithet to use, for what I have in mind is to test the probability of any allegation by asking how the person concerned would have behaved in the circumstances.

This can be illustrated by a reference to a case where the witness was in some difficulties because she was being taxed with the fact that, in a previous case, her evidence in court had conflicted with her statement to the police. Her explanation, when confronted with her previous aberrations and deviations from the path of utter accuracy, was to maintain that her evidence had been true and that she had not said what was recorded in her statement to the police. This, incidentally, provides the opportunity to apply the test by mental reaction twice. The actual question and answer are the following:

> Question: And you came to court and you told the magistrate that it is all not true, what you said in that statement?
> Answer: When the CID came to me he didn't ask me questions. Somebody told him that I was talking with [the accused] about the case, and he asked me what happened. So I told him that I told [the accused] the next

---

[30] Section 784 pp 873–4 quoting James *Principles of Psychology*.

morning that I couldn't remember what was said the night at the police station because of the injections, and [the accused suggested that I should go and see an attorney and put the case in front of him. That is what my words were to the CID and the CID put it in his statement '[a false statement]', which I never said.

In regard to the gentleman referred to as 'the CID' the test by mental reaction could then be applied in one or other or both of the following methods:

First method: Why should he want to write down something which you had not said?

Second method: If you told him that, how could he mistake it for an allegation that you had been asked to say that you had made a false statement?'

My own view is that both of these questions should be employed, and that the witness would be driven into making an unfounded and unacceptable attack on the police or else standing revealed as a liar. From this, moreover, the matter should develop into the second and distinct application of the test, with the following questions:

'You signed your statement after reading it over?'
'When you saw the words "[a false statement]" what did you think that they meant?'
'Did you point out to the CID that this was not what you said?'

From the test by mental reaction it is but a short journey to the test by improbability. For what is improbability but a mental reaction applied to any given set of facts? This is the mental reaction, not of the witness, nor of the subject of the testimony, but of the cross-examiner. Finally the test of probability will be applied by the court. It is for this latter reason that some degree of care must be exercised in suggesting that something is improbable. You may be distressed, when you are under full sail cross-examining a witness about the improbability of his testimony, to hear the judge remark to you: 'I find nothing improbable in that'. If misfortune of this nature should assail you, ask yourself whether the judge is right or wrong, and then do one of three things: either move on seamlessly as if nothing untoward happened because you realise the judge is right, or attack the point again because you realise that the reason why the judge is wrong is because you did not put your question clearly enough, or remember that there is always an appeal.

12.5.18 Cause to remember

One question which you should ask yourself while listening to the evidence-in-chief is: 'Why should he remember this?' From time to time the same question can usefully be put to a witness, the test being whether you are satisfied that no acceptable answer can be given.

Not quite in point but sufficiently close to be helpful is the following cross-examination which occurred when it became necessary to destroy the evidence of a witness who said that the accused had returned home at 4.15 am:

'You say that the accused came in at 4.15 am?'
  — 'It was about quarter past four in the morning.'
'Do you have a watch?'
  — 'No.'
'Is there a clock in your room?'
  — 'No.'
'Did anyone else in the room have a watch?'
  — 'No.'
'Then how can you say it was 4.15 am?'
  — 'Because the hooter blows at the steelworks at 4 am to tell the workers they must get up and I heard it a few minutes before.'

Followed by collapse of the cross-examination on this point!

So, too, you will catch a few Tartars and when you think that there is no conceivable reason why the witness should remember not only the facts but also the details of a conversation that took place five years previously he will come out with an answer as distressingly adequate as the one quoted. Remember, too, that your opponent may well have put the same question to the witness in consultation and it will be no surprise to him to find that he must justify his recollection.

The method which I recommend if this test is adopted, bearing in mind that this particular test can easily flow into that described in the next section, is to bring the transaction which you are examining into a position, if not of actual insignificance, then of almost daily routine. Ask yourself for example, to recall where you were on Tuesday night, three weeks ago. How good is your recollection on this point? Or try recalling the terms of a ten-minute discussion you had with the representative of a firm of legal publishers when you ordered a couple of textbooks from him. Alternatively, next time an exuberant motorist tries to arrange for your early demise as you are crossing the road try to recall the relative position of yourself and the car at all material times and then relate it to the traffic lights, if any.

To some extent the method under discussion was to be gleaned from the paragraph on closing off escape routes and from the example there given.[31] In essence you must discover where the witness's attention was focussed and what degree of concentration there would have been on the *res gestae*.

12.5.19 Test the witness on collateral matters

When you receive the treatment indicated in the previous paragraph, or when the witness deposes to a fact so simple that he cannot be shaken then a different technique must be used. The incidental advantage of this particular method is that it gains in effectiveness with the number of witnesses called against you, unless they are perfectly honest and reliable. What you do is to test the reliability of the witness's memory of the main fact by comparison with his memory of details. In most cases the main fact will be found to have been no

---

[31] See paragraph 12.5.10 above.

more noteworthy *at the time* than the accompanying circumstances. When the witness fails on the accompanying circumstances his memory of the main fact will have to be treated with some reserve. This may well be the time to disregard a few of the previous suggestions and to display some degree of forcefulness. It is in this context that questions should follow each other rapidly, giving the witness no time to improvise and imagine. A slightly more aggressive tone in the cross-examiner will force the witness on to the defensive, force him to rush out with ill-considered answers and perhaps cause him to manifest an uneasiness that will impress the court as indicative of untruthfulness.

For example, the witness says that your client made a certain admission. There were no other persons present. The problem is to destroy this. Your client's denial is not enough, because the mathematics of legal equilibrium results in the axiom that the positive is always greater than the negative. This axiom is not merely whimsy. It is very sound reasoning: an assertion receives an added quantity, being the improbability of invention, whilst a denial suffers a deduction, being the motive to deny. If you can establish facts that will counter the improbability of invention, that is entirely a different matter. The difficulty is to destroy the simple allegation without the facts which I have mentioned. It is here that you explore the circumstances, in the tone of voice and manner I have suggested. You will thus ask: What time of day was this? Where was it? Who got there first? Were you sitting or standing? Was my client sitting or standing? How long did the conversation last? Did anyone else come in while you were talking? What else was discussed? And fifty seven other rapidly-put questions to get the picture.

If possible you intend to return to this same theme later, and your preliminary purpose is to get the witness to commit himself to the surrounding details, details that he ought to remember if he is truthful but that he will have to improvise if dishonest. Also, if he is untruthful, your purpose of rapidity in the questioning is to give the witness as little time as possible to retain an impression on his memory of the answers given. When you return to this topic later you hope to get a substantially different picture and, perhaps, to test further some of the earlier answers which you did not allow to divert you from the immediate purpose but which merited more attention.

When dealing with conversations, where fabrication is so simple and denial so unconvincing, there are two vital questions. The one that should be put first in this particular group or on this particular subject is: How long did this conversation last? I rate this question so highly that I would say that it is often a 'sixty-four dollar question'. If the answer is 'a very short time' it leads to a later investigation, in appropriate cases, of why there should be a short conversation for the sole purpose of making an admission. If the answer indicates a lengthy or moderately lengthy discussion, you will exercise a respectful restraint and a judicious patience. Then, after you have subjected the witness to the barrage of questions which I have advised, you will invite him to tell you what else was discussed. If he is of average quality he will manage to mention about two minutes' worth of talk in a conversation lasting half an hour. Even the best of witnesses can seldom manage more than 20 per cent of the time which they have deposed to. Properly handled, this may be the method of discrediting the witness's testimony on a particular point under attack.

This technique must be used with some degree of caution or it may well be ineffective or futile. The various books that deal with cross-examination quote instances of witnesses whose evidence has been destroyed because, while they could depose early to the principal fact, they were unable to describe the surrounding or accompanying circumstances. But, as Moore remarks,[32]

> (I)t does not follow that the memory of a witness is not deserving of reliance in respect of a matter in which his mind was engaged, because it is defective as to secondary circumstances.

Thus, you will first ask yourself whether it is reasonable to expect the witness to have as equally clear a recollection of the secondary circumstances as he purports to have of the matter on which his mind was engaged. If you care to read the instances cited by Moore you will have some guidance, as good today as it was a century ago, on the cases in which this technique becomes useful.

12.5.20 Test by fact

The most effective and devastatingly destructive cross-examination is accomplished with the use of facts.

Not always will you have facts to use in the manner I am about to describe. In many cases you will be asked to knock down the coconuts without a ball to throw at them. You will be expected to sneak up when no one is looking and dislodge the coconut which will fall to the ground and shatter into small pieces. So you will understand the value of having something substantial with which to accomplish your task. The odd thing about these balls is that they don't often miss, in fact they are so easy to throw that if you do miss you had better conclude that law is not your profession. Another odd thing is that the successful throwing of balls seems to tempt even the judge to have a few shies for himself. As Wrottesley says,[33] using a different simile, counsel should:

> never continue the cross-examination of a witness if they saw the judge showed the disposition to do it himself. If they saw the judge, to use a somewhat sporting expression, in the least inclined to take up the running, let him do it.

However, elsewhere Wrottesley[34] complains that:

> (t)he benefits of cross-examination are sometimes defeated by the interposition of the court, to require an explanation of the motive and object of the questions proposed, or to pronounce a judgment upon their immateriality; whereas experience frequently shows that it is only by an indirect, and apparently irrelevant, inquiry that a witness can be brought to divulge the truth which he prepared himself to conceal.

---

[32] *Moore on Facts* (1908) s 806 at 900.
[33] Wrottesley *On the Examination of Witnesses in Court* 2 ed (Sweet & Maxwell, 1931) 91.
[34] Ibid at 150–1.

It would be cynically disrespectful to observe that it is all right if the judge is on your side. My own deferential comment is that the cause and course of justice are better served by judicial silence and restraint.

However, let us get back to technique in the use of facts. Facts are of many kinds: they are statements in documents, statements in the evidence of other witnesses, facts elicited by diligent inquiry and investigation and which cannot be proved in rebuttal, or facts which will be deposed to by subsequent witnesses. Naturally, the technique will vary in detail with the type of fact and it is not possible to set out a schedule or forms and precedents to be used in cross-examination in manner similar to forms and precedents of agreements, petitions or pleadings. The broad suggestion can be made that the degree of caution to be adopted in the use of facts must vary with the ease of proof of the fact itself. Thus, if you have a letter signed by a witness in which he says he was in Cape Town from 1 to 15 March, it is safe enough to put a question such as: 'I put it to you that you were not present at the meeting of the company in Johannesburg on 2 March.' He must concede it or be destroyed by his own hand. On the other end of the scale is a case such as *R v Burke*[35] where a witness gave his evidence in Irish through an interpreter. It was put to him that he could speak English, for he had used that very language in speaking to two persons at court. He denied this and evidence to contradict him was held to be inadmissible. It may fill in an idle ten or fifteen minutes if you were to try to work out how you would have handled the cross-examination in *R v Burke*, that is how you would establish the fact before putting the question, or how you would put the witness into a position where he could not make a false denial.

Where you are satisfied that the fact is properly capable of proof later, or where it has been proved by other witnesses already, it is often most effective to encourage the witnesses to give evidence directly contrary to the fact before putting the fact to him.

Generally speaking, this type of cross-examination is straightforward and it would be an exercise in lily-gilding were I to offer any suggestions on how to go about it. There is one word of advice that I might offer, however. It is this: when the witness is testifying, whether in-chief or cross-examination, you ought to be constantly on the alert for incongruities. If any statement does not reconcile with the facts, or with any other statement made by the witness, you must be instantly aware of it in order to exploit the inconsistency. When you find such a creature, incongruity, inconsistency or just plain discord, you are well on the way to achieving at least two of the objectives of cross-examination. Do not, however, read these paragraphs as referring only to incongruities. The instant theme is the use of facts; the testing of a witness by confronting him or her with facts.

An illustration of this (and of other points on the topic of cross-examination)

---

[35] (1858) 8 Cox CC 44.

is found in a case where a civil servant was dismissed for misconduct after an administrative inquiry presided over by, say, a Mr Ngobeni. The misconduct alleged was that he had submitted to 'higher authority' a document containing a number of false and scurrilous allegations about the head of his particular department, Mr Maluleke. At the administrative inquiry Mr Maluleke had given evidence dealing with and denying each of the specific allegations. Other witnesses had been called where it was considered necessary and the civil servant (subsequently to become the plaintiff) had cross-examined some of the witnesses. He had also himself given evidence. Whether due to ignorance, inexperience or other reasons which may be inferred, he had made little or no effort to establish the truth of the allegations in the document which he had signed. The result of the inquiry was that his dismissal had been recommended and later effected. He was, or considered himself to be, aggrieved by the decision, and brought an action for damages for wrongful dismissal.

At the trial the plaintiff testified in his own case and said that when Mr Maluleke entered the witness box he (the plaintiff) would 'prove every fact in the document'. He also said that this was not an impulsive statement, but one which he genuinely meant. Counsel then selected one particular allegation, selected it for the very reason that he knew beyond doubt that the allegation could be shown to be false, and asked the plaintiff why he had not attempted to prove this at the administrative inquiry. The answers on this point went as follows:

> 'Mr K, I shall not allow you to evade my questions. Tell me why you did not raise it if it was true.'
> — 'I just felt that at that particular inquiry I could not raise it.'
> 'Why not?'
> — 'Because of the fact that it was an administrative inquiry and I had no legal representative and I felt that at that stage I would not mention it.'
> 'Very well. We'll take that as your explanation for the present moment. Let's get back to your statement that should you be given the privilege of cross-examining Mr Maluleke you will establish every allegation in Exhibit 'R'.'

Some time later, when sufficient other matters had been dealt with, counsel turned to the task of destroying Mr K's testimony about the truth of the allegations in Exhibit 'R'. In this case he proposed to use facts. Now there were several facts which could be used, such as contrary evidence, an examination of books and vouchers, the absence of corroborative witnesses, but counsel decided to choose the one which allowed for no dispute or denial from the witness.

Counsel proposed to confront the plaintiff with the fact that, at the inquiry, he had made no attempt to prove, or even maintain the truth of, much less his belief in, the allegation in question. The witness knew what counsel was after. Counsel knew that the witness could not escape and that very little finesse was required on this topic. It will be seen how the witness was compelled to resort to indefensible and unsupportable allegations in his dilemma.

> 'Let us refer to the inquiry record, page 74. You said that the report, Exhibit 'R', was

drawn up by you and your associates in a hurry and that you in fact asked that this
paragraph be omitted. Did you say that?'
    — 'I did.'
'Is this true?'
    — 'It is perfectly true.'
'Is it the same as your evidence in court today?'
After a pause, 'It is.'
'Did you read the report?'
    — 'The report was read out by Green.'
'At your meeting?'
    — 'At our meeting.'
'Now Mr Ngobeni asked you: "but did you not read it?"—; and your answer was:
"I did not read it — we had no time." When you gave this answer what impression
were you trying to create in Mr Ngobeni's mind?'
    — 'It was read by Green, we all accepted it, and then we signed it and handed it
in.'
'Mr K, I am not easily diverted from my questions,[36] so try again, will you. What
impression were you trying to create?'
    — 'I cannot say what impression I was trying to create. I was just telling him
exactly what happened.'
'Were you trying to create the impression that you really didn't know that this
clause had been put in Exhibit "R" despite your insistence that it should be deleted?'
    — 'As I said before, my Lord, I knew it was Mr Green who read the complete
report to the meeting.'

After a few more questions the evidence proceeded:

'Your case there in effect was that you didn't know that this allegation remained in
the report; that was your case because you realized that the allegation couldn't be
supported?'[37]
    — 'No, m'Lord, I knew it was there when I signed the document. I didn't agree
with it.'
(Consider here, how this bears upon the witness's earlier statement that he would
'prove every fact in this document'.)

The process was not finished, however, and the following ensued:

'Would you tell his Lordship whether or not you knew that that paragraph was in
Exhibit "R" when you signed it.'
    — 'I have already admitted that.'
'Would you look at page 71 of the record where you were asked "What do you
mean you never had anything to do with it? You signed it" and you interrupted
saying "As far as I am concerned I signed it, but I didn't know he had included that,
because I asked him not to include it." Did you say that?'
    — 'I did m'Lord.'
'Was it true?'
    — 'No my Lord.'
'Did you know it was not true?

---

[36] See paragraph 12.5.33 below, in which the suggestion is made that the cross-examiner should
avoid indulging in empty rhetoric. Counsel need not have indulged in self-commendation.
[37] Not an elegant question because it is 'double-barrelled'.

— 'At the time I did.'

'You did! Why did you say something in evidence that was not true?'

— 'Because I had tried to have this taken off this particular document, but everybody else considered it should stay.'

'But you knew that you ought to speak the truth in placing your case before the presiding officer. Didn't you?'

— 'It is so.'

'And when you spoke an untruth, why did you do so? Was it to advance your case?'[38]

— 'It was not to advance my case.'

'Would you like to give any other reason why you spoke an untruth at the inquiry?'

—'At this stage of the trial, my Lord, I had no more further interest in the case. I realized then that I was going to be found guilty and that is why I said I knew nothing about it whatsoever.'

At this stage counsel made the pardonable error of allowing himself to be directed from his theme of confronting the plaintiff with the fact that he had not attempted to prove this one particular topic at the inquiry. The witness's statement that he knew that he would be found guilty was, however, subjected to the process of comparison with the facts, and effectively destroyed. Counsel then returned to the point as follows:

'Well, now, how dare you say that you had the impression that Mr Ngobeni had closed his mind to you, and that no evidence that you led would make any difference?'

No answer.

'Very well Mr K, there being no answer, I go back now to the record. You explained that you told an untruth to Mr Ngobeni because you realized that nothing you said was going to help. Why do you choose the untruth which helps your defence? Do you follow me?'

— 'I follow you.'

'Well, now will you explain this to his Lordship?'

— 'As I've already explained, that was the one point of the report that I was honestly not in favour of. I was not happy about that at any time.'

The plaintiff was painfully aware that he had committed himself to a statement that, as part of his case that he had been wrongfully dismissed, he was going to prove that his allegations against Mr Maluleke were true. He also knew that those allegations contained a point which we shall describe as X. He was further aware that counsel proposed to test his statement by examining point X in particular. Finally he was aware that he was weak on point X, if the epithet is not an understatement, because at the inquiry he had endeavoured strenuously to

[38] Another 'double-barrelled' question! A very bad one as the answer shows. The second question, an irresistible impulse, should have been kept in reserve. This aptly illustrates a statement in *Moore on Facts* (1908) section 1252 at 1395: 'Where a question addressed to a witness contains two interrogatories, a categorical answer should be construed with regard to the common habit of witnesses to ignore the earlier parts of a complex question, and to answer only the latter parts to which the attention is last directed.'

dissociate himself from point X. His problem, therefore, was to evade questions dealing with the inconsistent fact of what his conduct had been previously when he was given the opportunity to 'prove every fact in that document'. In the result he was completely unequal to the task which few witnesses indeed could have accomplished, and this enabled counsel to establish an ascendancy on the other points where no direct incongruity was available. Finally the plaintiff conceded that not a single one of the allegations in 'that document' had any substance in it.

The test by fact is applied by establishing the fact which is incongruous or inconsistent with the statement of the witness. In some cases he may be invited to explain the incongruity or inconsistency. Generally, however, that chance should not be afforded him, and the more effective question is to ask whether he still persists in the statement which you are attacking. If he says that he does, then you have material on which to argue that his evidence should not be accepted. If he says that he does not, do not spoil it for the sake of rhetoric. You will have destroyed the statement, and possibly the witness. If you carry it further you may destroy the point. It is very impressive and self-satisfying to ask a fine-sounding rhetorical question such as: 'Why did you try to mislead the court?' But all too often the witness is afforded a chance which is not deserved, and is enabled to wriggle out of the dilemma instead of being truly impaled on whichever of its horns you think the more effective.

In many cases, a little effective research will supply all sorts of devastating facts which can be thrown at the witness — more particularly if he is one of the parties. So if the plaintiff in a damages claim complains of the injuries to his back you can ask him how he manages, at the age of 70, to run up and down two flights of stairs when he visits his lady friend who has a flat on the second floor of a building in which there is no lift — and I haven't invented that illustration! Or if he is an estate agent who is suing for commission when your client says that someone else was the effective cause of the sale, you may ask him how many such cases he has had in the last ten years, how many he has lost and how many he settled by paying the costs — which also is not apocryphal. But the technique is to use facts, and only facts.

12.5.21 Previous inconsistent statements

One of the classic ways in which the credit of a witness may be impeached, is by reference to previous statements (whether oral or written) which differ from his testimony in court.

Cross-examination with reference to previous inconsistent statements, and the leading of evidence as to such statements, is permissible where the previous statements are relevant to the subject matter of the case.[39] The prior inconsistent statement is either proved through the evidence of the witness himself or, if he denies making the statement, by way of evidence.[40]

---

[39] See *Salzmann v Holmes* 1914 AD 471 at 477.

[40] If the cross-examining party has closed its case, it may apply to re-open same in order to lead the evidence in rebuttal. See *Sumesur v Dominion Insurance Co Ltd* 1960 (2) SA 801 (D).

The witness must be confronted with the prior inconsistent statement during cross-examination.[41] Cross-examination should be specific as to the time, circumstances and content of the earlier statement.

Cross-examining on a previous inconsistent statement involves three steps.

The first step involves putting the previous statement to the witness. The following is a suggested series of questions:

- You made a previous statement on this topic on another occasion.
- In which language did you make the statement?
- The statement was read back to you after it had been written down.
- This is the statement, is it not?
- This is your signature, is it not?
- The statement was read back to you before you signed it.
- You would not have signed it were you not satisfied with the correctness of its content.
- You took the oath before signing it.[42]

The second step is to place the inconsistent passages of the previous statement on record. The best method in this regard is to require the witness to read those passages aloud, and thus into the record.

The third step is to put the inconsistency to the witness.[43]

12.5.22 Attacking credibility

Before you embark on your career as a cross-examiner you must appreciate one fundamental matter. It may be once in a lifetime — or even less — that a witness will say to you:

> 'Stop! My answers are false. I concede that no reliance can be placed on my evidence.'

It may be twice in a lifetime — or even less — that the witness will be so overcome by your cross-examination that he will collapse in the witness-box.

Life, unfortunately, just doesn't work that way.

For the rest you will simply try to show, from surrounding circumstances, that the witness is not worthy of belief. You will examine his relationship with or bias towards the party who calls him to testify. You will look for personal motives which may incline him to misrepresent the facts. You will examine his antecedents, history and character. You will look for his prior statements in order to show contradictions or inconsistencies. Perhaps a few words on this topic or its various subdivisions would not be out of place.

---

[41] See paragraph 12.5.37 below, where the need to put one's case to a witness is dealt with.

[42] See paragraph 12.5.6 above. The questions should be put as leadingly as possible, so as to drive the witness into making the required concessions. See also the example of cross-examination of a lay witness in Appendix D, which involves cross-examination on a previous inconsistent statement.

[43] See, in general, with regard to cross-examination on previous inconsistent statements, D Zeffertt and A Paizes *The South African Law of Evidence* 2 ed 914 et seq, and PJ Schwikkard and S van der Merwe *Principles of Evidence* 3 ed 460–2. See also the example in Appendix D.

Certain factors bearing upon credibility need now be noticed.

• *Bias*

> The human mind practises singular delusions upon itself, and the faculties of observation and memory of biased witnesses are subject to peculiar aberrations for which allowance is constantly made without derogating from the veracity of the witness.[44]

Bias is often unrecognised by the witness and this can be easily understood when we consider the phenomenon of counsel, most learned in the law indeed, solemnly and earnestly arguing the contrary sides of a proposition, when we know that, were their briefs reversed, each would contend for the absurdity of that which is now being propounded. So, too, with the expert witnesses, men or women of the utmost integrity, who would be horrified at the thought that their opinions are in any whit affected by fealty. They are approached to provide evidence on facts often imperfectly stated and in circumstances where they must know what opinion their client desires. A little subtle cross-examination as to what they understood and what was said to them may often place their otherwise honest testimony in better perspective as to its impartiality.

In regard to this topic, it is useful to remember two principles of the law of evidence:

• It is permissible to ask a witness, other than a client or the legal representatives, what he or she said or did or what was shown to him or her (other than, a privileged document) at a consultation or interview with the client's legal advisers.[45]

• It is permissible to call evidence in rebuttal to prove bias on the part of a witnesses — this, I would suggest, means actual conscious bias.

It will be recognised that there are two aspects to this topic. The first is the bias of the honest witness who takes sides and in consequence allows his evidence to be affected; the second is the bias of the dishonest witness who has deliberately set out to assist the party who calls him.

The bias of the honest witness is difficult to demonstrate; it requires careful probing to elicit, careful investigation of the matters behind the testimony, investigation of the witness as a person, of his thoughts, desires and motives, investigation of the circumstances in which he comes to testify, investigation, in proper cases, of his opportunities of observation and of his judgment. All these matters must be carefully and tactfully examined without conveying an imputation of dishonesty.

One excellent example of unconscious bias is to be found where a pedestrian is knocked down by a bus. A host of fellow pedestrians will depose to the carefulness of the plaintiff and the carelessness of the bus-driver, while an equal

---

[44] *Moore on Facts* at 179–230.
[45] *International Tobacco Co (SA) Ltd v United Tobacco Cos (South) Ltd* (2) 1953 (3) SA 879 (W).

host of passengers on the bus can usually be found for the reverse proposition. The fact that neither group had cause to observe the incident adequately is one of the whimsies of litigation.

Where there is a deliberate bias, this usually being the case where rebutting evidence is available, the task of the cross-examiner is easier. The state of the witness's mind can be proved as a fact and his evidence tested in the light of the fact.[46] Often your task will be simplified, because this sort of bias may lead to exaggerations and improbabilities. These may be encouraged and stimulated to the point of self-destruction and with them will go the credibility of the witness.

- *Motive*

'Motive' is a word of wide signification in this context. It may be related to the previous topic of cross-examination by the test of mental reaction or it may be more closely the successor of the topic of 'bias'. In any event it is a matter to which you should look in cross-examination. You should ask yourself two questions on this topic: did the actors have a motive to act as the witness describes? Has the witness a motive to describe the action as he does?

When a motive is detectable, the principles on which to base cross-examination are those described previously. If it is a case of motive of the actors, then their alleged conduct must be tested in the light of the accepted motive and any incongruity should render the witness's testimony unacceptable. In the case of a motive to misrepresent on the part of the witness, cross-examination must be directed first to establishing the circumstances from which the motive would appear and then the witness must be taxed with his motives. If the circumstances have been adequately established, then a false denial of motive should be recognisable as such, while the enforced admission of a motive should weaken the acceptability of the evidence.

Obviously it is not practicable to enumerate all types of motives which may affect a witness in testifying. Almost every human failing can provide a motive, and human frailty and human failings are legion. Self-interest, self-protection, kinship, friendship, pride, conceit, self-righteousness, love, hate, envy, fear, are all factors which may colour or distort the evidence of a witness. Ignorance and obstinacy are others. If you have or acquire a feeling for human nature you may sense the motive as you listen to the evidence-in-chief. In other cases the motive must be pried out like the pearl from the oyster — or, perhaps more aptly, like the thorn from the flesh. Your cross-examination should be adapted to the circumstances and should be planned to expose the weakness which underlies the evidence. Matters such as kinship and friendship, if not candidly brought out during the evidence-in-chief, are the simplest to elicit, requiring only a question such as: 'How long have you known Mr X?' Others, such as

---

[46] This topic is fully dealt with in the textbooks on evidence. See for example Zeffertt and Paizes *The South African Law of Evidence* 2 ed at 920.

self-interest or self-protection are on the same plane, it being necessary to do little more than inquire how the witness might be affected by the judgment. Of more subtle aura are pride, conceit, self-righteousness and those factors which are essentially psychological in nature.

• *History*

It is permissible to discredit a witness by reference to his history or antecedents. This, however, is a weapon which I suggest should be used with as much eagerness as the Great Powers today desire to use the atom bomb. The average witness has no great desire to enter the witness-box and, often, no greater desire to testify falsely. It is a fact, regrettable but true, that the press is wont to report most prominently those passages in evidence which reflect adversely upon witnesses, clients or lawyers. The evidence which is of significance in the case is often so uninteresting or lacking in 'news value' as to be overlooked entirely. It may, in these circumstances, be unwarranted to attempt to discredit a witness by reference to his antecedents. Each case will have to be judged on its merits and counsel is entitled to show that a witness, by reason of previous convictions or any other matter likely to affect his character, is not worthy of credence. You should be particularly reluctant to attack a witness's character or reputation to satisfy the personal ill-will of your own client. Your first consideration should be whether the material at your disposal would in fact render the evidence unacceptable.

The answers of the witness when cross-examined on collateral matters which go only to credibility cannot be rebutted.[47]

The witness, it seems, may be asked whether his evidence has been rejected in other cases. Unless you know why the evidence has been rejected you take the chance that your fireworks are damp squibs. If it is lack of veracity or credibility that caused the court to reject the witness's testimony then there is good reason to ask the court to treat him with reserve in your own case, and there is good material for cross-examination along the lines of: 'Do you know the meaning of taking an oath? Do you regard it seriously? Does it in fact have any significance for you? I put it to you that you would be quite willing to give false evidence on oath if it suited you.' And so on. But if the court, in rejecting the witness's evidence, remarked that he was transparently honest but clearly mistaken or that 'from his imperfect position of observation he was not able to form a clear picture of what took place' it is difficult to see how he is not worthy of belief on any subsequent occasion that he enters the witness-box. Perhaps, however, this is merely an illustration of the advice given earlier never to ask a question unless you know the answer.

---

[47] *S v Sinkankanka* 1963 (2) SA 531 (AD). See, in general, Zeffertt and Paizes *The South African Law of Evidence* 2 ed 917–920.

• *Contradictions*

These may be contradictions in the course of the testimony, or contradiction by means of prior inconsistent statements, or contradictions between the *viva voce* evidence and the pleadings. I am not concerned with the law of evidence on the use of prior inconsistent statements but with the method of their utilisation.

The fact that the witness makes or has made contradictory or even inconsistent statements is of great value in the attack on credibility. It is therefore important that the contradiction or inconsistency be preserved and not destroyed. Destruction results from over-eagerness, impatience or inexpertness. The witness should not be invited to reconcile or explain contradictions or inconsistencies, the reason being that in most cases the witness will respond to the invitation, and often with no small measure of success. Yet of all the impulses that beset a cross-examiner, none is stronger than that to extend the forbidden invitation. But if you think a moment you will realise that the question is a gin, a trap, a snare and a delusion. It can achieve nothing.

> You ask: 'Mr K yesterday you told the court that the contract was in writing but you had lost the letter, today you say it was an oral one. How can you be telling the truth?'
>
> So Mr K answers: 'Yes, my Lord, I regret that I did not express myself clearly yesterday. I had in mind that a letter was written confirming the oral contract and I thought that the letter in fact would be the contract. I have lost the letter. But the contract was an oral one and I did not mean to convey anything else.'

The truth may well be that Mr K has found the letter overnight and doesn't like the look of it, or it may be anything else. However, the point no longer exists. How much better it is, when you get the reply that the contract was oral, to say nothing, to show nothing and to do nothing. Then you argue that there was a clear contradiction, and that no reliance should be placed on the witness on this point.

If you would object that your opponent may elicit the answer in re-examination then it must be conceded that the possibility exists — if he likes playing with fire. He does not — or should not — know what the explanation is, nor even whether there is an explanation. He will be reluctant to emphasise a contradiction that may well have gone unnoticed.

Internal contradictions, if I may call them that, may be born or may be made. They are born when the witness spontaneously utters a statement directly the opposite of what he has said previously. This does not necessarily result from any skill on your part; your skill consists in not wagging your tail — until you are sufficiently a master of cross-examination to pounce on the contradiction, hurl it back at the witness and beat him with it so that he does not recover. You also have to possess the skill to recognise which contradiction is so damning that it can be handled in this way. You must also learn to distinguish between contradictions and discrepancies, for discrepancies are liable to be used either as the hallmark of mendacity or of veracity as the mind of the judge dictates — and with equal justification, let it be conceded. When you next relate an anecdote, mark how there is a variation in detail as you inflict it on one friend after another — indeed it is almost as though some puckish imp were driving your thought processes in haphazard fashion so that the words tumble out as near as possible in sequence but jostled and pushed by one another. Why, then, should the thought process of a witness be given less latitude in the judgment passed on them? So the importance of discrepancies must not be over-estimated. When a witness swears falsely he will be sure of the fact on which he lies and unsure of details. Thus in undergoing the test of cross-examination he will testify differently on details and his evidence will be marked with discrepancies. So the importance of discrepancies must not be underestimated.[48]

This leads me to contradictions which are not born, but made. These indeed, to my mind, are the highest achievement of pure cross-examination. They are achieved by the application of logic to the evidence of the witness and, by that logical process, can lead to the destruction of that evidence. I call it 'pure cross-examination' because I doubt seriously whether an honest, truthful, candid witness can be led into serious self-contradiction. The process is a development of what I described as 'Test by Fact'. Instead of showing that the evidence is inconsistent with a fact, proven or to be proved, you show, in the process, that it is inconsistent with logic. In practice you will usually not directly start with questions directed towards the suspect statement, but with questions which will lead to final acceptance of a proposition directly contrary to that statement. You will put to the witness each successive step or proposition in your reasoning and compel his assent thereto, until finally there can only be a concession of your proposition. It is in this process that you should resort most lavishly to the leading question for, to strain a metaphor, you propose to lead the witness irresistibly to the goal you have chosen. When you have secured the final concession from him and established your contradiction you will remember all the advice that has been given in the preceding pages of this chapter. If the contradiction is in concept it may better be kept for argument. If it is in terms, in direct words, the witness may be confronted with it. By the phrase 'in terms' I mean, to take a simple example, something like 'I was there' and 'I was not there'.

One of the most effective ways of attacking credibility by contradiction lies in the use of letters written or statements signed by the witness. But, as Hamlet remarked regretfully, there's the rub. It does not often happen that the document which can be used to contradict the witness is entirely free of matter

---

[48] Wellman at 42: 'Avoid the mistake, so common among the inexperienced, of making much of trifling discrepancies'. Judge HC Nicholas said in his 1984 Olive Schreiner memorial lecture (reproduced in 1985 *SALJ* 32 at 42) that 'the daily experience of the courts . . . teach[es] us [that when]. . . . accounts of a transaction come from the mouths of different witnesses it is seldom that it is not possible to pick out apparent or real inconsistencies between them. These inconsistencies are studiously displaced by an adverse pleader, but oftentimes with little impression on the minds of the judges. On the contrary, a close and minute agreement induces the suspicion of confederacy and fraud.'

which can be used against your own client. If you cross-examine on a document which is otherwise inadmissible, you render the whole document admissible in re-examinations. How, then, does one use only the contradictory matter? It has been suggested that you should ask the witness whether he wrote the particular letter, or, I would add, signed a particular statement. The letter or statement is then produced to the witness and he is asked to read it over to acquaint himself with its contents. By this means he will observe the contradictory statement. When this has been done you ask him whether he still persists in the statement made in his testimony. 'And', says Wrottesley,[49] 'in the case of an honest witness', the result might very well be that he would qualify that statement in your favour.

Not a very encouraging comment, that is, and one which gives rise to a host of interesting queries. Should the desired result not eventuate and should the witness be cautious enough to content himself the answer 'Yes' instead of trying to extricate himself from a contradiction which he can see, and which he thinks the judge can also see, you are back where you started. You must now weigh up with unerring accuracy the advantage of proving the terms of the contradictory statement, against the prejudice which will result from other portions of the document.

Of course, with the proper use of rule 35 there should be no more documentary surprises in litigation, and the well-prepared witness will have an answer for everything. Contrariwise, as a character in literature once remarked, the damaging effect on one's own case may well be minimised because the opponents will know all about the document.

The principal point to look for is the distinction between contradiction and discrepancies. For one good, sound contradiction the risk may well be taken; for a couple of discrepancies it is stupid to risk proving, for example, a prior consistent statement.

An interesting example of the good, sound contradiction occurred in a case heard in the Witwatersrand Local Division a few years ago. The plaintiff was a passenger in a motorcar being driven by the second defendant on the main road from Johannesburg to Mbombela. On a winding section of the road near Machadodorp the car collided with a caravan which was being towed by a car proceeding in the opposite direction. The plaintiff was injured and she sued the second defendant as well as the insurers of the caravan. The second defendant's story was a simple one. He was travelling at a moderate speed when the combination vehicle came from the opposite direction. Because of the left hand bend and the different turning circles (to use a technical term) of the car and the caravan, the latter trespassed over the white line and struck his car. One of the allegations against him was that he was driving at an excessive speed. The plaintiff's legal advisers subpoenaed the claims manager of an insurance company which had issued the second defendant with a comprehensive

---

[49] Wrottesley *The Examination of Witnesses* 70.

motorcar policy and obtained the production of the claim form which the second defendant had submitted in connection with the damage to his car. In this claim form the second defendant had given a description of the accident which was entirely consistent with his evidence in court. Sad to say, however, the claim form required a statement as to the speed of the insured vehicle and, perhaps cautiously or perhaps incautiously, the second defendant had written '120 kph', qualifying this with cabalistic signs meaning 'approximately'. Well, 120 kph does seem to be a somewhat reckless speed to dash through a winding mountain road which is liberally ornamented with single and double white lines. In this case the prejudice of corroborating the second defendant's description of the accident was insignificant compared with the advantage of contradicting him on one of the elements of negligence urged against him. It might be remarked that the plaintiff herself could give no evidence as to speed because she was asleep at the time — it was well after sunset. The contradiction was used as a cudgel wherewith to beat the second defendant and to destroy, very effectively, his story of a reasonable speed which, in the witness box, showed signs of dropping well below 80kph.

Before leaving the topic of contradiction of witnesses I must recount one further illustration from an actual trial. It is what Shakespeare had in mind when he said that 'out of this nettle, danger, we pluck this flower, safety'.[50] It also shows that you never know what will impress a court and what effect your cross-examination is having either upon the witness or upon the judge. The case is one which has already been mentioned in this chapter and is the one where damages were claimed for wrongful dismissal. The defendant justified the dismissal upon the grounds of a false and defamatory report made by the plaintiff about his immediate superior. During the course of cross-examination of the plaintiff this gentleman took advantage of his privilege as a witness, and, despite warning by cross-examining counsel, gave utterance to further grossly defamatory remarks concerning the same superior officer. In brief he accused the latter of misappropriating public property, of receiving Christmas presents from individuals and companies who and which desired to receive favourable attention from this official and of taking possession of Christmas presents sent to the staff of his department, subsequently to sell those Christmas presents back to the staff at reduced prices, presumably to pocket the proceeds. These were unpleasant allegations, interesting enough to attract the attention of the gentlemen of the press who happened to be present. The statements could not be ignored, as they might have been in the average trial action which attracts no press publicity.

Up to this stage the cross-examination had been following, in the main, the lines which are to be discussed subsequently herein under the sub-title 'The half-truth'.[51] This means that counsel was more than satisfied with the answers, for the time being, while the apparent credibility of the witness was unshaken.

---

[50] Harry Hotspur in *Henry IV Part I* Act II scene iii.
[51] Paragraph 12.5.25.

But now it was no longer simply a question of the credibility of the witness. There was also the question of the integrity of the superior officer, with a variety of political overtones and implications. The first line of attack was obvious. There could possibly be a 'Test by Fact'.[52] Fact could not be a denial by the superior officer, because the issue was purely a collateral one, to credibility only, and rebutting evidence was inadmissible. Therefore the test had to take the narrower form of 'Test by Mental Reaction'.[53] It was not a simple 'What did you think?' but a more complex 'What did you do because of what you must have thought?'

The plaintiff was accordingly asked whether he had included this allegation in the document which led to his ultimate resignation. No danger in this question, because counsel knew the answer. Next came the more significant question: 'Did you ever report these matters to those in authority above him (your superior officer)?' Still not a very dangerous question because counsel had consulted with most of these people and he also knew that neither party had disclosed any document or copy of any document containing such a report.

The 'Test by Mental Reaction' now came into operation. The plaintiff had made no secret of his dislike of his superior officer and he knew that, consistently, his conduct would have been to report his complaints. He knew that if he said 'No' he would be discredited so he said 'Yes'. Here he gambled, because the official to whom he claimed to have made his report had resigned some time past and was not readily available as a witness. However, he also knew that this official would not have received an oral report, so he claimed to have submitted his information in writing.

Counsel now realised that to complete his test he would have to grasp the nettle before he could pluck the flower. He asked 'Do you have a copy of this report?' knowing full well that the plaintiff had kept typed copies of his relevant documents. Again the test by mental reaction compelled the answer 'Yes'.

'Could you please produce this copy after the lunch adjournment?'
— 'Yes, I can.'

The court intervened to ask whether the time allowed was adequate for the purpose but the witness said that it was.

Two days and 57 excuses later the document had still not been produced and the flower had duly been plucked. It should be noted that the witness could never answer any question on this topic other than affirmatively without exposing the falseness of his evidence.

Some time later counsel met the judge and thought to profit by learning how the latter had regarded the plaintiff as a witness. Counsel, it might be remarked, was always ready to learn from his own mistakes.

[52] Paragraph 12.5.20.
[53] Paragraph 12.5.17.

'Well', said the judge, 'I shall tell you. The plaintiff was not making a bad impression on me until you called for that document. When he could not produce it I started to disbelieve his whole story and I think it was that which made me see the whole of his evidence in a different light.'

I have cited this as an instance of contradiction, rather than as one of the other tests mentioned. I think it is a true contradiction. The plaintiff deposed that there was a document. He was forced to contradict himself not by words but by conduct. How effective that contradiction was appeared from the judgment.

12.5.23 The talkative witness

In dealing with the topic of 'Preparation for Trial' I ventured the suggestion that it was perfectly proper to advise your witnesses as to their manner of giving evidence. I also suggested that you should warn them against volunteering information or making speeches.[54] Now, as cross-examining counsel, what do you do when you encounter a witness whose loquacity exceeds, you think, his veracity?

Speeches by witnesses arise from several causes but there are two principal reasons to be considered. Often the speech is to give the witness a respite and enable him to think of an answer. On other occasions the objective is to divert the cross-examiner from the point.

Generally, I would advise you not to interrupt, provided that you can trust yourself to think of three things at once. You must remember your original question, you must remember the objective of your original question, and finally you must listen to and analyse the speech which the witness is making. All of which is not as easy in practice as it sounds in theory. An interruption may itself have three consequences. It may cause you to forget your question and objective because your mind is focussed on your interruption; it may cause the court either to reprove you or to get the impression that you are trying to suppress the witness's answer; or it may cause your opponent to put on a fine display of indignation, with many a loud cry of 'let him answer the question'. It is not that the display of indignation will hurt you but that it is nicely calculated to disrupt the tenor of your cross-examination.

When the speech is finished, a minor dilemma arises. Do you go back to your question, or do you follow the witness along the highways and byways of the answer? This I must leave to you, because no general advice can be given with any degree of confidence. In many cases you will dramatically ignore the speech and adopt the technique discussed in paragraph 12.5.26.[55] In other cases you will decide that the original question and objective may be held in abeyance or even abandoned while you attack the statements made in the speech.

---

[54] See paragraph 8.3.6 in chapter 8.

[55] The technique of repeating the question in response to an evasive answer is dealt with in paragraph 12.5.26 below.

Occasionally you will meet witnesses whose business or commercial experience has made them past masters of the diversionary speech. With Macbeth you may lament that it is a tale told by an idiot, full of sound and fury but signifying nothing. These witnesses must be treated with care and with respect, for to follow them on false scents may be calamitous. Rather, persist in the question until it is answered or until clearly it cannot be answered.

On the whole, however, I suggest that your policy should be to let the witness talk but yourself to remain in control.

Thus, in a recent case, a chairman of a company was being cross-examined on a matter relating to the re-organisation of the share capital of the company. Cross-examining counsel wished to emphasise what he believed to characterise the answers of the witness, a clever evasiveness and a reluctance to furnish direct replies. His questioning was the following:

> 'Was this deliberately omitted from the ultimate circular?'
> — 'It was omitted, consciously omitted, yes.'
> 'Very well. Would this fall under the description of full details of the scheme?'
> — 'I have pointed out that time had elapsed and circumstances had changed, and that there was only this choice before the shareholders at this time.'
> 'Mr X, you are experienced, I take it, in conducting company meetings as chairman?'
> — 'Yes.'
> 'You are experienced in dealing with questions from shareholders, good questions, bad questions, and difficult questions, are you not?
> — 'I have some experience.'
> 'And I suggest that you are trying to evade the question.'
> — 'What I am trying to establish is that the sort of thoughts that were in our minds when we drafted this premature notice to shareholders, which in fact was before there had been an acceptance of the merger by the state, the circumstances then were not the same as the circumstances surrounding the shareholders as a company as it was at 1 July.'
> 'I know that is what you are trying to say, but what I am trying to ask is: do you agree that what is set out in this particular paragraph on page 6 of Exhibit 30 comes under the description of full details of the scheme?'
> — 'It is not full details of the scheme, no. It is a sketchy outline of the scheme as it was at that time.'
> 'It is one of the details of the scheme?'
> — 'It is one of the details.'
> 'And do you agree that in giving full details of the scheme this would be included?'
> — 'If this was still correct.'
> 'Did it ever become incorrect?'
> — 'I am not able to say.'
> 'You are, Mr X. You know full well that up to 15 September 2003 the scheme in regard to the supply and production of ore never deviated from the terms of this paragraph. You know that, Mr X?'
> — 'Yes, that is true. But what I should perhaps have said was that the operation of the scheme, and the amount of profit allowed to the purchaser, had been differently defined.'

12.5.24 No answer: remember the record

It sometimes happens that you put a question to the witness which he is unable to answer. For want of anything better to do the witness remains silent. This must be regarded as profit, and the more questions that remain unanswered the greater your success as a cross-examiner. But the profits must not slip through your fingers, particularly if there is any possibility of an appeal. By the time it comes to the stage of argument, let alone appeal, much may have happened, and even the trial judge will have forgotten the details of the awkward silence. It is useless to rely on the operator/stenographer and worse than useless to rely on the transcript of an electronic recording.

Let us imagine that the defendant in a defamation case has published a statement that your client has failed properly to account for funds of a voluntary association of which he was the treasurer. The defence is one of privilege and the defendant says that he believed that his statement was true. He, himself, has never examined the books of account and he has had to concede this. Certain members of the committee have gone to the offices of the auditors to examine the books but, for some reason best known to themselves, they have not inspected the vouchers which reflect the money actually received by your client. You now have the witness in a corner as to the basis for his belief and you put the question in this form.

> 'I suggest you could never have believed that my client had failed to account for the money he received.'

The witness knows that the committee members did not examine the vouchers and he can hardly rely on any alleged information from them. He knows that he never had any other information about money received by your client. He cannot answer, and he does not. You pause for the effect and then proceed with your next question:

> 'How long after you resigned from the committee did you next see the plaintiff?'

The ultimate transcript, to your consternation, will read:

> 'I suggest that you could never have believed that my client had failed to account for the money he had received. How long after you resigned from the committee did you next see the plaintiff?'

You have made two mistakes and seriously jeopardised the destructive effect of the silence. In the first place, you should have asked a question and not made a statement. In the second place, you should have ensured that the silence was recorded. The transcript should have been in the following form on exactly the same points:

> 'On what information did you rely for your belief that my client had failed to account for the money he had received?'
> 'Very well, as there is no answer to that question, will you tell us when you next saw the plaintiff after you had resigned from the committee?'

On the first form of the transcript it could be argued that the witness did not understand your statement to be a question and he was still trying to puzzle it out when you went on to the next point. On the recommended form there can be no dispute because, unless both the witness and his counsel agreed that there had been no answer, someone would have protested. Therefore, when a sufficient interval has elapsed to justify your assumption you should state it in some unequivocal manner before leaving the point. You should not be afraid. If you are wrong in the assumption the witness is entitled to give his answer and you are entitled to ask him why he took so long.

I have dilated upon this topic because silences, as I have said, are the signals of success in cross-examination — if they are true silences, recognised and recorded as such.

12.5.25 The half-truth

The suggestion was made some years ago by the late Harold Hanson QC, who was an accomplished exponent of the art of cross-examination:

> 'I like', he said, 'to get the witness to tell a half-truth. I then leave it and go on to other topics. Later, I return to the question on which the witness has told half the truth. By that time he has forgotten what he said and has forgotten how much of the truth he has told. His answer is different — and usually inconsistent — and it is clear that the original answer was not truthful.'

This you can do with the defensive witness, with the witness who has to justify, with the witness who has to explain, with the witness who has something to hide. An immediate attack on a half-truth is less effective because the witness is still concentrating on the point and how much he can safely concede. The evasions will be more skilful and less inconsistent; after a half-hour or so he will be a little uncertain of what was said the first time. The only point on which I would venture to add anything is that you must be sure that the half-truth is in fact only half the truth, more or less. If it is the whole truth and nothing but the truth then you will get the same answer when you return to the topic and you will have done nothing for your client and a good deal for the opposition.

If you are looking for some authority which will tell you how to recognise a half-truth when you hear one then you will be sadly disappointed. Perhaps one could say that if the answer meets those facts which have already emerged during the evidence of the witness but does not meet other facts of which you are aware but which can be taken not to be present to his mind at the time of his answer then it is a half-truth. It is then a question of discretion whether, on returning to the topic, you present the first-mentioned or second-mentioned set of facts. Seemingly the latter is the better course, but you will always weigh up the circumstances and make what you think is the better decision in your own case with that particular witness.

12.5.26 Repetition of the question

> 'Mr Hanson, you have put that question ten times already', remarked his Lordship with a petulant pout.
> 'Yes m'Lord,' boomed Hanson in reply, 'and I shall put it fifteen times if my case requires it.'

Perhaps you haven't the personality of the late Harold Hanson QC (and the incident occurred before he took silk) but you can profit by his example. He was probably right in his attitude towards the court, because the relevant consideration is not always how many times a question is put. What is relevant is how many different answers it elicits.

There are four methods of using repetition as an instrument of cross-examination:

• When a question is a vital one and you suspect that it has not been satisfactorily answered, the witness having tailored the answer to the context of the question, in further cross-examination you bring different facts into the context, facts which will put a different complexion upon the transaction, but facts which the witness cannot dispute. In the new context you put the old question. The old answer is inadequate and even if the witness remembers the old answer he must realise its inadequacy in the new context. So you get a modified answer. You repeat the process for as long as the supply of fact holds out, presenting a little more each time, and receiving in exchange a slightly varied answer. This is most effective when the new facts can be utilised one by one in chronological sequence, and it was probably this that Hanson had in mind when he effectively disposed of the interruption.

• The second method is a variation of the first and is often useful to destroy a denial. Without going into any detail I can best illustrate this by the reference to the case discussed in paragraph 12.6.12 of this section. Counsel was trying to prove that there was no genuine belief in the truth of the scurrilous complaints which the plaintiff had made in regard to his superior officer, or in the allegations he made in the witness-box. Accordingly, duly inspired by his junior, he put the following questions, answered as shown:

> 'Mr K, are you an impulsive person?'
> — 'No my Lord.'
> 'Do you talk or act recklessly, without regard to the true facts?'
> — 'No my Lord.'
> 'Are you truthful in your allegations?
> — 'Yes my Lord.'
> 'Well, I suggest that you were impulsive, reckless or untruthful in making your last allegation.'
> — 'I was not my Lord.'

Here the matter had to rest for the nonce, for there was no point in becoming involved in a 'yes, you are/no I am not' quibble with the witness. As cross-examination progressed, however, and it could be shown that the witness had acted impulsively or had made unsupportable statements, the question was repeated:

> 'When you said (or did) that, were you being impulsive, reckless or untruthful?'

(Modified of course in the context.) With every denial, manifestly hollow, the falseness of every previous denial seemed to become more apparent. A judge, no less than the man in the street, could well first have thought it improbable that the plaintiff would make such serious allegations without some justification in fact. By the repetition of the question the improbability was rebutted, and counsel was enabled to argue that it was more probable that, with an imperfect knowledge of a few garbled facts, the plaintiff would impulsively make false allegations, undeterred by their gravity and potential consequences.

- The third method is simple and effective — when used with correct timing. If the timing is miscalculated the Bench will probably let you know all about it. It is simple — you ignore the answer and repeat the question. It is effective — you ought to get a completely different answer to each question, or else expose the inadequacy of the previously answer. The timing must be correct, or the Bench will point out that the witness has answered the question, and ask that you not waste time by repeating your questions.

This needs some explaining. You ask a question. The answer, or so you believe, is evasive because the witness cannot answer. Instead of prosaically suggesting that the answer does not properly deal with the question, you rather act as if no answer had been given. If you remonstrate with the witness you may get involved in a three or four sided wrangle as to how far the answer meets the question. Rather avoid this. Repeat the question and get another answer before anyone else has had time to gird up his loins and join the fray. I say it is simple, so let the example be equally simple.

The action is for damages by a jaywalker who has had a difference of opinion with a bus which was turning a corner. The plaintiff is being cross-examined:

> 'Is it possible to look at the robot without seeing the pedestrian light?'
> — 'I was not interested. I was interested only in the robot, I did not bother to look at the pedestrian light.'
> 'Is it possible to look at the robot without seeing the pedestrian light?'
> — 'When you are looking at one then I suppose so.'
> 'If you look at the robot you cannot avoid seeing the pedestrian light?'
> — 'I just know it was in my favour.'
> 'Do you agree with the proposition that if you look at the robot you cannot avoid seeing the pedestrian light?'
> — 'All right, I will agree.'

Counsel somewhat spoiled the dramatic effect of the cross-examination by modifying the final question, but since he got the answer he wanted I suppose that he may be forgiven.

- The fourth method is a variation on the third: you sternly ask the witness what the question was that you asked, causing the witness to repeat your question rather in the manner of a scolded child, and you then insist that he answer that question — as in, the previous example:

'Is it possible to look at the robot without seeing the pedestrian light?'
— 'I was not interested. I was interested only in the robot, I did not bother to look at the pedestrian light.'
'What was my question?'
— 'You asked me whether it is possible to look at the robot without seeing the pedestrian light.'
'Yes. Now please answer that question.'
— 'No, it isn't.'

12.5.27 Observe and listen

It is of the essence of cross-examination that you must remain in control of the witness. Not only must there be the control of the questioning which has already been mentioned, but there must be a psychological control. This is not achieved by looking down at your brief while you put a series of impersonal questions to the witness. You should look at the witness with each question you put and you should refer to your notes, if possible, only to refresh your memory as to the sequence of topics you propose to debate.

Lest you dismiss this as impractical theorising, something akin to Mesmerism or the Black Arts, let me turn to the more practical side of the matter. Witnesses are judged on demeanour — a shifting, uncertain, subjective basis of judgment, perhaps, but withal a popular one. If this is good enough for the Bench, it is good enough for you — provided that you have the discretion to keep your judgment to yourself, at least until the proper time. In the main, the signs of demeanour that you will observe will be subtle, so subtle that you may even doubt your own discernment, so subtle that they may not be detected by the judge whose eye is on his note, so subtle that they will defy formulation in the inadequacies of even the finest nuances of the English language. The coarser manifestations I can describe. I can tell you about the witness who, speaking through an interpreter, looks neither at you nor at the judge but alone at his ally, or the witness who, speaking without an interpreter, looks neither at you nor at the judge but alone at your opponent. The cause you may guess; the manifestation you may exploit. I can tell you about the witness who hangs his head and looks sheepish — a phenomenon dearly loved of those who deal with this topic, a phenomenon more often encountered in the books than in the witness-box. If you meet this witness you will clearly know how to exploit the awkwardness and embarrassment. More challenging is the witness with an air of defiance, perhaps boldly so if he is lying, perhaps almost imperceptibly so if he is apprehensively concealing what he would not have you know. These signs you must mark and interpret. Having interpreted them you must exploit. With the boldly defiant you may decide to attack, to antagonise and to turn the defiance into hostility. For if your questions are proper and your manner within the limits of fair behaviour hostility can usually tell only in your favour. With the more surreptitious defiance you may decide to probe and to press your questioning from a variety of angles so that you may uncover what is being concealed.

I have advised you to keep your observations to yourself until the proper time, that usually being the stage of argument when you will be better able to determine whether your judgments were justified. Naturally there are exceptions and quite often counsel will say to the witness: 'Just answer my question, don't look at [so-and-so] he can't help you.' This is a calculated risk and serves to draw the judge's attention to what he may not have noticed. If you are right — and make sure that you are — the witness will not deny the impeachment, thus making your point for you. If you are wrong just notch it up to experience, of which you will acquire plenty.

No less than the witness's demeanour, so the tone of voice and phraseology will tell you much. Sometimes you will listen to the evidence-in-chief and gain the impression that he has learnt his story by heart. The odd question in cross-examination will elicit a repetition in tone and phraseology and confirm your belief. In this case it might well be worth the gamble to start at the beginning and take him through his evidence as though you were leading the evidence-in-chief.[56]

In a recent criminal case the following passages occurred separately in the evidence of one of the state witnesses:

1. 'When D told him, whilst standing next to him, that you refused to allow him to do it, did he make any comments?'
   — 'He turned around the first time. *I forgot about that, that I left a piece out* he said to her the best thing for both of them to do is to take sleeping tablets and [Accused No 2] turned around and she said they can't do that.'
2. 'Who spoke to him, or did he speak?'
   — 'Just a while before he came there, the deceased came to the [shop] too, and Alfie left there and — *I am sorry, I was mistaken* — and he went and fetched Accused No 1, and when they came back they were all three sitting with the deceased, Accused No 1, and Alfie, were sitting talking in Alfie's car, and after a while the deceased left, and just a little while after that the Accused No 1 left too.'
3. 'Just before that, did [Accused No 2] say anything?'
   — 'I have made a mistake before in my statement, *which I have omitted two things*; it was twice that they had been at my home, under the same reasons, to go and fetch [Accused No 3] but the last time, on the day of the murder, that Monday, that is when the deceased said that he thinks it best if they took sleeping tablets.'

Now, this witness was testifying in regard to events which had occurred three years before. What inference should counsel then draw from the three phrases which are reported in italics? My own view is that there is a clear hint that the witness has memorised her story. It is remarkable that she would remember the details in these three short passages after a lapse of three years. But when she naively talks about leaving something out I suggest that the inference in regard to rehearsal or memorising becomes a strong one. It is in no spirit of

---

[56] Although repetition of the evidence-in-chief should, as a rule, be avoided (see paragraph 12.5.29 below), there is always the exception that proves the rule.

condemnation whatsoever, nor even of criticism, that I reproduce the actual questions which counsel for one of the accused put to the witness, and then offer my own suggestion. When I say 'my own' I do not take any personal credit for this technique. It is something I often observed employed by counsel who was regarded as one of the leading cross-examiners of his day; something I observed and at long last came imperfectly to recognise for its true worth.

The actual questions arose almost fortuitously out of a point in cross-examination:

> 'Now, you didn't mention this in your statement?'
> — 'No, I forgot about it. It didn't come into my mind at all.'
> 'And you also didn't make any mention of this in your evidence-in-chief?'
> — 'I beg your pardon.'
> By the court: 'Well she only mentioned it because you asked the question Mr W.'
> 'No, but it is important, m'Lord.'
> 'You didn't mention it in your evidence-in-chief either?'
> — 'Well I didn't. It is so long ago that everything happened, that there are things that I couldn't remember until only afterwards, and people started asking me questions.'
> 'You have had consultations before you came to give evidence? Is that correct?'
> — 'I beg your pardon.'
> 'Before you came to give evidence in court here today?'
> — 'Yes.'
> 'Did you have any consultations with the police? Did you see my learned friend [the prosecutor], in connection with this case?'
> — 'Yes, I have.'
> 'How many times?'
> — 'Well once.'
> 'And you had a full conversation with him?'
> — 'Well, not really. I came back afterwards, and I told him a few things that I forgot to tell him.'
> 'In other words, he asked you to remember as much as you could?'
> — 'Yes.'
> 'And you didn't remember this?'
> — 'No, I did not.'

Counsel must have had many considerations to weigh up in regard to his method of cross-examination, so what follows is merely an alternative suggestion, made, obviously, without full knowledge of those considerations. It might have been effective to commence the cross-examination with a question which, if not quite of the 'sixty-four dollar' class,[57] would create an atmosphere and disturb the witness. I cannot speculate as to answers, but the following is a possible line of questions:

> 'Miss B, I made a note of your answers given to my learned friend's questions and I have written this: "I forgot about that, and I left a piece out." Do you remember saying that?' Please assist me, because I have some difficulty in understanding what you meant by the words: "I left a piece out".'

---

[57] See paragraph 12.5.9 above.

Then similar use would be made of the phrase: 'I have omitted two things.' The other one, 'I am sorry, I was mistaken' requires far more delicate handling and would probably have to be held in reserve for a while. Indeed the whole process would be a test of finesse; for there is little doubt that the witness would not readily admit that she had committed her statement to memory. The pretext of misunderstanding, a legitimate pretext in my submission, is the device to lead the witness on, to encourage her into volunteering information with the object of getting her into a position where the denial of the direct question would be transparently false.

Clearly the witness would not like the phrase 'I left a piece out' and would say that what she meant was 'I forgot something'. You would then have to develop the incongruity between 'leaving out a piece' and 'forgetting something', the operative word being 'piece.' In all probability you would not be able to force an admission at this stage and would have to content yourself with accepting a half-truth. When the next passage was discussed you might find that the difference in phraseology would expose the half-truth for precisely what it was.

Often, of course, the clue is more difficult to detect and the nuance of phraseology more delicate than in these examples, but you should listen to the evidence-in-chief with regard to the manner of expression no less than with regard to the details of the story. If you remain uncertain you may test it in cross-examination not by asking the bold, direct question: 'Have you rehearsed your story?' but by casually putting the very question which elicited the response in chief. You listen for repetition or similarity beyond that which is inevitable when a story is being repeated. One or two similar tests may be applied later in cross-examination and when you are in position to quote three or four instances of unusual repetition you may tax the witness with having learned off or rehearsed his story.

Wrottesley[58] has the following comment on this point:

> If he [the witness] is cunning, he will endeavour to conceal his true feelings. The eye, the tones of the voice, and the mouth are the best indexes to the state of mind of a witness. A convulsive twitching of the muscles of the mouth will often betray agitation which the witness wishes to conceal, while the eye will reveal nothing as its expression may be changed to suit the purpose of the witness.

Myself I doubt whether you will ever encounter a witness as obliging as the one discussed by the learned author, and I can only advise that if you wait for such manifestations of a guilty conscience you may well sooner grow grey in the practice of the law. I do, with respect, agree with the author's subsequent advice that you should not divert your attention from the witness. I think, however, that the physical signs of untruthfulness will be far more subtle, so subtle, indeed, as to be no more than an aura.

Occasionally you will meet the witness with the disconcertingly direct stare.

---

[58] *The Examination of Witnesses* 79.

This may be his normal façade or it may be deliberately assumed in order to discomfort you and distract you in your cross-examination. Should you flinch then the witness will gain the ascendancy. I certainly do not recommend dealing with this sort of witness by adopting the manner nonchalant, that is, back half-turned to the witness and one leg casually perched on a chair so that there can be no doubt about your contempt for this creature.

Good cross-examination consists not in histrionics but in logic. Logic has no need of thunder to achieve its ends. It needs compulsion by its content and by the concentration of the cross-examiner, concentration mentally on the logic of the situation and physically on the subject of the cross-examination — the witness.

12.5.28 Cross-examination is not supposed to be a test of stamina

If you apply yourself to your task, and if you apply the techniques suggested in this chapter, then your cross-examination ought to be purposeful and incisive. As Nienaber JA put it at 699 of *Africa Solar (Pty) Ltd v Divwatt (Pty) Ltd*[59] (in the event, the successful appellant was ordered to pay a third of the costs on the attorney and client scale as a mark of disapproval of the inordinately lengthy cross-examination):

> Proper cross-examination does not consist, under the guise of testing credibility, of rehashing with a witness, repetitively and obstinately, his evidence-in-chief in an apparent attempt to wear him down so as to unearth discrepancies that can then become the source of a submission that the witness should for that reason be disbelieved. Cross-examination is not supposed to be a test of stamina. I do not believe that I am being unfair to counsel for the plaintiff if I say that his questioning of De Villiers and Pichulik . . . was the personification of that particular style of cross-examination. To a significant degree this contributed to an increase in both the duration and the record of the proceedings . . . Counsel for the respondent estimated that the trial was unnecessarily prolonged by at least one-third. That estimate is not, in my opinion, an exaggeration . . . .

Properly prepared and conducted, cross-examination should indeed not be 'a test of stamina', and you should heed the above warning. That said, a certain degree of latitude must be allowed and I know of no judgment in which this has been better described than that of Hardiman J of the Supreme Court of Ireland at 705–6 of *Martin Maguire and Others v Seán Ardagh and Others, and the Attorney General*:[60]

> Cross-examination is a special skill and usually an acquired one, of which a thorough knowledge of the facts of a particular case is merely the foundation. A person without experience of the art is very unlikely to be able to conduct an effective cross-examination . . . . As it happens, the greatest demonstration of the utility of cross-

[59] 2002 (4) SA 681 (SCA).
[60] [2001] IR 385 (SC)

examination of which I am aware is furnished by the case . . . of Parnell.[61] Mr Parnell had been accused of many heinous things, some on the basis of perjured evidence supported by forged documents, produced by a witness procured by his deep-pocketed political and commercial enemies. This . . . was destroyed in cross-examination of remarkable skill carried out over a period of several days by the great Irish advocate Sir Charles Russell QC. The witness was quite destroyed, did not attend for the fifth day of his cross-examination, made affidavits admitting perjury and forgery and committed suicide when the police came to arrest him. At a stroke, Parnell was transformed from a prisoner in the dock of public opinion to a vindicated accuser. This cross-examination took time and required the patience of the tribunal. It involved many passages (including one where the witness was made to write out a series of apparently randomly selected words) when the point being made must have been utterly obscure to the listeners. The tribunal was required to have faith in the advocate and the faith was of course fully justified . . . None of this would have been possible had Charles Russell been debarred from cross-examination, [or] limited in his time for that purpose.

One more reference will get the matter into perspective, and show that perhaps the judge must tolerate some loquacity in the interest of justice. Trollip JA stated:[62]

> It is true, as already remarked, that the cross-examination on the item of R14 000 was inordinately lengthy and, with some hindsight, it now appears to have been irrelevant. But generally, in regard to that complaint and others by the plaintiff about the manner in which the trial was conducted on defendant's behalf one should bear in mind that usually a wide latitude should be afforded a defendant in presenting his defence, especially when he is confronted with a substantial claim for damages. In such a case, I think that the defendant is usually entitled 'to put his back against the wall and to fight from any available point of advantage.' (Cf Kekewich J, in *Blank v Footman, Pretty & Co* 39 ChD 678 at 685, quoted with approval in *Nel v Nel* 1943 AD 280 at 288.)

12.5.29 Avoid simple repetition of the evidence-in-chief

I have said that you should cross-examine chronologically. The value of this is that an incongruity or unreality becomes easier to detect. On the other hand, it is a mistake, and a serious one at that, to allow the witness to repeat the evidence-in-chief. The story only gains by the repetition.[63]

What you would possibly do, chronologically, would be to select particular allegations from the witness's evidence and deal with them. Subject to all other suggestions I have recorded, you would proceed, for example, thus:

---

[61] The Parnell case is a celebrated case in Irish history. Charles Parnell was the leader of the Irish bloc in the British House of Commons. In 1889 the *London Times* attempted to blacken his name by linking him with the so-called Phoenix Park murders. A tribunal was set up to investigate the charges. The main witness against Parnell was one Richard Piggott who, it is said, showed every confidence when he concluded his examination-in-chief, but who was shown in cross-examination by Russell QC to be a liar and a forgerer.

[62] *Shatz Investments (Pty) Ltd v Kalovyrnas* 1976 (2) SA 545 (A) at 560F.

[63] See also *Africa Solar (Pty) Ltd v Divwatt (Pty) Ltd* 2002 (4) SA 681 (SCA) 699, as quoted in paragraph 12.5.28 above.

'Now, Mr Klitznit, you told the court that you were standing at your front gate.'
— 'Yes.'
'Who was with you?'
— 'Nobody.'
'Do you have children?'
— 'Yes. Three.'
'Where were they?'
— 'Playing in the garden.'
'How do you know?'
— 'I could hear them.'
'Did you see them?'
— 'Well, I suppose I must have turned to look at them, but it is a long time ago and I can't be sure.'
'What were you more interested in, the intersection fifty yards away from your gate or the children in the garden?'

And so each step in the story is tested in turn, without allowing the witness to repeat and confirm.

12.5.30 Use humour sparingly, if at all

There is limited room for humour in cross-examination.

Why do I say that? As usual I have three reasons: firstly, very few of us are the masters of wit that we fondly imagine; secondly, humour usually ill-becomes junior counsel who is making his way at the Bar; it elevates him to a self-assumed status of familiarity with the court; thirdly, should the sally come to grief it can only make counsel look ridiculous.

Be chary then of your puns and witticisms.

That said there is, particularly as you progress in your career, still some room for humour in this context. In the first place, gentle ridicule can sometimes be used to attack a witness so as to expose weaknesses in his story.[64] Also, where you do receive a reverse in cross-examination and are satisfied that the reverse is plain to all and irremediable, you might (I put it no higher than that) consider conceding it with good humour. Salhany[65] speaks of a colleague who, on receiving a damaging answer in cross-examination, smiled and said 'touché'. It was, he says,

> Most effective, because it broke that otherwise awkward silence that can be devastating; it added some humour; it diminished the impact of the answer; it suggested a slight injury, not a fatal blow, and it showed respect for the witness.

Summing up, I would suggest that humour has little part in litigation, unless used with sure timing and the touch of the master, not of the clown.

---

[64] As in the example quoted by Salhany *Cross-Examination* at 44 of the young Norman Birkett's politely enquiring of a cabdriver, after establishing how many people he had knocked down and how much destruction he had wrought after losing control of his allegedly slow-moving vehicle, 'Well, I wonder if you would like to estimate how much more damage you might have done if you had been going fast?'

[65] Salhany *Cross-Examination* 56.

12.5.31 Avoid aggravating the damages by your cross-examination

Reference has also been made to the case of *Joseph v Black and Others*[66] where the conduct of the defendant's case was taken into account in aggravation of damages. This introduces a nice problem into cross-examination, usually only in defamation actions where the defence of justification is pleaded. Counsel would hardly plead justification without being specifically instructed to do so. If justification is pleaded, the plaintiff, when he testifies, must be cross-examined in support of the plea. Should the plea not be established the persistent attack on the plaintiff might be held to have aggravated the damages. Therefore the cross-examination has aggravated the damages. Counsel conducted the cross-examination. Therefore counsel aggravated the damages. Do not trouble yourself to find the fallacy in this reasoning; I know that it is fallacious. But it is the reasoning of the press, the public and, all too often, the attorneys on whom counsel relies for support. Eventually it will also be the reasoning of the client too, for he will have convinced himself that all he wanted to do was to render an apology, and he will forget his vainglorious boast about the plaintiff 'He'll never dare to go to court.'

Nevertheless, counsel has a duty to perform, and that is to carry out the instructions of the client where these are based on proper and supportable premises. Cases of aggravation of damages through injudicious cross-examination, no doubt, do occur but they are not of frequent occurrence. You may derive some comfort from this fact, from the discussion in paragraph 2.10 above, and also from the judgment of Trollip J in *Guggenheim v Rosenbaum (2)*[67] where it was held that since the statements complained of were not connected with the plaintiff's cause of action and did not bear upon her delictual claim they did not have the effect of aggravating the damages.

Not only in your own interests, but also in those of your client, to which your own interests must be subordinated, you must be alert not to indulge in cross-examination which amounts to maintaining the delict of which the plaintiff complains unless there is satisfactory evidence to support your attack. The attack will be akin to the test by fact, and the essence of that attack is fact.

12.5.32 The subtle distortion in cross-examination is indefensible, if done deliberately

There is no doubt that subtle distortion is a most effective method of cross-examination.

There is equally little doubt that, when done deliberately, it is indefensible. There can be just as little doubt that what to you may appear to be the

---

[66] 1930 WLD 327.

[67] 1961 (4) SA 21 (W). See also *Salzman v Holmes* 1914 AD 471 at 482. An interesting study in tactics is to be found in the case of *Walton v Cohn* 1947 (2) SA 225 (N) which bears on this topic. As to the effect of looseness in the framing of a question relating to the plaintiff's alleged reputation for immorality see *Senkge v Bredenkamp* 1948 (1) SA 1145 (O) at 1152–3.

technique of establishing a contradiction by logical development may, to your opponent, appear to be the method of subtle distortion. I hesitate to illustrate this method not only because I think that it should be discouraged, but also because I know that fairly early in your career you will observe examples better than any I could quote. When you are shifting uneasily in your seat, longing to intervene but painfully conscious that your objection will be quite ineffectual, when you wonder how on earth your witness can so blithely agree to propositions which only superficially correspond with the evidence-in-chief then you are observing the subtle distortion. Perhaps, in truth, you will even become aware, during your own cross-examination, that something is amiss. Your opponent is muttering to himself and the witness is beginning to show signs of resentment. You then ask, with a clear conscience 'Mr K am I distorting your answers?' To your consternation the answer is 'Yes'. But, if your conscience is indeed clear, do not be distressed. You simply offer to start again and in nine cases out of ten when you carefully repeat your questions you arrive at the same conclusion. This time, however, you win. You win because you have invited the court to watch you; you win because, if there were to be a distortion, the court would intervene; you win because the protest of the witness was not a protest but a pretext. It is of the tenth case that you must beware, and you must be as wary as you would be of making an incautious submission in argument. At that latter stage the court would ask you: 'But, Mr Ngobeni, can that be correct?' And that simple question in argument would cause you to see your submission in truer perspective. So, too, if you would avoid the subtle distortion in cross-examination you must ask yourself in the fleeting seconds between an answer and the next question: 'But, Mr Ngobeni, can that be so?'

When you blunder, apologise. But the deliberate distortion should be no part of the practitioner's art.

12.5.33 Avoid empty rhetoric

Every question should have a purpose and should be designed to achieve a purpose. The oratorical flourish is a thing of the past. It might have impressed a jury in rural America but it serves merely to annoy a judge who has better use for his time. A popular method of cajoling a witness was to remind him that he was on oath. It still survives. It achieves nothing. If he is truthful he knows that he is truthful. If he is lying he will be as unimpressed as when he was first sworn in. If he is possibly mistaken he will say: 'Well, I am trying to give you a correct impression; I am certainly not trying to mislead anyone.' And all that you accomplish is the unenviable distinction of looking foolish.

On a similar basis was counsel's Parthian shot when he had spent an hour cross-examining a police constable without any degree of success. As counsel resumed his seat he put the final question: 'I put it to you that your evidence is a tissue of lies.' Since counsel had omitted to establish why the witness should indulge in the weaving of such tissues, and as he had failed signally to show any lies, the only effect was to incur the displeasure of the court. Nor do I exaggerate when I say that the aura of that suggestion persisted when his client subsequently entered the witness-box to testify on his own behalf.

12.5.34 Do not accept the answer: probe it

Your cross-examination may have been prepared with long and anxious considerations of each point which you will put to the witness. On the other hand you may have had opportunity only to make quick marks or notes in the margin of your examination book as you are recording the evidence-in-chief. In either event you will have some general plan of attack and a number of detailed topics for investigation. Strangely enough, what seemed so vulnerable when the point came to your mind acquires a degree of resistance when made the subject of question and answer. It is distressingly easy to lose the initiative when the witness has an answer for everything and when you see your points being blunted one after another.

This, however, is one of the tests of advocacy. While on your feet, in the stress of conflict, you must be able to analyse the answer just as you originally analysed the proposition. You do not simply accept a denial or an evasion and pass on to the next point. If you do this you are lost. The answer itself must be compared with the facts, with every fact in the case, in search of an incongruity. It must be considered in the light of logic, or by the test of mental reaction. All this you must learn to do with computer-like rapidity.

Too often counsel, on receiving an unfavourable answer, seems to go to pieces. He shows this by his very demeanour that the answer hurts. He falters, fumbles through the papers, whispers to the instructing attorney or to the client seeking solace in the guise of getting instructions. If counsel is to have a demeanour in these matters it should rather be that he does not for a moment believe anything that the witness says and that the answer is being received for what it is worth. Don't overdo it, but above all don't show your anguish. After all, did you really expect the witness to admit that the testimony was false or improbable or unacceptable? Keep on at the witness, for there are very few witnesses who will maintain a story when it is assailed from a number of points in succession. And in the very process of probing it with differently framed questions it will often happen that the weakness in the answer will be exposed, exposed by chance, but exposed nevertheless.

12.5.35 'Why?'; 'How?'

Beware exploring where you should not with questions beginning with 'Why', or 'How'. This has to an extent already been dealt with above,[68] but that the lesson has not yet been learned is shown by the following excerpt from an appeal record in our own courts. The charge was rape.

> Cross-examined by Mr X: 'And by what particular feature did you recognise the accused as one of your assailants?'

[68] See paragraph 12.5.11 above, dealing with the proposition that, as a general statement, one doesn't ask a question to which one doesn't know the answer.

— 'By an old scar on his nose.'
'And that is all?'
— 'Yes, that is all.'
The Court: 'Let the accused come up here to the Bench. We want to see the scar.'
The Witness: 'He also has a scar above one of his eyes. I am not certain now which eye it is.'
(Accused's face being inspected by the court.)
The Court: 'Let the witness come here and point out the scars.'
— 'Here they are, the one between the eyes and the one next to the left eye.'
'It can be recorded that there is a brown streak just between the eyes, and there is some mark on the left eyebrow.'
Mr X: 'So the only method by which you can identify the accused in any way is by certain marks which you say you remember on his face.'
— 'Not only those scars but his face as it is there as well.'

The court later questioned the accused to clarify the position:

'These marks that you have and which the complainant pointed out, did you have them on 21 December?'
— 'I had these marks.'
'Did the complainant see you anywhere outside this morning?'
— 'I did not notice.'
'And at the preparatory examination did she come close to you?'
— 'No, m'Lord.'

In the example just quoted, counsel should have been aware that his client's face bore the markings described. It must then be asked what he hoped to gain from the question: 'And by what particular feature did you recognise the accused?' To the outsider it would seem that he was taking a chance that the complainant had overlooked the scar even at the preparatory examination. It seems to have been an undue risk to invite identification of a person who bore easily identifiable marks on his face.

Of course, it is relatively simple to join in the chorus and condemn the 'How' and 'Why' class of question. They can be so dangerous as to be fatal; they seldom bring results because very few witnesses are stupid enough to give an answer that does not support their statement. At best, counsel becomes involved in a long running fight with the witness, trying now to destroy the 'Why' or the 'How' rather than the original statement. In practice, however, the problem of avoiding this class of question is less simple. You are obliged to challenge the witness on his statement for fear that the very lack of challenge or of testing may be warrant for the acceptance of what he says. To challenge without resorting to these impish little words is rather difficult. Nor is even the most experienced cross-examiner immune to the virus. It is sorely tempting to believe that the fatuity of a proposition can be exposed by inviting the proponent to justify it. If in fact you are sure that the first of my cautionary rules is satisfied then you may 'how' and 'why'. You may even 'where', 'when' and 'what'. But do you really know the answer to the question? Or are you really satisfied that you have the means of compelling the witness to proffer the answer you want him to give?

The object of cross-examination is not to establish the facts deposed to by the witness. It is to destroy these facts or to establish facts which render the witness's facts unacceptable. Thus, on identity, you do not ask 'How did you identify him?' You ask: 'Was it dark? Were you taken by surprise? Were you terrified? Did you struggle? Fiercely?' So you will tread with caution!

12.5.36 This isn't television

Don't, whatever you do, think that what you see on television, particularly American television, bears any resemblance to a South African court. Salhany[69] puts it as follows:

> Some counsel, raised on American TV court scenes, seem to think that they can compel only the answer 'yes' or 'no' to their questions. No self-respecting judge would permit such tactics. It is not only unfair to the witness, it gives an artificial air to the whole proceedings. A witness is entitled to give a full and complete answer to the questions put to him.

12.5.37 Always remember to put your case to the witness

If the witness has testified on a point on which you propose leading contradictory evidence, you must put that evidence to the witness.

If you intend arguing that the evidence of the witness on a particular point should not be accepted, you must put this to the witness.[70]

12.6 CROSS–EXAMINING EXPERT WITNESSES

Expert testimony may vary from a simple analysis in a running-down case through a complex medical discussion in a medical negligence case to an abstruse dissertation on matters of chemistry or engineering in patent cases. In this regard:

- Preparation is of course assisted by the provisions of rule 36(9), in terms of which you will always be entitled to a summary of the expert's evidence before he testifies.
- Your preparation, however, will generally precede receipt of the rule 36(9)*(b)* summary. If acting for the plaintiff you will, as pointed out in paragraph 6.17 above, generally be entitled to a copy of the expert's summary in terms of rule 36(8). If acting for the defendant, you will in any

---

[69] Salhany *Cross-Examination – The Art of the Advocate* 30 and 31. Of course, there are *some* questions that *do* require nothing more than a yes or a no for an answer, but that is not generally so.

[70] Failure to put your case to the witness is the equivalent of failure to cross-examine. See in this regard paragraph 12.3 above, and the authorities collected in fn 4. As the court said at 36J–37B of *President of the Republic of South Africa and Others v South African Rugby Football Union and Others* 2000 (1) SA 1 (CC): 'As a general rule it is essential, when it is intended to suggest that a witness is not speaking the truth on a particular point, to direct the witness's attention to the fact by questions put in cross-examination showing that the imputation is intended to be made and to afford the witness an opportunity, whilst still in the witness-box, of giving any explanation open to the witness . . . If a point in dispute is left unchallenged in cross-examination, the party calling the witness is entitled to assume that the unchallenged witness's testimony is accepted as correct.'

event have some idea of what type of expert the plaintiff is likely to call and what topics the expert is likely to address, and you will have enlisted the aid of your own expert or experts in the relevant field or fields to assist you in preparation.

• The keys, once you receive the summary of the expert's proposed evidence, are four. Firstly, you examine the witness's qualifications to satisfy yourself as to whether he is indeed sufficiently qualified and whether it would not be useful for you to take up with him a comparison between his qualifications and those of your expert.[71] Secondly, you look for language in the summary which you can exploit as over-stating or under-stating a position as the case might be, suggesting subjectivity. Thirdly, you look for factual assumptions on which opinions are based, to see whether you can successfully attack those assumptions, and with them the opinions.[72] And finally, you rely on your own experts to advise you in painstaking detail as to the witness's qualifications and the correctness or otherwise of the opinions expressed in the summary, so as to enable you to cross-examine with efficacy on those points.

• In preparing your cross-examination with the assistance of your experts, you must insist on reducing issues into understandable language, and understandable logic. Very often you will find that in consultation with your own experts, you understand neither the opinion of the opposing expert, nor your experts' criticism of his opinion, nor their explanations for that criticism. If so, it might of course be that this is all to be put down to your obtuseness. But if so, you will be no better equipped for trial if you don't insist on matters being explained to you until you understand them. More likely, the reason you understand nothing is because matters are being put in highly technical language which neither you nor the judge will understand. It is always best to assume that if you do not understand the point, nor will the judge. You should consequently be fearless in insisting that matters be explained to you until you understand them. And when they have been explained to you so that you understand them, you must insist on the explanation being reduced into understandable language. Remember that your purpose is ultimately to show flaws in the opinion of the opposing expert, and that the person to whom you must show these flaws is the judge. You are unlikely to achieve that if you and the expert fence in scientific and technical language which you did not understand until you had the benefit of hours of consultation, and which the judge still does not understand.[73]

---

[71] See, for example, the cross-examination of an expert in Appendix D.

[72] Munkman makes the valid point at 119 that 'An expert opinion consists of a conclusion drawn from facts which may or may not be true, by inferences which may or not be sound'.

[73] Salhany 109–10. Note also his point at 112 that '[i]f they [experts] are [in the course of cross-examination] compelled to speak in simple language, the myth or aura of invincibility will be pierced.'

- In most instances of cross-examination of expert witnesses you need have very little regard to the methods which have been discussed previously in this section. There may, of course, be a subconscious bias, better described as a partisanship, but this will usually be of little moment. The cross-examination will usually proceed on lines of pure logic or scientific analysis.

- Always examine the reliability of the factual assumptions on which the expert based his opinion. You will ascertain what factors the witness has taken into account in arriving at his opinion. Your own studies and instructions should have equipped you to judge whether one or more of these factors should have been disregarded, or whether other factors should also have been considered. Once an error in the premises is established, if it can be established, the inquiry is how far that error bears upon the result.

- The next attack, assuming the failure of the previous one suggested, is on the justification for drawing an inference or forming an opinion as the witness has done. In this context it is only the most thorough mastery of the subject that can ever enable you to assail the testimony. It is useless to say: 'I put it to you that, on these facts, your opinion is incorrect.' You will usually receive only one answer. If you seek to assuage your wounded feelings of self-esteem by asking 'Could one possibly come to a different opinion?' the witness will usually say that it is possible but most improbable. That, it may be remarked, can only add to the credibility of the witness in the eyes of the court. The honest witness, the skilled testifier, the competent expert, will seldom hesitate to concede the possibility that someone else might think differently, but may well take the opportunity of demonstrating convincingly to the court why that other opinion, although an understandable one, would not be the correct one.

  There was a particular medical witness — I shall not specify the field in which he specialised — who himself had a technique of confounding counsel on these lines. He would express his opinions, say, on a point of prognosis, giving a sketchy reason for his views. Counsel, somewhat emboldened by the apparent superficiality of the reasoning, would challenge the statement made, only to be met with chapter and verse, copiously supported by reference to textbooks, medical journals and the witness's own practical experience. From which emerges the moral that you must not merely be dissatisfied with the opinion; you must *know* that it is wrong and you must be able to show *why* it is wrong.

- A further point to bear in mind in the cross-examination of experts is the essence of the matter. For an illustration of this I turn again to the field of criminal law: The accused was charged with murder, it being alleged that he had shot the deceased with a pistol. The case for the prosecution was based on circumstantial evidence and also on the evidence of a ballistics expert who identified a cartridge found at the scene of the crime as having come from a pistol which belonged to the accused. In examining photographs of the 'crime' cartridge case and of 'test' cases the defence formed the theory that there was a discrepancy, apparently overlooked by the expert, in the relative positions of the firing-pin indentation and the marks caused by the ejector mechanism. At first considerable energy was devoted to obtaining evidence to show that the firing pin on that particular type of pistol was capable of rotation. The idea was to show that if these discrepancies existed, and if the pin rotated, the two sets of photographs could not be matched. In other words, if the indentation of the firing pin was not constant, then the relationship between that indentation and the ejector marks was capable of any amount of variation and one could never rely on that relationship to prove identity. It was as if 'the points of similarity' in finger-prints could be shown to vary spatially in different prints.

Prima facie this was an attractive line of reasoning, but it contained the seeds of destruction for the defence case. True enough, it would weaken portion of the case on identity, but it would render it *possible* that the 'crime' cartridge did in fact come from the accused's pistol because that pistol could then cause different firing-pin indentations on different cartridge cases. The ejector markings, in themselves, would then produce the necessary link and would reinforce the circumstantial evidence. The ejector marks, it should be remarked, were identical in both sets of photographs.

The essence of the matter lay in divorcing the 'crime' exhibit from the 'test' exhibit. If this could be done then the similarity of the ejector markings would have to be regarded as no more than coincidental. Counsel thus decided to reverse completely the theory on which the defence had been working, and he directed his cross-examination of the ballistics expert towards showing that the firing pin in that particular type of pistol, and in the accused's pistol especially, would always produce the same impression on the cartridge case. This was established, and from there counsel proceeded to his next proposition, namely that the photographs revealed the discrepancy which has been mentioned. That discrepancy, in turn, was ultimately conceded with the result that the defence proved that the accused's pistol could not have fired the fatal shot. On this proposition, the circumstantial evidence became valueless and the accused was acquitted.

- In collision cases, it might be noted in passing, the courts are not over-enthusiastic about basing their findings as to negligence on deductions made *ex post facto* by expert witnesses, where these deductions are inconsistent with credible eyewitness evidence. As Ogilvie Thompson AJ (as he then was) said in *Van der Westhuizen v SA Liberal Insurance Co Ltd*:[74]

---

[74] 1949 (3) SA 160 (C) at 168. See also *Diale v Commercial Union Assurance Co Ltd* 1975 (4) SA 572 (A) at 576–7, *Netherlands Insurance Co. Ltd v Brummer* 1978 (4) SA 824 (A) at 831, *Abdo NO v Senator*

> [T]he strictly mathematical approach, though undoubtedly very useful as a check, can but rarely be applied as an absolute test in collision cases, since any mathematical calculation so vitally depends on exact positions and speeds, whereas in truth these latter are merely estimates almost invariably made under circumstances wholly unfavourable to accuracy.

12.7 EXAMPLES

See Appendix D for an example of cross-examination of a lay-witness, and one of cross-examination of an expert. The point to observe in the former is the use of leading questions and the closing off of escape avenues. The point to observe in the latter is the efficacy of gently but firmly pinning the expert down to a comparison between his credentials and those of the questioner's experts.

See also paragraph 19.9, in chapter 19, dealing with cross-examination in the criminal context.

Insurance Co Ltd 1983 (4) SA 721 (E) at 725–6, *Motor Vehicle Assurance Fund v Kenny* 1984 (4) SA 432 (E) at 436–7, *Van Eck v Santam Insurance Co Ltd* 1996 (4) SA 1226 (C) at 1229–30, *Vergoedingskommissaris v Multilaterale Motorvoertuigongelukkefonds* [1998] 3 All SA 155 (O), *Nock v Road Accident Fund* [2000] 2 All SA 436 (W) at 443 and *GS Fouche Vervoer BK v Intercape Bus Service* [2006] 1 All SA 24 (C).

CHAPTER 13

Re-examination

13.1 THE PURPOSE OF RE-EXAMINATION

The purpose of re-examination is to clarify answers given in cross-examination.[1]

As with evidence-in-chief, only non-leading questions are allowed.

13.2 DO YOU, OR DON'T YOU?

The scope for re-examination is restricted, particularly because re-examining counsel is in no better position than when leading the witness in chief. Thus, he may not put leading questions, and one of the characteristics of re-examination is that it tends to develop into a series of objectionable leading questions. It is all very well to say to a witness:

> 'Will you explain why, in your evidence in chief, you omitted to tell the court such-and-such?'

The probability is that he will say something stupid, such as 'Well, I intended to do so but I forgot' when he ought to say 'I never for a moment imagined that it could have had anything to do with the case because my discussions with the plaintiff were on a basis radically different from that suggested to me in cross-examination.'

After you have suffered at the hands of a few of your own witnesses you tend to use this form: 'You did not mention such-and-such a point in your evidence-in-chief and my learned friend cross-examined you at length on it. Now did you think that this had anything to do with the case?' Even if you obtain the desired answer before your opponent can object it is not likely to carry very much weight with the court. Moreover, there are two chances, and the witness may well guess wrongly.

I have seen very few successful re-examinations. On the other hand, I have seen many failed re-examinations. In some instances, the very fact that re-examination is deemed necessary serves only to emphasise the damage that was wrought in cross-examination. If the egg of your witness's evidence was shattered in cross-examination, then that's the way it is and, as repair procedures go, far better to look to all the world as if nothing went wrong and then later argue that what might at first blush have looked like shattered pieces of eggshell was in fact, on closer examination, a sparklingly healthy wholesome egg that has never been better, than to be caught out in the open trying to stick pieces of shattered eggshell together! In most instances, where the re-examiner

---

[1] D Zeffertt and A Paizes *The South African Law of Evidence* 2 ed 921.

284

attempts to put Humpty Dumpty together again, the damage is only made worse by the witness doggedly clinging to the concessions made under cross. Conversely, where the witness reverts, in the safe harbour of re-examination, to his original version at odds with the concessions made in cross-examination, the effect is only to emphasise his loss of credibility.

Reverting to one of the sub-themes of this book, you should only attempt to re-examine if you have good reason to believe that the purpose of re-examination will be served, ie, that you will indeed be able to satisfactorily clarify something which needs clarification — otherwise, don't.[2]

13.3 TIPS FOR RE-EXAMINATION

To summarise, then, do not re-examine unless you have good reason to believe that you will succeed in clarifying something that was raised or muddied in cross-examination, and that the clarification is needed. If you are so satisfied, then the following tips might assist you:

* During cross-examination note on your record the points for re-examination, having regard also to the manner of your witness as indicating that he may desire to explain a particular topic more fully.
* Unless there is one fundamental point which is required to give perspective either to cross-examination or re-examination, it is easier to follow the sequence of the cross-examination.
* Confine re-examination to matters of substance, principally in regard to the issues in the case, or, where this can be done, important matters of credibility.
* Do not attempt to improve on favourable answers: associated matters that are unfavourable may emerge, or the witness may misunderstand your motives and recant with the speed of light.
* Where your opponent has been incautious in referring to otherwise inadmissible conversations or documents, exploit his error if you can gain thereby. Get the whole story before the court.
* Establish facts in preference to seeking explanations or excuses.
* Avoid rhetorical or futile questions, such as:

    'Have you any motive to mislead the court?'

    Sometimes, and rarely, however, it may be useful to ask:

    'Do you have any interest in the outcome of this case?'

* Repetition of the evidence-in-chief is usually unnecessary; what may be useful is amplification of that evidence to meet suggestions made in cross-examination.

---

[2] The Grays Inn guidelines to which reference was made in paragraph 11.6 above suggest, only slightly tongue-in-cheek, that '[t]he first rule of re-examination is don't re-examine [and that the] second and third rules are the same'.

- Avoid eliciting new matter which, if allowed as an indulgence, will confer a right of further cross-examination.
- Be wary of asking questions of which you do not know the answer, or of *which you are not sure that the witness knows the answer.*
- Be particularly careful in trying to reconcile contradictory statements — you may even get a third version,
- Regard each witness as an idiosyncratic case to be treated on his own merits in regard to the need for and nature of method of re-examination.
- In view of the delicacy of the restorative process, *your questions must be framed with a nicety of expression exceeding that required at any other stage of the evidence.*
- Re-examination requires you to be particularly astute in imparting assurance to the witness, not just through your careful formulation of the questions, but also your manner. As Evans puts it:[3]

> Don't do it at all unless you have to and unless you can be sure of doing it really well. Relax, stay calm, radiate quiet confidence. The Honest Guide is back in charge and about to restore sanity to the proceedings.

[3] Keith Evans *The Golden Rules of Advocacy* (Blackstone Press Limited, 1993) 117.

CHAPTER 14

Closing Your Case

14.1 INTRODUCTION

Although little needs to be said about this topic, it deserves a chapter of its own because of the potentially career-shattering implications of a premature closing.

What will be discussed in this chapter are: closing for the plaintiff; and closing for the defendant.

It needs, in this regard, to be emphasised that I am dealing with the normal run of cases, and will leave for other textbooks a discussion of the more complicated situation where there are multiple parties, or where the defendant bears the burden of proving some issues.[1]

14.2 CLOSING THE PLAINTIFF'S CASE

Your task is simple, but crucial.

The decision as to when to close your case is not one that you should take on the spur of the moment. You will have thought this issue through in your preparation for the case when you considered what issues the plaintiff needed to prove and through what witnesses and documents, etc, you proposed proving those issues. You will, throughout your case, be reflecting from time to time on whether you have *prima facie* established those issues which you need to prove, whether the witnesses you have called have been sufficient or whether you need take the risk of calling others, and so forth.[2]

If you are satisfied that you have led what evidence you can and need on those issues on which the plaintiff bears the burden of proof, and if you are satisfied that calling further witnesses is either unnecessary or inadvisable, then you close your case. You do so by the simple expedient of standing up, looking the judge in the eye and using words to the following effect:

> 'That is the plaintiff's case, my lord.'

---

[1] See, for the situation where the burden of proof on certain issues rests with the defendant, Uniform Rules 39(13) and 39(14), and Magistrate's Court Rule 29(9). Beware of utilising these provisions if you are for the plaintiff because of the sting in the tail of both provisions which provide that the plaintiff may only call rebutting evidence to the extent that the evidence already led by him did not touch on issues with regard to which the plaintiff does not bear the burden of proof. You might think yourself clever by utilising these provisions, and then find that you have inadvertently led evidence touching on the point (or are, at least, thought by the judge to have done so) and that you have, effectively, caught your own tail.

[2] The test at this stage, as will be more fully discussed in chapter 15, is not whether the evidence is such that the court *ought* to find in favour of the plaintiff, but whether it is such that a reasonable court *might* do so. There must, in other words, be sufficient evidence on those points on which the plaintiff bears the burden of proof that a reasonable court might find for the plaintiff. See the authorities referred to in chapter 15.

14.3 CLOSING THE DEFENDANT'S CASE

There are two stages at which you might close the defendant's case: after the plaintiff has closed his case and without your leading evidence, or after you have led evidence for the defendant.[3]

Your decision as to the former is dealt with in the ensuing chapter, dealing with applications for absolution from the instance. As to the latter, the considerations are much the same as those applicable to the plaintiff as outlined above: you ask yourself whether you need or want to risk calling more evidence for the defendant and, if your view is in the negative, you close your case in identical terms to those of your opponent, save that you are closing the defendant's case.

---

[3] See, for the distinction between the two, the judgment of Beadle CJ in *Supreme Service Station (1969) (Pty) Ltd v Fox & Goodridge (Pty) Ltd* 1971 (4) SA 90 (RAD) at 92. As His Lordship there said, 'it is perfectly competent for a court to refuse an application for absolution from the instance when the application is made at the close of the plaintiff's case, but to grant it if the defendant then promptly closes his case and renews the application without calling any evidence at all. There is no inconsistency in two such diametrically opposed orders . . . because the test to be applied when application is made before the defendant closes his case is "what *might* a reasonable court do", whereas the test to be applied when the application is made after the defendant has closed its case is "what *ought* a reasonable court to do".'

Applying for Absolution from the Instance

15.1 INTRODUCTION

There are two stages at which the defendant might apply for absolution from the instance: at the close of the plaintiff's case and before the defendant's case, and where the defendant closes his case without leading evidence.[1]

Because the latter is to all intents and purposes simply a matter of argument, which is the topic dealt with in the next chapter, I shall in this chapter restrict myself to the former, viz, applications for absolution from the instance at the close of the plaintiff's case.

15.2 DO YOU, OR DON'T YOU?

I can recall being told by counsel, who was one of the *dramatis personae,* of one of the shortest legal arguments on record. It was at the end of the plaintiff's case and came after an eloquent, persuasive argument by defendant's counsel in support of an application for absolution from the instance. Counsel for the plaintiff rose to reply.

> 'My learned friend', said he, 'may have absolution from the instance — at his peril.'

The application was quickly withdrawn.

What is known as 'the rule in *Gascoyne v Paul & Hunter*'[2] sets out the circumstances in which the court will grant absolution from the instance at the end of the plaintiff's case. This sort of application will not be granted when there is evidence on which a reasonable man *might* give judgment in favour of the plaintiff.

Applications for absolution from the instance stem from four possible causes:

* the actual failure by the plaintiff to make out a case;
* a failure to understand the rule in *Gascoyne v Paul & Hunter;*
* a desire to protect the defendant from cross-examination if possible;
* excessive zeal, which I am tempted colloquially to describe as a desire to be smart.

It is interesting to observe the remarks of Schutz JA on this topic:[3]

---

[1] See the discussion of the distinction between the two in para 14.3 of chapter 14, in particularly fn 3.

[2] 1917 TPD 170. Approved and described in those terms by Schreiner JA in *Gafoor v Unie Versekeringsadviseurs (Edms) Bpk* 1961 (1) SA 335 (A) at 340. See also *Claude Neon Lights Ltd v Daniel* 1976 (4) SA 403 (A), *Gordon Lloyd Page & Associates v Rivera and Another* 2000 (1) SA 88 (SCA) at 92E–93A and *De Klerk v ABSA Bank Limited and Others* 2003 (4) SA 315 (SCA) at 320I–321A.

[3] In *De Klerk v ABSA Bank Limited and Others* 2003 (4) SA 315 (SCA) at 320I–321A.

Counsel who applies for absolution from the instance at the end of a plaintiff's case takes a risk, even though the plaintiff's case be weak. If the application succeeds the plaintiff's action is ended, he must pay the costs and the defendant is relieved of the decision whether to lead evidence and of having his body of evidence scrutinised should he choose to provide it. But time and time again plaintiffs against whom absolution has been ordered have appealed successfully and left the defendant to pay the costs of both the application and the appeal and with the need to decide what is to be done next. The question in this case is whether the plaintiff has crossed the low threshold of proof that the law sets when a plaintiff's case is closed but the defendant's is not.

Before you ask for absolution at the close of the plaintiff's case you must ascertain into which of the four categories suggested your application falls. The only one which is safe, of course, is the first. The second needs a consideration of what amounts to a *prima facie* case, which varies from one case to the next. The third is a calculated risk about which I have already said something; it is not highly recommended. The fourth means you ought to be on the stage rather than at the Bar.

Assuming in your favour that the fourth instance will never arise, the real question is how one determines when to make such an application, and what the consequences of an error of judgment may be? Firstly, of course, there are the cases in which absolution has been sought and refused. If you study some of these[4] you will find a fair amount of guidance. You will not waste everybody's time by asking the court to 'sift all the evidence led and say what [it] is prepared to accept and what not'. Nobody can tell you when, in any hypothetical set of circumstances, it is safe or even wise to apply for absolution at the end of the plaintiff's case. There must be hundreds, even thousands, of cases where this has been done, properly and successfully. A few of them are reported and are available to serve as examples.[5]

Your cautious approach to such applications should be dictated more by the consequences of success, than of failure. Should you fail, the worst that can happen is that your client will pay the wasted costs — if any. In the nature of things those costs ought not to be intolerable (which is, of course, not to say that you should chance such an application where you yourself are satisfied that there are no prospects of success: there are no advantages that I can think of in gratuitously making an ass of yourself). If you succeed when you should have failed your client may face the prospect of an appeal. *De Klerk v ABSA Bank*, quoted above, shows that even a judge may be held to have erred in granting absolution from the instance, while there are many more reported cases where magistrates have done so, and the appeal courts have held them to have been wrong.

---

[4] Such as *Gandy v Makhanya* 1974 (4) SA 853 (N) and *De Klerk v ABSA Bank Limited and Others* 2003 (4) SA 315 (SCA).

[5] Such as *De Villiers NO v Summerson* 1951 (3) SA 75 (T), *Langham Court (Pty) Ltd v Mavromaty* 1954 (3) SA 742 (T), *Van Zyl v Niemann* 1964 (4) SA 661 (A), *Van der Merwe v Austin* 1965 (1) SA 43 (T) and *Naboomspruit Munisipaliteit v Malati Park (Edms) Bpk* 1982 (2) SA 127 (T) 138.

You should always ask yourself what is to be gained as well as what can be lost, for the costs of a successful appeal may be considerable. If your witnesses will give evidence which may bolster up the plaintiff's case, or if your client cannot face cross-examination, these are very relevant considerations in deciding upon your tactics. Another consideration is that if the plaintiff has not made out a *prima facie* case, but if he may derive support from your witnesses you can close your case without leading evidence and be no worse off.

If your witnesses do not help the plaintiff — subject to the unexpected — then it is always safe to give the plaintiff the benefit of the doubt and to assume that he has made out enough of a case to call for an answer. If you are wrong you may lose the case through your error of judgment, but far more often would the error lie in any contrary assumption.

15.3 ESOTERICA OF APPLICATIONS FOR ABSOLUTION

Note the following:

• Absolution is unlikely to be given at the close of the plaintiff's case where several defendants are sued, jointly or in the alternative. This is so even if one of those defendants can rightly argue at the close of the plaintiff's case that no case has been made out against him. The reason for this is the possibility of injustice if the subsequent evidence of the other defendant or defendants might point to blame on the part of that defendant.[6]

• Likewise, absolution is unlikely to be granted at the close of the plaintiff's case where the case involves claim and counterclaim arising out of the same facts. The reason for this is the possibility of injustice should the evidence on the defendant's counterclaim disclose a case for the plaintiff on his claim.[7]

• There is no room for absolution from the instance where the burden of proof rests with the defendant. The defendant will in such an event only be entitled to judgment if he discharges that burden (in which event the judgment will, in the nature of things, be a dismissal, and not an absolution), and if he fails therein the plaintiff will be entitled to judgment.[8] Thus, the plaintiff in such a situation is in effect faced with the choice discussed in paragraph 14.3 in chapter 14 above: if he believes that the defendant has not discharged the burden of proof resting on him, he closes his case, whereas if he suspects that the defendant might have done sufficient to discharge that burden of proof, he leads his evidence. There is no scope for a defendant being absolved from the instance: there will either be judgment for the plaintiff, or dismissal of the plaintiff's action, ie, judgment for the defendant.

[6] See *Mazibuko v Santam Insurance Co Ltd and Another* 1982 (3) SA 125 (A).
[7] *Atlantic Continental Assurance Company of SA Ltd v Vermaak* 1973 (2) SA 525 (E) at 526.
[8] See *Arter v Burt* 1922 AD 303 at 306, *Ramnath v Bunsee* 1961 (1) SA 394 (N) at 400 and *Sentraalwes Personeelondernemings (Edms) Bpk v Nieuwoudt* 1979 (2) SA 537 (C) at 546A–B.

CHAPTER 16

The Argument

16.1 INTRODUCTION

As to the charge, I do not think twelve guineas was excessive, having regard to the importance of the case . . . It is a mistake to estimate a fee simply upon the basis of the time occupied in court. There are other circumstances to be considered — the importance of the case, and the time and attention given to its preparation. The most effective arguments are often the shortest, and sometimes the most ineffective are the longest. The more care and trouble counsel take in the preparation of a case, probably the more concise and effective will the arguments be. Speaking for myself the arguments which most frequently appeal to me are the shorter, crisp, well-prepared, rather than the long, discursive ones.[1]

It is in the field of argument that the distinction between jury-centred systems (such as for example in the United States) and judge-centred systems becomes most apparent. It is one thing to argue before a jury whose emotions may sometimes cloud the individual sense of logic of each of its twelve members; it is another thing entirely to address a judge. Judges are (or at least most judges are) human, but their humanity is a far cry from the emotional humanity of a jury.

16.2 THE OBJECTS OF ARGUMENT

I suggest that the objects of argument can be stated in seven categories:

* to advance your case in accordance with your case theory, by defining the issues and outlining the burden of proof with regard to those issues;
* to summarise and collate the evidence pertinent to your case. If acting for the plaintiff, to perform this exercise in respect of each issue of fact required to be resolved in your favour for the establishing of your cause of action. If acting for the defendant, to do so firstly in regard to your answer to the plaintiff's cause of action, and then in regard to issues of fact required to be resolved in your favour for the establishing of any particular defence;
* to advance reasons why the evidence of witnesses against you should be rejected, and the evidence of your own witnesses accepted;
* to draw attention to, and urge the acceptance of, probabilities which will resolve any issue of fact or conflict of evidence in your favour;
* to anticipate your opponent's case, and to advance reasons why his case should be rejected;
* to draw the court's attention to any principles of law and to the authorities from which those principles are to be gleaned;

---

[1] Per Bale CJ in *Landers v Vogel* (1906) 27 NLR 590 at 591.

- to draw the court's attention to factors relevant to the exercise of any discretion, the making of any assessment (such as damages) or the determination of any other issue in general.

16.3 THE APPROACH TO ARGUMENT

Throughout this book I have been at pains to emphasise one aspect of technique which overshadows all others. That aspect is the pursuit of the essence. Now, as the trial nears its end and when there is no going back because the course you have navigated has for ever been swallowed in the oceans of history, now comes your final effort. From a crowded cargo of fact and principle you must select the essence. You must unload and arrange your cargo, arrange it so that your voyage can be seen for what it is. James Elroy Flecker wrote lines which you might adapt to my metaphors and my thesis:

> We travel not for trafficking alone.
> By hotter winds our fiery hearts are fann'd.
> For lust of knowing what should not be known
> We take the golden road to Samarkand.

In your argument the golden road is your path, Samarkand your objective and the hotter wind is still your quest for the essence. That wind, that lust and the knowledge are to be found in the quest for the essence.

And from poetry to the prosaic paragraphs of a judgment, the words of Curlewis JA in *Peimer v Finbro Furnishers (Pty) Ltd*:[2]

> I desire to make some observations on the issues in this matter, which, though quite simple as appears from the judgment of Centlivres J in the court below, have become involved in some obscurity and confusion owing to the line of argument adopted before us by counsel for the appellant.

Mark you, when that selfsame counsel later became a judge he was famed not only for learning and understanding, but also for directness and incisiveness of thought.

Your approach to the argument will be decided before you are called upon to speak. Your view of the essence of the matter will have been formed through consultations, pleading and advising on evidence. The last exercise is to orient your argument to the essence. Points are not to be made for the sake of making points but because they point to the essence. But perhaps it is idle for me to attempt to gloss the passage last quoted.

While I have to some extent decried emotion or emotionalism in the arguing of civil cases, and while I do not advocate the fiery rhetoric of earlier days, I would not like to suggest that you argue your case like a radio announcer reading the stock exchange prices. I believe that personality plays a powerful

[2] 1936 AD 177 at 188.

part in the presentation of cases. With due modifications indicated by differences in legal climate, I largely agree with Du Cann[3] when he says:

> This kind of derogatory dismissal [of eloquent speeches] is far too common. It is largely founded on the belief that emotion is an unreliable guide to a true decision on fact, and that there is therefore something suspect in evoking or displaying emotion. This both distorts reality, for most human action is prompted by feeling and not by facts, and supposes that there is an infallibility about fact which produces verdicts with the accuracy of a Pythagorean equation.

In an earlier chapter I gave the instance of the apologetic advocate whose timorousness did not stand in the way of success. From that illustration I do not wish to depart. I do say, however, that particularly on issues of fact, the object must be to persuade no less than to dissect, analyse, collate and expound. In the process of persuasion you will be well served by personality and persistence.

When you set out to attain one or more or all of the seven objectives I have suggested it matters not only *what* you are doing but also *how* you do it. That *how* is the subject of the ensuing paragraphs.

16.4 PREPARATION

For a good many years, in those cases where you appear for a plaintiff, a mild form of panic will strike you when your opponent closes his case and the judge says to you: 'Yes, Ms Ntshingila [or whatever it may be]?'

There will be some cases where you can, with justification, ask for an adjournment to prepare argument, but asking is one thing, and receiving may be another. It is well, therefore, to prepare yourself mentally for the argument stage as well as doing whatever physical preparation time will allow. Of course, a carefully planned advice on evidence and careful preparation before trial will facilitate your task on argument.

As the case progresses, you perform the functions of a computer to resolve what your general plan will be when you are called upon. If your case is one that depends primarily on the determination of an issue of law you may decide to argue that issue first, and then to deal with the facts which have to be found to establish your client's right to relief on the principle of law for which you contend. More often, however, the law comes in at the end of the argument, when the facts have been dealt with and the requisite elements of the cause of action established. Your determination of the essence and the realisation of that essence during the trial are matters which will influence profoundly the sequence of your argument. Generally speaking, if you can prepare so as to confine your argument to the essence you will have gone a good way towards framing your submissions in the form which will please the Bench. Counsel often underrates the intelligence of the Bench and its ability to grasp and understand the submissions made. I do not dispute that at times judges seem to be a little obtuse, although it is not for me to say where the fault may lie. But if

---

[3] *The Art of the Advocate* (Pelican Books) 156.

you prepare an argument on the basis of confining yourself to the essence and omitting the non-essential details, you will most infrequently regret your decision.

One thing that you must accept is that you are going to omit some point or other — unless you are able to sit down with a transcript of the evidence and with adequate time to prepare a full list of points and details. You will often reproach yourself for not having said this, that or the other. Probably you may console yourself with the thought that if there was so much merit in the point then you would never have overlooked it or else the judge must have seen it. But you don't want to miss these points, and so your trial technique must be designed not to do so.

The preliminary preparation provides you with your notes on the points and considerations pertinent to the issues. Your notes of evidence must do the rest. The technique which I suggested for picking up points for cross-examination can be used for the purpose of argument. The difficulty is that counsel will hardly be in a position to mark relevant passages occurring in the notes of his own cross-examination, while an attorney appearing alone in a case is in a worse position. If you can evolve a system of making quick notes as points arise, without disrupting the flow and effect of the cross-examination, then you will succeed where so many others have failed.

Where literally no time exists for preparation of an argument it is well to work on preparatory notes and to fit into these your comments on the witnesses, point by point. If you adopt the line of least resistance, that is taking notes of evidence and reading through them, making your submissions point by point as your notes of evidence proceed, you will present an argument, but you may find that you have handed to the court a jigsaw puzzle in 500 pieces instead of a complete picture.

If I might try to coin an epigram I would offer this: prepare where possible but always be prepared.

16.5 ADMISSIONS

The stage of argument is fascinating to those who value the aesthetics of the law. The winnowing is a process of submissions by counsel and comments by the judge, with the blowing away of the chaff and leaving of the grain. You will find that counsel is often, in this procedure, compelled to concede propositions which fall from the Bench with a degree of authority difficult to resist. Nor does that degree of authority necessarily ensure the correctness of any given proposition. In these circumstances it might be comforting to know that concessions made by counsel during argument are not usually held to be binding on the client.[4] Perhaps even the casual concession of a fact may be

---

[4] *Paddock Motors (Pty) Ltd v Igesund* 1976 (3) SA 16 (A) at 23, *Prinsloo & Viljoen Eiendomme (Edms) Bpk v Morfou* 1993 (1) SA 668 (T) at 669–70, and *National Police Service Union v Minister of Safety and Security* 2000 (3) SA 371 (A) at 379.

withdrawn where it is not intended to amount to a formal admission whose object is to dispense with evidence on a particular point.

The question of admissions or concessions is one which presents no small degree of difficulty. Apart from the question of tactical denials in pleadings and admissions to shorten the proceedings there are two schools of thought. One is: 'Never admit anything; the opposition may fail or forget to prove it.' The other is: 'Never deny anything that is going to be proved anyway.' In the long run, and probably even in the short, you will show more profit on the latter policy.

Lest you wonder what this has to do with forensic eloquence let me at once unto the breach. In argument it is usually better policy to concede the indefensible, thus:

> During discussion at the Bar, however, counsel correctly admitted that such onus is discharged on a preponderance of probability.[5]

There is one precaution to be observed, however. Your view of the indefensible may not necessarily coincide with that of the judge, and the view of the judge may not necessarily coincide with that of the appeal court. However, you must have sufficient courage and confidence to concede what is insupportable because to argue such matters may well cause contamination of contentions that are of more substance and of more value to your case.[6]

16.6 WRITTEN HEADS OF ARGUMENT, AND STARTING WITH A ROAD MAP

If you can furnish written heads of argument, even if these only be in the form of a skeletal outline of your argument, so much the better: it shows the degree of your preparation, it avoids the court having to note each and every authority to which you refer in your argument, it leaves the judge with a written memorial to which he will, hopefully, refer again and again in drafting his judgment and, every once in a while, you might receive the compliment of seeing your heads transformed into the judge's judgment.[7]

In either event, ie, whether you are able to hand up written heads or have to rely on your oral skills alone, it is best to start by giving the Bench a roadmap of where you want to go.

Start, in other words, by telling the judge what points you propose covering, and the order in which you propose covering them. We are more comfortable

---

[5] Per Van den Heever JA in *Northview Properties (Pty) Ltd v Lurie* 1951 (3) SA 688 (A) at 696B.

[6] There is a no-doubt apocryphal anecdote about Sir Hartley Shawcross arguing before the House of Lords in England. The story goes that Sir Hartley began by announcing that he had four points to make, two of which were bad, one arguable and one unanswerable. The obvious retort that fell from the bench was that he should indicate which was which, to which his response was 'That's for me to know, and for you to find out'. Keep this as an anecdote only. If a point is bad, abandon it. Concentrate on your good points.

[7] Your preparation of the heads of argument should begin when the trial brief lands on your desk, and should be well advanced by the time the trial begins. You will by then have identified the legal points in issue and the relevant authorities, in order to structure your case accordingly. As the trial proceeds, so in the evenings will your heads proceed.

travelling when we know the route we are going to follow and have some idea of the destination. You will be amazed at how much more at ease a judge is listening to your argument when he knows what topics you are going to cover, than when he wonders whether you are ever going to get to the points he might be particularly eager to discuss with you.

16.7 THE STRUCTURE OF YOUR ARGUMENT, GENERALLY

As a general statement, your argument (heads of argument, oral argument) should be structured as follows:

- Define the issues, and offer your road-map of the order in which you intend dealing with them.
- The facts. Deal with the facts. The law can only be discussed properly in the context of the facts.
- The law. Having dealt with the facts, discuss the legal conclusions to be reached on the strength of those facts.
- Costs.
- Conclusion. What do you ask?

16.8 DICTION AND MANNER

Speak clearly. Speak naturally. Speak as though you believe in the justice of what you are arguing. With all this, however, there are as many styles of address as there are successful advocates at the Bar — or attorneys at the Side-Bar. Subject to that, you must ensure that you are heard, that you are understood and that you leave an impression. You need not renounce eloquence, though you will avoid dramatics. Does the following speech become any less convincing, in a claim for damages by a man who has lost the use of his legs as a result of a motor accident, because it is addressed to a judge rather than to a jury?

> What life lies in store for the plaintiff for the next 40-odd years? When he is not in hospital for treatment he may be employed as a telephonist. His life will be a monotonous existence in a wheel-chair, shuttling between his switchboard and his monastic cell. The highlight of his existence is that his sympathetic employers have fixed a monkey-chain in his bathroom, so that he can swing himself from his wheel-chair into his bath without assistance.
>
> He is impotent. He will probably never know the companionship of a wife, the joy of the first-born child. For him there is not to be parenthood, whose cares and responsibilities are counted for nothing against the delights of one's own children. Nor in his older age, when his children are grown, will he live again those early years of parenthood in the coming of his grandchildren.

Of course, you do not argue the interpretation of a contract in these phrases; you select your occasion — and you select your judge. When in doubt, be guilty rather of understatement than the contrary. If the statement is sound it will not suffer from being presented in 'low key'. To use the photographic metaphor again, many of the most dramatic presentations are those with subtle variations of low tones and undertones.

There is the inevitable word of caution, if you would learn from the mistakes of others before making your own. Don't overdo the emotional addresses and the purple passages. Often enough has a judge been heard to admonish counsel for addressing him as though he were a jury. Nor do I see any reason why magistrates should be subjected to any different form of address. Both owe their position to their knowledge of the law and, usually, to their experience in trials. Yours is not the first case they have heard. If you study the quotation I have given on this topic you will see that there is no appeal for an emotional decision, the appeal is for a decision on the facts stated in an emotional form.

What you say may be affected not only by its impact on the ear, but also by your impact on the eye. The drama of your speech may suffer if you slouch, if your stance and style are slovenly, if you shuffle your papers restlessly back and forth.

Stand up, look the judge in the eye and use your body as a weapon of persuasion as much as you use logic and words, leaning forward to emphasise a point, and using your hands whether it be in the form of anchoring them to the lectern or upturned briefcase in front of you, or pointing to a passage, etc. Do not underestimate the importance of conveying your conviction not just in the words that you use, but in your manner.

With a judge of fact the psychological motivation is different and far more subtle than I would think it is with a jury. Nevertheless it is there. Precisely what it is may be difficult to define. Perhaps there is the need to convey a sense of conviction in your cause. Perhaps it is to compel ('request' might be a better word) the attention of the court. Perhaps it is something quite ineffable. Whatever it may be, the value of the personal communication is very real and never to be overlooked.

16.9 DISCUSSING THE EVIDENCE

When the trial has lasted three days you cannot spend another three days repeating the evidence for the benefit of the court. Nor can you expect the judge to be mindful of every phrase uttered by every witness, no matter how comprehensive his own notes. Nor yet should you expect the judicial officer to see the significance of the nuances of expression which bear upon your case or condemn that of your adversary. So you set about your argument on the evidence, quoting no more than is necessary but overlooking nothing that is vital.

I have already suggested as a convenient procedure the method of argument by starting by telling the judge what points you propose covering and the order in which you propose covering them, and then on each point dealing with the facts before dealing with the law. Now, that theme must be made the subject of a variation. The variation is an *obbligato* played on the personality of the witnesses. On each issue some or other witness will have said something, and you must tell the court what testimony should be accepted and what rejected.

You must always bear in mind that should you fail in this task there is, in ordinary circumstances, no appeal. For, as has been said:

> It is true that an appeal is a rehearing of the case, but as said by Lord Sankey in *Powell and wife v Streatham Manor Nursing Home* ((1935) AC 243 at 249):
>
>> 'It is perfectly true that an appeal is by way of rehearing, but it must not be forgotten that the court of appeal does not rehear the witnesses. It only reads the evidence and rehears the counsel. Neither is it a re-seeing court . . . On an appeal against a judgment of a judge sitting alone the court of appeal will not set aside the judgment unless the appellant satisfies the court that the judge was wrong and that his decision ought to have been the other way. Where there has been a conflict of evidence the court of appeal will have special regard to the fact that the judge saw the witnesses.'
>
> Lord Sankey quotes with approval the remarks of *Lord Shaw in Clarke v Edinburgh Tramways Co* (1919 SC 35 (HL) 36) where he says:
>
>> 'In my opinion the duty of an appellate court in those circumstances is for each judge of it to put to himself, as I now do in this case, the question: "Am I — who sit there without those advantages sometimes broad and sometimes subtle — which are the privileges of the judge who heard and tried the case, in a position, not having those privileges to come to a clear conclusion that the judge who had them was plainly wrong?" If I cannot be satisfied in my own mind that the judge with those privileges was plainly wrong, when it appears to me to be my duty to defer to his judgment.'
>
> I quote the above because it is a very recent and forceful expression by the House of Lords of a principle which this court has adopted in the several cases quoted from the bar, eg, *National Employers Mutual General Insurance Association v Gany* (1931 AD 187 at 199); *Estate Kaluza v Brauer* (1926 AD 243).[8]

In regard to each witness whose evidence you want rejected you must be prepared, therefore, with the facts and contentions on which the court will be asked to find in your favour. The grounds on which testimony may be rejected are capable of almost infinite variation. Nor need you establish that the witness is not worthy of belief, for no more is to be accepted the evidence of he who errs while trying to speak truthfully than of he who lies knowing that he swears falsely. But, whatever you do, say something; for, if you can find no reason to advance as to why the word of a particular witness should not be accepted, the court will not find it for you.

It may help if you cast your mind back to the suggestions which were offered on cross-examination, for the failure of the witness on one or more of the tests propounded in that chapter may be a reason for disbelieving him or not accepting his testimony.[9] There are many other matters, of course, which were

[8] Per Wessels CJ in *Bitcon v Rosenberg* 1936 AD 380 at 395–6. See also *R v Dhlumayo* 1948 (2) SA 677 (A) at 705 and *Marine & Trade Insurance Co Ltd v Mariamah and Another* 1978 (3) SA 480 (A) at 486E.

[9] See particularly paragraphs 12.5.15–22 of chapter 12. A good starting point would be the *dictum* in *SFW Group Limited and Another v Martell et Cie and Others* 2003 (1) SA 11 (SCA) referred to in paragraph 4.3.4 in chapter 4. But be careful in the argument *'falsum in uno, falsum in omnibus'* in which regard see *S v Mtsweni* 1985 (1) SA 590 (A) at 593–4 (although the *dictum* that, because a witness lied on one point he is not necessarily to be disbelieved on another, ought not to be taken too literally: a lie on one point can, and usually will, blight the witness's credibility, impacting on all of his evidence: see *Cooper and Another v Syfrets Trust Limited* 2001 (1) SA 122 (SCA) 132).

not dealt with previously but which relate to this topic. Evasiveness on the part of the witness, hedging, lacking of candour, inconsistency, an undue time taken in answering questions, feigned forgetfulness, a pretended need for an interpreter are some of the principal lines of attack which supplement the tests already discussed.[10] I would say that, demeanour apart, one of the best grounds for asking the court to reject the evidence of a witness is that he fails the test by mental reaction. That, however, is purely a personal view, for the ordinary test by fact could well be regarded as the acid test of testimony. However, you will be able from the foregoing to gather how cross-examination forms the basis of the subsequent argument on credibility.

As I have said before, judges and magistrates are inclined to rely very strongly on demeanour when weighing up the words of the witnesses. Demeanour, of course, includes all the matters such as evasiveness, hedging and so on, which I mentioned in the previous paragraph. It includes also the more subtle aura of the witness, the expressible or sometimes ineffable impression he or she makes on the court and it includes his or her physical mannerisms in the witness-box. In the course of your argument you will, no doubt, have a few observations on demeanour, but here again I have a word of caution. You will remember the discussion on expert witnesses and you will encounter gentlemen, eminent in their field, expressing diametrically opposite views arising out of any given set of facts. The same phenomenon arises in the case of counsel's contentions on credibility or his digressions on demeanour. His view of the witness is affected by the colour of the spectacles he is wearing, varying from a tasteful rosy hue to a jaundiced yellow-green. For this reason be conservative in your assessment, and refrain from being dogmatic in your manner.

It is usually well to deal with the topic of credibility first, because your submissions on the issues will inevitably stand or fall with your submissions on the acceptability of the witnesses.

It is in this attack on the credibility of the opposing witnesses that the most painstaking attention to detail is required and the need for careful preparation arises. You must be most careful to select what is of moment and to discard what is merely plausibly attractive but of no real substance. Attention to detail is required because it is outside the witness's theme, usually, that one finds the material on which to base an argument as to credibility. It is the hundred and one little circumstantial matters which enable you to attack the stoutly defended citadel of the main theme. The comparison process is one which usually pays dividends. Of course, that very process renders you susceptible to the alluring false scents of which I spoke in chapter 4. You will learn how an argument or comparison which shone like a beacon at midnight may pale with the morning sun and be so dull as to be almost invisible at noontide. It is for this

---

[10] See, in general, dealing with demeanour of witnesses, *President of the Republic of South Africa and Others v South African Rugby and Football Union and Others* 2000 (1) SA 1 (CC) at 43, *Santam Beperk v Biddulph* 2004 (5) SA 586 (SCA) at 594C–H, and *Medscheme Holdings (Pty) Ltd and Another v Bhamjee* 2005 (5) SA 339 (SCA) at 345.

very reason that I say that you must be selective in your submissions. Often the insupportable will weaken the good. An unwarranted attack on a witness may cause the court to entertain a feeling of resentment and to defend the witness in its judgment when really he or she ought to be castigated. If there is a point of substance state it, hammer it if necessary, don't be talked out of it. But don't spoil it with a lot of nonsense about minor discrepancies which don't take the matter further anyway.[11]

From your discussions of the credibility of the witnesses you are able to proceed with the issues, now armed with the reasons why you say that the court should make particular findings on particular points relevant to individual issues.

My last suggestion flows from the first sentence of this section. The degree of detail in your discussion should be dictated by the demands of the essential submissions, discarding the dross and retaining the pure metal of which your weapons will be formed.

16.10 ILLUSTRATION AND ANALOGY

I group these two aspects of technique together because, for all their differences, they are really the same form of argument. You make your point by going outside the facts of your own case. You may, when employing the method of illustration, use a biblical story, you may employ anecdotes or you may occasionally use the odd humorous story or apt quote. That is what I mean by illustration and I believe that no argument ever loses by illustration, *carefully chosen and properly handled*. You will, of course, adapt your illustration to the sophistication of the tribunal and remember again that judges don't like being addressed as though they were juries.

16.11 LET THE COURT FIND THE POINT?

Many writers advocate this technique. Many of the leading advocates at the Bar employ it — or claim to do so.

Nobody says what you are to do when the court fails to find the point.

I suggest that you must get to know your judges. With many you can safely indulge in a large degree of understatement, secure in the knowledge that the judge will be quick to see the significance of what you are saying. With others you may safely assume that a question put to you — or your opponent — by the judge will be the basis of the ultimate decision.

My own view is that this approach has nothing whatsoever to recommend it. Argument in a lawsuit is not a game of poker where the judge must guess what sort of hand you are holding. He may guess wrongly. Concise and comprehensive statement of the essential facts and principles of law will cost you nothing, and will risk nothing.

---

[11] See the discussion of contradictions in paragraph 12.5.22 above, particularly in fn 48. It is important to learn the distinction between material and immaterial discrepancies.

16.12 IMPOSE THE ESSENCE OF THE CASE

Far better, in my view, than deliberately understating your case in the fond hope that the court will seize successfully on your tantalising hints, to establish for yourself in your thinking beforehand what the essential points are that you want to make and which in your view constitute the reasons why the court should find in your favour, and then to make those points firmly, and clearly, planting them as pillars before the court such that judge or opponent will have to demolish them if you are to fail.

16.13 BREVITY

Judges like brevity.

Brevity saves the good points from becoming obscured with a mass of facts, issues, submissions, arguments, contentions, considerations.

Brevity, however, does not mean that you should speak quickly: the judge must be given the opportunity to take on board the points which you make and, to that end, you should, if anything, deliberately slow your delivery so as to give him adequate opportunity to do so.

16.14 REPETITION

Judges do not like repetition.

If a point is a good one and stated concisely the judge should understand it. If it is a bad point then there is nothing in it. It takes only an elementary mathematical calculation to show that ten times nothing is worth no more than one times nothing.

Don't misunderstand this, however. Persistence may be needed, even if this involves some degree of repetition. It often happens that a court will resist or reject a point, wrongly, for want of understanding of the submission which is being made. The location of the blame is irrelevant. You will find that, in consultation or in discussions, you cannot follow a line of reasoning until it is restated in different words. So let it be with your arguments. Persist with the good points — until the court is aware of what you are saying and why you are right in your contention.

16.15 CITING AND READING FROM AUTHORITIES

It may seem trivial to you, but the judge does like to be able to note the authorities which you quote. *Smith v Smith* is simple, but not all cases are Smith cases. Ensure, therefore, odious though the word 'ensure' is when used as an imperative, that you cite your authorities in such a manner that the court may note the names and the reference. When in doubt, spell.

From this it is but a short journey to a similar comment on the reading of the authorities and the delivery of the address generally.[12] For some reason counsel often has a subconscious fear that people are getting crotchety when he is reading from authorities. In consequence the speed increases. Possibly, this results from the further subconscious reasoning that, having noted the reference, the judge will not make notes of what is read, but will be able to consult the authority itself when giving judgment. This is an error. The important thing is to convey the reasoning to the judge during the course of the argument, particularly when subsequent contentions depend upon the proposition established by your citation. If anything, therefore, the authority should be read with more deliberateness than adopted in other portions of the address. How often will you find, when working in the calm of your chambers, that you have to read a passage in a judgment two or three times in order to appreciate its essential message? Why should the judge be of such high mental ability that he can understand, appreciate, analyse and apply a hastily gabbled quotation from a turgid judgment?

The trick, when reading from authorities in the course of your argument, is four-fold: first, tell the judge why the passage is important, second select only so much of the passage as is necessary for you to get your message across, third deliberately slow your address and finally, as you were hopefully taught at school, maintain a measure of eye contact with the judge by looking up from the text from time to time to ensure that the connection between you and the judge is not being lost.

More difficult to discuss is the question of whether, when reading a rather lengthy extract, you should interrupt it with comments pertinent to the matter under consideration as they arise logically from what you are reading. On the whole I would suggest that this method should be rejected. The matter of moment is to convey the essence and trend of whatever authority you are quoting. An interruption may prejudice the smooth, coherent presentation of a line of logic. It is better, therefore, to return to the specific sentence after you have read the whole extract, and then to make your point based on that sentence.

The next problem is how many authorities to quote. The answer is not always simple. One may be enough if it is in point and binding upon the court. If the authorities are persuasive but not binding then multiplication adds to the persuasive effect.

There is one suggestion which I might diffidently make regarding authorities — a suggestion which I believe to be important. You will recall that, in dealing with pre-trial consultations, I advised you never to accept as accurate anything that your client or witnesses may tell you, but to test the accuracy of each statement. Authorities are witnesses as to the law. Whether the authority is for or against you, before you quote it you should subject it to the same testing.

---

[12] See the suggestions about reading in 'Matters of Style, Address and Manners', in Appendix B.

If you are sceptical, pick up a volume of law reports and look for cases which have subsequently been dissented from or held to have been wrongly decided. There is nothing more embarrassing to counsel than to be exposed in open court relying on a case which has since been overturned.

Nor, in general, is it profitable to rely upon the citation of authorities in textbooks. Authors — or some of them — are human beings and err with the best of us. Use the textbook as your source from which to seek the authorities. But do not shirk, nor skimp, nor scrape, nor save. Read each authority and judgment to decide whether it properly justifies the proposition for which it is cited. Equally you should exercise caution in citing the views of contemporary textbook writers in support of your contentions. Many are treated with respect, but even among those limited few, Homer will be found occasionally to nod. You will find in the law reports many instances where passages cited from leading text books have been disapproved.

All this latter discussion can be summarised by saying that you should be satisfied, in quoting authority, not only that the authority supports your proposition, but also that the authority is rightly decided.

It is said of the late Greenberg JA that on one of his own decisions[13] being cited some thirteen years later in an appeal[14] where he was one of the five judges hearing the matter, he inquired of counsel who relied upon that decision: 'But, Mr X, was I right?' And in his judgment he said:

> As at present advised, I see no reason for departing from the guarded statement made in *Van der Merwe v Union Government* 1936 TPD 185, which seems to me to be supported by the law in regard to duties imposed on the users of a level crossing.

For counsel who contemplates quoting authorities in support of his submissions there is a valuable lesson in those few phrases. Your mental attitude should not be one of elation that you have found a judgment that says, somewhere or other, what you want it to say. You should, indeed, welcome the judgment and feel a proper degree of self-satisfaction for having found it. You should read it. Strange as it may seem, I am convinced that many counsel do not read beyond the first paragraph of the headnote — indeed I *know* that that happens. So you perform your final analytical process on the judgment, in search of an essence, asking yourself eight questions:

- How did the jurisdiction of the court which pronounced the judgment compare with that of the court in which I am to argue?
- On what facts was the judgment based?
- Does the headnote correctly reflect the facts, the reasoning and the decision of the court?
- For what reasons did the court in truth arrive at its decision?
- Was the reasoning of the court correct?

---

[13] *Van der Merwe v Union Government* 1936 TPD 185.
[14] *Moore v Minister of Posts & Telegraphs* 1949 (1) SA 815 (A) at 817.

- Is the passage in the judgment on which I wish to rely an *obiter dictum*[15] or is it part of the actual decision?
- Are the authorities on which the decision is based also correct?
- Has the judgment been subsequently applied, criticised or overruled?

From this — if from nothing else — you will realise the limitations which the practice of law places upon ordinary social activity.

In regard to the last point you will find that, thanks to the excellent noter-up service now provided, there are an ever increasing number of annotations upon a great many cases — an overwhelming number upon some. Whether you follow them all to their bitter end is something for you to determine. Since many judgments deal with a number of points you will find that some 90 per cent of the annotations are useless for the purpose of your particular problem. All I can say is: happy hunting!

16.16 HUMOUR

In the main, I adhere to what I said about humour in discussing the outline of the case and cross-examination. By argument stage, however, some slight relaxation is usually permissible. Sometimes it may be beneficial — provided the case is one that lends itself to humour. Claims for damages for bodily injuries do not often fall into this category if the complaints are genuine,[16] nor do matrimonial actions.

16.17 ARGUE, RESPOND, REPLY

As a general statement,[17] the plaintiff commences with argument, the defendant answers, and the plaintiff then replies.

The plaintiff's argument should be directed towards all of the above objects, including anticipation of the defendant's case.

The defendant's argument should be directed towards advancing the defendant's case, and answering the plaintiff's submissions.

The plaintiff's reply should be limited to new matter raised in the defendant's argument.

16.18 IN CONCLUSION

If you appear for the plaintiff, your argument must conclude with a résumé of the relief which your client seeks. For example:

---

[15] *Pretoria City Council v Levinson* 1949 (3) SA 305 (A) at 316–7. See also Hahlo, HR and Kahn, Ellison *The South African Legal System and Its Background* (Juta 1968) at 260–1, 270–2 and 275–6.

[16] That said, I fondly recall the sardonic humour of leading counsel for the plaintiff in a personal injuries case (he now adorns the Bench) who, on rising to reply, remarked with a smile that his friend the leading counsel for the defendant had, in his argument, 'borne the plaintiff's pain with admirable stoicism'!

[17] See rule 39(23): the parties may confer with the judge in chambers as to the form and duration of the addresses.

> M'Lord or M'Lady, I ask for judgment for the plaintiff in the sum of R2 475 000,00. I also ask an order that the defendant forthwith deliver to plaintiff the 1 000 shares in the company known as XYZ Ltd, the share certificates to be accompanied by transfer forms duly signed in favour of the plaintiff (and whatever other orders may be necessary to cover failure to transfer the shares). I ask that preparation fees be allowed in respect of the architect, Mr A, the accountant, Mr B, and the quantity surveyor, Mr C, and that Mesdames D, E and F be declared to have been necessary witnesses. I ask for an order that the defendant pay the plaintiff's costs.

If judgment is in fact being sought in terms of certain specific claims in the combined summons or declaration it is sufficient to mention only those claims in a formula such as:

> I ask for judgment in terms of claims (a), (b), (c), (d), (e), (f) and (h) of the particulars of claim.

When you appear for the defendant this very onerous task is lightened and you may simply have to ask for 'absolution from the instance with costs', or that 'the plaintiff's claim be dismissed with costs' or whatever else may be appropriate.

Needless to say, if you are asking for some special order bearing on costs, you should be armed with the necessary authorities in support of your point. It is possible that your opponent will concede matters such as preparation fees or the costs of two counsel. It would be too sanguine if you were to anticipate that he would not oppose vehemently a request for attorney- and client costs in the event of your being successful, or disallowance of portion of his costs should he end up with the laurels of victory.

If I may be forgiven a little disrespect and a little repetition I would conclude with two suggestions:

- If you are heckled, give the court a patient hearing, but try not to be diverted from your theme. All too often the court's interruptions arise from an incomplete grasp of the issues; when the judge is presented with the full picture he may realise that his *prima facie* view needs modification.
- Present your argument with sufficient deliberateness to enable the judge to make adequate notes of your submissions. He cannot be expected to do it full justice if you are already developing the second and third points while he is still noting the first.

CHAPTER 17

Applications

17.1 INTRODUCTION

Applications are of three kinds: unopposed, urgent and opposed. The problems which arise are a result of the tendency of the first two kinds to develop into the third. Junior counsel will find that unopposed applications form a substantial portion of his practice in his early years at the Bar. As that practice develops, or as complications set in, he will also find that there is always someone waiting to take advantage of his mistakes. Attorneys will be made even more painfully conscious of this phenomenon, because in the majority of cases the initial labour and responsibility will be theirs.

In the field of application work you may well think that the scope for advocacy is so limited that any discussion is unnecessary. There is no advice on evidence, very little pre-trial procedure, no examination of witnesses[1] and perhaps very little in the way of forensic fireworks in the argument. Nevertheless applications impose demands upon the technique of the practitioner in two principal respects, being respectively drafting and argument. The consequences of bungling are, more often than not, irredeemable, with the result that applications can be more expensive for the client than the average trial action.

For the purposes of this discussion I make the assumption that every unopposed and every urgent application will develop into an opposed matter. I suggest that you do the same.

17.2 THE INITIAL APPROACH

17.2.1 The primary question

Rule 6(1) of the Uniform Rules of Court provides that applications are to be brought upon notice of motion supported by affidavits.[2]

The primary question is accordingly whether the case is a proper one for proceeding by way of application. True enough, in modern practice almost any form of relief may be sought in motion proceedings, but there is always a degree of risk attached to an over-enthusiastic response to the invitation which

---

[1] Subject to rule 6(5)(*g*) in appropriate cases.

[2] Applications to the Constitutional Court have a similar definition: see rule 11(1) of the Constitutional Court Rules. The Petition Proceedings Replacement Act 35 of 1976 provides that where a statute or rule provides for proceedings by way of petition, this must be construed as a reference to proceedings by way of notice of motion. Thus, for example, the reference in s 9 of the Insolvency Act 24 of 1936 to a petition for provisional sequestration is to be construed as a reference to an application for sequestration by way of notice of motion.

might be read into the judgment of Murray AJP in the *Room Hire* case.[3] There are innumerable annotations on that case, which show firstly the importance of the case, secondly that opinions differ on what is a proper subject for motion proceedings, and thirdly that some practitioners have not troubled to study the judgment and have not learnt to treat it with the respect required when handling explosives.

The negative is relatively simple to state: do not employ motion procedure in claims for damages, in matrimonial matters or in any case where the applicant's right to relief depends on a fact which is disputed by the respondent or which may reasonably be expected to be disputed.[4] The *Room Hire*[5] case explains that a genuine dispute of fact may arise in one or more of the following manners:

- The respondent may deny one or more of the material allegations made on the applicant's behalf and produce positive evidence to the contrary or apply for the leading of oral evidence to show the contrary.
- The respondent may admit the applicant's evidence but allege other facts which the applicant disputes.
- The respondent while conceding that he has no knowledge of one or more material facts may deny them and put applicant to the proof, and may himself propose to give evidence to show that the applicant is biased, untruthful or unreliable and that certain facts upon which the applicant relies are untrue.

The consequences of discovering too late that you are embroiled in a factual dispute and ought not to have proceeded by way of application can be disastrous. Although the court has the power to direct that oral evidence be heard on any particular issue which is in dispute, it is never certain that the court can be persuaded.[6]

17.2.2 The particular court's practice directives

A further aspect to bear in mind is that if you intend launching an application in a court in which you do not normally appear, you will be well advised to study the particular court's rules and practice directives before launching the application.[7]

---

[3] *Room Hire Co (Pty) Ltd v Jeppe St Mansions (Pty) Ltd* 1949 (3) SA 1155 (T) at 1162.

[4] A relatively simple method of establishing whether a real dispute of fact exists is to address a letter of demand to the respondent and to examine the respondent's reply thereto. See also the discussion of factual disputes in application proceedings in paragraph 17.9.4 below.

[5] At 1163.

[6] See, in this regard, the discussion of factual disputes and the court's various options, in paragraph 17.9.4 below.

[7] Erasmus *Superior Court Practice* contains some of the different courts' rules and practice directives. (Erasmus does not contain the North West High Court's practice directives.) In some divisions the practice directives change almost every term. A simple expedient is to telephone a colleague in that particular division and ask him what the practice is.

17.3 DRAFTING THE FOUNDING AFFIDAVIT

17.3.1 Think

The theme is: think first and save costs later. The thought process is set out in more detail hereunder, but it may be summarised as follows:

- What relief does your client require?
- Does he have *locus standi?*
- In order to obtain that relief, what is your client's cause of action?[8]
- Does your client have the necessary evidence to support his cause of action?
- Are the documents you intend to use relevant?
- Are you about to approach the correct court? In other words, does the court have jurisdiction?
- Is your client's case urgent?
- What is the respondent's case, and how can you meet it in the applicant's founding affidavit?
- Is there a foreseeable dispute of fact?

17.3.2 Your plan of campaign

It is not necessary to embark upon an elaborate or tedious analysis of draftsmanship. It will afford a useful guide if you roughly equate the notice of motion to the particulars of claim and the founding affidavit to a mongrel, bred of the inter-marriage of the particulars with the evidence in chief in a trial action.

Your general plan of campaign in drafting applications, therefore, will be that discussed in previous chapters in this book, namely:

- Extracting the essence (chapter 4)
- Pleadings (chapter 5)
- Advice on evidence (chapter 7)
- The leading of witnesses (chapter 11)

The reason for including the third item is that the technique required in preparing an advice on evidence should be used to breed the mongrel which I have mentioned. In other words, that technique effects the union between the particulars of claim and the evidence led in proof of those particulars. Application proceedings eliminate completely the distinction between those two stages of procedure and it is the advice on evidence, or a modification thereof, which ensures that your case is properly presented in your affidavits.

For fear that I have obscured the subject with verbiage, I would briefly recapitulate:

---

[8] See *Johannesburg City Council v Bruma Thirty-Two (Pty) Ltd* 1984 (4) SA 87 (T) 91C–F. See also *Schiebler v Kiss* 1985 (3) SA 489 (SWA) 494J–495B, where the applicant obtained a rule nisi for an attachment *ad confirmandum* and on the return date sought an interdict preventing the alienation of assets.

- Determine the issues material to your cause of action (as in pleadings). Include in your affidavits allegations on each issue which you have determined (as in the leading of witnesses and in proving your cause of action).
- The basic allegations will cover the parties, the applicant's *locus standi*, the jurisdiction of the court, and finally the cause of action. But what is required is evidence and not merely averments.
- As with the leading of evidence, ensure that the affidavit (or affidavits) tell/s the story as cogently, chronologically and persuasively as possible. It should begin with an introduction in which the parties, *locus standi* and the facts establishing jurisdiction are sufficiently described; it should then go on to outline the essence of the application; this should be followed by the story in logical sequence; and it should end with the conclusion, outlining what the applicant seeks and recapitulating why the applicant suggests that he is entitled to that relief.

17.3.3 The law of evidence

Although some practitioners appear a little sceptical on this point, the law of evidence applies no less to applications than to actions. True enough, for reasons of convenience and practicality, some degree of relaxation is permitted in urgent applications where a *status quo* must be preserved. An applicant may then set out his information or belief as to the existence of certain facts, where he cannot conveniently obtain the affidavit of the actual witness. All too often this indulgence is carried over into matters where the element of urgency is absent, and then there is trouble. There may also be trouble in the urgent matters. Your technique should be to avoid trouble. Even the permissible use of hearsay statements carries with it the virus, as may be gauged from the words of Schreiner J:[9]

> Where hearsay statements are permissibly inserted in or attached to a petition [application] in an urgent matter the fact that they would lose such weight as they may possess through being contradicted is not, in my opinion, a ground for striking them out. But where they were in the first instance improperly inserted or attached our practice is to strike them out, at least where they are of sufficient importance to be embarrassing (*Maudsley v Maudsley's Trustees* 1940 WLD 166).

Much time and money is wasted on striking-out applications, the parties being less interested in the forensic flourishes and fencing of their lawyers than in obtaining a decision on the merits. Perhaps the time is approaching where the consequences of such disregard of the laws of evidence should be visited on the legal advisers and not on the trusting clients.[10]

---

[9] In *Mia's Trustee v Mia* 1944 WLD 102 at 105–6. See also *Galp v Tansley NO and Another* 1966 (4) SA 555 (C) and *Padongelukkefonds v Van Den Berg en'n ander* 1999 (2) SA 876 (O) 881F–882I.

[10] See for example *Simoes v Hasewinkel* 1966 (1) SA 579 (W) 583–4, which deals with the overburdening of the record with documents.

Apart from the limited indulgence granted in urgent applications, practice sometimes allows the exposition of hearsay evidence for a further limited purpose. Where a person has given a party information which was material to the latter's case, but has declined to make an affidavit, it is competent to set out the details of the information for the purpose of applying to the court for a subpoena against the reluctant informant.[11] Rule 6(5)(g) gives the court power to direct:

> that oral evidence be heard on specified issues with a view to resolving any dispute of fact and to that end may order . . . any other person to be subpoenaed to appear and be examined and cross-examined as a witness.

However, bear in mind the remarks of Price J:

> It would be deplorable if a litigant were allowed to come to court on vague rumours and hearsay statements and then claim the right to have *viva voce* evidence heard about these rumours so that he could subject witnesses on the other side to cross-examination on the off chance that he might be able to show that the vague rumours and hearsay statements were true.[12]

All this may be summarised by saying that every statement of fact in an application must be proved by a witness exactly as though it were a fact to be proved in a trial action, with the limited exception allowed in cases of urgency.

17.3.4 The case must be made out in the founding affidavits

It follows from the preceding discussion that skeletons, mortal or otherwise, should be kept in their appropriate closets and not be brought under the scrutiny of a jaundiced opponent and a cynical court. So it has sometimes been stated that it is not competent to present the skeleton of a case in the application, filling in by means of the replying affidavit those portions which the respondent places in issue by denial or contradictory evidence.[13] Your founding affidavit is the only chance which you will have to place your case before the court, unless you wish to take the risk of the court's being as indulgent as in *Registrar of Insurance v Johannesburg Insurance Co Ltd (1)*[14] where Hiemstra J said:

---

[11] Eg *Ecker v Dean* 1937 SWA 1, *Oertel NO v Pieterse* 1954 (3) SA 364 (O), *Khumalo v Director-General of Co-Operation and Development and Others* 1991 (1) SA 158 (A) 167E–J and *Campbell v Kwapa* 2002 (6) SA 379 (W) 382B–D.

[12] *Garment Workers Union v De Vries and Others* 1949 (1) SA 1110 (W) 1132–3.

[13] Cf *Kleynhans v Van der Westhuizen NO* 1970 (1) SA 565 (O) 568E–569D. See also, with regard to the principle that a case must be made out in the founding affidavits, *Titty's Bar and Bottle Store (Pty) Ltd v ABC Garage (Pty) Ltd and others* 1974 (4) SA 362 (T) 368B–369A, *Shephard v Tuckers Land & Development Corporation (Pty) Ltd (1)* 1978 (1) SA 173 (W) 177G–178A, *Director of Hospital Services v Mistry* 1979 (1) SA 626 (A) 636A–636F, *Skjelbreds Rederi A/S and Others v Hartless (Pty) Ltd* 1982 (2) SA 739 (W) 742D, *Port Nolloth Municipality v Xhalisa and Others* 1991 (3) SA 98 (C) 111E, *Nick's Fishmonger Holdings (Pty) Ltd and Another v Fish Diner in Bryanston CC and Others* 2009 (5) SA 629 (W) 646I and Herbstein & Van Winsen *The Civil Practice of the High Courts of South Africa* 5th ed (Vol 1) 440–441.

[14] 1962 (4) SA 546 (W) 547.

> I am not prepared to allow the rules of procedure to tyrannise the court where an important matter has to be thrashed out fully and all the facts have to be put before the court. In this particular case, because the case is complex and it cannot be fairly expected from the petitioner to have all the facts at his disposal before he launches his petition, which was in fact launched in the public interest, I will overlook the fact that an important part of the petitioner's case was put in after his original petition.

You would probably be wise to regard this as a special case and to approach every application on the basis that, if you fail to make out a case in your founding affidavits, you will suffer the equivalent of absolution from the instance. A replying affidavit should be no more than its title; it should not try to be a supplementary affidavit. To put it in another way, you must stand or fall by your notice of motion and founding affidavits.

17.3.5 Confirmatory affidavits

From the judge's point of view it is useful if you set out the whole of your case in the main founding affidavit, making reference to the supporting affidavits wherever necessary. In his way the court can obtain a picture of the whole case by reading through the main founding affidavit. I have judicial assurance that '[i]t is most exasperating if the nature of the case can only be ascertained by having to read and piece together various affidavits or documents.' If a particular allegation would be hearsay as far as the applicant himself is concerned, it could be dealt with as follows:

> On 24 February 2008 the respondent withdrew the sum of R1 579 from the banking account of the partnership, as appears from annexure 'G' hereto, being the confirmatory affidavit of the former bookkeeper to the partnership Mr. Ignatius Flavius Brown.

That said, where the fact or facts in question are particularly important, you would be well advised to support them with more than a bland confirmatory affidavit. Deal with them in detail in the main founding affidavit, confirm in that affidavit that the facts are themselves affirmed in the confirmatory affidavit, and then have the deponent to the confirmatory affidavit not just confirm, but go into some detail in the course of that confirmation.

17.3.6 Rule 6

No doubt you will study carefully the various sub-rules comprising rule 6, in order to master the practical aspects of application proceedings. These are dealt with in the books on practice and procedure and I do not propose to embark upon any detailed analysis of their provisions.[15] However, there are certain sub-rules and aspects relating to rule 6 that must be highlighted:

•   Rule 6 provides specific time periods for the filing of an answering and a replying affidavit. If you are out of time, you should file an application for condonation which complies with the requirements for condonation.

---

[15] See inter alia *Herbstein & Van Winsen The Civil Practice of the High Courts of South Africa* 5th ed, Erasmus *Superior Court Practice*, and Harms *Civil Procedure in the Supreme Court.*

- In terms of sub-rule (7) a respondent is entitled to launch a counter-application, and to join any party to the same extent as if he were a defendant in an action.
- Sub-rule (8) provides that any person against whom an order has been granted *ex parte* may anticipate the return day upon delivery of 24 hours' notice.
- Sub-rule (11) provides that interlocutory and other incidental applications may be brought on notice. 'Notice' does not mean notice of motion.[16]
- Sub-rule (12)*(c)* provides that where an order has been granted in a party's absence in an urgent application, that party may by notice set the application down for reconsideration of the order.[17]
- In terms of sub-rule (13) special time periods apply to the State as a respondent, unless a court has authorised a shorter period.
- Sub-rule (14) provides that the provisions relating to joinder, consolidation, intervention of parties, third party procedure and tenders shall also apply to applications.
- One last point that you should bear in mind: in appropriate cases, rule 35(12) (which deals with the production of documents for inspection and copying) applies to motion proceedings, while rule 35(13) may entitle you to invoke the provisions of rule 35 relating to discovery.

17.3.7 Temperate language

Do not let your emotions rule your choice of language. Points can and should be made firmly, but without using intemperate language. See the judgments of Botha JA in *Administrator, Transvaal and Others v Theletsane and Others*[18] and *Noel Lancaster Sands v Eksteen en andere*,[19] where the judge remarked upon the unnecessarily harsh language used by the respondents in countering the allegations contained in the founding affidavits.

17.4 URGENT APPLICATIONS

17.4.1 Generally

The potential applications of urgent motion proceedings are almost limitless. These, mainly, are designed to preserve a *status quo*, but include matters such as rule 43 applications, and sequestration and liquidation proceedings. They may relate to the removal or threatened removal of children, to the impending and precipitate departure of a debtor, or to the preservation of funds to which the applicant has a claim. As variegated as may be human beings and their

---

[16] This means that the short form is to be used as contemplated in Form 2 of the Uniform Rules of Court. See *SA Metropolitan Lewensversekeringsmaatskappy Bpk v Louw NO* 1981 (4) SA 329 (O) 332H and *Nasionale Aartappel Koöperasie Bpk v Price Waterhouse Coopers Ing en andere* 2001 (2) SA 790 (T).
[17] *ISDN Solutions (Pty) Ltd v CSDN Solutions CC* 1996 (4) SA 484 (W) 486H–I.
[18] 1991 (2) SA 192 (A).
[19] 1974 (3) SA 688 (T) 693.

relationships one to another, so diversified may be the subject matter of urgent applications.

Sometimes they are necessary. Where there is any prospect of avoiding them, they should be treated as potential Pandora's boxes. Once they are opened, who knows what ills may fly out? Litigation at leisure is a perilous enough procedure without adding the hazards of haste. Let us consider some of the hazards of urgent applications.

17.4.2   Your client may not tell you the whole story

You may find that your client doesn't tell you the whole story. 'Why then,' you may exclaim, 'he has only himself to blame if he conceals things from his attorney! After all, an attorney is like a doctor, and should be told everything.' But soft, you are observed. The patient does not and cannot tell the doctor everything; the medical gentleman gets half the story from his instruments. The patient tells only his complaints. So, too, with the attorney; the client tells only his complaints. If the attorney bases his diagnosis (an urgent application) only upon the complaints, then he runs the risk of grievous error.

In a previous chapter I discussed the technique of pre-trial consultations. If my suggestions in paragraph 17.3 of the present chapter are valid, then the same procedure should be applied in regard to the consultation preceding an urgent application. To that extent, therefore, there need be no repetition of my suggestions. The simple objective should be to get the whole story, for and against, so that nothing is overlooked when the papers are drafted, so that you may know where to anticipate an attack, and so that you may know where to seek support. Experience shows that it is almost inevitable, if the drafting occurs at or immediately consequent upon the first consultation, that something will be overlooked. You may miss no more than the odd little fact that prods the subconscious sense of misgiving, but with not sufficient insistence to goad that sense into activity. Strange creatures these little facts, akin to the elf in their coyness, like the imp in their capacity to tantalise, and the very devil to deal with when they are fed by the respondent and his lawyers. All that I can say is that you must sensitise yourself into receptivity of these messengers through the subconscious, and when you detect them you must stop. Stop abruptly. Get the thing out into the open and examine it. From there onwards you are on your own.

17.4.3   The consequence of non-disclosure

If the affidavits omit to disclose something which might affect the court's decision, the court may, on the return day of any rule nisi or at the appropriate stage in the proceedings, discharge the rule or set aside the order which it granted as a matter of urgency.[20] It is said that in *ex parte* applications the utmost good faith must be shown. However, it would be safer to put the proposition

---

[20] See *Schlesinger v Schlesinger* 1979 (4) SA 342 (W) 348E–350C and *MV Rizcun Trader (4); MV Rizcun Trader v Manley Appeldore Shipping Ltd* 2000 (3) SA 776 (C).

on the basis that 'in *ex parte* applications it is the duty of the applicant to lay all relevant facts before the court, so that it may have full knowledge of all the circumstances of the case before making its order'.[21]

It is a wise precaution, in consulting with the client on the drafting of his affidavit, to conclude by asking: 'Is there any document or fact which might be relevant to either party's case and about which you have not yet told me?' You can make it a little less stilted, if necessary, or you could make it even more formal.

I suggest you will err on the side of safety, if error it be, by making it a practice to explain to your client that he is expected to disclose facts which operate against him and by telling him of the possible consequences of non-disclosure. If he then discloses a fact which is destructive of his case, the application is one which should never be brought in any event. If the fact is not in that category, then it is capable of exposition and explanation, and nothing will be lost by dealing with it at the earliest possible stage. In the rare case where your client is abusing the process of the court and bringing his application for an ulterior purpose, the consequences of non-disclosure will be on his head and not yours.

Documents, for the purposes of this topic, must be regarded as facts. Even, I would suggest, a self-serving letter written by the respondent should be attached to the application, so that the court may be able to judge what the issues will be and whether it is proper to grant your client the relief which he seeks at that stage. While I have known of many cases where interim orders have been discharged for non-disclosure of material facts subsequently placed on record by the respondent, I do not know of a case where the disclosure of such material containing adverse facts has led to the refusal of an order. Careful explanation by the applicant of adverse facts lends strength to his own evidence. After all, the burden of disproof rests more heavily than the burden of proof, and to acquit oneself of the former is so much the more impressive.

17.4.4 Is the matter urgent?

On the assumption that you have been able to put the whole story on paper, together with whatever documents may be involved, you turn to consider the next problem. Is the matter urgent? This question is often the rock on which the hastily launched application comes to grief.

If the application is, in your opinion, one that cannot wait, then that opinion must be brought home to the court, not as an opinion but as a matter of fact. Rule 6(12)*(a)* affords relief from the time limits, forms and stipulations as to service laid down by the rules in cases of urgency. In the enthusiasm sometimes engendered by that sub-rule you should not lose sight of rule 6(12)*(b)* which provides that an 'applicant is to set forth explicitly the circumstances which he avers render the matter urgent and the reasons why he claims that he could not

---

[21] Per Solomon JA in *Estate Logie v Priest* 1926 AD 312 at 323.

be afforded substantial redress at a hearing in due course'. This signifies that there must be a prayer for urgency in the notice of motion, and the question of urgency must be specifically dealt with in the founding affidavit.[22]

Rule 6(5)*(a)*, which has been held to be peremptory, requires that every notice of motion be as near as may be in accordance with Form 2(a) and requires the applicant to nominate the dates by which the respondent is to deliver a notice of intention to oppose and answering affidavit.[23] A respondent must then comply with the rules laid down by the applicant, and may object when the matter is called in court.

The sub-rule does not call for a certificate of urgency by counsel but, of course, the practice of any particular division of the High Court may require such certificate before the court is to be troubled with the matter.[24] Should this be so then counsel will have to discharge his duty to the court as well as to the client. He should consider the matter again carefully, as objectively as possible and with regard to the remarks of judges in the past concerning such certificates.

In brief, what your founding affidavit must establish is that the applicant will suffer some form of prejudice or harm, and probably irreparably at that, if relief is not afforded him *instanter*.[25] The grounds of such prejudice are infinitely variable as, for example, the removal of children outside the Republic of South Africa, the impending departure of a debtor together with his spouse, their passports and your client's money, a threatened sale of a motor vehicle held on credit purchase, or a pending sale in execution to the prejudice of creditors who have not yet taken judgment. Sometimes urgent orders are sought and granted restraining a husband from harassing his estranged wife. Be careful, however, not to confuse the element of harm with that of urgency. It is such confusion that leads the court to ask: 'Ms Brown, is this matter urgent?'

Well, let me give a simple and true example to show why the matter is urgent and why the judges might well be a little more forbearing in their challenges of urgency, even at 4 o'clock on a Friday afternoon.

This incident took place in the middle of the 1940s, when the Johannesburg morning newspaper of a Tuesday would publish the day's motion roll.

Counsel was consulted a day or so before motion day by an attorney whose client was experiencing matrimonial problems, not the least of which was a

---

[22] See, for an excellent exposition of the approach to be adopted to urgent applications with reference to time limits etc, the 'Memorandum to Practitioners Re: Procedure in the Pretoria Urgent Motion Court' dated 12 February 2007 of Judge Southwood, reprinted at D5–33 to D5–37 of Erasmus *Superior Court Practice*. Although the memorandum contains detail which is particular to the Pretoria urgent court, it outlines principles which would apply in any urgent court, and is well worthwhile studying, whatever division you practise in.

[23] *Gallagher v Norman's Transport Lines Ltd* 1992 (3) SA 500 (W) 502E–G.

[24] See para 10.1 of the Practice Manual: KwaZulu-Natal and the Eastern Cape: Rules of Practice para 12*(a)*(i) for examples of where a certificate of urgency is required.

[25] See *I L & B Marcow Caterers (Pty) Ltd v Greatermans SA Ltd and Another* 1981(4) SA 108 (C), where Fagan J deals with what constitutes urgency at 112H–113H.

marriage in community of property. Another problem was £2 000 in a building society account. The third problem, of course, was the husband — and which of us isn't? Well, it seems that the attorney was about to issue summons for a judicial separation, alternatively a restitution of conjugal rights (failing compliance wherewith a decree of divorce), this being the standard technique in dealing with problem husbands in those days. What the attorney wanted was an urgent interdict restraining the husband from drawing and the building society from paying the £2 000 that I have mentioned.

'Why', asked counsel, emulating his betters although he will never grace the Bench, 'is the matter urgent?'

Said the attorney: 'Because when he gets our summons he will draw the money and my client will never see it again.'

'Yes,' said counsel, 'what evidence do you have that he will do this?' 'My client says so.'

'Indeed,' said counsel, still at his judicial best, 'on what does she base that statement?'

The attorney could not supply the necessary information and counsel advised against an urgent application, stating that these were no grounds of urgency. He did relent, however, to the extent that he was willing to countenance an application without notice if it were set down for hearing in the motion court in the ordinary course. And so it was done.

Now it happened on the Tuesday that the problem husband sat in the train on the way to Pretoria, he being a clerk in the accounts section of the Defence Force which was then in the last stages of the termination of hostilities. And he read his morning newspaper. So tedious was the journey that he even read the motion roll. And lo, there, written as large as life, was his own name. At the next station he disembarked and soon he was on his way back to the metropolis of crime — Johannesburg. Whether he urged the engine-driver towards greater speed I do not know, but before the court could grant an interdict a certain building society account no longer had £2 000 in it.

How could counsel have convinced the court that the matter was urgent by saying: 'My client *knows* that her husband will withdraw all the money as soon as he knows that she is commencing proceedings against him?' Perhaps it is well to let the learned judge make the decision, notwithstanding the multitude of judicial utterances about the absence of urgency. I must confess that in a great many cases I am at a loss to understand the tender solicitude for absent respondents. If the matter proves not to have been urgent at all there are so many sanctions available that respondents can be protected and reckless applicants adequately punished. It seems to me that if a party or his legal advisers really believe a matter to be urgent the court, unless an abuse of its process is apparent, should allow them to take the risk. The question 'Why is this matter urgent?' would remain unlamented if it disappeared from the judicial anthology.

17.4.5   Notice to respondent

Urgency apart, I would suggest that in every case the respondent should be given such notice of the hearing of the application as may be practicable. Of course, there are many cases where the giving of such notice will defeat the very object of the proceedings. In such cases, it is imperative that you show in your founding affidavit why notice is not being given.

17.4.6   Administrative arrangements

The technical side of urgent applications is something that bears most heavily on the attorney. Usually the affidavits and notice of motion have to be typed at the weirdest hours of the day or night. The matter becomes ready for presentation when the registrar of the court has gone into hibernation. Fortunately enough, most judges are tolerant and resigned to their fate, with the result that even on Saturday nights a matter may be heard if urgent. Then arises the problem of service, for the sheriff acquires an elusiveness that would be envied by many of those on whom he usually effects service.

What I am trying to say is that the attorney must plan his campaign and make his administrative arrangements before they are to be put into effect. Nothing is more frustrating than to be granted an urgent order and to have no means of serving it upon the respondent. Yet, under the pressure of consulting, drafting, typing, copying and briefing counsel, I have known cases where attorneys have not given a single thought to the problem of how to bring their work to the stage of practical effectiveness, by service by the sheriff upon the person of the respondent.

17.4.7   Draft order

It should not be overlooked that the order in an urgent application may differ in form from that which would be granted consequent upon a hearing in due course. It would seem logical to modify your notice motion to suit the realities of the situation or, at the very least, to have available a draft of the order which the court will be asked to grant as a matter of urgency. Although there does not appear to be any need specifically to give the respondent leave to anticipate a return day (because rule 6(8) provides for this) many judges insist that a prayer be inserted in the draft order in these terms, so as to apprise the respondent of his rights.

17.5   DRAFTING THE ANSWERING AFFIDAVIT

17.5.1   Generally

Once again the technique is to combine pleading, advice on evidence and the leading of evidence in a single document. There are problems, of course, but they are easy to recognise, simple to state and capable of control.

17.5.2   The first inquiry

The first inquiry is whether the applicant has made out a case for the relief which he seeks. It may be very little more than a passing inquiry at this stage, for you are not required of necessity to elect whether to oppose the application on this basis only or whether to file affidavits. There may be cases so clear that the court will say that you ought not to have incurred the costs of further affidavits, but these will be rare indeed, so rare in fact that in 30 years or more of practice you may not encounter even one of them. Usually you answer the evidence and leave the sufficiency of the applicant's case for determination at the hearing.[26]

Nevertheless, if the case is dependent purely on a question of law, you need not file any affidavits and may rely upon a notice in terms of rule 6(5)(d)(iii), setting out the question of law on which you intend to reply.

17.5.3 The second inquiry

The next inquiry is whether the application contains inadmissible evidence or any matter which is 'scandalous, vexatious or irrelevant'.[27] Allegations or statements falling into any one of these categories may be struck out, but a complication arises. If the plaintiff attempted to lead inadmissible evidence in the course of a trial action, you would object. The court would hear argument and rule on the admissibility of the evidence. The defendant would then know to what extent it would be necessary to deal with the evidence in the course of his case. In application proceedings the evidence is on record until struck out, although the necessity of answering it cannot be determined until the respondent has closed his case (in effect) and the stage of argument has been reached. If the application to strike out should fail, and the allegations remain unanswered, then no further opportunity may be afforded to file whatever affidavits may be required. A good deal will be said in argument, should you try to remedy such an omission, about cherries and the number of bites permitted to a respondent whose legal advisers err in their view of the law of evidence. You will be, or may be, a little distressed at the latitude which seems to be allowed to applicants in their affidavits despite what I said previously in regard to hearsay and other inadmissible evidence.

The solution is not too difficult to find. If you can answer the allegation apart from the question of admissibility, then you should so do. Nevertheless, together with your answering affidavit, you should consider filing a notice of application to strike out the passages to which you object.[28]

Guidance on the proper procedure can be found in *Elher (Pty) Ltd v Silver*,[29] where Price J held that an application to strike out must be made at the time

---

[26] *Bader and Another v Weston and Another* 1967 (1) SA 134 (C).

[27] Rule 6(15). The rule is not exhaustive as to the grounds on which a court will strike out allegations.

[28] Rule 6(11) renders it unnecessary to comply with the formalities of rules 6(1) to 6(5).

[29] 1947 (4) SA 173 (W) 176–178, referred to in *Molebatsi v Magasela* 1953 (4) SA 484 (W), *Meinert (Pty) Ltd v Administrator of South West Africa in Executive Committee* 1959 (2) SA 498 (SWA), *Bezuidenhout v Reitz Waardasiehof en 'n ander* 1964 (1) SA 838 (O), *Madzimbamuto v Lardner-Burke NO and Another* 1966 (2) SA 445 (RS) and *Wiese v Joubert en andere* 1983 (4) SA 182 (O).

when the matter is before the court on the merits. In the course of his judgment the learned judge said:

> A great waste of time, energy and expense is involved in the procedure which Mr M has followed. First of all, there must be a full-dress argument or, at any rate, very considerable argument on the merits in order to enable the court to decide whether the passages objected to are or are not relevant. Then a decision as regards the relevancy of various passages must be given. Then more evidence is to be filed by the petitioner, and finally the merits must be argued again before the court which hears the application. I do not agree that Mr M's client is entitled, at this stage, to a decision on this issue. It is evident that what the petitioner is really seeking is legal advice from the court. The court asked Mr M why he himself could not advise his client to ignore those allegations which he considered were irrelevant or based on hearsay evidence, and he indicated that if his advice turned out to be erroneous his client would be at a disadvantage. The petitioner wishes to be told by this court that he need not deal with certain facts alleged, but this court is not trying the merits of the dispute and those facts may turn out to be important when all the evidence is before the court and full argument has been heard, or may be so regarded by the court that does ultimately hear the application. There is authority for this view. In the case of *Gilbert v Comic Opera Company* (16 ChD 594) the identical question arose and Bacon VC said:
>
>> '. . . Until the hearing I cannot tell whether the affidavits objected to are really in reply or not. I have nothing to guide me at this stage of the proceedings. If they are not strictly in reply the court will not regard them at the hearing, but that is a question which cannot now be decided.'
>
> Furthermore, at this stage of the proceedings the contents of those affidavits are not tendered as evidence. The evidence is merely being collected in the form of affidavits to be tendered later on to the court that hears the application. It follows from such cases as that of *Kingswell v Argus Co Ltd* and *Kingswell v Robinson* 1913 WLD 129 that the contents of such documents as affidavits are not before the court as evidence until the actual hearing of the case.
>
>> 'The affidavits objected to are not now before me as evidence in the application; they are merely documents filed with the registrar to be used later as evidence, when the application is heard.'
>
> Two illustrations will show some of the inconvenience involved in the procedure now attempted to be followed: Mr M contends — *inter alia* — that certain evidence of alleged duress does not amount to duress and he asks the court to decide that as there is no proper evidence of duress all the evidence directed to the proof of duress should be struck out. The court which is to decide this is not hearing the application, but merely a preliminary objection to evidence, nevertheless it is asked to decide some of the issues raised in the main application. Mr M also contends that a certain contract which is in issue between the parties is a contract in writing and that certain evidence tendered in relation to that contract is inadmissible and should be struck out because it seeks to vary the terms of the contract. Mr I's reply is that the contract is ambiguous, that it is partly in writing and partly oral, and that in any case the evidence objected to does not contradict the writing but explains it. These are all issues that will have to be decided by the court that hears the application, but Mr M claims the right to have them decided in advance by the expedient of applying to strike out certain evidence. Such a practice would produce grave difficulties and I am unable to sanction it by ordering the deletion of any of the passages objected to whether on the ground that they are irrelevant or that they are hearsay evidence.

The way in which the objection was taken to the various passages in the affidavits calls for comment, namely:

*   Neither the court nor, as far as I know, the respondent was notified of the intention to make such an application. When such an application is intended to be made the passages objected to should be precisely indicated in a proper notice in terms of rule 6(15). The notice should identify specifically the passages to which objection is taken, and should specify the grounds on which those passages are attacked. The court should not be expected to take a written note of each passage as it is read out, nor should it be necessary for the court to mark the record.

*   The striking-out application must itself be based upon timeous written notice, as was stated in *Abromowitz v Jacquet and Another*,[30] failing which the court may disregard your protests. Roper J was prepared to recognise that:

> There may be cases where it is impracticable to give such notice, for instance where affidavits are filed at the last moment and it would be impossible to give notice without delaying the proceedings and so causing prejudice to one or other of the parties. In such a case the court would obviously not insist on notice of the nature described. . . .

Applications for the striking out of matter which is 'scandalous, vexatious or irrelevant' should be made only if your client will be prejudiced thereby. In this regard, and in regard to technical objections to the admissibility of evidence in your opponent's affidavits, you might well remember the words of Margo AJ in *Jones v John Barr & Co (Pty) Ltd*[31] where he stated:

> In a proceeding before a judge alone an occasional item of inadmissible evidence ordinarily creates no prejudice, for the court simply ignores it or gives it no weight. There may be cases where prejudice does result from such evidence, but this is not one of them.

17.5.4   Drafting the answering affidavit itself

Having decided the preliminary technicalities, you then proceed with the affidavit itself.

Bearing in mind that your purpose is to persuade, it is best to commence the answering affidavit (after dealing with the customary formalities as to who the deponent is and so forth) with an outline of the defence, in sufficient detail to apprise a court thereof. Thereafter you will deal with the allegations contained in the founding affidavit paragraph by paragraph.

---

[30] 1950 (2) SA 247 (W) 252 and *Karpakis v Mutual & Federal Insurance Co Ltd* 1991 (3) SA 489 (O).
[31] 1967 (3) SA 292 (W) 296. See also *Western Bank Ltd v Thorne NNO and Others NNO* 1973 (3) SA 661 (C).

In the majority of cases your task should be no more complicated than asking the respondent to comment on each allegation of fact in the application. His denial or explanation then becomes his evidence. Avoid moulding his affidavit into that archaically stilted and turgid language which is so often revelled in by those who have anything to do with the drafting or settling of affidavits.

Be that as it may, the point to bear in mind is that the affidavit is your client's evidence supported, if necessary, by the affidavits (evidence) of other witnesses and by documents properly identified in somebody's affidavit.

17.6 DRAFTING THE REPLYING AFFIDAVIT

17.6.1 Generally

An applicant is permitted to reply to the respondent's answering affidavit.[32] Replying affidavits are liable to be objectionable in two principal respects. In the first place, the applicant should not seek to supplement his original affidavits and to remedy omissions, nor may he introduce new evidence in support of his case. In the second place, many practitioners mistakenly think that the weight of an allegation is enhanced by its repetition in a later affidavit. Thus they seek unnecessarily to reply to the respondent by putting in issue what is already in issue, or by placing on record what is really argument based on facts already on record. Perhaps they wish to ensure that counsel (on the other side) gets the point. What is to be gained by letting the respondent know in advance what you think are the weaknesses in his case?

17.6.2 The purpose of the replying affidavit

The purpose of replying is 'to reply to averments made by the respondent in his answering affidavits' and by doing so refute the evidence deposed to by the applicant.[33] Subject to this general principle, the textbooks and judgments help mainly in approaching the matter negatively—what not to do. The negative propositions I have already mentioned in the first paragraph of this section. The applicant, naturally, must answer those statements of fact which he denies, or he may place on record further facts which would show that the respondent's allegations are false, are incomplete or do not give a true reflection of the actual position. In doing this the applicant may himself create a state of affairs where the matter cannot be determined on paper but must go to trial. Therefore you will endeavour to find a means of dealing with the respondent's case without this unfortunate result, with its possibility that your client may be ordered to pay all the wasted costs. Let me then essay a formulation of some precepts in the hope that they may be of assistance to you.

*   *Usually*, the respondent's bare denials require no reply.

---

[32] You are again advised to study the rule applicable to your particular application. For example Rule 43 does not permit a replying affidavit.

[33] *Bayat and Others v Hansa and Others* 1955 (3) SA 547 (N), per Caney J at 553. See also Herbstein & Van Winsen *The Civil Practice of the High Courts of South Africa* vol 1 5 ed 429.

- In preparing your client's replying affidavit, you should not work from the respondent's affidavit alone. It may double the labour, but in considering every single statement made by the respondent you should refer as well to your client's own statement in his founding affidavit. Neglect of this elementary rule may cause your client to place on record two inconsistent statements on the same point. This, to say the least, is hardly calculated to advance his case and may well lead to a precipitate and uneconomical settlement. In fact, you should never draft *any* affidavit without being aware of every preceding affidavit and *every* relevant letter or document.

- If you attempt to supplement an inadequate founding affidavit, you may find that the additional material is struck out because it should have been in the initial founding affidavit.[34] The other possibility is that the respondent will seek and perhaps obtain leave to file a fourth set of affidavits. This topic will be discussed in the next paragraph, but before we get there it might be useful to distinguish between new evidence and a new deponent, as was done by Erasmus J in *Brenda Hairstylers (Pty) Ltd v Marshall*[35] where the learned judge said:

> I shall deal with this application first. Miss Kalil's affidavit was annexed to the replying affidavit in order to reiterate a point made by the applicants in this application which has been denied by the respondent in her opposing affidavit. It is to the effect that a large percentage of lady customers usually follow a hairdresser when she accepts employment in another salon. Whatever may be said by the applicants about such an affidavit in similar circumstances, two facts remain undisputed. Firstly it is a new deponent tendering evidence (cf *Elher (Pty) Ltd v Silver* 1947 (4) SA 173 (W) at 176) and secondly, the evidence tendered is merely a repetition of the evidence already before the court. As to the first point, it is conceivable that the respondent may, if she prefers, object to such evidence by a new deponent for reasons of impartiality, fraud and the like, but such a course, if permissible, is wholly unnecessary for the evidence itself is not new and the case must be distinguished from those instances where new or fresh evidence is tendered in a replying affidavit. As the familiar evidence thus tendered already stands denied by the opposing affidavit and a court cannot on motion proceedings in such a case decide where the truth lies, it follows in my view that a further affidavit by another deponent to the same effect serves no purpose, but merely runs up costs. I accordingly ordered that Miss Kalil's affidavit be struck out with costs.

17.7 FURTHER AFFIDAVITS

The number of sets of affidavits allowed in application proceedings is normally three, but the court has a discretion whether to allow further sets of affidavits.[36]

If you want to know what constitutes a 'set of affidavits' you might refer to a

---

[34] See paragraph 17.3.4 above.

[35] 1968 (2) SA 277 (O) 278–9.

[36] Rule 6(5)(e). It has been said that a court has a discretion to allow further affidavits and will allow a further set of affidavits only in 'exceptional circumstances' or where a court considers such a course advisable. See Erasmus *Superior Court Practice* B1–47.

judgment of Williamson J[37] where it was held to be permissible to file additional affidavits setting out facts discovered after the original affidavits had been filed but before the opponent had replied to them. Such additional affidavits, in proper cases, would be regarded as part of the original set.

If you represent the party desiring to file a fourth—or fifth—set of affidavits, there is one point you should bear in mind in the drafting of those affidavits. Since you rely on the discretion of the court in obtaining leave to file your affidavits you must be prepared with material on which to persuade the court to act in your favour. Often this will appear from the last set of affidavits filed by your opponent; if not it will have to be placed before the court on affidavit. I suggest that it would be excessively technical to file one affidavit explaining why you want to file additional affidavits and then to tender those affidavits separately. Particularly since the court would be entitled to look at the substantive affidavit in determining whether to grant leave, it would seem more practical to combine the two; that is to say, the additional set of affidavits themselves should set out the facts on which leave is sought. Nor are you entitled, strictly speaking, to file the additional affidavit before obtaining leave of the court. I mention this because I have encountered cases where an attorney has simply filed the additional affidavit and appeared affronted when told that he has erred. Judges are very tolerant, but one day you will meet a martinet.

If you act for the party against whom the new affidavits are tendered you may be in a tactical dilemma. Naturally the affidavits will be designed to counter or destroy some matter of substance in your own affidavits. To that extent your instinct is to object to their admission. But usually they arise because some feature of the presentation of your own case has deprived your opponent of the chance of placing his case on record earlier. This dilemma is one which may confront junior counsel in the earlier years of his practice when his lack of experience may lead him to make the wrong decision.

If you would see how this works in practice you might refer to the case of *Mundy v Mundy.*[38] In that case a wife came into possession of a notice issued to her husband by a gold-mining company informing him, as was the practice in those days, that it had received a transfer deed purporting to be signed by him and reflecting the sale by him of shares in the company. The parties were already engaged in matrimonial proceedings and the husband, through his attorneys, had given an undertaking not to dispose of the assets of the joint estate. When she received this notice the wife inferred that the husband was acting in breach of his undertaking. She applied urgently for an interdict restraining her husband from disposing of any further assets in the joint estate pending the determination of the action between the parties. She was granted a rule *nisi* operating as an interim interdict.

In due course the husband filed an answering affidavit, to which he attached a broker's note showing that the shares had in fact been sold before his attorneys

---

[37] *Transvaal Racing Club v Jockey Club of South Africa* 1958 (3) SA 599 (W).
[38] 1946 WLD 280.

gave the undertaking. This evidence, of course, effectively destroyed the inference that the husband was disposing of assets in breach of his undertaking.

The wife in her replying affidavit set out evidence to show:

- that her husband was possessed of shares and assets other that those admitted in his answering affidavit;
- that her husband was untruthful and in the habit of making untruthful statements;
- that he had made threats to conceal from her the assets in the joint estate and had tried to apply pressure on her to withdraw her action by saying that unless she did so he would not give her any information about these assets.

The husband, in turn, sought leave to file a fourth set of affidavits to deal with the new allegations made by the wife in her replying affidavit. The affidavit which he wished to file consisted mainly — if not entirely — of denials of the wife's statements. In tendering this affidavit, his counsel said that if the wife did not consent to its admission he would apply to strike out the new matter referred to.

At this stage counsel for the wife had to weigh up the fourth set of affidavits against the striking-out and against the strength of his original case. In the result he decided not to agree to the filing of the affidavits, fearing that the husband's denials would destroy the effectiveness of the 'new material', and thinking that there was a reasonable prospect of successfully opposing the striking-out application or, at least, of succeeding on a legal aspect arising from the application.

The decision, unfortunately, was wrong. Had the fourth set of affidavits been allowed in, it seems most probable that the court would have held that the dispute of fact could not be decided on paper, but that the balance of convenience favoured the granting of an interdict *pendente lite*.[39] Also he was wrong in his assessment of the law. The 'new matter' was struck out and the rule nisi discharged.

If I can offer any useful suggestion based on this case, I would say that in the majority of cases it might be more prudent to let your opponent place on record whatever can fairly be said to be an answer to something your own client has raised, and then to look for a 'quintessence'[40] which will enable the court to decide the matter in your favour notwithstanding, or perhaps because of, the conflict of fact involved.

---

[39] In *Gool v Minister of Justice and Another* 1955 (2) SA 682 (C) at 688C–E, the test for an interim interdict was considered as follows: the applicant's right need not be shown on a balance of probabilities; and it is sufficient if such a right is *prima facie* established, though open to some doubt. The court's approach is to take the facts set out by the applicant together with the facts set out by the respondent which the applicant cannot dispute and to consider, having regard to the inherent probabilities whether the applicant should on those facts obtain final relief at the trial. The facts set up in contradiction by the respondent should then be considered, and if serious doubt is thrown upon the case of the applicant he should not succeed. See also *LAWSA* vol 11 2 ed p 420 para 404.

[40] See chapter 4.

In any event, on whatever side of the fence you may be, study a few of the reported cases in order to ascertain the principles on which the court will exercise its discretion[41] and give long and earnest thought to the tactical considerations involved.

17.8 PREPARATION

Preparing for an opposed application differs radically from preparing for trial or from preparing your argument in a trial action. Even if you, as counsel, have been responsible for settling your client's affidavits you will experience a feeling of oppression when you are handed a brief containing some two or three hundred pages of affidavits and annexures with the information that the matter has been set down for hearing on such and such a date. There is obviously more ways of preparing for an opposed application than that proposed in this paragraph. In time you will develop your own method.

Well, you must find out what it is all about. Not only that, but when the judge says to you 'Mr Brown, what does the respondent say about such-and-such a point?' you must be able to tell him. Without sounding pedantic, it is assumed that you have been briefed with an application that has been indexed and paginated. If not, then you will firstly have to arrange that the papers are indexed and paginated. Secondly, you must equip yourself with some coloured pencils and coloured Post-it flags. It may be useful if you commence your preparation by reading the notice of motion and founding affidavit as an entity. As you read though the founding affidavit and you encounter a reference to an annexure, write down the page reference of the annexure in the founding affidavit in one of your chosen coloured pencils and then flag the annexure with its name so that you can find the annexure easily in court. Of course, in reading the applicant's founding affidavit you will, in the appropriate places, refer to and study whatever annexures are quoted in support of the applicant's case and at the same time you will make a note on a notepad developing a skeleton of the applicant's case. Once you have finished reading the founding affidavit you should have a succinct note in your best manuscript of the applicant's case. Now you know what the applicant's case is about. If you want to continue reading then by all means do so. If it makes you dizzy and totally confused then you are normal.

The next step is to appreciate not only the case but the issues. I suggest that you find it convenient to take your brief to pieces and to divide it into the three main affidavits, namely: founding, answering and replying affidavits. You will then flag each affidavit so that when you are in court on your feet you can find the affidavit easily. You will then take your coloured pencils and choose one which you will use to represent your own client, one to represent the opponent

---

[41] Particularly *James Brown & Hamer (Pty) Ltd v Simmons NO* 1963 (4) SA 656 (A) 660 citing *Zarug v Parvathie NO* 1962 (3) SA 872 (D). Also *Highfield Milling Co (Pty) Ltd v A E Wormald & Sons* 1966 (2) SA 463 (E), a case relating to provisional sentence.

and one to mark those passages in the (opponent's) affidavits which seem to be worthy of condemnation. From here the preparation becomes a matter of intense study, concentration and analysis. To proceed with my suggested method, you should start with the first disputed paragraph in the applicant's founding affidavit. Side by side with this you should read the respondent's answer and also the applicant's reply. Often you will find it sufficient to write on the side of the paragraph in the applicant's affidavit, whether the allegation is admitted or denied, a brief note of the respondent's explanation and the page and paragraph reference to the respondent's answer, using whatever coloured pencil has been bestowed upon that individual. In the answering affidavit you would at the relevant paragraph note a reference to the founding affidavit and a reference to the applicant's reply in the replying affidavit. There is no reason why the notations should be endorsed only on the answering affidavit and you would bring about the necessary notations on the applicant's founding affidavit as well. Then a similar notation is made on the applicant's reply. You would then make a short note in your notepad referring to all the references relating to that specific allegation.

All this may make you wonder whether I think you are in grade 4 at primary school. I do not think that. However, I do know the problems that counsel has in memorising a brief and finding his way around a mass of papers while on his feet in court trying to answer a judge's question. I assure you that by the time you have read the brief in the manner suggested not only will you have a full understanding of the issues, but you will be able to trace anyone's statement on a topic without fumbling or scratching in your brief.

Naturally, you will have prepared the legal issues involved and your final stage is to combine your preparation of the facts with the authorities in support of your contentions. On this point you certainly do not need any suggestions from me. All these preparations will be recorded in your notepad and from your preparations you should be able to dictate your heads of argument.[42]

There is one further aspect of the matter that will never cease to trouble you, even after you have taken silk and theoretically know all about these matters. I refer to the decision as to the method in which your argument is to be presented. Presumably you will prepare notes. Presumably these notes will contain an analysis of facts followed by the authorities to be quoted in order to support your propositions. Whether you are appearing for the applicant or respondent, however, you will err if you condition your mental approach to a fixed, rigidly formulated argument.

If you appear for the applicant, the judge may say to you: 'Mr Brown, I have read the papers and you need not trouble to go through the facts unless there is anything to which you particularly want to draw my attention.' If your thinking is geared to a detailed analysis of fact followed by submissions on what the court should find on the facts and thereafter the submissions of law,

---

[42] Perhaps, you will have typed all your notes onto your laptop computer. You should then, with the necessary changes, be able to click the print icon to produce an elegant set of heads of argument.

supported by cases, you may find that this announcement is apt to create a vacuum. Sometimes the mind does not function in a vacuum. The only practical suggestion I can offer is that your argument must not be made to be utterly dependent on a point-by-point discussion of the facts.

Of course, this unexpected development (be it windfall or trap) need not unduly disturb you if you are in the habit of asking yourself the preliminary question: what is the essence of the matter? It does, I agree, require complete mastery of your brief to enable you to respond to the judge in terms such as:

'My Lord, in those circumstances I submit that it appears from the papers that . . .'[43]

Here you state the conclusion of fact upon which your argument rests, and then, provided the court lets that pass, you develop your thesis on what happens in consequence of that conclusion. Sounds simple! But if you intended to develop your submissions on the facts or law in the course of your taking the court through the affidavits, you will be in trouble.

If this embarrassment befalls you then you might have a second glance at chapter 4 and apply it by being prepared for the future to deal with opposed applications in four segments, each of which will have a clear thesis: the facts; issues arising from the facts; law on the issues arising from the facts; conclusions. In following this thesis, perhaps the best way to stay out of trouble is to refer the judge to the relevant paragraph in your heads of argument dealing with issues arising from the facts and then to develop the argument from your heads.

From the respondent's point of view the matter is a little more difficult. You can prepare an argument on whatever lines you can possibly think of, but it is in the highest degree unlikely that you will ultimately present it to the court in that same form. The reason is that the applicant's counsel will also make submissions. Dictates of logic and convenience require you to deal with his contentions at the same time as you are making your own submissions on any point. The simplest way of dealing with this problem is to make a note of your opponent's argument at the relevant paragraph of your heads of argument to remind you of his argument when you reach that part of the argument. You should have had the advantage of having studied his heads of argument and you should have anticipated the thrust of his main arguments. Of course you can press on with your prepared notes and then at the end deal with additional points arising from your learned friend's argument. Somehow or other this does not seem to have the same force or carry the same conviction. Moreover, you may easily fall into the trap of arguing inconsistently. All in all, you should prepare your notes in such a way that you preserve sufficient flexibility to enable you to add comments on what your opponent has said, and you should not commit your mind to a predetermined course.

---

[43] See Appendix B on how to address judges in the Constitutional Court and in the Supreme Court of Appeal.

17.9 ARGUMENT

17.9.1 A preliminary word of caution

It is only in three respects, after a preliminary word of caution, that there need be any further discussion on the topic of argument.

The word of caution is that a greater degree of deliberateness is required in arguing opposed applications than in trials, perhaps even than in appeals. Certainly in trial actions the judge has a strong impression of the facts, evidence and issues after hearing an opening address, reading the pleadings and listening to the witnesses. In opposed applications the atmosphere is different, for the judge usually has to perform simultaneously the tasks of assimilating the evidence and evaluating the argument. To this extent his notes of the argument may have to be more comprehensive. He therefore requires more time to make those notes. Should you not allow for this you may find that some of your contentions are imperfectly remembered and not as lucidly understood as they might have been. Your argument must be a masterpiece of logic, not eloquence. It must appeal to the mind, not the emotions. If you pause for a minute between sentences while the judge make notes your argument will have gained in strength, not lost. In fact, strive during argument to enable the judge to grasp your argument and allow him to make a prefect note of it. Allow him sufficient time to make a cross-reference from his court book to your heads of argument or vice versa.

The three matters peculiar to motion proceedings are preliminary points (points *in limine*), arguing points of law and disputes of fact.

17.9.2 Preliminary points (points *in limine*)

Rule 6(5)(*d*)(iii) stipulates the procedure which a respondent must follow when he wishes to oppose an application on a point of law only. A preliminary point, however, may be a point of fact or it may be a point of law which remains even after all the affidavits have been filed.[44] The rules do not specify the procedure for such cases and it seems reasonable to assume that a respondent who wishes to apply for the dismissal of the application on such a point would probably have to serve and file a notice of his intention. Certainly he should do so when his objection does not appear *ex facie* the papers.[45] The Bar's ethical rules require you to inform your opponent before argument that you intend taking a preliminary point.[46]

17.9.3 Arguing points of law

Subject to what is stated above, it appears to be settled law that either party may argue any point of law which arises from the facts disclosed in the affidavits,

---

[44] By filing affidavits a respondent does not forfeit his right to raise an objection on a point of law to the granting of the relief claimed. See *Choonora v Rahim* 1960 (2) SA 504 (W) and *Nasionale Party, Suidwes-Afrika, en andere v Konstitusionele Raad en andere* 1987 (3) SA 544 (SWA).

[45] *Turkstra v Friis* 1952 (2) SA 342 (T).

[46] See Uniform Rules of Professional Conduct rule 4.28.3.

notwithstanding that his affidavits do not expressly refer to such point of law.[47]
It should not be overlooked, as stated previously, that any concession as to the
law made by counsel during argument will not be binding on his client nor,
probably, any concession as to inferences to be drawn from the facts.

17.9.4 Disputes of fact

Your approach to this topic in argument will, not surprisingly, depend on
whether you are arguing the matter for the applicant or the respondent. In
these circumstances I shall briefly outline the principles which arise and
indicate some of the authorities, leaving you to take your choice and to refer to
the textbooks for further guidance.

In the first place the court will 'examine the alleged dispute of fact and see
whether in truth there is a real dispute of fact which cannot be satisfactorily
determined without the aid of oral evidence'.[48] Respondents ought to be
prevented from raising fictitious disputes of fact and thus delaying the applicant
in his right to the relief claimed. As Price JP said in *Soffiantini v Mould*:[49]

> If by a mere denial in general terms a respondent can defeat or delay an applicant who
> comes to court on motion, then motion proceedings are worthless, for a respondent
> can always defeat or delay a petitioner by such a device. It is necessary to make a
> robust, common-sense approach to a dispute on motion as otherwise the effective
> functioning of the Court can be hamstrung and circumvented by the most simple and
> blatant stratagem. The Court must not hesitate to decide an issue of fact on affidavit
> merely because it may be difficult to do so. Justice can be defeated or seriously
> impeded and delayed by an over-fastidious approach to a dispute raised in affidavits.

Where there is in truth a dispute of fact making it impossible to decide the
matter on affidavit there arises, I suggest as respectfully as I can, a kaleidoscopic
pattern built of the reflections of three mirrors: possible orders, possible orders
as to costs, and judicial personality. Now, what that pattern is based on appears
from rule 6(5)(g) which empowers the court, if the matter cannot be decided on
affidavit, to:

1. dismiss the application; or
2. make an appropriate order with a view to ensuring a just and expeditious
    decision; or
3. direct that oral evidence be heard on specified issues;[50] or

[47] *Allen v Van der Merwe* 1942 WLD 39 at 47, *Van Rensburg v Van Rensburg en andere* 1963 (1) SA 505
(A) 509–10 and *Kruger v Die Land- en Landboubank van SA en andere* 1968 (1) SA 67 (GW) 65G–77B.
[48] Per Watermeyer CJ in *Peterson v Cuthbert & Co Ltd* 1945 AD 420 at 428. See also *Room Hire
Company (Pty) Ltd v Jeppe Street Mansions (Pty) Ltd* 1949 (3) SA 1155 (T) 1162, *Soffiantini v Mould* 1956
(4) SA 150 (E) 154, *Administrator, Transvaal and Others v Theletsane and Others* 1991 (2) SA 192 (A) 197,
Grobbelaar v Freund 1993 (4) SA 124 (O) 130 and *South Peninsula Municipality v Evans and Others* 2001
(1) SA 271 (C).
[49] 1956 (4) SA 150 (E) 154, Jennett and Wynne JJ concurring.
[50] A court will adopt this approach where the factual dispute is a narrow one and can be disposed of
expeditiously. An example of an order referring a matter to oral evidence can be found in *Metallurgical
and Commercial Consultants (Pty) Ltd v Metal Sales Co (Pty) Ltd* 1971 (2) SA 388 (W) 396H.

4. refer the matter to trial with appropriate directions as to pleadings or definition of issues, or otherwise,[51] or

5. in an appropriate case the court may grant an order if the facts alleged by the respondent, together with those facts alleged by the applicant which are admitted by the respondent, justify the making of such order.[52]

Superimposed on these courses is the court's general discretion as to costs, where there are four possibilities:

6. the applicant may have to pay the costs;

7. costs may be ordered to follow the ultimate event (costs in the cause);

8. costs may be reserved for decision by the court ultimately hearing the matter (costs reserved); or

9. the respondent may be directed to pay the costs, if the court can be persuaded in terms of 5 above.

From respondent's counsel's point of view it will be argued that the applicant should have anticipated a dispute of fact and that the proper combination of orders is, on the preceding list, 1 and 6.[53] From the applicant's counsel point of view he will, no doubt, first rely upon *Peterson v Cuthbert & Co Ltd*[54](that there is no genuine dispute of fact) and that he is entitled to 5 and 9, failing this, 3 and 7.

From the respondent's point of view, again, a second choice would doubtless be 4 and 8. In selecting order 6 in regard to costs rather than 7 counsel would, no doubt, have in mind a possible failure at the ultimate trail, in which event it might still be possible to save something from the wreckage by showing that the applicant should not have proceeded by way of application in the first place.

The applicant's second choice would be 4 and 7, but at a pinch he would no doubt settle for 4 and 8.

It could hardly be denied that the fate of many applications depends on the personality of the judge. The secret, from the applicant's point of view, is to know your judge and to know what type of appeal will rescue your client from the tangled web of disputed facts into which he has landed himself. A good deal depends on the equities of the case and on your ultimate prospects of success. If you can narrow the disputed issues to one fundamental point, you have every prospect of getting an order combining 3 and 7 or 3 and 8.

---

[51] An example of an order referring a matter to trial can be found in *Haupt t/a Soft Copy v Brewers Marketing Intelligence (Pty) Ltd* 2006 (4) SA 458 (SCA) 469J.

[52] *Plascon-Evans Paints Ltd v Van Riebeeck Paints (Pty) Ltd* 1984 (3) SA 623 (A) 634I, which sets out the test for a final order. In *National Director of Public Prosecutions v Zuma* 2009 (2) SA 277 (SCA) at 290D (para 26) Harms DP applied the same test, but prefaced it by stating that '[m]otion proceedings, unless concerned with interim relief, are all about the resolution of legal issues based on common cause facts.' For exceptions to the general rule see Herbstein & Van Winsen *The Civil Practice of the High Courts of South Africa* vol 1 5 ed 469–70.

[53] See especially *Room Hire Co (Pty) Ltd v Jeppe St Mansions (Pty) Ltd* 1949 (3) SA 1155 (T) 1162, *Mashaoane v Mashaoane* 1962 (2) SA 684 (D) 688A–D and *Joubert en 'n ander v Stemment en andere* 1965 (3) SA 215 (O) 219C. But see *Van Aswegen v Drotskie* 1964 (2) SA 391 (O).

[54] 1945 AD 420 at 428. See also *Da Mata v Otto NO* 1972 (3) SA 858 (A) 867G–870C.

If the dispute of fact ranges far and wide, then your objective must be to establish that there is reason to believe that the dispute will ultimately be decided in favour of your client, and that the equities are strongly in his favour. Then the applicant's approach should be 4 and 7, or alternatively 4 and 8.

The respondent's approach is so simple that I need do no more than refer to the cases cited before.

Both parties should bear in mind that the court is not bound by any dispute of fact and may, for example, reject allegations made by one of the parties because these are in conflict with the documents attached to the papers or with the general probabilities. In such cases the fact that one of the parties does not ask for the hearing of *viva voce* evidence will cause the court to decide the matter on the affidavits before it, and may cause the court to find against that party.[55]

17.10 MOTION COURT

It is in unopposed applications that you, as counsel, will probably gain your first introduction to the High Court. When you make your first appearance you will find yourself acutely conscious of the presence of your black-robed and disapproving colleagues. You will feel that your every word is being analysed and your every fault magnified.

Depending on your personal degree of conceit, this feeling should be experienced for some five to 15 years.

Apart from the psychology of the motion court, where I cannot offer any useful advice, there is also the practical side, where I can try to do so.

- Study your brief before you go to court. Some counsel do not trouble with this preliminary, and one day a judge will say something about it in open court.
- Ensure that the papers comply with the rules of court. To which end, it is always a wise approach also to study the relevant rules of court again.
- Where service is necessary, verify that there has been *proper* and *timeous* service upon the respondent. To which end it is a wise plan to study the rules of court again. Satisfy yourself that the proper proof of service has been placed before the court and that the return has been signed by the sheriff.
- Ask yourself whether the court may require authority to be cited in support of any proposition relevant to your case. Thus if yours is an unopposed application to presume death, for example, the court will want to be told on what principles the presumption will be made. You should thus be in a position to quote authorities, not only on the general

---

[55] *Gulf Oil Corporation v Rembrandt Fabrikante & Handelaars (Edms) Bpk* 1963 (2) SA 10 (T) 28C, *Broadway Pen Corporation v Wechsler & Co (Pty) Ltd* 1963 (4) SA 434 (T) 449F–G, *Du Plessis en 'n ander v Tzerefos* 1979 (4) SA 819 (O), *Joh-Air (Pty) Ltd v Rudman* 1980 (2) SA 420 (T) 429A–H, *Dekro Paint and Hardware (Pty) Ltd v Plascon-Evans Paints (Tvl) Ltd* 1982 (4) SA 213 (O) 224D and *LAWSA* Vol 3 2 ed Part 1 p 86 para 150.

principles, but also by way of comparison with your own case. If you are involved in a complicated or prolix case, consider preparing heads of argument to assist the court and ensure that they are filed timeously.

- Ask yourself whether your case is one in which the court is required to call for a report from a State official or where it does so as a matter of practice. Instances of the former are applications for rehabilitation under the Insolvency Act or involving transactions in a Deeds Registry; of the latter are applications affecting minors. In these cases you should be sure that the papers have been timeously served upon the official concerned, that he has reported to the court, and that you have a copy of his report. It sometimes happens that there is some adverse statement in the report and that you deem it advisable to file an affidavit dealing with that statement. In such cases you should remember that a copy of your affidavit must be served upon the same official so that he may report further if he so desires.

- After all these preliminaries have been attended to, you appear in court to await the calling of your matter (or, hopefully, your matters).[56] What to say at this stage is always a problem of some degree. Of course the judge may say: 'I have read the papers, what order do you want?' Then you simply refer to the notice of motion and specify which of the prayers is required. In the absence of such indication you will not err if you adopt a routine of first telling the court the nature of the application, eg an application for a provisional sequestration order, or a default judgment and so on. Your next utterances depend on the simple application of the analytical processes which have so often been suggested in this book. You ask yourself what are the constituent elements of the cause of action on which your case is based, and then, in turn, refer the court to the page and paragraph where the evidence of each element appears. To take a simple and frequent example: your address to the court in an application for provisional sequestration:

> M'Lord, this is an application for the provisional sequestration of the respondent's estate. The application was served on the respondent personally on such-and-such a date and the sheriff's return of service is before your Lordship at p 10 of the paginated papers. It appears from p 2 para 4 that the applicant is a creditor in the sum of R5 790. This is a liquidated amount being in respect of goods sold and delivered. The respondent has admitted this liability as appears from a letter written by him, being annexure 'A' to the founding affidavit. The application is also based upon the fact that the respondent is factually insolvent, and your Lordship will see from p 3 that the respondent had a discussion with the applicant, giving full information as to his financial position. The respondent admitted that his assets total R187 600 while his liabilities are R428 100, this appears from para 7 at p 4 of the founding affidavit. The sequestration will be to the advantage of creditors, as appears from para 9 on p 5 in that creditors will receive a dividend of 15 cent in the rand after payment of the administration costs. This calculation

---

[56] If you have never appeared before the particular judge, ensure that you introduce yourself to him before the hearing.

appears at para 10 of the founding affidavit. The applicant holds no security for his claim. The applicant has provided security as required by the Act, and the Master's certificate is attached as annexure 'D'. The application has also been furnished to the respondent's employees, the registered trade union and to the South African Revenue Services. Under the circumstances, I move for a provisional order of sequestration returnable on such-and-such a date.

If you analyse this little harangue you will find that it refers to each material fact which must be established in an application for a provisional sequestration order. It also refers to the nature of the applicant's case on each point. Unless something particularly calls for such a course it is not necessary to read out whole paragraphs or annexures. It is usually sufficient to summarise the effect of the allegation made.

• It sometimes happens that the order which you will actually seek differs in some degree from that set out in the notice of motion. In these cases it will be convenient, for the court and all others concerned, if you prepare a draft of the order you want, and hand it up when the matter is heard. This expedites the proceedings of the court and, more important, affords you adequate time for considering the effect and phraseology of the order. If it has to be hammered out during the hearing of the matter, there is a fair prospect that it will be unsatisfactory in some respect. On handing up a draft order, you should explain to the court in what respects the draft order differs from the notice of motion.

• Remember that, in unopposed applications, it is your duty to draw the court's attention to defects in the papers or obstacles in the way of the relief sought. To some extent the court marks its recognition of counsel's fulfilment of this duty by accepting without question any assurance that may be given or statement made from the Bar.

• As a matter of courtesy to the court, do not walk out as soon as your own matter has been disposed of. Wait until the next matter has been called and counsel is on his feet. Apart from the courtesy, this has a practical side because often a point will occur to the judge after you have sat down which he may want you to clarify.

CHAPTER 18

Technique in Appeals

18.1 CIVIL APPEALS

This chapter deals with civil appeals only. Criminal appeals are dealt with elsewhere.[1]

18.2 THE DECISION AS TO WHETHER TO APPEAL OR NOT

Appeals are strange phenomena. In those cases where you have every hope of righting an injustice the client runs out of money or enthusiasm, while in those where you are hard pressed to agree that the matter is even faintly arguable the client is determined to fight. This makes the appeal always something of a problem child — for the appellant. The respondent is in a different and better position, and should there be signs of illegitimacy he has but to abandon the offspring of the litigation.

There is no right of appeal in civil matters heard by the High Court. Section 20 of the Supreme Court Act[2] requires the leave of the trial court or, where that court refuses leave, the leave of the Supreme Court of Appeal on application to it. I do not propose to discuss the provisions of the Act, as this is somewhat outside my purpose in the present work. However I direct your attention to s 20 and leave you to find your own way through its labyrinthine provisions.

One of the important aspects in regard to an appeal, as far as the potentially unsuccessful party is concerned, is the issue of costs. The additional costs involved in an application for leave to appeal may not be very substantial, but the costs of the appeal (if leave is granted) will no doubt be a fairly unwelcome burden on the loser. This is but one of the factors which must be borne in mind when one decides whether or not to seek leave to appeal. There are, of course, other factors, primary amongst which is the question of whether one is entitled to seek to appeal at all.

The test to be applied in considering both whether a judgment is appealable and whether there are any prospects of success on appeal appears from the judgment in *Westinghouse Brake & Equipment (Pty) Ltd v Bilger Engineering (Pty) Ltd*.[3]

The following are the considerations to which thought must be directed when deciding whether to apply for leave to appeal or not:

• Is the judgment final or interlocutory?
• Is the issue one of fact?

---

[1] See paragraph 19.14 in chapter 19.
[2] Act 59 of 1959.
[3] 1986 (2) SA 555 (A) at 560I.

- If it is fact were there findings on credibility leading to the decision?
- If issues of credibility are involved, to what extent is the decision based on demeanour or the court's impression of the witnesses?
- If the factual decision is based upon probabilities, is the court's evaluation of the probabilities correct?
- Was the judgment one of absolution from the instance and, if so, at what stage was it granted?
- If the judgment is based upon law, can you find the precise point in the reasoning where the error lies?
- Was any authority overlooked?
- Do the authorities relied upon in fact support the judgment?
- What is the relative force of the authorities for and against the proposition?
- Can any authority upon which the judgment was based be shown to be wrong?
- Is the judgment an exercise of judicial discretion or a decision as to the rights of your client?

I shall not attempt a detailed discussion of each of these topics, for I regard it as a checklist to be followed before take-off. Some of the topics can usefully be commented upon, with references to only a few of the cases.

As to the first point, the question of whether the judgment was final or interlocutory, s 20 draws no distinction between interlocutory and final judgments — although the distinction may affect the grant of leave.[4]

The problems which arise in appeals on fact have already been mentioned[5] and these are particularly pressing problems where the judgment has been based in large measure on credibility. Seldom will it occur that the trial judge has so descended into the arena that the appeal court will disregard his findings and determine the issues for itself on the recorded evidence.[6] Moreover, in consequence of the need to obtain his leave to appeal, a suggestion in an application for such leave that there has been undue participation in the proceedings may well provoke an 'equal and opposite reaction'.[7] It is to be hoped that judicial detachment will reassert itself if — in the exceptional case — it has been lost.

---

[4] See *Zweni v Minister of Law and Order* 1993 (1) SA 523 (A) at 531B–532A: where the judgment or order in question, whether interlocutory or final, does not dispose of all the issues between the parties, leave will be refused unless the balance of convenience favours a piecemeal resolution of the case. In the nature of things, this is a factor that will generally weigh more heavily against the applicant for leave to appeal where the judgment was interlocutory.

[5] See paragraph 16.9 above, and *R v Dhlumayo and Another* 1948 (2) SA 677 (A). But see also *Protea Assurance Company Ltd v Casey* 1970 (2) SA 643 (A) at 648, *Commercial Union Insurance Co of SA Ltd v Wallace NO* 2004 (1) SA 326 (SCA) at 338I and *Santam Beperk v Biddulph* 2004 (5) SA 586 (SCA) at 589F–I.

[6] As in *Solomon and Another NNO v De Waal* 1972 (1) SA 575 (A).

[7] See, for example, *MEC for Public Works, Roads and Transport, Free State v Esterhuizen and Others* 2007 (1) SA 201 (SCA), where the appeal court marked its disapproval of the making of unwarranted allegations against the trial judge by awarding costs on the attorney-client scale.

A complicating factor may arise in cases where the judge has held an inspection *in loco* and relied on his observations for the purpose of his decision.[8] The procedure is usually for the court to make a full note of its observations and, in appropriate cases, this may be as complete for appeal purposes as was the actual inspection for purposes of the trial. Where the probabilities depend on impressions gained at the inspection an appellant has considerable difficulties to meet.

In regard to probabilities it must be shown that the court lost sight of factors so important that if they had not been overlooked the decision would have been the other way.[9]

All of this adds up to the proposition that if your checklist shows positive answers to all of the second, third and fourth points (the matter was decided on the facts, credibility findings were made and, in making those findings, the trial court based its decision largely or entirely on its impression of the witnesses' demeanour) you should advise against an appeal unless there is a powerful negative answer to the fifth point (evaluation of the probabilities). If that is also positive you will have to hope for better luck on the seventh to eleventh points (the legal points).

Where the judgment appealed from is one of absolution from the instance[10] not only will the plaintiff have failed to discharge the onus, but, *ex hypothesi*, there may be further evidence available and he will not have been deprived of his cause of action. Barring issues of prescription, you will have to choose between instituting action anew and appealing. Unfortunately, given that if the wheels of law do not grind exceedingly fine, they certainly grind slowly, issues of prescription will usually bar the first option.

As to the law, again I wish to voice a word of caution. Legal purism could well be tempered with a measure of common sense in regard to how the law will fare on appeal.

In regard to the seventh point, whether in the case of a matter turning on a legal point the court's reasoning was erroneous, if the answer is 'no' you realise that you will have a difficult appeal. All the others are permutations and computations, in which you learn from experience.

The aforegoing having been said, and all other things being equal, appeals on law are more readily to be advised than appeals on fact.

As to the twelfth point, no matter how aggrieved your client may be, nor how much you think that the court has erred, take the precaution of inquiring of yourself whether the judge made a determination of rights (for or against your client) or whether he was entitled to exercise a judicial discretion and

---

[8] *Sampson v Pim* 1918 AD 657 at 662.

[9] *Maitland & Kensington Bus Service (Pty) Ltd v Jennings* 1940 CPD 489 at 493. You might, with advantage, see the practical application of this proposition in *Germani v Herf and Another* 1975 (4) SA 887 (A) per Trollip JA at 903A–904F.

[10] See, as to absolution at this stage, *New Zealand Construction (Pty) Ltd v Carpet Craft* 1976 (1) SA 345 (N) at 348–9 and *Mills Litho (Pty) Ltd v Storm Quinan t/a 'Out of the Blue'* 1987 (1) SA 781 (C) at 786G–I.

purported to do so. The test is simple: given all the facts upon which the judgment was based and assuming the court's view of the law to have been sound, did the court have any option but to give judgment or make an order precisely as it did? If there was room for a judgment or order which could conceivably vary from judge to judge, then the matter is one of judicial discretion and the scope for appeal is limited.[11]

Always remember that although it is sometimes possible to raise new points or arguments on appeal,[12] there are limitations, and you will not readily be allowed to rely upon a point which has been specifically abandoned in the court below.[13] Nor is it easy to obtain an amendment of pleadings,[14] the main problem being the difficulty of showing that the point has in fact been fully canvassed in evidence.

Note, finally, the obvious, important and oft-overlooked point that one appeals against, or supports as one's misfortune or fortune might dictate, only the *outcome* (the substantive order made) and not the *reasoning* by which the trial judge arrived at that outcome.[15] Thus, the successful party need not cross-appeal in order to argue that the judgment must be upheld on other grounds than those contained in the judgment itself.[16]

18.3 THE DECISION AS TO WHETHER TO CROSS–APPEAL OR NOT

The vagaries of legal life are such that the apparent victor might be as (or almost as) dissatisfied with the result as his vanquished opponent.

Or the victor might be satisfied, but convinced that he can do still better on appeal.

The decision as to whether to cross–appeal or not is as difficult as, and perhaps even more difficult than, the decision as to whether to appeal.

The starting point is to remember that which has already been mentioned in paragraph 18.2 above: one appeals only against a substantive order on the basis that one wants to change it, and not against the reasoning which led to the order.[17] From there, much the same considerations apply as in paragraph 18.2 above, subject to the important *caveat* that it is often best to simply defend what one has rather than to risk losing all in reaching out for more. A bird in the hand is, after all, usually better than two in the bush.

---

[11] *Tjospomie Boerdery (Pty) Ltd v Drakensberg Botteliers (Pty) Ltd and Another* 1989 (4) SA 31 (T), *Caxton Limited and Others v Reeva Forman (Pty) Ltd and Another* 1990 (3) SA 547 (A) at 566, and *Ciba-Geigy (Pty) Ltd v Lushof Farms (Pty) Ltd en 'n Ander* 2002 (2) SA 447 (SCA) at 462.

[12] *Sentrale Kunsmis Korporasie (Edms) Bpk v NKP Kunsmisverspreiders (Edms) Bpk* 1970 (3) SA 367 (A).

[13] *Gcayiya v Minister of Police* 1973 (1) SA 130 (A).

[14] *Standard Trading Co 1960 (Pty) Ltd v Lacey Knitting Mills Ltd* 1972 (3) SA 392 (A) at 395B–E.

[15] See *Administrator, Cape, and Another v Ntshwaquela and Others* 1990 (1) SA 705 (A) at 715D.

[16] *S v Boesak* 2000 (3) SA 381 (A) at 393A–B.

[17] See the authorities quoted in fnn 15 and 16 above.

18.4 POINTS OF PROCEDURE

The points of procedure relating to appeals are mainly to be borne in mind by attorneys, for counsel's function at this stage is merely to do what he is told and to speak when he is spoken to.

There is, as pointed out in paragraph 18.2 above, no automatic right of appeal against a judgment or order of a provincial or local division sitting as a court of first instance, nor against judgments or orders in respect of a judge's appeal, or finally a judgment or order of a provincial or local division given on appeal to it.

The position in regard to appeals from the magistrate's court remains unaltered. The rules of both the magistrate's court and the High Court are sufficiently clear, and it is simply required to study and peruse the relevant rules each time when it is intended to embark upon an appeal. It is suggested that particular attention be paid to the following:

- the time limits imposed;
- the filing of a power of attorney;
- security;
- preparation of the record;
- applying for a date for the hearing;
- the filing of the prescribed number of copies of the record, and the manner in which it is to be presented;
- the time limits stipulated for filing of the heads of argument.

18.5 APPEALS TO THE CONSTITUTIONAL COURT

The purpose of this paragraph is not to deal extensively with appeals to the Constitutional Court. This aspect is covered in detail in tomes dealing with the subject.[18] The golden rule is to study the rules and practice directives of the Constitutional Court and, of course, to follow the techniques advocated in this chapter.

Although the Constitutional Court is primarily a court of appellate jurisdiction limited to constitutional matters, it can also act as a court of first instance where it is in the interests of justice for it to do so.[19]

You should, as in all other appellate courts, in fact prepare two arguments, the one being your written heads and the other being the oral argument which you propose presenting on your feet.[20]

Applications for leave to appeal are made directly to the Constitutional Court.[21] An application for leave to appeal must contain the following:

---

[18] S Woolman et al *Constitutional Law of South Africa* 2 ed (Juta OS November 2007) ch 5.

[19] See rule 18 of the Constitutional Court rules.

[20] Constitutional Court rule 13(3)*(b)* states that parties should assume that all the judges have read the written arguments, and that there is no need to repeat what is set out therein.

[21] The procedure is set out in Constitutional Court rule 19.

- the decision against which the appeal is sought to be brought, and the grounds upon which such decision is disputed;
- a statement setting out clearly and succinctly the constitutional matter or matters which are proposed to be raised in the appeal;
- such supplementary information or argument as the applicant considers necessary;
- a statement indicating whether the applicant intends applying for leave to appeal to any other court.

Applications for leave to appeal may be dealt with summarily, or the Court may order that the application be set down for argument before it.

Generally, the factors that the Court will take into account in deciding whether or not to grant leave to appeal are:

- the importance of the issue raised;
- the prospects of success (although it has been emphasised that this is not necessarily determinative[22]);
- the public interest in a determination of the constitutional issues raised;
- the accuracy of the pleadings. The Court has emphasised that constitutional litigation requires accurate identification of the statutory provisions in question.[23]

The actual procedure on appeal is dealt with in the rules of the Constitutional Court. Rule 21 makes provision for a practice note where additional information must be furnished to the registrar. Rule 30 provides that certain provisions of the Supreme Court Act are also applicable to the Constitutional Court. The Court's powers on hearing appeals are regulated by s 22 of the Supreme Court Act.

18.6 PREPARING THE ARGUMENT

One of the most tedious exercises in the advocate's practice is preparing his argument in appeals, particularly burdensome because heads of argument must be filed before the appeal.

In one sense the load is lightened because the judgment and the notice of appeal itself will have served to delimit the matters to which attention is to be directed. In another sense the load is increased because the heads of argument will be constrained by the grounds of appeal. The labour which follows consists of reading and analysing the record and of noting cross-references or comparisons in the evidence. In the original argument — in trial matters at least — a great deal of this cataloguing is done by an impromptu statement of what the witnesses have said. There is no opportunity for a detailed dissection, and,

---

[22] *De Reuck v Director of Public Prosecutions, Witwatersrand Local Division and Others* 2004 (1) SA 406 (CC), *Fraser v ABSA Bank Limited (National Director of Public Prosecutions as Amicus Curiae)* 2007 (3) SA 484 (CC) and *Phumelela Gaming & Leisure Limited v Gründlingh and Others* 2007 (6) SA 350 (CC).

[23] *Shaik v Minister of Justice and Constitutional Development and Others* 2004 (3) SA 599 (CC) and *Crown Restaurant CC v Gold Reef City Theme Park (Pty) Ltd* 2008 (4) SA 16 (CC).

moreover, the facts are fresh in your memory. On appeal, after some months (and usually a year or more) have elapsed, not only do you have to refresh your memory, but you must also be able to support your argument by specific references to the relevant passages in the record. The clerical work in noting these references in the heads of argument is time-consuming and sometimes soul-destroying. Inevitably there is a tendency to make the analysis more refined and more meticulous than was possible in the court below. This may have the merit of allowing a more scientific dissertation on the facts, but over-refinement may be self-destructive because it loses touch with the broad effect of the evidence in the court a quo, where minutiae were seen as such. The stark black and white of print does not admit of the half-tones and shadows in which evidence is truly to be observed. Nor will the appeal court be unaware that any detailed analysis is inconsistent with the true atmosphere of the trial. Also, time will be wasted on slavery to detail.

The basic principles of preparation are set out in chapter 16 which deals with argument, but as a general plan I suggest that every argument on appeal, whether for appellant or respondent, must take cognizance of three main topics:

- the principles adopted by appeal courts in the exercise of their functions. By this I mean matters such as judicial discretion, the approach to appeals on fact (having regard especially to onus, credibility or probabilities) as well as principles or maxims such as *stare decisis;*
- the analysis of and submissions on fact, leading to the conclusion for which you contend;
- the investigation of and submissions on principles of law, leading to the proposition you seek to establish.

The second and third items may be reversed, depending on the exigencies of any particular appeal.

In drafting your heads of argument it is wise to see that each paragraph, as a matter of logic and sound technique, follows directly upon and is consistent with the submission or exposition in the previous paragraph. There must be a coherent, smooth-flowing evolution of a thesis. Missing links are for anthropologists, not for advocates.[24] And, through all the accumulation of arguments and contentions, must be discernible the true essence of the matter. You will not be the worse off if you make a practice of testing each of your propositions in the context of the essence.

There is a lot to be said for spending some time trying to capture the essence of the appeal, ie, the essence of the reason why you say that the appeal should either be allowed or dismissed depending upon where you sit, in as succinct but striking a sentence or two as you can, and opening your heads with this

---

[24] See *Caterham Car Sales & Coachwork Ltd v Birkin Cars (Pty) Ltd* 1998 (3) SA 938 (SCA) at 955B–C. What must be contained in your heads of argument are *points* of argument, and not an entire dissertation.

sentence or two in paragraph form. It does not harm to try to grab the imaginations of the judges of appeal at first opportunity.[25]

The tedious part of preparation is that, the facts usually being new or no longer fresh in your memory, you have to acquaint yourself with every fact and every statement in the record. This trite, almost contemptible, point is one you should not dismiss too airily. It is always a trifle disconcerting to be in the middle of an elaborate and elegantly reasoned argument and to hear the reproving question from the Bench:

> 'Mr Brown, that is a very interesting proposition, but doesn't your own witness, Klitznit, say the exact opposite at 278?'

This can be avoided by the plan which follows, a plan which can be of the utmost value in the dissection of facts where a factual argument is involved. There will, inevitably, be a number of topics that you will have to discuss. You can call them points, steps in the analysis, links in the chain or whatever else you fancy. Now you prepare your plan, your framework, your sequence or, again, whatever metaphor you select. The whole analysis of fact, be it from an historical or a syllogistic approach, is a sequence with a beginning and leading to an end. So now you write down each element in the history or syllogism. Of course, you have studied the record, extracted an essence, and given a modicum of thought to what case you intend to present to the court on appeal. This has equipped you for the first act of preparation. You write your historical or syllogistic list. To each item in the list you assign a letter. I hope that the alphabet is adequate. Then you embark upon the tedious part. You read the record again, carefully, critically and regardless of time. As you find a reference to one of the topics in your list you perform two exercises: in the margin of the record you note your reference letter next to the passage of evidence or whatever it may be; on your list, there being of course ample space for this, you note the name of the witness and the page reference.

When you come to the last stage of preparation, writing out your heads of argument, the task is almost a clerical one if your analysis has been done properly. You have all the points; you have all the cross-references; really you have the whole case.

---

[25] See John Munkman *The Technique of Advocacy* 143, where the author suggests that one should try to introduce one's argument in a fashion that arouses interest and attention. An interesting case which illustrates this point well can be found in the best-selling author John Grisham's book *The Innocent Man* (Century Press, 2006). *The Innocent Man* is the true story of Ron Williamson, who was condemned to death for the brutal rape and murder of a woman but who was in fact completely innocent. His innocence was proved by DNA evidence, once the technology became available. Williamson would have been executed had a *habeas* petition not succeeded at the eleventh hour. It succeeded before a judge who did not have a record of granting such petitions, but whose attention was pertinently drawn to the merits of the matter by his clerk. Grisham writes on p 271 that the clerk 'was captivated by the opening paragraph: "This case is a bizarre one about a dream that turned into a nightmare. . . ."'. Williamson's case is, perhaps, the most striking example one can imagine of the possible advantages of a pithily succinct opening paragraph to a document. It is probably not an overstatement to say that it literally meant the difference between life and death.

Researches into the law receive similar treatment — a syllogistic list of propositions and a note of all the authorities under each point.

Finally you get down to drafting, having regard to the relevant rules of court, and also to how those rules are applied in practice in the particular Division to which you are appealing, whether that be the SCA, the Concourt, or a Provincial Division.[26]

You find yourself in a dilemma of sorts: brevity or 'adequacy'? The tendency seems to be not to file 'heads' of argument, but to file the very argument itself. I have known counsel (two seniors plus a most significant junior, let me say) spend ten to fifteen minutes polishing up a single word and exhausting the whole gamut of synonyms to express a single concept (they did not triumph in the appeal.) The merit is that, in the detached atmosphere of chambers, each point is given full consideration with the certainty that where a proposition is evolved the thought that led to that proposition is preserved. To state the proposition barely and to rely on memory for reconstruction of the reasoning is sometimes perilous procedure. Nor, if there is no inordinate prolixity, will the tribunal itself find fault with this method, for it enables the argument to receive more effective consideration in advance. The drawback is that the argument on appeal often takes the form of a recitation of the heads. It can sound stilted and even ineffectual. However, in the first place you ought with sufficient skill to be able to overcome this by not reading from your heads and, in the second place, force of rhetoric seldom wins appeals, for where judgment is reserved the impact of rhetoric is etched out and fades, leaving the lines of the written notes standing as the picture of the argument.

My last suggestion is to counsel for the appellant. If you are to have the last word, take an advantage which you probably did not have in the court below. Devote a little time to study of the respondent's heads and prepare for your reply. I leave out of consideration the other question: shall I anticipate or shall I reply? Usually the former, but adequate preparation will leave you a degree of flexibility which is utterly essential to enable you to cope with the reaction of the court.

18.7 TAKE TIME TO THINK

When preparing for the hearing of an appeal (preferably before you even draft your heads but, if that luxury was not afforded to you, at least before arguing the appeal), *take time to think.*

Start with a long view of the case. Ignore all the minutiae. Ask yourself why you won or lost as the case might be, and what the answer or answers to that victory or defeat might be? Re-examine your analysis of the essence of the matter. If this thought process leads to discouragement, so be it: at least you now have some idea of what you are up against, and can deal with it. If it leads

---

[26] Here you will have to pay regard to any practice directions applicable in the particular Division. You will find these collected in the relevant text books on civil procedure.

to encouragement, ask yourself what type of questions you might face, and think through your responses to those questions.

You will find that *time spent simply thinking is never time wasted*.

18.8 THE APPEAL HEARING ITSELF: YOUR APPEALING WAYS

A trite maxim for appeals is: expect the unexpected. If you are respondent, expect that your opponent will not be called upon and that you will have to begin. If you are the appellant you ought to entertain two apprehensive expectations: that the court will floor you with a surprise blow as you come out of your corner fighting; that you may never be able to exercise your right to reply because your opponent will not be called upon.

If you are the appellant I could venture a suggestion that seems valid at least for the Supreme Court of Appeal and Constitutional Court. It is this: beware of the early question. The judges are wont to study the record before they go into court — and not merely a halfhour before. They are also wont to study counsel's heads of argument, and will have formed some views on what ought to be discussed during the argument. One's heads of argument usually have a few introductory remarks which formally outline the issues. Then one normally goes to the basic propositions which are to be established in argument or upon which the following submissions are to be based. This, experience has shown me, may often be the critical stage in the whole operation. The countdown, to use the modern idiom, is over and you have a lift-off. Your whole craft (figuratively as well as an abstract noun) is now delicately poised to take direction. Often, verily as a ground-to-air missile and sometimes no less devastating, comes that question. Ask me not what the actual question is. All too often, if you will forgive my trifling with language, it is the epitome of the quintessence of the matter. It may seem innocuous, gentle, almost as a mild correction. However, watch it. Wait for it. Before you answer, however, think about it and assess its effect on your thesis.

As an example of this type of question let me refer you to counsel's submissions in *Peila v Peila*.[27] The law has changed since *Peila*, but the point to be made relates not to the law but to the technique. The plaintiff wife had admittedly been guilty of adultery on several occasions. She alleged malicious desertion by her husband and sought a divorce by reason thereof. For the husband it was contended, following authority, that her adultery was an absolute bar to her action, while the husband's counterclaim for a divorce by reason of that adultery was unassailable. In these circumstances, after dealing with the introductory matter, the heads of argument contained the assertion that the court has no power to condone a party's adultery so as to deprive the other party of a defence or a cause of action based thereon.

---

[27] 1972 (1) SA 399 (A). Counsel for the appellant was Eric Morris SC, the author of the first three editions of this work.

Perhaps this submission was deliberately pitched high in order to evoke a response. If so it succeeded only too well. As counsel reached this particular proposition the gentle question came from on high:

> 'Mr X, if the court hears the cases of both parties and decides in favour of the plaintiff, does it really deprive the defendant of a defence?'

I am not sure that counsel immediately appreciated what thinking motivated the question. That question, however, held the essence of the appeal, and the next question showed this:

> 'Doesn't the court really weigh up the conduct of the parties and decide which one of them really caused the break-up of the marriage?'

In some cases, on a question such as the first being put, you may well have to abandon your planned argument entirely (or at least in large part) and, duly equipped thereto with a complete mastery of the facts and the law, debate that first question in order, if possible to refute it.

In other cases you may decide that the question is in fact answered or can be answered during the course of your argument on the heads filed. If so make your reply and the court will wait as patiently as possible for the answer. The Supreme Court of Appeal is usually more patient than a Provincial Division.

If the question is one which you recognise as what is politely called 'a stinger' and you cannot think of any satisfactory answer you may say:

> 'My Lord, may I return to that later?'

So you do not return to it later — or at all. You will not have fooled anybody — except perhaps yourself. And when it is all over it may be a profitable study to consider where that question fits in the list of pre-appeal considerations set out at the commencement of this chapter. If the appeal was noted or opposed on your advice you should ask yourself whether that advice should have been different, whether you yourself should have asked that question before the matter went further. The next time you will, or so you resolve, ask yourself the question before the court does. Somehow, the question is vastly different next time. So much for the unexpected.

The next proposition is pithily phrased as: *timeo Danaos et donas ferentes.* It happens during argument that your opponent is put a number of questions by one or other of the judges of appeal — sometimes by the whole lot of them jointly, severally, jointly and severally or even simultaneously. It is disrespectful to refer to these questions as a heckling. You will, no doubt, derive great encouragement from this process, and be most appreciative of the gifts coming from the Bench. Again, vigilance is your watchword. All may be well. But it may be that among the questions is one that is an overstatement or a misconception. Your opponent may miss it. You must not, for when your turn arrives you can be sure that that same question will emerge. This time, since the questioning is from a different angle, even diametrically opposed, that question will be seen without its facade and will stand exposed for what it is. You for your part must already have decided whether the question may safely be put aside as mere overstatement, or whether it must be met in order to show that its refutation does not carry with it an element of danger in that the opposite becomes established. Equally must you appraise your opponent's answers, for it sometimes happens that counsel, thinking while on his feet, can enunciate only a portion of the true proposition. The court, however, adopting a different posture, may very well develop and amplify the answer. So you must be prepared to meet not only what your opponent said, but what he might have said.

For the rest it seems to me that the technique of arguing appeals is little different from a combination of what I have suggested in chapter 16 in regard to trials and chapter 17 in regard to opposed applications.

There are, however, one or two points which bear mention. Your first appearance in the Supreme Court of Appeal is one of them. If you spend a day bathed in perspiration, you are merely normal. It does not mean that your appeal is a bad one, that your heads of argument are defective or that you are arguing like an incoherent tongue-tied bucolic. You will have questions put to you, so it will seem, from all points of the compass. In fact there are only three or five of them — judges, I mean, not points of the compass. Bear with them and soon you will emulate counsel who said to the judge on the extreme left:

> 'Wait a minute, I'm still answering his question; then I'll deal with you. I can only answer one at a time.'

'*His* question' referred to the question from the judge on the extreme right.

Another point is this: You are not shackled to your heads of argument. If you want to argue different points, argue them; if you want to quote different or additional authorities, quote them. If you want to hand in additional heads of argument, do so. The more difficult the appeal, the more ready the court will be to listen to your submissions. I have known counsel — very junior and very inexperienced — to become terror-struck when an Olympian voice boomed:

> 'Is that in your heads of argument?'

The learned judge in fact merely wanted to know whether he should make his own note of the point or whether it was already there for his reference.

CHAPTER 19

Criminal Cases

Revised by Johann Engelbrecht SC
(Member of the Pretoria Bar)

19.1 AN INTRODUCTION TO CRIME

> Remember that in a criminal trial the odds are against you, that you are a fool and your client is a rogue.[1]

This may have been the position when this pungent advice was penned. With the new dispensation in South Africa came the Constitution.[2] Section 35 now confers certain inalienable rights on any person arrested or detained and ensures a fair trial for every accused.[3] To ensure a fair trial, presiding officers in criminal trials must ensure that all constitutional rights were rigidly adhered to during the investigation stage, at the time of the arrest, during detention and during the trial. In general, the blanket legal professional privilege that attached to the contents of the police docket made way for the right of the accused to ask for discovery of all the statements in the police docket as well as the documentary evidence on which the state relies, providing a most useful weapon in the hands of the cross-examiner: inconsistencies or contradictions between the statement made to the investigator and the evidence of the witness during the actual trial can now be readily exposed. On the other hand, it must be remembered that police efficiency has increased. So too has science. So too, various amendments to the Criminal Procedure Act 51 of 1977 (the Act) have made it most difficult to take advantage of the technical defects that could oft times be found to invalidate a summons, charge or indictment and so to nullify a conviction. Last, and by no means least, the ingenuity of a generation of our predecessors has taught prosecutors a technique of efficiency that might have been lacking in past days.

Perhaps too many guilty people are acquitted for all I know. Perhaps, moreover, it never happens that innocent people are convicted. Perhaps all investigating officers and all public prosecutors scrupulously perform their duty of placing before the court all available evidence, even if it assists the accused. Perhaps it has never happened that an investigating officer or a public prosecutor has coached and rehearsed a state witness. All these things remain matters of sheer speculation. All that I can say with any degree of certainty, is that as the war between criminals and society becomes more intense, both sides

---

[1] From *The First Forty Years* by H H Morris KC. All other quotations in this chapter, where not otherwise specified, are from the same book.

[2] Constitution of the Republic of South Africa, 1996.

[3] *S v Zuma* 1995 (2) SA 642 (CC), 1995(1) SACR 568 (CC).

tend to extremes. If your client is innocent it will require all your ability to secure an acquittal, for some very capable people will believe the opposite and will be working to secure a conviction. They will be working, moreover, in a procedural system which is constantly being refined to aid them in their task.

The procedure at a summary trial is now stipulated in s 115 of the Act which requires the judicial officer, if the accused pleads not guilty, to ask him if he wishes to make a statement indicating the basis of his defence. If the accused does not make such a statement, or if he makes a statement that requires clarification, the court may then put questions to the accused in order to ascertain the basis of his defence. If the explanation contains admissions, these admissions may then be recorded, with the consent of the accused, as formal admissions in terms of s 220 of the Act. Such admissions provide sufficient proof of the facts admitted and the state need not prove those facts.[4] Section 115 does not remove the right of the accused to remain silent during the plea stage of the trial. As far as the legal 'adviser' is concerned he may reply on behalf of the accused, who must then be asked whether he confirms what has been stated on his behalf.

The object of these provisions is obviously to expedite the proceedings, and to dispense in some cases with witnesses whose evidence would not be disputed. From the point of view of the state the business of the prosecution is facilitated; from the point of view of the accused the advantages of the section may be regarded as dubious—probably from the point of view of the prosecution and the demands of justice, the procedure is to be recommended.

To obtain an acquittal in a criminal case you yourself must be a master of every branch of technique — or just plain lucky. You will have been taught that in our law, an accused person is presumed to be innocent until he is proved to be guilty. At the back of your mind may lurk a belief that this contrasts most equitably with the law of France where an accused must prove his innocence — and Devil's Island take the hindmost. In practice you may sometimes wonder in frustration whether you have confused the two systems. When you think this, however, it is time to take a long hard look, not at the system of justice in South Africa, for all its faults, but at your client or, perhaps, at yourself. Courts err. Appeal courts err, too. Sometimes, however, the court does not err. Not every accused person is a Dreyfus.[5] On the laws of chance alone you might expect a conviction in 50 per cent of your criminal defences. But these laws do not apply, for reasons already suggested. If you are engaged in a game, which is open to some doubt, it is a game of skill — about the 'chance' aspect there will be some mention made later. So your client's conviction may be due to the

---

[4] *S v Seleke* 1980 (3) SA 745 (A) 754G.

[5] Captain Alfred Dreyfus was a French soldier who was court-martialled in France in the 1890s for allegedly selling military secrets to Germany. Found guilty and sentenced to life imprisonment on the notorious Devil's Island penal colony in French Guiana, his unfair trial and conviction — which many felt was spurred by anti-semitism — became a cause celebré. The real spy is now generally considered to have been one Esterházy.

plain simple exigencies of the case or, in a few cases, to the lack of skill of his counsel or attorney. Whence, then, springs your sense of frustration? The answer becomes my first proposition.

Criminal law involves persons, emotions and tragic consequences. Without a feeling for those factors you will do less than your best. Although you should realise these humanistic aspects and conduct your case with their realisation, you must at the same time preserve a degree of detachment that will leave your judgment keen and unclouded.

> Do not make your client's case your own. If you do, you have to handle two bad cases. He has bought your services and not your emotions.

As you proceed on a career involving the defence of persons charged with crime you will become painfully conscious of one of the characteristics of clients. By the time they become clients they do not need an advocate but a necromancer. They will usually have killed their defence stone cold dead. You will demolish witnesses and wait in keen anticipation for the magic words to float through the court: 'Not guilty.' But finally there is the evidence of the investigating officer who confides to the court that your client has indulged in a few statements and explanations that make your flesh creep. Many years ago, in a moment of frankness, a detective once confided to counsel that the police might 'volunteer' a little evidence if they knew the accused was guilty and they couldn't quite prove it. But that was many years ago and, after a succession of cases where the accused does not dispute the statements ascribed to him, you will realise that the tongue is the most powerful weapon in the fight against crime.

In this lies my second proposition. Anything that your client can do, you can do better. In argument there is not much danger arising from counsel's oral indiscretions. At all other stages of the case you must weigh your words as though they were gold — whether you are cross-examining a witness, objecting to evidence or making an application. The less you say the less you may err.

My third proposition is more consoling. Previously, dealing with civil litigation, we suggested that someone waits to take advantage of any mistake that you may make. In criminal law, subject to the second proposition I have stated, it is your turn to wait for mistakes. When you find one take the same advantage of it that others would take of yours. Beware, however, of impetuosity. If you show your hand too soon the mistake may be rectified. It is only experience, and a thorough knowledge of the law and rules of evidence, that will enable you to detect the mistake when it occurs. Many amendments to the law result from the fact that counsel knew a mistake when he saw one and bided his time before capitalising on it. One example was, in a negligent driving case, where the prosecution failed to prove that the offence was committed on a public road.[6] The law reports and the biographies of successful counsel will disclose others. This is the element of 'chance' of which I spoke earlier.

[6] *S v H* 1988 (3) SA 545 (A) and *S v Kruger en andere* 1989 (1) SA 785 (A).

If I may suggest a philosophy of crime it is this: from the moment that your client is arrested and charged, everything that happens is profit. Things can get no worse, for the very act of charging him manifests his liability to punishment, whatever that punishment may be. There is a reason behind this philosophy. I have known counsel to debate long and earnestly in chambers as to whether a point of law in a criminal case was a 'good' point or not. To my mind that is not the test. Arguing a bad point will not make the case any worse — but remember, 'bad cases make bad law'. If the point has substance it has a potential for profit. The successful criminal lawyer is one who sees the profit and seizes it before it eludes his grasp. Anything may be profit — as I said before.

19.2 *PRO DEO* OR LEGAL AID DEFENCES

Junior counsel, in his early days at the Bar, may well have gleaned his experience of crime from *pro Deo* and 'dock' defences. These have now been replaced by Legal Aid defences. The observations to be made, however, remain valid. There has been some criticism of the fact that the defence of persons charged with one of the most serious of crimes — murder — should so often be entrusted to the most inexperienced of counsel. Until the economics of the matter can be adjusted it must remain so. And when the economics are adjusted the taxpayer will by no means welcome the adjustment.

Yet I doubt whether the unfortunate accused does suffer quite as much prejudice as the critics say. The Legal Aid brief is usually prepared with more thoroughness than counsel, in later years, will devote to cases involving large sums of money and abstruse principles of law. If you err as your predecessors have done, it will be an error that you will hopefully not have cause to regret. If counsel appears to be inept, the court will inevitably come to the assistance of the accused.

Counsel's duty to interview his client, and the consequences of failure to do so, are dealt with in *S v Majola*[7] where counsel in a *pro Deo* matter had not ascertained whether his client wished to give evidence. The following passage from the judgment of Trollip AJA is relevant:[8]

> Secondly, that an act or omission by a legal representative of one of the parties to criminal litigation (in contradistinction to one by the trial Court itself) can constitute an irregularity vitiating the proceedings appears from *S v Twopenny and Others* (AD, delivered on 8 September 1981), and cf *S v Mushimba and Others* 1977 (2) SA 829 (A). Here, due to a *bona fide* misunderstanding by appellant's counsel of his duty towards his client, appellant was not afforded the opportunity of discussing, considering and deciding whether or not to testify on his own defence, and of terminating the mandate of his counsel if, contrary to his wishes, the latter insisted that he should not testify. That constituted an irregularity in the proceedings. I agree that *Matonsi's* case, 1958 (2) SA 450 (A), is therefore distinguishable on the facts. That the irregularity resulted in a failure of justice, justifying this Court making the above-mentioned

---

[7] 1982 (1) SA 125 (A).
[8] At 133D–G.

orders (cf s 322(1) of the Act) is amply borne out by the facts that the Court *a quo*, in convicting the appellant, relied heavily and repeatedly on his failure to testify and the appellant was aggrieved by not having been afforded the opportunity of testifying.

The right of an accused to a fair trial can under circumstances lead to a postponement of the trial when the accused is dissatisfied with the *pro Deo* advocate who had been appointed on his behalf, if the dissatisfaction is not feigned or unreasonable.[9]

Marcus AJ pointed out in *S v Ntuli*[10] that the South African system of criminal procedure is adversarial in nature and that in such a system, legal representation for the accused becomes indispensable. Unless counsel properly represents his client, the right to a fair trial and the right to a fair appeal may be negated.

You will interview your client and take his statement — twice as carefully because there is no attorney to do the spadework for you. You will read and analyse the authorities on 'intention to kill' and whatever other facet of the crime may arise in your case. You will prepare yourself with authorities to support whatever contention you may decide to make. When you have done this, although you may not present or conduct your case with the sure touch and skill of someone ten years your senior, you will at least succeed in placing before the court most of what could possibly be said for your client. If you have done your job conscientiously, it is but rarely that the court will let your client suffer for your want of experience.

I hope that I shall be forgiven if I now add a few of the lines which follow the passage quoted at the beginning of this chapter:

> You will need all the assistance you can get, and there are many in court that can help you. Be courteous to everyone — even to the judge. Get on friendly terms with everyone associated with your trial. In the end most of them will be out to help you . . . . One of the most important persons at a trial is the prosecutor. He can help you in a variety of ways. He may take a plea that suits your client. On your conviction he may say a few words in your favour. He can always meet you in the matter of dates. His very demeanour in the case may be of assistance to you. The court orderly and the interpreter may be useful. A shorthand-writer once put me on to a point I had not seen. That point saved my client. Courtesy pays dividends.

The Legal Aid defence imposes a duty on counsel which, to some extent, can be more easily discharged with a liberality of courtesy.

Counsel becomes not only his client's defender, but also his attorney. Very often the defence involves the calling of witnesses other than the accused. In such cases counsel — you — must personally take steps to secure the attendance of those witnesses.

Since you do not have an instructing attorney (other than the Legal Aid Board), you should request the Registrar of the High Court, or when on circuit the clerk of the magistrate's court, the judge's registrar or the court itself to

---

[9] *S v Dangatye* 1994 (2) SACR 1 (SCA) at 23*a–c*.
[10] 2003 (4) SA 258 (W), 2003 (1) SACR 613 (W).

arrange for the issue of a subpoena or to otherwise arrange for the attendance of the witness. This is not much of a practical difficulty. Simply hand any one of them a list of the witnesses and their addresses. If the Director of Public Prosecutions, in cases of urgency, requests the investigating officer to bring the witness to court, that officer, I am told, is instructed not to enter into any discussions with the witness. Whether this instruction is complied with remains an open question.

Since you may, as your preparation of the case develops, come across additional points which need be put to your client you should not hesitate to arrange to see him as often as you need. You can, of course, go to the prison where he is being detained, but it is often better to have him brought to the court where the services of an interpreter will be made available to you — subject to the exigencies of the service. The chief clerk in the Director's office is (in theory) the official who will assist in arranging for the availability of the accused.

It does happen, rarely perhaps, that your own resources are inadequate for the proper preparation of your case — and I do not mean to imply that you do not possess the requisite skill. Such an instance occurred in what was then the Witwatersrand Local Division, some years ago. There were three sets of counsel because of the conflicting interests of the accused. Accused Nos 1 and 3 were defended *pro Deo* whilst accused No 2 had instructed her own attorney and counsel. During the course of their preparation *pro Deo* counsel found that it was necessary to investigate the history of a particular shop in Johannesburg. This involved the examination of building plans and records, as well as the tracing of witnesses who might be able to give whatever evidence was necessary. All of this is work not normally performed by counsel — even *pro Deo* counsel. When the difficulty was put to the deputy attorney-general he suggested that application should be made to court for the appointment of attorneys to act *pro Deo* for accused No 1 and No 3 respectively. The application was made and granted.

Accordingly, in a proper case, where the work required is, as I have said, beyond your resources, you may consider following a similar procedure. Also you may deem this to be essential in cases where there is a good reason to maintain secrecy in regard to the identity of witnesses whom you desire to subpoena and where you do not wish to disclose the information. In such a case, I suggest, the court would not require you to disclose the identity of the witnesses in your application, but would accept your statement from the Bar as to the difficulty that had arisen. Naturally, you will exercise the highest degree of responsibility in giving the court your assurance — if you don't, you may subsequently gain the impression that the ceiling has collapsed on you.

Finally, on this topic, I venture to suggest that, in a case where counsel desires to have attorneys appointed to assist him on a similar basis, the court would not require a formal application but would probably act on an oral application by counsel, brought before it at a time arranged with the prosecution. Again, you will have to exercise a high degree of responsibility in making any such application.

Presently counsel (*pro Deo*) is appointed by the Judicial Care Centre and a brief will only be handed to legal representative if he is registered with the centre. The onus is on the legal representative to ensure that he is so registered.

19.3 DEFENDING THE GUILTY

Second only to the 'should a doctor . . .?' line of fatuities is the one which goes, more or less, 'should a lawyer defend a man whom he knows to be guilty'? Much has been written on this topic, learnedly, superficially or even flippantly. Perhaps an illustration will convey the answer.

Junior counsel, a man of some experience — or so he thought — had been instructed to defend a person charged with murder. It was the common *pro Deo* case: a gambling-room in a township, a tin full of skokiaan or some other hell's-brew, an argument about money settled with a quick stroke of the knife before the victim knew what it was all about. Counsel duly interviewed his client and found, to his mild surprise, that the defence was not intoxication but an alibi. I say 'mild' because in those less enlightened days under the Liquor Act of 1928 many black people were reluctant to admit drinking. Counsel then proceeded to investigate the alibi and to seek for supporting witnesses. The accused provided some names and counsel then took the necessary steps to have them traced. After a few days he received a telephone call from the investigating officer, to say that the witnesses could not be found and that, indeed, the police had been trying for some time to trace them at the instance of the accused. This latter statement alone should have caused counsel to think. But experience, let it be remarked, is a series of lessons. By the day of the trial the missing witnesses had not been traced, and counsel had no doubt that they did not exist. Accordingly he sought out the Crown prosecutor and discussed the acceptance of a plea of guilty of culpable homicide — the basis being that the accused's state of intoxication rendered him incapable of forming the intention to kill which is required in cases of murder.[11] The Crown prosecutor agreed to accept the plea, and counsel proceeded to interview his client and tell him the good news. Somewhat to counsel's this time more profound surprise, the accused was not overjoyed at the prospect of receiving a sentence of some four years' imprisonment with hard labour and declined to plead guilty to the lesser charge. His defence, he insisted, was an alibi. An alibi meant he wasn't there. If he wasn't there, he didn't do it. In these circumstances the trial proceeded. The Crown called its first witness and counsel proceeded with his cross-examination designed to establish circumstances which would reduce the crime from murder to culpable homicide. When this witness had furnished enough information, counsel addressed the court, craving a short adjournment in order to discuss the prospect of a plea of guilty of culpable homicide. The

---

[11] *R v Ndhlovu* 1945 AD 369.

adjournment was granted, but the accused remained adamant and uninfluenced by the prospect of the death penalty, a prospect rendered a little remote as a result of the evidence thus far given, but a prospect nevertheless. When all argument and persuasion had failed, counsel shrugged his shoulders, both literally and metaphorically, and the trial proceeded. So did the cross examination of the first witness. Counsel deemed it inadvisable to ask the simple question 'I put it to you that the accused wasn't there', because he thought that was a stupid question and that the witness would, as the Bible says, answer a fool according to his folly. Accordingly he probed a little, seeking either to draw the witness into a contradiction or to close up some escape routes in the methods previously described. To his surprise, the third and most profound in the case, the witness commenced to give evidence inconsistent with that given at the preparatory examination. In a short time the evidence of this gentleman was demolished. That left two more eyewitnesses, but with these counsel wasted no time on the mitigatory points — which indeed had already been established if needed. He proceeded straight to the point of identification and, within a short time, there were three descriptions of the perpetrator and the deed, all so utterly irreconcilable that the accused was not even put on his defence.

Not for a moment do I venture to suggest that the accused was as innocent of this crime as a babe unborn. The truth will forever remain locked in the conscience of one person only, and will die with him. What I do suggest is that counsel erred in presuming to judge guilt of his client, even though three eyewitnesses said upon oath 'I saw the accused stab the deceased to death and run away'. The lesson to be learned from this is that you are there to fight the case on the facts your client presents to you.

It is not your function actually to pronounce upon the guilt of your client. Equally it is not your function mentally to judge of his guilt or innocence. Just as, emotionally, you should not make his case yours, no less should you abstain from condemning him in your own mind. In the jargon of the American underworld, you are his 'mouthpiece'; sometimes a little less in that you may not be able to say what he tells you, sometimes a little more in that, unlike the ordinary mouthpiece, you are to superimpose skill and technique upon his utterances.

Where you are a little less than a mouthpiece it is because your client has said a little more than he ought.[12] Where he confesses his guilt the scope for defending him is drastically curtailed. The first limitation is that you may not call your client as a witness to testify as to his innocence or, I would remark, even to say anything inconsistent with what he has told you. This is an instance of your duty to the court overriding your duty to your client. The second limitation is felt in the cross-examination of witnesses because you may not suggest to them anything inconsistent with what your client has told you

---

[12] But see *S v Moseli* (1) 1969 (1) SA 546 (O).

though you may cross-examine on credibility. If I might essay a crude example I would take the same case described in this section and assume that instead of raising an alibi the accused said 'I stabbed him, but you just have to get me off,' counsel would not be entitled, in cross-examination, to say to a witness:

'I put it to you that the accused did not stab the deceased.'

He would, however, be entitled to cross-examine the witness as to the conditions of visibility, the number of people present, everybody's particular state of intoxication and excitement, as well as the witness's own opportunity of observation. Then, I venture to suggest, it would not be impermissible to put the following question or an appropriate variant:

'How, then, can you possibly say who stabbed the deceased?'

I was once placed in a similar situation. My client, during consultation, admitted that he was at the murder scene that night driving his car. He was adamant however that he was alone. A witness testified that a car similar to that of my client entered the premises the particular night. The evidence was further that apart from the driver, who was not identified, there was a passenger in the car. I was entitled to put it to the witness that my client never entered the premises accompanied by another person.

In argument, similarly, it could be submitted that although the accused might have done the deed, yet, on the evidence, it could equally have been the act of someone else and that the accused should be given the benefit of the doubt. The judge might then say to you: 'Mr Brown, if the accused did not do so, why didn't he go into the witness-box and tell us this?'

This, of course, is a very difficult question to escape and one which the court might be entitled to put to you. Yet it should be sufficient response to say: 'M'Lord, the onus is on the state. If the evidence for the state leaves the matter in doubt then the accused is entitled to the benefit of that doubt and there is no onus upon him to say anything in order to obtain that benefit.'

However, in all cases where your client has made a rash confession to you, you should carefully explain the limitations imposed upon your own conduct of his case. He should also be informed that such limitations would not apply were he to brief other counsel and refrain from making a similar confession to him. It is then for him to decide whether he thinks that his inventive faculty will provide him with an answer to the charge.

Where your client elects to continue to repose his trust in you there is a further aspect to his defence. You may well assume that miracles will not happen, that the prosecutor will not fail to prove an element of his case, that the state witnesses will not contradict each other (for are they and your client not *ad idem* already?) and that a conviction is a very strong probability. In this case the final picture depends in large measure upon the angle of the lighting. Your client may stand out in bold relief or he may be lost in such an intricacy of light and shade that the court must be impelled rather to condemn the harshness of fate in selecting him as its sacrificial offering. The chiaroscuro of circumstance and causation is no creature of chance. Neglected, it may be lost and the whole background may blend into nothingness with one promontory — your client. It is your task to create that chiaroscuro. It is a task that commences when, having confessed to you, your client desires you still to defend him. Perhaps, however, the generalised suggestions which I can offer as a guide will better be gleaned from the sections which follow, particularly those dealing with consultations, pleading guilty and admissions, cross-examination, argument and mitigation. Of all these I regard consultation as paramount.

19.4 CONSULTATION

19.4.1 Consulting criminally, generally

Counsel's preparation starts before the consultation. Before a consultation is arranged counsel must insist on a brief that contains full particulars of the charge (in the lower courts) or the indictment (in the High Court), copies of all the statements in the police docket as well as the documentary evidence. As a general rule the defence is entitled to these documents.[13] Counsel must study these documents in preparation for the consultation. As a junior counsel with little or no experience I found it a salutary practice (and as a silk with much more experience I still cling to this habit) to compile a strategic plan. My strategic plan is the basis on which I conduct the trial. The strategic plan contains a definition of the crime(s) levelled against the accused by the state, so that the elements of the crime are always available to me. The relevant case law must be studied and a reference to the leading judgments on each of the elements is noted. The same applies *mutatis mutandis* where statutory crimes are involved. The elements of the crime are gleaned from the relevant statutory provision that was contravened. It is of the greatest of importance to study the relevant case law in order to ascertain the interpretation given to the section by the relevant judgments.

Counsel's moment of truth, if I may be pardoned that journalistic cliché, comes when his instructing attorney and the client sit opposite him at his desk. With his homework done counsel will feel comfortable and ready to set about the business of defence. To a large degree the result will be affected by the conduct of the consultation.

It is a very simple matter to take pen and paper and to write down what your client says. The attorney can do this too, with as little effort and probably with more imagination. Counsel's task is far more complex than that. If counsel has been briefed, it is because he is deemed to be a specialist in the field of defence. He should approach the case with the knowledge, skill and thoroughness of a specialist. He thus conducts his consultation according to a system, with definitive objectives in view. These objects are already tabled in the strategic

---

[13] *Shabalala and Others v Attorney-General of Transvaal and Another* 1996 (1) SA 725 (CC), 1995 (2) SACR 761 (CC).

plan[14] and during consultation the need may arise to amplify or change your strategic plan ie, the defence is an alibi or necessity, etc. Of course, then you will as soon as possible study the relevant case law on these topics. It is not, positively not, one of those objectives to ascertain whether your client is guilty.

19.4.2 Six suggestions

Your investigations will be shaped to one or more of the following ends, bearing in mind that you have already ascertained the case against your client:

- to ascertain what statements or admissions your client has made;
- to ascertain your client's defence;
- to ascertain what factors bear upon the conduct of the defence;
- to ascertain what factors must be established in order to paint the best possible picture of your client in the event of a conviction;
- to examine the difficulties in your client's case;
- to be careful about asking tactless questions.

The first problem, obviously, is to reconcile the case against your client and your client's defence. If you say to your client: 'Tell me what happened', he may well reply: 'The police arrested me but I don't know what it is all about.' That's fine, because you then proceed on the lines I have mentioned. However, the reply may be 'Well, these two chaps came with ten diamond rings which they said they had swiped from some jeweller-chap and they said we could split it fifty-fifty if I would sell them.' This story can be told with any degree of colloquialism and in a wide variety of accents. It immediately creates the problem of defending the client who has confessed to you. Perhaps, then, it would be well to take the above topics in turn and to offer brief suggestions on each.

19.4.3 Ascertain what statements or admissions your client has made

A technique employed some years ago by one of the outstanding criminal lawyers of his time seems to be remarkably simple and effective. He would ask his client 'tell me, what do the police say happened?' This would enable the client to give a fair picture of the case against him without committing himself to a confession. It may not always be necessary to go as far as this because in many cases the charge will speak for itself or can be made to speak a little more plainly by means of a request for further particulars. One way or another, however, you must find out precisely what case your client has to meet.

I have already commented, with sadness, on the loquacity of clients when arrested or interrogated. You should have a healthy respect for the police force, both as detectives and as psychologists. Seldom does a client consult his lawyer before the police approach him and invite him to 'assist' or 'explain' or to 'make

---

[14] See chapter 4, where one's approach to cases in general, and extracting the essence of cases in particular, was discussed.

a statement'. If he did take a wise preliminary step he would no doubt be advised to say nothing and sign nothing. It is thus your business to find out how much damage your client has done, and on this point there is no need to be so afraid of tactless questions. You should investigate every occasion on which your client met or spoke to a member of the police force between the date of the offence and the consultation with yourself. You need memorise precisely two simple questions, no less and (whatever you do) no more. The questions are:

> 'What did he say?'
> 'What did you say?'

You repeat these questions as often as the occasion demands. Do not, at this stage, start your own private cross-examination with questions such as:

> 'Why did you say that?'
> 'Why didn't you tell him such-and-such?'

True enough, you may have to investigate these matters, but your function is to ascertain and not to demolish. At this stage, therefore, you classify these latter questions as 'stupid'.

19.4.4 Ascertaining your client's defence

From this preliminary investigation you have sufficient to appreciate your client's difficulties. You therefore invite him to tell you his defence. Sometimes he will invite you to tell him. In most cases you could do a lot better than him. In all cases you will decline.

It may be well, before extending your invitation, to point out to your client the manner in which you will be handicapped should he elect to admit his guilt. However, the decision must be his, for you have no interest in influencing him to adopt any particular line of defence.

Let us pause here, for this is an important aspect of your practice, requiring some degree of skill and a great degree of care. Some cases are simple, so simple that you could go into court after a ten-minute talk with your client. Others, such as fraud charges, have some complexity and require consultations extending over days.

It is not enough to say: 'Tell me all about it' and to switch on your tape recorder. No client, unless he has a string of previous convictions, can really appreciate what is important and what is not. As a result he often omits matter which is relevant and significant. Nor will he necessarily remember all the details of his story if allowed to tell it in his own fashion. In short, as each sentence is noted or recorded, you are testing it, weighing it, looking for both causation and consequence, and considering its probability or improbability. All of these considerations may have to be discussed before you proceed to the next event in the chronology. Most important of all is to watch for omission of some intermediate fact. This may be due to a 'screening' process — conscious or subconscious — by your client. Not for the sake of idle curiosity alone will you ask about the missing factor. These unconsidered trifles have the habit of turning up at disconcerting moments during cross-examination of your client, usually under the title of 'Why wasn't this put to the state witnesses?' Coupled with a sub-title of 'Your counsel can't be quite the fool he looks, so you must be a liar?' Of course when the prosecutor asks: 'Did you tell this to your counsel?' you will object. The objection will be upheld, but the damage is absolutely unavoidable.

If I dilate at inordinate length on this topic it is in an attempt to make one point of such significance that in years to come you may even forgive me. The point is that nothing must be allowed to come as a surprise to you.

The ascertainment of the identity of state witnesses is made simple by the fact that you are in possession of their statements. Where the evidence of a state witness differs from the defence version a question along the following lines can be asked: 'Why would he falsely implicate you?' The purpose of this inquiry is a continuation of your ascertainment of the state case, and also to assist in the preparation of cross-examination. The matter requires to be developed by investigation of the circumstances pertaining to each potential witness, both from the personal aspect and also as a witness. By 'personal aspect' I mean all circumstances extraneous to his evidence which might be used in cross-examination to attack his evidence on grounds of credibility, bias and so on. These will include, in appropriate cases, points such as opportunity for observation and other material bearing on the acceptance or rejection of his story.

Factors affecting the case or bearing upon the conduct of the defence are infinitely variable. Your purpose is to avoid being taken by surprise at the trial. The pleadings (the summons, charge or indictment as well as the list of substantial facts) will be as cryptic as the prosecutor can make them and as the law allows. Litigation, we are often told by the courts, is not a game of chance and it seems to be the purpose of the civil Uniform Rules of Court to eliminate the element of surprise. The Act does not reflect any comparable tendency, and without thorough preliminary investigation you may be unprepared to meet some or other aspect of the state case.

The importance of consultations and investigation cannot be over-emphasised. They are the very foundation of the proper conduct of criminal cases.

It is at this stage that you weigh up every aspect of your client's statement, investigating further what may be obscure and asking yourself the implications of particular topics or points. Each topic or point may then call for more detailed discussion in greater or lesser degree.

At this stage, too, you commence to consider your client's previous incautious utterances and the effect of what he said or did not say. Since you are not cross-examining him, it may be wiser to point out to him that what he said (or did not say) raises problems in the light, say, of the defence now raised in consultation.

If there is an inconsistency between what was said to the police and what is now raised as the defence, that inconsistency must be examined and explained else it will founder the whole defence, for few courts are inclined to overlook such inconsistencies. While, it is true, an accused person is at present under no obligation to speak when he is interrogated or charged, if he does talk, he may in cross-examination be asked to explain any omission which later becomes apparent as a result of the conduct of his defence. In other words, if he does speak, he may legitimately be expected to speak fully and anything added later can euphemistically be used against him in a court of law.

When your client's attention is directed to considerations of this nature he will no doubt ask you:

> 'What shall I say if the prosecutor asks me this in cross-examination?'

While you may well discuss the implications of any particular answer, you should carefully avoid suggesting how your client could meet the difficulty. Apart from the ethical considerations there are a few pragmatic problems:

If your client relies upon counsel's suggestion and not his own knowledge, he will possibly remember only a portion of that suggestion. The prosecutor may, then, in cross-examination, adopt the technique previously discussed in chapter 12 under the heading of 'The Half-truth', with disastrous results — for you. Inevitably there will be factors unknown to you and of which your suggestion does not take cognisance. Keep your ingenuity then for better causes. If you need further argument on this theme, ask yourself how, when your suggested answer is further tested in cross-examination, your client will fare in explaining, say, 'his' mental processes on which that answer is based.

19.4.5 Consulting in the presence of others

A further point in regard to consultation with your client is that, throughout, you will be vigilant in your watch for witnesses whose words will add weight to his own.

From this it seems logical to consider the question of consulting with the supporting witnesses. Generally speaking, your methods and objectives are the same as those mentioned previously. There is, however, one vital cautionary rule and there is one modification. As a cautionary rule I would advise that you should not consult with your client in the presence of his supporting witnesses, and *vice versa*. While legal professional privilege attaches as between yourself and your client, it does not extend to outsiders who are at the consultation. This includes witnesses and, in fact, all who attend the consultation otherwise than in the exercise of a duty, such as a stenographer, an interpreter or the legal representatives. Consequently, not only should you generally consult with witnesses out of the presence of your client, but you should be careful about what you disclose to them with regard to the defence of your client, if you disclose anything to them at all, lest they blurt anything out in the witness-box.

For the modification, fortunately, my suggestions proceed in the direction of relaxation. I say, therefore, that you need not tread so warily, nor need you fear the consequences of tactlessness. Indeed, the more tactless you are the better you can judge whether the witness is an ally or a Trojan horse. Ask him anything or everything; you then have a measure of his potential for damage if he is called by the defence. But do not allow yourself to be misled by an apparent strength and confidence or a manifest pusillanimity on his part. Particularly by the former, for, as has been remarked before in this context: 'Gym form and ring form are often two very different things.'

19.4.6 Having an eye on possible mitigation

During the course of the trial you will, in cross-examining the state witnesses, have an eye to a possible finding of guilty, and will try to establish facts which reduce the gravity of the offence or which mitigate the guilt of your client. Of course, you will tread softly, because the average judicial officer is by no means insensitive to the atmosphere of the case and must not be allowed to think that your sole objective is to reduce the severity of the sentence. The facts which you will try to establish, however, as I have tritely remarked in other contexts, vary infinitely and cannot even be analysed into categories. In this regard, you share my own difficulty. I cannot tell you what those facts are. Nor do you know what they may be in any particular type of case. That means that only your client can tell you.

Next problem on the list, therefore, is how to elicit these facts from your client so that you have at least some idea of where you are going. Before you set about the process, however, you should spare at least a passing glance for the following topic, dealing with tactless questions. Having done this, you can ask your client a few questions. It may be found most useful, in this context, sometimes to put aside any discussion of the merits of the case entirely. Ask him about himself, his family, background, history, employment and problems. If, out of all this, you are unable to find some line that will warrant exploration then either there is nothing to be said for your client or else you should stick to opinions and pleadings.

By this time you know what the case against your client will be; you know his defence; you know the human being who is involved in the conflict. Here, then, you apply your client's personality to the state case, and you should be able to judge how far you may safely go in asking your client questions on this topic.

19.4.7 Preparing your client to testify, and for the decision as to whether he will testify

It will be necessary to prepare your client for the ordeal in the witness-box. The word 'prepare' must not be misunderstood because, as was pointed out earlier on, the intention is to convey to your client the problems that may arise and not to tell him how to answer them.

The first question that must be considered, but not necessarily decided, is whether your client will in fact give evidence at all. The final decision can only be made after the close of the state case. Naturally, you are well aware of the authorities on the effect of the failure of the accused to answer the state case. In this regard there is a distinction between direct evidence implicating the accused in the commission of the crime and circumstantial evidence. In *S v Chabalala* [15] it was held:

> The appellant was faced with direct and apparently credible evidence which made him the prime mover in the offence. He was also called on to answer evidence of a similar nature relating to the parade. Both attacks were those of a single witness and capable of being neutralised by an honest rebuttal. There can be no acceptable explanation for him not rising to the challenge. If he was innocent appellant must have ascertained his own whereabouts and activities on 29 May and been able to vouch for his non-participation. He was also readily able to confirm that the complainant indeed placed his hand on someone else's shoulder. To have remained silent in the face of the evidence was damning. He thereby left the *prima facie* case to speak for itself. One is bound to conclude that the totality of the evidence taken in conjunction with his silence excluded any reasonable doubt about his guilt.

The reasoning is somewhat different where the accused is confronted only with circumstantial evidence. In *S v Parrow* Holmes JA stated the approach as follows:[16]

> I pause here to refer briefly to the so-called doctrine of recent possession of stolen property. In so far as here relevant, it usually takes this form: On proof of possession by the accused of recently stolen property, the Court may (not must) convict him of theft in the absence of an innocent explanation which might reasonably be true. This is an epigrammatic way of saying that the Court should think its way through the totality of the facts of each particular case, and must acquit the accused unless it can infer, as the only reasonable inference, that he stole the property. (Whether the further inference can be drawn that he broke into the premises is a charge such as the present one, will depend on the circumstances). The onus of proof remains on the state throughout. Hence, even if, after the closing of the cases for the state and the defence, it is inferentially probable that the accused stole the property, he must be acquitted unless the only reasonable inference is that he did so; for the law demands proof beyond reasonable doubt.

We seem to have progressed a long way over the centuries, from the position where the accused was not competent to testify in his defence, to the position — or so it might seem-where, if he does not, he might as well plead guilty. Nevertheless in every case you must debate with the accused the desirability or necessity of his entering the witness-box. You need not, of course, be as cynical as I have been, but your client must be made to realise the consequences of failing to testify. In this regard you can only advise your client what to do-the final decision remains with him.

It is not an unreasonable assumption to make that your client will not be a good witness. In fact, he may be a very bad witness. Yet that is his problem, not yours. If he wishes to give evidence, it is my view that you should not dissuade him. I have already discussed one aspect of this topic in paragraph 2.5 above, so I refer again to that paragraph and the cases cited. If your client does not wish to

---

[15] 2003 (3) SACR 134 (SCA) para 21. See too *S v Boesak* 2001 (1) SA 912 (CC), 2001 (1) SACR 1 (CC).
[16] 1973 (1) SA 603 (AD) at 604.

testify, again, he probably has a very good reason for this attitude. It might be well cautiously to investigate those reasons and, at the same time, point out the limitations that will be placed on cross-examination of the state witnesses and on argument should he not enter the witness-box. I have known cases where counsel has asked for written instructions when told that the client does not wish to testify.

19.4.8 Examining the difficulties in your client's case

Let us assume, however, that the client wishes to testify or, at least, that no final decision is to be made until the end of the state case. It now becomes necessary to consider what difficulties will arise in the defence case which may call for explanation under cross-examination. I have already partially described the process in paragraph 19.3 above. Now it must be taken further. When you find a difficulty, or an inconsistency, it must be put to your client.

I think that it is not improper to say, for example: 'Well, you say XYZ. Now if that is so the prosecutor will put to you ABCD because that does not seem to be consistent with XYZ. If he does this what is your answer?' Nor does it appear wrong, when your client says that the answer is KLMN, to point out that the answer is unsatisfactory, because, for example, K contains A or B or C or more than one of them.

This is what I mean by 'preparing' your client for cross-examination. In the process, you prepare yourself, because you recognise the problems and you prepare to meet them, either in argument, or by the exercise of restraint and caution in the cross-examination of the state witnesses. The latter technique, if you are lucky, may result in the problem being completely overlooked by the prosecutor when the client does in fact give evidence. Usually this is the best course; I repeat that anything your client can do, you can do better — with particular reference to the ill-considered utterance. Therefore, if you can divert attention from a problem and avoid arousing it, so much the better. If you don't anticipate it, you have neglected your consultation.

It is no part of your function to provide answers, explanations or reconciliations. In effect you will conduct a cross-examination of your client at this stage, not with the object of coaching him in the answers to be given later — because he wouldn't remember them anyway — but to find out whether there are answers and to give your client time to think over the explanations tendered. On this latter basis it might be advisable in fact to give him time to reflect on his answers by adjourning the consultation to another day. Always remember that there is nothing in the book to say that you are limited to one consultation.

Do not forget that, in terms of s 335 of the Act, your client is entitled to a copy of any written statement he may have made to the police. Get this and subject it to the treatment I have suggested.

19.4.9 Do not ask tactless questions

I have already, in paragraph 19.3 above, indicated what the consequences of tactless questions may be. Perhaps, then, I could again attempt an epigram to convey my meaning: in a civil case you must be told everything; in a criminal case you must know everything but be told only what is good for you.

Your knowledge of everything will come from many sources. You may get pieces of the jigsaw puzzle from defence witnesses. You may draw shrewd deductions from comparing the statements of the state witnesses (which your will have read on receipt of the docket contents) with your client's version. With this knowledge behind you, you must judge what questions may safely be put to your client in consultation. As a rough and ready guide you can, moreover, take a tactless question to be one which might cause your client to make a confession of his guilt or to make a statement inconsistent with his defence. This is not pure sophistry, neither is it cynical sophistry. Every accused person is, as a matter of public policy I would suggest, entitled to defend himself against a criminal charge. If an accused is entitled to defend himself he should be in no worse position because he has engaged an expert to do it. To some extent he is in a worse position because he may defend himself untrammelled by a secret knowledge of his own guilt. If he is defended by an expert the latter's code of conduct will not allow him that degree of freedom of action which the client enjoys. The expert, therefore, must maintain the fullest possible freedom of action by not seeking the key to his client's conscience.

You are the expert. It might also be added that if you cannot learn how to avoid asking your client tactless questions then you may not be able to avoid asking such questions of witnesses.

I remember an incident when an attorney was defending an accused person. That attorney was one of the most skilled and devastating exponents of the art of cross-examination. The cross-examination of one of the state witnesses had proceeded, and very effectively at that. When the attorney sat down the magistrate who was trying the case looked puzzled. He paused for a few moments and looked at the attorney. He then turned to the witness and asked a question, a significant question let it be remarked, receiving an answer completely favourable to the accused. The attorney then rose to his feet and said:

'Thank you, your Worship, that is the question I was afraid to ask.'

That was the truth. A man of his ability would not overlook a vital question. Yet the answer was uncertain and, if unfavourable, could have done the client harm. It was more profitable, therefore to maintain a tactful silence and rely upon what success had already been achieved.

I am well aware that this illustration is out of context. It made a profound impression on me at the time and I include it now, rather than later, because the message it carries is as applicable at this stage as at the stage of cross-examination.

19.5 PREPARATION

19.5.1 Criminal preparation, generally

In the main, preparation for a criminal case differs very little from preparation for a civil trial. The first essential is a thorough acquaintance with the facts. Your brief should therefore contain copies of all the statements filed in part A of the police docket (statements of all the state witnesses), part B (copies of all the documentary evidence in possession of the state), and the indictment (in the High Court) or charges (in the lower court) preferred against your client. The indictment will include amongst others a list of the names of the state witnesses. I find it prudent to refer in more detail to the judgment in *Shabalala*[17] where the court made the following order:

A. 1. The 'blanket docket privilege' expressed by the rule in *R v Steyn* 1954 (1) SA 324 (A) is inconsistent with the Constitution to the extent to which it protects from disclosure all the documents in a police docket, in all circumstances, regardless as to whether or not such disclosure is justified for the purposes of enabling the accused properly to exercise his or her right to a fair trial in terms of s 25(3).

2. The claim of the accused for access to documents in the police docket cannot be defeated merely on the grounds that such contents are protected by a blanket privilege in terms of the decision in *Steyn's* case.

3. Ordinarily an accused person should be entitled to have access to documents in the police docket which are exculpatory (or which are prima facie likely to be helpful to the defence) unless, in very rare cases, the State is able to justify the refusal of such access on the grounds that it is not justified for the purposes of a fair trial.

4. Ordinarily the right to a fair trial would include access to the statements of witnesses (whether or not the State intends to call such witnesses) and such of the contents of a police docket as are relevant in order to enable an accused person properly to exercise that right, but the prosecution may, in a particular case, be able to justify the denial of such access on the grounds that it is not justified for the purposes of a fair trial. This would depend on the circumstances of each case.

5. The State is entitled to resist a claim by the accused for access to any particular document in the police docket on the grounds that such access is not justified for the purposes of enabling the accused properly to exercise his or her right to a fair trial or on the ground that it has reason to believe that there is a reasonable risk that access to the relevant document would lead to the disclosure of the identity of an informer or State secrets or on the grounds that there was a reasonable risk that such disclosure might lead to the intimidation of witnesses or otherwise prejudice the proper ends of justice.

6. Even where the State has satisfied the Court that the denial of access to the relevant documents is justified on the grounds set out in paragraph 5 hereof, it does not follow that access to such statements,

---

[17] *Shabalala and Others v Attorney-General of Transvaal and Another* 1996 (1) SA 725 (CC) at 790.

either then or subsequently must necessarily be denied to the accused. The Court still retains a discretion. It should balance the degree of risk involved in attracting the potential prejudicial consequences for the proper ends of justice referred to in paragraph 5 (if such access is permitted) against the degree of the risk that a fair trial may not enure for the accused (if such access is denied). A ruling by the Court pursuant to this paragraph shall be an interlocutory ruling subject to further amendment, review or recall in the light of circumstances disclosed by the further course of the trial.

B. 1. Insofar and to the extent that the rule of practice pertaining to the right of an accused or his legal representative to consult with witnesses for the State prohibits such consultation without the permission of the prosecuting authority, in all cases and regardless of the circumstances, it is not consistent with the Constitution.

2. An accused person has a right to consult a State witness without prior permission of the prosecuting authority in circumstances where his or her right to a fair trial would be impaired, if, on the special facts of a particular case, the accused cannot properly obtain a fair trial without such consultation.

3. The accused or his or her legal representative should in such circumstances approach the Attorney-General or an official authorised by the Attorney-General for consent to hold such consultation. If such consent is granted the Attorney-General or such official shall be entitled to be present at such consultation and to record what transpires during the consultation. If the consent of the Attorney-General is refused the accused shall be entitled to approach the Court for such permission to consult the relevant witness.

4. The right referred to in paragraph 2 does not entitle an accused person to compel such consultation with a State witness: —
   (a) if such State witness declines to be so consulted; or
   (b) if it is established on behalf of the State that it has reasonable grounds to believe such consultation might lead to the intimidation of the witness or a tampering with his or her evidence or that it might lead to the disclosure of State secrets or the identity of informers or that it might otherwise prejudice the proper ends of justice.

5. Even in the circumstances referred to in paragraph 4(b), the Court may, in the circumstances of a particular case, exercise a discretion to permit such consultation in the interest of justice subject to suitable safeguards.

The onus resting on the state to make proper discovery was reiterated in *Crossberg v S.*[18]

---

[18] *Crossberg v S* 2008 (2) SACR 317 (SCA).

You will now have a good idea of the potential witnesses and a method of approach for each witness. To achieve this I suggest that during consultation your enquiry should develop along the following lines: 'Do you know witness A? He says . . . . Why would he falsely implicate you?' The list is not exhaustive and your questions would differ according to the factual dispute, eg, where identity is in dispute you will investigate in detail how your client was dressed, any facial characteristics and compare this with any descriptions given by the witness.

In many criminal cases there is a further aspect of preparation to which you might profitably direct your attention. In this highly civilised society of ours crime is no longer necessarily something that hurts your neighbour. It would be laughable indeed to compare the Ten Commandments with the statute law of any self-respecting society. And when we throw in rules, regulations, proclamations, ordinances and by-laws for good measure, we have a welter of precept the comprehension of which, let alone its recollection, is well nigh impossible. When, therefore, your client's sins lie in the contravention of one of these enactments, it is essential to have a look at the enactment itself. There are two good reasons for this:

Firstly, it is well to know what the case is all about. Not only will you know when — if ever — the state fails to prove one of the elements of the crime (you will know this from the information contained in your strategic plan) but also you will in some exceptional cases find that, unhappily, the onus is cast upon the accused to prove his innocence.[19] In such a case you should have a sound knowledge of the judgments of the Constitutional Court (and other courts) regarding presumptions. Where a statutory enactment places a true reverse onus on the accused, such a presumption is unconstitutional.[20] Before a presumption is unconstitutional, it must be such that it is inconsistent with the presumption of innocence in that a true reverse onus is placed on the accused to prove his innocence. As part of this aspect of the matter I would remark that it is necessary to study not only the regulation or section under which your client is charged, but also the whole of the regulations and the enabling statute. It is not uncommon for a statute to provide for the proof of the offence or certain essential elements thereof by means of presumptions. As part of your preparation you should study the constitutionality of the presumption. If you don't and the presumption is not unconstitutional and you are unaware of the presumption you may be embarrassed, and your client may be prejudiced for want of rebuttal of something that you thought the State was obliged to prove but had not.

Secondly, a close study of the relative enactments, principal or subsidiary,

---

[19] That would usually be upon a balance of probabilities. See *Ex parte Minister of Justice: In re R v Bolon* 1941 AD 345 and the numerous annotations thereto. Such cases will in the present dispensation be very rare indeed.

[20] *S v Manamela and Another (Director-General of Justice intervening)* 2000 (3) SA 1 (CC) and the noter-up thereon, which abounds with examples.

may afford a legal defence such as *ultra vires*. From which you turn to study authorities on that topic, sadly to find that what seemed so clear becomes somewhat opaque when you try to ascertain and apply the tests laid down by the courts.

No small part of preparation is to take the latest copy of one of the standard textbooks on criminal law and reread the chapter in which your type of case is discussed. Find a few of the relevant decisions, read a few of the annotations, and never neglect the odd moment of introspection of which was referred to in chapter 4. From the reported cases you will learn many lessons; from your introspection you will find how to follow them.

It will probably be only later in your career that you will have cause to consider my next topic, by which time you will probably know more about the technique than I can offer. However, from time to time there will be cases in which the decision will depend upon matters such as ballistics, graphology, toxicology or some other obscure science. I have already dealt with the cross-examination of expert witnesses. I repeat that, if there is to be a decisive — or important — issue based on expert evidence, you must be as much a master of the topic as the witness who will be put up against you. You must recognise that scientific investigation and scientific criminal investigation have improved enormously in South Africa and you will probably not have the good fortune to meet an expert who claims to have measured a distance of one ten-thousandth of an inch 'with my eye'.

Your preparation will consist in a study of the relevant textbooks on firearms, questioned documents or whatever your problem may be. You might also look for biographies or autobiographies which contain accounts of similar cases. I would suggest that the textbooks on cross-examination would help, but you should be on your guard against assuming that experts are all as stupid as is suggested in some of the 'classics' on the topic.

At the earlier stage of your career your may find yourself involved— professionally only, I hope — in cases of negligent driving, or of driving under the influence of alcohol. Now, in these cases you may meet two classes of expert witnesses — those who deal with motorcars and those who deal with persons. The trouble, it seems, arises when the motorcars are not kept away from the persons, or rather vice versa. Since you may expect quite a few of these cases, it is worth your while to acquire at least a background of the technical knowledge on which they are to be approached. What I mean is that you should make a study of motorcars as mechanical objects and driving as a science. Most people drive — or fondly believe they drive — without much knowledge of what makes a car go, much less what makes it stop. From a lawyer's point of view braking, steering and lighting systems merit particular study. The other aspect, the personal, is dealt with in the textbooks on medical jurisprudence. One way of dealing with questions of intoxication is to make an appointment with an expert in the field (usually a physician), and to discuss your problems with him so that you can gain a better understanding of the issues. A few discussions with your more experienced colleagues will also teach you how to set about the preparation of your cross-examination of the policeman, the indignant citizen and the district surgeon.

At this stage you finalise your tactical plan that goes hand-in-hand with your strategic plan. Your tactical plan will include topics such as the names of the witnesses that should be called on behalf of the defence and the tenor of their evidence as well as that of the state witnesses, what is in dispute and topics (not questions) which should be addressed during cross-examination in order to get the defence version accepted at the end of the day. The list is not exhaustive and each case will present its own tactical plan. As an example, where the defence is an alibi and identity is in dispute you will from your strategic plan know what questions should be put during cross-examination in order to destroy the reliability of such identification.[21] This you will get after a study of the judgments pertaining to identity. The same applies to the cautionary rules if applicable.

19.5.2 Preparing witnesses

I have already dealt with this to some extent in paragraph 19.4 above.

At the outset you must remember that the court was not there. It is your primary function to place the defence version coherently and chronologically before the Court. Consider yourself as the director of the film, the witness as the actor, the facts as the script, and the court as the audience. From this it logically follows that you must direct and control the flow of the evidence. I interpose to remark that confidence boosts confidence: self-assuredness boosts self-assuredness. Remember your witness looks up to you — your behaviour influences his testimony.

At the outset the witness must be told to always tell the truth, to take his time to answer a question especially during cross-examination, to make sure the question is understood and if unsure ask that the question be repeated, to only answer the question and not to volunteer facts, to use plain language, not to lose his temper and lastly not to improvise or guess — if he does not know the answer he says so or that he cannot remember. It is also important that you tell the witness not to argue with the cross-examiner and to make and keep eye contact with the court. I prefer that my witnesses stand whilst testifying and that they are properly dressed. The former is a matter of personal preference. The latter is non-negotiable.

Then follows the next phase. At this stage you as legal representative of the accused have already consulted with the accused and potential witnesses, and your trial plan is at hand. Each witness must then be prepared for his testimony. The witness must know the chronological order in which his testimony will be presented. It is essential that the witness is *au fait* with the facts that he has to testify about, and in what form the questions will be put and how to react to a question. Then the court situation should be simulated and the witness must be

---

[21] See for example *R v Mputing* 1960 (1) SA 785 (T) and *S v Mehlape* 1963 (2) SA 29 (A).

taken through his evidence with due regard to the basic principles of how to conduct examination in chief. Possible problem areas, ie, previous inconsistent statements, family ties, improbabilities in the version of the witness, etc. must be addressed and explained.

19.6 SEPARATE TRIALS

If fortune makes strange bedfellows, crime makes uncomfortable ones. The camaraderie that prevailed at the time of the (alleged) offence wears thin with the passing of time and the loquacity of the less resolute of the (alleged) wrongdoers. Solace may be sought in the judicial separation authorised in terms of s 157(2) of the Act. Although this section provides that a court may, on application of the prosecutor or any of the accused, direct separate trials of persons who are charged jointly, it is in practice not with any degree of alacrity that the courts will exercise these powers.

If your client's co-accused has become an incubus you may decide to make the application. If he may become a chink in the armour you should start to consider how to get rid of him.

You will, or course, refer to the reported cases, to find out where you are going and how, and also to learn what problems will arise.

No doubt, as Van den Heever JA expressed it in *R v Bagas*,[22]

> It is expedient that persons charged with the same offence should be tried together.

But your concern is not expediency. You have only one purpose in mind: the defence of your client, to the point of acquittal if possible. Thus, whenever your client's co-accused is an existing or potential threat, you should consider an application for a separation of trials. Thus the *Mallalieu* case,[23] a *cause celebre* in its time, affords a diverting exercise in speculation as to how the verdict would have gone had the court not (quite rightly) ordered a separation of trials and had it not (not so rightly) ordered that the case of the male of the pairing Mr Mallalieu, should be heard first. Miss Tolputt's alleged confession might well have prejudiced *Mallalieu* in the minds of the jurors. In *Kritzinger's* case, however, it was suggested that where the court refuses a separation of trials because the prejudice to the State would outweigh the prejudice to the accused, it should 'avoid the possibility of prejudice to the accused' by careful explanation to the jury as to how the evidence can be used.[24] Without a jury the problem is purely psychological.

As a starting point you can consider the judgment in *S v Ntuli and Others*:[25]

> Now s 155 (now s 157(2)) of the Code endows the trial Court with a discretion to direct, if it thinks fit, that persons jointly charged with the same offence should be tried separately (see *R v Bagas* 1952 (1) SA 437 (A) at 441F; *R v Nzuza and Another*

---

[22] 1952 (1) SA 437 (A) at 441.
[23] *R v Mallalieu & Tolputt* 1932 NPD 80.
[24] *R v Kritzinger* 1952 (4) SA 651 (W), per Ramsbottom J at 654C.
[25] 1987 (2) SA 69 (A) at 72H–73G.

1952 (4) SA 376 (A) at 380A, 381 E). It follows that appellate interference with the exercise of that discretion will only be justified on one of the recognised, restricted grounds, that is that the trial Court committed an irregularity or misdirection of such a kind, or acted so unreasonably or improperly, that its decision was thereby vitiated (cf *Bagas*'s case supra at 441F–H; *Nzuza's* case supra at 380D). And, even if one or more of those grounds is established on appeal, this Court will not set aside the conviction in question unless it is satisfied that a failure of justice has resulted there from (s 369(1) of the Code).

In exercising its discretion the trial Court has to weigh up the likelihood of prejudice to the applicant accused resulting from a joint trial against the likelihood of prejudice to the other accused or the State if their trials are separated, and decide whether or not, in the interests of justice, a separation of trials should be granted. 'Prejudice' there means prejudice in the sense that no injustice should be caused to the party concerned, including the State. (These principles are culled from the cases of *Bagas, Nzuza* (supra) and *R v Heyne* 1956 (3) SA 604 (A) at 630A.) The weight to be given to each of the relevant factors in the adjudication of this issue is for the trial Court to assess in the exercise of its discretion.

Before an application for separation of trials will succeed the applicant must show that he will suffer substantial prejudice.[26] The mere fact that a co-accused made a confession implicating your client would not automatically provide a ground for a separation of trials.[27] Section 219 provides that a confession is only admissible against the person who made the confession.

In *S v Makeba and Another*[28] the court held:

> The use of Mbongqi's confession as corroboration for Skhumbuzo's evidence was a fatal flaw in the assessment of his evidence. Section 219 of the Criminal Procedure Act 51 of 1977 forbids it. That section provides:
>> 'No confession made by any person shall be admissible as evidence against another person.'

Even indirect use of the confession for purposes of corroboration is not permitted. In *Makeba* an accused had made a confession and the trial Court in convicting the other accused had excluded from its consideration the statements in the confession which had directly implicated the other accused, but had used the confession to establish an essential part of the chain of circumstantial evidence leading to their conviction. On appeal it was held that the trial Court had relied on inadmissible evidence and the appeal was allowed. It follows, therefore, that no reliance should have been placed on Mbongqi's confession as corroboration for Skhumbuzo's evidence, either directly or indirectly. That misdirection was fundamental to the credibility finding in favor of Skhumbuzo on which the conviction essentially depended. (It is of course unnecessary in this case to consider the admissibility of a co-accused's

---

[26] *R v Kritzinger* supra fn 23 at 654F.
[27] Section 219; *S v Makeba and Another* 2003 (2) SACR 128 (SCA).
[28] 2003 (2) SACR 128 (SCA) para 14.

extra-curial admission — as opposed to a confession.) This approach received the imprimatur of the Constitutional Court.[29]

In view of the decision in *R v Matsinya*[30] which affirms that the order in which the separated trials are to be heard is a matter to be decided by the Director of Public Prosecutions, you should not lose sight of the possibility that the co-accused may be tried first and called as a witness against your client. Of course, even if the trial proceeds jointly, he may testify in his own defence and so become a witness against your client — or he may not.

On balance I would express the view that wherever a co-accused has made a confession or admission, or where there is a possibility of prejudice to your client for any other reason, you should apply for a separation of trials. The cases in which your decision will be wrong are so few as to be negligible. If your application fails you will have lost nothing. If it succeeds and your client is tried first you will have gained something, for even judges of appeal have expressed doubts as to whether a trial judge can so completely disregard inadmissible evidence of this nature as to avoid any possibility of prejudice.[31] If your application succeeds and the co-accused is tried first, subsequently to be called as a state witness against your client, then at least you will have been provided with some material for cross-examination. In this regard I suggest you refer to my parting words in paragraph 19.1 above.

19.7   THE INDICTMENT, SUMMONS OR CHARGE

Even a criminal case must have pleadings, in order to tell the court what the issues are. The indictment, summons or charge (to which I shall simply refer as *the indictment*) serves also to tell the accused what case he has to meet. You should not be reluctant to use it for that purpose.

Section 87 provides for the delivery of particulars before or at the trial, in any event before evidence has been led. The sooner you obtain particulars, the more expeditiously can you set about the preparation of your case. Usually the prosecutor will furnish further particulars upon the filing of a proper request without waiting for an order of court, which is another reason for not delaying your request. The details which you will seek must vary according to circumstances, but you should always have regard to the provisions of the relevant sections of the Act, which may restrict the degree of particularity to which your client is entitled.

As in civil cases, the object of further particulars is to limit the issues, and not to broaden them perhaps to the extent of obscurity. Thus, in the case of *S v Sadeke*[32] Dowling J said:

> The function of particulars is not to enlarge the issues. These particulars which I have
> read out appear to me to be intended to embrace every possible form of negligence in

[29] *Molimi v S* 2008 (3) SA 608 (CC), 2008 (2) SACR 76 (CC).
[30] 1945 AD 802.
[31] Eg Watermeyer JA in *R v Kohlinfila Qwabe* 1939 AD 255 at 262–3.
[32] 1964 (2) SA 674 (T) at 675–6.

> driving a motor vehicle. And I go so far as to say that no prosecutor, having the record of evidence he intends to lead before him, could in the circumstances of this case *bona fide* have offered the defence those particulars.
>
> The practice to me presents itself as an abuse of process which should be discontinued forthwith; *and particulars should be given with regard to the evidence which is intended to be led.*

The State is bound by the further particulars supplied.

When the question of particulars has been disposed of, or perhaps even without the necessity of asking for particulars, you will turn to consider the formal validity of the indictment. You will ask yourself whether it is open to objection or whether there should be an exception or motion to quash, in which case the appropriate application must be made before the accused pleads.[33] It is in this context that your study and analysis of any relevant statutory provisions becomes important, although there is no reason why such application should not be made in appropriate cases where the indictment charges an offence under common law. Bear in mind, however, that you are obliged to give reasonable notice to the Director of Public Prosecutions or prosecutor of your intention to except or move to quash the charge.[34]

You may find, in the majority of cases, that your victory upon an exception or motion to quash will be Pyrrhic. Usually it will be possible to amend the indictment or to re-indict. However, there will be cases, such as where the provisions upon which the state relies are *ultra vires*, where there is no possibility of reframing the charge, and that will be the end of the matter. In this context you might remember that the validity of a regulation may long have been accepted without challenge — until the first time —and yours may well be that first time.[35]

In terms of s 86 the court can also order an amendment of the charge or indictment. It does not authorise amendments to charges that bring about the substitution of a new charge. The concept of 'amendment' implies a degree of retention of that which is to be changed.[36]

19.8 PLEADING GUILTY AND MAKING ADMISSIONS

The question of whether to allow your client to plead guilty is a vexed one. If he insists on doing so you should hesitate to dissuade him, although the courts have often said that the sentence should not be more severe because the accused has denied his guilt. That means, logically, that he should not be given a more lenient sentence as a reward for having pleaded guilty. On the other hand my own view is that you should never encourage your client to enter such a plea. It is on this point that many practitioners think differently. Perhaps I could

---

[33] Section 85, read with ss 86 and 87.

[34] Section 106(3).

[35] Compare, however, *Commissioner for Inland Revenue v Lazarus' Estate* 1958 (1) SA 311 (A) at 322B.

[36] *S v Kruger en Andere* 1989 (1) SA 785 (A).

illustrate my point by referring to a case — unreported — that occurred some forty years ago or more.

By reason of a series of unhappy and extraneous coincidences the police stopped a motorcar which was proceeding from Johannesburg to Durban. The occupants were all arrested and placed in a police van for conveyance to the police station at the town *en route*. The next step was the discovery in the police van of a paper bag containing lumps of unwrought gold. The senior occupant of the car, who was the head of the family which was travelling therein, was duly charged with the possession of this gold, it being alleged that in fact the paper bag came from his clothing. Bail was arranged and the accused proceeded to consult his attorney. Subsequently the accused appeared before the magistrate of the town in question. What passed between the accused and his attorney is veiled in obscurity, but a plea of guilty was entered on the record. There was an address in mitigation, after formal evidence had been led of the arrest of the accused and the finding of the gold. The accused then found, to his consternation, that not only was a substantial fine imposed, but also his car was forfeited to the State because it had been used as a means of conveyance in the commission of the offence. The fine was paid, the car was retained by the state and the accused returned to Johannesburg, sadder and poorer. He then consulted another attorney who briefed counsel to advise on the matter. By a stroke of good fortune the proceedings were defective, in that the plea of guilty had been uttered not by the accused but by his legal representative. The Supreme Court set aside the proceedings as irregular, and in due course the accused reappeared in the same town, before a different magistrate, on the same charge. This time the plea was one of 'not guilty'. The defence then proceeded to establish that the accused and his companions had been in the custody of a police constable when they were being taken to the police station by van. When they alighted the constable got out of the van first in order to shepherd his flock to the charge office. Only after they had all been locked in the cells was the bag containing the lumps of gold found — on the floor of the van. The constable was unable to say which of the arrested persons, four or five in number, had placed or dropped it on the floor. Thus there was no evidence that the particular accused had ever been in possession of that gold. The result was an acquittal, a refund of the fine and restoration of the car.

Perhaps the accused had confessed his guilt to his first legal representative. We shall never know. I think, however, that the message is plain enough to see and for this reason I counsel against advising your client to plead guilty. By calling on the state to prove its case he has nothing to lose and everything to gain.

If at the end you decide to plead guilty, make sure that the 'act' of the accused which you admit on his behalf falls within the parameters of the offence charged.

On the topic of making admissions I have merely a concise quotation — the underlying reasoning being similar:

> Never make an admission unless it pays you or the point is entirely immaterial. It pays
> you when it dispenses with a witness who might be dangerous.

Should you decide to plead guilty, you should consider utilising the provisions of s 105A, which provides for a sentence agreement that is entered into by the accused and the state. In practice you will approach the representative of the state with the proposal that a sentence agreement be entered into, and a suggestion as to what a just and proper sentence would be having regard to all the relevant facts. This is where you must be realistic because at the end of the day the court's *imprimatur* must be placed on the agreement. If the court does not confirm the agreement you simply withdraw from the agreement and the trial starts *de novo* before another court. Nothing contained in the agreement may be used in the subsequent trial. You also have the choice not to withdraw from the agreement and to proceed with the sentencing process.

19.9 CROSS–EXAMINATION

19.9.1 Cross-examining criminally, generally

The objectives in cross-examination are those which were discussed in chapter 12. The cautionary rules are the same. The manner in which you go to work is the same. The consequences of error, however, are more drastic and it behoves you to tread even more warily. Let me make a few additional suggestions:

* If the witness has not given any evidence adverse to your particular defence think twice before you cross-examine at all. As it has been so succinctly stated:

  > Don't let your client invite you to give the state witness hell just because he is a
  > state witness and therefore a witness against your client.

  It is essential that before accepting or rejecting the invitation to cross-examine a witness, you analyse the testimony of the witness. I suggest that you apply the following analysis:

  ▪ Is there any evidence in the testimony of the witness that corroborates the defence version? If the answer is in the affirmative do not cross-examine the witness on those aspects. You may well find that during cross-examination this version changes to your detriment. The golden rule is that you do not highlight that which is already in your favour.

  ▪ You will be in possession of the statement the witness made to the police. Is there any evidence contained in that statement that corroborates the defence version that was not elicited by the State during examination-in-chief? If the answer is yes then that is an area for cross-examination. From your preparation you will also know whether such facts exist. You have observed the witness during his testimony and if you are satisfied that he is an honest witness try and elicit those facts by adroit cross-examination.

  ▪ Does any part of his evidence contradict any part of the state's case against your client? Leave that unchallenged.

- From the information contained in the witness' statement or the information at your disposal are there facts not elicited during evidence in chief that will contradict the state's version? That is then the area for cross-examination. Elicit those facts.
- Can you destroy the credibility of the witness by showing a conflict between his evidence and more objective evidence or that his evidence is improbable because it conflicts with the probabilities?
- Can the credibility of the witness be destroyed because of the witness's perception, memory or ability to communicate?
- Can the credibility of the witness be destroyed because of a previous inconsistent statement or conduct inconsistent with his evidence?
- Can the credibility of the witness be destroyed by reason of interest, bias or bad character?
- A proper preparation would enable you to immediately recognise whether or not the evidence establishes the jurisdictional pillars on which a conviction can follow for the particular crime, eg, was the accused legally found 'in possession',[37] did the witness lay a foundation for the admissibility of a confession,[38] etc. If the evidence does not, leave this aspect for argument. If the evidence does, try and destroy the credence of this evidence during cross-examination.
- If applicable, where the cautionary rules of evidence apply to the witness, highlight the reason for the rule during cross-examination and apply that to the witness. If you are dealing with the evidence of a child bear in mind the factors that a court must take into account to determine the competency of that child as a witness. Direct your cross-examination along these lines.

- If the witness is rude, offensive or resentful, suffer him patiently and do not follow him into the gutter.
- Do not cross-examine crossly. You will not cross-examine efficiently if you do so. A modicum of righteous indignation at the right moment may do a little more good and may even infect the court with the right virus.
- If necessary, postpone your 'sixty-four dollar question' until you have got all that you want from the witness.[39] Seek his co-operation. Be friendly. Criminal cases differ vitally from civil because the former are so intensely personal. You must not forget that one of your objectives throughout is to paint the best possible picture of your client and of the facts. You can often do this with the co-operation of the state witnesses. A state witness who has had a 'sixty-four dollar question' thrown at him hardly feels like co-operating. Remember, moreover, that the witness does not know what is in your mind. Usually he did not want to be a witness in the first place. He has been inconvenienced by having to attend court and he has

[37] Sections 36 and 37 of the General Law Amendment Act 62 of 1955.
[38] Section 217 of Act 51 of 1977.
[39] See the discussion of 'The attack, and the sixty-four dollar question', in paragraph 12.5.9 above.

not been mollified by having to wait his turn to enter the witness-box. Nor, in the magistrates' courts, will his temper have been improved by a series of remands while the state was trying to get some coherence into its case. So when you rise to cross-examine you just assume until the contrary is proved that the witness is hostile. Not necessarily hostile to your client; more probably he wishes he had never seen or heard of your client in the first place. He is hostile to you, because you are going to keep him in the witness-box, you are going to humiliate him, and you are going to 'try to make him out a liar'. The witness resents you, distrusts you, fears you, and will defend himself against you.

- When you have got all this into your head, you can start your work. And your first task is to make the witness into a witness for the defence. If he is rude, smile — praying that it may be the smile on the face of the tiger. If he is reluctant, coax. If he is defensive, reassure.

  Then, when you have got all you can, decide quickly what is left against your client. If nothing is left, why then, there is nothing more to do. If there is a residue, the time may have come to show the witness that his first-formed opinion of you was more accurate than the later impression. Then is the time for the 'sixty-four dollar questions', inconsistent statements, irreconcilable facts, credibility, character or whatever else you have against this particular witness.

- One more word of warning. It would be a mistake to assume that the investigating officer is necessarily hostile to your client. The man has a duty to perform. Very seldom — I shall not say never, because these things do happen — has he a motive to misrepresent. More often than in the case of the average witness does he have cause to remember. Worse still, the investigating officer has a thing called a 'docket'. On this docket he makes notes when the matters are fresh in his memory. He does not have to refresh his memory from the docket when he is in the witness-box; he has been working with it for so long that he knows it by heart. All of which means that it is safer to secure his co-operation than to try to discredit him.

19.9.2 Remember to always put the defence version

During cross-examination you must always put the defence version to the state witnesses. When and how this should be done is succinctly stated in *S v Scott-Crossley*:[40]

[26]   The court *a quo* held against the appellant the fact that his full version as to everything that had transpired on the day in question was not put to certain State witnesses. The court reasoned:
'At the stage that the version of accused 3 was put to Mnisi for the first time as aforestated, the following witnesses on the facts had already testified and were cross-examined: Forget Ndlovu, Sergeant Ferreira, Zodwa Mathebula and Thuli Siwela. Accordingly the case or version of accused 3 was not put to these witnesses.

[40] 2008 (1) SACR 223 (SCA).

The principle as stated in *S v Van As* 1991 (2) SACR 74 (W) is that the failure of the accused to put his version or case to state witnesses will in an appropriate case justify an adverse inference being drawn against such an accused when assessing or evaluating the credibility of his version.

But it is not necessary for an accused's version to be put in all its detail to every witness who takes the stand to give evidence for the state. The limits of the obligation to put the defence version to state witnesses appear from the following passage in Phipson *Evidence* 7 ed 460 quoted in *R v M*:[41]

'As a rule a party should put to each of his opponent's witnesses in turn *so much of his own case as concerns that particular witness*,[42] or in which he had a share. . . . If he asks no questions he will, in England, though not perhaps in Ireland, generally be taken to accept the witness's account. . . . Moreover, where it is intended to suggest that the witness is not speaking the truth upon a particular point, his attention must first be directed to the fact by cross-examination, so that he may have an opportunity of explanation. . . . Failure to cross-examine, however, will not always amount to an acceptance of the witness's testimony, e.g. if the witness has had notice to the contrary beforehand, or the story is itself of an incredible or romancing character. . . .'.

It must also be emphasised that the failure to put a version, even where it should have been put, does not necessarily warrant an inference that the accused's version is a recent fabrication. The words 'in an appropriate case' taken by the trial judge from *S v Van As* are important. As Davis AJA said of the passage in Phipson just quoted: 'These remarks are not intended to lay down any inflexible rules even in civil cases, and in a criminal case still greater latitude should usually be allowed.'

The learned judge went on to say [at 1028–9]:

'That at that stage the girls should have been cross-examined I have no doubt; indeed, I have difficulty in imagining why this was not done. Whatever the reason it was certainly unfortunate that he [the attorney for the accused] did not do so. But in the circumstances of this case I am unable to draw any inference adverse to the accused from his failure. When Lydia was recalled it must again be said that he should have taken advantage of the opportunity to cross-examine; but then it is only fair to say that the prosecutor, or at least the magistrate, should have put the story to her at that stage. And he might well also have recalled the complainant; compare *Rex v Filanius* (1916 TPD 415 at 418), per Mason, J. The learned Judge, who delivered the judgment of the Court *a quo*, gave a number of points on which "severe criticism can be directed to the evidence of the appellant (the accused) and his witness (Campher)". The first is the failure to put the defence case to the two girls; this he describes as "most significant". But significant of what? Significant, as I would suggest under the circumstances of this particular case, of nothing but an error of judgment on the part of the attorney.'

The adverse inference drawn by the court against the appellant for the failure to put the full defence version to the witness Ndhlovu was not justified and a misdirection. He was at no stage at the scene on the farm. The same applies to the evidence of Siwela — she did not testify on the events which occurred on that fatal night as she was not present, having left shortly after 13:00 — and to the other witnesses

---

[41] 1946 AD 1023 at 1028. See also *Small v Smith* 1954 (3) SA 434 (SWA) at 438E–G and *S v Van As* 1989 (3) SA 881 (W), 1991 (2) SACR 74 (W) at 108c–h.

[42] Emphasis supplied.

mentioned in the judgment of the trial court, who were never at the farm on the day in question.

19.9.3 Previous inconsistent statements

Cross-examining a witness on his previous inconsistent statement will only be effective and of value if the following guidelines are observed:

> As I have mentioned, in the present matter the cross-examination of the state witnesses, insofar as it was directed at the contents of their police statements, was done properly. In each instance the witness was asked to confirm that he had made a statement to the police. The witness was then asked whether that which he told the policeman was written down; whether it was read back to him; whether he was asked to confirm the correctness thereof; and whether, having done so, he was asked to sign, or place his mark, or thumb-print, on the statement. The witness was then asked to identify, with reference to his signature or mark (except, obviously, where a thumb-print had been placed on the statement), that the statement in question was in fact the statement he made. Once confirmation of this had been obtained, counsel proceeded to go through the whole statement with the witness. After each sentence, or on occasion after a whole paragraph, had been read to the witness he was asked whether he had in fact said to the police what had been read to him (and therefore written down). Sometimes the answer was in the affirmative, other times not. Having gone through this exercise, the witness was then referred to differences between such witness' earlier evidence and those portions of the police statement which he had confirmed reflected what he had told the police. In some instances these differences were marked, in others the differences could be described as subtle. Where appropriate, the witness was asked why certain facts mentioned during his evidence did not appear in the statement, with it being suggested that the reason there for was that he had not told the police. The witness was asked why there were such contradictions and/or omissions, thereby being afforded an opportunity to provide an explanation.[43]

If the witness denies either making the statement or the reliability thereof, eg, he denies that the statement was read back to him or that something was said, call the police officer who recorded the statement to testify — such officer will never concede that he falsely recorded information.

19.9.4 Cross-examining on the opening statement

It is permitted, depending upon the statements made by the prosecutor in his opening address, to cross-examine a witness in regard thereto. In this regard the judgment of Erasmus J in *S v Mbata and Others*[44] can be referred to.

19.9.5 The criminal trap

In criminal cases you will encounter a special type of witness, whose very function is to observe and to remember, with the object of later testifying as to his observations. He is the trap. In fact, in some instances, he may instigate the particular incident which he observes.

---

[43] *S v Govender and Others* 2006 (1) SACR 322 (E) at 327*b–f*.
[44] 1977 (1) SA 379 (O) at 380.

The simplest form of trap is that instituted to discourage motorists from speeding. As a matter of passing interest, if you ever have occasion to cross-examine traffic officers in this type of case, you might care to refer to an article written by a layman, as well as to the cases where electronic devices have been involved.[45]

Perhaps of greater moment are cases of trapping persons for contraventions, or alleged contraventions, of the laws relating to gold and diamonds. It seems that the same type of witness is involved in all these cases, and the same techniques in cross-examination appear to be called for. In some instances, of course, there will be no reason to doubt the integrity of the witnesses, and the attack must be on observation, reliability and memory. In regard to traps of a particular type I would quote from a judgment of Claassen J:[46]

> The trap usually received one-third of the money which is seized. See *R v Zahlen* 1951 PH (1) H69. This is a large and easy source of income for the trap, and accordingly he will not be particular about his victim, as also appears from the evidence of the messenger of the court, Myburgh, ie, that the trap Vlok in a loud voice offered him diamonds for sale. This was done so that the interest of the said Sander, who heard it and who also apparently acted as inciter in his own interest, was aroused. Where such persons are paid and act off their own bat serious thought must be given to this and the courts must discourage it with all their might. It amounts to a prostitution of the police force, and it approaches the prostitution of our courts. I personally regard it as degrading to have to listen to such evidence. I cannot describe it in any wise as an honourable procedure. I have difficulty with the evidence of detectives who bring this sort of case to consummation. At one stage their conduct is entirely mendacious, fraudulent and full of false pretences and then afterwards from a certain stage it is submitted that they are honest and upright persons. It is contradictory of any concept of moral principles. It is said that in the case of such an official there can be no wrong motive, as, for example, in the case of the trap. I do not agree, because before arrest of the victim their only purpose is, by means of deceit, to do everything to persuade an ordinary member of the public to commit an offence, to get their hands on his money and then to arrest him. I emphasise that I am now speaking of cases where innocent persons land in trouble through the activities of detectives, and such cases are not unknown.

You will, of course, study this and other cases on the topic more fully and, before you set out with all flags flying, you will tactfully find out what you can about your client's background and the circumstances in which he found himself the victim of a trap. In any event, I am sure that you will benefit from a circumspect application of the learned judge's *dicta* to your own case. See also

---

[45] De Jongh, HM 'The Gatsometer and Stopwatch Speed Checking' *Tydskrif vir Hedendaagse Regsgeleerheid* Vol 31 (1968) at 147 and 253. The cases are *S v Margolis* 1964 (4) SA 579 (T), *S v Dawson* 1966 (1) SA 259 (N), *S v Du Plessis* 1966 (1) SA 607 (C) and *S v Lucas* 1968 (2) SA 592 (E). In order to get further assistance in these cases I suggest that you refer also to *S v Currin* 1961 (4) SA 393 (O) and *R v Peche* 1967 (4) SA 252 (RAD).

[46] *R v Vlok and Vlok* 1954 (1) SA 203 (SWA) at 206.

S v Sellem[47] in regard to the court's approach to sentence where a 'trap' is involved. I suggest, apart from what was set out in chapter 12, two methods of testing the reliability of the evidence given:

- If two or more persons have participated as a trap — your client should be able to tell you this — it is reasonable to suppose that they will tell the same story in their evidence-in-chief. They must then, in cross-examination, be taken outside the essential features of their common narrative and the results compared. The process is laborious, it is frustrating and it might tire the patience of the court. Those considerations must take second place. In cross-examination of the first witness you take his evidence-in-chief and examine it point by point. As examples of rudimentary questions you might take this approach:

> 'When you entered the room where was the accused'?
> 'Was he standing or sitting?'
> 'Was he alone?'
> 'Did you notice the furniture in the room?'
> 'Next to what piece of furniture did you find the accused?'
> 'How was he dressed?'
> 'What was he doing when you came in?'
> 'What did he do then?'
> 'Who spoke first?'

Now, whatever you do, do not elevate these specific questions into a praetorian formula. Modify, adapt and improve on them. And do not expect spectacular results from the first witness.

It is when the second witness testifies that you will find out whether you have succeeded. You put exactly the same questions on details, looking for a different set of answers. I repeat that this is no abracadabra; but I have known traps to give such radically different stories that the magistrate has acceded to an application for discharge at the end of the state case. On the other hand, there are more convictions than acquittals.

If you are fortunate enough to get a substantial discrepancy in questioning the second witness you will experience an almost irresistible urge to ask the following question:

> 'But the previous witness said X, Y and Z on this point. Is he wrong or are you wrong?'

What possible benefit is there in such a question? The discrepancy exists. It is for the court to say who is wrong. Will the witness say: 'I am wrong?' Will he say 'the last witness is wrong?' Neither of these two courses will appeal to him. You do not know what he will say; probably he will try to reconcile his own version with X, Y and Z. By the time you have finished chasing him through his reconciliation, you will have destroyed the discrepancy and lost the theme of your cross-examination. I know that I

[47] 1992 (2) SA 795 (A).

have made this point previously,[48] and I make it again, because, despite all that is written in the books on cross-examination, this is one of the most difficult lessons to learn.

• With regard to the second method of testing evidence — when a police officer testifies as to his own observations, subject to what I stated previously in paragraph 19.4.9, you should make it an invariable rule to call for the notes which he made at the time of the observations. Sometimes he has used the back of a cigarette box and later written the notes into the docket before discarding the cigarette box. Why no court appears to have commented strongly on this practice is a little difficult to understand. However, if entries were made in a pocket-book, call for this document. If it is not at court, persist in your application so that you can examine the original entries. Perhaps you will draw a blank, but there has been more than one case where a policeman's notebook contained *ex post facto* erasures and alterations.

You might also remember, particularly in the case of motor accidents and traffic offences, that the notebook or original document is a source of potential profit. For one reason or another original measurements and observations seem to be highly susceptible to error, sometimes to such an extent as to make the later plan or evidence totally unacceptable. Thus, in one case, all measurements were taken from 'fixed point-fencing pole'. An inspection *in loco* showed a row of 'fencing poles' all similar and indistinguishable one from another, with nothing to identify the one selected.

Where the nature of the evidence against your client comes from a trap or the use of an undercover operation the provisions of s 252A of the Act should be remembered and canvassed during cross examination. These provisions are:

(a) whether, prior to the setting of a trap or the use of an undercover operation, approval, if it was required, was obtained from the director of public prosecutions to engage such investigation methods and the extent to which the instructions or guidelines issued by the director of public prosecutions were adhered to;

(b) the nature of the offence under investigation, including —
    (i) whether the security of the state, the safety of the public, the maintenance of public order or the national economy is seriously threatened thereby;
    (ii) the prevalence of the offence in the area concerned; and
    (iii) the seriousness of such offence;

(c) the availability of other techniques for the detection, investigation or uncovering of the commission of the offence or the prevention

---

[48] See paragraphs 12.5.13 and 12.5.14 above, dealing with the need to avoid arguing with the witness, and to restrict your cross-examination to facts, not conclusions.

thereof in the particular circumstances of the case and in the area
concerned;

(d) whether an average person who was in the position of the accused,
would have been induced into the commission of an offence by the
kind of conduct employed by the official or his or her agent concerned;

(e) the degree of persistence and number of attempts made by the
official or his agent before the accused succumbed and committed
the offence;

(f) the type of inducement used, including the degree of deceit,
trickery, misrepresentation or reward;

(g) the timing of the conduct, in particular whether the official or his
agent instigated the commission of the offence or became involved
in an existing unlawful activity;

(h) whether the conduct involved an exploitation of human
characteristics such as emotions, sympathy or friendship or an
exploitation of the accused's personal, professional or economic
circumstances in order to increase the probability of the commission
of the offence;

(i) whether the official or his agent has exploited a particular
vulnerability of the accused such as a mental handicap or a substance
addiction;

(j) the proportionality between the involvement of the official or his
agent as compared to that of the accused, including an assessment of
the extent of the harm caused or risked by the official or his agent as
compared to that of the accused, and the commission of any illegal
acts by the official or his agent;

(k) any threats, implied or expressed, by the official or his agent against
the accused;

(l) whether, before the trap was set or the undercover operation was
used, there existed any suspicion, entertained upon reasonable
grounds, that the accused had committed an offence similar to that to
which the charge relates;

(m) whether the official or his agent acted in good or bad faith; or

(n) any other factor which in the opinion of the court has a bearing on
the question.

The information so obtained may either show that the accused will not
receive a fair trial if the evidence of the trap is admitted, or will serve as
mitigating factors when sentence is considered.

19.9.6 Cross-examination as to identity

Identity is often the most important point in a criminal case. You should study
the cases where the courts have discussed the topic,[49] because you can gather

---

[49] For example *R v Shekele and Another* 1953 (1) SA 636 (T), *R v Nyende* 1956 (2) SA 55 (T), *R v Mokoena* 1958 (2) SA 212 (T) at 215–7, *S v Mehlape* 1963 (2) SA 29 (T) at 33–4, *S v Mthetwa* 1972

from the reports what particular line of cross-examination should be pursued in the defence of your client. I might remark in passing that 'identity' is often concomitant with an alibi, a subject which is considered later in this chapter.

The method I suggest now can be described either as a variation of closing escape routes or as test by fact.[50] In essence you do not challenge identity in the manner of bulls at gates. Instead you investigate the topics which bear on ability to identify, and then, if you have the witness encompassed with negative circumstances such as no lighting, great excitement, lapse of time, fleeting observation, no abnormal features,[51] you put the vital question. However, you should not ask:

'Why do you say it was the accused?'

That is a stupid question, and you will receive an answer according to your folly.

It might be almost as stupid to say:

'I put it to you that, in these circumstances, you could not possibly identify the accused.'

It is in all probability enough if you put no more than:

'I put it to you that it was not the accused.'

In reply you will receive the answer 'it was' — spoken in tones ranging from indignant to petulant. But take the least possible risk of provoking an item of identification which you had not thought of. It is useful to remember the words of Van den Heever JA[52] on this topic:

The positive assurance with which an honest witness will sometimes swear to the identity of an accused person is in itself no guarantee of the correctness of that evidence. One often finds that a woman who was totally unable to point out her assailant on an identification parade will, when the accused is arrested on the strength of other evidence, swear positively at the trial that she recognises him as her assailant.

19.9.7 Identification parades

From identity it is but a short step to identification parades, designed to establish that a complainant or other witness can in fact select the right person as the accused. It is part of your function to test the fairness and reliability of this form of parade, over which neither the accused nor his attorney has any degree of control.

Your investigation will take place in cross-examination of every witness who identifies the accused and also of the police officer who arranged and

---

(3) SA 766 (A) at 768A–C and *S v Sithole* 1999 (1) SACR 585 (W) at 591. Also see annotations on the reports of these cases. Compare, however, *S v Sinkankanka* 1963 (2) SA 531 (A) at 543D. Also refer to *Wills Circumstantial Evidence* 7 ed 192–205.

[50] See paragraphs 12.5.10 and 12.5.20 above.
[51] Compare *R v Schoombie* 1945 AD 541 at 544.
[52] *R v Masemang* 1950 (2) SA 488 (A) at 493.

conducted the parade. You should first read the cases[53] in order to see what weaknesses have been found in this method of proof and, then, test the following points:

- how many people were presented at the parade;
- the physical appearance of other persons on the parade;
- comparison of the facial and other appearance of those persons with the accused;
- the attire of other persons on the parade;
- comparison of the attire of those persons with that of the accused; information given to the witnesses who were asked to identify the 'suspect';
- what those witnesses were asked to identify;
- what opportunity the witnesses had of observing the mustering of the parade; what opportunity the witnesses had of discussion before and after the parade; discussions between the witnesses *inter se* or with the police;
- whether anything happened, whether deliberately or unintentionally, from which the witness could draw an inference as to the state of mind of the police officer who arranged or supervised the parade.

Of course, despite my critical remarks at the commencement of this subparagraph, an identification parade is of the greatest assistance to the accused where the witness fails to point out the correct — or any — person.

19.9.8 Cross-examination on identification by voice

From the recognition of an accused person on an identification parade it is but a short step, in the official mind, to identification by voice. I do not take as my theme the proposition that it is not possible to recognise voices. But just try to pass the time in the motion court by trying to identify your colleagues by their voices — you will find that you are, to say the least, not always successful. My contention is that the identification of an utter stranger by some real or fancied vocal timbre is so fraught with danger that it should be treated with the utmost reserve. You can study the relevant cases[54] and perhaps direct your cross-examination along the following lines:

- time for which the criminal's voice was heard;
- circumstances in which it was heard, including agitation on the part of the witness;
- competing sounds and so on;
- circumstances in which the accused's voice was tested; other voices tested;
- time for which the voice was tested;
- competing sounds at time of test.

---

[53] For example *R v Olia* 1935 TPD 213, *R v W* 1947 (2) SA 708 (A), *R v Masemang* 1950 (2) SA 488 (A), *R v Nara Sammy* 1956 (4) SA 629 (T), *R v Y and Another* 1959 (2) SA 116 (W), *R v Mputing* 1960 (1) SA 785 (T) and *S v Khumalo* 1991 (4) SA 310 (A).

[54] Such as *R v Gericke* 1941 CPD at 211, *S v M* 1963 (3) SA 183 (T) at 185 and *R v Chitate* 1966 (2) SA 690 (RAD).

It may be permissible in this context to ignore some of my previous advice *but only when you are satisfied that you know the answer before you put the question.* You may ask the witness whether there was any special characteristic by which he recognised the accused's voice. Before you ask this question you will have consulted with the accused at length, listening carefully for any such characteristic. It may be a deep voice, or a shrill one, or there may be a lisp, or a slurred 'r', perhaps a rolling 'r' or even one or other of the many accents to be heard in this country. But until you are satisfied that there is no feature of identification, however slight, do not ask the question and do not ask the witness to describe the voice.

19.9.9 Cross-examining fingerprints

Identification by means of fingerprints is popularly reputed to be infallible, and if it is your misfortune to have one of these cases your problem will be well nigh insuperable.[55]

However, you will obtain a fair idea of how to approach the topic by reading the few cases I have quoted, together with others you will find, and from the general discussion of the topic by *Wills*.[56] Perhaps the most fruitful line of cross-examination, also of argument, is the investigation of the time at which the accused's fingerprint could have been placed where it was found.[57]

Fingerprint evidence must not overawe you, and I quote from the judgment in *Nksatlala's* case at 546: [58]

> Where, as here, there is only one fingerprint, where it does not appear to be an ideally clear one and where the points of resemblance that are visible are near to the minimum in number, it is of the greatest importance that the expert evidence, whether it is that of one or more witnesses, should be closely scrutinized to eliminate, as far as is humanly possible, all risk of error.
>
> In the present case, however, there was no cross-examination of the expert on the question of identity and it was not challenged on appeal. It must accordingly be accepted that the appellant's fingerprint was found on the window of the car on the day of the robbery.

19.9.10 Cross-examining DNA

Identification by means of DNA evidence *is* infallible, provided that the paper-trail is accurate and complete. Your attack must thus be concentrated on the accuracy and reliability of the paper-trail.

---

[55] *R v Morela* 1947 (3) SA 147 (A), *R v Smit* 1952 (3) SA 447 (A), *S v Kimimbi* 1963 (3) SA 250 (C), *S v Nala* 1965 (4) SA 360 (A) and *S v Malindi* 1983 (4) SA 99 (T). In regard to the different points of view dealing with comparative charts, see *S v Van Wyk* 1982 (2) SA 148 (NC) and *S v Nyathe* 1988 (2) SA 211 (O).

[56] *Circumstantial Evidence* 7 ed 205–23.

[57] As in *R v Du Plessis* 1944 AD 314 at 322 and 323, and *R v Nksatlala* 1960 (3) 543 (A) at 551.

[58] Compare *S v Kimimbi* 1963 (3) SA 250 (C).

19.9.11 Cross-examining handwriting

Evidence as to the identification of an accused person by his handwriting is not as acceptable as fingerprint evidence,[59] and your task in cross-examination is somewhat easier. What you will look for are:

* an examination, with the expert, of the training he has received in his science;
* the possible sources of errors in identification generally;
* the variations that exist in the handwriting of persons with no motive to disguise;
* the impossibility of being certain as to identity;
* the effect of the use of different types of writing instrument on the question of comparison or identification;
* dissimilarities between the disputed document and any 'test' document.

No doubt you will also be watchful for problems of spelling, whether these affect the State witnesses or the accused.

19.9.12 Test by fact

Perhaps one short illustration will be of value in the context of cross-examination in criminal cases. It is the cross-examination of the complainant in an attempted rape case, but might serve as a general model for applying the 'test by fact'. It comes from a source often quoted in this chapter.

The complainant alleged that, while her husband was away working a night shift, the accused, their lodger, entered her room and attempted to rape her. She said that she managed to push him out of the room and he left the house.

There were two relevant facts known to the accused: the husband had a mistress; and a quarrel had taken place between the husband and wife on the morning after the attempted rape.

The cross-examination proceeded:

'When your husband left you that night he kissed you?'
'Yes.'
'You and he parted on the usual terms of affection?'
'Yes.'
'After he left you had no visitors?'
'That is so.'[60]
'When he returned next morning you had a tremendous row with him?'
'Yes.'
'You were shouting at him and abusing him?'
'Yes.'
'That was not because the accused had attempted to rape you?'
'Oh, no.'
'It was because of something your husband had done?'

[59] *R v T* 1958 (2) SA 676 (A), *R v Chidota* 1966 (3) SA 428 (RAD) and *R v Mayahle* 1968 (2) SA 801 (RAD). See also Osborn *Questioned Documents* 2 ed (1946) as an example of textbooks on the topic.
[60] Thus closing an escape route. Cf paragraph 12.5.10 in chapter 12.

'Yes.'

'And that "something" you found out after he had gone on night shift?'

'Yes.'[61]

'And you told us you had no visitor that night?'

'Yes.'

'There was only one person who could have told you that "something", and that was the accused?'

'Yes.'

'So he did not go out that night?'

'I made a mistake.'

'He told you that while you were in England your husband had been carrying on with another woman?'

'Yes.'

'Did you tell your husband that you had found out that he had been carrying on with another woman?'

'Yes.'

'Did you tell your husband that it was the accused who had told you this?'

'Yes.'

'Your husband then asked you where this took place and you told him it was in your bedroom?'

'Yes.'

'It was after this that you told him for the first time that the accused had attempted to rape you?'

'Yes.'

At this stage the State's case collapsed.

19.9.13   Cross-examination as to character

The consequences of cross-examining a state witness or co-accused as to his character are well known. It is necessary for my purposes merely to remind you of the relevant section of the Act[62] and to refer you to the textbooks on evidence and criminal law for the necessary discussion.

The advice is so elementary that I almost apologise for giving it. However, there is a trap, so it may be that I shall be forgiven. The advice is that your consultation should have been so thorough that, if your client has an Achilles heel, you should be aware of it. In other words, unless he cannot be attacked on the aspect of character you will studiously, albeit regretfully, refrain from attacking the State witnesses on this point. Of course, you may well be inclined to take the well-known 'calculated risk' and content yourself with submitting in argument that even your client's disreputable past does not mean that he is guilty of the offence wherewith he is charged. I cannot, however, conscientiously recommend this procedure.

The trap lurks in the case where you represent more than one accused, one of whom, perhaps, may be vulnerable to the provisions of the section. In such

---

[61] This is a vital question. It permits of only one answer.
[62] Section 227.

a case it has been held[63] that an incautious attack on the character of a state witness will allow cross-examination of that one unfortunate accused as to his character, although his co-accused may have nothing to fear. It was suggested in the judgment, perhaps only by implication, that the position might possibly be different where counsel, in cross-examining the state witness as to character, indicates that he does so on behalf of one or other of the accused who is not vulnerable to a retaliatory attack as to his own character. This, of course, poses problems.

Firstly, the cross-examination, one might legitimately suppose, ought to be of such a nature that it could reasonably be accepted that the instructions did in fact come from the accused person who enjoyed an unsullied character.

Secondly, the moment you suffer a split personality of the nature indicated, you automatically tell the court that there is something wrong with one of your clients.

Thirdly, it looks like a 'stunt' and, for some reason, South African courts do not appear to like stunts (the position may be different where the dollar holds sway). The true solution to this dilemma is separate representation of the accused but, in criminal cases, funds do not always permit the luxury of a plurality of pleaders.

19.10 OBJECTIONS TO EVIDENCE

While your client is under cross-examination it is, of course, your function to see that he is protected from inadmissible or improper questions. Particularly you should be on the watch for questions such as 'Why did you not tell the police what you now tell the court?' It has been held that this is not proper, because, when arrested, an accused is, or ought to be, warned that he is not obliged to say anything.[64]

In ordinary circumstances, if inadmissible evidence is tendered counsel objects to it. As often as not the court itself will raise a query even before counsel's thought processes have galvanised him into activity. At one time a little inadmissible evidence was a windfall, because it could lend substance to an otherwise tenuous appeal. The modern trend, however, legislative and judicial, is not to uphold such appeals unless there has been a failure of justice[65] or real substantial prejudice. This being so, it would seem advisable to object to improper questions and inadmissible evidence.

An interesting case on this topic, and one whose study is well worth your while, is *R v Noorbhai*.[66] In that case the accused appeared before a judge and jury, charged with the crime of murder. It was what Davis AJA described as 'a most unusual crime'. The accused was alleged to have shot his enemy, the deceased, 'in cold blood' in the presence of his servant, and then to have

---

[63] *R v Heyne en Andere* (2) 1958 (1) SA 612 (W).
[64] *R v Patel* 1946 AD 903 at 908, citing *R v Mashelele and Another* 1944 AD 571 at 583–5.
[65] *R v Patel* 1946 AD 903.
[66] 1945 AD 58.

obtained the services of two other persons to dispose of the body. The attorney-general, for some reason which does not appear ever to have been fully elucidated, had prepared a list of books borrowed by the accused from a local library. The list categorized the books into 'Crime' or 'Western Crime' with one volume described as 'War'. Davis AJA dryly observes in parentheses: 'How "Holy Deadlock", presumably by A P Herbert, comes to be described as "Crime" was not explained.' The list was put in by consent and the accused was cross-examined upon the list without objection being made by counsel. I shall not venture to inquire whether counsel blundered or whether he took a calculated risk (a carefully calculated risk). If it was a calculated risk it is well to see how the point was dealt with by the judge *a quo* as well as by Davis AJA on appeal.

The judge *a quo* stated (quoted at 66):

> Exhibit 'G' was then put in, I gathered, by consent. I was at that time quite in the dark as to the nature of the books to which it referred, or as to the purpose of the evidence it provided, and having regard to [counsel's] attitude, I felt under no duty to inquire.

In giving the judgment on appeal Davis AJA said at 76:

> In the present case it is possible that counsel allowed the documents to be put in by inadvertence, thinking that an admission was only being asked of the correctness of a list of books, under s 318, to save the calling of the librarian, and it may be that, once having wrongly let it go in, he thought that the less attention he drew to it, by objections to cross-examination, the better for his client. Still, the fact that he did allow it to go in by consent and that he raised no objection to the cross-examination of the accused thereon, has not been lost sight of by this court in considering whether the appeal, based upon this irregularity, should be allowed.

At 76 to 79 of the report is a discussion of the suggested bases of admissibility in regard to the list, the learned judge of appeal finding ultimately that the list was inadmissible and prejudicial to the accused. Nor, as he remarks, were the jury warned to dismiss it from their minds. The remainder of the judgment, as far as it is relevant for present purposes, reads as follows (at 80):

> Had I any doubt whether this evidence was capable of having influenced the verdict of the jury and whether it may in fact have done so, my doubt might have been resolved against the prisoner by counsel's consent to the document being put in and his lack of objection to the cross-examination. But I have none. It was contended that the evidence against the accused was so overwhelming that the jury must in any case inevitably have convicted. But there were difficulties in the case for the Crown; it contained curious features-for instance, the strangeness of the story told by Amos, and the unsatisfactory and contradictory character of the medical evidence. It cannot therefore be said that, without the inadmissible evidence, and having regard only to the rest of the evidence, strong as it undoubtedly was, the jury would inevitably have convicted and that no reasonable men could have done otherwise (cf *R v De Villiers* 1944 AD 493). Nor can the fact that, in spite of this inadmissible evidence, one juryman disagreed with the verdict of the majority, be left out of consideration. 'By itself' it is not of great importance-cf *Tshingumuzi & another v Attorney-General of the Colony of Natal* [1908] AC 248—but, in the circumstances which are now under consideration, it does not stand alone and should not be left out of account.

> For these reasons the accused in my opinion suffered at his trial actual and substantial prejudice from this irregularity, which constituted a failure of justice in terms of the decision in *R v Rose* (1937 AD 467).

The warning is plain to see. The courts are not readily going to penalise an accused person for want of objection by his counsel,[67] but where the abstention is shown to be deliberate there may be a first time.

19.11 THE DEFENCE CASE

19.11.1 The accused

It is trite law that the onus is on the State to prove the guilt of the accused beyond reasonable doubt. Then arises a problem. If at the close of the case for the prosecution there was no evidence that your client had committed the offence charged or any offence of which he can be convicted on the charge, you will probably have applied, successfully, for the discharge of your client. If your application was unsuccessful then you have reached the point of no return, for a decision has to be made whether your client is to give evidence in his defence.

> If the State had succeeded in proving a *prima facie* case, then the fact that the accused failed to go into the witness-box to refute this case would have transformed this *prima facie* proof into proof beyond a reasonable doubt that she had committed the offence.[68]

The use of the phrase '*prima facie* case' is unfortunate. It is only when the evidence produced calls for an answer that one can say that there is *prima facie* proof, which in the absence of an answer becomes conclusive proof.[69] It frequently happens that an accused is acquitted despite the fact that a discharge was refused at the end of the state case. The reason is obvious if regard is had to the level of proof required which, at the end of the case, is proof beyond a reasonable doubt. At the end of the State case the question is whether there is evidence on which a reasonable court can convict.[70]

That these remarks (in *Swartz*) were obiter and possibly a little overstated is not the problem. What is of utmost concern is, at the least, that your client's failure to testify is a factor to be taken into account and may transform *prima facie* proof into proof beyond reasonable doubt. You might have regard to the words of Malan JA in a minority judgment[71] later applied by the Appellate Division[72] as a correct exposition of the juristic process involved:

> If an assault-using the term in its widest possible acceptation-is committed upon a person which causes death either instantaneously or within a very short time thereafter and no explanation is given of the nature of the assault by the person within

[67] Compare *S v Sinkankanka and Another* 1963 (2) SA 531 (A) 538F.
[68] Per Van Zyl J in *S v Swartz* 1966 (2) SA 333 (C) at 334F.
[69] *Ex parte Minister of Justice: In re R v Jacobson and Levy* 1931 AD 466 at 478.
[70] *S v Ndlangamandla* 1999 (1) SACR 391 (W).
[71] *R v Mlambo* 1957 (4) SA 727 (A) at 737.
[72] *S v Rama* 1966 (2) SA 395 (A) at 400-1.

whose knowledge it solely lies, a court will be fully justified in drawing the inference that it was of such an aggravated nature that the assailant knew or ought to have known that death might result.

Particularly where the accused's state of mind is relevant should he be called as a witness, for[73] —

> where a question of the state of mind of an accused person is in issue, it is not easy for a court to come to a conclusion favourable to the accused as to his state of mind unless he has himself given evidence on the subject.

A further matter to bear in mind is that while it may seem an attractive proposition to suggest in argument that there are possible explanations for the facts which are consistent with the innocence of the accused, and that the accused should accordingly be given the benefit of the doubt, there are limits to the validity of such an argument. The court will 'not speculate on the possible existence of matters upon which there is no evidence, or the existence of which cannot reasonably be inferred from the evidence.'[74]

On the strength of all these authorities you will, no doubt, come to the conclusion that it will only be rarely that you will not call your client as a witness in his own defence. That there are such cases, however, equally does not admit of doubt. If he will inevitably convict himself different considerations may apply and other tactics must be considered.

19.11.2   The wife, relatives and friends of the accused

If you are hesitant about calling the accused's wife as a witness because she may be thought to be biased, reflect that she can be no more biased than your client himself. And, who knows, you may even encounter a prosecutor with a profound sense of chivalry. Nowadays, I warn, many women have turned to prosecuting.

Similar reasoning, as to bias, if not to chivalry, applies to other relatives and to friends of the accused. I offer only one word of caution — or precaution. If you do call a relative or friend to support the defence case be sure that, immediately the witness has identified himself, he tells the court fully about the relationship or friendship. If it comes out only in cross-examination the resulting odour will attach not only to the witness, but also to the accused; and not only to the accused, but also to his legal representatives.

Never put into the witness-box a witness whom you have not interviewed. Never rely on the *ipse dixit* of your client that 'So-and-so can confirm this' or whatever so-and-so is alleged to be capable of saying.

19.11.3   Alibis

Alibis are very popular defences.

---

[73] *R v Mohr* 1944 TPD 105, per Schreiner J at 108. See also *R v Deetlefs* 1953 (1) SA 418 (A) at 422F, *S v Khola* 1966 (4) SA 322 (A) at 327F–G and *S v F and Others* 1967 (4) SA 639 (W) at 644F–G.
[74] *R v Ndhlovu* 1945 AD 369 at 386 and *R v L* 1946 AD 190 at 196.

If your defence is a sound alibi you should inform the court or the authorities of its nature as soon as possible so that the State may investigate your story. If you disclose it for the first time at your trial you may considerably weaken your defence.

However, s 93 provides that where the defence of an accused is an alibi and the court before which the proceedings are pending is of the opinion that the accused may be prejudiced in making such defence if proof is admitted that the act or offence in question was committed on a day or at a time other than the day or time stated in the charge, the court shall reject such proof notwithstanding that the day or time in question is within a period of three months before or after the day or time stated in the charge, whereupon the same consequences shall follow as are mentioned in proviso (b) of s 92 (2).

There is no onus on the accused to prove his alibi. At the end of the day the evidence is evaluated in toto to determine whether the version of the accused is reasonably possibly true. It was succinctly put as follows in *S v Trainer*:[75]

> [9] A conspectus of all the evidence is required. Evidence that is reliable should be weighed alongside such evidence as may be found to be false. Independently verifiable evidence, if any, should be weighed to see if it supports any of the evidence tendered. In considering whether evidence is reliable, the quality of that evidence must of necessity be evaluated, as must corroborative evidence, if any. Evidence, of course, must be evaluated against the onus on any particular issue or in respect of the case in its entirety. The compartmentalised and fragmented approach of the magistrate is illogical and wrong.

Bear in mind that few alibis are sound.

Not always will you be briefed in time to follow this advice—even if your alibi is sound.

Beware, I would add, of the alibi that grows with the passage of time. I remember a case some years ago when the two accused wished to prove an alibi for eleven o'clock on a particular Saturday night. They alleged that they were outside their home in Jeppe, Johannesburg, at the precise moment when, according to the prosecutor, they were engaged in committing a rape in a plantation some distance away from. They obligingly provided counsel with two alibi witnesses. In cross-examination, however, a loophole appeared in the alibi. Nothing daunted, they provided two more witnesses to plug the loophole. The process of opening up and resealing loopholes continued until the defence had thrown thirteen witnesses into the breach. Counsel for the accused now believes that thirteen is an unlucky number.

What ought to be remembered in the case of the first alibi witnesses is that the prosecutor will have a classic opportunity to cross-examine on the lines of 'cause to remember'. Usually the accused will have been arrested only some days-even weeks — after the offence. Usually the need for alibi witnesses will have become apparent only at the stage of preparation for trial. Prosecuting counsel seldom has it so easy!

[75] 2003 (1) SACR 35 (SCA) para 9.

When the second alibi witness is called not only will the prosecutor repeat the process, but he will doubtless invoke a technique similar to that discussed in paragraph 19.9.5 of this chapter. Moreover, if one witness is open to attack on the 'cause to remember' theme, it would seem that the effectiveness of the attack will increase by process of geometric and not of mathematical progression.

A quotation from *R v Ndhlovu*[76] may conclude the topic:

> It is true that the accused, as I have already mentioned earlier, gave no explanation of what occurred. This must, of course, be taken into account against him — indeed, I have done so. But it must be remembered that once he decided to say, quite untruthfully, that he was not there at all, he could thereafter give no explanation. And his deciding to do so is not altogether surprising in an ignorant native, who felt that he would be involved in serious trouble, no matter what he said, if once he admitted that he was there.

Perhaps the more sophisticated clients will have their false alibis treated less considerately.

19.11.4 Specific defences and witnesses

Both at common law and under many statutes, there are specific defences open to an accused person. In such instances the onus will ordinarily be upon the accused. Thus at common law he will have to establish the defence of insanity. On the other hand, though, the state bears the onus to prove all the elements of the crime.

Perhaps the existence of a general onus on the State to prove guilt beyond a reasonable doubt tends to obscure the task of the defence in cases of the type I have mentioned, but I am not sure that practitioners always approach their task with what I suggest is the proper state of mind. Your attitude must be no different from what it would be if you were acting for the plaintiff in a civil case. If you fail in a civil case, your client, the plaintiff, will probably suffer absolution from the instance. If you fail in a criminal case your client may find himself in a place where there is no absolution. I am not suggesting a formalised approach such as advice on evidence but I do suggest that there must be a similar approach in preparation, while the defence should be conducted along the lines suggested in chapters 4 to 8.

In other words, an analysis must be made of the issues on which proof is required and of the witnesses available to prove the elements of such issues. Often it will be necessary to call expert evidence — and this, too, apart from those instances where the onus is on the accused. It is well, in presenting your case, to remember that in criminal matters that there are three distinct divisions in regard to the onus which has to be discharged by an accused and, should an appeal eventuate, you may regret any economy in the calling of supporting witnesses. The categories are:

---

[76] 1945 AD 369 at 387–8.

- Ordinary cases where the onus is on the state to prove its case beyond reasonable doubt[77] and the accused must be given the benefit of the doubt; i e if his story may reasonably be true he is entitled to an acquittal.[78]
- Cases where a special defence must be proved by the defence, on a balance of probabilities.
- Cases where a special defence must similarly be proved on a balance of probabilities, but the acceptance of that defence is a matter of judicial discretion, so that an appeal court will not ordinarily interfere, even if it does not agree with the views of the trial judge.[79]

It may be that, in practice, these distinctions are of academic importance, because ideally you will call whatever witnesses are available to support each element of your case.

19.12 ARGUMENT

19.12.1 Generally

Even in these cynical times it would be well not to neglect the art of oratory, which has for centuries been regarded as the highest attribute of advocacy. It will not be your lot to sway a jury with an exposition of eloquence so moving that none could resist it. You may read the books to which I have from time to time referred,[80] and find many fine examples of addresses to juries in both civil and criminal cases. From these examples you can learn much, once you have mastered the fundamental principles of knowing what you are after and on what foundations your oratory must stand.

Whether you address a magistrate, a judge or a judge and assessors, your argument will not prevail by sheer eloquence of rhetoric alone. Did the jury trial differ in any marked degree? In the words of counsel who argued cases before juries for some 40 years:

> An address by itself in a jury trial will rarely secure an acquittal. Modern juries are more sophisticated and better informed than they were, say, fifty years ago. Besides, any judge who is worth his salt will easily dispose of any hot air that you may talk. . . . Let your address be eighty per cent cold analysis of the evidence and twenty per cent rhetoric.

The same counsel had one further piece of advice:

> Do not talk to the jury about their intelligence. If they have any you will only sicken them. If they haven't the flattery will not help you.[81]

---

[77] But compare the judgment of Malan JA in *R v Mlambo* 1957 (4) SA 727 (A). See also *S v Steynberg* 1983 (3) SA 140 (A) and *S v Van Niekerk* 1981 (3) SA 787 (T).

[78] *Heslop v S* 2007 (4) SA 38 (SCA), 2007 (1) SACR 461 (SCA).

[79] Compare *S v Nell* 1968 (2) SA 576 (A) and cases cited at 577 and 580, and *S v Van der Berg* 1968 (3) SA 250 (A).

[80] Donovan *Skill in Trials* and *Tact in Court*, Harris *Illustrations in Advocacy* and *Hints on Advocacy*, and Du Cann *The Art of The Advocate* at 154 and 167.

[81] See also Judge J W Donovan *Tact in Court* 45 and 67–8.

On these lines you may well approach a judge, or a judge and assessors.

19.12.2 A few pointers

- No case ever suffered because counsel reminded the court of the incidence and nature of the onus, the reminder being either direct or oblique as suited the nature and sophistication of the tribunal.
- It is empty rhetoric, however, to talk of 'beyond reasonable doubt' and 'benefit of the doubt' unless you can show the court where the doubt is to be found.
- A court may convict upon the evidence of a single witness provided the witness is a competent one.[82] Merely because there are two, three or fifty witnesses in a case does not take it out of this category, where the surplus witnesses do not relate to the question of guilt,[83] eg, an ambulance driver who conveyed the deceased to hospital.
- Ask yourself whether the case is one in which corroboration is required, and, if so, what corroborative evidence has been tendered. If yours is such a case it may be convenient to present the argument on the following lines:
  - authorities as to the general principle;
  - evidence of the complainant;
  - evidence tendered as corroboration; effect of cross-examination;
  - authorities where similar corroborative evidence was tendered;
  - the accused's evidence[84] in denial.
- Attempt to destroy the cogency of the State case, bearing in mind that the more damage you can do the easier will it be for you to argue and the court to find that the explanation of the accused 'may reasonably be true'.[85]

19.12.3 Planning and structure

In whatever way you present your argument, at least have a plan. Quote the law first if you will, or else discuss the evidence and then the law, but do not flit from point to point like a butterfly. An argument is cogent and compelling if it confirms to the following precepts:

- It must be logical.
- It must be coherent.
- It should be brief.
- It should not be repetitive.

---

[82] Section 208 of the Act. See also *R v Mokoena* 1932 OPD 79, *R v Mokoena* 1956 (3) SA 81 (A), and *S v Artman* 1968 (3) SA 339 (A).

[83] See, however *R v Abdoorham* 1954 (3) SA 163 (N) and *Swarts v R* 1954 (2) PH H107 (O), which latter case considers the existence of 'real' evidence in addition to the single witness.

[84] On this topic, particularly the last point made, see *S v Snyman* 1968 (2) SA 582 (A), especially at 589H–590D, and also *S v Artman* 1968 (3) SA 339 (A).

[85] *R v Difford* 1937 AD 370.

To attain these ends you might consider the following as a blueprint, bearing in mind that the first point must always come first, while the second and third points are reversible:

- In your own mind look for and determine the essence of the matter. Your subsequent argument will be designed to establish that essence in your own favour.
- Determine what principles of law will arise on the merits of the case. Be prepared with your notes of authorities on each point.
- Discuss the evidence. The easy way is to go through the evidence of each witness and make your comments. The more difficult is to take a series of points and discuss the evidence on each point. The topic has been discussed in chapter 16.
- Remember that your discussion of each point of evidence must be teleological — to show either that it does not lead to the inference of guilt, or to show that it leads to the opposite conclusion and to the acquittal of your client.
- Beware of misleading yourself by a painstaking dissection and destruction of the *minutiae* of the State case without regard to the cumulative effect of those *minutiae*.[86]

19.12.4 Never, never, never surrender

During the course of argument the court may criticise some of your submissions. There is no merit in abandoning any point which you may have made — in any event, it belongs to your client, and you have no right to abandon it. After all, the court may be wrong and you may be right.

19.13 MITIGATION

I do not propose to provide an exhaustive analysis of what constitutes mitigating factors. Nor do I propose to refer to the dozens of reported cases on sentence. I doubt whether one really achieves very much, from a positive point of view, by referring to the sentence imposed for a similar offence in another case. I say this because the question of sentence is intimately bound up with the nature and circumstances of the offence and of the personality and situation of the accused — *your* client, in *his* case. Although I have decried the quoting of authorities on the question of sentence, I do suggest that you refer, in support of the proposition I have just made as well as for the general guidance on mitigating factors, to a judgment of Van Heerden J in a case on appeal,[87] where the learned judge discusses the factors affecting the accused personally, the factors relating to the offence itself and the factors pertaining to public policy. Of course, you will find many other equally valuable judgments.

---

[86] See *R v De Villiers* 1944 AD 493 and cases annotated against that report, as also *S v Snyman* 1968 (2) SA 582 (A) at 589H and cases there cited.

[87] *S v Pillay* 1968 (3) SA 21 (N) at 24–5.

The court is entitled, in terms of s 112(3) and s 274 of the Act, to 'receive such evidence as it thinks fit in order to inform itself as to the proper sentence to be passed'. This evidence must be on oath[88] or the court may well be entitled to disregard it. Somehow or other one tends to gloss over the business of mitigation and to rely on one's own eloquence to save one's client from the undue rigours of the law. Let me in no wise decry that eloquence or attempt to discourage your oratory, but without a foundation of fact, it is futile. There have, it must be noted, been decisions to the effect that the court is not obliged to hear argument in mitigation, but it would be only on very rare occasions that a court would deny you a further hearing. As to mitigation, there may be some uncertainty as to the incidence or nature of the onus. It would seem that the accused must establish mitigating factors on a balance of probabilities, although a court might be inclined sometimes to give him the benefit of the doubt.[89]

Do not allow your efforts on the topic of mitigation to be coloured by the defeat you have sustained on the merits of your defence. I have tried, in these short notes, to make the point that mitigation of sentence is a separate issue, a new trial, and it should be approached with the same care and energy as any other trial.

The accused must, at some stage, have the opportunity of adducing evidence in mitigation, and the failure to afford him such opportunity amounts to an irregularity.[90]

You will only do justice to your client in this regard if you bear in mind:

> What has to be considered is the triad consisting of the crime, the offender and the interests of society.[91]

In a most illuminating judgment on the triad,[92] one of South Africa's most distinguished judges, Judge Friedman (as he then was), analysed the correct approach to the assessment of a proper and individualised sentence. I quote this judgment in detail because it sets out what evidence should be placed before the sentencing officer to enable him to pass a proper and individualised sentence, and what the relevant sentencing pillars are that receive recognition. The following quotation, although long, is deserving of careful study:

> According to Winston Churchill in *English Prisons and Borstal Systems* (1952):
> 'The mood and temper of the public in regard to the treatment of crime and criminals is one of the most unfailing tests of the civilization of any country. A calm and dispassionate recognition of the rights of the accused against the State, and even of convicted criminals against the State, a constant heart-searching by all charged with the duty of punishment, a desire and eagerness to rehabilitate in the world of industry all those who have paid their dues in the hard coinage of punishment, tireless efforts towards the discovery of curative and regenerating

---

[88] *R v Njinema and Another* 1951 (2) SA 183 (C), and *S v Van Rensburg* 1968 (2) SA 622 (T).

[89] *S v Shepard* 1967 (4) SA 170 (W). See also *S v Cooke* 1968 (3) SA 159 (E).

[90] *S v Leso en 'n Ander* 1975 (3) SA 694 (A).

[91] *S v Zinn* 1969 (2) SA 537 (A) at 540.

[92] *S v Banda* 1991 (2) SA 352 (BG).

processes, and an unfaltering faith that there is a treasure, if you can only find it, in the heart of every man—these are the symbols which in the treatment of crime and criminals mark and measure the stored-up strength of a nation, and are the sign and proof of the living virtue in it.'

The above quotation contains an eloquent distillation of the essential elements in the imposition of punishment by a court.

It is a truism that sentence is 'pre-eminently a matter for the discretion of the trial Court', and this discretion must be 'judicially and properly exercised'. See *S v Giannoulis* 1975 (4) SA 867 (A) at 868F–H.

The Court, in imposing sentence, must have due regard to the facts of the case, and in addition thereto, must apply certain well-established legal principles relating to the extent and magnitude of punishment. An awesome responsibility is thereby vested in the Court.

In ancient history retaliation and physical abuse were utilised to punish an offender for his crimes. With the advance of society, and its humanistic values, a movement developed to redress the wrongs of the past in this regard. Ancient principles of punishment have been considerably ameliorated and indeed save for a few countries have been jettisoned in favour of a more human and just approach towards the question of punishment.

In determining a proper sentence the lapidary words of Holmes JA in *S v Rabie* 1975 (4) SA 855 (A) at 861A–862F contain a comprehensive and useful guideline of the principles to be applied in imposing sentence and are applied by the Courts in this country.

After a careful analysis of the principles applicable to this subject, Holmes JA summed up at 862G, in general, and with admirable brevity, as follows, and I quote:

'Punishment should fit the criminal as well as the crime, be fair to society, and be blended with a measure of mercy according to the circumstances.'

In the same case Corbett CJ (then JA), after agreeing with the reasons given by Holmes JA, stated at 865G–866C and I quote:

'In his *Commentary on the Pandects* 5.1.57 Voet writes of the need for Judges to be free from hatred, friendship, anger, pity and avarice. In a note on this section in his Supplement to the Commentary (published in 1973) Van der Linden makes interesting reference to the views of a number of writers, classical and otherwise, as to the proper judicial attitude of mind towards punishment. (A translation of this particular note conveniently appears in the *Selective Voet* – Gane's translation vol 2 at 72.) The note (quoting Gane's translation) commences:

"It is true, as Cicero says in his work on Duties bk 1 ch 25, that anger should be especially kept down in punishing, because he who comes to punishment in wrath will never hold that middle course which lies between the too much and the too little. It is true also that it would be desirable that they who hold the office of Judges should be like the laws, which approach punishment not in a spirit of anger but in one of equity."

Van der Linden further notes that among the most harmful faults of Judges is, *inter alia*, a striving after severity (*severitatis affectatio*). Apropos this, a passage is quoted from Seneca on Mercy, including the declaration: "Severity I keep concealed, mercy ever ready" (*severitatem abditam, clementiam in promptu habeo*). Van der Linden concludes with a warning that misplaced pity (*intempestiva misericordia*) is no less to be censured.

Despite their antiquity these wise remarks contain much that is relevant to contemporary circumstances. (They were referred to, with approval, in *S v Zinn* 1969 (2) SA 537 (A) at 541). A judicial officer should not approach punishment in a spirit of anger because, being human, that will make it difficult for him to achieve that delicate balance between the crime, the criminal and the interests of society which his task and the objects of punishment demand of him. Nor should he strive after severity; nor, on the other hand, surrender to misplaced pity. While not flinching from firmness, where firmness is called for, he should approach his task with a humane and compassionate understanding of human frailties and the pressures of society which contribute to criminality. It is in the context of this attitude of mind that I see mercy as an element in the determination of the appropriate punishment in the light of all the circumstances of the particular case.'

Kotzé AJA who concurred in the judgment of Holmes JA stated at 866D–E:

'In regard to what has been termed the "approach of mercy", I merely wish to say that I have always understood it to be the duty of a judicial officer, called upon to impose punishment upon an offender, to consider to what extent the particular circumstances of a given case require that justice should be tempered with mercy.'

I respectfully agree with what has been stated by the learned Judges in *Rabie's* case with reference to the guidelines adumbrated therein.

In determining the sentence to be passed on the accused I am guided by the following:

(a) The acknowledged objects and purpose of criminal punishment are deterrent, preventive, reformative and retributive.

    (i) Deterrent, this may be general (i.e., discouraging others than the accused from committing the crime), special (discouraging the specific offender from doing it again), or both.

    (ii) Preventive, to protect the public from further criminal conduct by the accused. This may arise out of incapacitation as a result of confinement to prison.

    (iii) Reformative, concerning the rehabilitation of the offender by educational or other correctional treatment in the most effective manner.

    (iv) Retributive, the exaction of a penalty which reflects the seriousness of the offence, to promote respect for the law, and to provide appropriate punishment for the offender.

According to Gordon *Criminal Law of Scotland* (1967) at 50:

'The retributive theory finds the justification for punishment in a past act, a wrong which requires punishment or expiation. . . . The other theories, reformative, preventive and deterrent, all find their justification in the future, in the good that will be produced as a result of the punishment.'

Schreiner JA observed in *R v Karg* 1961 (1) SA 231 (A) at 236A, while accepting the importance of the element of deterrence, that 'the retributive aspect has tended to yield ground to the aspects of prevention and correction'. See also *S v Rabie* (*supra* at 862A); *Modern Criminal Law* by Wayne R La Fave at 2–3.

(b) What must also be considered is the triad consisting of the crime, the offender and the interests of society. See *S v Zinn* 1969 (2) SA 537 (A) at 540G; *S v Scheepers* 1977 (2) SA 154 (A).

I am in respectful agreement with what has been stated in these cases. See also *S v Somo* 1980 (3) SA 143 (T) at 145E–F.

The elements of the triad contain an equilibrium and a tension. A court should, when determining sentence, strive to accomplish and arrive at a judicious counterbalance between these elements in order to ensure that one element is not unduly accentuated at the expense of and to the exclusion of the others. This is not merely a formula, nor a judicial incantation, the mere stating whereof satisfies the requirements. What is necessary is that the Court shall consider, and try to balance evenly, the nature and circumstances of the offence, the characteristics of the offender and his circumstances and the impact of the crime on the community, its welfare and concern. This conception as expounded by the Courts is sound and is incompatible with anything less.

The guidelines that I have referred to stem from the importance of the legal principles applicable in sentencing an offender.

Therefore all the elements of the triad, although not identical, are indissociable.

(c)   In considering the offender, due regard must be had inter alia to the following:
  (i)   his/her age and background;
  (ii) level of education, attainment, and position in society;
  (iii) family circumstances, whether married or not, and the question of dependants;
  (iv) motive in committing the offence, whether for personal gain or for reasons of avarice, or being actuated by some moral or laudable objective;
  (v)   whether the offender stood to gain by the offence;
  (vi) the question of the accused being a first offender;
  (vii) the effect of punishment on the offender, and more particularly if a sentence of imprisonment is imposed;
  (viii) the prospects of reformation and correction, and becoming a useful member of society;
  (ix) the presence or absence of remorse or contrition;
  (x)   whether instead of imprisonment an alternative method of punishment would not be appropriate in the circumstances;
  (xi) a perceptive understanding of the accused's human frailties as effected by the circumstances surrounding the commission of the offence in question and a balancing of those frailties against the evil of the offender's deed. See *S v Sigwahla* 1967 (4) SA 566 (A) at 571E–F.
  (xii) Influence or encouragement of another. See *S v De Boer* 1968 (4) SA 866 (A); *S v Lehnberg en 'n Ander* 1975 (4) SA 553 (A); *S v Van Rooi en Andere* 1976 (2) SA 580 (A); *S v Khubeka en Andere* 1980 (4) SA 221 (O).

The above list is not exhaustive, but I believe that it contains pragmatic tests for the truth of the assertion of considering the position of the offender.

(d)   The crime. In passing sentence the trial court must take into account the moral and ethical nature of the crime, and the gravity of the offence. It is accepted and is indeed logical that a more serious crime will carry with it a greater moral blameworthiness than a minor or less serious offence. This involves a moral and value judgment. A process of arid intellectualism is insufficient. Mere theorising is not sufficient. What matters finally is how the Court views the crime on its own merits, and all the relevant proven facts and circumstances must be carefully considered and assessed.

Merely to find that a crime is by itself serious without regard to its setting and its factual context, and thereby concluding that the crime committed by the offender is therefore also serious, is not appropriate, and may result in a serious misdirection. The Court does not and cannot rely on a catalogue of crimes. To do so would result in a purely mechanistic approach, whereby the Court, in its judicial discretion, would fail to pay due regard to the facts and circumstances of the particular crime.

Conjoined to the nature of the crime are also the consequences of the crime. If the consequences are serious or indeed incalculable, the aggravating circumstances will be viewed more seriously by the Court. On the other hand, if there were no serious consequences or results flowing from the crime, the aggravating circumstances recede.

The sentence therefore must be commensurate with the gravity or otherwise of the crime, and is a necessary concomitant of punishment. See Du Toit *Straf in Suid Afrika* at 89–91; *S v Zinn (supra)*; *S v Haasbroek* 1969 (1) SA 356 (E).

(e)   The interests of the community. The Court fulfils an important function in applying the law in the community. It has a duty to maintain law and order. The Court operates in society and its decisions have an impact on individuals in the ordinary circumstances of daily life. It covers all possible ground. There is no sphere of life it does not include. The Court must also by its decisions, and the imposition of sentence, promote respect for the law, and in doing so must reflect the seriousness of the offence, and provide just punishment for the offender while taking into account the personal circumstances of the offender.

The feelings and requirements of the community, the protection of society against the accused and other potential offenders must be considered, as well as the maintenance of peace and tranquillity in the land needs to be taken into account. See *Du Toit (op cit* at 91–2).

A weighty consideration in imposing sentence is also the protection of the community. If an offender is a psychopath or a danger to society, society needs to be protected, and the Court has a bounden duty to protect society by imposing an appropriate sentence. In this respect the prospects of rehabilitation or reformation of an offender must be given due weight.

The nature of the crime is of considerable importance. It may be of such significance or so far reaching that imprisonment is the only adequate punishment. See *S v Maarman* 1976 (3) SA 510 (A); *S v Holder* 1979 (2) SA 70 (A) at 77–8.

While considering the interests of society as a factor in determining sentence, the interests of society should not be over-stressed to the detriment of the personal factors of the accused. As has already been indicated, a balance should be maintained between the different elements of the triad.

While it is clear that in crimes which impinge on the peace and tranquillity of society the interests of society come to the fore and may result in a recession of the personal circumstances of the offender, nevertheless the interests of society must not be over-emphasised at the expense of the personal circumstances of the accused. Due weight must be given to the personal circumstances of the accused throughout the process of sentencing. See *S v Quandu en Andere* 1989 (1) SA 517 (A); *Du Toit and Others Commentary on the Criminal Procedure Act* at 28–7.

(f)   As a general principle equal punishment for equal offences is to be imposed unless the personal characteristics of the respective accused make such differentiation necessary. See *S v Giannoulis (supra)*; *S v Marx* 1989 (1) SA 222 (A) at 225–6.

(g)   Mercy is regarded as a concomitant of justice. In *S v Rabie (supra* at 861D *et seq)* Holmes JA stated:

> 'Then there is the approach of mercy or compassion or plain humanity. It has nothing in common with maudlin sympathy for the accused. While recognising that fair punishment may sometimes have to be robust, mercy is a balanced and humane quality of thought which tempers one's approach when considering the basic factors of letting the punishment fit the criminal, as well as the crime, and being fair to society.'

The concept of mercy has been recognised by the Courts of this country. As has been said: 'Justice must be done but mercy, not a sledgehammer, is its concomitant.'

See *S v Harrison* 1970 (3) SA 684 (A) at 686A; *S v Sparks and Another* 1972 (3) SA 396 (A) at 410G.

These guidelines clearly spell out how the question of sentence should be approached. A mere *ex parte* statement from the bar is insufficient. Evidence is needed that will include expert testimony of, for example a forensic criminologist, psychologist, psychiatrist or a social worker.

In *S v Lewis*[93] Hefer JA said:

> A probation officer's report is something to which considerable importance is attached (cf *S v Adams* 1971 (4) SA 125 (C) at 127 and *S v Jansen and Another* 1975 (1) SA 425 (AD) at p 428 (both dealing with juveniles; *S v Maxaku* 1973 (4) SA 248 (C) at 254), for it usually provides the Court with all available information which will assist in understanding the problems of the accused (*S v H and Another* 1978 (4) SA 385 (ECD) at 386) and in determining the most appropriate form of punishment. Such a report always require careful consideration and often critical analysis in order to ensure that the views of a probation officer are not simply substituted for the Court's own views (*S v H and Another* loc cit). But if the recommendations contained therein are not followed, the accused and a Court of appeal is entitled to know why.

The same applies to the report of any other expert, for example the evidence of a forensic criminologist. A word of caution: without a proper and in depth consultation with the expert you can not lead the evidence of the expert with confidence. It is essential that you understand the content of the report and are comfortable with the technical terms of the discipline of the expert — remember the court is not an expert in the particular discipline and must be made to understand the evidence.

Bear in mind that mitigating factors are not synonymous with the term 'substantial and compelling circumstances' that appears in s 51 of the Criminal Law Amendment Act 105 of 1997, dealing with prescribed minimum sentences.[94]

In *S v Malgas*[95] the court considered the phrase 'substantial and compelling circumstances', and expressed itself as follows:

> [25] What stands out quite clearly is that the courts are a good deal freer to depart from the prescribed sentences than has been supposed in some of the previously decided cases and that it is they who are to judge whether or not the circumstances of any particular case are such as to justify a departure. However, in doing so, they are to respect, and not merely pay lip service to, the Legislature's view that the prescribed periods of imprisonment are to be taken to be ordinarily appropriate when crimes of the specified kind are committed. In summary —
> A.   Section 51 has limited but not eliminated the courts' discretion in imposing sentence in respect of offences referred to in Part I of Schedule 2 (or imprisonment for other specified periods for offences listed in other parts of Schedule 2).

---

[93] 1986 (2) PH H 96 (A).

[94] See in general, as to prescribed minimum sentences, *S v Malgas* 2001 (2) SA 1222 (SCA), 2001 (1) SACR 469 (SCA), and *Vilakazi v S* [2008] 4 All SA 396 (SCA).

[95] 2001 (2) SA 1222 (SCA), 2001 (1) SACR 469 (SCA).

B.   Courts are required to approach the imposition of sentence conscious that the Legislature has ordained life imprisonment (or the particular prescribed period of imprisonment) as the sentence that should ordinarily and in the absence of weighty justification be imposed for the listed crimes in the specified circumstances.

C.   Unless there are, and can be seen to be, truly convincing reasons for a different response, the crimes in question are therefore required to elicit a severe, standardised and consistent response from the courts.

D.   The specified sentences are not to be departed from lightly and for flimsy reasons. Speculative hypotheses favourable to the offender, undue sympathy, aversion to imprisoning first offenders, personal doubts as to the efficacy of the policy underlying the legislation, and marginal differences in personal circumstances or degrees of participation between co-offenders are to be excluded.

E.   The Legislature has however deliberately left it to the courts to decide whether the circumstances of any particular case call for a departure from the prescribed sentence. While the emphasis has shifted to the objective gravity of the type of crime and the need for effective sanctions against it, this does not mean that all other considerations are to be ignored.

F.   All factors (other than those set out in D above) traditionally taken into account in sentencing (whether or not they diminish moral guilt) thus continue to play a role; none is excluded at the outset from consideration in the sentencing process.

G.   The ultimate impact of all the circumstances relevant to sentencing must be measured against the composite yardstick ('substantial and compelling') and must be such as cumulatively justify a departure from the standardised response that the Legislature has ordained.

H.   In applying the statutory provisions, it is inappropriately constricting to use the concepts developed in dealing with appeals against sentence as the sole criterion.

I.   If the sentencing court on consideration of the circumstances of the particular case is satisfied that they render the prescribed sentence unjust in that it would be disproportionate to the crime, the criminal and the needs of society, so that an injustice would be done by imposing that sentence, it is entitled to impose a lesser sentence.

J.   In so doing, account must be taken of the fact that crime of that particular kind has been singled out for severe punishment and that the sentence to be imposed in lieu of the prescribed sentence should be assessed paying due regard to the bench mark which the Legislature has provided.

19.14 CRIMINAL APPEALS

The technique of appeals is dealt with in chapter 18, but that chapter does not specifically deal with criminal appeals. Chapter 18 however contains useful hints on how to handle yourself in the appeal court and how heads of argument should be prepared and argument presented.

There is no longer an automatic right of appeal from a lower court to a higher court in criminal cases. Section 309B of the Criminal Procedure Act provides that any accused, other than a person contemplated in the first proviso to s 309(1)*(a)*, who wishes to note an appeal against any conviction or against any resultant sentence or order of a lower court, must apply to that court for leave to appeal against that conviction, sentence or order within 14 days[96] after the passing of the sentence or order following on the conviction; or within such extended period as the court may on application and for good cause shown, allow.

Every application for leave to appeal must set forth clearly and specifically the grounds upon which the accused desires to appeal. If the accused applies orally for such leave immediately after the passing of the sentence or order, he must state such grounds, which must be recorded and form part of the record.

If any application referred to in this section is refused, the magistrate must immediately record his or her reasons for such refusal.

An application for leave to appeal may be accompanied by an application to adduce further evidence (hereafter referred to as an application for further evidence) relating to the conviction, sentence or order in respect of which the appeal is sought to be noted.

An application for further evidence must be supported by an affidavit stating that:

- further evidence which would presumably be accepted as true, is available;
- if accepted the evidence could reasonably lead to a different decision or order; and
- there is a reasonably acceptable explanation for the failure to produce the evidence before the close of the trial.

Section 309C provides that if any application
- for condonation,
- for further evidence, or
- for leave to appeal,

is refused by a lower court, the accused may by petition apply to the Judge President of the High Court having jurisdiction to grant any one or more of the applications in question.

Any petition must be made

- within 21 days[97] after the application in question was refused or
- within such extended period as may on an application accompanying that petition, for good cause shown, be allowed.

An accused who submits a petition must at the same time give notice thereof to the clerk of the lower court where the conviction or sentence or order was made.

When receiving the notice the clerk of the court must without delay submit to the registrar of the High Court concerned copies of —

---

[96] Note that because these are days as prescribed in an Act as opposed to a rule, they are calendar days and not court days. In other words, Saturdays, Sundays and public holidays are included.

[97] Calendar days. See fn 96.

- the application that was refused,
- the magistrate's reasons for refusal of the application and
- the record of the proceedings in the magistrate's court in respect of which the application was refused provided that
  - if the accused was tried in a regional court and was legally represented at the trial, or
  - if the accused and the Director of Public Prosecutions agree thereto, or
  - if the prospective appeal is against the sentence only, or
  - if the petition relates solely to an application for condonation, and
- acopy of the judgment, which includes the reasons for conviction and sentence shall suffice for the purposes of the petition.

There is one exception where there is an automatic right to appeal. Section 309(1)*(a)*(ii) provides that if a person was sentenced to imprisonment for life by a regional court under s 51(1) of the Criminal Law Amendment Act 105 of 1997, an appeal may be noted without having to apply for leave to appeal.

CHAPTER 20

'Gods, Graves and Scholars'

From archaeology to law is a far enough cry, although in these enlightened days there are many who would fain relegate the latter to the category of the former. The instant theme, however, is not altogether archaeological, or even archaic. It is modern and pragmatic. The gods of this chapter are the judges before whom you will appear, with a passing mention of the demi-gods — or magistrates. The category of graves seems to me to be an apt ascription for arbitration. Scholars? Well, I shall conclude my work with my views on scholars.

20.1 GODS

Judges, in one's first few years of practice, are awesome beings of foreboding mien and overwhelming presence. It is no chance freak of architecture that ensconced them in lofty eyries from which their eagle eyes survey the ranks of juniors below. When you have been in practice a good many years and find your contemporaries, yea, even your juniors, adorning the Bench, judges seem to lose a good deal of their terror and presence, but forever do they look down on you.

It is not my purpose unduly to criticise the judiciary, and, if what I write seems to suggest that there are failings on the part of judges, it may well be that my own imperfections have led me into misconception. However, Harris[1] has the following to say:

> It has often happened that a learned judge with an irritable temperament has interrupted counsel repeatedly before he has had an opportunity of opening his case, and interrupted the witness while giving his evidence as well as the cross-examination because he has not understood its points, so that everybody has been either unnerved or irritated in turn.

It is to be observed that in 1945 the English court of appeal used language which showed that it is not only the irritable and short-tempered judge who may unduly hamper the course of justice:[2]

> The part which a judge ought to take while witnesses are giving their evidence must, of course, rest with his discretion. But with the utmost respect to the judge it was, I think, unfortunate that he took so large a part as he did ... I can find no trace whatever of any tendency to take sides or to press a witness in any way which could be considered undesirable. It is quite plain to me that the judge was endeavouring to

---

[1] Richard Harris KC *Illustrations in Advocacy* 5 ed (Stevens & Haynes, 1915) 254.
[2] *Yuill v Yuill* [1945] 1 All ER 183 (CA) at 185.

ascertain the truth in the manner which at the moment seemed to him most convenient. But he must, I think, have lost sight of the inconveniences which are apt to flow from an undue participation by the judge in the examination of witnesses . . . it is for counsel to decide at what stage he will put the question, and the whole strength of the cross-examination may be destroyed if the judge, in his desire to get what seems to him to be the crucial point, himself intervenes and prematurely puts the question himself.

Lest it be thought that South African judges do not err in this respect let me quote from a judgment of the Appellate Division:[3]

> The learned Judge-President, no doubt with good intent, appears to have been anxious that a case, which at the outset did not appear to him to present any real difficulties, should not be dragged on too long. He sought from time to time to expedite the hearing of the matter by virtually taking over from counsel both the examination and cross-examination of witnesses. In doing so, it appears that he may at times have overlooked the judge's usual role in our system of civil trial procedure, and to have associated himself too closely with the conduct of the case, thereby denying himself the full advantage usually enjoyed by the trial judge who, as the person holding the scale between the contending parties, is able to determine objectively and dispassionately, from his position of relative detachment, the way the balance tilts.

It is a matter of some regret that Wessels JA in delivering this judgment, did not quote the powerful phraseology of Lord Denning in *Jones v National Coal Board*,[4] although he did refer to that case with approval. Lord Denning's words so lucidly and with such mastery of language and phrase express the duties of judges and counsel that it would have been well to repeat them for the guidance of our own courts and practitioners.

In the hope of heartening counsel in his task, and mindful of many other cases where judges, often with equally good intent, appear to have transgressed, I therefore quote what should not be allowed to pass into the limbo of forgotten things.

> In the system of trial which we have evolved in this country, the judge sits to hear and determine the issues raised by the parties, not to conduct an investigation or examination on behalf of society at large, as happens, we believe, in some foreign countries. Even in England, however, a judge is not a mere umpire to answer the question 'How's that?' His object above all is to find out the truth, and to do justice according to law; and in the daily pursuit of it the advocate plays an honourable and necessary role. Was it not Lord Eldon LC who said in notable passage that '*truth is best discovered by powerful statements on both sides of the question*' . . . and Lord Greene MR who explained that justice is best done by a judge who holds the balance between the contending parties without himself taking part in their disputations? . . . And it is for

---

[3] *Hamman v Moolman* 1968 (4) SA 340 (A) at 344 citing *R v Roopsingh* 1956 (4) SA 509 (A) and *Jones v National Coal Board* [1957] 2 All ER 155 (CA). See also the authorities cited by counsel in *Roopsingh's* case at 510, and *Rondalia Versekeringskorporasie van SA Bpk v Lira* 1971 (2) SA 586 (A), *Solomon and Another NNO v De Waal* 1972 (1) SA 575 (A), and *Vilakazi v Sanlam Assuransie Maatskappy Bpk* 1974 (1) SA 23 (A). Also *Olivier v Die Kaapse Balieraad* 1972 (3) SA 485 (A).

[4] [1957] 2 All ER 155 (CA) at 158–160.

the advocate to state his case as fairly and strongly as he can, without undue interruption, lest the sequence of his argument be lost. . . . The judge's part in all this is to hearken to the evidence, only himself asking questions when it is necessary to clear up any point that has been overlooked or left obscure; to see that the advocates behave themselves seemly and keep to the rules laid down by law; to exclude irrelevancies and discourage repetition; to make sure by wise intervention that he follows the points that the advocates are making and can assess their worth; and at the end to make up his mind where the truth lies. *If he goes beyond this, he drops the mantle of a judge and assumes the robe of an advocate; and the change does not become him well.* Lord Bacon spoke right when he said that:

'Patience and gravity of hearing is an essential part of justice; and an overspeaking judge is no well tuned cymbal.'

Excessive judicial interruption inevitably weakens the effectiveness of cross-examination . . . for at one and the same time it gives a witness valuable time for thought before answering a difficult question, and diverts cross-examining counsel from the course which he had intended to pursue, and to which it is by no means easy, sometimes, to return.

To reproduce these passages in the pages of a textbook is easy. To bring them to the notice of a judge in the hurly-burly of a trial is difficult and delicate, for judges vary in their temperament and even the most mild-mannered judge has the last, and most effective, word. If he persists in so doing you may console yourself with the thought that the court of appeal will no doubt put the matter into proper perspective — if your client can afford an appeal. For this reason you must square your shoulders and brace yourself against judicial wrath by insisting upon your rights and persisting in your protestations. This will take a lot of courage, but without that courage you will be runner-up more often than you take the laurel wreath of victory.

It is often thought that it is unwise to antagonise the judge by quarrelling with him, or by opposing him in his personal views. There are three possibilities: the judge may already be antagonistic; the judge may resent your express or implied criticism of his conduct; the judge may determine fairly and objectively whether you are right or he is. In the first and third events you have nothing to lose. What then of the second? There lies the problem, for it is only the self-opinionated and arrogant man or woman who should be resentful of just criticism, fairly stated and founded at least on a reasonable cause of complaint. The descent 'into the arena',[5] one would imagine, would be easier for a judge who has the qualities which I have just stated. So if your assessment of your judge is that he is self-opinionated or arrogant then, in theory at least, it would seem that the consequences of judicial wrath might extend even to your client. In such a case it might be well to temper courage with caution — but not too little courage nor too much caution. It might be well to bide your time until you are certain that you have not misjudged the situation and then make your submissions, with firmness and without offensiveness. You will, of course, bear in mind that there are limits to the freedom that counsel enjoys in resisting

[5] Per Lord Greene MR in *Yuill v Yuill* [1945] 1 All ER 183 (CA) at 189B.

the court. My own view is that the courts could well exercise a far greater forbearance than is sometimes the case. Counsel must not be disrespectful or contemptuous, it is true, but how is he to meet what he genuinely believes to be transgressions on the part of the judicial officer? Two examples of cases where the legal practitioner came to grief are *R v Silber*[6] and *R v Rosenstein*.[7] And if one expresses respectful agreement with the decision in the former case one may be pardoned, I hope, for having serious misgivings as to the correctness of the judgment in the latter. Bearing in mind that the judge who delivered the judgment of the court on appeal in *Rosenstein's* case was Ramsbottom J, whose name was synonymous with patience and fairness, it is manifest that if counsel is to discharge his duty to his client he must inevitably run the risk of judicial displeasure becoming unjudicial pique. Of course, if the courts did exercise more tolerance in regard to counsel's grievances then a state of mind would exist in which there would probably be less cause for criticism. But I must largely leave it to you to work out when or how to stop the judge when he embarks on a detailed examination or cross-examination in the middle of your interrogations.

The human mind, or so it would seem to the layman, functions in three ways. In the first place the brain is activated by a host of instincts which have evolved in the echoing aeons since humanity emerged from the world of beasts. Secondly, there are behaviour patterns superimposed by years of individual training or conditioning. These patterns are infinitely variegated, embracing such manifestations as the salute accorded by a soldier to a commissioned officer, the post-prandial cigar, the fear of thunder and a thousand and one other characteristics and oddities. In the third place the mind thinks, it cerebrates. It evaluates. It considers. It ponders. It cogitates. It analyses. It reaches its conclusion purely on a digestion of the data afforded it, unaffected by its instincts and undiverted by its behaviour patterns.

Nothing is known to warrant the conclusion that the judicial mind functions in any other way.

I dismiss from consideration the process described as inspiration. I do not deny it. I cannot dispute that it may be method of mind-function. All I wish to say about inspiration is that if it is a pure mind-function then it is possibly a combination or interaction of instinct and subconscious analysis. If, however, inspiration comes from without then, beyond any doubt, I am not qualified to take the discussion further.

I return to the judicial mind. Ideally the judicial mind should function in the third manner which I have described. Naturally enough, the judicial mind is affected by its instincts. This is understandable, unavoidable and acceptable within limits. The greatest problem of the practitioner is the judicial mind whose reasoning process is dominated or even influenced by its behaviour patterns. Let there be no misunderstanding here. By behaviour patterns I do

---

[6] 1952 (2) SA 475 (A).
[7] 1943 TPD 65.

not mean something like the courteous gesture of the gentleman raising his hat when he encounters a lady. I mean the way of thinking that is engrained on every single mind as a result of its schooling, its environment, its associations and its own personal life-history. I include the plethora of prejudices with which almost every one of us is plagued. He is indeed a great judge who can put behind him his behaviour patterns and can process the data afforded him almost as impersonally as does a computer.

It is no criticism of the *bona fides* or honesty of purpose of the Bench to point to the problem which arises when the judge's own conditioning dominates his demeanour and affects his judgment. Examples are not difficult to find. A judge may, for example, have difficulty in doubting the truthfulness and honesty of a member of his or her own particular social sphere. He or she may have had a somewhat unhappy matrimonial life and for that very reason may have some conditioned antipathy towards wives or husbands or co-defendants. On the other hand he or she may have good reason for believing that being a co-defendant is merely one of the unfortunate quirks of fate. Of course, it can be only in the rarest of cases that the judge would consciously permit his cerebration to be affected by the behaviour pattern imposed on him by his circumstances. But do we not all think as we have been trained to think? And if portion of our training is to regard a particular factor with favour or disfavour then our thinking, when that factor is a datum, must almost inevitably lead us to regard it as we have been trained to do, believing that in the process we are making an impartial assessment.

While this form of subconscious orientation is a problem, the more pressing question is how to deal with it. Without knowing his entire background and personal history it is a matter of no small difficulty to recognise that a set of circumstances exists in which a particular judge's consideration and analysis of the data is likely to be faulty. Assuming, in any given case, that counsel (or an attorney) does believe that some particular circumstance in the case may evoke a behaviour pattern in the court's mind, the question of coping with the problem is an exercise in tact and tactics. Counsel cannot bluntly say 'I know that you don't like people of my client's ethnic group but I want you to dismiss that from consideration when considering his evidence'. That is contempt.

Perhaps, from years of experience, something will emerge which will enable you to recognise the dominance of a behaviour pattern and perhaps you may develop a method of dealing with the manifestation. It is a very real problem, the answer to which often eludes even the most capable advocate.

How real counsel's problem is can be ascertained from the case of *Solomon and Another NNO v De Waal*[8] where, despite its earlier decision of *Hamman v Moolman*,[9] the appeal court again was asked to consider interventions by the learned Judge-President. The judgment contains the following remarks:

[8] 1972 (1) SA 575 (A) at 580E–H.
[9] 1968 (4) SA 340 (A).

> However, by descending into the arena of the conflict between the parties in that manner the learned judge might well have disabled himself from assessing with due impartiality the credibility of the witnesses, the probabilities relating to the issues, and the amount of the general damages sustained by plaintiff. Even if that were not so, such interventions might well have created the impression, at least in the minds of defendants, that he had so disabled himself and that he was favouring or promoting the plaintiff's cause and prejudging the case against defendants. In that regard it must be born[e] in mind that justice should not only be done but should manifestly and undoubtedly be seen to be done.

The first lesson you should learn in regard to judges is that they are not necessarily right. As you yourself progress along the road of the law you will pass through many consultations. In how many of those consultations will you find that you have started off by misconceiving the position for want of hearing or appreciating some fact or other? So it is with judges. Not all the skill and experience in the world will provide an assurance that there will never arise a blind spot, or that some fact will not be overlooked. It is for this reason that you must ensure that the judge has the facts, and all the facts, brought to his attention; while you must know the law, and all the law.

Often it is not easy to withstand judicial dominance, but if the interests of your case demand it you have to resist, your conduct being a combination of courtesy, respect and firmness.

In regard to magistrates the problems which you will encounter are perhaps different in degree only. Magistrates are appointed from the ranks of prosecutors and often appear in their thinking to be oriented more to the psychology of prosecution than to that of defence. What this demands, in the majority of cases, is greater care and precision on your part. It is not that the magistrate will not see your case, it is not that he does not want to see your case, it is not that he has closed his mind to your case. It is simply that, just as your training in criminal matters was to secure acquittals, so his original training was to secure convictions. In so doing he viewed matters from the point of view of a criminal investigation, prosecution and conviction. Let it not be thought for a moment that magistrates do not know what a reasonable doubt is. All you have to do is to read your newspapers any day to see cases where some very dubious characters have been given the benefit of the doubt in the magistrate's court. If one can rely on these reports, it is usually because the evidence for the state was confused and contradictory. Therein lies the lesson, so plainly that I need not expound on it.

Nor should you delude yourself into the belief that the magistrate's background does not qualify him to appreciate abstruse arguments in civil cases. Here again the reports belie the belief, for you will find countless cases where the Appellate Division or the Supreme Court of Appeal has reversed the decision of a provincial division and restored the magistrate's judgment. Which shows how perplexing is the practice of the law.

Magistrates, no less than judges, must be treated with courtesy and respect. I make no mention of firmness because it seems that magistrates are less likely to essay domination of the course of the matters which they are trying. In place, therefore, of firmness, I would substitute circumspection, for the reasons I have already given.

One final word: It is counsel's practice to introduce himself to a judge before whom he is to appear for the first time. There seems to be no reason why a magistrate should not be accorded a similar courtesy. This formality sometimes leads to unexpected windfalls as a result of the awkward silence that often follows the preliminary handshake, and so you should never be reluctant to pass the time of day. Your client can restrain his impatience for a few minutes longer while you learn a few things for his benefit.

An important point of technique in magistrate's court trials is to remember that the record must often be written in longhand. Now you want your gems of cross-examination recorded for the benefit of the appeal court, if necessary. The magistrate wants to keep a proper record for his own sake as well as that of the appeal court. That leaves only the opposition. The opposition may not regard your words in the same light as you do. For that reason we dismiss the opposition from consideration. If you want your cross-examination properly recorded you will have to restrain your impatience. Often the most effective method of cross-examination is to put the questions in rapid succession denying the witness time to invent answers and excuses. Before a magistrate that may be impossible. Moreover, if you put question B while he is still recording question A he will not be able to appreciate — or even to hear — answer B. This means that question B has to be repeated, by which time the witness has invented a new answer and says that you misunderstood the original one which he did not give anyway.

20.2 GRAVES

The great Lord Denning commenced one of his judgments:[10]

> When I was young, a sandwich-man wearing a top-hat used to parade outside these courts with his boards back and front proclaiming 'Arbitrate, don't litigate'. It was very good advice so long as arbitrations were conducted speedily, as many still are in the City of London. But it is not so good when arbitrations drag on forever.'

Let me set out the possible problems with arbitrations, in order that you may realise why I suggest that 'graves' might not be an unfitting description:

* The costs to the loser are greater, because the loser has to pay the arbitrator's fees as also the costs of the venue and of transcription, as well as those for which he would be liable in ordinary litigation. If there have to be two arbitrators and an umpire the expense can well be double that of a hearing by the court.[11]

---

[10] *Bremer Vulken Schiffbau and Maschinenfabrik v South India Shipping Company* [1980] 1 Lloyds Rep 255 (CA) at 270.
[11] That said, when arbitrations work they can be more expeditious than litigation, offsetting these additional costs.

- By the time dates have been arranged to accommodate the arbitrator and the legal representatives of both parties, arbitration is often little more expeditious than litigation, if it is more expeditious at all.
- Where the arbitrator is not a lawyer, he is liable to all the imperfections of an untrained mind—a single, *unappealable*, untrained mind — dealing with the complexities of law and fact that arise in a trial.[12]
- For all practical purposes there is no appeal from a bad or erroneous decision.[13] You can (and in many cases do) specifically agree on a right of appeal, but in that event the agreement might itself lead to disputes and, in addition, the losing party now finds himself having to pay for the cost of the appeal arbitrators, usually numbering three.

Sometimes attempts are made to avoid the first three objections to arbitration listed above. Agreements provide, with a wealth of specification, that any arbitration is to be held informally, without pleadings, without legal representation and (piously enough) without delay. In similar manner do captains of cricket teams decide which eleven is to bat first. I have seen one such agreement which stipulated not only that the rules of evidence and procedure were not to apply, but also that the matter was to be decided without regard to the principles of law. You should have heard counsel argue the meaning of that one! Rules of procedure, the law of evidence and the principles of law have been evolved over many centuries of application of trial and failure, of experience and of expense.

It is only right to tell you that my views on this point do not accord with judicial thinking. Corbett J in the case of *Dipenta Africa Construction (Pty) Ltd v Cape Provincial Administration*[14] held quite the contrary, and his views are reported in these words:[15]

> (T)he arbitration is likely to give rise to technical issues of considerable difficulty and complexity . . . In the circumstances . . . I have come to the conclusion that the interests of the parties will best be served by the appointment of an engineer as arbitrator.
>
> I find my viewpoint reinforced to some extent by the following consideration. This decision, as I see it, turns largely upon an assessment of the technical complexities and difficulties involved in the case . . . If these complexities and difficulties are under-estimated and an advocate be appointed, the disadvantages following from that are in my view likely to be far greater than if these complexities and difficulties are over-estimated and an engineer be appointed. The general balance

---

[12] Why a layman should be asked to act as a judge is a puzzle. The theory is often advanced that an architect, engineer or quantity surveyor is better equipped to understand the technicalities of disputes in building or engineering cases. This may be so, but it must be the more carefully weighed against his lack of skill in legal or evidentiary matters. Nor do I for a moment concede that the technique of building of houses, offices, roads or bridges is so esoteric that the average judicial officer is at any disadvantage in considering technical evidence on the points involved.

[13] See, for the limited grounds on which an arbitration award can be reviewed, *Telcordia Technologies Incorporated v Telkom SA Limited* 2007 (3) SA 266 (SCA).

[14] 1973 (1) SA 666 (C). (Note the report on appeal: 1973 (3) SA 47 (A).)

[15] At 672D–H.

of utility and convenience would therefore seem to favour an engineer appointment in this particular case.'

Let me give you a view of the other side. In the case of *Phame (Pty) Ltd v Paizes*[16] the cause of action was based on a contract containing an arbitration clause which provided that if any dispute that arose was a matter of law counsel was to be appointed as an arbitrator, while if it was a matter of accountancy an accountant was to arbitrate. The plaintiff alleged that as a result of a misrepresentation he had been induced to pay more than the true value of the property and he claimed a reduction of the purchase price. Whether this was a matter of law or accountancy need not trouble one. Let us assume that an accountant had been appointed as arbitrator in terms of a further clause which dealt with such states of uncertainty. If you read the reported judgment which establishes that the *actio quanti minoris* is available to a purchaser of incorporeals who claims a reduction of the purchase price because of a non-fraudulent misrepresentation you will see why neither party could really be satisfied to have the matter decided by any arbitrator, especially by one not trained in the law.

There are, of course, some arguments in favour of arbitration:

- There is no press publicity in the case of private arbitrations and hence no reputations ruined to make a Roman holiday.[17]
- The parties may select their own judge with an eye to qualities which they consider of value in their own dispute. The advantages of this factor should not be under-estimated. Choose someone whose knowledge in the particular field or fields the parties will respect, who will be able to exercise authority over the proceedings, and who will be able to give a quick award.
- Finality can be assured, with no appeal and no question of absolution from the instance. This is quicker and may be cheaper in the long run, even if the loser has to swallow his disgruntlement.
- When dates have been arranged there is no question of parties and witnesses having to waste valuable days because the rolls are congested and no court is available.
- Arbitrations, being capable of informality, are also capable of flexibility and offer scope for tactical exercises that would be impossible in a court.
- Having no inherent jurisdiction, it is the function of the arbitrator to listen to evidence and to argument. He has no power to form a view of the case simply by reading the pleadings and then to suggest — even command —

---

[16] 1973 (3) SA 397 (A).

[17] Arbitrations are in any event supposed to be confidential. See D Butler and E Finsen *Arbitration in South Africa – Law and Practice* (Juta, 1993) 213–4, *Ali Shipping Corporation v Shipyard Trogir* [1998] 2 All ER 136 (CA), *City of Moscow v The Bankers Trust Company and Another* [2004] BLR 229 (CA) and *Emmott v Michael Wilson & Partners Ltd* [2008] 1 Lloyd's Rep 616 (CA). But see *Replication Technology Group and Others v Gallo Africa Ltd* 2009 (5) 531 (GSJ) 547.

that the parties arrive at a settlement. And he has less of a tendency to descend into the arena.

As far as technique is concerned, you must recognise the need to adjust the conduct of your case to the particular qualifications of the arbitrator. Where the arbitrator is a specialist in his field, the fine points of tactics and cross-examination may be blunted by the emphasis on the technical facts in dispute, and the powers given by s 14 of the Arbitration Act 42 of 1965 are perhaps less likely to be useful implements of procedure than when you appear before counsel. It may then be that inspection, examination and qualified witnesses are all-important, and your presentation of the matter must be shaped by your own expert advisers. Where, however, you have a lawyer as arbitrator only slight modification of your trial technique may be called for.

Peace be with you.

20.3 SCHOLARS

Scholars! 'Who', you may ask, 'are the scholars?' As I near the end of my thesis and as I recall some 45 years in which my stumbling footsteps have traced the path I offer you for your journey I feel that I can now answer that question. I am a scholar. As I write, I must think, and I must reason the why and the wherefore. And if I pretend to teach, it is no more than a whimsical impertinence on my part. For in the writing and in the thinking and in the evolving of the why and the wherefore, I am teaching — teaching myself. Nor yet do I consider my lessons to have been well learned. Nor yet have I met a colleague who himself is learned beyond learning. Nor yet, least of all, can I be sure that what I advise is free of folly. I trust that I write with humility when I record that even in the greatest have I seen error. And is error anything more than a lesson yet to be learned?

In every case, every consultation, every opinion, is to be found something to be learned. There is law to be learned, and foresight, and knowledge of humanity. If from these teachers you do not learn you may well fall by the wayside.

May you, too, be one of the scholars.

Skeletal Advice on Evidence for the Plaintiff

ADVICE ON EVIDENCE FOR THE PLAINTIFF

1. INTRODUCTION

Every story has to start somewhere: a brief outline of how the case came about, and when it is on the roll. For example, in a collision matter, you might say that two vehicles collided with one another within the intersection of whatever streets on whatever day, that arising out of this A sued B for the damage to his vehicle, B in due course counter-claimed for his own damage and the matter is enrolled for trial on whatever day and, finally, that you have been asked to furnish A with an Advice on Evidence.

2. ANALYSIS OF THE PLEADINGS

2.1 Common cause issues

List them, point for point.

2.2 Disputed issues

List them also, point for point. Some of them might be quite immaterial and if so, you can say so. Some of them will be easily established in the evidence of the plaintiff, and you can say so here and not deal with them again. But the usefulness of this part of the Advice is that you force yourself to establish precisely what issues are in dispute, and which are material.

You might already at this stage, when dealing with disputed issues, have made notes for yourself further on under following sub-headings. For example, in a collision case where *locus standi* is in dispute, you might now already have made a note under 5.1 to obtain and discover the documentation relating to the credit purchase of the vehicle and under 6 to give rule 35(9) notice thereof.

3. DISCUSSION OF THE ISSUES, AND OF THE BURDEN OF PROOF

A logical point-by-point discussion of the material issues:

Firstly, discuss who bears the burden of proof? (In some cases that is so obvious it really seems foolish even to mention it, but in other cases not).

Secondly, how do you propose going about proving those issues on which you bear the burden of proof?

Thirdly, discuss what tactics the defendant's will probably adopt? (In some instances it is pointless or simply too speculative to deal with this, but in other cases it is imperative to bear in mind that there are witnesses C, D and E who the defendant probably will want to call. What will they likely say? How will you counter what they say? How credible are they likely to be).

Fourthly, discuss not only the issues and their likely outcome, but also steps that need to be taken in order to investigate those issues and prepare thereon which will not necessarily be dealt with under the other sub-headings or which in any event are best logically also discussed here. In a collision case, it is usually best to visit the scene and consult there with witnesses. If so, say so, say more or less when you think the inspection should be arranged for, and who should be present. If experts are necessary, describe which experts, and make recommendations. If a range of people have to be consulted with, identify who needs to be consulted with, whether they should be best consulted with alone or together with other witnesses, and make recommendations in this regard.

The aim is that when your attorney — and if he so decides, the client — has finished reading your discussion in paragraph 3, he will have a good idea how the matter looks, and how it is likely to pan out. You might for example find yourself here ending with the conclusion that the case is bad and should be settled at best. If that is the way it is, the sooner your attorney — and the client — knows, the better. If you are acting for the defendant this may be the appropriate stage to discuss the possibility of making a tender.

4.   SEPARATION OF ISSUES IN TERMS OF RULE 33(4)

Your discussions at 2.2 and 3 will lead you to the conclusion here. Should issues be separated or not? If so, what issues? If you don't want to separate but the other side do and launch an application, how likely are you to defeat that application? All of this needs to be considered here.

See in this regard the question of duration as discussed in paragraph 8 below.

5.   DISCOVERY

5.1   Discovery by the plaintiff

Your discussion at 2.2 and 3 above will have led you, while dealing with that, to making points of specific documents that need to be discovered. You will list them here.

Remember, discovery is generally the key to postponement. You want to impress on your attorney the importance of timeous and comprehensive discovery.

It might be that your attorney has already made discovery. If so, study the discovery, compare it with your notes as to what needs to be discovered and advise him (invariably) as to what needs to be supplementarily discovered.

While making a note of the items that need to be discovered, it will also be a good idea that under 6 below you are also making a note of those items of which rule 35(9) notice should be given.

5.2   Discovery by the defendant

This is not a matter of doing the defendant's work. There might be documents that you would want to inspect that will be in the possession of the defendant. Here you list only those documents that are important to your client. If the defendant has already made discovery but has not included them or all of them, then:

- to the extent that they are discovered, request your attorney to ask for copies from the other side or the right of inspection;
- to the extent that they are not discovered, point out that they should have been and refer to 6 below where you will list a rule 35(3) notice. Point out that it must be insisted that the answer to the rule 35(3) notice must be on oath. Cases have been lost through ill-considered rule 35(3) answers under oath, bearing in mind that it is generally the litigant who will have to depose.

If the defendant has not yet made discovery, a rule 35(3) notice is not appropriate. Request your attorney to address a letter to the other side calling upon them to make discovery and to include the documents in question therein, and tell your attorney that should they then make discovery and not include all of those documents, those that they do discover must be inspected/copied, and those that they don't must be dealt with by way of rule 35(3).

6. NOTICES

6.1 Rule 36(10). See the discussion of this rule in chapter 6 above. Consider whether a rule 36(10) notice is required, and if so, of what documents. List them. It is no guide for you to simply suggest that the attorney should give rule 36(10) notice. You must tell him *what he must give rule 36(10) notice of.*

6.2 Rule 35(9). The same comments apply. Do not simply suggest that rule 35(9) notice be given. Stipulate of what documents it must be given.

6.3 Section 22 of the Civil Proceedings Evidence Act 25 of 1965. Again, be specific.

6.4 Section 30 of the Civil Proceedings Evidence Act 25 of 1965. Be specific.

6.5 Rule 35(3). Be specific.

6.6 Rule 36(9). Be specific.

6.7 There might be other rules to which you would want to refer. Whether that is so or not ought generally to arise out of your discussion of the issues in paragraph 3.

7. WITNESSES

Deal with the witnesses you propose calling. Some you will say ought to be reserved and might or might not be called depending on how others do. Deal with the order of witnesses so that your attorney can arrange things with them. Deal with which witnesses need to be subpoenaed, and which need merely to be reserved. Deal with subpoenae *duces tecum* in terms of rule 38(1). Go so far as to suggest which subpoenae need to be accompanied by a nice letter explaining the need for the evidence, apologising for the inconvenience and perhaps offering to accept copies of the documents rather than forcing the recipient to deliver them to the registrar etc., and which do not. Ultimately, the aim is to win, and recalcitrant and angry witnesses generally don't help you win.

8. ESTIMATED DURATION OF THE HEARING

Your discussion in paragraphs 3 and 7 above will have given you some idea of how long the trial is likely to take. Now you can say how long the trial is likely to last.

In some Divisions (such as for example Pretoria and Johannesburg), early and advance notice must be given to the DJP if a trial is likely to last longer than a certain number of days, and a judge might well not be allocated if that notice is not given. In yet other Divisions, matters are set down for a specific number of days — which, if you represent the defendant and if the plaintiff will have to begin, might be advantageous in that you will have forced the plaintiff to lay his cards on the table before the matter runs out of time and has to be postponed. But part-heard matters are expensive and inconvenient, and if it is clear that the matter will definitely run for longer than the allocated number of days, the sooner this is known and dealt with, the better.

9. PRE–TRIAL CONFERENCE

Do you want an early pre-trial conference, or one closer to the date? I am perhaps nothing more than a creature of habit, but my experience has been that early pre-trial conferences usually achieve nothing because neither party has all the chess pieces on the board yet.

In each instance, the particular practice of the particular Division has to be borne in mind.

10. RECOMMENDED STEPS

Attorneys are generally as busy as counsel, even more so. Your attorney should carefully study your advice, but he might not. Apportioning blame afterwards doesn't help. It's useful to have a final paragraph like this where you list the steps that need to be taken in the order they need to be taken. In 2.2, for example, you might have said that you have drafted (and enclose) a rule 21(2) request for further particulars aimed at forcing the defendant out of cover on a number of issues. Then that will be repeated here ('The enclosed rule 21(2) request for further particulars for purposes of trial must be served and filed as soon as possible and a timeous and proper answer thereto enforced. A copy of the answer must please be furnished to me as soon as same is received by my instructing attorney'). In 3 you will have listed steps that need to be taken in preparation for trial (consult with this person and that person, go to the scene with this and that person, take photographs, draw up a sketch plan, bring in this-and-this expert, etc.). While you were doing that, list those points here so that there is a point-by-point outline of *precisely* what must be done, more or less in the chronological order in which it must be done. In 4 you might have suggested that your instructing attorney address a letter to the other side insisting upon a separation and notifying the other side that if they don't agree within a specified time, a substantive application will be brought. Then list it here. And so on.

You might find it more useful, rather than listing the steps in a paragraph, to have a separate annexure listing in point form what is required of the attorney. Whatever route you take, it should be the one that you believe is most suited to the aim of the advice, which is to timeously and practically advise your instructing attorney as to what needs to be done in order to prepare properly for trial in the matter.

DATED at JOHANNESBURG on this the 15th day of DECEMBER 2009.

Matters of Style, Address and Manners

1. MATTERS OF STYLE

There are many things you can do to improve on the impact you make in court. What follows are a few diffident suggestions:

- Speak well. An advocate is far more than just a performer, but he is *also* a performer. Your job is to persuade, and the better you have prepared, the better you marshal your case and your arguments, and the better you *speak*, whether that be to witnesses or to the court, the better you will be performing.

  This is a particularly sensitive point in South Africa, where you might find yourself seldom if ever speaking in your mother tongue. If that is so then, regrettable though that might be, the sooner you master the language in which you will find yourself speaking in court so that you can use it effectively and persuasively, the better.

- Try to avoid the 'ums', 'ahs' and other sounds which betray nervousness and detract from the force of your speech. Try, in the beginning of your career, to consciously replace those nervous mannerisms with pauses. You will find the impact on your presentation is immeasurable. Nervousness is replaced with *gravitas*.

  Listen, if you can, to the speeches of Winston Churchill and Barack Obama. Each, you will find, has practised the habit of *pausing* when the rest of us would betray our doubts as to the next choice of words with an 'um'.

- Related to the previous point is the excessive use of 'my Lord'. Subject to the esoterics (dealt with below) of 'Justice' and so forth, you address the judge as 'your Lordship' (where you would otherwise have said 'you'), and you refer to 'my Lord' as a mark of respect where you would otherwise have paused (as in 'if I may, my Lord, refer to page 12 of the bundle').

  Nervousness often betrays itself in repetitious 'my Lords'. Be conscious of that, and keep it to the necessary minimum.

- Do not speak too quickly. Speak in measured tones. Pause deliberately and ensure that the judge has written down and grasped the point you have made. You might find that you need to deliberately slow your delivery. Nervousness makes us speak quickly. A person who speaks too quickly betrays nervousness and is less easily followed. A person who speaks in measured tones shows command. Which would you rather show?

- *We do not think, we submit.*

  As in 'I submit that. . . .', as opposed to 'I think that'.

  The distinction is important, and was adverted to in paragraph 9.2 of chapter 9. Your task is to represent a party to the best of your ability. To that end, you are not just perfectly entitled, but indeed obliged, to make submissions with which you might not personally agree.[1]

---

[1] Indeed, much lies at the heart of this distinction between 'I think' and 'I submit'. You are not only entitled, but obliged, to *make a submission* which is as far removed from what you actually *think* as Cape Town is from Lusaka. By the same token, and within reason (because an absurdity remains an absurdity for all that it is contained in a submission and not an opinion), you are entitled to be treated with respect by the court no matter how contemptuous it might be of the content of your submission

I think it was the late Judge Greenberg who caustically remarked to counsel: 'Mr Brown, I am not in the least interested in what you think about the matter. Make your submissions.' Even very experienced counsel fall into the trap from time to time. The expression jars on the sensibilities and detracts from the effectiveness of an argument.

- Use plain words, but avoid slang or colloquialisms.
- Where a lectern is available in court on which you can place your hands and the documents which you are using, so that there is a free and easy space between your eyes, the documents and the witness or judge whom you are addressing, use it: it will improve your body language, and your body language communicates as much, if not more, than the words you use.[2]

  If no lectern is available, consider using your briefcase, if it is large and solid enough.
- Remember that we communicate through our body language as well as through our mouths. Apply the SOLER principles: Shoulders square, Open stance, Leaning slightly forward, making Eye contact, with a sufficiently Relaxed posture.
- Take time to go over your argument before you deliver it. Additional points, or better ways of demonstrating the points, will come to mind.

  If possible, always provide written heads of argument. You should start drafting your heads long before the trial starts. Your advice on evidence should be the blueprint for your heads. As the trial proceeds, spend time each evening amending your heads as the evidence develops.
- When on your feet, whether in argument or leading or cross-examining a witness, read only what you have to and, when reading, slow your delivery and maintain eye-contact.

  If you have to read, either in examining or cross-examining a witness, or more likely in argument, limit your reading to the minimum necessary, and deliberately slow your delivery whilst reading, ensuring that you keep eye contact by looking up from that which you are reading from time to time. We are all inclined when we find ourselves reading something aloud in court firstly to wonder, halfway through, why we ever chose to read this passage and how we are ever going to extricate ourselves from it, and secondly to read too fast, presumably because of our hope that if we read quickly, our purgatory will the sooner be over.

  You can achieve this by means of planning. You should generally know what you intend to read (either to a witness or to the judge in argument), and in your planning you should ruthlessly limit that which you read to only that which is relevant. And whilst doing so, be aware of the human tendency to speed up one's delivery whilst reading. Deliberately counteract that tendency by slowing down and maintaining eye-contact by reading, pausing whilst making eye-contact, returning to the text and so forth. The maintaining of eye-contact will itself slow the delivery, achieving both ends.
- Whether you are reading to the witness in the course of the evidence, or (more likely) to the judge in the course of argument, your communication will be so much more effective if you ensure that all concerned have before them that from which you are reading, so that they can not only listen to you, but follow with their eyes.[3]

---

precisely because it is a submission which you make on behalf of a client whose case you are fearlessly fighting, and not necessarily an opinion you actually hold.

[2] See the point made in paragraph 9.13 in chapter 9, to the effect that human beings are more video than they are audio.

[3] This, as with so much else, links up with the point made in paragraph 9.13 in chapter 9. Human beings follow much more effectively that which they both see and hear, than only that which they hear.

- When reading a passage in argument, explain to the court beforehand why that passage is relevant. A good technique is to pause when you arrive at the most relevant portion of the passage, and reiterate why it applies to your case.

    The lesson to be learnt is to be very careful of the passages you choose to read in court.
- Have all the authorities that you are going to rely on flagged and marked in court before you argue. The modern practice appears to be to prepare a bundle of authorities for the judge (with, of course, a copy for your opponent) containing all the case law and articles you will refer to (or at least the most relevant). This is particularly useful if you are relying on foreign authorities.
- Be aware of not interrupting the judge. When the judge speaks, listen intently, make it plain through your body language and your eye contact that this is what you are doing and that you welcome the interruption as an opportunity for you to learn the judge's thinking, and wait for the judge to finish before you respond. In fact, the very act of waiting will enable you better to marshal your thoughts for the response.
- Remember the jack-in-the-box routine described in paragraphs 9.3 and 9.8 of chapter 9: as a general statement, and unless either the judge is addressing you and your opponent together (the question of what date to adjourn the matter to, for example), or you and your opponent are rising at the commencement or close of proceedings, only one of you should be on your feet. If you are speaking to the judge, then you should be on your feet and he in his seat. If he rises for any reason to interrupt you, you take your seat. And *vice versa*.
- *Never forget* that the law, and advocacy, is an honourable profession. By your words and your conduct, convey your awareness of this fact. You will find that the more your opponents and your judges respect you for your integrity, the better you will be for it.

2. MODES OF ADDRESS

- One suspects that all our courts will, in time, adopt the examples of the Constitutional Court and the Supreme Court of Appeal. But for the moment, one must distinguish between modes of address in:
    - The Constitutional Court and Supreme Court of Appeal.
    - The High Courts.
    - The Magistrates' Courts.
    - Other tribunals.
- In the Constitutional Court and Supreme Court of Appeal, one speaks not of 'judge', but of 'justice' (as in 'Justice Sachs', or 'Justice Farlam'), and not of 'my lord' or 'my lady', but of 'Justice Sachs', or 'Justice Farlam' (as in 'as pointed out by 'Justice Sachs', as opposed to 'as pointed out by 'his Lordship Mr Justice Sachs').[4]
- In the High Court, for the moment, the mode of address remains that of 'my Lord', 'your Lordship', or 'my Lady' or 'your Ladyship'.
- As pointed out above, you address the judge as 'your Lordship' (where you would otherwise have said 'you'), and you might refer to 'my Lord' as a mark of respect where you would otherwise have paused (as in 'if I may, my Lord, refer to page 12 of the bundle').
- Magistrates (regional or ordinary) are addressed, irrespective of gender, as 'your worship'.
- Arbitrators are referred to as 'Mr Arbitrator' or 'Mrs Arbitrator' (where you would otherwise have said 'you'). Proceedings in arbitrations being somewhat less formal

---

[4] See, for the Constitutional Court, Practice Direction 1 of 1995 (replicated for example at D1–1 of Erasmus *Superior Court Practice*) and, for the Supreme Court of Appeal, the practice direction of 17 August 2007 replicated at 2007 (6) SA 1.

than in open court, there is more scope for you to refer to the arbitrator also as 'you' (as in 'if I may ask you to turn to p.12 of the bundle').

- From there onwards, the mode of address is as varied as is the type of tribunal. You might find yourself referring to 'Mr Chairman', 'Madam Chair', etc.
- When do you refer to 'Jones J', and when to 'his lordship Mr Justice Jones'?

Where one is referring in one's *written heads of argument* to a reported case, one refers to 'Jones J' (as in 'Jones J held . . .'). But where one is on one's feet, one refers to 'his Lordship Mr Justice Jones' (or 'her Ladyship Madam Justice Jones').[5]

3. MATTERS OF MANNERS

- How do we refer to the client?

An advocate should, I suggest, never refer to 'my client'. He should maintain the distance created by the intervening fact of his attorney by referring either to 'the plaintiff', or to 'Mr Smith'.

An attorney, on the other hand, can refer to 'my client'. But it is suggested that he, too, would benefit from referring to 'the plaintiff', or 'Mr Smith'. Distance breeds objectivity, or at least the appearance of it.

- How do we refer to our opponents?

Glissan[6] suggests (he is very diffident about this, but I like what he says) that one begins with reference to one's opponent as 'my learned friend', and then goes on simply to refer to 'my friend'.

One might criticise this form of address as outmoded ('my learned friend' containing, it has been observed, three contradictions in one phrase). But, as has been emphasised throughout this work, there should be a purpose to what one does, and there is a purpose to these forms of address. As was pointed out in paragraph 3.7.5 in chapter 3, the law is an honourable profession and we are, as trial lawyers, all members of a brotherhood and sisterhood who can drink and laugh together after the best of fights.[7] These modes of address help us to remember that.

- Remember to always introduce yourself to the presiding officer beforehand, if you have not before made his or her acquaintance in the capacity in which he or she sits.

If you have met the judge at a dinner party, but not in court, you have not made his acquaintance, and must introduce yourself. If the judge is an acting judge and you have met him many times as an opponent but never on the bench, courtesy requires you to meet him beforehand in this new guise of his.

Whether your opponent has made the acquaintance of the judge before or not, he must accompany you so that there can be no question of discussions between the judge and the one party in the absence of the other.

Preliminary introductions in the case of appeals are more complex, because of the numbers involved. Full Bench appeals usually involve the two or three judges (as the case might be) gathering in the chambers of the senior judge at least a quarter of an

---

[5] Save, as pointed out above, in the Constitutional Court and Supreme Court of Appeal, where the reference is to 'Justice'.

[6] *Cross-examination – Practice and Procedure* (Butterworths Australia, 1991) 12.

[7] There is, in this regard, a wonderful vignette written by the Chief Justice of Ireland, Ronan Keane, in a preface to a book written by his colleague and, in their days at the bar, often opponent, Eamon Walsh, published posthumously after the latter's death:

'Splendid battles, and never a cross word!' he said to me once, his head cocked quizzically in that familiar manner. That was over breakfast on an autumn morning in Galway with a driving wind blowing the rain against the windows and just a hint of sun behind the clouds . . . A few days later, I heard that he was dead.

hour beforehand, and the best thing would be for you to arrange with the senior judge's registrar to take you and your opponent in when that happens. Practice in the Supreme Court of Appeal and the Constitutional Court involves you and your opponent being taken through to the most senior judge sitting on the appeal (and not the others) beforehand (whether you have made his or her acquaintance before or not). Thus, in the Supreme Court of Appeal and Constitutional Court, you need not ensure that you introduce yourself to each and every judge, whether you have made their acquaintance beforehand or not.

Leading Witnesses

1. EXAMPLE OF THE LEADING OF A LAY WITNESS

(a) Note that in the following example, when counsel commences he puts the witness at her ease by asking leading questions about non-contentious issues, and then switches to non-leading questions as soon as the evidence approaches the contentious issues. Note also the use of the techniques described in paragraph 11.6 of chapter 11.

The example assumes that the authenticity of the plan is not admitted and has to be established.

This is an example, and not a precedent. You might find that you would prefer to lead the evidence differently. You might, for example, prefer introducing the plan earlier in the evidence, or whereas the leader of the evidence in the example is about to return to the plan in order to take the witness through the run-up to the collision, you might have preferred dealing in more detail at an earlier stage with that which is depicted on the plan. No matter. So long as the result is effective.

(b) The example:

Counsel:	Mrs Smith, you are the plaintiff in this action?
Plaintiff:	Yes, that's correct.
Counsel:	You are an architect, and you live in Morningside, in Enahleni?
Plaintiff:	Yes, that's correct.
Counsel:	This case relates to a collision in which you were involved on a Friday, the 15th of July 2006, in Vause Road in Enahleni.[1]
Plaintiff:	Yes.
Counsel:	At the time, you lived at the same address in Morningside as you do now?
Plaintiff:	Yes.
Counsel:	That's at 11:35 Oscar Road, in Morningside?
Plaintiff:	Yes.
Counsel:	And your practice, that is and at the time was, in the Berea, in the Musgrave Centre?
Plaintiff:	Yes.
Counsel:	Can you tell the court, at approximately what time of the day did the collision occur?
Plaintiff:	It was in the afternoon, at about half past three.
Counsel:	And where were you on your way to?
Plaintiff:	I was on my way home, from work.
Counsel:	What vehicle were you driving?
Plaintiff:	A Mercedes Benz.
Counsel:	Who was the owner of the Mercedes Benz?
Plaintiff:	I was.
Counsel:	When you say that you were the owner, do you mean that you were the full owner, or was the vehicle under lease or credit purchase?

---

[1] Comment: one assumes that this was admitted on the pleadings. Even if it wasn't, a court is hardly likely to view it as contentious. Hence the acceptably leading nature of the question.

Plaintiff:	No, it was fully paid off. I was the owner.
Counsel:	And can you tell the court what type of Mercedes it was, and what year of manufacture?
Plaintiff:	It was fairly new, a 2005 model, a 240E. I had bought it new.
Counsel:	The registration detail?
Plaintiff:	ND 12345.
Counsel:	To return to the collision, you had told us that you were on your way home from work. . . .
Plaintiff:	Yes.
Counsel:	Was Vause Road on your normal route home from work?
Plaintiff:	Yes.
Counsel:	Were you in any sort of a hurry?
Plaintiff:	No, not at all. I was simply going home from my practice. I had no prior appointments.
Counsel:	In front of you there is a bundle of documents, marked 'A'. Can I ask you to please turn to p 7? [Plaintiff, judge, and sundry other role-players all turn to p 7. Counsel for the plaintiff will of course already have his bundle open on p 7].[2]
Counsel:	Can you tell the court what this document is?
Plaintiff:	Yes, it's a plan of the collision scene.
Counsel:	Do you know who the author of the plan is?
Plaintiff:	Yes; I drew it up.
Counsel:	When did you draw it up?
Plaintiff:	The day after the accident. You must remember that I am an architect. I thought it best that I should use my skills to draw a picture of the scene whilst it was still fresh in my mind. I also went back to the scene to take measurements.
Counsel:	Is the plan before you an original, or a copy?
Plaintiff:	It's the original.[3]
Counsel:	There are measurements on the plan. Are they yours?
Plaintiff:	Yes.
Counsel:	How did you take these measurements?
Plaintiff:	I used a tape measure.
Counsel:	And is the plan according to scale?
Plaintiff:	Not perfectly, but being an architect, I couldn't help but draw the plan as

---

[2] Note the points made in paragraphs 6.10, 6.11 and 6.25 in chapter 6 relating to the status of documents, and either proof thereof or agreement thereon. In practice, agreement on the use of a bundle or bundles of documents and on the status of those documents will usually have been reached at the pre-trial conference. For purposes of this example, it is assumed that the defendant declined to admit the plan, necessitating proof thereof.

[3] The so-called best evidence rule requires the original document to be produced where the content of the document is directly in issue. See *Welz and Another v Hall and Others* 1996 (4) SA 1073 (C) at 1079. As stated by Conradie J in *Welz*, '[t]he rule is a very ancient one. It goes back to the Dark Ages . . ., before faxes and photocopying machines, when making copies was difficult and such copies as were made often inaccurate. Under those circumstances Courts, naturally, insisted upon production of the original document as being the most reliable evidence of its contents. Nowadays, a Court can be asked to permit the use of a copy if the original of a document is not available'. Outdated and irrelevant as the rule might generally be, it still exists and, where agreement has not been reached at the pre-trial conference to the effect that 'copies of documents may be used instead of originals', it is best to prove the document by way of proof of the original, as in this example.

	accurately as I could, so I would think that the dimensions are more or less accurate.[4]
Counsel:	Can you describe for us what we see on this plan?
Plaintiff:	Well, you will see that Vause Road runs from south to north and is a double carriageway. [Follows a description, prodded from time to time by questions from counsel, of that which is depicted on the plan, without as yet dealing with the actual route which the plaintiff took].[5]
Counsel:	Now, with reference to the plan, please tell the court what route you took from the point of your leaving your office in the Musgrave Centre.
Plaintiff:	Yes, if you look at the plan, I left the Centre, and turned into. . . . [followed by a description of the route taken by the plaintiff, until she turned into Vause Road, leading up to the collision].
Counsel:	And when you turned into Vause Road out of Mkhize Road, as we can see on the plan on p 7 of the bundle, can you tell us what the traffic conditions in Vause Road were like? Was it busy?
Plaintiff:	No, not at all. It was early afternoon, well before the rush-hour.
Counsel:	What was the weather like?
Plaintiff:	It was a fine day. Dry.
Counsel:	We can see on the plan that. . . .

2.   EXAMPLE OF THE LEADING OF AN EXPERT WITNESS

(a)   Note that the leading of the evidence of an expert witness is facilitated by the fact that a summary of the expert's evidence will have been delivered in terms of rule 36(9)*(b)*.

(b)   The example:

Counsel:	Ms Klitznit, you are a theoretical physicist, and you practise as such from premises in Johannesburg, is that correct?
Klitznit:	Yes, that's correct.
Counsel:	You brought out a report for the plaintiff in this matter, is that correct?
Klitznit:	Yes, that's correct.[6]
Counsel:	Before you there is a bundle of documents, marked 'B', which contains all of the expert summaries. Can I ask you to turn to p 3467 of that bundle?
Klitznit:	Yes, I've got it.
Counsel:	That is the first page of your report?
Klitznit:	Yes.
Counsel:	The report is dated 31 August 2009, is that correct?
Klitznit:	Yes.
Counsel:	And in bundle 'B' it extends over pp 3467 to 4922, is that so?
Klitznit:	Let me see . . ., yes, you're correct.
Counsel:	Before I turn to the report itself, can I ask you to turn to p 4923?

---

[4] Note how the plan has been proven by means of non-leading questions. Of course, in most instances the plan will have been admitted, and there will be no need to prove it in this fashion. However, the accuracy of the measurements will likely not be admitted, so that one might still need to prove that.

[5] When using a plan, it is best to first orient the court as to what is depicted on the plan.

[6] Even experts need to be eased into their task — thus the odd but obvious leading question to begin with. Moreover, the aim remains not to waste time by asking non-leading questions on uncontentious issues. The expert has brought out a report. The report is there for all to see. Save when it comes to opinions and reasons for those opinions, you can and should ask leading questions.

Klitznit:	Yes, I have it.
Counsel:	This, extending from p 4923 to p 4987, is your *curriculum vitae*, is that correct?
Klitznit:	Yes.
Counsel:	Is this an up-to-date CV?
Klitznit:	Yes.
Counsel:	Can I ask you to briefly take us through your CV?
Klitznit:	Certainly [followed by the expert taking the court through the CV, prodded from time to time by questions from counsel. What counsel will do is to concentrate on those aspects of the CV which are particularly relevant to the issues at hand, such as pausing to concentrate on a particular book written by the expert touching on the pertinent issues in the case, and so forth].[7]
Counsel:	Now, reverting to p 3467 and the start of your report, do you confirm the report? [8]
Klitznit:	Yes.
Counsel:	Does it contain your views on the matters that you were asked to consider, and the reasons for those views?
Klitznit:	Yes.
Counsel:	In the first paragraph of your summary, you deal with the documentation which you studied in the course of bringing out your report. Is that correct?
Klitznit:	Yes.
Counsel:	Can you take us through that list of documents?
Klitznit:	Yes, certainly [and proceeds to do so. Once again, counsel will if necessary prod with questions on particularly pertinent aspects].
Counsel:	Turning to the second paragraph of your report, you say the following [proceeds to quote the essential aspect of the paragraph]. Would you mind elaborating on that?
Klitznit:	Yes, certainly. You see I . . . [proceeds to explain to the court the particular opinion, and the reasons for the particular opinion. Again, prodded from time to time by questions from counsel where this is appropriate].[9]
Counsel:	Now, your opposite number for the defendant in this matter is Mr Saunderson, not so?
Klitznit:	Yes.
Counsel:	Mr Saunderson's report begins on p 22343, and the portion of his report dealing with the same topic as you and I have just dealt with, is his paragraph 97 on p 22429. Could I ask you, whilst keeping the bundle open on p 3468 where we were, to turn to p 22429?

---

[7] It is strictly speaking necessary to 'qualify' your witness, ie to prove his or her expertise. Your opponent will often lean over and tell you that he admits the expert's expertise, or will stand up and tell the court this. Beware of taking that concession too much at face value, and skipping over the expert's qualifications. Where expertise is admitted, you can reduce the amount of questions needed, but it might still be useful to highlight for the court the *particular* expertise and experience of the witness.

[8] This catch-all question has limited usefulness, but it still serves to encompass those minor issues of the expert's summary which you might omit to deal with in the course of the oral evidence.

[9] Note the point already made above, to the effect that the rule 36(9)*(b)* summary of an expert witness facilitates your leading of the evidence.

Klitznit: Yes, I have it.

Counsel: Would you please take the court through Mr Saunderson's views in this regard, and your comments on his views?[10]

---

[10] It is essential that your expert deals not only with her views and the reasons for those views, but also with the hopefully entirely illogical views of the opposing expert.

Cross-examining Witnesses

1. EXAMPLE OF CROSS-EXAMINATION OF A LAY WITNESS

(a) Note the use of leading questions only, and the technique of closing off escape routes beforehand.

(b) Example:

Counsel: Sergeant Msibi visited you the next day at your home to take a statement, didn't he?

Witness: Yes.

Counsel: You knew that he was taking a statement from you so that you could record what had happened.

Witness: Yes.

Counsel: He spoke to you in Sesotho, not so?

Witness: Yes.

Counsel: You and he are both Sesotho-speaking?

Witness: Yes.

Counsel: But you are both also conversant in English?

Witness: Yes, we also spoke English to one another.

Counsel: He asked you in Sesotho what had happened, and you told him?

Witness: Yes.

Counsel: And as you told him, he wrote it down?

Witness: Yes.

Counsel: You have a grade 12 qualification?

Witness: Yes.

Counsel: You can read English, can't you?

Witness: Yes, I can.

Counsel: Although he and you spoke in Sesotho, he wrote what you told him down in English?

Witness: Yes.

Counsel: And when he had finished writing it all down, he read to you in English what he had written down, didn't he?

Witness: Yes.

Counsel: And when he had finished reading it to you, he gave it to you, and you read it yourself, not so?

Witness: Yes, I think I remember that. . . .

Counsel: And you can of course read.[1]

Witness: Yes, I can read, I read in my job.

Counsel: He then asked you if you were satisfied that he had written down what you told him?

Witness: Yes.

Counsel: And you then signed it?

---

[1] Note that this question, essentially a repeat of a prior question establishing the ability to read English, could be safely put, given that this had already been established. That said, the question could as easily have been done without.

Witness:	Yes.
Counsel:	Turn to the bundle, p7 [witness pages, and finds the page].
Counsel:	That is your signature, isn't it?
Witness:	Yes.
Counsel:	There, on pages 5 to 7 of the bundle, is your statement to Inspector Msibi, not so?
Witness:	Let me see. . . . Yes.
Counsel:	Now, remember you told us about this other car which veered into your path, causing you to veer out into the path of the plaintiff?
Witness:	Yes, that's what happened. . . .
Counsel:	Read through the statement. Take your time. Can you find any mention of this other vehicle in that statement?[2]
Witness:	[Takes time laboriously to read, scratches his head, begins to sweat]. No.
Counsel:	I am going to put to you why there isn't any mention of that vehicle in your statement.
Witness:	Why?
Counsel:	Because there never was such a vehicle.
Witness:	No, there was.
Counsel:	Because you made up that story, as an excuse for your losing control.
Witness:	No, there was such a vehicle.
Counsel:	But you hadn't yet dreamed it up when Inspector Msibi came to see you.
Witness:	No, it happened.
Counsel:	That's why you never mentioned such an important thing in your statement.
Witness:	No, I tell you, there was such a vehicle.

2.   EXAMPLE OF CROSS–EXAMINATION OF AN EXPERT WITNESS

These were the opening questions of cross-examination, aimed at attacking the expert's credentials and in any event comparing those credentials with those of the experts for the defendant:[3]

Counsel:	Mr Klitznit, in your CV I saw no mention of publications. What works have you published?
Klitznit:	Well, my reports and research work have been under contract and under confidentiality agreements so I have no work that has been published in the public domain.
Counsel:	So you have not published anything in scientific journals?
Klitznit:	No, I have not.
Counsel:	You have not been peer reviewed once?
Klitznit:	I am peer reviewed in most of the work that I produce for clients.

---

[2] This is an open-ended and not a leading question. The question could of course have been put in a leading fashion ('You do not find any mention of this other vehicle in the statement'), but the trap has by now been sprung, the witness can no longer escape from it, and an open-ended question of this nature arguably has more impact.

[3] Beware of unnecessarily attacking an expert's expertise. Such an attack should only be made if it is warranted. An unwarranted attack on the expert's credentials is counter-productive, will serve only to irritate the judge, and might well depending upon the extent of the attack, constitute a breach of ethical rules. See for example the Uniform Rules of Professional Conduct for Advocates insofar as they relate to cross-examination, as outlined in para 18.6.5.7 of PJ Schwikkard and S van der Merwe *Principles of Evidence* 3 ed 371.

Counsel:	I mean in public scientific journals.
Klitznit:	No, I have not.
Counsel:	The expert summaries of [the experts for the defendant] contain details of publications in the public domain. Do you remember them?
Klitznit:	I don't recall all of them, but I do know that they have published a lot.
Counsel:	Both of them have published quite widely. Would you agree with that?
Klitznit:	I agree.

Index